Keep this book. You will need it and use it throughout your career.

About the American Hotel & Lodging Association (AH&LA)

Founded in 1910, AH&LA is the trade association representing the lodging industry in the United States. AH&LA is a federation of state lodging associations throughout the United States with 11,000 lodging properties worldwide as members. The association offers its members assistance with governmental affairs representation, communications, marketing, hospitality operations, training and education, technology issues, and more. For information, call 202-289-3100.

LODGING, the management magazine of AH&LA, is a "living textbook" for hospitality students that provides timely features, industry news, and vital lodging information.

About the Educational Institute of AH&LA (EI)

An affiliate of AH&LA, the Educational Institute is the world's largest source of quality training and educational materials for the lodging industry. EI develops textbooks and courses that are used in more than 1,200 colleges and universities worldwide, and also offers courses to individuals through its Distance Learning program. Hotels worldwide rely on EI for training resources that focus on every aspect of lodging operations. Industry-tested videos, CD-ROMs, seminars, and skills guides prepare employees at every skill level. EI also offers professional certification for the industry's top performers. For information about EI's products and services, call 800-349-0299 or 407-999-8100.

About the American Hotel & Lodging Educational Foundation (AH&LEF)

An affiliate of AH&LA, the American Hotel & Lodging Educational Foundation provides financial support that enhances the stability, prosperity, and growth of the lodging industry through educational and research programs. AH&LEF has awarded hundreds of thousands of dollars in scholarship funds for students pursuing higher education in hospitality management. AH&LEF has also funded research projects on topics important to the industry, including occupational safety and health, turnover and diversity, and best practices in the U.S. lodging industry. For information, call 202-289-3180.

HOSPITALITY INDUSTRY FINANCIAL ACCOUNTING

Educational Institute Books

UNIFORM SYSTEM OF ACCOUNTS FOR THE LODGING INDUSTRY
Tenth Revised Edition

RESORT DEVELOPMENT AND MANAGEMENT
Second Edition
Chuck Y. Gee

PLANNING AND CONTROL FOR FOOD AND BEVERAGE OPERATIONS
Sixth Edition
Jack D. Ninemeier

UNDERSTANDING HOSPITALITY LAW
Fourth Edition
Jack P. Jefferies/Banks Brown

SUPERVISION IN THE HOSPITALITY INDUSTRY
Third Edition
Raphael R. Kavanaugh/Jack D. Ninemeier

MANAGEMENT OF FOOD AND BEVERAGE OPERATIONS
Fourth Edition
Jack D. Ninemeier

MANAGING FRONT OFFICE OPERATIONS
Seventh Edition
Michael L. Kasavana/Richard M. Brooks

MANAGING SERVICE IN FOOD AND BEVERAGE OPERATIONS
Third Edition
Ronald F. Cichy/Philip J. Hickey, Jr.

THE LODGING AND FOOD SERVICE INDUSTRY
Sixth Edition
Gerald W. Lattin

SECURITY AND LOSS PREVENTION MANAGEMENT
Second Edition
Raymond C. Ellis, Jr./David M. Stipanuk

HOSPITALITY INDUSTRY MANAGERIAL ACCOUNTING
Sixth Edition
Raymond S. Schmidgall

PURCHASING FOR HOSPITALITY OPERATIONS
William B. Virts

MANAGING TECHNOLOGY IN THE HOSPITALITY INDUSTRY
Fourth Edition
Michael L. Kasavana/John J. Cahill

MANAGING HOSPITALITY ENGINEERING SYSTEMS
Michael H. Redlin/David M. Stipanuk

BASIC HOTEL AND RESTAURANT ACCOUNTING
Sixth Edition
Raymond Cote

ACCOUNTING FOR HOSPITALITY MANAGERS
Fourth Edition
Raymond Cote

CONVENTION MANAGEMENT AND SERVICE
Seventh Edition
Milton T. Astroff/James R. Abbey

HOSPITALITY SALES AND MARKETING
Fourth Edition
James R. Abbey

MANAGING HOUSEKEEPING OPERATIONS
Second Edition
Margaret M. Kappa/Aleta Nitschke/Patricia B. Schappert

DIMENSIONS OF TOURISM
Joseph D. Fridgen

HOSPITALITY TODAY: AN INTRODUCTION
Fifth Edition
Rocco M. Angelo/Andrew N. Vladimir

MANAGING BAR AND BEVERAGE OPERATIONS
Lendal H. Kotschevar/Mary L. Tanke

ETHICS IN HOSPITALITY MANAGEMENT: A BOOK OF READINGS
Edited by Stephen S. J. Hall

HOSPITALITY FACILITIES MANAGEMENT AND DESIGN
Third Edition
David M. Stipanuk

MANAGING HOSPITALITY HUMAN RESOURCES
Fourth Edition
Robert H. Woods

FINANCIAL MANAGEMENT FOR THE HOSPITALITY INDUSTRY
William P. Andrew/Raymond S. Schmidgall

HOSPITALITY INDUSTRY FINANCIAL ACCOUNTING
Third Edition
Raymond S. Schmidgall/James W. Damitio

INTERNATIONAL HOTEL MANAGEMENT
Chuck Y. Gee

QUALITY SANITATION MANAGEMENT
Ronald F. Cichy

HOTEL INVESTMENTS: ISSUES & PERSPECTIVES
Fourth Edition
Edited by Lori E. Raleigh and Rachel J. Roginsky

LEADERSHIP AND MANAGEMENT IN THE HOSPITALITY INDUSTRY
Second Edition
Robert H. Woods/Judy Z. King

MARKETING IN THE HOSPITALITY INDUSTRY
Fourth Edition
Ronald A. Nykiel

CONTEMPORARY HOSPITALITY MARKETING
William Lazer/Roger Layton

UNIFORM SYSTEM OF ACCOUNTS FOR THE HEALTH, RACQUET AND SPORTSCLUB INDUSTRY

CONTEMPORARY CLUB MANAGEMENT
Edited by Joe Perdue for the Club Managers Association of America

RESORT CONDOMINIUM AND VACATION OWNERSHIP MANAGEMENT: A HOSPITALITY PERSPECTIVE
Robert A. Gentry/Pedro Mandoki/Jack Rush

ACCOUNTING FOR CLUB OPERATIONS
Raymond S. Schmidgall/James W. Damitio

TRAINING AND DEVELOPMENT FOR THE HOSPITALITY INDUSTRY
Debra F. Cannon/Catherine M. Gustafson

UNIFORM SYSTEM OF FINANCIAL REPORTING FOR CLUBS
Sixth Revised Edition

HOTEL ASSET MANAGEMENT: PRINCIPLES & PRACTICES
Edited by Paul Beals and Greg Denton

MANAGING BEVERAGE SERVICE
Lendal H. Kotschevar/Ronald F. Cichy

FOOD SAFETY: MANAGING THE HACCP PROCESS
Ronald F. Cichy

UNIFORM SYSTEM OF FINANCIAL REPORTING FOR SPAS

FUNDAMENTALS OF DESTINATION MANAGEMENT AND MARKETING
Edited by Rich Harrill

ETHICS IN THE HOSPITALITY AND TOURISM INDUSTRY
Karen Lieberman/Bruce Nissen

HOSPITALITY AND TOURISM MARKETING
William Lazer/Melissa Dallas/Carl Riegel

HOSPITALITY INDUSTRY FINANCIAL ACCOUNTING

Third Edition

Raymond S. Schmidgall, Ph.D., CPA
James W. Damitio, Ph.D., CMA

EDUCATIONAL INSTITUTE
American Hotel & Lodging Association

Disclaimer

This publication is designed to provide accurate and authoritative information in regard to the subject matter covered. It is sold with the understanding that the publisher is not engaged in rendering legal, accounting, or other professional service. If legal advice or other expert assistance is required, the services of a competent professional person should be sought.
—*From the Declaration of Principles jointly adopted by the American Bar Association and a Committee of Publishers and Associations*

The authors, Raymond S. Schmidgall and James W. Damitio, are solely responsible for the contents of this publication. All views expressed herein are solely those of the authors and do not necessarily reflect the views of the Educational Institute of the American Hotel & Lodging Association (the Institute) or the American Hotel & Lodging Association (AH&LA).

Nothing contained in this publication shall constitute a standard, an endorsement, or a recommendation of the Institute or AH&LA. The Institute and AH&LA disclaim any liability with respect to the use of any information, procedure, or product, or reliance thereon by any member of the hospitality industry.

Editor: Jessica Miller

Contents

Preface xiii

About the Authors xiv

1 **Introduction to Accounting** 3

Accounting Defined 4

Bookkeeping versus Accounting

Branches of Accounting 4
Organizations Influencing Accounting 6
Forms of Business Organization 7

*Sole Proprietorships • Partnerships • Limited Partnerships •
Limited Liability Companies • Corporations • S Corporations*

The Accounting Function in the Hospitality Industry 10
Principles of Accounting 13

*Cost • Business Entity • Continuity of the Business Unit (Going
Concern) • Unit of Measurement • Objective Evidence • Full
Disclosure • Consistency • Matching • Conservatism •
Materiality*

Overview of Financial Statements 19

Balance Sheet • Income Statement • Statement of Cash Flows

Cash versus Accrual Accounting 22
The Fundamental Accounting Equation 23

Effects of Transactions on the Accounting Equation

Summary 28
Endnotes, Key Terms, Review Questions 29
Problems 32

2 **Accounting for Business Transactions** 41

Accounts 41

Asset Accounts • Liability Accounts • Owners' Equity Accounts

Debit and Credit   44

Mechanics of Double-Entry Accounting • Recording Changes in Assets, Liabilities, and Owners' Equity • Recording Changes in Revenues and Expenses • Recording Owner's Withdrawals • Determining Account Balances • Normal Balances

General Ledger   49
Journalizing   50

Standard Account Forms • Posting • The Trial Balance • Compound Journal Entries

Comprehensive Illustration—Journalizing, Posting, and
    Preparing a Trial Balance   58
Summary   63
Endnotes, Key Terms, Review Questions   67
Problems   68

3   Accounting Adjustments **79**

The Need for Adjustments   79
Cash versus Accrual Accounting   80
Classification of Adjusting Entries   81
Deferral Adjustments Illustrated   82

Prepaid Insurance/Insurance Expense • Depreciation Expense • Unearned Revenues

Accrual Adjustments Illustrated   85

Accrued Wages Payable • Accrued Utilities • Accrued Assets

Failure to Prepare Adjustments   88
Comprehensive Illustration—Adjustments   89
Summary   94
Key Terms, Review Questions   96
Problems   97

4   Completing the Accounting Cycle **107**

The Accounting Cycle   107

Adjusted Trial Balance • Preparation of Financial Statements • Closing Entries • Post-Closing Trial Balance

The Worksheet   116
Reversing Entries   120
Comprehensive Illustration—Completing the Accounting Cycle . .   121
Summary   125
Key Terms, Review Questions   127
Problems   128

5 Income Statement **141**

Major Elements of the Income Statement 141
Relationship with the Balance Sheet 143
Sales 143
Cost of Goods Sold 144
Expenses 146
Gains and Losses 147
Income Taxes 148
Extraordinary Items 149
Earnings per Share 149
Income Statements for Internal and External Users 150
Uniform System of Accounts 152
Internal Income Statements—A Contribution Approach 152

> *Contents of the Summary Operating Statement*

Departmental Statements 157
Uniform System of Accounts for Restaurants 160
Statement of Retained Earnings 162
Summary 163
Endnotes, Key Terms, Review Questions 164
Problems 166
Chapter Appendix—Departmental Schedules 175

6 Balance Sheet **201**

Purposes of the Balance Sheet 201
Limitations of the Balance Sheet 203
Balance Sheet Formats 204
Content of the Balance Sheet 204

> *Current Accounts • Noncurrent Receivables • Investments •*
> *Property and Equipment • Other Assets • Long-Term Liabilities •*
> *Owners' Equity • Footnotes • Consolidated Financial Statements*

Summary 217
Endnotes, Key Terms, Review Questions 217
Problems 219
Chapter Appendix—Hilton Consolidated Financial Statements ... 228

7 Specialized Journals and Subsidiary Ledgers **261**

Control Accounts and Subsidiary Ledgers 261
Specialized Journals 264

> *Sales Journal • Cash Receipts Journal • Purchases Journal • Cash*
> *Disbursements Journal*

General Ledger 274
General Journal 274

Payroll Journal 274
Specialized Journals for Lodging Operations 278
Computerized Systems 280

> *Hardware • Software • Hotel Computer Systems*

Summary 281
Key Terms, Review Questions 282
Problems 283

8   Cash **295**

Internal Control of Cash 295
Voucher System 297

> *Preparation of a Voucher*

Petty Cash 299
Bank Reconciliation 301

> *Preparing a Bank Reconciliation • Illustration of a Bank Reconciliation*

Gross Method of Recording Purchases 305
Net Method of Recording Purchases 306
Credit Card Sales 307
Integrated Cash Management for Multi-Unit Operations 308
Summary 308
Key Terms, Review Questions 309
Problems 310

9   Receivables and Payables **317**

Uncollectible Accounts Expense (Bad Debts) 318

> *Direct Write-Off Method • Allowance Method*

Using Debit and Credit Cards to Manage Receivables and Credit . 322
Notes Receivable 323

> *Interest-Bearing Notes*

Notes Payable 326

> *Non-Interest-Bearing Notes*

Summary 329
Key Terms, Review Questions 330
Problems 331

10   Inventory **337**

Periodic versus Perpetual Inventory Systems 337

> *Taking a Physical Inventory • Consigned Goods • Transportation Costs*

Inventory Valuation Methods 341
 Comparison and Evaluation of Inventory Valuation Methods

Estimating Ending Inventory and Cost of Goods Sold 343
 The Retail Method • The Gross Profit Method

Lower of Cost or Market (LCM) 345
Perpetual Inventory System 345
Summary 347
Key Terms, Review Questions 347
Problems 348

11 Property, Equipment, and Other Assets **355**

Property and Equipment 355
 Lump Sum Purchase • Depreciation of Property and Equipment

Intangible Assets 364
Other Assets 365
Summary 365
Endnotes, Key Terms, Review Questions 366
Problems 369

12 Current Liabilities and Payroll **375**

Notes Payable 376
Accounting for Payroll-Related Liabilities 378
 Payroll Records • Regular Pay and Overtime Pay • Payroll Journal
 Entries • Reporting Tips

Other Current Liabilities 391
 Property Taxes

Summary 392
Key Terms, Review Questions 392
Problems 394

13 Partnerships **401**

Advantages of Partnerships 401
 Ease of Formation • No Partnership Taxes • Synergy

Disadvantages of Partnerships 402
 Limited Life • Mutual Agency • Unlimited Liability

General versus Limited Partnerships 402
Partners' Capital and Drawing Accounts 403
Formation of a Partnership 403
 Division of Income

Admission of a New Partner 406
Withdrawal of a Partner 409
Liquidation of a Partnership 409
Summary 412
Key Terms, Review Questions 412
Problems 414

14   Corporate Accounting **421**

Financial Statements 421
Advantages and Disadvantages of the Corporation 421
Taxes 422
Organizational Structure 422
Forming a Corporation 423
Common Stock 423
Dividends 424
Retained Earnings 425
Stock Subscription Plan 426
Preferred Stock 427
Cash Dividends Compared to Stock Dividends 428
Stock Splits 429
Treasury Stock 429
Book Value Per Share of Common Stock 430

Book Value versus Market Value per Share

Summary 431
Key Terms, Review Questions 432
Problems 433

15   Bonds, Leases, and Mortgages Payable **439**

Disadvantages and Advantages of Bond Financing 440

Disadvantages of Bond Financing • Advantages of Bond Financing

Classifying Bonds 441
Other Features of Bonds 443
Journal Entries for Issuance of Bonds 443

Bonds Sold between Interest Payment Dates

Market Value Versus Face Value 444

Bonds Issued at a Discount • Bonds Issued at a Premium

Year-End Adjusting Entries for Bonds Payable 446
Effective Interest Rate Method of Bond Amortization 447
Bond Sinking Fund 448
Convertible Bonds 448
Retirement of Bonds 449
Leases 449

Pensions 450
Mortgages Payable 451
Summary 451
Key Terms, Review Questions 452
Problems 454

16   Investments in Corporate Securities 459

Accounting for Investments 459

*Investments in Debt Securities • Short-Term Equity Investments •
Long-Term Equity Investments*

Valuation of Investments 465

*Held-to-Maturity Securities • Trading Securities • Available-for-
Sale Securities*

Summary 468
Key Terms, Review Questions 468
Problems 470

17   Statement of Cash Flows 477

The Purpose of the Statement of Cash Flows 477
Classification of Cash Flows 479
Conversion of Accrual Income to Net Cash Flows from
   Operations 482

Direct and Indirect Methods

Preparing the SCF 484

*Step 1: Determining Net Cash Flows from Operating Activities • Step
2: Determining Net Cash Flows from Investing Activities • Step 3:
Determining Net Cash Flows from Financing Activities • Step 4: Presenting Cash Flows by Activity on the SCF • Interpreting the Results*

Accounting for Other Transactions 493
Summary 495
Key Terms, Review Questions 496
Problems 497

18   Analysis and Interpretation of Financial Statements 509

Analysis of Financial Statements 509
Horizontal Analysis 512
Vertical Analysis 514
Trend Analysis 515
Ratio Analysis 517

*Ratio Standards • Purposes of Ratio Analysis • Average versus
Ending Value • Classes of Ratios*

Liquidity Ratios   520

Current Ratio • Acid-Test Ratio • Operating Cash Flows to Current Liabilities Ratio • Accounts Receivable Turnover • Average Collection Period

Solvency Ratios   525

Debt-Equity Ratio • Long-Term Debt to Total Capitalization Ratio • Number of Times Interest Earned Ratio • Fixed Charge Coverage Ratio • Operating Cash Flows to Total Liabilities Ratio

Activity Ratios   528

Inventory Turnover • Property and Equipment Turnover • Asset Turnover • Paid Occupancy Percentage and Seat Turnover • Complimentary Occupancy • Occupancy Percentage • Average Occupancy Per Room • Multiple Occupancy

Profitability Ratios   535

Profit Margin • Operating Efficiency Ratio • Return on Assets • Return on Owners' Equity • Earnings per Share • Price Earnings Ratio • Viewpoints Regarding Profitability Ratios

Operating Ratios   541

Mix of Sales • Average Daily Rate • Revenue per Available Room • Gross Operating Profit per Available Room • Average Food Service Check • Food Cost Percentage • Beverage Cost Percentage • Labor Cost Percentage • Limitations of Ratio Analysis

Summary   548
Endnotes, Key Terms, Review Questions   548
Problems   554

Index   565

Preface

Hospitality Industry Financial Accounting, Third Edition, is designed for individuals wishing to learn the fundamentals of financial accounting through hospitality industry examples. The illustrations and examples in this text cover all areas of the hospitality industry including hotels, restaurants, and clubs.

All 18 chapters in this book include review questions and problems that reinforce the key points in the respective chapters. Several new problems have been added to each chapter for this edition. Chapter 1 provides an introduction and overview of financial accounting. The organizations that affect accounting are discussed in this chapter along with the basic accounting principles.

Chapter 2 explains accounting for basic business transactions. The five basic groups of accounts are introduced along with numerous transactions that involve many specific accounts in these groups. Chapter 3 illustrates the basic accounting adjustments that are necessary at the end of accounting periods.

Chapter 4 covers the procedures for the closing of the books and summarizes the entire accounting cycle. The chapter introduces the concept of the worksheet and demonstrates the preparation of the balance sheet and the income statement.

Chapters 5 and 6 cover in detail the most common financial statements: the income statement and the balance sheet. These financial statements are discussed in the context of the *Uniform System of Accounts for the Lodging Industry,* the *Uniform System of Financial Reporting for Clubs,* and the *Uniform System of Accounts for Restaurants.*

Chapter 7 focuses on the special journals and related subsidiary ledgers typically used in the hospitality industry. Chapter 8 begins a section of the book that covers in detail the accounting for specific items on the balance sheet. The chapter explains the specific accounting procedures for cash, including petty cash funds and bank reconciliations.

Chapter 9 covers both receivables and payables, while Chapter 10 describes inventory procedures. Property, equipment, intangibles, and other assets are discussed in Chapter 11, and Chapter 12 covers current liabilities and payroll.

Chapter 13 covers the major aspects of partnership accounting, including formation of a partnership, procedures for profit sharing, and dissolution of a partnership entity.

Chapter 14 introduces accounting procedures used in the most complex form of business, the corporation. Chapter 15 focuses on the issuance of bonds and accounting for leases and long-term mortgages.

Investments in corporate securities are discussed in Chapter 16. The cost and equity methods are discussed, and consolidated financial statements are introduced. The statement of cash flows, now mandated by the Financial Accounting Standards Board, is explained in Chapter 17. The text concludes with Chapter 18, which offers a detailed discussion of the analysis and interpretation of financial statements.

About the Authors

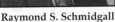

Raymond S. Schmidgall   James W. Damitio

Raymond S. Schmidgall is a professor in *The* School of Hospitality Business at Michigan State University. He holds a B.B.A. in accounting from Evangel College and an M.B.A. and a Ph.D. in accounting from Michigan State University. He is also a Certified Public Accountant. He has published articles in *Lodging, Club Management, The Bottomline, The Consultant, Restaurant Business,* and the *Cornell Hotel and Restaurant Administration Quarterly.* Dr. Schmidgall has also written or co-written five accounting textbooks oriented to the hospitality industry, including basic texts on financial management, financial accounting, and managerial accounting. He conducts workshops and seminars for the Club Managers Association of America, American Hotel & Lodging Association, International SPA Association, National Automatic Merchandising Association, Hospitality Financial and Technology Professionals, Golf Course Superintendents Association of America, and Meeting Professionals International. Dr. Schmidgall is Secretary of the Association of Hospitality Financial Management Educators, a member of the AH&LA's financial management committee, a member of International CHRIE's finance committee, a member of HFTP's communications and CHAE committees, serves on the editorial board of CHRIE's *Journal of Hospitality and Tourism Research,* and is a member of several professional accounting associations.

James W. Damitio is a professor in the School of Accounting at Central Michigan University, where he is also Director of the Perry Schools of Banking and Director of the Entrepreneurship Program. He received a B.S. in accounting from Central Michigan University and an M.B.A. in Finance and a Ph.D. from Michigan State University. He is a Certified Management Accountant, and is a member of the Institute of Management Accountants and Hospitality Financial and Technology Professionals.

He has published articles in the area of hospitality accounting, management accounting, and ethics in journals such as *Internal Auditing, Management Accounting,* the *Cornell Hotel and Restaurant Administration Quarterly, Real Estate Review, Florida International Review,* the *Journal of Hospitality Financial Management,* and the *Journal of Hospitality and Tourism Research.*

He is the coauthor of two textbooks, *Hospitality Industry Financial Accounting* and *Accounting for Club Operations,* and is a contributing author of *Financial Management for the Hospitality Industry.* Dr. Damitio has worked for Ernst & Young and was a self-employed retailer for 14 years.

Chapter 1 Outline

Accounting Defined
    Bookkeeping versus Accounting
Branches of Accounting
Organizations Influencing Accounting
Forms of Business Organization
    Sole Proprietorships
    Partnerships
    Limited Partnerships
    Limited Liability Companies
    Corporations
    S Corporations
The Accounting Function in the Hospitality
    Industry
Principles of Accounting
    Cost
    Business Entity
    Continuity of the Business Unit (Going
        Concern)
    Unit of Measurement
    Objective Evidence
    Full Disclosure
    Consistency
    Matching
    Conservatism
    Materiality
Overview of Financial Statements
    Balance Sheet
    Income Statement
    Statement of Cash Flows
Cash versus Accrual Accounting
The Fundamental Accounting Equation
    Effects of Transactions on the
        Accounting Equation

Competencies

1. Define *accounting* and distinguish it from bookkeeping. (pp. 3–4)

2. Describe the six branches of accounting. (pp. 4–6)

3. Identify and describe organizations that have influenced hospitality accounting practices. (pp. 6–7)

4. Describe basic forms of business organization and their advantages and disadvantages. (pp. 7–10)

5. Describe the responsibilities of a hospitality firm's accounting department. (pp. 10–12)

6. Apply generally accepted accounting principles to hospitality situations. (pp. 13–19)

7. Describe the major types of financial statements: balance sheets, income statements, and statements of cash flows. (pp. 19–23)

8. Describe the fundamental accounting equation and apply it to accounting situations. (pp. 23–27)

1

Introduction to Accounting

ACCOUNTING is simply a means to an end. Businesses, governments, and other entities use it as a means to account for their activities. Generally, this is accomplished through the use of numbers; thus, many people associate accounting with mathematics. However, accounting is much more than numbers.

Accounting assists in providing answers to many questions that hospitality managers raise, such as the following:

- How much cash is available to pay bills?
- What was the total payroll last pay period?
- What amount of property taxes did we pay this year?
- What amount of interest did we pay on long-term debt last year, and how much must be paid during the current year?
- How much does a current guest owe the hotel?
- What were the total food sales for the dinner period last night?
- What amount of food inventory was on hand at the beginning of the month?
- When did we purchase the kitchen range, and how much did it cost?
- How much do we owe the bank on the mortgage?
- What are payroll costs as a percentage of room sales?
- What amount of dividends did we pay to stockholders this past year?
- What is the ratio of food and beverage sales to room sales this past month?
- How much do we owe the meat purveyor?
- When is the utility bill, received yesterday, due?
- How was this hotel corporation financed?

The list of such questions is endless. Hospitality operations, whether hotel, motel, resort, club, restaurant, airline, or hospital, perform a multitude of activities each day. They sell assorted products as well as provide a variety of services. The need to keep track of these many activities has produced modern accounting systems.

Accounting Defined

The American Accounting Association defines **accounting** as "the process of identifying, measuring, and communicating economic information to permit informed judgments and decisions by users of the information."[1] The economic information is generally financial and is stated in monetary terms. For example, room sales for the period were $1,500,000 and net income was $150,000. The accounting process includes observing events in order to identify the events that are of a financial nature. These events must be measured in monetary terms; that is, a monetary value is placed on the observed activity. For example, a meal is sold to a guest. This activity is of a financial nature and is measured by the sales price of the meal. Next, accounting requires recording, classifying, and summarizing the economic events, such as food sales. In the case of the above example, the sale is recorded on a sales slip. This sale is then classified as a food sale as opposed to other types of sales and, at the end of the accounting period, will be summarized in a financial statement along with other economic events. The accounting process continues as financial statements and other reports are provided to users.

A key element of accounting is communication. In other words, not only must information be accumulated and properly summarized, it must be communicated in a way that users understand. The statement of cash flows (SCF) is an example of a report that communicates accounting information. For many years, cash flow information was communicated indirectly at best. Now the SCF provides details of cash inflows and outflows. This information is considerably more useful than what has been communicated in the past.

Bookkeeping versus Accounting

There is a difference between bookkeeping and accounting, though many think they are the same thing. **Bookkeeping** is only a part of accounting—that of recording and classifying transactions. Accounting also includes summarizing and interpreting, which is beyond the scope of bookkeeping.

A bookkeeper records and classifies transactions, usually a routine, clerical task, whereas an accountant supervises the work of the bookkeeper, summarizes the accounting information, and interprets the financial statements. The accountant must also be able to survey a business's transactions, determine how its accounting data are to be used, and so on, and then be able to design an accounting system to fit the business. After the designed system is installed, the accountant must be able to supervise the bookkeeper's work, review it for accuracy, and report to management and others, in quantitative terms, the firm's activity for the period and its financial position at a given time. Thus, the demands on an accountant are much greater than those on the bookkeeper, and the required training is more extensive.

Branches of Accounting

Accountants classify accounting activities in various ways. However, most accountants agree that there are distinct but overlapping branches of accounting. These include financial accounting, cost accounting, managerial accounting, tax accounting, auditing, and accounting systems.

Financial accounting refers to accounting for revenues, expenses, assets, and liabilities. It involves the basic accounting processes of recording, classifying, and summarizing transactions. This area is often limited to the accounting necessary to prepare and distribute financial reports. Financial accounting is historical in nature; that is, it deals with past events. Managerial accounting, on the other hand, deals with proposed events.

Cost accounting is the branch of accounting dealing with the recording, classification, allocation, and reporting of current and prospective costs. Cost accountants determine costs by departments, functions, responsibilities, and products and services. The chief purpose of cost accounting is to help operations personnel control operations.

Managerial accounting is the branch of accounting designed to provide information to various management levels in the hospitality operation for the purpose of enhancing controls. Management accountants prepare performance reports, including comparisons to the budget. One major purpose of these reports is to provide in-depth information as a basis for management decisions. Although managerial accounting may vary among segments of the hospitality industry and certainly among different establishments, many management accountants use various management science techniques and tools. Algebra and forecasting are examples of these techniques.

Tax accounting is the branch of accounting relating to the preparation and filing of tax forms with government agencies. Tax planning to minimize tax payments is a significant part of the tax accountant's work. Tax accounting usually focuses on income tax at the federal, state, and local levels, but may also include sales, excise, payroll, and property taxes. Many hospitality operations employ tax accountants, while some operations contract the services of tax accountants employed by certified accounting firms.

Auditing is the branch of accounting involved in reviewing and evaluating documents, records, and control systems. Auditing may be either external or internal. It is most often associated with the independent, external audit called a **financial audit.** The external auditor reviews the financial statements of the hospitality operation, its underlying internal control system, and its accounting records (journals, vouchers, invoices, checks, bank statements, and so forth) in order to render an opinion of the financial statements. Financial audits may be conducted only by certified public accounting firms who generally also provide recommendations for strengthening the operation's internal controls.

Over the past several years, hospitality operations have increasingly employed internal auditors, whose primary purpose is to review and evaluate internal control systems. Many large hospitality firms have a full staff of internal auditors who conduct audits at individual properties to help management maintain the internal control system.

The final branch of accounting is **accounting systems.** Accounting systems personnel review the information systems of hospitality organizations. Information systems include not only the accounting system but other elements such as reservations. Because many hospitality operations are now computerized, many accounting systems experts are electronic-data-processing specialists, such as programmers and systems analysts. The trend toward larger accounting systems staffs in hospitality organizations continues as the information revolution continues into the twenty-first century.

Organizations Influencing Accounting

Several organizations have influenced the accounting practices used in the hospitality industry. Most have affected accounting in general, while Hospitality Financial and Technology Professionals is hospitality specific. Each organization has contributed in a different way.

The *American Institute of Certified Public Accountants (AICPA)* consists *only* of certified public accountants (CPAs). It was the dominant organization in the development of accounting standards in the United States through 1973. Its Committee of Accounting Procedure issued 51 *Accounting Research Bulletins* recommending generally accepted accounting principles (often referred to by the acronym *GAAP*). The Committee of Accounting Procedure's successor, the Accounting Principles Board (APB), issued 31 Opinions from 1959 to 1973 that established GAAP. In addition, the AICPA influences accounting development through its research division and other committees.

The *Financial Accounting Standards Board (FASB)* replaced the APB in 1973 as an independent, seven-member, full-time board to issue statements on financial accounting standards (principles). The FASB is the major influence in the private sector in the development of these standards, and it was this board that required the recently mandated statement of cash flows.

The *Securities and Exchange Commission (SEC)* was created by Congress when it passed the *Securities and Exchange Act of 1934*. It administers laws dealing with the interstate sale of stocks and bonds. The SEC has been empowered by Congress to prescribe accounting principles for U.S. companies whose capital stock or bonds are sold publicly. For all practical purposes, this involves most major hospitality lodging and food service companies. Even though the SEC has the authority to develop accounting standards for publicly listed companies, it works closely with the FASB, generally adopting the FASB standards as appropriate to companies under its jurisdiction.

The *Internal Revenue Service (IRS)* is the federal government agency charged with enforcing federal tax laws. Many *smaller* companies generally keep their records on an accounting basis that facilitates the preparation of their tax returns. Therefore, the IRS has indirectly influenced their accounting practices. Larger companies in essence keep two sets of books: one that follows GAAP and another that follows the Internal Revenue code.

Hospitality Financial and Technology Professionals (HFTP), formerly known as the *International Association of Hospitality Accountants (IAHA)*, consists primarily of financial executives of hospitality companies. Its major purpose is to enhance financial management and technology in the hospitality industry. HFTP's professional certifications are the Certified Hotel Account Executive (CHAE) and the

Certified Hotel Technology Professional (CHTP).[2] HFTP is responsible for developing and upgrading the *Uniform System of Accounts for the Lodging Industry*, which is published by the Educational Institute of the American Hotel & Lodging Association in conjunction with the Hotel Association of New York City.

Forms of Business Organization

A business organization, generally referred to as a *business entity*, is any business existing separately from its owners. A diner, a motel, and a travel agency may be small businesses, but they are separate businesses and must be accounted for separately from the records of their owners. For example, assume the fictitious Barbara Collins owns a 30-unit lodging property. She may drive her car to and from her motel; however, her car is her personal asset. Assume her motel has a van to provide transportation service for its guests. The van is equipment belonging to the motel and should be properly accounted for by the business, not by the owner of the business.

There are four basic forms of business organization: sole proprietorships, partnerships, limited liability companies, and corporations. There are also some hybrid forms, such as limited partnerships and S corporations. Each is discussed briefly in the following sections.

Sole Proprietorships

In terms of sheer numbers, the **sole proprietorship** form of business organization is the most frequently encountered in the hospitality industry. However, revenues from corporate lodging businesses total nearly two-thirds of the lodging revenue across the United States.[3]

As the name implies, a sole proprietorship is a business owned by a single individual who generally (but not necessarily) manages the business. Its popularity stems from the ease with which it is formed. Establishing a sole proprietorship may simply require filing an assumed business name statement with the proper authorities, such as the county government.

From a legal viewpoint, the owner of a sole proprietorship is not separable from the business and is held legally responsible for all debts of the business. For accounting purposes, the business is a separate business entity.

The owner of a sole proprietorship is not paid a salary or wage by the business, but simply withdraws cash from it. These withdrawals are not considered an expense of the business, nor are they deductible for tax purposes. The business does not pay income taxes, but the income or loss from the business is reported on the owner's personal income tax return.

Furthermore, medical insurance and other fringe benefits are deductible for tax purposes only if they benefit employees. Since the owner is not an employee, any payments made by the business to benefit the owner are accounted for as withdrawals by the owner.

In addition to the nondeductibility of benefits, disadvantages include unlimited liability of the owner for the debts of the business, and the difficulty the owner may have in raising large amounts of cash for use by the business.

The sole proprietorship may be an ideal form of organization if the anticipated risk is minimal and is covered by insurance, if the owner is either unable or unwilling to maintain the necessary organizational documents and tax returns of more complicated business entities, and if the business does not require extensive borrowing.

Partnerships

A **partnership** is a business owned by two or more people joined together in a non-corporate manner for the purpose of operating a business. Partnerships are created by either oral or written agreement. The written agreement is better because it provides a permanent record of the terms of the partnership. The written agreement should include the duties and initial investment of each partner, and the sharing of profits and losses. Each partner is responsible for the debts of the partnership and the actions of other partners acting within the scope of the business.

The advantages of a partnership are as follows:

1. Greater financial strength is provided since there is more than one owner. The added capital can provide greater resources for expansion of the business.

2. Businesses organized as partnerships do not pay any income taxes. Income or losses from the business are distributed to the partners according to the partnership agreement. The owners then include the income or losses on their own personal tax returns.

Major disadvantages of the partnership form of operation are as follows:

1. Partners are taxed on their share of the profits regardless of whether cash is distributed to them.

2. Partners may become frustrated in sharing the decision-making process, which can prove cumbersome. Partners may hold different opinions, and, theoretically, each has an equal right to manage the business.

3. Partners generally have unlimited legal liability for obligations of the business. This can be a significant factor where uninsurable business risks exist. This disadvantage may be partially overcome within the partnership form by the use of a limited-partnership form of organization.

Limited Partnerships

A **limited partnership** is a form of partnership that offers the protection of limited liability to its **limited partners.** In order to have limited liability, limited partners may not actively participate in managing the business. In addition to at least one limited partner, a limited partnership must have at least one **general partner** who is responsible for the debts of the partnership—that is, the general partner has unlimited liability. Unlike a general partnership agreement, which can be oral, the limited partnership must be in writing, and the certificate of limited partnership must be filed with the proper government authorities. Most states regulate the public sale of limited partnership interests. Furthermore, public offerings must be filed with the Securities and Exchange Commission; thus, sizable legal fees may be incurred. Smaller private issues generally seek an exemption from registration.

The major unique feature of limited partnerships is the limited liability afforded to limited partners. The extent of limited partners' liability is limited to their investments. However, to ensure limited liability, limited partners cannot actively participate in controlling or managing the hospitality business.

In recent years, the limited partnership has become an attractive financing vehicle for the expansion of hospitality operations. Limited partnerships have been formed for specific projects, with the hospitality establishment acting as the general partner and investors as the limited partners. Thus, the use of the limited partnership enables the hospitality establishment to obtain needed capital and still maintain control over operations.

The basic tax advantages available to general partners are also available to limited partners. Nontax advantages include limited liability and the fact that, within certain limits, the limited partners' interests may be transferred to others without prior approval of the general partners. The latter option is available only to limited partners, not to general partners.

Limited Liability Companies

A **limited liability company (LLC)** is a relatively new form of business organization. The LLC has been gaining in popularity because it combines the corporate feature of limited liability with the favorable tax treatment of partnerships and sole proprietorships. The LLC, unlike the S corporation, may have an unlimited number of owners (who are referred to as *members*) and is not restricted to one class of stock. Further, the members are not restricted to individuals and may include such nonindividuals as corporations. Unlike a partnership, the LLC may have a single owner.

Corporations

A **corporation** is a legal entity created by a state or another political authority. The corporation receives a charter or articles of incorporation and has the following general characteristics:

1. An exclusive name
2. Continued existence independent of its stockholders
3. Paid-in capital represented by transferable shares of capital stock
4. Limited liability for its owners
5. Overall control vested in its directors

While hospitality businesses organized as sole proprietorships account for the largest number of businesses, hospitality corporations account for the greatest volume in terms of sales, assets, profits, and employees. Several hospitality corporations, such as Holiday Corporation, Marriott Corporation, and McDonald's Corporation, have annual sales in excess of $2 billion.

The major advantages of the corporate form over other forms of business organization include the following:

1. Its shareholders' liability is normally limited to their investment.

2. Owners are taxed only on distributed profits.

3. Employees can be motivated by equity participation, such as stock bonus plans and stock options, and by certain tax-favored fringe benefits.

4. Equity capital can be raised by selling capital stock to the public.

5. Tax rates are generally lower for small corporations than they are for individuals.

6. The corporation's life continues irrespective of the owners' lives.

As with other forms of business organization, there are disadvantages of the corporate form. The major disadvantage is **double taxation,** which means that corporate profits are taxed twice. First, they are taxed on the corporation's own income. Then, any profits paid out as dividends are considered taxable income to the individual stockholders.

In addition, with many corporations, stock is sold to new but unknown stockholders. If these stockholders are able to buy a sufficient quantity of stock, the original owners may lose control of their business. Of course, this can be precluded by maintaining more than 50 percent ownership of the corporation's stock.

S Corporations

Double taxation, a major drawback of the corporate form of operation, can be overcome if the corporation files as an **S corporation** for tax purposes. In essence, this allows the corporation to be taxed like a partnership.

The philosophy behind the S corporation provisions of the Internal Revenue Code is that a firm should be able to select its form of organization free of tax considerations. The S corporation is a hybrid form allowing limited liability for owners but avoiding the corporate "curse" of double taxation.

To qualify as an S corporation, the corporation must meet several tests, including, but not limited to (1) having 100 or fewer stockholders and (2) having only one class of stock.

This form of organization can be very useful when corporate losses are anticipated and owners have taxable income that can absorb the losses. It can also be very useful when corporations are profitable without having uses for extra capital that may be taxed on accumulated earnings. Since profits are passed through to stockholders, they are not taxed as accumulated earnings.

The Accounting Function in the Hospitality Industry ———

The accounting function in hospitality industry properties is provided by a group of specialists ranging from bookkeepers to executives with such titles as Executive Vice President and Controller (or Comptroller). Chief accounting executives are

Exhibit 1   Responsibilities of Hotel Controllers

Area	Percentage Reporting Responsibility
Accounts Receivable	100%
Accounts Payable	99
Payroll	95
Night Auditors	94
Cash Management	86
Food Controls	78
Cashiers	77
Computer System—Accounting	77
Purchasing	77
Receiving	66
Storage	66
Computer System—Front Office/Reservations	65
Tax Returns	61
Internal Auditors	46
Investments	40
Risk Management	37
Security	25

Source: A. Neal Geller, Charles Ilvento, and Raymond S. Schmidgall, "The Hotel Controller: Revisited," *The Cornell Hotel and Restaurant Administration Quarterly,* November 1990, p. 94.

responsible for typical accounting functions such as receivables, payables, payroll, and, in some cases, storage and security. Exhibit 1 summarizes a survey of 319 hotel *property* (as opposed to *corporate*) controllers and shows a wide range of reported responsibilities. Exhibit 2 shows the responsibilities of club controllers.

The sizes of accounting staffs may vary widely, from one part-time bookkeeper in a small ten-room motel to several hundred people in a large hotel or restaurant chain. For example, the accounting staff at a certain major worldwide hotel firm totals approximately 190, while the corporate accounting staff (accounts payable, payroll, internal audit, tax, etc.) at a major food service corporation's headquarters totals 138. A large hotel corporation's accounting staff covers many areas, as reflected by the sample organization chart in Exhibit 3.

The size of the accounting staff at an individual property depends on the size and diversity of the hotel's operations. The accounting staff at hotels with more than 1,000 rooms ranges from 30 to 50 people, consisting of personnel ranging from receiving clerks to the hotel controller. Exhibit 4 is a sample organization chart for the accounting function at a large hotel.

The accounting function within a lodging property is information oriented; that is, its major role is providing information to users. For external users such as financial institutions, accounting usually communicates through financial statements. Internally, accounting provides a wide variety of financial reports, including

Exhibit 2   Responsibilities of Club Controllers

Area	Percentage Reporting Responsibility
General Accounting	99.0%
Computer System—Accounting	98.5
Accounts Payable	98.5
Accounts Receivable	98.0
Payroll	97.5
Cash Management	91.5
Computer System—Club Operations	80.9
Human Resources	79.9
Tax Returns	78.4
Club Security	75.9
Investments	68.8
Food Controls	49.7
Beverage Controls	48.2
Risk Management	43.7
Purchasing	43.2
Cashiers	35.2
Receiving	26.1
Storage	25.6
Income Auditors	24.1
Internal Auditors	24.1
Night Auditors	12.1

Source: Raymond S. Schmidgall and Ronald F. Cichy, "Club Controller Requirements: Skills, Knowledge, and Responsibilities," *The Bottomline*, December/January 1998, pp. 15–18.

operating statements. Exhibit 5 lists various management reports generally prepared by accounting department personnel. The operating statements are formatted to reflect revenues and related expenses according to areas of responsibility. In addition to reports on the income of the property as a whole, statements are prepared for each department that generates revenues and incurs expenses, such as rooms, food and beverage, and telecommunications. The accounting department also prepares separate statements for service centers such as marketing and property operation and maintenance.

Regardless of the size of an operation's accounting department, the diversity of its responsibilities, or the number and types of reports produced, the accounting staff is responsible for providing *service*. The accounting staff must work closely with operating management and other service departments if the hospitality property is to meet its objectives.

Exhibit 3   Sample Organization Chart for Large Corporate Accounting Staff

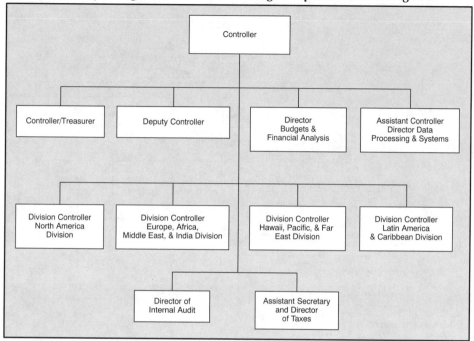

Principles of Accounting

In order to understand accounting methods, you must understand basic accounting principles. These generally accepted accounting principles provide a uniform basis for preparing financial statements. Although not "etched in stone" by boards of accountants, accounting principles have become accepted over time through common usage and also through the work of such major accounting bodies as the American Institute of Certified Public Accountants, the American Accounting Association, and the Financial Accounting Standards Board (FASB).

Students of hospitality accounting may wonder why an accounting transaction is recorded in a particular way at a particular time or why some asset value is not changed at some point. Generally, the reasons relate to accounting principles. For example, a fixed asset may have cost $10,000 but may have a suggested value per the manufacturer's catalog of $12,000. The cost principle dictates that the fixed asset be recorded on the books at its cost of $10,000 rather than at the suggested value of $12,000. A second example is the accrual of payroll at the end of the month. Assume that employees have worked the last few days of the month and that the next pay date falls in the following month. The matching principle dictates that the unpaid payroll for the period be recognized both as an expense during the current accounting period and as a liability.

The following sections briefly discuss several generally accepted accounting principles.

Exhibit 4   Controller's Department Organization Chart

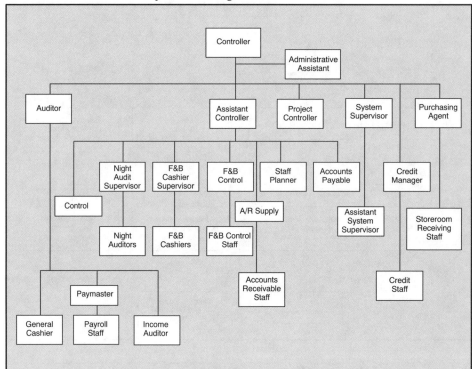

Cost

The **cost principle** states that when a transaction is recorded, it is the transaction price (cost) that establishes the accounting value for the product or service purchased. For example, if a restaurateur buys a dishwasher, the agreed-upon price between the restaurant and the supplier determines the amount to be recorded. If the agreed-upon price is $5,000, the dishwasher is initially valued at $5,000 in the restaurant's accounting records. The supplier may have acquired the dishwasher from the manufacturer for $4,000 and the restaurant may receive an offer of $5,500 for it the day it is purchased; however, it is the cost that establishes the amount to be recorded. If amounts other than cost (such as estimates or appraisals) were used to record transactions, accounting records would lose their usefulness. When cost is the basis for recording a transaction, the buyer and seller determine the amount to be recorded. This amount is generally an objective and fair measure of the value of the goods or services purchased.

When the value of a *current* asset is clearly less than the cost recorded on the books, it is acceptable to recognize this decline in value. Thus, the *conservatism principle* (to be discussed later in this chapter) overrides the cost principle. For example, many properties carry inventory at the *lower* of cost or current market value. On the other hand, property and equipment (also frequently called *fixed*

Exhibit 5   Management Reports

Report	Frequency	Content	Comparisons	Who Gets It	Purpose
Daily Reports of Operations	Daily, on a cumulative basis for the month, the year to date.	Occupancy, average rate, revenue by outlet, and pertinent statistics.	To operating plan for current period and to prior year results.	Top management and supervisors responsible for day-today operation.	Basis for evaluating the current health of the enterprise.
Weekly Forecasts	Weekly.	Volume in covers, occupancy.	Previous periods.	Top management and supervisory personnel.	Staffing and scheduling; promotion.
Summary Report-Flash	Monthly at end of month (prior to monthly financial statement).	Known elements of revenue and direct costs; estimated departmental indirect costs.	To operating plan; to prior year results.	Top management and supervisory personnel responsible for function reported.	Provides immediate information on financial results for rooms, food and beverages, and other.
Cash Flow Analysis	Monthly (and on a revolving 12-month basis).	Receipts and disbursements by time periods.	With cash flow plan for month and for year to date.	Top management.	Predicts availability of cash for operating needs. Provides information on interim financing requirements.
Labor Productivity Analysis	Daily, weekly, monthly.	Dollar cost; manpower hours expended; hours as related to sales and services (covers, rooms occupied, etc.).	To committed hours in the operating plan (standards for amount of work); and to prior year statistics.	Top management and supervisory personnel.	Labor cost control through informed staffing and scheduling. Helps refine forecasting.
Departmental Analysis	Monthly (early in following month).	Details on main categories of income; same on expense.	To operating plan (month and year to date) and to prior year.	Top management and supervisors by function (e.g., rooms, each food and beverage outlet, laundry, telephone, other profit centers).	Knowing where business stands, and immediate corrective actions.
Room Rate Analysis	Daily, monthly, year to date.	Actual rates compared to rack rates by rate category or type of room.	To operating plan and to prior year results.	Top management and supervisors of sales and front office operations.	If goal is not being achieved, analysis of strengths and weaknesses is prompted.
Return on Investment	Actual computation, at least twice a year. Computation based on forecast, immediately prior to plan for year ahead.	Earnings as a percentage rate of return on average investment or equity committed.	To plan for operation and to prior periods.	Top management.	If goal is not being achieved, prompt assessment of strengths and weaknesses.
Long-Range Planning	Annually.	5-year projections of revenue and expenses. Operating plan expressed in financial terms.	Prior years.	Top management.	Involves staff in success or failure of enterprise. Injects more realism into plans for property and service modifications.
Exception Reporting	Concurrent with monthly reports and financial statements.	Summary listing of line item variances from predetermined norm.	With operating budgets.	Top management and supervisors responsible for function reported.	Immediate focusing on problem before more detailed statement analysis can be made.
Guest History Analysis	At least semi-annually; quarterly or monthly is recommended.	Historical records of corporate business, travel agencies, group bookings.	With previous reports.	Top management and sales.	Gives direction to marketing efforts.
Future Bookings Report	Monthly.	Analysis of reservations and bookings.	With several prior years.	Top management, sales and marketing, department management.	Provides information on changing guest profile. Exposes strong and weak points of facility. Guides (1) sales planning and (2) expansion plans.

Source: *Lodging,* July 1979, pp. 40–41.

assets) normally are carried at cost less the depreciated amounts and are not reduced to market value as long as management plans to retain them for their useful lives. This treatment of property and equipment is based on the *going-concern principle* (also discussed later in this chapter).

Business Entity

Accounting and financial statements are based on the concepts that (1) each business is a **business entity** that maintains its own set of accounts, and (2) these accounts are separate from the other financial interests of the owners. For example, if a hotel owner decides to take some food home from the hotel for personal use, it should be properly charged to the owner's account. Recording a business activity separately from the owner's personal affairs allows a reasonable determination of the property's profitability. Not only does separate recording provide excellent information for managing the business, it is also necessary for properly filing tax returns. Whether the hospitality business is organized as a sole proprietorship, partnership, or corporation, separate tax forms or portions of forms must be filed for the business.

Continuity of the Business Unit (Going Concern)

According to the **continuity of the business unit principle**, in preparing the accounting records and reports, it is assumed that the business will continue indefinitely and that liquidation is not a prospect—in other words, that the business is a **going concern**. This assumption is based on the concept that the real value of the hotel or motel is its ability to earn a profit, rather than the value its assets would bring in liquidation. According to this concept, the market value of the property and equipment need not appear on the financial statements, and prepaid expenses are considered assets. If there is a reasonable chance the hospitality property may be unable to continue operations in the near future, allowance for this future event should be reflected in the financial statements. This may be best accomplished by reducing asset values to their market values.

Unit of Measurement

The financial statements are based on transactions expressed in monetary terms. Thus, in the United States, the **unit of measurement** is the U.S. dollar. The monetary unit is assumed to represent a stable unit of value so that transactions from past periods and the current period can be included on the same statement. However, there have been significant changes in price levels in the United States in recent years, and the dollar is not as stable as it has been in the past.

In the late 1970s and early 1980s, inflation, as measured by the Consumer Price Index, exceeded 10 percent. The FASB responded by requiring large hospitality firms to show current replacement costs of their property and equipment in footnotes to their financial statements. For some lodging properties, the current values of property and equipment exceeded twice the amount of the fixed assets carried on the books. Since inflation has been relatively low for the past few years, the FASB has rescinded this reporting requirement.

Exhibit 6   Types of Disclosure and Examples

Type of Disclosure	Example
Accounting methods used	Straight-line method of depreciation
Change in the accounting methods	A change from depreciating a fixed asset using the straight-line method to using the double declining balance method
Contingent liability	A lawsuit against the company for alleged failure to provide adequate security for a guest who suffered personal injury
Events occurring after the financial statement date	A fire destroys significant uninsured assets of the hotel company one week after the end of the year
Unusual and nonrecurring items	A hotel firm in Michigan suffers significant losses due to an earthquake

Objective Evidence

Accounting transactions and the resulting accounting records should be based as much as possible on **objective evidence.** Generally this evidence is an invoice or a canceled check. However, estimates must be assumed in the absence of such objective evidence. For example, suppose that the owner of a restaurant contributes equipment, purchased several years ago for personal use, to a restaurant corporation in exchange for 100 shares of stock. Further assume that there is no known market value for the restaurant corporation's stock. The owner may believe the equipment is worth $1,000, while the original catalog shows the cost several years ago of $1,400, and an appraiser appraises the equipment at $850. In this example, the most objective estimate of its value today would be the appraiser's estimate of $850.

Full Disclosure

The financial statements must provide information on all the facts pertinent to the interpretation of the financial statements. This **full disclosure** is accomplished either by reporting the information in the body of the financial statements or in the footnotes to the financial statements. Footnote disclosures might include the accounting methods used, changes in the accounting methods, contingent liabilities, events occurring after the financial statement date, and unusual and nonrecurring items. An example of each type of disclosure is presented in Exhibit 6.

Consistency

Several accounting methods are often available for reporting a specific kind of activity. Management selects the method most appropriate under the circumstances. For example, there are several ways to determine inventory values, and there are several methods of depreciating fixed assets. The **consistency principle** requires that once an accounting method has been adopted, it should be followed from period to period unless a change is warranted and disclosed. The consistency principle allows a user of financial information to make reasonable comparisons between periods. Without consistent accounting, trends indicated by supposedly comparable financial statements might be misleading. When it becomes necessary to change to another method, the change must be disclosed and the dollar effect on earnings or on the balance sheet must be reported.

The consistency principle does *not* dictate that a hospitality operation must or even should use the same accounting methods for preparing tax returns that it uses for preparing financial statements for external users. The principle does not even require that a method selected for one element of a company be used for all similar elements. For example, the straight-line method of depreciation may be used to depreciate one hotel, and an accelerated method of depreciation may be used to depreciate another hotel owned by the same company.

Matching

The **matching principle** refers to relating expenses to revenues. For example, suppose that a hotel purchases a computerized reservations system that will benefit the hotel for several years. The cost is therefore recorded as a fixed asset and the cost of the system is written off over the system's life. The result is a partial write-off of the cost of the fixed asset each year against the revenues generated in part by using the system. This process is referred to as *matching* and is the basis for adjusting entries at the end of each accounting period. The matching principle is used when transactions are recorded on an accrual basis rather than a cash basis. The accrual basis and cash basis of accounting are discussed later in this chapter.

Conservatism

The **conservatism principle** calls for recognizing expenses as soon as possible, but delaying the recognition of revenues until they are ensured. The practical result is to be conservative (low) in recognizing net income in the current year. It is not proper to deliberately understate net income; however, many accountants wish to be cautious in recognizing revenues and "generous" in recognizing expenses.

A good example of this is the accounting treatment of lawsuits. If a hotel is a plaintiff in a lawsuit and its legal counsel indicates the case will be won and estimates the amount of settlement, the amount is not recorded as revenue until a judgment is rendered. On the other hand, if the same hotel is a defendant in a lawsuit and its legal counsel indicates the hotel will lose the lawsuit and most likely will pay a stated amount, the "expense" should be recognized immediately.

Conservatism is apparent in the valuation of inventory at the lower of cost or current market value and the recognition of nonrefundable deposits for future banquets as a liability until the banquet is catered.

Materiality

According to the **materiality principle,** events or information must be accounted for if they "make a difference" to the user of the financial information. An item is material in comparison to a standard. Some accountants have attempted to establish materiality by rules of thumb; for example, an item must be recognized if it exceeds a certain percentage of total assets or total income. However, this approach fails to address an item's relative importance over time. In addition, several immaterial items may be material when viewed collectively.

The materiality principle is often applied to fixed assets. Tangible items with useful lives beyond one year are commonly recorded as fixed assets. However, when such items cost less than a certain amount (specified by the board of directors of the purchasing organization), they are expensed because the cost is considered immaterial. An example would be a wastebasket. A $39 wastebasket might have a useful life of ten years, but since it costs less than the (for example) $100 limit for recording expenditures as fixed assets, it is expensed. In this case, the expenditure was immaterial to record as a fixed asset.

When a hospitality property provides footnotes to supplement the body of its financial statement, only material or potentially material items are presented.

Overview of Financial Statements

Hospitality enterprises often have several objectives, such as being profitable, being a leader in the marketplace, and growing in size, as in adding more restaurants or lodging operations. However, three basic objectives of every hospitality business are solvency, profitability, and having a positive cash flow. *Solvency* is the ability to pay debts on time, which is reflected in part by the enterprise's balance sheet. *Profitability* is the ability to generate net income, which is shown on a firm's income statement. *Cash* is used to pay the firm's bills as they come due. The cash flow of the hospitality enterprise is shown on the statement of cash flows.

Balance Sheet

The **balance sheet** is also called the *statement of financial position*, because it reflects the financial position at a point in time. The balance sheet consists of things the business owns, called **assets,** and claims to those assets, called *liabilities* and *equities*. Assets include cash and equipment used in the business. The claims to assets by parties external to the business are called **liabilities,** while claims by owners are referred to in general terms as **owners' equity.**

To illustrate the relationships among assets, liabilities, and owners' equity, consider Kathy's Catering Service. Kathy Spring purchased a van for the business, paying $3,000 cash and financing the remaining amount of $12,000 with a loan from the bank. Further, she purchased service equipment for the company for $500. The balance sheet for Kathy's Catering Service would show assets of $15,500

Exhibit 7   Sample Simplified Balance Sheet

Kathy's Catering Service
Balance Sheet
December 31, 20X1

ASSETS

Cash	$ 1,000
Accounts receivable	2,000
Van	15,000
Equipment	500
Total Assets	**$18,500**

LIABILITIES AND OWNER'S EQUITY

Liabilities:	
Accounts payable	$ 2,000
Notes payable	12,000
Total Liabilities	14,000
Owner's Equity	
Kathy Spring, Capital	4,500
Total Liabilities and Owner's Equity	**$18,500**

(van, $15,000; equipment, $500), liabilities for $12,000 (the amount the business owes the bank), and owner's equity of $3,500 (the amount Kathy has invested in her business).

All financial statements have headings that include (1) the name of the hospitality business, (2) the title of the financial statement, and (3) the date of, or period covered by, the financial statement. Exhibit 7 is a simplified balance sheet for Kathy's Catering Service at the end of its first year of operation. Assets consist of cash of $1,000, accounts receivable (amounts due from customers for services provided) of $2,000, the van at its cost of $15,000, and service equipment that cost $500. Liabilities consist of accounts payable (amounts due to suppliers of food and operating supplies) of $2,000, and the notes payable due the bank of $12,000. Owner's equity consists of $4,500. This is calculated by subtracting total liabilities of $14,000 from the total assets of $18,500 to equal $4,500.

The balance sheet of Kathy's Catering Service reflects the financial position on December 31, 20X1. However, the balance sheet does not reflect the enterprise's profitability or its cash flow for 20X1. These will be shown on the income statement and the statement of cash flows, respectively.

Income Statement

The **income statement** shows the results of operations (that is, revenues and expenses) for a period of time. The period of time covered by the income statement usually ends at the date of the balance sheet. The income statement is generally

Exhibit 8   Sample Simplified Income Statement

Kathy's Catering Service
Income Statement
For the year ended December 31, 20X1

Revenues:
Catering services $120,000

Expenses:
Cost of food	$36,000	
Wages	75,000	
Other operating expenses	8,000	
Total expenses		119,000

Net Income $ 1,000

Note: This is a simplified income statement, since neither depreciation expense nor interest on the notes payable with the bank
are shown.

prepared monthly for management's purposes and generally less frequently for outside users. For example, the information in the income statement is provided annually to the Internal Revenue Service. The income statement has various other names, such as the *earnings statement, profit and loss statement (P&L)*, and *statement of income and expenses.*

The income statement shows both revenues and expenses of the hospitality enterprise for a period of time. **Revenue** is an inflow of assets (such as cash) resulting from the sale of goods or services to customers, while an **expense** is the use of assets to produce revenues. When revenues exceed expenses for a period of time, the hospitality enterprise earns a profit commonly referred to as *net income.* If expenses exceed revenues, a net loss is incurred.

Exhibit 8 shows the income statement for Kathy's Catering Service for the year ended December 31, 20X1. The income reflects catering revenue of $120,000 and expenses of $119,000, resulting in net income of $1,000.

The net income of $1,000 is added to the amount of Kathy's original investment of $3,500 to equal owner's equity of $4,500, as shown on the balance sheet. This process is called the *closing process.*

The income statement reflects the profitability of a hospitality business. However, the cash flows of Kathy's Catering Service are not shown on either the balance sheet or the income statement, so we proceed to the statement of cash flows.

Statement of Cash Flows

The **statement of cash flows (SCF)** reflects the cash inflows and outflows for a period of time. Cash inflows come from a number of sources, such as cash sales, collection of accounts receivable, infusions of cash from owners, and bank loans. Cash outflows result from the purchase of equipment, the payment of wages, the

Exhibit 9   Sample Statement of Cash Flows

Kathy's Catering Service
Statement of Cash Flows
For the year ended December 31, 20X1

Cash inflows:		
Invested by owner		$ 3,500
Proceeds from bank loan		12,000
Cash sales		118,000
Total cash inflows		133,500
Cash outflows:		
Purchase of van	$15,000	
Purchase of service equipment	500	
Payment for food	34,000	
Payment of wages	75,000	
Payment of operating expenses	8,000	
Total cash outflows		132,500
Increase in cash		$ 1,000

purchase of food, and so on. When cash inflows exceed cash outflows for the period, the result is an increase in cash flow. When cash outflows exceed cash inflows for the period, there is a decrease in cash flow.

Exhibit 9 shows a simplified statement of cash flows for Kathy's Catering Service. Cash inflows of $133,500 come from Kathy's investment of $3,500, proceeds from the bank loan of $12,000, and cash sales of $118,000. (The cash sales from customers is the net result of $120,000 of sales and accounts receivable of $2,000.)

Cash outflows of $132,500 include the purchase of the van for $15,000 (cash of $3,000 and the notes payable of $12,000), purchase of service equipment of $500, the payment of $34,000 for food (which is the cost of food sold of $36,000 less the $2,000 owed suppliers and shown on the balance sheet as accounts payable), payment of wages of $75,000, and payment of other operating expenses of $8,000.

The SCF shows the cash flow for the period. Remember, bills are paid with cash, not with profits. Hospitality enterprises often have cash flows that are different from their net incomes as shown on their income statements.

The balance sheet, the income statement, and the SCF are the three major financial statements prepared periodically by hospitality enterprises. A key to excellent communication is to provide this information in sufficient detail to be useful to the reader of the financial statements.

Cash versus Accrual Accounting

The cash and accrual bases of accounting are two methods of determining when to record a transaction.

Cash basis accounting recognizes an accounting transaction at the point of cash inflow or outflow. For example, cash received in 20X2 for rooms sold in 20X1 would be treated as 20X2 revenues. Likewise, expenses incurred in 20X1 for which cash was disbursed in 20X2 would be treated as 20X2 expenses. Because of these improper assignments of revenues and expenses, cash basis accounting is generally not a fair reflection of business operations. Cash basis accounting usually violates the generally accepted accounting principles discussed earlier. However, using this method is acceptable if the results do not differ materially from those that accrual basis accounting would produce. Although cash basis accounting is the simpler of the two methods, its use is generally limited to very small hospitality operations where the owner is also the manager.

The more commonly used **accrual basis accounting** recognizes all revenues according to the accounting period in which they were earned, and, similarly, records all expenses incurred to earn the revenues in that same period. Since revenues earned, whether or not they have been received, and expenses incurred, whether or not they have been paid for, are all recognized within the accounting period, expenses are matched with revenues. At the close of any accounting period, accrual basis accounting allows a more meaningful evaluation of the business's operation because it matches expenses with revenue.

Under accrual basis accounting, procedures must be set up to record all transactions relating to a particular time period during that same period. For instance, a telephone bill for June may arrive late in July, yet the expense must be recognized in June, when it actually occurred. Another problem is that some expenses, such as payroll, do not exactly match the accounting period. Payrolls are paid periodically on a certain day of the week. Only occasionally would that date correspond to the end of the accounting period. It is necessary, therefore, to adjust payroll costs to the accounting period.

Other kinds of transactions receive special treatment under accrual basis accounting. Purchases of furniture and equipment are not considered expenses only of the period in which they were purchased. Instead, a pro rata share of the cost in the form of depreciation expense is charged to each accounting period during the useful life of long-lived purchases. Inventory purchase transactions are another example. Only when the inventory is sold does it become a cost in determining operating performance. Calculation of the cost of goods sold involves beginning and ending inventories plus purchases. For example, $2,000 of beginning food inventory plus $10,000 of food purchases during the accounting period less $2,500 of ending food inventory equals cost of food sold of $9,500.

Accrual basis accounting requires a number of **adjusting entries** at the end of each accounting period. Once the adjusting entries have been recorded, the income and expense for the period will provide a reasonable basis for measuring the business's financial and operating progress.

The Fundamental Accounting Equation

In accounting, a business's properties are called its *assets,* and ownership rights to these assets are called *equities.* Therefore, assets must equal equities. For example, if Kathy Spring establishes a catering business separate from her personal effects and invests $3,500 in it, the business, Kathy's Catering Service, will show assets of $3,500 and equities of $3,500. In this case, the assets of $3,500 are cash, and the equities of $3,500 are the ownership rights to assets. The accounting value of the ownership rights of the proprietor in the assets of the business enterprise is commonly shown under the name of the proprietor followed by the word *Capital*, as shown below.

ASSETS	=	EQUITIES
Cash, $3,500	=	Kathy Spring, Capital, $3,500

As Kathy Spring acquires assets such as a van and equipment for the business, she may find that she is unable to finance all the assets acquired with her personal resources. She will finance these additional assets by borrowing money from others and then purchasing the assets, or by buying the assets on account, that is, buying with a promise to pay at a later date. The businesspeople from whom Kathy Spring buys assets on account are known as *creditors*. The creditors of a business also have a claim to the assets of the business.

Assume that Kathy's Catering Service purchases a van for $15,000 for its catering business by paying $3,000 down and obtaining financing from First Bank for $12,000. Kathy signs a promissory note that indicates, among other things, the amount, the due date, and the interest rate. The accounting equation is now expanded.

ASSETS		=	LIABILITIES	+	OWNER'S EQUITY	
Cash	$ 500		$ —			
Van	15,000	Loan	12,000		Kathy Spring, Capital	$3,500
	$15,500	=	$12,000	+		$3,500

The accounting equation now shows that there are two types of claims on assets: the claims of the owner, Kathy Spring, and the claims of the creditor, First Bank. If Kathy Spring does not pay First Bank the amount due when required per the loan agreement, First Bank has the right to force sale of the van to secure its money.

The equation Assets = Liabilities + Owners' Equity is the **fundamental accounting equation** upon which all double-entry bookkeeping is based. The equation may be rearranged as:

Assets − Liabilities = Owners' Equity

Assets − Owners' Equity = Liabilities

The balance sheet, a basic financial statement that expresses the business's financial position at a point in time, is an expression of the basic accounting equation: Assets = Liabilities + Owners' Equity. The balance sheet for Kathy's Catering Service after the first two transactions would be:

Kathy's Catering Service
Balance Sheet

Assets		Liabilities & Owner's Equity	
Cash	$ 500	Notes payable	$12,000
Van	15,000	Kathy Spring, Capital	3,500
Total Assets	$15,500	Total Liabilities and Owner's Equity	$15,500

Before introducing more transactions and their effects on the accounting equation, let us define what we have so far. *Assets,* simply stated, are anything of value owned by a business. They include cash, investments, accounts receivable, food inventory, beverage inventory, buildings, equipment, prepaid insurance, and so forth.

Liabilities are obligations to pay money or other assets, or to render services, to an outside party (a person or a business enterprise) either now or in the future. Liabilities represent claims that nonowners have on the firm's assets. Liabilities include accounts payable, loans payable, wages payable, rent payable, unearned revenue, bonds payable, notes payable, and so on.

Owners' equity is the excess of assets over liabilities. The claims of the firm's owners to the firm's assets are represented by owners' equity. Owners' equity is also called *net worth* at times.

Equities, then, are all claims to assets. This term includes both liabilities (the claims of creditors), and owners' equity (the claims of the owner).

Effects of Transactions on the Accounting Equation

The previous discussion of the accounting equation included two transactions:

1. Kathy Spring, owner, invested $3,500 in the business.

2. She purchased a van for the business for $15,000 by paying $3,000 from the business and borrowing $12,000 from the First Bank.

Each transaction affects the elements of the accounting equation. As previously shown, assets were increased from $–0– to $3,500 when the proprietor invested in the business. Further, assets were increased when the van was purchased. The effects of these two transactions on the accounting equation are shown again below. Note that the equation remains in balance after each transaction.

	ASSETS				LIABILITIES		OWNER'S EQUITY
	Cash	+	Van	=	Notes payable (First Bank)	+	Kathy Spring, Capital
(1)	$ 3,500		$ —		$ —		$3,500
(2)	– 3,000		15,000		12,000		—
	$ 500	+	$ 15,000	=	$ 12,000	+	$3,500

Then four more transactions followed:

3. The business purchased service equipment for $500 cash.

4. Kathy invested $2,000 more in the business.

5. The business purchased on account $200 worth of operating supplies from Gordon Food Service.

6. The business paid one month's rent of $1,000 on its office building.

The effects of these transactions are shown in Table I.

Table I

	Assets					=	Liabilities		+	Owner's Equity
Cash	+	Operating Supplies +	Prepaid Rent +	Equip- ment +	Van	=	Accounts Payable (Gordon Food Service) +	Notes Payable (First Bank)	+	Kathy Spring, Capital
(1) $3,500	$—	$—	$—	$—		$—	$—		$3,500
(2) – 3,000				15,000			12,000		
500				15,000			12,000		3,500
(3) – 500	—	—	500			—			
0			500	15,000			12,000		3,500
(4) 2,000	—	—				—			2,000
2,000			500	15,000			12,000		5,500
(5)	200	—				200			
2,000	200		500	15,000		200	12,000		5,500
(6) – 1,000		1,000							
$1,000 +	$200 +	$1,000 +	$500 +	$15,000	=	$200 +	$12,000 +		$5,500

Transaction 3 results in the exchange of one asset, Cash, for another asset, Equipment. Liabilities and owner's equity remain the same.

Transaction 4 increases an asset, Cash, and owner's equity.

Transaction 5 results in the increase of an asset, Operating Supplies, and the increase of a liability account, Accounts Payable.

Transaction 6 results in the increase of an asset, Prepaid Rent, and the decrease of an asset, Cash.

Kathy Spring's primary objective in investing her resources in the catering business is to increase her owner's equity by earning profits. She will accomplish this objective by selling food to customers. Profits will be earned only if the revenue from selling food is greater than the expenses incurred. To illustrate the effect of revenues and expenses on owner's equity, consider three additional transactions:

7. Kathy's Catering Service catered a dinner party for Walter Adams and received $800.

8. The business paid employees $300 to work on the dinner party.

9. The cost of food purchased for cash and used totaled $300.

The effects of these transactions on the accounting equation are found in Table II.

Table II

| | | | | | | = | Liabilities | | + | Owner's Equity |

	Cash	+	Operating Supplies +	Prepaid Rent +	Equip-ment +	Van	=	Accounts Payable (Gordon Food Service) +	Notes Payable (First Bank) +	Kathy Spring, Capital
(1)	$3,500		$—	$—	$—	$—		$—	$—	$3,500
(2) –	3,000		—	—	—	15,000		—	12,000	—
	500					15,000			12,000	3,500
(3) –	500				500					
	0				500	15,000			12,000	3,500
(4)	2,000		—					—		2,000
	2,000				500	15,000			12,000	5,500
(5)			200	—				200		
	2,000		200		500	15,000		200	12,000	5,500
(6) –	1,000			1,000						
	1,000		200	1,000	500	15,000		200	12,000	5,500
(7)	800									800
	1,800		200	1,000	500	15,000		200	12,000	6,300
(8) –	300									– 300
	1,500		200	1,000	500	15,000		200	12,000	6,000
(9) –	300									– 300
	$1,200	+	$ 200	+ $1,000 +	$ 500	+ $15,000	=	$ 200	+ $12,000 +	$5,700

$17,900

$17,900

Transaction 7 results in an increase in cash, an asset, of $800, and an increase in owner's equity of $800. The claim to the $800 received is by Kathy Spring, proprietor, since the $800 was paid for services rendered to the customer, Walter Adams. The $800 collected from the customer is known as a *revenue*. In this illustration, a **revenue** is an inflow of cash, accounts receivable, or other asset in exchange for food and services.

Transaction 8 is an example of an expense. This transaction results in an equal decrease of assets and owner's equity by $300. The $300 paid to employees for their services reduces cash and owner's equity by the same amount.

Transaction 9 is another example of an expense. In this illustration, $300 was paid for food used to cater the dinner party for Walter Adams. The result is a decrease in cash and a similar decrease in owner's equity. All expenses decrease owner's equity and either decrease assets or increase liabilities.

After Transaction 9, the assets of $17,900 equal the liabilities of $12,200 plus the owner's equity of $5,700. Thus, the accounting equation remains in balance after the nine transactions.

Summary

All types of business entities use accounting to "account" for their business activities. Accounting is the process of identifying, measuring, and communicating economic information to permit users of the information to make informed judgments and decisions. Accounting differs from bookkeeping in that accounting includes summarizing and interpreting information, while bookkeeping simply involves recording and classifying transactions.

There are several distinct yet overlapping branches of accounting. They are financial accounting, cost accounting, managerial accounting, tax accounting, auditing, and accounting systems.

Accounting is regulated and influenced by several different organizations. The Financial Accounting Standards Board (FASB) issues statements regarding generally accepted accounting procedures and financial statements. The Securities and Exchange Commission (SEC) and the Internal Revenue Service (IRS) administer various laws dealing with stock sales and income taxes, respectively. Hospitality Financial and Technology Professionals (HFTP) enhances accounting in the hospitality industry, and several of its members were members of the AH&LA's Finanacial Management Committee, which periodically updates the *Uniform System of Accounts for the Lodging Industry.*

Businesses can be organized in several different ways. The four major types are sole proprietorships, partnerships, limited liability companies, and corporations. There are also hybrid forms, such as S corporations and limited partnerships. Two major concerns when choosing a business form are the legal responsibility for the debts of the business and the method of taxation used.

In a hospitality firm, the accounting function is performed by several specialists who oversee many activities such as receivables, payables, and payroll. Sizes of accounting departments can vary considerably, depending on the sizes and degrees of complexity of their host organizations.

Generally accepted accounting principles are guidelines that help to keep all businesses' accounting records consistent. These are not laws but the basis for accounting methods. The principles include the cost principle, the matching principle, the business entity principle, the going concern principle, the unit of measurement principle, the objective evidence principle, the full disclosure principle, the consistency principle, the matching principle, the conservatism principle, and the materiality principle.

Three major financial statements required for most businesses are the balance sheet, the income statement, and the statement of cash flows. The balance sheet is a statement of financial position on a certain date. The balance sheet shows the relationship of the fundamental accounting equation. The fundamental accounting equation is the basis of all double-entry accounting. It states the relationship between assets of the business and the claims to those assets, namely liabilities and owners' equity. The equation is Assets = Liabilities + Owners' Equity.

The income statement is a statement of the revenues and expenses of a business over a certain period of time. The income statement is a statement of profitability, since the difference between revenues and expenses is net income or profit.

The statement of cash flows shows a business's cash inflows and outflows over a certain period of time. This statement differs from the income statement when accrual basis accounting is used rather than cash basis accounting. In accrual basis accounting, the revenues and expenses of a business are recognized when they are actually earned or incurred, rather than when actual cash inflow or outflow occurs. The statement of cash flows enables its users to know the various types of cash flows and related amounts.

Endnotes

1. *A Statement of Basic Accounting Theory* (Evanston, Ill.: American Accounting Association, 1966), p. 1.

2. The Educational Institute of the American Hotel & Lodging Association has developed a study guide used by candidates who are preparing to take the CHAE examination.

3. Albert Gomes, *Hospitality in Transition* (Houston, Texas: Pannell Kerr Forster, 1985), p. 92.

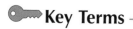

Key Terms

accounting—The process of identifying, measuring, and communicating economic information to permit users to make informed judgments and decisions.

accounting systems—The branch of accounting that covers the review of a firm's entire information system, not just the accounting system.

accrual basis accounting—System of reporting revenues and expenses in the period in which they are considered to have been earned or incurred, regardless of the actual time of collection or payment.

adjusting entries—Entries required at the end of an accounting period to record internal adjustments of various accounts due to the matching principle of accounting.

assets—Resources available for use by the business—that is, anything owned by the business that has monetary value.

auditing—The branch of accounting that examines a firm's financial statements and internal controls for the purpose of expressing opinions regarding the financial statements.

balance sheet—Statement of the financial position of the hospitality establishment on a given date, giving the account balances for assets, liabilities, and ownership equity.

bookkeeping—The recording and classification of transactions.

business entity principle—An accounting principle that requires that a business maintain its own set of records and accounts that are separate from other financial interests of its owners.

cash basis accounting—System of reporting revenues and expenses at the time they are collected or paid, respectively.

conservatism principle—An accounting principle that requires accounting procedures that recognize expenses as soon as possible, but delay the recognition of revenues until they are ensured. For example, nonrefundable deposits for future services should be recognized as liabilities until the service is actually performed.

consistency principle—An accounting principle that requires that once an accounting method has been adopted, it should be followed from period to period in the future unless a change in accounting methods is warranted and disclosed.

continuity of the business unit principle—The assumption in preparing the accounting records and reports that the business will continue indefinitely and that liquidation is not a prospect—in other words, that the business is a going concern.

corporation—A form of business organization that provides a separate legal entity apart from its owner or owners.

cost accounting—The branch of accounting dealing with the recording, classification, allocation, and reporting of current and prospective costs in order to aid operations personnel in controlling operations.

cost principle—An accounting principle that requires recording the value of transactions for accounting purposes at the actual transaction price (cost).

double taxation—This occurs when both corporate profits and dividends paid to stockholders are taxed.

expenses—Costs incurred in providing the goods and services offered.

financial accounting—A branch of accounting dealing with recording, classifying, and summarizing transactions involving revenues, expenses, assets, and liabilities.

financial audit—An independent, external audit.

full disclosure principle—An accounting principle that requires that a business's financial statements provide information on all the significant facts that have a bearing on their interpretation. Types of disclosures include the accounting methods used, changes in the accounting methods, contingent liabilities, events occurring subsequent to the financial statement date, and unusual and nonrecurring items.

fundamental accounting equation—The equation upon which all double-entry bookkeeping is based: Assets equal liabilities plus owners' equity. This equation is a balance to be tested and proven, not a formula to be calculated.

general partner—The member(s) of a limited partnership who has (have) unlimited liability for the debts of the partnership.

going concern principle—An accounting principle that requires the preparation of accounting records and reports under the assumption that the business will continue indefinitely and that liquidation is not a prospect; also referred to as *continuity of the business unit principle*.

income statement—A report on the profitability of operations, including revenues earned and expenses incurred in generating the revenues for the period of time covered by the statement.

liabilities—Claims to a business's assets by parties external to the business.

limited liability company—An unincorporated business entity that is not restricted to one class of stock and may have any number of owners. It combines the corporate feature of limited liability with the favorable tax treatment of partnerships and sole proprietorships.

limited partner—The member(s) of a limited partnership who has (have) limited liability. Limited partners may not actively participate in managing the business.

limited partnership—A partnership in which one or more of the partners have limited liability; that is, their liability is limited to the amount of their investment in the partnership and their personal assets are not vulnerable to their business's creditors. Every partnership must have at least one general partner, and there are several criteria that must be met in the case of a limited partnership.

managerial accounting—The branch of accounting that provides information to various management levels for the enhancement of controls, usually in the form of budgets.

matching principle—An accounting principle that requires that expenses and revenues be matched to the period in which they were incurred or earned regardless of when they are actually realized.

materiality principle—An accounting principle that states that only items that are "material" or that "make a difference" should be presented in financial statements. For example, materiality may be established by a rule of thumb that states that an item is recognized if it exceeds a certain percentage of total assets or income.

objective evidence principle—An accounting principle that states that all accounting transactions and the resulting accounting records should be based on objectively determined evidence to the greatest extent possible.

owners' equity—Financial interest of the owners of a business in that business—equal to assets minus liabilities.

partnership—An unincorporated business owned by two or more individuals. The partners co-own all the assets and liabilities of the business and share in some manner in its profits or losses.

revenues—Inflows of assets resulting from sales of goods or services to customers.

S corporation—A type of corporation in which profits are taxed in the same manner as those of a partnership; S corporations thus avoid double taxation.

sole proprietorship—An unincorporated business entity that is owned by a single individual.

statement of cash flows—A statement that reflects the cash inflows and outflows of a business for a period of time. It explains the change in cash by showing the effects on cash of a business's operating, investing, and financing activities for the accounting period.

tax accounting—The branch of accounting dealing with the preparation and filing of tax forms with the various governmental agencies.

unit of measurement principle—The accounting principle that requires financial data to be recorded with a common unit of measure. In the United States that common unit is the dollar.

Review Questions

1. How are bookkeeping and accounting different?
2. What are the various fields of accounting and how do they differ?
3. What are the major advantages and disadvantages of the corporate form of organization?
4. If a firm did not use the continuity of the business unit principle, what effect would this have on its financial statements?
5. Why should accountants adhere to the conservatism principle?
6. What are the differences among the three major financial statements?
7. How does cash basis accounting differ from accrual basis accounting?
8. How would *liabilities* be defined in terms of the basic accounting equation?
9. Why are footnote disclosures in financial statements necessary, and what forms do they take?
10. How do room sales transactions on account affect elements of the accounting equation?

Problems

Problem 1

Fill in the following blanks with the accounting principle that best applies.

a. Cost
b. Business Entity
c. Going Concern
d. Unity of Measurement
e. Objective Evidence

f. Full Disclosure
g. Consistency
h. Matching
i. Conservatism
j. Materiality

1. A fire occurred in your hotel during the previous year. The estimated loss due to a pending lawsuit is recorded because of the _____ principle.
2. You purchased a new dishwasher from Mike's Machines for $1,250, and, because of the _____ principle, it is recorded at $1,250, even though you could now sell it for $1,500.
3. Although the last biweekly pay period ended December 26, your employees have worked through the end of December. The unpaid salaries and wages are accrued as of December 31 because of the _____ principle.
4. Your firm is the defendant in a major lawsuit. Your attorney believes you may lose. Although the attorney is unable to estimate the potential loss, the lawsuit is briefly mentioned in a footnote to the financial statements because of the _____ principle.

5. In the past, you have depreciated furniture in your hospitality firm using the straight-line method. You are going to change to an accelerated method, even for the furniture you previously depreciated using the straight-line method. Changing depreciation methods violates the _____ principle.

Problem 2

Complete the sentences below regarding basic accounting principles.

1. The upward valuation of land subsequent to its purchase violates the _____ principle.
2. Keeping records for a business separate from the owner's personal affairs is in keeping with the _____ principle.
3. Assuming a business will continue until the assets are fully utilized is in accordance with the _____ principle.
4. Using an invoice, rather than the seller's opinion of the value, to document the value of equipment, is based on the _____ principle.
5. Providing necessary details regarding depreciation methods in footnotes to financial statements is based on the _____ principle.
6. Changing inventory valuation methods year after year violates the _____ principle.
7. Recording accrued payroll at the end of the month is based on the _____ principle.
8. Expensing the purchase of a filing cabinet (useful life of 10 years) rather than recording it as equipment is most likely based on the _____ principle.

Problem 3

Indicate which branch of accounting would likely be most involved with each activity listed below. Consider the branches of financial accounting, cost accounting, managerial accounting, tax accounting, auditing, and accounting systems.

1. Preparing the firm's federal income tax return.
2. Reviewing procedures for purchasing, receiving, and issuing food stocks.
3. Processing the payroll for the biweekly pay period.
4. Evaluating the need for upgrading the point-of-sale system in the restaurant.
5. Working closely with the hotel's general manager and department heads in preparing the five-year budget for the hotel.
6. Recording food service charge sales in the restaurant and posts the charges to the guests' accounts.

Problem 4

The following are balance sheet accounts for Blair's Catering:

Accounts payable	$ 5,000
Accounts receivable	4,000
Blair Douglas, Capital	15,000
Cash	1,000
Equipment	10,000

Food supplies	2,000
Prepaid rent	3,000

Required:

Prepare a simplified balance sheet. Consider following the example of Kathy's Catering Service shown in the chapter.

Problem 5

You have been hired as a bookkeeper by Henry Holiday, owner of Henry's Inn. During your first week on the job, the following transactions occur:

1. New furniture costing $10,000 was purchased with a loan from the bank.
2. Mr. Holiday contributed $5,000 to the business as new capital.
3. Cash of $1,000 was paid on the $10,000 loan.
4. Office supplies of $50 were bought on account from Stu's House of Office Supplies.
5. A new computer costing $1,500 was paid for with cash.

Required:

Show and describe how the transactions affect the fundamental accounting equation, Assets = Liabilities + Owner's Equity.

Problem 6

Cody Bryan opened his food service establishment (Cody's Place) as a sole proprietorship and recorded the following activity during his initial month of business:

1. Cody invested $20,000 in his business.
2. The business purchased $100,000 of equipment. It paid $20,000 down and borrowed the remainder.
3. Cody's Place sold 3,000 meals at an average price of $15 each. Ninety percent of the sales were for cash. The remainder were on credit. No credit sales were collected in the first month.
4. The business recorded a cost of food sold equal to 30 percent of the total food sales.
5. Cody's Place recorded the purchase of $20,000 of food inventory and paid $5,000 to suppliers during its first month.
6. The business incurred other expenses of $8,000 and paid cash for each.
7. Cody's tax rate is 28 percent. Taxes will be paid in the following month.

Required:

Prepare an income statement for Cody's Place for its first month of business. Remember to show revenues earned and expenses incurred only.

Problem 7

Based on the information in Problem 6, prepare a list of cash inflows and outflows for Cody's Place for its first month of operations.

Problem 8

Dwayne Kent on January 1, 20X1, opened the Double K Inn, a ten-room lodging facility. During the first three days the following transactions were completed.

a. He invested $50,000 of his personal cash in a bank account opened in the name of Double K Inn.

b. He paid $2,000 for the month of January to lease a building containing the ten guest-rooms.

c. He rented rooms for the three days and collected an average of $50 per room for the 15 rooms that were "sold." Treat this activity as a single transaction to keep things simple.

d. He purchased guest supplies on account from Hotel Suppliers, Inc., for $300.

e. He paid an advertising bill of $500.

Required:

1. Arrange the following asset, liability, and proprietorship titles in an expanded accounting equation like that shown in the chapter: Cash, Guest Supplies, Prepaid Rent, Accounts Payable, and Dwayne Kent, Capital.

2. Show by additions and subtractions the effects of each transaction on the assets, liabilities, and proprietorship of the Double K Inn. Show net totals for all items after each transaction.

Problem 9

Natalie Ray's lodging business (she is a sole proprietor) had the following activity:

1. She invested $50,000 in the business.

2. The lodging business purchased a van, paying $5,000 down and borrowing $20,000 from the bank.

3. The business purchased operating supplies for $1,000.

4. The business prepaid $2,000 for rent for the first month.

5. The business prepaid $2,000 for insurance for the year.

6. The business purchased additional operating supplies on account from RM Wholesale, Inc. for $5,000.

7. The business purchased several pieces of equipment for $30,000 cash.

Required:

Prepare a table similar to Table I (page 26) and show the impact of these activities on the following accounts:

- Cash
- Operating supplies
- Prepaid insurance
- Prepaid rent
- Equipment
- Van

- Accounts payable
- Bank loan
- Natalie Ray, Capital

Problem 10

Melvin Dwight owns a small catering business called M.D.'s Catering. At the beginning of the current month, the business had the following assets: cash, $2,500; food inventory, $500; beverage inventory, $2,500; office supplies, $200; and delivery truck, $2,000. M.D.'s owed $500 to Lawrence Supply Co., and $1,500 on a note to First Auto Bank. On the first day of the month, M.D.'s Catering completed the following transactions:

a. Melvin invested $500 more in M.D.'s Catering.
b. Food costing $250 was purchased on account from Lawrence Supply Co.
c. Twenty dinners were served to L&M Trucking Co. Board of Directors, and L&M was charged $5.50 for each dinner. Cash was received from L&M. The costs of food and beverages served were $40 and $15, respectively.
d. Melvin paid $20 for repair work to the delivery truck. (Note: This expenditure should be considered an expense.)
e. Melvin paid J.D. Hill $15 for labor services received.
f. Melvin paid First Auto Bank $450 on account.
g. Melvin withdrew $300 from the firm for personal use.

Required:

1. Arrange the asset, liability, and proprietorship titles in an expanded accounting equation like that shown in Table II in this chapter.
2. Enter the assets and liability of M.D.'s under the titles of the equation. Determine Melvin Dwight's equity and enter it under the title of Melvin Dwight, Capital.
3. Show by additions and subtractions the effects of each transaction on the elements of the equation. Show new totals after each transaction.

Problem 11

Using the account names and account balances from Problem 10, create a balance sheet (dated December 31, 20X2) for M.D.'s Catering. Follow the example given in Exhibit 7.

Problem 12

Charlie Reps owns the Spring Valley Motel. It is the end of the year 20X5 and he has asked you to help him prepare his balance sheet. His account balances are as follows:

Accounts receivable	$ 300
Inventory	50
Notes payable	2,500
Cash	250
Prepaid insurance	50

Accounts payable	200
Building	5,000
Wages payable	150
Owner's equity	?????

Required:

1. Find the missing account balance, using the fundamental accounting equation.
2. Prepare Charlie's balance sheet for 20X5, using the form shown in Exhibit 7.

Problem 13

Melanie Anastor is the owner and manager of Mel's Diner, a popular eatery and gathering place. She believes things are going very well, but she needs to have an income statement prepared for the IRS for 20X7. She has hired your consulting firm to prepare one.

Melanie's sales from food and beverages for the year were $575,000. Labor costs for her cooks, servers, and buspeople were $190,000. Cost of food used was $165,000. General maintenance and upkeep costs for the year were $20,000. Other operating costs (including your consulting fee of $10,000) came to $90,000.

Required:

Prepare an income statement for 20X7 for Mel's Diner according to Exhibit 8.

Problem 14

Nathan Thom's catering business (Nathan Catering) has just completed its first month of operations (January 20X5), and he is trying to put a balance sheet together. He provides you with the following information.

1. Cash—the bank says he has $1,200 in his account. However, Nathan knows that checks #115 and #116 have not cleared the bank. They were written for $120 and $85, respectively.
2. Several customers have not paid amounts owed to Nathan Catering as follows:

Adam Base	$350
Ben Fence	200
Carl Home	420
Della Line	148
Ernst Plate	390

3. The business purchased $12,000 of food during January 20X5 and the physical inventory revealed that $2,000 of food is on hand on January 31, 20X5.
4. The business owed three suppliers at the end of January 20X5 as follows:

Full Bones, Inc.	$950
Good Foods	480
Harry's Beverage	200

Required:

Prepare a balance sheet for January 31, 20X5, for Nathan Catering.

Problem 15

Juan and Wendy Carlos own a small roadside motel called the Carlos Inn. They prepare their own financial statements and are learning about the importance of the statement of cash flows. They desire your assistance in preparing a statement of cash flows for the Carlos Inn.

The following series of transactions occurred at the Carlos Inn during 20X3:

- It paid cash for wages to employees of $60,000.
- It acquired a loan from Lone Star Bank for $25,000. Used the loan to buy new shuttle van for $30,000.
- It paid cash for cleaning supply purchases of $2,000.
- It had sales (no credit sales are made at the Carlos Inn) of $155,000.
- It paid operating expenses with cash of $45,000.
- It paid fees for a reservation system of $5,000.
- The owners withdrew cash of $10,000.

Required:
1. Prepare a statement of cash flows for the Carlos Inn for 20X3.
2. Assuming there is a surplus in cash, suggest some ways in which it could be used.

Chapter 2 Outline

Accounts
    Asset Accounts
    Liability Accounts
    Owners' Equity Accounts
Debit and Credit
    Mechanics of Double-Entry
        Accounting
    Recording Changes in Assets,
        Liabilities, and Owners' Equity
    Recording Changes in Revenues and
        Expenses
    Recording Owner's Withdrawals
    Determining Account Balances
    Normal Balances
General Ledger
Journalizing
    Standard Account Forms
    Posting
    The Trial Balance
    Compound Journal Entries
Comprehensive Illustration—Journalizing,
    Posting, and Preparing a Trial Balance

Competencies

1. Explain the functions of accounts and T-accounts, and classify accounts into the major account categories. (pp. 41–44)

2. Define the terms *debit* and *credit*, explain the basis of the double-entry accounting system, and identify the normal balances of commonly used accounts. (pp. 44–49)

3. Define *general ledger*, distinguish between balance sheet and nominal accounts, and describe the relationship between general ledger accounts and the chart of accounts. (pp. 49–50)

4. Demonstrate how to journalize and post accounting entries, and prepare a trial balance for accounts. (pp. 50–67)

2

Accounting for Business Transactions

IN THIS CHAPTER, we introduce the T-account, the concepts of debits and credits, the journal, the recording process of journalizing, the ledger, the process of posting, and the trial balance. These tools are all basic to a double-entry accounting system.

Business transactions are the raw data of accounting. First, business events are observed and those of an economic nature are identified. For example, suppose a customer purchases a meal for $12.00. From the seller's viewpoint, the purchase of the meal is a business event of an economic nature. The seller exchanges food and service for $12.00. An example of an event that is not of an economic nature is "a potential guest has entered our hotel." No goods or services have been provided yet; thus, the event is insignificant from an accounting viewpoint.

In the first example, the sale of food and accompanying services for $12.00, an economic event has occurred. The measure of this transaction is the sales price of $12.00, which must be recorded as a sale and as a receipt of cash. At the same time, the provision of food and use of labor have occurred. These activities must also be recorded, but the detail of this recording will be provided later.

Accounts

Economic events, such as those in the preceding illustration, are reflected in accounts. An **account** is the basic element used in an accounting system to classify and summarize business transactions. Think of the account as a basic storage unit for data. Thus, accounts must be established for each separate classification. For example, each business will have a cash account, as well as accounts to record different types of sales and expenses.

To illustrate accounts, we start with a **T-account** that has three basic parts: the title, the left side, and the right side. The T-account's name is derived from its appearance. A T-account looks like the letter *T*, as shown below:

(Name of Account)	
(left side)	(right side)

Increases in accounts are recorded on one side of the account, and decreases are recorded on the other side. Which side (left or right) is used for increases and which is used for decreases depends on the type of account. For example, let us consider Cash, an asset account. Assume $100 is received and $50 is disbursed in two separate transactions. This cash activity would be shown as follows:

Cash			
Received	100	Disbursed	50

Notice that the increase in cash is shown on the left side, while the decrease in cash is shown on the right side. This is generally true for all asset accounts.

The decreases are subtracted from the increases in our Cash account to yield the account balance. In this example, the Cash account has a $50 balance:

Cash			
Received	100	Disbursed	50
Balance	50		

Future cash activities would be recorded in the Cash account in a similar fashion, except the balance would reflect both increases and decreases.

Hospitality businesses have many accounts. The general classifications include assets, liabilities, and owners' equity. Under the owners' equity classification, there are capital, revenue, and expense accounts.

A few of the more common accounts are described in the next sections.

Asset Accounts

Cash. Cash includes cash on hand in the custody of cashiers and other employees, plus the cash on deposit with banks. Accountants generally maintain a separate cash account for each cash fund and for each account with the bank.

Notes Receivable. A formal written promise to pay a sum of money at a fixed future date is called a *promissory note*. Businesses refer to these notes as *notes receivable* when they receive them from debtors. Generally, the Notes Receivable account contains only notes receivable from debtors who maintain open accounts with the enterprise. Notes receivable from officers, employees, and affiliated companies are shown in separate accounts.

Accounts Receivable. Goods or services are often sold to guests on the basis of the guests' oral or implied promises to pay in the future. Such sales are known as *sales on account*, and the promises to pay are known as *accounts receivable*. Accounts receivable are segregated by type of debtor. Accounts receivable from guests would be shown in one account, while amounts due from officers, employees, and companies affiliated or associated with the business would be shown in separate accounts.

Accrued Interest Receivable. This account consists of interest earned on interest-bearing assets that the business has not yet received at the date of the balance sheet.

Marketable Securities. Securities (stocks and bonds) that are purchased as short-term investments and are thus readily convertible to cash are classified as marketable securities.

Inventories of Merchandise. Several accounts will be maintained for the inventory of goods for sale, including but not limited to Beverage Inventory, Food Inventory, and Gift Merchandise Inventory.

Office Supplies. Postage stamps, stationery, paper, pencils, and similar items are known as *office supplies*. They are assets when purchased. As they are used in the business, they become expenses.

Other Prepaid Expenses. Prepaid expenses are items that are assets when purchased but become expenses as they are used. Prepaid items include prepaid rent, unexpired insurance, and prepaid taxes. Each type of prepaid expense is accounted for in a separate account.

Investments. Investments in securities of affiliated or associated companies and other securities purchased as nontemporary investments are included in an investment account.

Property and Equipment. This class of assets includes land, buildings, furniture, carpets, linen, china, glassware, and uniforms. A separate account is maintained for each type of property and equipment.

Liability Accounts

Notes Payable. This account includes promissory notes given to creditors. Promissory notes given to banks may be shown separately from notes to other creditors.

Accounts Payable. An account payable is an amount the business owes to a creditor, resulting from an oral or implied promise to pay at some future date.

Taxes Charged to Guests and Withheld from Employees. All taxes collected from guests or withheld from employees are generally recorded in separate accounts, such as Sales Taxes Payable, FICA Payable, Federal Income Taxes Withheld, State Income Taxes Withheld, and City Income Taxes Withheld.

Income Taxes Payable. The firm will record the amount of federal, state, and city income taxes due for prior fiscal years in separate accounts. The estimated liability for income taxes on the current year's net income to date will also be recorded in these accounts.

Accrued Expenses. Expenses for a period not yet paid at the end of the accounting period (such as wages, salaries, interest, and utilities) are recorded as well as the liability. A separate account is maintained for each item.

Advance Deposits. This is the unearned portion of revenue resulting from cash received from a guest for a period following the end of the accounting period. Deposits on banquets and room reservations may also be shown as advance deposits.

Mortgage Payable. A mortgage payable is a long-term debt for which the creditor has a secured prior claim against one or more of the hospitality firm's assets.

Owners' Equity Accounts

Many transactions affect the owners' equity of a business enterprise, including the investment of a proprietor, withdrawal of assets by a proprietor, and revenues earned and expenses incurred by the organization. So that an accountant can readily obtain information on the various kinds of increases and decreases in owners' equity, a different account is used for each type of increase or decrease.

Capital Account. When an individual invests in a business organized as a sole proprietorship, the investment is recorded in an account bearing the investor's name. All other capital accounts will be "closed" into this account periodically. If the firm is incorporated, the Capital account is replaced by two types of accounts: (1) Capital Stock, in which different accounts are maintained for different types of stock; and (2) Retained Earnings, in which net income or loss (the results of operations less dividends declared) is recorded.

Revenue and Expense Accounts. Revenues increase owners' equity, whereas expenses decrease it. The prime objective of a business enterprise is to earn a profit. If the enterprise is to succeed, detailed information regarding the kinds of revenues and expenses must be supplied to management on a timely basis. This information is maintained in a separate account for each revenue and expense item. Common revenue and expense accounts include the following:

Revenues	Expenses
Room Sales	Beverage Expense
Food Sales	Food Expense
Beverage Sales	Wages Expense
Gift Shop Sales	Payroll Taxes
Green Fees	Office Supplies
Pro Shop Sales	Rent
Banquet Sales	Cleaning Supplies
Interest Income	Electricity
Dividend Income	Fuel
	Insurance
	Interest
	Advertising Expense
	Travel Expenses
	Property Taxes
	Depreciation Expense
	Income Taxes

The kind of revenue or expense recorded in each of these accounts is reasonably evident from its title, as is true of most revenue and expense accounts.

Debit and Credit

The left side of any account is always called the **debit** side and the right side is always called the **credit** side, as arbitrarily established by accountants. Debit and credit are abbreviated "dr" and "cr," respectively. To *debit* an account is simply to record an amount on the *left* side of the account; to *credit* an account is to record an amount on the *right* side. The difference between the total debits and credits of an account is called the **account balance**. Thus, an account may have either a **debit balance** or a **credit balance**. Accounting personnel will often use the term *charge* in place of *debit*.

When Michael Miller invests $10,000 in his lodging business, cash is increased (debited) for $10,000, and the $10,000 is recorded on the left side of the Cash T-account. The account Michael Miller, Capital is also increased (credited in this account) for the $10,000. This is recorded on the right side of the account, as shown:

Cash		Michael Miller, Capital	
10,000			10,000

When Michael Miller invested $10,000 in his business, both cash and Michael Miller's proprietorship increased. Observe, however, that the cash increase is recorded on the left side of the Cash account, while the owners' equity increase is recorded on the right side of the Michael Miller, Capital account. This results from the mechanics of double-entry accounting.

Mechanics of Double-Entry Accounting

In **double-entry accounting**, every transaction affects and is recorded in at least two accounts, and the debits of the entry must equal the credits of the entry. Since every transaction is recorded with equal debits and credits, the sum of the debits recorded must equal the sum of the credits recorded. When the accounts are balanced, each account has either a debit or credit balance. The equality of debit and credit accounts is tested by preparing a trial balance, discussed in detail later in this chapter. The equality of these two groups of accounts provides some assurance that the arithmetic of the transaction recording process has been properly completed.

Equal debits and credits in recording transactions result under a double-entry system because the system is based on the fundamental accounting equation, Assets = Liabilities + Owners' Equity. Increases in assets are recorded with debits, and decreases in assets are recorded with credits. Increases in liabilities and owners' equity are recorded with credits, while decreases are recorded with debits. These rules are shown below:

Assets		=	Liabilities		+	Owners' Equity	
+	−		−	+		−	+
dr	cr		dr	cr		dr	cr

The rules can be restated in this way:

1. Asset accounts are increased by debits and decreased by credits.

2. Liabilities and owners' equity accounts are increased by credits and decreased by debits.

Applying these two rules keeps the accounting equation in balance; that is, assets equal liabilities plus owners' equity.

Recording Changes in Assets, Liabilities, and Owners' Equity

The following three transactions from the hypothetical Mable Motel will illustrate these concepts.

For Transaction 1, assume that Molly Mable invests $100,000 in her lodging enterprise, the Mable Motel. The Mable Motel records the $100,000 that Molly invests as follows:

Cash		Molly Mable, Capital	
(1)	100,000	(1)	100,000

This transaction increases cash of the Mable Motel and also increases Molly Mable's equity in her business. Since Cash is an asset account, it is debited for the $100,000 received. Molly Mable, Capital is an owner's equity account, so it is increased by a credit entry of $100,000. Recording this transaction as shown results in debits equaling credits and assets equaling owner's equity. At this point there are no liabilities.

For Transaction 2, assume that Molly Mable borrows $50,000 from First Bank. She signs a note, which in this case is a written promise to pay the bank the $50,000 in three years. The transaction is recorded as follows:

Cash		Notes Payable—First Bank	
(2)	50,000	(2)	50,000

The asset account Cash is increased with a debit for the $50,000 cash received. The liability account, Notes Payable—First Bank, is increased with a credit for the $50,000 of cash borrowed. First Bank has claims to the Mable Motel's assets of $50,000. The above recording results in debits equaling credits, and assets (cash) of $150,000 equaling liabilities of $50,000 and owner's equity of $100,000.

Transaction 3 for this lodging enterprise is the purchase of $80,000 worth of furniture by the Mable Motel. The transaction is recorded as follows:

Furniture		Cash	
(3)	80,000	(3)	80,000

The asset account Furniture is increased (debited) for $80,000, while another asset account, Cash, is decreased (credited) for $80,000. This transaction is recorded, as all transactions must be, with debits equaling credits. Further, the accounting equation of $A = L + E$ is in balance, as follows:

Assets	
Cash	$ 70,000
Furniture	80,000
Total	$ 150,000
Liabilities and Owner's Equity	
Notes Payable—First Bank	$ 50,000
Molly Mable, Capital	100,000
Total	$ 150,000

Recording Changes in Revenues and Expenses

In theory, revenues and expenses can be recorded directly in the Owners' Equity account. However, in the real world, revenues and expenses are recorded in separate accounts to facilitate the communication of this information in the income statement. Revenues increase owners' equity, so increases in revenues are recorded with credits. Expenses decrease owners' equity, so increases in expenses are recorded with debit entries. The expanded accounting equation, including the debit and credit rules for each account classification, is as follows:

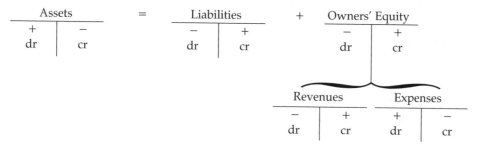

Note: At the end of the accounting period, revenue and expense accounts are closed to the Owners' Equity account.

Two transactions (Transactions 4 and 5) of the Mable Motel will illustrate the rules of debit and credit for revenue and expense accounts. Transaction 4 is the receipt of $50 for a room rented to Susan Smith, a guest. The transaction is recorded as follows:

Cash		Room Revenues	
(4) 50			(4) 50

Cash and Room Revenues are increased by the rental of a room for one night and Susan Smith's payment of $50. The Cash account is debited for $50 to reflect the increase, while the revenue account, Room Revenues, is increased (credited) for $50.

Transaction 5 is a $30 cash payment to Jason Jones for work performed for the motel. The transaction is recorded as follows:

Wages Expense		Cash	
(5) 30			(5) 30

Wages Expense is increased with a debit of $30, while Cash is decreased with a credit entry of $30.

Recording Owner's Withdrawals

The owner of an unincorporated business such as the Mable Motel may decide to withdraw cash from his or her business. Withdrawals reduce the owner's equity in the business and have the same effect as an expense on the owner's equity. The drawing account is not an expense account, however. Owners' withdrawals are recorded in a drawing account that is a subclassification of the owners' equity account, similar to revenue and expense accounts. Since withdrawals reduce owners' equity, the drawing account is increased with debits and decreased with credits in the same way expense accounts are increased and decreased.

Transaction 6 for the Mable Motel illustrates the withdrawal of $100 by Molly Mable from her business. The transaction is recorded as follows:

Molly Mable, Drawing		Cash	
(6) 100			(6) 100

The drawing account is increased with a debit entry of $100, while the cash account is decreased with a credit of $100.

Determining Account Balances

The difference between the sum of the debits and the sum of the credits of each account results in the account balance. When the debit total exceeds the credit total, the account has a debit balance. When the credit total exceeds the debit total, the account has a credit balance. For example, the Cash account for the Mable Motel has a debit balance of $69,920, since the sum of the debit entries of $150,050 exceeds the sum of the credit entries of $80,130, by $69,920:

	Cash		
(1)	100,000	(3)	80,000
(2)	50,000	(5)	30
(4)	50	(6)	100
	150,050		80,130
Debit Balance	69,920		

The balance of the Molly Mable, Capital account is a credit balance, since the credit entry of $100,000 exceeds debits which, in this case, are zero:

	Molly Mable, Capital	
	(1)	100,000
	Credit Balance	100,000

Normal Balances

The **normal balance** of an account is the kind of balance, either debit or credit, that an account generally shows. This balance results from increases in the account, and only on occasion does the balance of an account result from an excess of decreases over increases. The major classes of accounts have the following normal balances:

Type of Account	Normal Balance
Asset	Debit
Liability	Credit
Owners' Equity:	
Capital	Credit
Revenue	Credit
Expense	Debit
Drawing	Debit

Accountants know the normal balance of every account of the accounting system of their lodging business and are skeptical of an account with a balance opposite from normal. Investigating accounts with suspicious balances will usually show either an error or an unusual transaction. For example, if the Furniture account has a credit balance, an error has most certainly been made. On the other hand, a credit balance in a guest's account would probably not attract attention, because such credits occur whenever the guest makes a deposit with his or her reservation.

General Ledger

A group of accounts is defined as a *ledger.* The **general ledger** is the group of general accounts that includes accounts for assets, liabilities, owners' equity, revenues, expenses, and owner's drawing. The **balance sheet accounts**, also called *real accounts* since they are permanent accounts and are never closed, include the asset, liability, and owners' equity accounts. The remaining accounts are temporary accounts and are often called **nominal accounts.** These accounts include revenue, expense, and drawing accounts, which are closed at the end of each year into the Owners' Equity account. The general ledger may be a binder housing all accounts, or, if the general ledger is computerized, all accounts may be printed on a continuous form.

Each hospitality business should have a complete listing of all accounts. This is called a **chart of accounts.** The chart of accounts lists all account numbers and account titles. The major purpose of the chart of accounts is to guide accountants as they record business transactions.[1] Rather than invent new accounts, accountants generally record all transactions in accounts that are listed in the chart.

Accounts are numbered according to their classification. For example, a chart of accounts for a lodging firm might look like this:

Classification	Account Numbers	Examples of Accounts	
Assets	100–199	Cash on Hand	100
		Petty Cash	101
		.	
		.	
		.	
		Furniture	151
		.	
		.	
		.	
		Building	171

Liabilities	200–299	Accounts Payable	200
		Notes Payable	201
		.	
		.	
		.	
		Mortgage Payable	249
Owner's Equity and Drawing	300–399	Owner's Name, Capital	300
		Owner's Name, Drawing	301
Revenues	400–499	Rooms Revenue	400
		Food Revenue	401
Expenses	500–599	Wages Expense	500
		Supplies Expense	501
		.	
		.	
		.	
		Depreciation	550

Exhibit 1 is the Assets section from the sample chart of accounts from the ninth edition of the *Uniform System of Accounts for the Lodging Industry*. The suggested three-digit account numbers for each classification are listed here:

Assets	100–199
Liabilities	200–280
Equity	281–299
Revenue	300–399
Cost of Sales	400–499
Payroll and Related Expenses	500–599
Other Expenses	600–699
Fixed Charges	700–799

Thus, this system has four separate classifications of expenses from "cost of sales" through "fixed charges." Many lodging operations use a very extensive chart of accounts like this to classify and summarize business activity and facilitate financial reporting.

Journalizing

Thus far, we have recorded transactions directly in the T-accounts. Each account reflects only the activity affecting that account. For example, the Mable Motel's Cash account reflects only the cash portion of the cash transactions. The Cash account shows only the changes in cash and does not reveal the sources of cash receipts or the uses of cash disbursements.

In actual practice, transactions are seldom recorded directly in ledger accounts for three reasons:

1. There is not room for much detailed information in a ledger account. Accounts are mainly for classifying and summarizing financial information. If an

Exhibit 1   Assets Section from a Sample Chart of Accounts

ASSETS

100 Cash
    101 House Funds
    103 Checking Account
    105 Payroll Account
    107 Savings Account
    109 Petty Cash
110 Short-Term Investments
120 Accounts Receivable
    121 Guest Ledger
    122 Credit Card Accounts
    123 Direct Bill
    124 Notes Receivable (Current)
    125 Due from Employees
    126 Receivable from Owner
    127 Other Accounts Receivable
    128 Intercompany Receivables
    129 Allowance for Doubtful Accounts
130 Inventory
    131 Food
    132 Liquor
    133 Wine
    135 Operating Supplies
    136 Paper Supplies
    137 Cleaning Supplies
    138 China, Glassware, Silver, Linen, and Uniforms (Unopened Stock)
    139 Other
140 Prepaids
    141 Prepaid Insurance
    142 Prepaid Taxes
    143 Prepaid Workers' Compensation
    144 Prepaid Supplies
    145 Prepaid Contracts
    146 Current Deferred Tax Asset
    147 Barter Contracts Asset
    149 Other Prepaids
150 Noncurrent Receivables
155 Investments (not short-term)
160 Property and Equipment
    161 Land
    162 Buildings
    163 Accumulated Depreciation—Buildings
    164 Leaseholds and Leasehold Improvements
    165 Accumulated Depreciation—Leaseholds
    166 Furniture and Fixtures
    167 Accumulated Depreciation—Furniture and Fixtures
    168 Machinery and Equipment

(continued)

Exhibit 1 *(continued)*

ASSETS

169 Accumulated Depreciation—Machinery and Equipment
170 Information Systems Equipment
171 Accumulated Depreciation—Information Systems Equipment
172 Automobiles and Trucks
173 Accumulated Depreciation—Automobiles and Trucks
174 Construction in Progress
175 China
176 Glassware
177 Silver
178 Linen
179 Uniforms
180 Accumulated Depreciation—China, Glassware, Silver, Linen, and
    Uniforms
190 Other Assets
   191 Security Deposits
   192 Deferred Charges
   193 Long-Term Deferred Tax Asset
   196 Cash Surrender Value—Life Insurance
   197 Goodwill
   199 Miscellaneous

Source: *Uniform System of Accounts for the Lodging Industry,* 9th rev. ed. (Lansing, Mich.: Educational Institute of the American Hotel & Lodging Association, 1996), pp. 191–192. ©Hotel Association of New York City.

    account includes all the details, it does not serve well as a device for classifying and summarizing.

2. Account entries fail to record a complete record of each transaction in any one place, since a ledger has many accounts, each located on a separate page. As noted, each transaction affects at least two accounts.

3. If transactions are recorded directly in the accounts, errors are easily made and are difficult to locate.

    Therefore, rather than recording directly in the accounts, the accountant records the transaction first in a journal. This process is called **journalizing.** The information recorded in the journal is then "transferred" to the ledger accounts.

    A journal is commonly called a *book of original entry,* since the transaction is first recorded there, while the ledger is referred to as a *book of final entry.*

    Firms in the hospitality industry maintain several kinds of journals. However, the simplest and most flexible is the general journal. A general journal provides for recording:

1. Date of the transaction (in the date column).

2. Titles of the accounts used (in the account titles and explanation column).

3. Explanation of the transaction (in the account titles and explanation column).

Exhibit 2   Transactions 1 and 2 for the Mable Motel

			General Journal			Page 1	
Date		**Accounts/Explanation**	**Post. Ref.**	**Debit**		**Credit**	
20X1							
Jan.	1	Cash		1 0 0 0 0 0			
		Molly Mable, Capital				1 0 0 0 0 0	
		To record investment by Molly					
		Mable in the Mable Motel.					
Jan.	1	Cash		5 0 0 0 0			
		Notes Payable—First Bank				5 0 0 0 0	
		To record amount borrowed from					
		First Bank.					

4. Page numbers of ledger accounts to which the debit and credit amounts of the transaction are "transferred" (in the Post. Ref. [posting reference] column).

5. Debit and credit effects of the transaction on the accounts listed (in the debit and credit columns).

Exhibit 2 shows how Transactions 1 and 2 for the Mable Motel are recorded in the general journal. The date of the transactions, January 1, 20X1, is recorded for each. Then the account titles and amounts and an explanation for each transaction are recorded. Note that the account title for the credit entry of each transaction is indented. The account numbers in the posting reference column are recorded when the amounts are transferred from the journal to general ledger accounts. Generally, dollar signs, commas, and decimal points are not used in lined journals or ledgers. Also, when amounts are in even dollars, the accountant may leave the cents column blank or simply draw a dash across the column.

Standard Account Forms

T-accounts are commonly used in teaching, since details are eliminated and the student can concentrate on ideas. Hospitality businesses, however, do not use T-accounts to record transactions. Exhibit 3 illustrates the account form that businesses with manual accounting systems most often use.

Exhibit 3   Account Form Used with Manual Accounting Systems

Account Title Cash			Account No.					

Date		Accounts/Explanation	Post. Ref.	Debit	Credit	Balance
Jan.	1	Initial investment		1 0 0 0 0 0		1 0 0 0 0 0
	1	Loan from bank		5 0 0 0 0		1 5 0 0 0 0

In Exhibit 3, the Cash account is not divided into two sides as is the T-account. Instead, it has debit and credit columns next to each other. Further, this account has a balance column so the balance of the account can be maintained at all times. After the two transactions mentioned before are recorded in the Cash account, the balance is $150,000.

The balance column in Exhibit 3 does not indicate whether the Cash account has a debit or credit balance, since the balance of an account is always assumed to be the normal type unless otherwise indicated. Therefore, the Cash account will have a debit balance. If a transaction causes an opposite balance, such as a credit balance in the Cash account, the accountant indicates it by entering the balance in red, by circling the balance, or by enclosing the balance in brackets or parentheses.

Posting

The process of transferring amounts recorded in the general journal to ledger accounts is called **posting.** Posting is done periodically, sometimes daily, but always by the end of an accounting period. When the accountant posts the amount to the ledger account, he or she completes the posting reference column in the general journal by indicating the account number to which the amount is posted. In the posting reference column of the corresponding ledger account, the accountant lists the general journal page where the posted amount was journalized. Journal debits are posted as ledger account debits and journal credits as ledger account credits.

Exhibit 4 shows Transactions 1 and 2 recorded in the Mable Motel's general journal on January 1, 20X1, and the posting of these amounts in the general ledger accounts. The relationships are shown with arrows for the first transaction, as follows:

1. The date of the journal entry in the general journal (January 1, 20X1) is shown on both the Cash account and the Molly Mable, Capital account.

2. The $100,000 cash received and recorded in the general journal is posted to the Cash account.

3. In the posting reference of the general journal, the Cash account number 100 is written to indicate the completion of the posting.

Exhibit 4 Illustration of Relation of Journal and Ledger Accounts

General Journal — Page 1

Date	Accounts/Explanation	Post. Ref.	Debit	Credit
20X1				
Jan. 1	Cash	100	1 0 0 0 0 0	
	Molly Mable, Capital	300		1 0 0 0 0 0
	To record investment by Molly			
	Mable in the Mable Motel.			
Jan. 1	Cash	100	5 0 0 0 0	
	Notes Payable—First Bank	220		5 0 0 0 0
	To record amount borrowed from First Bank.			

General Ledger Accounts

Account Title Cash   **Account No.** 100

Date	Accounts/Explanation	Post. Ref.	Debit	Credit	Balance
Jan. 1	Initial investment	GJ 1	1 0 0 0 0 0		1 0 0 0 0 0
1	Loan from bank	GJ 1	5 0 0 0 0		5 0 0 0 0

Account Title Molly Mable, Capital   **Account No.** 300

Date	Accounts/Explanation	Post. Ref.	Debit	Credit	Balance
Jan. 1	Initial investment	GJ 1		1 0 0 0 0 0	1 0 0 0 0 0

Account Title Notes Payable—First Bank   **Account No.** 220

Date	Accounts/Explanation	Post. Ref.	Debit	Credit	Balance
Jan. 1	Loan from bank	GJ 1		5 0 0 0 0	5 0 0 0 0

4. In the posting reference column of the general ledger Cash account, the source and page (*GJ 1* for *general journal,* page *1*) are recorded.

5. The posting of $100,000 to the Molly Mable, Capital account is shown, including the posting reference of the account number 300 for Molly Mable, Capital in the general journal and GJ 1 as the posting reference in the Molly Mable, Capital account.

The recording of account numbers in the general journal and page numbers from the general journal in the general ledger accounts at the time of posting is called *cross-indexing.* It allows accountants to check and trace the origins of the transactions.

The Trial Balance

The trial balance of accounts, generally shortened to just **trial balance**, is a listing of the accounts and their debit and credit balances. The trial balance is prepared to test the equality of debits and credits. Accountants prepare the trial balance using the following procedure:

1. Determine the balance of each account in the ledger.

2. List the accounts and show debit balances in one column on the left and credit balances in a separate column to its right.

3. Add the debit balances.

4. Add the credit balances.

5. Compare the totals of the debit and credit balances.

When the total of the debit balance accounts equals the total of the credit balance accounts, the trial balance is in balance. If the trial balance does not balance, someone erred in recording the transactions, in determining the balances of each account, or in preparing the trial balance. However, a balanced trial balance is not proof that all transactions have been recorded properly. For example, an accounting employee may mistakenly record the payment of advertising expense by debiting Wages rather than Advertising. The trial balance would still be in balance, yet the amount of wages and advertising will have been incorrectly recorded. The trial balance, if correct, indicates only that debits equal credits.

Exhibit 5 shows the balance of each account of the Mable Motel after Transactions 1 through 6 were recorded. The exhibit also shows the Mable Motel's trial balance. Since the total of debit balance accounts of $150,050 equals the total of credit balance accounts of $150,050, the trial balance is in balance.

Compound Journal Entries

Up to this point, all transactions used in illustrations have affected only two accounts. Business transactions will often involve three or more accounts. Journal entries recording these transactions are called **compound journal entries.** As with all journal entries, debits must equal credits.

Exhibit 5   Mable Motel Accounts and Trial Balance

ASSETS	=	LIABILITIES	+	OWNER'S EQUITY

Cash

(1) 100,000	(3) 80,000
(2) 50,000	
(4) 50	(5) 30
	(6) 100
150,050	80,130
69,920	

Furniture

(3) 80,000	
80,000	

Notes Payable— First Bank

	(2) 50,000
	50,000

Molly Mable, Capital

	(1) 100,000
	100,000

Molly Mable, Drawing

(6) 100	
100	

Room Revenues

	(4) 50
	50

Wages Expense

(5) 30	
30	

Mable Motel
Trial Balance

	Debit	Credit
Cash	$ 69,920	
Furniture	80,000	
Notes Payable—First Bank		$ 50,000
Molly Mable, Capital		100,000
Molly Mable, Drawing	100	
Room Revenues		50
Wages Expense	30	
Total	$ 150,050	$ 150,050

To illustrate a compound journal entry, consider the Mable Motel's purchase of office supplies from Kay's Business Supplies. The motel paid $50 and charged $50 for the purchase of $100 of office supplies. The transaction would be recorded as follows:

		Dr	Cr
20X1			
Jan. 1	Office Supplies	100	
	Cash		50
	Accounts Payable—Kay's Business Supplies		50
	To record the purchase of office supplies.		

This journal entry shows $100 debited to office supplies and $50 credited to two accounts: Cash and Accounts Payable—Kay's Business Supplies.

Comprehensive Illustration—Journalizing, Posting, and Preparing a Trial Balance

This last major section of the chapter contains a comprehensive illustration of the accounting process from journalizing through the preparation of a trial balance. The hypothetical hospitality enterprise is Carson Catering, owned by Don Carson. Since the business is new, only a few transactions are incurred during the first month of operations. Each will be fully analyzed, explained, and journalized in the general journal.

The chart of accounts and a description of each account for Carson Catering is as follows:

Account No.	Account Title	Description
100	Cash	Cash in the bank and on hand
105	Accounts Receivable	Amounts due the company from customers
110	Operating Supplies	Supplies to be used in catering parties for customers
120	Van	Vehicle used in catering business
200	Accounts Payable	Amounts owed suppliers for items purchased on account
210	Notes Payable—Big Motors Acceptance Corporation (BMAC)	Amount due BMAC from loan for van
300	Don Carson, Capital	Owner's equity in the business
301	Don Carson, Drawing	Amount of withdrawals by owner
400	Catering Revenue	Amounts earned from catering parties
500	Wages Expense	Wages paid to employees of the business
501	Advertising Expense	Cost of advertising purchased
502	Food Expense	Cost of food catered to customers
503	Gas Expense	Cost of gas, oil, and so on, used in van

Each business transaction incurred during December 20X1 will be provided and analyzed using T-accounts, and a brief explanation will be given.

Transaction 1:   Don Carson forms Carson Catering on December 1, 20X1, and invests $5,000 of his personal funds in the business. The accounts affected are as follows:

Cash		Don Carson, Capital	
(1) 5,000			(1) 5,000

Cash is increased with a debit entry, and Don Carson, Capital is increased with a credit entry.

Transaction 2:   On December 5, Carson Catering pays $500 for advertising in the local paper. The accounts affected are as follows:

Advertising Expense		Cash	
(2) 500			(2) 500

Advertising Expense is increased with a debit entry, while Cash is decreased with a credit entry.

Transaction 3:   In anticipation of catering events, Carson Catering purchases a van on December 8, 20X1, costing $15,000. A down payment of $3,000 is made, and the remainder ($12,000) is financed through Big Motors Acceptance Corporation (BMAC). The transaction is analyzed as follows:

Van		Cash		Notes Payable—BMAC	
(3) 15,000			(3) 3,000		(3) 12,000

With the purchase of the van, the Van account is increased with a debit for its cost of $15,000. Cash is reduced by $3,000, which is the amount of the down payment, so Cash is credited. The difference between the cost of $15,000 and the down payment of $3,000 is financed by BMAC. Don Carson signs a note that requires 12 quarterly payments starting April 1, 20X2. The note for $12,000 is recorded with a credit to the Notes Payable—BMAC account.

Transaction 4:   On December 12, 20X1, Carson Catering purchases food costing $200 to be served at a party for M.J. Jolly.

Food Expense		Cash	
(4) 200			(4) 200

Food Expense is increased by $200 with a debit entry, while Cash is decreased with a credit entry of $200. In many hospitality food service businesses, the purchase of food is recorded in an asset account, Food Inventory, and, as the food is used, the Food Expense account is charged and Food Inventory is credited. However, since Carson Catering is purchasing only the food necessary for a particular catered event, Food Expense is charged directly.

Transaction 5:   On December 13, 20X1, Carson Catering purchases $300 of operating supplies on account from Supplies, Inc. These supplies will be used for several catered events over the next few months. The transaction will affect the accounts as follows:

Operating Supplies		Accounts Payable (Supplies, Inc.)	
(5)	300	(5)	300

An asset account, Operating Supplies, is increased with a debit entry for $300, and Accounts Payable is increased with a credit by $300. The debit is made to an asset account rather than an expense account, since the operating supplies purchased will be used during catered events beyond the current period. If the operating supplies purchased were expected to be used in their entirety in December, an Operating Supplies expense account would have been charged. The terms of sale require Carson Catering to pay the amount due Supplies, Inc., on December 28.

Transaction 6: On December 13, Carson Catering caters the party for M.J. Jolly and receives payment of $800. The transaction is analyzed as follows:

Cash		Catering Revenue	
(6)	800	(6)	800

Cash is debited by the increase in cash of $800, and Catering Revenue is increased with a credit to the account for $800.

Transaction 7: On December 19, 20X1, Carson Catering purchases food for a party to be catered for Mary Chris Smith. The accounts affected are as follows:

Food Expense		Cash	
(7)	300	(7)	300

This transaction is the same as Transaction 4. Food Expense is increased by (debited for) $300, and Cash is decreased by (credited for) $300.

Transaction 8: On December 20, 20X1, Carson Catering caters the party for Mary Smith for $1,000. She pays $300, and Carson agrees to allow Mary two weeks to pay the remainder due of $700. Thus, three accounts are affected as follows:

Cash		Accounts Receivable (Mary Smith)		Catering Revenue	
(8)	300	(8)	700	(8)	1,000

Cash is debited for the $300 increase, while Accounts Receivable is increased with a debit for $700. Catering Revenue is increased with a credit for the total cost to the customer of $1,000.

Transaction 9: On December 22, 20X1, Carson Catering purchases $25 of gasoline for its van. The transaction is analyzed as follows:

Gas Expense		Cash	
(9)	25	(9)	25

Gas Expense is increased by (debited for) $25, and Cash is decreased by (credited for) $25. Quite possibly, Carson Catering will not use the entire amount of gasoline purchased during the rest of the month. However, it is impractical to account for gasoline put into the van as an asset and account for it on a usage basis. Further, the $25 is also an immaterial amount, so the expedient way to account for this expenditure is to expense it.

Transaction 10: On December 28, 20X1, Carson Catering pays $400 to part-time employees who assisted with the two catered events. The accounts affected are as follows:

Wages Expense		Cash	
(10) 400			(10) 400

Wages Expense is increased by (debited for) $400, and Cash is decreased by (credited for) $400.

Transaction 11: On December 28, 20X1, Carson Catering pays Supplies, Inc., the $300 due. Two accounts are affected as follows:

Accounts Payable (Supplies, Inc.)		Cash	
(11) 300			(11) 300

The payment to Supplies, Inc., of $300 decreases the Accounts Payable account so that account is debited, and Cash is decreased with a credit for the $300.

Transaction 12: On December 28, 20X1, Don Carson withdraws $200 from Carson Catering for his personal use. The Cash and Drawing accounts are affected as follows:

Don Carson, Drawing		Cash	
(12) 200			(12) 200

The withdrawal by the owner of Carson Catering is accounted for by increasing (debiting) Don Carson, Drawing for $200. The Cash account is credited for $200, since cash is reduced by the amount of the owner's withdrawal.

The T-accounts used in the preceding 12 transactions are shown only for analysis purposes. In the real world, the transactions are recorded first in a journal. For illustrative purposes, Exhibit 6 contains the general journal that shows how each of the 12 transactions are journalized.

Exhibit 7 contains the general ledger of accounts for Carson Catering. The 12 transactions recorded in the journal (Exhibit 6) have been posted to the appropriate ledger accounts. The posting reference column indicates the source of the amount, which is either page 1 or 2 from Carson Catering's general journal.

Exhibit 8 shows the trial balance of Carson Catering at the end of the month. The balance of each general ledger account has been placed in the appropriate debit and credit columns, and the columns each add up to $18,800. Therefore, the trial balance at December 31, 20X1, for Carson Catering is in balance.

Exhibit 6   General Journal, Carson Catering

		General Journal Carson Catering				Page 1
Date		Accounts/Explanation	Post. Ref.	Debit	Credit	
20X1						
Dec.	*1*	*Cash*	*100*	5 0 0 0		
		Don Carson, Capital	*300*		5 0 0 0	
		To record Don Carson's investment in				
		Carson Catering.				
	5	*Advertising Expense*	*501*	5 0 0		
		Cash	*100*		5 0 0	
		To record advertising expense.				
	8	*Van*	*120*	1 5 0 0 0		
		Cash	*100*		3 0 0 0	
		Notes Payable—BMAC	*210*		1 2 0 0 0	
		To record purchase of van.				
	12	*Food Expense*	*502*	2 0 0		
		Cash	*100*		2 0 0	
		To record food expense.				
	13	*Operating Supplies*	*110*	3 0 0		
		Accounts Payable (Supplies, Inc.)	*200*		3 0 0	
		To record the purchase of operating				
		supplies on account.				
	13	*Cash*	*100*	8 0 0		
		Catering Revenue	*400*		8 0 0	
		To record catering revenue.				
	19	*Food Expense*	*502*	3 0 0		
		Cash	*100*		3 0 0	
		To record food expense.				
	20	*Cash*	*100*	3 0 0		
		Accounts Receivable (Mary Smith)	*105*	7 0 0		
		Catering Revenue	*400*		1 0 0 0	
		To record catering revenue.				
	22	*Gas Expense*	*503*	2 5		
		Cash	*100*		2 5	
		To record gas expense.				

Exhibit 6 *(continued)*

Date		Accounts/Explanation	Post. Ref.	Debit	Credit
		General Journal **Carson Catering**			Page 2
20X1					
Dec.	28	Wages Expense	500	4 0 0	
		Cash	100		4 0 0
		To record wages expense.			
	28	Accounts Payable (Supplies, Inc.)	200	3 0 0	
		Cash	100		3 0 0
		To record payment on account.			
	28	Don Carson, Drawing	301	2 0 0	
		Cash	100		2 0 0
		To record cash withdrawal by Don			
		Carson.			

Summary

Accounting is based on transactions that occur in the business world. Many transactions occur every day in a major organization. Double-entry accounting is designed to classify and summarize these transactions.

An account is the basic unit of accounting. It is represented in this chapter by a T-account, which is a simple tool used to teach accounting.

Accounts have two sides. Increases in the accounts are recorded on one side, while decreases are recorded on the opposite side. There are several different classifications of accounts such as asset, liability, and owners' equity. Owners' equity accounts are subclassified as capital accounts, revenue accounts, and expense accounts.

The left side of an account is defined as a *debit,* and the right side is defined as a *credit.* The account balance is the difference between the sum of the debits and the sum of the credits. When total debits exceed total credits, the account has a debit balance. When credits exceed debits, the account has a credit balance. In general, different account classifications have different balances, which are called *normal balances.* For example, an asset account under normal circumstances will have a debit balance, and a liability will have a credit balance.

In double-entry accounting, every transaction affects and is recorded in at least two accounts, and the debit entry must equal the credit entry. This is tested with the preparation of a trial balance. If each transaction has been recorded with equal debits and credits, the account balances should equal. This does not ensure, however, that all transactions have been recorded correctly; it simply shows that the transactions have been recorded with balanced debits and credits.

Exhibit 7   General Ledger, Carson Catering

Account Title _Cash_   **Account No.** _100_

Date		Accounts/Explanation	Post. Ref.	Debit	Credit	Balance
20X1						
Dec.	1	Investment in Carson Catering	GJ 1	5 0 0 0		5 0 0 0
	5	Payment, advertising expense	GJ 1		5 0 0	4 5 0 0
	8	Partial payment on van	GJ 1		3 0 0 0	1 5 0 0
	12	Payment of food expense	GJ 1		2 0 0	1 3 0 0
	13	Catering revenue	GJ 1	8 0 0		2 1 0 0
	19	Payment of food expense	GJ 1		3 0 0	1 8 0 0
	20	Receipt of cash—catering				
		revenue	GJ 1	3 0 0		2 1 0 0
	22	Payment of gas expense	GJ 1		2 5	2 0 7 5
	28	Payment of wages	GJ 2		4 0 0	1 6 7 5
	28	Payment on account	GJ 2		3 0 0	1 3 7 5
	28	Withdrawal by D. Carson	GJ 2		2 0 0	1 1 7 5

Account Title _Accounts Receivable (Mary Smith)_   **Account No.** _105_

Date		Accounts/Explanation	Post. Ref.	Debit	Credit	Balance
20X1						
Dec.	20	Partial charge sale	GJ 1	7 0 0		7 0 0

Account Title _Operating Supplies_   **Account No.** _110_

Date		Accounts/Explanation	Post. Ref.	Debit	Credit	Balance
20X1						
Dec.	13	Purchase of operating supplies	GJ 1	3 0 0		3 0 0

Account Title _Van_   **Account No.** _120_

Date		Accounts/Explanation	Post. Ref.	Debit	Credit	Balance
20X1						
Dec.	8	Purchase of van	GJ 1	1 5 0 0 0		1 5 0 0 0

Exhibit 7 *(continued)*

Account Title	Accounts Payable (Supplies, Inc.)	Account No.	200				
Date	**Accounts/Explanation**	**Post. Ref.**	**Debit**		**Credit**	**Balance**	
20X1							
Dec. 13	Purchase of operating						
	supplies on account	GJ 1			3 0 0	3 0 0	
28	Payment on account	GJ 2	3 0 0			- 0 -	

Account Title	Notes Payable—BMAC	Account No.	210				
Date	**Accounts/Explanation**	**Post. Ref.**	**Debit**		**Credit**	**Balance**	
20X1							
Dec. 8	Loan for van	GJ 1			1 2 0 0 0	1 2 0 0 0	

Account Title	Don Carson, Capital	Account No.	300				
Date	**Accounts/Explanation**	**Post. Ref.**	**Debit**		**Credit**	**Balance**	
20X1							
Dec. 1	Investment in Carson Catering	GJ 1			5 0 0 0	5 0 0 0	

Account Title	Don Carson, Drawing	Account No.	301				
Date	**Accounts/Explanation**	**Post. Ref.**	**Debit**		**Credit**	**Balance**	
20X1							
Dec. 28	Withdrawal of cash	GJ 2	2 0 0			2 0 0	

Account Title	Catering Revenue	Account No.	400				
Date	**Accounts/Explanation**	**Post. Ref.**	**Debit**		**Credit**	**Balance**	
20X1							
Dec. 13	Receipt of cash for catering						
	revenue	GJ 1			8 0 0	8 0 0	
20	Record catering revenue—						
	M. Smith	GJ 1			1 0 0 0	1 8 0 0	

Account Title	Wages Expense	Account No.	500				
Date	**Accounts/Explanation**	**Post. Ref.**	**Debit**		**Credit**	**Balance**	
20X1							
Dec. 28	Payment of wages	GJ 2	4 0 0			4 0 0	

(continued)

Exhibit 7 *(continued)*

Account Title		_Advertising Expense_			Account No.		_501_				
Date		**Accounts/Explanation**	**Post. Ref.**	**Debit**				**Credit**		**Balance**	
20X1											
Dec.	5	Payment of advertising expense	GJ 1	5	0	0				5 0 0	

Account Title		_Food Expense_			Account No.		_502_				
Date		**Accounts/Explanation**	**Post. Ref.**	**Debit**				**Credit**		**Balance**	
20X1											
Dec.	12	Payment of food expense	GJ 1	2	0	0				2 0 0	
Dec.	19	Payment of food expense	GJ 1	3	0	0				5 0 0	

Account Title		_Gas Expense_			Account No.		_503_				
Date		**Accounts/Explanation**	**Post. Ref.**	**Debit**				**Credit**		**Balance**	
20X1											
Dec.	22	Payment of gas expense	GJ 1		2	5				2 5	

Exhibit 8   Trial Balance of Carson Catering

Carson Catering
Trial Balance
December 31, 20X1

Account Numbers		Debits	Credits
100	Cash	$ 1,175	
105	Accounts Receivable	700	
110	Operating Supplies	300	
120	Van	15,000	
200	Accounts Payable		$ —0—
210	Notes Payable—BMAC		12,000
300	Don Carson, Capital		5,000
301	Don Carson, Drawing	200	
400	Catering Revenue		1,800
500	Wages Expense	400	
501	Advertising Expense	500	
502	Food Expense	500	
503	Gas Expense	25	
	Totals	$ 18,800	$ 18,800

A group of accounts is defined as a *ledger*. The most common ledger is the general ledger, which includes the general accounts such as cash, accounts receivable, and accounts payable. All transactions are eventually recorded in these accounts; however, each account shows only one part of the transaction. For this reason, accountants record the entire transaction in a journal. This keeps track of all transactions and preserves the details of them. It also makes finding mistakes much easier. After transactions are recorded in the journal, they are posted to the proper accounts. After all transactions are posted, the trial balance is prepared.

It is also possible for a transaction to affect more than two accounts. This results in a compound journal entry. For example, cash sales may be paid partially in cash and partially on account. In this case, the debits would be to the Cash account and the Accounts Receivable, and the credit would be to Sales.

Endnotes

1. Generally, bookkeepers record and classify transactions, while accountants supervise the bookkeepers' work, summarize accounting information, and interpret financial statements.

Key Terms

account—The basic element in an accounting system used for classifying and summarizing business transactions.

account balance—The difference between the sum of the debits and the sum of the credits in an account.

balance sheet accounts—Accounts that are never closed, such as asset, liability, and owners' equity accounts.

chart of accounts—A listing of the titles (names) of all the accounts used by a particular business's accounting system. A chart of accounts should be sufficiently flexible to allow individual owners or managers to add or delete accounts to meet the specific needs of their properties. A company's chart of accounts defines the amount of detail that may be shown on its financial statements.

compound journal entries—Entries in the general journal that involve more than two accounts.

credit—Decrease in an asset or increase in a liability or capital—entered on the right side of an account; such amounts are said to be *credited* to the account.

credit balance—A balance in which the sum of the credits is greater than the sum of the debits.

debit—Increase in an asset or decrease in a liability or capital—entered on the left side of an account; such amounts are said to be *debited* or *charged* to the account.

debit balance—A balance in which the sum of the debits is greater than the sum of the credits.

double-entry accounting—A system of accounting in which every transaction affects and is recorded in at least two accounts, and the debits of the entry must equal the credits of the entry.

general ledger—The principal ledger, containing all of the balance sheet and income statement accounts (including assets, liabilities, owners' equity, revenues, expenses, and owners' drawing).

journalizing—The recording of transactions in a journal before they are entered in a ledger; the journal keeps a record of details of the transactions.

nominal accounts—Temporary accounts that are closed after each accounting cycle, such as revenue and expense accounts.

normal balance—The kind of balance, either debit or credit, that an account usually has.

posting—The process of transferring amounts recorded in the journal to the appropriate ledger accounts.

T-account—A representation of an actual account; it consists of a title, a right side, and a left side.

trial balance—A listing of the general ledger accounts and their debit and credit balances in order to test the equality of the balances.

Review Questions

1. How do revenues and expenses affect the owners' equity account?
2. Why are revenues and expenses recorded separately from the owners' equity accounts?
3. What is the difference between the terms *debit* and *credit?*
4. What is the normal balance of each major class of accounts?
5. What is the difference between balance sheet accounts and nominal accounts? What are some examples of each?
6. What are three reasons for journalizing?
7. What is the difference between a journal and a ledger?
8. What is the posting process?
9. What is the purpose of preparing a trial balance?
10. Does an "in-balance" trial balance ensure that the bookkeeper has performed flawlessly? Why or why not?

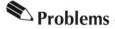 # Problems

Problem 1

Several accounts of Jacob's Inn are as follows:

- Cash

- Accounts Receivable

- Rent Expense

- Jacob, Capital

- Accounts Payable

- Room Revenue

- Interest Income

- Wages Expense

- Taxes Expense

- Water Expense

- Notes Payable

- Laundry Expense

Required:

Indicate the normal balance of each account.

Problem 2

D&G Inn has experienced several transactions on April 1 as follows:

   a. Cash received from cash sales totaled $1,750.20.
   b. Cash paid to the IRS for payroll taxes equaled $2,430.00.
   c. Check #8752 was written to Statewide Electric for $2,419.22.
   d. Sales on account for the day equaled $3,690.00.
   e. An insurance refund of $180.26 was received.
   f. Checks received in the mail and deposited in the firm's checking account totaled $5,100.00.
   g. Food supplies totaling $942.15 were purchased on account.

Required:

Determine the balance of the cash account at the end of April 1. Assume a cash balance of $6,700.00 on March 31.

Problem 3

Ryan Harris, owner of the Harris Café, has received cash and checks for his food service operation and has written several checks for the Café as follows:

   Feb. 1— Wrote check #181 in payment of accounts payable (Murphy Foods) for $230.00
   Feb. 2— Wrote check #182 to purchase equipment costing $536.00
   Feb. 3— Checks and cash totaling $2,428.36 received as cash sales were deposited in the Harris Café checking account.
   Feb. 4— Wrote check #183 for $352.00 to pay wages to his assistant
   Feb. 5— Wrote check #184 to Battlefield Utilities to pay the electric bill of $228.52

Required:

Determine the balance of the cash account at the end of the day on February 5. Assume the beginning checking account balance was $850.10 on February 1.

Problem 4

The following transactions have occurred at the Litchfield Inn:

   a. A new computer was purchased by paying 30 percent down and signing a bank note for the remainder.
   b. Salaries for the month were paid from cash.
   c. Kati Litchfield, the owner, withdrew cash for her personal use.
   d. Office supplies were purchased on account. The supplies will be expensed.
   e. Sales to guests were made on account.
   f. Excess cash was invested in temporary investments.
   g. A supplier was paid on account for supplies purchased 20 days ago.
   h. Rent for the following month was paid out of cash.

Required:

For each of the transactions, state which accounts are affected, state the normal balance for each account, and indicate whether the transaction is a debit or credit to that account. Set up your answers in columns, as indicated below:

Accounts Affected	Normal Balance	Debit or Credit

Problem 5

In order to better analyze revenue and expenses, accountants classify all revenues and expenses in separate accounts. Below is a list of revenue and expense account balances.

Wages Expense	$ 2,000
Food Sales	5,500
Rent Expense	700
Beverage Sales	400
Cost of Food Sales (Expense)	1,700
Cost of Beverage Sales (Expense)	100

Required:

   1. Create T-accounts for the revenue and expense accounts.
   2. Enter the account balances in the T-accounts (be sure to enter them on the correct side of the account).

Problem 6

You are a temporary bookkeeper hired by the Three-Ring Circus Company for the busy season. Your job is to journalize transactions that occur. The food service operation is run by Barney Bailey. He has given you the following transactions:

a. Purchase of food (hot dogs and popcorn) with cash, $75. All of this food will be sold this month.

b. Purchase of equipment on account from Circus Supply for $150.

c. Cash food sales of $300.

d. Payment of wages in cash, $110.

e. Beverage sales of $100.

f. Purchase of beverages, $12. These beverages will be sold this month.

g. Payment on account to Circus Supply for $10.

Required:

Prepare the necessary journal entries showing the debit and credit entries. In addition, provide a brief explanation of each entry.

Use the following account names: Cash; Equipment; Accounts Payable (Circus Supply Co.); Food Sales; Beverage Sales; Wage Expense; Food Expense; Beverage Expense.

Problem 7

The Turner Café has a general ledger with only twelve accounts. It is the end of the month and Josie Turner (owner) needs a trial balance in order to prepare the month's financial statement. The following are the general ledger accounts:

Cash	$ 3,500
J. Turner, Capital	10,500
Food Inventory	4,500
Prepaid Expenses	700
Accounts Payable	2,100
Equipment	15,400
Notes Payable	7,400
Sales	42,000
Cost of Food Sold	14,000
Rent Expense	2,000
Wages Expense	16,000
Other Expenses	6,900

Required:

Prepare a trial balance for the Turner Café.

Problem 8

Tyler Motel's general budget accounts at the end of December 31, 20X5, were as follows:

Cash	$ 12,400
Accounts Receivable	40,500
Inventory	18,300
Prepaid Insurance	2,100
Land	150,000
Buildings	2,400,000
Accumulated Depreciation, Buildings	1,250,000
Equipment	900,000
Accumulated Depreciation, Equipment	235,000

Accounts Payable	35,000
Notes Payable	846,000
Tyler Wray, Capital	28,600
Room Revenue	2,350,000
Wages Expense	751,000
Laundry Expense	50,000
Advertising Expense	36,000
Utilities Expense	52,000
Insurance Expense	22,000
Property Taxes Expense	20,000
Interest Expense	82,000
Depreciation Expense	115,000
Supplies Expense	33,000
Maintenance Expense	64,500

Required:

Prepare the trial balance for the Tyler Motel.

Problem 9

The following alphabetically arranged accounts and their balances were taken from the ledger of Chuck's Supply Company on December 31 of the current year:

Accounts Payable	$ 2,400	Office Equipment	1,600
Accounts Receivable	4,500	Office Supplies	85
Building	25,500	Prepaid Insurance	160
Cash	2,000	Prepaid Interest	15
Chuck Franko, Capital	18,300	Revenue	35,950
Delivery Equipment	2,500	Store Equipment	5,450
Interest Expense	200	Store Supplies	155
Interest Payable	150	Taxes Payable	250
Land	8,200	Telecommunications Expense	110
Merchandise Inventory	9,500	Truck Repairs	130
Mortgage Payable	6,500	Wages Expense	4,420
Notes Payable	1,200	Wages Payable	75
Notes Receivable	300		

Required:

Without changing the alphabetical arrangement of the accounts, prepare a trial balance for the company. That is, leave the account names in the same order, and arrange debits and credits in their proper columns. Then prepare the trial balance.

Problem 10

The following is an excerpt from the general journal of Mary's Motel:

		Dr	Cr
20X1			
Oct. 2	Cash	12,000	
	Equipment	10,000	
	Mary Ramaker, Capital		22,000
Oct. 3	Prepaid Rent	1,000	
	Cash		1,000
Oct. 3	Food Expense	2,000	
	Beverage Expense	500	
	Accounts Payable (Bixbie Food)		2,500
Oct. 4	Cash	500	
	Accounts Receivable	200	
	Food Sales		600
	Beverage Sales		100
Oct. 4	Wages Expense	195	
	Wages Payable		195
Oct. 6	Cash	100	
	Accounts Receivable		100

Required:

1. Write a general journal explanation for each of the foregoing entries.
2. Open the following T-accounts: Cash; Equipment; Mary Ramaker, Capital; Prepaid Rent; Accounts Payable (Bixbie Food); Accounts Receivable; Food Sales; Beverage Sales; Food Expense; Beverage Expense; Wages Expense; Wages Payable.
3. Post the journal entries to the proper accounts.

Problem 11

Jeremy Wayne has an account with Lee's Restaurant. He owed the restaurant $480.00 at the beginning of June. During June, Jeremy incurred several transactions with the restaurant as follows:

June 6	He purchased three meals on account for $34.00 and wrote "add 15% tip" at the bottom of the bill.
June 8	Jeremy sent Lee's Restaurant a check for $300.00 to pay down his account.
June 12	He purchased breakfast for himself on account and signed the check totaling $12.42, including tip.
June 15	Jeremy took a friend to lunch and charged the two lunches for $24.15. On the bottom of the bill, he wrote "add 20% tip."
June 21	Jeremy sent a check for $100.00 to the restaurant to pay down the account.
June 28	He visited the restaurant to celebrate his 30th wedding anniversary. The bill was for $480.00, not including the service charge or sales tax. The automatic service charge is 15 percent and 6 percent sales tax was added to the $480.00 plus service charge.

Required:

Determine how much Jeremy owed the restaurant at the end of June.

Problem 12

The trial balance of Stephanie's Steakhouse at the beginning of the day, July 1, 20X1, was:

Cash	$ 1,500	
Marketable Securities	5,000	
Accounts Receivable (Erica Lee)	20	
Accounts Receivable (Monica Ray)	15	
Office Supplies	2,250	
Cleaning Supplies	500	
Furniture	1,000	
Equipment	2,000	
Accounts Payable (Stacie Supply, Inc.)		$ 400
Notes Payable (Mineral State Bank)		1,500
Stephanie Smith, Capital		2,085
Food Sales		25,000
Beverage Sales		7,000
Food Expense	10,000	
Beverage Expense	2,000	
Wages Expense	8,000	
Utilities Expense	1,000	
Rent Expense	2,000	
Insurance Expense	500	
Office Supplies Expense	100	
Advertising Expense	100	
	$ 35,985	$ 35,985

Transactions for July 1, 20X1, were as follows:

  a. Received cash on account from Erica Lee, $10.
  b. Paid rent for the month of June, $200.
  c. Purchased food (to be expensed) on account from Stacie Supply, Inc., $250.
  d. Paid utilities bill for June, $100.
  e. Paid advertising bill for newspaper advertisement for July 1, $5.

    f. Paid temporary help for their labor for the day, $20.

    g. Sales on account to Monica Ray, $5 ($4 for food and $1 for beverages).

    h. Cash food sales for the day and beverage sales for the day, $250 and $60 respectively.

Required:

1. Set up T-accounts for each account listed in the trial balance of Stephanie's Steakhouse. Record the balance in each T-account per the trial balance. (Be sure to record the amounts on the proper side of the account.)
2. Record the transactions for July 1, 20X1. Identify each amount by its transaction letter.
3. Prepare a trial balance for July 1, 20X1 (end of day).

Problem 13

Bryan Wilson opened a coffee house using the name of BW's. During the first week, several transactions were completed:

    a. Bryan invested cash of $5,000 and contributed several assets at their fair market values: furniture, $5,000; equipment, $50,000; land, $100,000; and building, $450,000.

    b. Purchased operating supplies costing $400 on account from Stockwell's Wholesale.

    c. Purchased additional equipment costing $800 with cash.

    d. Paid an advertising bill for $150 using cash.

    e. Paid wages for the week of $450.

    f. Purchased food and beverage supplies on account of $1,200 and $400, respectively from Joe's Supplies. (Record this purchase in inventory).

    g. Paid utility bill for $80.00 with cash.

    h. Deposited $2,400 of cash received from customers for food and beverage sales.

Required:

1. Set up the following T–accounts: Cash, Food and Beverage Inventory, Furniture, Equipment, Land, Building, Accounts Payable, B. Wilson, Capital, Food and Beverage Sales, Operating Supplies Expenses, Advertising Expenses, and Wages Expenses.
2. Record the transactions in the accounts with each amount identified by the transaction letter.
3. Prepare a trial balance.

Problem 14

Paul Olivia opened a pizza business under the name of Olivia's Pizza Parlor, and during the first week completed the following transactions:

    a. Invested cash of $2,000 and the following assets at their fair market values: furniture, $2,000; equipment, $3,000; and building, $8,000.

    b. Purchased food and beverages on account, costing $500 and $100, respectively, from Edgar's Food Supply.

    c. Purchased a typewriter with cash, $200.

    d. Paid for newspaper advertising, $30.

e. Paid utility bills, $50.

f. Paid wages for the week, $250.

g. Paid for cooking supplies used during the week, $10.

h. Paid $100 on account to Edgar's Food Supply.

i. Received $900 from customers for pizza and beverages sold. Pizza sales amounted to $750, the remainder was beverage sales.

Required:

1. Set up the following T-accounts: Cash; Furniture; Equipment; Building; Accounts Payable (Edgar's Food Supply); Paul Olivia, Capital; Food Sales; Beverage Sales; Advertising Expense; Utilities Expense; Wages Expense; Cooking Supplies Expense; Food Expense; Beverage Expense.

2. Record the transactions in the accounts with each amount identified by its transaction letter.

3. Prepare a trial balance.

Challenge Problem

Problem 15

Jack Wicks is the owner and manager of the Rodeside Motel, which caters to family travelers. He has hired you to do his bookkeeping. The following transactions occurred in August:

a. Cash of $1,000 was paid on August 15 for September's rent.

b. Cash room sales of $15,000.

c. Room sales on account, $250.

d. Purchase of cleaning supplies for cash, $290.

e. Purchase of office supplies on account from Bing's Office Supply Hut, $150.

f. New investment by owner of $1,000.

g. Payment on account (Bing's), $50.

h. Rental income from vending machines, $75.

i. Payment of wages with cash, $5,700.

Further, he has account balances for the beginning of August as follows:

Cash	$ 3,120
Accounts Receivable	200
Cleaning Supplies	30
Office Supplies	100
Accounts Payable, Bing's Office Supply Hut	50
Notes Payable	400
Jack Wicks, Capital	3,000

Required:

1. Enter the transactions into the general journal, showing debits and credits, and an explanation for each.

2. Open T-accounts for each balance sheet account as well as for the revenue and expense accounts. Enter the beginning balances.

3. Post the August transactions to the T-accounts. Determine the ending balance for each account.

4. Prepare a trial balance for August 31, 20X3.

Chapter 3 Outline

The Need for Adjustments
Cash versus Accrual Accounting
Classification of Adjusting Entries
Deferral Adjustments Illustrated
    Prepaid Insurance/Insurance Expense
    Depreciation Expense
    Unearned Revenues
Accrual Adjustments Illustrated
    Accrued Wages Payable
    Accrued Utilities
    Accrued Assets
Failure to Prepare Adjustments
Comprehensive Illustration—Adjustments

Competencies

1. Explain the need for and timing of accounting adjustments, and distinguish between cash basis accounting and accrual basis accounting. (pp. 79–81)

2. Describe the major classes of accounting adjustments and use them to classify adjustments. (pp. 81–82)

3. Demonstrate how to enter deferral adjustments, and use straight-line depreciation for adjusting depreciation expense. (pp. 82–85, 89–95)

4. Demonstrate how to enter accrual adjustments. (pp. 85–88, 89–95)

5. Explain how a failure to make accounting adjustments affects financial statements. (pp. 88–89)

3

Accounting Adjustments

AT THE END of an accounting period, a trial balance of the general ledger accounts is taken. However, during the accounting period, certain assets are partially consumed but not recorded as expenses, and some liabilities are incurred but not recorded as expenses. Such "activities," along with others to be described in this chapter, must be recorded with journal entries called *adjustments* or **adjusting entries.**

The Need for Adjustments

The time period principle of accounting states that the life of an enterprise is divided into segments of time generally as short as a month, and the operations for the period and the financial position at the end of the period are reported in the financial statements. The income statement, which shows revenues and expenses, reports operations of the business enterprise, while the balance sheet reports the financial position at the end of the accounting period. Even though all transactions have been properly recorded and posted, several accounts must be adjusted to reflect the proper balances and to ensure that the financial statements prepared therefrom are reasonably accurate. Think of the adjusting process as a "fine-tuning" of the books. With the adjusting process, accountants attempt to make financial statements more accurate. Notice two things that are common to every adjusting entry: (1) Each entry involves a balance sheet account and an income statement account; and (2) no adjusting entry involves cash.

The matching principle is the major reason for adjustments. Expenses incurred must be *matched* with revenues generated. Two examples illustrate this requirement:

1. A vehicle is purchased at a cost of $21,600 and recorded in the Equipment account (a fixed asset). Assume the vehicle has a three-year life, after which it will be useless and worth $–0–. The expense related to this equipment is depreciation; therefore, each month the accountant records $\frac{1}{36}$ of the vehicle cost as depreciation expense. In this case, then, depreciation expense of $600 is recorded monthly via an adjusting entry. Not only are expenses increased monthly by $600, but fixed assets are reduced monthly by $600 to reflect the reduction in the value of the vehicle.

2. Assume a lodging firm pays $24,000 on January 1, 20X1, for fire insurance protection for the year. Since the firm benefits beyond one month from this expenditure, the entire amount is recorded as Prepaid Insurance (an asset) for

$24,000. However, at the end of January 20X1, the firm must recognize the expense for the month and reduce the value of the asset (Prepaid Insurance). This is accomplished with an adjusting entry of $2,000. Insurance Expense is debited and Prepaid Insurance is credited for the $2,000. The continuous using up of insurance coverage is referred to as a *continuous event*, and the expense relating to this item could be recognized continuously as time passes. However, accountants customarily record the adjusting entries to recognize insurance expense just before preparing the financial statements. Therefore, if the financial statements are prepared monthly, a monthly adjustment is made; if the firm issues statements quarterly instead of monthly, a quarterly adjustment is made.

When making adjustments, accountants must also consider how material or significant an item is. For example, a large firm may store great amounts of office supplies in inventory to ensure that the supplies are on hand when someone needs them. This way, the firm would not have to order an item each time someone needs to use it. Theoretically, office supplies should be recorded as assets and expensed as they are used. However, the accountant might not record office supplies expense every time an item is removed from inventory for usage. Instead, he or she might wait until the end of the accounting period to make a single entry to recognize the entire office supplies expense for the period. The cost of making an entry each time an item is removed from inventory is greater than the benefit realized from any accuracy achieved. In addition, perhaps the office supplies expense in total is quite immaterial in relation to the firm's activities. When the expense is insignificant, the item (office supplies in this case) may simply be expensed when purchased, with no asset recognized.

Cash versus Accrual Accounting

Cash basis accounting recognizes an accounting transaction at the point of cash inflow or outflow. This method of accounting does not require the adjustments discussed in the previous example of the vehicle. Instead of accounting for depreciation expense, this method of accounting would expense the vehicle one time only: when it was purchased. Similarly, the fire insurance coverage would be expensed only once in cash basis accounting: when the invoice was paid. Although cash basis accounting is simpler than accrual basis accounting, its use is generally limited to the smallest of hospitality firms.

Accrual basis accounting recognizes expenses when they are incurred regardless of when payment is made, and recognizes revenue when it is earned regardless of when cash is received. At the end of an accounting period, accrual basis accounting allows a more meaningful evaluation of the business's operation because it more accurately matches expenses with revenue.

Under accrual basis accounting, procedures must be set up to record all transactions relating to a particular time period during that period. That is, costs must be recorded when they are actually incurred and revenues recorded when they are actually earned, regardless of when cash actually changes hands. For instance, the electric bill for April may arrive late in May, yet the expense must be recognized in

April when it actually occurred. In addition, some expenses, such as payroll, do not exactly match the accounting period. Payrolls are paid periodically on a certain day of the week. Only occasionally would that date correspond to the end of the accounting period. Therefore, it is necessary to adjust payroll costs to the accounting period.

Other kinds of transactions receive special treatment under accrual basis accounting. For example, purchases of buildings are not considered expenses only of the period in which they are purchased. Instead, a pro rata share of the cost in the form of depreciation expense is charged to each accounting period during the useful lives of long-lived purchases. Inventory purchase transactions present another example. Only when the inventory is sold does it become a cost in determining operating performance. Calculation of the cost of goods sold involves beginning and ending inventories plus purchases.

Classification of Adjusting Entries

Adjusting entries consist of two major classifications: deferrals and accruals. **Deferrals** include adjustments for amounts previously recorded in accounts, while **accruals** include adjustments for which no data have been previously recorded in the accounts.

Deferred items include the following two types of adjustments:

Type of Adjustment	Example
Previously recorded assets become expense	Prepaid insurance (an asset) becomes insurance expense as time elapses
Previously recorded liabilities become revenue	Deferred service revenue (a liability) becomes revenue as services are provided

Accrued items include the following two types of adjustments:

Type of Adjustment	Example
Assets and revenues not previously provided	Recording a service provided but not previously recorded as a receivable (an asset) and a revenue
Liabilities and expenses not previously recorded	Recording the amount due the utility company (liability) and the corresponding expense

First, we will illustrate adjustments for deferral items. The asset/expense adjustments will include insurance and depreciation, while the liabilities/revenue adjustment will include the recognition of services provided.

Then, we will illustrate the adjustments for accrual items with liability/expense adjustments for accruing payroll and accruing utility expenses. We will illustrate the second type of accrual adjustment, the asset/revenue adjustment, with accrual of assets.

We will use the hypothetical rooms-only Michaels Motel to illustrate adjusting entries. The Michaels Motel records monthly adjustments and has a fiscal year-end of December 31.

Deferral Adjustments Illustrated

Prepaid Insurance/Insurance Expense

Assume the Michaels Motel paid a one-year fire insurance premium of $12,000 on January 1, 20X2. The payment was initially recorded in the Prepaid Insurance account (an asset account) since the benefit from the insurance payment lies in the future. Cash (another asset) was reduced by the amount of payment. At the end of January 20X2, an adjusting entry must be prepared to recognize the expiration of the asset (Prepaid Insurance) and to recognize Insurance Expense. The journal entry on January 31, 20X2, is recorded as follows:

Insurance Expense	$1,000	
Prepaid Insurance		$1,000
To record insurance expense for January.		

The T-accounts for Prepaid Insurance and Insurance Expense for the January 1 payment and the end of the month adjustment would appear as follows:

Prepaid Insurance

Jan. 1 (payment)	12,000	Jan. 31 (adjustment)	1,000
Jan. 31 (balance)	11,000		

Insurance Expense

Jan. 31 (adjustment)	1,000	

The Prepaid Insurance account now reflects the amount of unexpired insurance of $11,000, which is 11 months of insurance at $1,000 per month, or the amount for 12 months of $12,000 less the expired insurance cost of $1,000. The Insurance Expense account reflects the amount of insurance expense for January, which is $\frac{1}{12}$ of the annual insurance premium of $12,000.

Remember, the major reason for making this adjustment is so that the financial statements will properly reflect results of operations for the month and the financial position at the end of the month. Therefore, the income statement for the month would show $1,000 of insurance expense, and the balance sheet would include prepaid insurance of $11,000 as an asset.

Depreciation Expense

Just as prepaid insurance indicates a gradual continuous use of an asset, so depreciation is the expense of a depreciable asset. There are major differences between the two. First, prepaid insurance is written off over its relatively short life (generally one year), while the costs of property and equipment are expensed over long useful lives (often ranging up to 40 years). Second, the cost of property and equipment is generally relatively large compared to the cost of insurance. Still, the adjustment process involves an asset being expensed in both cases.

Depreciable assets are property and equipment such as buildings, furniture, vehicles, and equipment that have lives in excess of one year and are used in the business to generate revenues. The reduction in the value of depreciable assets is simply called *depreciation*. There are several different methods of accounting for depreciation; this chapter will present only the simplest, the straight-line method. The following three elements are involved in computing depreciation expense using the straight-line method:

1. **Cost of the asset.** This is the amount the enterprise pays to purchase the depreciable asset. In our illustration, the Michaels Motel was purchased on January 1, 20X2, at a cost of $3,500,000.

2. **Estimated useful life.** This is the estimated useful life of a depreciable asset. Unfortunately, since we are dealing with the future, we cannot be completely sure of the life of any depreciable asset. In our illustration, we will assume the building (the motel) has a useful life of 25 years.

3. **Estimated salvage value** (sometimes called *residual value*). This is the estimated market value of the depreciable asset at the end of its useful life. In our illustration, we estimate the motel will be worth $500,000 at the end of 25 years.

The equation for determining the depreciation expense for the accounting period is as follows:

$$\text{Depreciation Expense} = \frac{C - SV}{n}$$

$$\text{where } C = \text{Depreciable asset cost}$$
$$SV = \text{Estimated salvage value}$$
$$n = \text{Number of periods of useful life}$$

Therefore, the monthly depreciation expense of the building for January 20X2 is $10,000, determined as follows:

$$\text{Monthly Depreciation Expense} = \frac{\$3,500,000 - \$500,000}{300 \text{ months}}$$

$$= \underline{\$10,000}$$

The depreciation expense for January 20X2 is recorded with an adjusting entry:

Depreciation Expense	$10,000	
Accumulated Depreciation, Building		$10,000
To record depreciation expense of the building		
for January.		

The T-accounts after the recording and posting of this adjusting entry would appear as follows:

Depreciation Expense

Jan. 31 (adjustment) 10,000	

Accumulated Depreciation, Building

	Jan. 31 (adjustment) 10,000

Depreciation Expense will be reported on the income statement while the Accumulated Depreciation, Building, will be shown on the balance sheet as a deduction from the Building account.

The Accumulated Depreciation account is a contra-asset account that contains the total depreciation recorded on the building through the balance sheet date. This account normally carries a credit balance. The balance of this account is subtracted from the Building account to report the *net* book value (or *carrying value*) of the building on the balance sheet. Thus, the Michaels Motel would show the net book value of $3,490,000, determined as follows:

Cost of building	$3,500,000
Less: Accumulated depreciation	10,000
Net book value	$3,490,000

Unearned Revenues

A liability/revenue adjustment involving **unearned revenues** generally covers instances in which a guest pays cash for future services. In a lodging enterprise, a customer may pay for banquet space in advance. This payment would be recorded as a liability until the hotel rendered the service, thereby earning the revenue. To illustrate this type of adjustment, assume James Bell, a guest of the Michaels Motel, checks into a room on January 17 for 30 days. The Michaels Motel records the $600 it receives from Bell on January 16 as advanced deposits. Since Bell will not be charging any amounts to his account, his record is not kept at the front desk. Instead, it is placed in monthly rentals, which Michaels Motel's accountants adjust at the end of the month or at check-out, whichever comes first. James Bell stays at the Michaels Motel through the rest of January, which is 15 days. Therefore, of the

$600 deposit, $300 should be recognized as revenue at the end of the month, since $\frac{15}{30}$ times $600 equals $300.

At the end of January, the adjustment to record the revenue and reduce the liability account would be recorded in this way:

Advanced Deposits	$300	
Room Revenues		$300
To record reduction in advanced deposits		
account of James Bell.		

The T-accounts after the entry is recorded and posted would appear as follows:

Advanced Deposits

		Jan. 17 (cash received)	600
Jan. 31 (adjustment)	300		
		Jan. 31 (balance)	300

Room Revenues

		Jan. 31 (balance before adjustment)	65,000
		Jan. 31 (adjustment)	300
		Jan. 31 (balance)	65,300

The Advanced Deposits account is shown as a liability on the balance sheet dated January 31, 20X2. The room revenue of $65,300 earned in January will be reported on the firm's income statement.

All deferral adjustments are made to financial data already recorded in an enterprise's asset and liability accounts.

Accrual Adjustments Illustrated

Accrual adjustments are made for business data that have not yet been recorded on the firm's accounting records. Accrual adjustments include two types: liability/expense adjustments and asset/revenue adjustments. The liability/expense adjustments to be illustrated with the hypothetical Michaels Motel include the accrual of wages payable and the accrual of utilities expense. The asset/revenue adjustment includes the accrual of interest income on investments owned by the motel.

Accrued Wages Payable

Wages are paid periodically to employees, generally weekly, biweekly, or monthly; however, the pay period seldom ends—and employees are seldom paid—on the last day of the month, unless employees are paid on a monthly basis. Therefore, to record all wages for the month, wages must be accrued using an adjusting entry. The accrual recognizes both Wages Expense and the liability Accrued Wages Payable.

Assume the Michaels Motel pays its employees every two weeks, and the last payday in January is January 24. Therefore, wages for the period of January 25–31 must be accrued. For simplicity's sake, let us assume that all employees' wages total $10,000 every 14 days. Since the January 25–31 period covers seven days, the accrual should be $5,000, according to this calculation:

$$\$10,000 \times \frac{7}{14} = \$5,000$$

The adjustment would be recorded as follows:

Wages Expense	$5,000	
Accrued Wages Payable		$5,000
To record accrued wages at the end of January.		

The T-accounts after posting from the journal would appear as follows:

Wages Expense

Jan. 24 (balance)	17,143		
Jan. 31 (adjustment)	5,000		
Jan. 31 (balance)	22,143		

Accrued Wages Payable

	Jan. 31 (adjustment)	5,000

The income statement would reflect the Wages Expense of $22,143 for January, while the balance sheet would include the liability of $5,000 for Accrued Wages Payable.

Accrued Utilities

The Michaels Motel must record additional liability/expense adjustments at the end of the month, since the motel has not yet received invoices for utility services it has used, such as telephone, electricity, and water. To illustrate this type of adjustment, we will show how the Michaels Motel would accrue the electricity expense.

Assume the Michaels Motel is billed on the fifth day of the month for service it received the previous month; that is, on February 5, the motel receives the January electric bill. However, this hospitality enterprise wishes to record all of its adjustments on January 31 and prepare its financial statements as soon as possible.

Therefore, the Michaels Motel must estimate its January electric bill. There are several ways to do this; however, the Michaels Motel's accountant simply reads the electric meter and multiplies the kilowatt hours (kwh) of electricity used by the electric rate. For the month of January, assume the Michaels Motel used 71,050 kwh. The electricity expense for January based on the kwh used and the assumed electric rate of $.06 per kwh is calculated as follows:

$$71{,}050 \quad \times \quad .06 \quad = \quad \underline{\underline{\$4{,}263}}$$

The adjustment to accrue electricity expense is recorded in this way:

Electricity Expense	$4,263	
Accrued Expenses Payable		$4,263
To accrue electricity for January.		

The T-accounts after the accrual is posted would appear as follows:

Electricity Expense

Jan. 31 (adjustment) 4,263	

Accrued Expenses Payable

	Jan. 31 (adjustment) 4,263

Thus, the electricity expense for the period is recorded in keeping with the matching principle. In addition, the corresponding liability, the amount the Michaels Motel will owe the electric company, is recorded.

The income statement would reflect the Electricity Expense of $4,263, while the balance sheet would show the Accrued Expenses Payable of $4,263 as a liability.

Accrued Assets

Accrued assets are assets that exist at the end of the accounting period but have not yet been recognized. These assets reflect the right to receive future cash payments, and the corresponding revenue recognizes earnings. Examples of accrued assets include unbilled services and accrued interest receivable. The following example will illustrate the recording of accrued interest receivable for the Michaels Motel.

Assume the Michaels Motel invests $50,000 in a certificate of deposit on January 16, 20X2. The six-month certificate will generate $2,000 in interest at an annual interest rate of 8 percent. The Michaels Motel will receive the investment of $50,000 plus the interest of $2,000 on July 15, 20X2. Even though the Michaels Motel received no interest at the end of January 20X2, it has earned interest and records it with an adjusting entry.

The amount of interest earned is determined using the following equation:

$$\text{Interest} = P \times R \times T$$

$$\text{where } P = \text{Principal (the amount invested)}$$
$$R = \text{Annual interest rate}$$
$$T = \text{Portion of year covered by time of investment}$$

Therefore, the Michaels Motel should record $164.38 interest, which is calculated in this way:

$$\text{Interest} = \$50,000 \times .08 \times \frac{15}{365}$$
$$= \underline{\underline{\$164.38}}$$

The T element of the equation includes the number of days in January during which the $50,000 was invested, divided by the number of days in the year. Incidentally, the day the investment was made, January 16, is not included in the count of 15 days, so we assume the certificate was purchased at the end of the business day.

The adjusting entry would record the interest income in the following way:

Accrued Interest Receivable	$164.38	
Interest Income		$164.38
To record interest earned for January.		

An asset account, Accrued Interest Receivable, reflects the amount due the Michaels Motel at the end of January, while the revenue account, Interest Income, reflects the interest earned for January.

The T-accounts after the accrual was posted would be as follows:

Accrued Interest Receivable

Jan. 31 (adjustment)	164.38		

Interest Income

		Jan. 31 (adjustment)	164.38

The Accrued Interest Receivable is reported on the balance sheet as an asset, while Interest Income is shown on the income statement as revenue.

Failure to Prepare Adjustments

The failure to prepare and record adjusting entries will affect both the balance sheet and the income statement. Exhibit 1 shows the impact this failure would have on each statement. As Exhibit 1 shows, each type of adjusting entry not recorded has a different impact on the balance sheet and the income statement. In addition to the adjustments discussed in this chapter, many more adjustments are possible. The adjustments presented in this chapter serve simply as examples.

Exhibit 1 Impact on Financial Statements of Failure to Prepare Adjustments

Type of Adjustment	Example	Impact on Balance Sheet			Impact on Income Statement		
		Assets	Liabilities	Owners' Equity	Revenue	Expenses	Net Income
Deferral— Asset/ Expense	Depreciation	over	none	over	none	under	over
Deferral— Liability/ Revenue	Advanced Deposits	none	over	under	under	none	under
Accrual— Liability/ Expense	Wages Accrual	none	under	over	none	under	over
Accrual— Asset/ Revenue	Accrued Interest Receivable	under	none	under	under	none	under

Note: "Over" indicates *overstated*, "under" indicates *understated*, "none" indicates *no change*.

Comprehensive Illustration—Adjustments

We will use Carson Catering to provide a comprehensive illustration of adjustments. Assume that Carson Catering had just been formed and had a few transactions during its first month, December 20X1. Now we find Carson Catering on
November 30, 20X2, at the end of its first fiscal year of operations. The chart of
accounts includes the following:

Account Number	Account Title	Description
100	Cash	Cash in the bank and on hand
101	Certificate of Deposit	Investments in certificates of deposit with First Bank
105	Accounts Receivable	Amounts due the company from customers
107	Accrued Interest Receivable	Account for recording interest accrued but not received
110	Operating Supplies	Supplies to be used in catering parties for customers
115	Prepaid Rent	Account for recording rent paid in advance
120	Van	Vehicle used in catering business

121	Accumulated Depreciation, Van	Account for accumulating depreciation on van
125	Equipment	Account for recording equipment purchases
126	Accumulated Depreciation, Equipment	Account for accumulating depreciation on equipment
200	Accounts Payable	Amounts owed suppliers for items purchased on account
201	Accrued Wages Payable	Account for accruing unpaid wages
202	Accrued Interest Payable	Account for accruing unpaid interest
210	Notes Payable— Big Motors Acceptance Corporation (BMAC)	Amount due BMAC from loan for van
300	Don Carson, Capital	Owner's equity in the business
301	Don Carson, Drawing	Amount of withdrawals by owner
400	Catering Revenue	Amounts earned from catering parties
410	Interest Income	Account for recording interest earned
500	Wages Expense	Wages paid to employees of the business
501	Advertising Expense	Cost of advertising purchased
502	Food Expense	Cost of food catered to customers
503	Gas Expense	Cost of gas, oil, and so on, used in van
504	Rent Expense	Account to charge for rent expense
505	Supplies Expense	Account to charge for supplies expense
506	Interest Expense	Account for recording interest expense
507	Utility Expense	Account for recording utility expense
508	Depreciation Expense	Account for recording depreciation expense

Carson Catering's trial balance, which was figured at the end of its last business day and doesn't yet include any adjustments, is shown in Exhibit 2.

The following adjustments for Carson Catering at the end of November 30, 20X2, are required:

Adjustment	Explanation
1. Accrued Interest Receivable/Interest Income	No interest income has been accrued on the certificate of deposit that was purchased on July 1. The annual interest rate is 8 percent.
2. Prepaid Rent/Rent Expense	On July 1, 20X2, an office was leased for 12 months for $12,000. The rent for the 12 months was paid on July 1, 20X2. Prepaid Rent and Rent Expense have been adjusted for July through October, but not for November.

Exhibit 2   Trial Balance before Adjustments

Account Number	Title	Debits	Credits
	Carson Catering		
	Trial Balance (Before Adjustments)		
	November 30, 20X2		
100	Cash	$ 3,000	
101	Certificate of Deposit	10,000	
105	Accounts Receivable	6,200	
110	Operating Supplies	500	
115	Prepaid Rent	8,000	
120	Van	15,000	
125	Equipment	10,000	
200	Accounts Payable		$ 5,500
210	Notes Payable—BMAC		9,385
300	Don Carson, Capital		25,000
301	Don Carson, Drawing	8,000	
400	Catering Revenue		137,418
410	Interest Income		500
500	Wages Expense	37,000	
501	Advertising Expense	10,000	
502	Food Expense	60,000	
503	Gas Expense	2,200	
504	Rent Expense	4,000	
505	Supplies Expense	2,100	
506	Interest Expense	1,003	
507	Utilities Expense	800	
	Total	$177,803	$177,803

3. Operating Supplies/ Supplies Expense

A physical inventory of operating supplies on November 30, 20X2, reflects $250 in operating supplies on hand at the end of the fiscal year. This amount differs from the Operating Supplies balance of $500.

4. Depreciation of Equipment and Van

Depreciation expense has not been calculated on either the van or the equipment. The straight-line method will be used. The van was purchased for $15,000 on December 8, 20X1, so it will be depreciated for one full year. Its expected useful life is 4 years, and the estimated salvage value is $1,000.

The catering equipment was purchased on January 1, 20X2, and it will have a useful life of 5 years. Further, it will have a zero salvage value. The equipment will be depreciated for 11 months.

5. Accrued Wages Expense/
   Accrued Wages Payable

   Wages expense of $2,500 related to November 20X2 were not paid by the end of November 20X2.

6. Accrued Interest Payable/
   Interest Expense

   The last payment to BMAC was on October 1, 20X2. Two months of interest will be accrued. The annual interest rate is 12 percent, and the amount owed BMAC after the last payment is $9,385.

7. Utilities Expense/Accrued
   Expenses

   Carson Catering has not received the electricity bill for the month of November. A reading of the electric meter reveals 2,000 kwh were used, and the electric rate is $.08 per kwh.

Exhibit 3 shows (1) the calculation of the amount to be recorded with an adjusting entry, and (2) the journal entry. All adjusting entries are rounded to the nearest dollar to reduce the detail in this illustration.

Adjustment 1 records interest earned on the $10,000 certificate of deposit purchased July 1. No interest earned had previously been recorded. The interest is calculated for the five-month period of July through November 20X2. The effect on the financial statements is to increase Interest Income shown on the income statement and to increase Accrued Interest Receivable included on the balance sheet.

Adjustment 2 records rent expense for the month of November 20X2. Each month since July, this adjustment has been prepared to recognize the monthly rent expense of $1,000. So Rent Expense to be shown on the income statement is increased by $1,000, and the asset, Prepaid Rent, shown on the balance sheet, is reduced by $1,000.

Adjustment 3 records the difference in the operating supplies per the accounting records and the physical inventory of operating supplies at the end of November 20X2. Carson Catering's accounting procedure for operating supplies is to record purchases in the asset account Operating Supplies, and to determine the usage (expense) for the month by subtracting the dollar amount of the physical inventory of operating supplies from the amount shown in the asset account. The amount shown on the trial balance for Operating Supplies is $500. Since the physical inventory reveals only $250, Operating Supplies must be reduced by $250 and Supplies Expense increased by $250. The impact of this adjustment on the financial statements is an increase in the income statement's Supplies Expense of $250 and a reduction of the balance sheet's asset Operating Supplies by $250.

Adjustment 4 records depreciation expense on the van and the equipment for the year. Like many small businesses, Carson Catering waits until the end of the year to record its depreciation expense. The compound journal entry shows depreciation expense of $5,333 and increases in the two contra-asset accounts by a total of $5,333. Even though the van was not purchased on December 1, depreciation expense is calculated for the entire year. The difference between December 1, 20X1 (the first day of the fiscal year), and the purchase date of December 8, 20X1, is deemed to be insignificant. On the other hand, depreciation expense on the equipment is calculated for 11 months, since the equipment was purchased one month into the fiscal year.

Exhibit 3 Adjusting Entries

Carson Catering
Adjusting Entries
November 30, 20X2

Adjustment No.	Type of Adjustment	Calculation	Journal Entry		
1	Accrued interest	Interest = Principal × Rate × Time = 10,000 × .08 × 5/12 = $333	Accrued Interest Receivable Interest Income To record interest income earned through November, 20X2.	333	333
2	Rent expense	Monthly Rent = Annual Rent × 1/12 = 12,000 × 1/12 = $1,000	Rent Expense Prepaid Rent To record rent expense for November 20X2.	1,000	1,000
3	Operating supplies	Operating supplies per books $500 Physical count of operating supplies 250 Reduction in operating supplies $250	Operating Supplies Expense Operating Supplies To record the reduction in operating supplies on hand.	250	250

4	Depreciation expense	Depreciation of Van
		Depreciation = (C − SV)/n
		= (15,000 − 1,000)/4
		= $3,500
		
		Depreciation of Equipment
		Annual depreciation = $10,000/5
		= 2,000
		Depreciation for 11 months = 2,000 (11/12)
		= $1,833
			Depreciation Expense
			    Accumulated Depreciation, Van
			    Accumulated Depreciation, Equipment
			To record depreciation expense for the year.
				5,333	3,500
					1,833

5	Accrued wages	Simply $2,500	Wages Expense Accrued Wages Payable To record accrued wages at November 30, 20X2.	2,500	2,500
6	Accrued interest expense	Interest = Principal × Rate × Time = 9,385 × .12 × 2/12 = $188	Interest Expense Accrued Interest Payable To record interest expense since last debt payment.	188	188
7	Utilities expense	Expense = kwh × Cost/kwh = 2,000 × .08 = $160	Utilities Expense Accrued Expense Payable To accrue utilities expense (electricity) for November 20X2.	160	160

The impact of this adjustment is that depreciation expense of $5,333 is shown on the income statement, and the same amount is shown as a reduction of the two depreciable assets on the balance sheet.

Adjustment 5 records unpaid wages at the end of November 20X2. Employees worked during November; however, the pay period during which the $2,500 in unpaid wages were earned ends during December 20X2 and will be paid then. Still, because of the matching principle, the expense is recognized with this adjustment as well as the liability Accrued Wages Payable. This adjustment results in an increase in Wages Expense to be shown on the income statement and an increase in Accrued Wages Payable, a liability account, which is shown on the balance sheet.

Adjustment 6 is prepared to record interest expense on the unpaid balance owed to BMAC. When the van was purchased, $12,000 of its cost was financed with a loan from BMAC. Since the last payment was made on October 1, 20X2, interest expense must be accrued for the two months of October and November 20X2. The interest expense is determined based on the balance due BMAC after the last payment. This adjustment results in an increase in the Interest Expense account of $188 to be reflected on the income statement. Accrued Interest Payable is a liability account that will be included on the balance sheet.

Adjustment 7 is recorded to recognize the electricity used during November 20X2. Utilities Expense is shown on the income statement, while the Accrued Expenses account is a liability that will be reflected on the balance sheet.

Exhibit 4 lists Carson Catering's revenue and expense accounts. The pre-adjustment balances of revenue accounts total $137,918, while pre-adjustment balances of expense accounts total $117,103. The difference of $20,815 is Carson Catering's preliminary net profit for the fiscal year ended November 30, 20X2. However, seven adjusting entries were required to reflect the proper amounts in revenue and expense accounts. Each of the adjustments affects one revenue or expense account. The net impact of the seven adjustments is the reduction of net profits by $9,098 to $11,717 for the year. Thus, the failure to record these adjustments would have shown an overstatement in net profits of $9,098, which is 77.6 percent of the net profit for the year.

Summary

In an accrual basis accounting system, the goal is to produce an accurate picture of revenue, expenses, and therefore net income. Revenues are recorded when earned, and expenses are recorded when incurred. However, because the financial statements of a business are produced at the end of arbitrary time periods (months, for example), certain adjustments must be made to accounts to ensure that account balances are accurate for each time period. For example, certain assets may have been used and should be expensed although the entry has not been made, or a liability may have been incurred but not recorded. These entries are called *adjusting entries*. Adjusting entries always involve an income statement account and a balance sheet account. Adjusting entries never involve cash.

There are two types of adjusting entries: deferrals and accruals. Deferrals are adjustments for amounts previously recorded in accounts, while accruals are

Exhibit 4   Impact of Adjustments on Carson Catering's Net Profits

Revenue/ Expense Accounts	Pre-Adjustment Balances Debits	Credits	Adjustments Debits	Credits	Adjusted Balances Debits	Credits
Revenue:						
Catering Revenue		$137,418				$137,418
Interest Income		500		(1) $333		833
Expenses:						
Wages Exp.	$ 37,000		(5) $2,500		$ 39,500	
Adv. Exp.	10,000				10,000	
Food Exp.	60,000				60,000	
Gas Exp.	2,200				2,200	
Rent Exp.	4,000		(2) 1,000		5,000	
Supplies Expense	2,100		(3) 250		2,350	
Interest Expense	1,003		(6) 188		1,191	
Utilities Expense	800		(7) 160		960	
Depreciation Expense	–0–		(4) 5,333		5,333	
Totals	$117,103	$137,918	$9,431	$333	$126,534	$138,251

Pre-Adjustment Total Revenues	$ 137,918	Total Adjustments to Revenue	$ 333	Adjusted Total Revenue	$ 138,251
Pre-Adjustment Total Expenses	117,103	Total Adjustments to Expenses	9,431	Adjusted Total Expenses	126,534
Pre-Adjustment Net Profit	$ 20,815	Total Adjustment to Net Profit	$9,098	Adjusted Net Profit	$ 11,717

adjustments for which no data have been previously entered. Depreciation is a special adjustment designed to match expense to revenue from the use of property and equipment.

Unearned revenues occur when a guest pays for services before they are actually rendered. Such unearned revenues are actually liabilities of the business until the revenues are earned.

If adjusting entries are not prepared, the revenue and expenses will not be accurate. Therefore, net income will not be accurate. In addition, some balance sheet accounts will be overstated or understated. Adjusting entries must be recorded if businesses are to achieve reasonably accurate financial statements.

Key Terms

accrual basis accounting—System of reporting revenues and expenses in the period in which they are considered to have been earned or incurred, regardless of the actual time of collection or payment.

accruals—Adjusting entries made for business data that have not yet been entered into accounts.

adjusting entries—Entries required at the end of an accounting period to record internal adjustments of various accounts due to the matching principle.

cash basis accounting—Reporting of revenues and expenses at the time they are collected or paid, respectively.

cost of asset—Amount paid by a business to purchase an asset.

deferrals—Adjusting entries made for business data that have already been recorded in other accounts.

depreciable assets—Property and equipment owned by a business that last more than one year and are used to generate revenue.

estimated salvage value—The estimated market value of a depreciable asset at the end of its useful life.

estimated useful life—The estimated length of time that a depreciable asset will be used to help generate revenue.

unearned revenues—The offset for cash received for services before they are rendered.

Review Questions

1. What is the purpose of adjusting entries?

2. Are adjusting entries used in an accrual basis accounting system or in a cash basis accounting system? Why?

3. What are two examples of an accrual adjusting entry?

4. What are two examples of a deferral adjusting entry?

5. Why do adjusting entries never involve cash?

6. Why does each adjusting entry involve both a balance sheet account and an income statement account?

7. What is the relation between the matching principle and adjusting entries?

8. What is unearned revenue? When does it occur? How is the advanced deposits account classified?

9. In what situation would it be necessary to record accrued wages?

10. What method is used to adjust prepaid expenses to account for partial use?

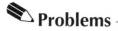**Problems** ——————————————————————————————————

Problem 1

Kathy's Kitchen bought a van to deliver Kathy's famous pies. The van cost $20,000. Kathy estimates that, with the hard use the van will get, it will be of use for four years. At the end of the four years, it will be sold for parts for $2,000.

Required:

1. Determine the monthly depreciation expense using the straight-line method.
2. Make the journal entry to record depreciation expense for January.

Problem 2

Kylie's Kitchen purchased several pieces of equipment during 20X6. The purchase date, item, cost, useful life, and salvage value are as follows:

Date	Item	Cost	Useful Life	Salvage Value
January 1	Cash register	$ 1,800	5 years	$ 500
March 1	10 8-top tables	2,500	10 years	500
July 1	Van	30,000	5 years	3,000
September 16	Range	4,500	7 years	800

Required:

Determine the depreciation expense for the year of 20X6 for each piece of equipment purchased. Use the straight-line method of depreciation.

Problem 3

Dave Townsend paid the fire insurance premium of $1,200 for the Townsend Café on April 24. The insurance coverage is from May 1 through October 31. Monthly financial statements are prepared for the Townsend Café.

Required:

1. Record the payment on April 24 for $1,200.
2. Based on the information above, what is the amount of insurance expense for April?
3. What is the monthly insurance expense for each month over the insurance coverage period?
4. What is the balance of the Prepaid Insurance account at the end of June?

Problem 4

Cassie Café is open each day of the year. The annual payroll for hourly employees is $182,500. The café pays wages on a biweekly basis on Friday for the pay period ending on Thursday. The last day of the month is on Wednesday. The last pay period ended on the prior Thursday.

Required:

1. Determine the payroll accrual at the end of the month.
2. Prepare the journal entry to record the accrual.

Problem 5

The Valley Catering Company has been contracted by a wedding planner to cater wedding and rehearsal dinners. Valley Catering requires an advance deposit of $200 for all engagements. On June 15, the wedding planner sends a check to Valley Catering for $400 ($200 for the wedding and $200 for the rehearsal dinner). The rehearsal dinner is on July 2, and the wedding is on July 3. The total cost for the rehearsal dinner is $300 and for the wedding, $800.

Required:

1. Make the journal entry to record the receipt of the deposit check on June 15.
2. Make the adjusting entries for July 2 and 3 to record the actual revenue earned and to adjust the advanced deposits account.

Problem 6

The Justin Fine Hotel borrowed $80,000 from the Convenience Bank on June 4, 20X6. The interest rate is 100 basis points (1 percentage point) above the LIBOR rate. The LIBOR rate on June 4 was 5 percent. On August 1, the LIBOR rate increased to $5\frac{1}{2}$ percent and on December 1 the LIBOR rate increased again by 50 basis points.

Required:

1. Determine the interest expense for June 20X6 and prepare the adjusting entry.
2. Determine the interest expense for the second half of 20X6.
3. Prepare the adjusting entry for December 20X6 to record the interest expense for December.

Problem 7

The Hilltop Inn pays its employees on a biweekly basis. The last day of the pay period for January is the 25th. The biweekly gross pay for Hilltop's employees has averaged $4,200. Assume a biweekly pay period covers 14 workdays.

Required:

1. Estimate the amount of wages payable at the end of January.
2. Record the adjusting entry for January.

Problem 8

The following are examples of adjusting entries in the general journal of Diane's Diner. Identify the accounts that are affected by each entry, and state whether it is a deferral or accrual entry.

1. Adjusting entry for wages that have been earned by workers but not yet paid or recorded
2. Adjusting entry for revenue that has now been earned, but was paid for previously
3. Adjusting entry to record periodic depreciation expense
4. Adjusting entry to record the use of one month's worth of prepaid rent
5. Adjusting entry to record interest earned on an investment but not yet received
6. Adjusting entry to record the cost related to electricity expense used, but not yet paid for

Problem 9

Diane Ososki owns O's Place. On March 1, O's Place borrowed $5,000 from the Poulan Bank. The annual interest rate is 8 percent. At the end of each quarter, O's Place must pay $500 on the debt plus the interest on the loan for the quarter. Assume interest is due only on the unpaid amount of the loan.

Required:

1. Determine the interest accrual for March 31.
2. Make the adjusting entry to record the interest accrued on March 31.
3. Make the adjusting entry to record the interest accrual as of April 30.
4. Record the payment due May 31.

Problem 10

Prepare adjusting entries in the general journal from the following information pertaining to the accounts of Eastpointe Inn as of December 31, 20X6 (the end of its fiscal year):

1. The prepaid insurance account shows a balance of $15,000 representing the March 31, 20X6, premium payment for one-year fire insurance coverage from April 1, 20X6, through March 31, 20X7.
2. Equipment costing $80,000 is being depreciated using the straight-line method and an estimated useful life of five years. (Assume salvage value is $10,000.) Annual depreciation has not been recorded.
3. Wages earned by employees for December 26–31, 20X6, have not been recorded. Weekly wages (for seven days) amount to $2,100.
4. Interest expense on a note payable of $50,000 has not been recorded during 20X6. The amount was borrowed on November 1, 20X5. The annual rate of interest is 8 percent.
5. The Guest Deposit account (a current liability account) has a balance of $2,000 before adjustments. Of these deposits, $800 were earned during December 20X6.

Problem 11

State (1) whether the following failures to record adjusting entries will understate or overstate net income, and (2) what the effect on the balance sheet accounts will be.

1. Not recording depreciation expense
2. Not adjusting unearned revenue when revenue is earned

3. Not adjusting prepaid rent when rent is used
4. Not recording accrued interest on investments
5. Not recording accrued interest on loans
6. Not recording services rendered, but not yet billed
7. Not recording accrued wages
8. Not recording the electric expense used but not yet paid for

Challenge Problems

Problem 12

Don Donuts, owned by Donald Weeks, has annual accounting periods ending each December 31. On December 31, 20X3, after all transactions were recorded, the bookkeeper prepared the trial balance of accounts:

Don Donuts
Trial Balance
December 31, 20X3

Cash	$ 2,500	
Supplies	1,250	
Prepaid Insurance	1,000	
Food and Beverage Inventory	2,000	
Equipment	10,000	
Accumulated Depreciation, Equipment		$ 4,000
Building	40,000	
Accumulated Depreciation, Building		6,000
Land	3,000	
Accounts Payable		600
Mortgage Payable		20,000
Donald Weeks, Capital		12,750
Donald Weeks, Drawing	4,000	
Food and Beverage Sales		85,000
Cost of Food and Beverage Sales	26,600	
Salaries Expense	30,000	
Advertising Expense	1,000	
Utilities Expense	3,000	
Supplies Expense	2,000	
Interest Expense	2,000	
	$128,350	$128,350

Required:

1. Open the following T-accounts: Supplies; Prepaid Insurance; Food and Beverage Inventory; Accumulated Depreciation, Equipment; Accumulated Depreciation, Building; Salaries Payable; Cost of Food and Beverage Sales; Salaries Expense;

Depreciation Expense, Equipment; Depreciation Expense, Building; Supplies Expense; Insurance Expense.

2. Prepare and post adjusting journal entries based on the following information.

   a. The physical count of the food and beverage inventory at December 31, 20X3, is $1,650.

   b. Insurance expired during the year, $500.

   c. Estimated depreciation of equipment for the year, $1,500.

   d. Estimated depreciation of the building for the year, $2,500.

   e. Salaries earned by workers between December 28 (payday) and December 31, $200.

   f. Physical count of supplies at December 31, 20X3, $1,100.

Problem 13

The general ledger of Reilly Restaurant shows the following accounts and balances (presented in random order) on October 31, 20X6:

Cash	$ 3,000
Accounts Receivable	5,000
Food Inventory	6,000
Equipment	25,000
Accumulated Depreciation	5,000
Prepaid Insurance	6,000
Accounts Payable	4,000
SR, Capital	20,000
SR, Withdrawals	4,000
Sales	200,000
Salaries and Wages Expense	70,000
Cost of Food Sold	60,000
Advertising Expenses	10,000
Other Operating Expenses	40,000

The adjustment data for the year ended October 31, 20X6 are as follows:

a. The balance in the Prepaid Insurance account represents a two-year insurance policy purchased on November 1, 20X5.

b. An inventory of food showed $2,000 worth of food supplies on hand on October 31, 20X6.

c. The equipment, purchased three years ago, is depreciated using the straight-line method and the estimated useful life is five years (salvage value $5,000).

d. Salaries and wages for the 10-day pay period ended Friday, November 7, 20X7. $2,700 will be paid on that day. (Assume the restaurant is open Monday–Friday only.)

Required:

1. Prepare a trial balance for the Reilly Restaurant.

2. Prepare the four adjusting entries.

3. Prepare an adjusted trial balance after making the adjusting entries.

Problem 14

The following is the December 31, 20X3, trial balance for Norm's Diner.

Norm's Diner
Trial Balance
December 31, 20X3

Cash	$ 6,750	
Accounts Receivable	1,400	
Food and Beverage Inventory	3,400	
Office Supplies	900	
Prepaid Rent	800	
Furniture	26,000	
Accumulated Depreciation, Furniture		$ 3,000
Equipment	60,000	
Accumulated Depreciation, Equipment		8,000
Accounts Payable		4,300
Unearned Revenue		300
Notes Payable		32,700
Norm Kamp, Capital		48,500
Food and Beverage Revenue		87,000
Cost of Food and Beverage Sold	35,880	
Wages and Benefits	29,000	
Rent Expense	8,800	
Office Supplies Expense	1,000	
Repairs and Maintenance	7,000	
Interest Expense	1,500	
Advertising Expense	1,370	
	$183,800	$183,800

Required:

Using the information in the trial balance, make the journal entries for the following transactions. You will need to use these additional accounts: Accrued Wages, Interest Payable, and Depreciation Expense.

1. Food and Beverage inventory was taken on December 31 after closing. The physical inventory was $2,650. (Hint: use Cost of Food and Beverage Sold as the expense account.)

2. A physical inventory of office supplies shows $810.

3. The furniture was bought last year. At that time, it had a useful life of six years and a salvage value of $8,000. Determine this year's depreciation using the straight-line depreciation method.

4. The equipment was bought two years ago. At that time, it had a useful life of 12 years and a salvage value of $12,000. Determine this year's depreciation using the straight-line depreciation method.

5. Norm paid his entire rent for the year on January 1. He has used the expense for 11 months in equal amounts. Determine the rent expense for December.

6. The last payday of the year falls on December 24. Determine the accrued wages for the staff. Average daily wages are $150.

7. Norm has a note payable with the Wooden Nickel Savings and Loan for part of his equipment. The payment is made every six months and is due on January 1 and July 1. The annual interest rate is 8.5 percent. Determine the amount of interest payable to WNSL (round to the nearest dollar).

8. Norm hires an independent firm to tend to the repairs and maintenance. However, the bill for December has not yet arrived. Norm's accountant expects repairs and maintenance to be about 6 percent higher than November due to the extensive holiday decorations Norm likes. November's expense was $600.

9. Norm catered a dinner on New Year's Eve for which he had received an advance deposit of $300. The dinner was paid for at the end of the night for a total of $525. The $225 in cash received has already been recorded as cash receipts. Record the advance deposit as earned revenue.

Problem 15

The following is the trial balance for the Mason Motel as of December 31, 20X2.

Mason Motel
Trial Balance
December 31, 20X2

Cash	$ 5,650	
Marketable Debt Securities	10,000	
Accounts Receivable	8,000	
Cleaning Supplies	2,500	
Prepaid Insurance	4,500	
Interest Receivable	300	
Furniture	40,000	
Accumulated Depreciation, Furniture		$ 20,000
Equipment	10,000	
Accumulated Depreciation, Equipment		5,000
Building	300,000	
Accumulated Depreciation, Building		100,000
Land	20,000	
Accounts Payable		5,000
Unearned Revenue		650
Notes Payable		5,000
Mortgage Payable		54,000
Melvin Mason, Capital		103,000

Room Revenue		146,800
Manager's Salary	15,000	
Housekeeper's Wages	15,000	
Cleaning Supplies Expense	2,000	
Office Supplies Expense	1,000	
Utilities Expense	5,000	
Advertising Expense	500	
	$439,450	$439,450

Required:

Using the information in the trial balance, make the journal entries for the following transactions. You will need to use these additional accounts: Accrued Wages, Insurance Expense, Interest Income, and Depreciation Expense.

1. Mason Motel bought a three-year insurance policy on July 1, 20X2, for the period of July 1, 20X2, through June 30, 20X5. Determine the insurance expense for 20X2.

2. A physical inventory shows $1,000 of cleaning supplies. Determine cleaning supplies expense for the year.

3. The furniture was bought two years ago. At that time, it had a useful life of four years and no salvage value. Determine this year's depreciation using the straight-line method.

4. The equipment was bought five years ago, and, at that time, had a useful life of ten years and no salvage value. Determine this year's depreciation using the straight-line method.

5. The building was bought five years ago, and the estimated useful life was 10 years. The salvage value is expected to be $100,000. Determine this year's depreciation using the straight-line method.

6. The last payday of the year falls on December 27. Determine the accrued wages for the housekeeper. There is one housekeeper on the staff who works eight hours a day. The housekeeper's hourly wage is $6.25.

7. Mason has owned the marketable debt securities since October 1, 20X2. The annual interest rate is 7 percent. Determine the amount of interest receivable on this investment.

8. Mason's utilities bill has not yet arrived. Mason's accountant estimates the utilities expense to be $500.

9. Mason owes $240 to an advertising firm. However, the advertising firm has not sent the bill yet.

10. Mason had guests whose rooms were paid for with an advance deposit of $650. The guests are now gone, and the entire deposit was earned.

11. Mason has guests who are staying at the hotel and will not leave until after December 31. They have three rooms, each costing $20. The guests have been at Mason's since December 27. Mason has not yet billed these guests. Calculate the amount of unbilled revenue to December 31.

Chapter 4 Outline

The Accounting Cycle
    Adjusted Trial Balance
    Preparation of Financial Statements
    Closing Entries
    Post-Closing Trial Balance
The Worksheet
Reversing Entries
Comprehensive Illustration—Completing
    the Accounting Cycle

Competencies

1. Explain the steps in the accounting cycle. (pp. 107–108, 121–127)

2. Explain the purpose of the adjusted trial balance and the relationships between the adjusted trial balance, the balance sheet, the income statement, and the statement of owners' equity. (pp. 108–110)

3. Describe the closing process, and explain the function of the post-closing trial balance. (pp. 110–116)

4. Describe the worksheet and explain its function. (pp. 116–120)

5. Explain the purpose of reversing entries and identify the circumstances under which they can be used. (pp. 120–121)

4

Completing the Accounting Cycle

IN THIS CHAPTER, we discuss the accounting cycle, focusing on the last five steps of the cycle as follows:

- Journalizing and posting adjusting entries
- Preparing an adjusted trial balance
- Preparing the income statement and the balance sheet
- Journalizing and posting closing entries
- Preparing a post-closing trial balance

In addition, this chapter will present a worksheet approach for adjusting entries and preparing the income statement and the balance sheet. Finally, the chapter will discuss reversing entries.

The Accounting Cycle

The **accounting cycle** consists of the many steps the accounting staff follows, beginning with analyzing transactions and ending with preparing a post-closing trial balance.

Exhibit 1 lists the ten steps in the accounting cycle. The length of the cycle depends on how often the business prepares financial statements. Most businesses prepare monthly financial statements. For these businesses, the cycle is one month long. However, for smaller businesses that prepare only annual financial statements, the accounting cycles last one year. Regardless of its length, the cycle starts when the accountant analyzes source documents to determine how to record the business transaction. Thus, the basic input of the accounting cycle consists of the various source documents, including sales invoices, purchase invoices, and time cards for hourly employees. The output from the accounting cycle consists of the financial statements.

Only the three basic financial statements (the income statement, the balance sheet, and the statement of owners' equity) are discussed in this chapter. In addition to the basic statements, accountants must prepare explanations called *notes to the financial statements* to accompany the financial statements.

The remaining steps in the accounting cycle involve the processing of accounting data that will generate the information included in the financial statements.

Exhibit 1 Steps in the Accounting Cycle

Step	Explanation
1. Analyzing transactions	Examining source documents such as sales invoices
2. Journalizing transactions	Recording transactions in a journal
3. Posting	Transferring the debits and credits from journals to the ledger accounts
4. Preparing a trial balance	Summarizing the ledger accounts to prove the equality of debits and credits
5. Preparing adjusting entries	Determining the adjustments and recording them in the general journal
6. Posting adjusting entries	Transferring the adjusting entries from the journal to the ledger accounts
7. Preparing an adjusted trial balance	Summarizing the ledger accounts to prove the equality of debits and credits after the posting of the adjusting entries
8. Preparing the financial statements	Rearranging the adjusted trial balance into an income statement and a balance sheet
9. Recording and posting closing entries	Journalizing and posting entries that close the revenue and expense accounts for the period to the capital account
10. Preparing a post-closing trial balance	Summarizing the asset, liability, and owners' equity accounts to prove the equality of debits and credits

Only journalizing and posting take place day after day during the accounting cycle. In theory, accountants prepare the various trial balances and prepare, record, and post adjusting and closing entries on the last day of the accounting cycle. In practice, accountants make adjusting entries and close accounts a few days into the following month or cycle, but record them as of the last day of the previous accounting period.

Adjusted Trial Balance

Adjustments are recorded in the general journal at the end of each accounting period, generally as of the last date of the month. The recorded amounts are then posted to the general ledger accounts as of the last day of the accounting period.

Accountants record and post adjustments in the same way that they record and post business transactions. The difference is only one of timing: business transactions occur every business day, but adjusting entries are recorded and posted on the last day of the accounting period. After posting the adjustments, the accountant prepares an **adjusted trial balance** to prove the equality of debits and credits.

Exhibit 2   Adjusted Trial Balance

Mason Motel
Adjusted Trial Balance
December 31, 20X1

	Debits	Credits
Cash	$ 5,000	
Marketable Securities	10,000	
Accounts Receivable	8,000	
Cleaning Supplies	1,800	
Prepaid Insurance	3,000	
Furniture	40,000	
Accumulated Depreciation, Furniture		$ 24,000
Equipment	10,000	
Accumulated Depreciation, Equipment		6,000
Building	300,000	
Accumulated Depreciation, Building		110,000
Land	20,000	
Accounts Payable		5,000
Notes Payable		5,000
Accrued Wages		150
Mortgage Payable		100,000
Melvin Mason, Capital		113,000
Melvin Mason, Drawing	10,000	
Room Revenue		150,000
Manager's Salary	15,000	
Assistant Manager's Salary	7,500	
Room Attendants' Wages	15,150	
Payroll Taxes	3,000	
Cleaning Supplies Expense	2,700	
Office Supplies	1,000	
Utilities	5,000	
Advertising	500	
Repairs and Maintenance	9,000	
Insurance Expense	1,500	
Depreciation Expense, Furniture	4,000	
Depreciation Expense, Equipment	1,000	
Depreciation Expense, Building	10,000	
Property Taxes	22,000	
Interest Expense	8,000	
Total	$ 513,150	$ 513,150

Remember that, before the accountant records adjusting entries, he or she will have prepared a trial balance; the only difference between that trial balance and the adjusted trial balance is the adjustments.

Exhibit 2 shows the adjusted trial balance for the Mason Motel, prepared at the end of the accounting period, which, for this illustration, is December 31, 20X1. Notice that the sums of the debit and credit columns are equal: both total $513,150.

Preparation of Financial Statements

The adjusted trial balance is used to prepare the income statement and the balance sheet. The revenue accounts make up the revenue (or sales) of the hospitality enterprise, while the expense accounts make up the expenses of the business. The difference between the revenues and expenses is either net income or net loss. Net income results when revenues exceed expenses, while a net loss results when expenses exceed revenues. The relationship between the adjusted trial balance for the Mason Motel and its income statement is shown in Exhibit 3. The net income for the year for the Mason Motel is $44,650, since revenues of $150,000 exceed expenses of $105,350.

A **statement of owners' equity** is a financial statement that summarizes transactions affecting the owners' capital account. The accountant prepares this schedule using information—the balances of the owners' capital and drawing accounts—from the trial balance. The accountant also takes the net income (or net loss) for the period from the income statement. The statement of owners' equity shows the following:

Owners' Equity—beginning of period	$ XXX
Plus: Net income for the period	XX
Less: Owner withdrawals for the period	(XX)
Owners' Equity—end of period	$ XXX

If a net loss is incurred for the period, the net loss would be subtracted in preparing the statement of owners' equity.

Exhibit 4 shows the statement of owner's equity for the Mason Motel for 20X1. During 20X1, Melvin Mason's capital account increased from $113,000 to $147,650 as the net result of net income for the Mason Motel of $44,650 and his withdrawals of $10,000.

The statement of owners' equity serves as a link between the income statement and the balance sheet, since the net income for the period, in essence, is transferred from the income statement to the balance sheet via this statement.

Exhibit 5 shows the Mason Motel's balance sheet dated December 31, 20X1. As expected, assets of $257,800 equal the sum of owner's equity (proprietorship) and liabilities, $257,800. (The balance sheet is the embodiment of the fundamental accounting equation.) Rather than tracing the Melvin Mason, Capital and Drawing accounts from the adjusted balance, the accountant simply takes the balance for the Melvin Mason, Capital account from the statement of owner's equity shown in Exhibit 4.

Closing Entries

Revenue and expense accounts are nominal accounts, since they are subclassifications of owners' equity. Accountants separate revenue and expense accounts to get more detailed information for use in preparing the financial statements. Once the financial statements are prepared, the accountant closes the revenue and expense accounts, clearing the accounts to zero by transferring the balances to the

Exhibit 3   Adjusted Trial Balance and the Income Statement

Mason Motel
Adjusted Trial Balance
December 31, 20X1

	Debits	Credits
Cash	$ 5,000	
Marketable Securities	10,000	
Accounts Receivable	8,000	
Cleaning Supplies	1,800	
Prepaid Insurance	3,000	
Furniture	40,000	
Accumulated Depreciation, Furniture		$ 24,000
Equipment	10,000	
Accumulated Depreciation, Equipment		6,000
Building	300,000	
Accumulated Depreciation, Building		110,000
Land	20,000	
Accounts Payable		5,000
Notes Payable		5,000
Accrued Wages		150
Mortgage Payable		100,000
Melvin Mason, Capital		113,000
Melvin Mason, Drawing	10,000	
Room Revenue		150,000
Manager's Salary	15,000	
Assistant Manager's Salary	7,500	
Room Attendants' Wages	15,150	
Payroll Taxes	3,000	
Cleaning Supplies Expense	2,700	
Office Supplies	1,000	
Utilities	5,000	
Advertising	500	
Repairs and Maintenance	9,000	
Insurance Expense	1,500	
Depreciation Expense, Furniture	4,000	
Depreciation Expense, Equipment	1,000	
Depreciation Expense, Building	10,000	
Property Taxes	22,000	
Interest Expense	8,000	
Total	$513,150	$513,150

Mason Motel
Income Statement
For the Year Ended December 31, 20X1

Room Revenue	$150,000
Manager's Salary	$15,000
Assistant Manager's Salary	7,500
Room Attendants' Wages	15,150
Payroll Taxes	3,000
Cleaning Supplies Expense	2,700
Office Supplies	1,000
Utilities	5,000
Advertising	500
Repairs and Maintenance	9,000
Insurance Expense	1,500
Depreciation Expense, Furniture	4,000
Depreciation Expense, Equipment	1,000
Depreciation Expense, Building	10,000
Property Taxes	22,000
Interest Expense	8,000
	105,350
Net Income	$ 44,650

Exhibit 4 Statement of Owner's Equity

Mason Motel
Statement of Owner's Equity
For the year ended December 31, 20X1

Melvin Mason, Capital, January 1, 20X1	$113,000
Plus: Net Income for 20X1	44,650
Less: Melvin Mason, Withdrawals	10,000
Melvin Mason, Capital, December 31, 20X1	$147,650

---

owners' equity capital account. The accountant closes these accounts with **closing entries** that must be recorded in the general journal and then posted to the general ledger accounts.

The revenue and expense accounts are often closed to the capital account through a **clearing account** called Income Summary. Thus, the balance of the Income Summary account after the closing of all revenue and expense accounts is the net income or net loss for the period. This balance is then closed to the Owners' Capital account, resulting in a zero balance in the Income Summary account. The closing process transfers revenues and expenses to the Owners' Equity account, and also reduces the revenue and expense accounts to zero to prepare them for receiving data during the following accounting period.

The Owners' Drawing account is also closed at the end of the accounting period, but not to the Income Summary account. Instead, it is closed directly to the Owners' Equity account.

The three basic steps of the closing process are as follows:

1. Close the revenue and expense accounts to the Income Summary account.

2. Close the Income Summary account to the Owners' Equity account.

3. Close the Owners' Drawing accounts to the Owners' Equity account.

Exhibit 6 shows the flow of the amounts from the revenue and expense accounts through the Income Summary to the Capital account. This exhibit also shows the closing of the Drawing account to the Capital account.

In closing entry 1 (CE#1), the amounts from the expense accounts (A and B) are transferred to the Income Summary account. Each expense is credited for the amount of its previous debit balance, and the total of $220 is debited to the Income Summary account.

CE#2 effectively closes the revenue account (R) to the Income Summary account by debiting Revenue R by $250 and crediting the Income Summary account by $250.

CE#3 transfers the balance of the Income Summary account of $30 to the Capital account by debiting the Income Summary account and crediting the Capital account.

Exhibit 5 Adjusted Trial Balance and the Balance Sheet

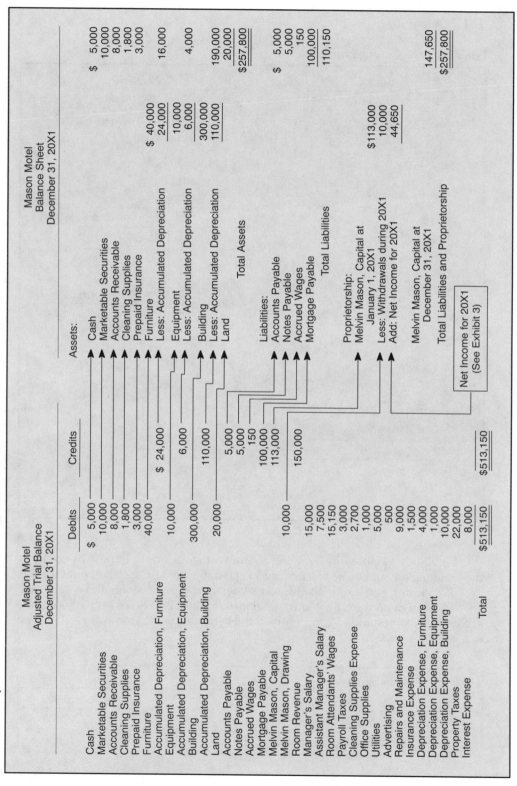

Mason Motel
Adjusted Trial Balance
December 31, 20X1

	Debits	Credits
Cash	$ 5,000	
Marketable Securities	10,000	
Accounts Receivable	8,000	
Cleaning Supplies	1,800	
Prepaid Insurance	3,000	
Furniture	40,000	
Accumulated Depreciation, Furniture		$ 24,000
Equipment	10,000	
Accumulated Depreciation, Equipment		6,000
Building	300,000	
Accumulated Depreciation, Building		110,000
Land	20,000	
Accounts Payable		5,000
Notes Payable		5,000
Accrued Wages		150
Mortgage Payable		100,000
Melvin Mason, Capital		113,000
Melvin Mason, Drawing	10,000	
Room Revenue		150,000
Manager's Salary	15,000	
Assistant Manager's Salary	7,500	
Room Attendants' Wages	15,150	
Payroll Taxes	3,000	
Cleaning Supplies Expense	2,700	
Office Supplies	1,000	
Utilities	5,000	
Advertising	500	
Repairs and Maintenance	9,000	
Insurance Expense	1,500	
Depreciation Expense, Furniture	4,000	
Depreciation Expense, Equipment	1,000	
Depreciation Expense, Building	10,000	
Property Taxes	22,000	
Interest Expense	8,000	
Total	$513,150	$513,150

Mason Motel
Balance Sheet
December 31, 20X1

Assets:		
Cash		$ 5,000
Marketable Securities		10,000
Accounts Receivable		8,000
Cleaning Supplies		1,800
Prepaid Insurance		3,000
Furniture	$ 40,000	
Less: Accumulated Depreciation	24,000	16,000
Equipment	10,000	
Less: Accumulated Depreciation	6,000	4,000
Building	300,000	
Less: Accumulated Depreciation	110,000	190,000
Land		20,000
Total Assets		$257,800
Liabilities:		
Accounts Payable		$ 5,000
Notes Payable		5,000
Accrued Wages		150
Mortgage Payable		100,000
Total Liabilities		110,150
Proprietorship:		
Melvin Mason, Capital at January 1, 20X1	$113,000	
Less: Withdrawals during 20X1	10,000	
Add: Net Income for 20X1	44,650	
Melvin Mason, Capital at December 31, 20X1		147,650
Total Liabilities and Proprietorship		$257,800

Net Income for 20X1
(See Exhibit 3)

Exhibit 6   The Closing Process

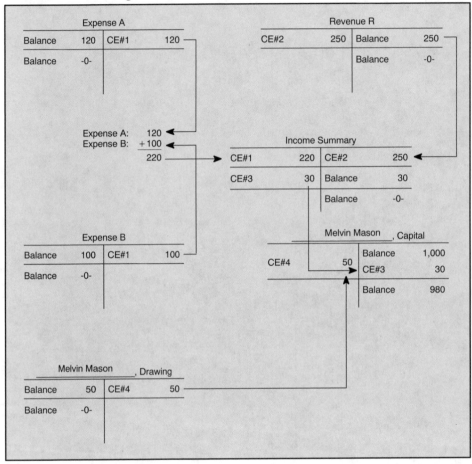

Finally, CE#4 closes the Drawing account into the Capital account by crediting the Drawing account by its balance of $50 and debiting the Capital account for $50.

The closing entries for the Mason Motel's expense accounts have debit balances as shown on the adjusted trial balance (Exhibit 2). Therefore, to close these accounts, a compound closing entry debits Income Summary and credits each expense account.

Dec. 31	Income Summary	$105,350	
	Manager's Salary		$15,000
	Assistant Manager's Salary		7,500
	Room Attendants' Wages		15,150

Payroll Taxes	3,000
Cleaning Supplies Expense	2,700
Office Supplies	1,000
Utilities	5,000
Advertising	500
Repairs & Maintenance	9,000
Insurance Expense	1,500
Depreciation Expense, Furniture	4,000
Depreciation Expense, Equipment	1,000
Depreciation Expense, Building	10,000
Property Taxes	22,000
Interest Expense	8,000
To close the expense accounts at year-end.	

The Room Revenue account, as shown in Exhibit 2, has a credit balance. Therefore, to close and clear this revenue account, the account must be debited for the balance and the Income Summary account must be credited for the same.

Dec. 31	Room Revenue	$150,000	
	Income Summary		$150,000
	To close the Room Revenue account at year-end.		

When a firm's revenue and expense accounts are closed into the Income Summary account, the balance reflects the result of the year's operations as either net income or net loss. After the two previous closing entries, the Mason Motel's Income Summary T-account has a credit balance of $44,650, the amount of net income earned for 20X1.

Income Summary			
CE#1	105,350	CE#2	150,000
		Balance	44,650

To close and clear the Income Summary account for the Mason Motel, the account is debited for $44,650 and Melvin Mason, Capital is credited for $44,650. The journal entry is recorded as follows:

Dec. 31	Income Summary	$44,650	
	Melvin Mason, Capital		$44,650
	To close the Income Summary account		
	at year-end.		

Finally, the Drawing account is closed to the Capital account. Since the Melvin Mason, Drawing account has a $10,000 debit balance, it is credited by $10,000 and the Capital account is debited for $10,000 as follows:

Dec. 31	Melvin Mason, Capital	$10,000	
	Melvin Mason, Drawing		$10,000
	To close the Drawing account at year-end.		

After the closing entries have been posted, the revenue and expense accounts, the Drawing account, and the Income Summary account have zero balances. The Melvin Mason, Capital account has been increased from $113,000 to $147,650, as shown in the statement of owner's equity (Exhibit 4).

Post-Closing Trial Balance

After the accountant records and posts the closing entries, the only accounts with balances that remain in the general ledger are the balance sheet accounts. These accounts must be in balance; that is, the total of debit balance accounts must equal the total of credit balance accounts. To test this equality and to check the accuracy of the closing process, the accountant prepares a **post-closing trial balance**. As with the trial balance prepared before the closing process, account balances are listed in debit and credit columns and totaled to ensure that debits equal credits.

Exhibit 7 shows the post-closing trial balance of the Mason Motel as of December 31, 20X1. The account balances have been taken from the ledger accounts for inclusion on this trial balance. Note that no revenue, expense, or drawing accounts are included, because they have been closed for the accounting period to the Melvin Mason, Capital account through the closing entries.

The Worksheet

The accountant may use a **worksheet** in the adjusting process and in completing the accounting cycle. A worksheet is a columnar sheet of paper on which accountants list the general ledger accounts before making adjustments and preparing the income statement and balance sheet. It is only a tool and is not part of the formal accounting records. Accountants generally use it to reduce the chance of errors in adjusting accounts and producing the financial statements. The worksheet helps the accountant accomplish the following:

1. Prepare the trial balance.

Exhibit 7   Post-Closing Trial Balance

	Mason Motel Post-Closing Trial Balance December 31, 20X1	
	Debits	Credits
Cash	$ 5,000	
Marketable Securities	10,000	
Accounts Receivable	8,000	
Cleaning Supplies	1,800	
Prepaid Insurance	3,000	
Furniture	40,000	
Accumulated Depreciation, Furniture		$ 24,000
Equipment	10,000	
Accumulated Depreciation, Equipment		6,000
Building	300,000	
Accumulated Depreciation, Building		110,000
Land	20,000	
Accounts Payable		5,000
Notes Payable		5,000
Accrued Wages		150
Mortgage Payable		100,000
Melvin Mason, Capital		147,650
Total	**$ 397,800**	**$ 397,800**

2. Adjust the accounts without immediately having to post adjustments to the ledger accounts. Instead, the adjusting entries can be journalized and posted after the worksheet is completed.

3. Prepare the adjusted trial balance.

4. Segregate the adjusted account balances into columns for preparing the income statement and the balance sheet.

5. Determine the net income or loss for the accounting period.

To reiterate, the worksheet is merely an accountant's tool; it is neither published nor given to management to use. Each individual accountant decides whether or not to use a worksheet. He or she must weigh the advantage of reducing the chance of errors and the time required to prepare the financial statements (since recording and posting of the adjustments can be done later) against the disadvantage of the additional time required to prepare the worksheet.

The worksheet for the Mason Motel for the end of 20X1 is shown in Exhibit 8. Observe the following concerning this worksheet:

1. Column 1 lists the Mason Motel's accounts. These were taken from general ledger accounts, except for the five located at the bottom of the list. They result from adjustments.

Exhibit 8 Worksheet

Mason Motel
Worksheet
For the year ended December 31, 20X1

(1) Account Title	(2) Trial Balance Debit	(3) Trial Balance Credit	(4) Adjustments Debit	(5) Adjustments Credit	(6) Adjusted Trial Balance Debit	(7) Adjusted Trial Balance Credit	(8) Income Statement Debit	(9) Income Statement Credit	(10) Balance Sheet Debit	(11) Balance Sheet Credit
Cash	5,000				5,000				5,000	
Marketable Securities	10,000				10,000				10,000	
Accounts Receivable	8,000				8,000				8,000	
Cleaning Supplies	2,500			(b) 700	1,800				1,800	
Prepaid Insurance	4,500			(a) 1,500	3,000				3,000	
Furniture	40,000				40,000				40,000	
Accumulated Depreciation, Furniture		20,000		(c) 4,000		24,000				24,000
Equipment	10,000				10,000				10,000	
Accumulated Depreciation, Equipment		5,000		(d) 1,000		6,000				6,000
Building	300,000				300,000				300,000	
Accumulated Depreciation, Building		100,000		(e) 10,000		110,000				110,000
Land	20,000				20,000				20,000	
Accounts Payable		5,000				5,000				5,000
Notes Payable		5,000				5,000				5,000
Mortgage Payable		100,000				100,000				100,000
Melvin Mason, Capital		113,000				113,000				113,000
Melvin Mason, Drawing	10,000				10,000				10,000	
Room Revenue		150,000				150,000		150,000		
Manager's Salary	15,000				15,000		15,000			
Assistant Manager's Salary	7,500				7,500		7,500			
Room Attendants' Wages	15,000		(f) 150		15,150		15,150			
Payroll Taxes	3,000				3,000		3,000			
Cleaning Supplies Expense	2,000		(b) 700		2,700		2,700			
Office Supplies	1,000				1,000		1,000			
Utilities	5,000				5,000		5,000			
Advertising	500				500		500			
Repairs and Maintenance	9,000				9,000		9,000			
Property Taxes	22,000				22,000		22,000			
Interest Expense	8,000				8,000		8,000			
	498,000	498,000								
Insurance Expense			(a) 1,500		1,500		1,500			
Depreciation Expense, Furniture			(c) 4,000		4,000		4,000			
Depreciation Expense, Equipment			(d) 1,000		1,000		1,000			
Depreciation Expense, Building			(e) 10,000		10,000		10,000			
Accrued Wages				(f) 150		150				150
			17,350	17,350	513,150	513,150	105,350	150,000	407,800	363,150
							44,650			44,650
							150,000	150,000	407,800	407,800

2. Columns 2 and 3 show the trial balance that the accountant prepared before making any adjustments. The total of the debit column (column 2) of $498,000 equals the total of the credit column (column 3) of $498,000. If the Mason Motel accountant had not used a worksheet, he or she would have prepared a separate trial balance.

3. Columns 4 and 5 list six adjustments, as follows:

Adjustment	Amount	Purpose
a	$ 1,500	To record insurance expense for 20X1.
b	700	To record additional cleaning supplies used as expense for the year.
c	4,000	To record depreciation expense of furniture for the year.
d	1,000	To record depreciation expense of equipment for the year.
e	10,000	To record depreciation expense of the building for the year.
f	150	To accrue unpaid wages at the end of 20X1.

Notice that each adjusting entry has a debit and a credit. The total of the debits of $17,350 equals the total of the credits of $17,350. When the accountant completes the worksheet and prepares the financial statements, he or she records the adjusting entries in the general journal and then posts them to the ledger accounts.

4. Columns 6 and 7 show the adjusted trial balance. As discussed previously in this chapter, the adjusted trial balance is simply the trial balance of ledger accounts after adjustments have been prepared. As with all trial balances, the total of the debit column should equal the total of the credit column. Further, the totals of columns 6 and 7 equal the totals of the Mason Motel's adjusted trial balance that is shown in Exhibit 2. This adjusted trial balance is simply a duplicate of that shown in Exhibit 2. However, remember that if the Mason Motel accountant had decided to use a worksheet in completing the accounting cycle, the trial balance on the worksheet would have sufficed, and he or she would not have prepared a separate adjusted trial balance.

5. Columns 8 and 9 include only the revenue and expense accounts, since these are the only accounts for which amounts are shown on an income statement. The amounts in columns 8 and 9 are those shown on the income statement as provided in Exhibit 3. In actual practice, a more detailed income statement is generally prepared for management's internal use, and a less detailed income statement is prepared for external uses. Room revenue of $150,000 is the only revenue account and, since it has a credit balance, it is shown in the credit column. All the amounts from the expense accounts in column 6 are written in column 8, since they represent debit balances. The difference between the totals of columns 8 and 9 (that is, expenses and revenue) equals the net income for the accounting period. The Mason Motel's net income for 20X1 is $44,650.

6. Columns 10 and 11 include the remaining accounts, those that are shown on the balance sheet. The total of the debit column (column 10) exceeds the total of the credit column (column 11) by $44,650, which is the same amount as the net income earned in 20X1 by the Mason Motel. The net income figure thus serves as a "balancing amount" for the balance sheet columns of the worksheet.

After the worksheet is completed, the accountant would prepare the formal income statement and balance sheet as shown in Exhibits 3 and 5, respectively, for the Mason Motel. If the accountant used a worksheet, he or she would complete the accounting cycle in the following way:

*   Record and post adjusting entries.

*   Record and post closing entries.

*   Prepare a post-closing trial balance.

Reversing Entries

Reversing entries are journal entries made the first day of an accounting period to reverse the effects of adjusting entries made on the last day of the previous accounting period. The sole purpose of reversing entries is to simplify the first journal entries related to the same items during the next accounting period.

For example, on December 31, 20X1, the Mason Motel recorded accrued wages payable of $150 as adjusting entry (f). If the Mason Motel's accountant uses reversing entries, this adjustment is reversed on January 1, 20X2, with the following entry:

Accrued Wages	$150	
Room Attendants' Wages		$150
To reverse the accrual of Room Attendants' Wages.		

After this reversing entry is recorded, the expense account (Room Attendants' Wages) has a credit balance of $150. This credit will be more than offset when the Mason Motel records the first payroll in January 20X2. Assume the first payroll is paid on January 12, 20X2, and the total room attendants' wages are $1,350. Of the $1,350, $150 relates to the employees' work performed during 20X1 and $1,200 is for work performed in 20X2. The matching principle requires that expenses for each period be *recorded* in that period, though not necessarily paid in the separate periods. The $150 for 20X1 was recorded in 20X1 using an adjusting entry. The Mason Motel would record the payroll in January as follows:

Room Attendants' Wages	$1,350	
Cash		$1,350
To record the payroll for Room Attendants' Wages.		

It appears that the entire $1,350 is expensed in January 20X2. However, because of the reversing entry, the net effect is that only the $1,200 of expense pertaining to 20X2 is reflected as the balance. At this point, the Room Attendants' Wages T-account would look like this:

Room Attendants' Wages

Jan. 12 Pay period	1,350	Jan. 1 Reversing	150
Balance	1,200		

If the Mason Motel had not used reversing entries, the accountant would still have recorded the proper amount in the Room Attendants' Wages expense account by using the following compound entry when the first payroll in January was paid:

Room Attendants' Wages	$1,200	
Accrued Wages	150	
Cash		$1,350
To record the payroll for Room Attendants' Wages.		

Generally only those adjusting entries that are accruals of assets and liabilities may be reversed. For example, the accrual of interest income and the related interest receivable, as well as the accrual of interest payable and the related interest expense, may be reversed. On the other hand, certain adjustments, such as the adjustment of prepaid insurance to recognize insurance expense at the end of the accounting period, may *not* be reversed. In this case, there is no transaction in the following period to offset a reversing entry as there is for the accrual of assets and liabilities. Thus, the end result in the ledger accounts is the same, regardless of whether or not reversing entries are used. It is up to the accountant to decide which approach is easier to use, since the use of reversing entries has no effect on the financial statements.

Comprehensive Illustration—Completing the Accounting Cycle

After adjusting entries are recorded and posted, an adjusted trial balance is prepared. Exhibit 9 shows the adjusted trial balance for Carson Catering on November 30, 20X2. The total debits of $186,317 equal the total credits of $186,317, so the accounts are in balance. The next step is preparing the income statement, the statement of owner's equity, and the balance sheet for Carson Catering. Exhibits 10 through 12 show these financial statements.

The income statement (Exhibit 10) covers the entire fiscal year for Carson Catering of December 1, 20X1, through November 30, 20X2. Revenues total $138,251, while expenses total $126,534, giving a net income of $11,717. (This particular income statement is very simplistic.)

Exhibit 9   Carson Catering Adjusted Trial Balance

Carson Catering
Adjusted Trial Balance
November 30, 20X2

Account Number	Account	Debits	Credits
100	Cash	$ 3,000	
101	Certificate of Deposit	10,000	
105	Accounts Receivable	6,200	
107	Accrued Interest Receivable	333	
110	Operating Supplies	250	
115	Prepaid Rent	7,000	
120	Van	15,000	
121	Accumulated Depreciation, Van		$ 3,500
125	Equipment	10,000	
126	Accumulated Depreciation, Equipment		1,833
200	Accounts Payable		5,500
201	Accrued Wages Payable		2,500
202	Accrued Interest Payable		188
203	Accrued Expenses Payable		160
210	Notes Payable—BMAC		9,385
300	Don Carson, Capital		25,000
301	Don Carson, Drawing	8,000	
400	Catering Revenue		137,418
410	Interest Income		833
500	Wages Expense	39,500	
501	Advertising Expense	10,000	
502	Food Expense	60,000	
503	Gas Expense	2,200	
504	Rent Expense	5,000	
505	Supplies Expense	2,350	
506	Interest Expense	1,191	
507	Utilities Expense	960	
508	Depreciation Expense	5,333	
	Total	$186,317	$186,317

The statement of owner's equity (Exhibit 11) reflects Don Carson's initial capital investment of $5,000 in Carson Catering on December 1, 20X1, and also his additional investment of $20,000 during the fiscal year ended November 30, 20X2. This statement also reflects the net income for the year as well as Don Carson's withdrawals of $8,000 during the year. The final balance of $28,717 will be carried over to the balance sheet and shown as Don Carson, Capital as of November 30, 20X2.

The balance sheet (Exhibit 12) reflects the financial position of Carson Catering as of the last day of the accounting period, November 30, 20X2. Assets total $46,450, while liabilities and owner's equity total $46,450. This statement reflects

Exhibit 10   Carson Catering Income Statement

Carson Catering		
Income Statement		
For the year ended November 30, 20X2		
Revenue:		
Catering Revenue		$ 137,418
Interest Income		833
Total		138,251
Expenses:		
Wages	$ 39,500	
Advertising	10,000	
Food	60,000	
Gas	2,200	
Rent	5,000	
Supplies	2,350	
Interest	1,191	
Utilities	960	
Depreciation	5,333	126,534
Net Income		$ 11,717

Exhibit 11   Carson Catering Statement of Owner's Equity

Carson Catering	
Statement of Owner's Equity	
For the year ended November 30, 20X2	
Don Carson, Capital, December 1, 20X1	$ 5,000
Plus: Capital investment during the year	20,000
Plus: Net income for the year	11,717
Less: Don Carson, Withdrawals	$ 8,000
Don Carson, Capital, November 30, 20X2	$ 28,717

the fundamental accounting equation: assets equal liabilities plus owner's equity. Notice that Don Carson, Capital reflects the $28,717 from the statement of owner's equity rather than the $25,000 as shown on the adjusted trial balance (Exhibit 9) for Don Carson, Capital. This particular form of the balance sheet is very simplistic. Discussion of the proper balance sheet form is beyond the scope of this chapter.

Now Carson Catering's accountant begins closing the nominal accounts (the revenue, expense, and drawing accounts). The revenue and expense accounts will be cleared and closed through the Income Summary account. The closing entries for Carson Catering are as follows:

Exhibit 12   Carson Catering Balance Sheet

Carson Catering
Balance Sheet
November 30, 20X2

Assets

Cash	$ 3,000
Certificate of Deposit	10,000
Accounts Receivable	6,200
Accrued Interest Receivable	333
Operating Supplies	250
Prepaid Rent	7,000
Van	15,000
Less: Accumulated Depreciation, Van	(3,500)
Equipment	10,000
Less: Accumulated Depreciation, Equipment	(1,833)
Total Assets	**$ 46,450**

Liabilities and Owner's Equity

Accounts Payable	$ 5,500
Accrued Wages Payable	2,500
Accrued Interest Payable	188
Accrued Expenses Payable	160
Notes Payable—BMAC	9,385
Don Carson, Capital	28,717
Total Liabilities and Owner's Equity	**$ 46,450**

1. Closing Entry #1: Revenue Accounts

Catering Revenue	$137,418	
Interest Income	833	
Income Summary		$138,251
To close the revenue accounts.		

2. Closing Entry #2: Expense Accounts

Income Summary	$126,534	
Wages Expense		$39,500
Advertising Expense		10,000
Food Expense		60,000

Gas Expense	2,200
Rent Expense	5,000
Supplies Expense	2,350
Interest Expense	1,191
Utilities Expense	960
Depreciation Expense	5,333
To close the expense accounts.	

3. Closing Entry #3: Income Summary

Income Summary	$11,717	
Don Carson, Capital		$11,717
To close the Income Summary account.		

4. Closing Entry #4: Drawing Account

Don Carson, Capital	$8,000	
Don Carson, Drawing		$8,000
To close the Drawing account.		

After the closing entries are posted from the general journal to the general ledger accounts, all the nominal accounts have zero balances and are ready for posting of activity for the following accounting period.

The last step in the accounting cycle is preparing the post-closing trial balance. Exhibit 13 shows Carson Catering's post-closing trial balance for November 30, 20X2. The total debits of $51,783 equal the total credits of $51,783, thus proving the equality of debits and credits.

Summary

The accounting cycle consists of a set sequence of steps the accounting staff performs during each fiscal period. The accounting cycle begins when the accountant analyzes transactions and ends when he or she prepares a post-closing trial balance.

At the end of the accounting period, after making, journalizing, and posting adjusting entries, the accountant prepares an adjusted trial balance to prove the equality of debits and credits. Because the accountant prepared a trial balance before making adjustments, the only differences between that trial balance and the adjusted trial balance should be the adjustments themselves. The accountant uses the adjusted trial balance in preparing the income statement and balance sheet, taking account balances directly from the adjusted trial balance.

Exhibit 13   Carson Catering Post-Closing Trial Balance

Carson Catering
Post-Closing Trial Balance
November 30, 20X2

Account Number	Account	Debits	Credits
100	Cash	$ 3,000	
101	Certificate of Deposit	10,000	
105	Accounts Receivable	6,200	
107	Accrued Interest Receivable	333	
110	Operating Supplies	250	
115	Prepaid Rent	7,000	
120	Van	15,000	
121	Accumulated Depreciation, Van		$ 3,500
125	Equipment	10,000	
126	Accumulated Depreciation, Equipment		1,833
200	Accounts Payable		5,500
201	Accrued Wages Payable		2,500
202	Accrued Interest Payable		188
203	Accrued Expenses Payable		160
210	Notes Payable—BMAC		9,385
300	Don Carson, Capital		28,717
	Totals	**$ 51,783**	**$ 51,783**

The statement of owners' equity is prepared using information from the income statement and the trial balance. The statement of owners' equity is a summary of the transactions affecting the owners' equity account. Net income is added to owners' equity from the beginning of the period, and then owners' drawing accounts are subtracted, resulting in owners' equity at the end of the period. The statement of owners' equity is a link between the income statement and the balance sheet, since net income is essentially transferred from the income statement to the balance sheet through this statement.

After the accountant prepares financial statements, he or she closes revenue and expense accounts. The accountant closes these accounts with closing entries that he or she records in the general journal and then posts to the general ledger accounts. In a very simple accounting system, revenues and expenses may be reflected directly in the owners' equity account. However, to more clearly see the amounts that lead to net income, the accountant records revenue and expenses in separate temporary equity accounts. These accounts are closed at the end of a fiscal period and the balances are brought to zero. The accountant often does this by transferring the balances to a clearing account called Income Summary. Once all revenue and expense accounts are closed to Income Summary, the balance in the Income Summary account should be net income. This balance is then closed out to the Owners' Equity account. After all closing entries are journalized and posted, only balance sheet accounts are left with balances. At this time, the accountant prepares a post-closing trial balance to prove the equality of debits and credits of the permanent accounts, and the accounts are ready for the start of a new fiscal period.

The worksheet is a tool that an accountant may use in the adjustment process and in completing the accounting cycle. A worksheet is used to list general ledger accounts in columns by debit and credit.

Reversing entries are journal entries made at the beginning of an accounting period to reverse the effects of adjusting entries made in the previous period. This is done to simplify the first journal entry related to that same item during the new period. Reversing entries can usually be made only on accruals of assets or liabilities. Reversing entries are not mandatory, so each firm must weigh the benefits and costs in deciding whether to prepare them.

Key Terms

accounting cycle—The sequence of principal accounting procedures of a fiscal period: transaction analysis, journal entry, posting to ledger accounts, trial balance, adjustments, adjusted trial balance, preparation of periodic financial statements, account closing, and post-closing trial balance.

adjusted trial balance—The trial balance prepared to prove the equality of debits and credits after adjusting entries have been posted to accounts.

clearing account—An account used to temporarily store information as part of an accounting procedure.

closing entries—Journal entries prepared at the end of the period (normally yearly) to close the temporary proprietorship accounts into permanent proprietorship accounts.

post-closing trial balance—The trial balance prepared after closing entries have been posted to accounts to prove the equality of debits and credits in the permanent accounts.

reversing entries—Journal entries made on the first day of an accounting period to reverse the effects of adjusting entries made on the last day of the previous accounting period.

statement of owners' equity—A financial statement that summarizes transactions affecting the owners' capital account(s).

worksheet—A working paper used as a preliminary to the preparation of financial statements.

Review Questions

1. What are the differences between a trial balance, an adjusted trial balance, and a post-closing trial balance?

2. What is the purpose of a worksheet?

3. What are closing entries? When are they prepared?

4. What is the Income Summary account? When is it used?

5. What are the ten steps in the accounting cycle?

6. What is a reversing entry?

7. Why would an accountant prepare reversing entries?

8. How is the owner's drawing account closed?

9. What are the three main steps in the closing process? What are the features of each?

10. Why do only balance sheet accounts have balances in the post-closing trial balance?

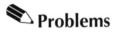

Problems

Problem 1

The following is a list of some accounts used by a food service business:

a. Food Inventory	i. Equipment
b. Prepaid Insurance	j. Notes Payable
c. Food Sales	k. A.M. Smith, Drawing
d. Utility Expenses	l. Income Summary
e. Cash	m. Wages Expense
f. Accounts Receivable	n. Operating Expenses
g. Accounts Payable	o. Depreciation Expense
h. A.M. Smith, Capital	p. Accumulated Depreciation

Required:

For each account:

1. State what type of account it is (permanent, temporary, clearing).

2. State whether it is closed during closing entries (yes/no).

3. If it is closed during closing entries, state to which account it is closed.

Problem 2

The Roadhouse Inn's activities for 20X1 and 20X2 that affect the Emily Road, Capital account are as follows:

	20X1	20X2
Net income for the year	$55,000	$58,500
Withdrawals by Emily Road	$20,000	$25,000
Investment by Emily Road	–$0–	$10,000

In addition, the balance of the Emily Road, Capital account on January 1, 20X1, was $52,500.

Required:

1. Prepare a statement of owner's equity for the Roadhouse Inn for 20X1.
2. Determine the balance of the Emily Road, Capital account as of the end of 20X2.

Problem 3

The Haslett Hotspot's activities for 20X4 and 20X5 affecting the Malorie Haslett, Capital account are as follows:

	20X4	20X5
Net Income (Loss)	($2,000)	$10,000
Withdrawals by Malorie	15,000	20,000
Investment by Malorie	40,000	–0–

In addition, the balance of the Malorie Haslett, Capital account on December 31, 20X5, was $50,000.

Required:

1. Determine the balance of the Malorie Haslett, Capital account at the beginning of years 20X4 and 20X5.
2. Prepare a statement of owner's equity for the Haslett Hotspot for 20X5.

Problem 4

The following is an income statement for Chuck's Steakhouse:

Chuck's Steakhouse
Income Statement

Food and Beverage Revenue		$ 474,500
Expenses:		
Wages	$ 142,350	
Cost of Food Sold	156,585	
Advertising Expense	9,490	
Repairs and Maintenance	40,333	
Rent Expense	33,215	
Depreciation Expense	15,000	
Utilities Expense	18,980	415,953
Net Income		$ 58,547

The balance of the Owner's Equity account is $96,000 at the beginning of the period. During the year, the owner has drawn out 5 percent of his equity (use beginning Owner's Equity to calculate this).

Required:

Prepare a statement of owner's equity for Chuck's Steakhouse.

Problem 5

The following is a trial balance for the Albatross Motel:

Albatross Motel
Trial Balance
December 31, 20X2

Cash	$ 6,100	
Short-Term Investments	15,000	
Accounts Receivable	2,900	
Prepaid Insurance	2,250	
Equipment	10,000	
Accumulated Depreciation, Equipment		5,000
Building	275,000	
Accumulated Depreciation, Building		100,000
Land	130,000	
Accounts Payable		5,000
Advance Deposits		200
Notes Payable		7,000
Mortgage Payable		49,000
Melvin Mason, Capital		217,050
Room Revenue		98,500
Manager's Salary	19,000	
Housekeepers' Wages	15,000	
Office Supplies Expense	1,000	
Utilities Expense	5,000	
Advertising Expense	500	
	$481,750	$481,750

Required:

1. Post the following adjusting entries to the proper T-accounts.

Adjusting Entries

a.	Dec. 31	Insurance Expense	$ 325	
		Prepaid Insurance		$ 325
b.	Dec. 31	Depreciation Expense	$ 1,000	
		Accumulated Depreciation, Equipment		$ 1,000
c.	Dec. 31	Depreciation Expense	$20,000	
		Accumulated Depreciation, Building		$20,000
d.	Dec. 31	Housekeepers' Wages	$ 130	
		Accrued Wages, Housekeepers		$ 130
e.	Dec. 31	Utilities Expense	$ 500	
		Accounts Payable		$ 500
f.	Dec. 31	Unearned Revenue	$ 200	
		Room Revenue		$ 200

2. Prepare an adjusted trial balance.

Problem 6

The following is an adjusted trial balance for Tinker's Motel:

Tinker's Motel
Adjusted Trial Balance
December 31, 20X1

Cash	$ 15,900	
Supplies	3,400	
Accounts Receivable	8,000	
Furniture	100,000	
Accumulated Depreciation, Furniture		$ 20,000
Building	250,000	
Accumulated Depreciation, Building		140,000
Accounts Payable		6,090
Mortgage Payable		57,900
Tinker Bell, Capital		81,000
Room Revenue		219,000
Wages	43,800	
Utilities Expense	19,710	
Insurance Expense	15,330	
Supplies Expense	32,850	
Depreciation Expense	35,000	
	$523,990	$523,990

Required:

1. Prepare the journal entries to close the revenue and expense accounts to the Income Summary account.

2. Prepare the journal entry to close the Income Summary account to the Owner's Equity account.

Challenge Problems

Problem 7

The following is an adjusted trial balance for Steven's Motel for the month of November. Steven's accountant has prepared the trial balance and adjusting entries. Now the financial statements must be prepared from the adjusted trial balance.

Steven's Motel
Adjusted Trial Balance
November 30, 20X1

Cash	$ 2,300	
Accounts Receivable	200	
Equipment	35,000	

Accumulated Depreciation, Equipment		$ 5,000
Building	$ 77,000	
Accumulated Depreciation, Building		19,000
Accounts Payable		2,000
Note Payable		4,500
Mortgage Payable		10,000
Steven Schultz, Capital		72,598
Steven Schultz, Drawing	1,450	
Room Revenue		6,045
Wages	1,028	
Payroll Taxes	242	
Repairs and Maintenance	302	
Utilities Expense	121	
Depreciation Expense	1,500	
	$119,143	$119,143

Required:

From this adjusted trial balance, prepare (1) the income statement, (2) the balance sheet, and (3) the statement of owner's equity.

Problem 8

Tuma's Place is a food service operation with a December 31 year end. The adjusted trial balance is as follows:

Tuma's Place
Adjusted Trial Balance
December 31, 20X4

Cash	$ 12,500	
Food Inventory	15,200	
Prepaid Expenses	4,300	
Equipment	35,800	
Accumulated Depreciation, Equipment		$ 12,000
Accounts Payable		3,600
Notes Payable		20,200
Molly Tuma, Capital		45,000
Molly Tuma, Withdrawals	30,000	
Food Sales		180,600
Wages Expense	54,000	
Cost of Food Sold	46,800	
Advertising	6,200	
Utilities Expense	3,800	
Supplies Expense	8,500	
Rent Expense	24,000	
Depreciation Expense	4,300	
Insurance Expense	6,400	
Interest Expense	1,800	
Other Expenses	7,800	
Total	$ 261,400	$ 261,400

Required:

1. Prepare an income statement.
2. Prepare a balance sheet.
3. Prepare the closing entries. Use the income summary account as needed.

Problem 9

Beth Krainz opened Krainz Catering on June 1, 20X7. The adjusted trial balance for June 30, 20X7, follows:

Krainz Catering
Adjusted Trial Balance
December 31, 20X7

Cash	$ 8,400	
Food Inventory	1,200	
Prepaid Expenses	800	
Equipment	15,000	
Accumulated Depreciation, Equipment		$ 500
Accounts Payable		1,000
Notes Payable		10,000
Beth Krainz, Capital		10,000
Sales		18,300
Wages	5,500	
Cost of Food Sold	4,500	
Supplies Expense	800	
Other Expenses	3,600	
Total	$39,800	$39,800

Required:

1. Prepare an income statement.
2. Prepare a balance sheet.
3. Prepare the closing entries. (Use an income summary account as needed.)
4. Prepare a post-closing trial balance.

Problem 10

The following is an adjusted trial balance for Mary's Miracle Pastries, a successful coffee shop. Mary's accountant has prepared the trial balance and adjusting entries. Now the financial statements must be prepared from the adjusted trial balance.

Mary's Miracle Pastries
Adjusted Trial Balance
December 31, 20X3

Cash	$ 32,522
Short-Term Investments	12,000
Accounts Receivable	17,000

Food and Beverage Inventory	$ 9,200	
Equipment	35,000	
Accumulated Depreciation, Equipment		$ 5,000
Building	167,000	
Accumulated Depreciation, Building		40,000
Accounts Payable		7,000
Accrued Wages		600
Note Payable		15,000
Mortgage Payable		79,000
Mary Ramaker, Capital		58,999
Mary Ramaker, Drawing	4,600	
Pastry Revenue		361,350
Cost of Food Sold	126,473	
Wages	108,405	
Advertising Expense	14,454	
Repairs and Maintenance	18,068	
Insurance Expense	7,227	
Depreciation Expense	15,000	
	$566,949	$566,949

Required:

From this adjusted trial balance, prepare (1) the income statement, (2) the balance sheet, and (3) the statement of owner's equity.

Problem 11

The trial balance and adjusted trial balance for Twyla's Diner are as follows:

Twyla's Diner
Trial Balance and Adjusted Trial Balance
December 31, 20X3

	Trial Balance		Adjusted Trial Balance	
Cash	$ 7,750		$ 7,750	
Accounts Receivable	1,400		1,400	
Food Inventory	3,400		2,800	
Office Supplies	900		800	
Prepaid Rent	800		–0–	
Equipment	75,000		75,000	
Accumulated Depreciation,				
Equipment		$ 8,000		$ 12,000
Accounts Payable		4,230		4,230
Notes Payable		28,200		28,200
Accrued Wages		–0–		1,000
Twyla Kamp, Capital		48,500		48,500
Food Revenue		80,500		80,500
Cost of Food Sold	35,880		36,480	
Wages and Benefits	31,000		32,000	
Rent Expense	8,800		9,600	

	Trial Balance		Adjusted Trial Balance	
Office Supplies Expense	$ 1,000		$ 1,100	
Interest Expense	3,500		3,500	
Depreciation Expense	–0–		4,000	
	$169,430	$169,430	$174,430	$174,430

Required:

By analyzing the differences between the figures in the trial balance and the adjusted trial balance, determine the adjusting entries that recorded (1) adjustment of food inventory, (2) office supplies, (3) depreciation expense, (4) adjustment of prepaid insurance, and (5) accrued unpaid wages.

Problem 12

Greg Dempster owns and operates the Hilltop Inn, a rooms-only lodging facility. On December 31, 20X8, the trial balance was as follows:

Hilltop Inn
Trial Balance
December 31, 20X8

Cash	$ 8,500	
Cleaning Supplies	2,400	
Prepaid Insurance	4,800	
Equipment	118,500	
Acc. Depr.—Equipment		$ 20,000
Accounts Payable		3,000
Interest Payable		–0–
Notes Payable		60,000
Rent Payable		–0–
Greg Dempster, Capital		30,000
Sales		200,000
Wages Expense	75,000	
Cleaning Supplies Expense	6,000	
Utilities Expense	7,500	
Rent Expense	24,000	
Laundry Expense	10,000	
Advertising Expense	17,000	
Other Expense	2,000	
Maintenance Expense	19,300	
Depreciation Expense	11,000	
Insurance Expense	1,500	
Interest Expense	5,500	
Total	$313,000	$313,000

Required:

1. Enter the account balances from the trial balance in the Trial Balance columns of a worksheet.
2. Enter the adjusting entries in the worksheet based on the following information:
   a. Cleaning supplies on hand at year end total $1,600.

b. Unexpired insurance at the end of 20X8 equals $1,200
c. Depreciation expense for December (not recorded) totals $1,000.
d. Interest expense for December (not recorded) totals $500. Record the amount due as interest payable.
e. The rent expense for the year is based on 13 percent of total sales. Two thousand was paid on the first day of each month. Any remaining rent due must be recorded.

3. Extend the numbers over to an adjusted trial balance columns on the worksheet.
4. Complete columns on the work sheet for both the income statement and balance sheet.

Problem 13

1. Using the adjusted trial balance from the solution of Problem 11, prepare the proper closing entries for Twyla's Diner. Close all revenue and expense accounts to Income Summary.
2. Close Income Summary to the Owner's Equity account.
3. Prepare a post-closing trial balance for Twyla's Diner.

Problem 14

The following is an adjusted trial balance for Fleischer's Motel as of December 31, 20X2. The accountant for Fleischer's needs to close out the temporary revenue and expense accounts to Income Summary, and then to the Owner's Equity account.

Fleischer's Motel
Trial Balance
December 31, 20X2

Cash	$7,100	
Accounts Receivable	700	
Supplies	1,300	
Prepaid Insurance	4,500	
Investments	15,000	
Accounts Payable		$ 200
Note Payable		3,000
Mark Fleischer, Capital		13,000
Room Revenue		47,900
Rental Revenue		670
Wages	13,740	
Supplies Expense	2,000	
Utilities Expense	5,960	
Rent Expense	9,760	
Insurance Expense	4,500	
Interest Expense	210	
	$64,770	$64,770

Required:

1. Open the T-accounts for the revenues and expenses as well as the Income Summary and Owner's Equity accounts.

2. Prepare the journal entries necessary to close out the temporary accounts to Income Summary, and post the entries to the proper T-accounts.

3. Close the Income Summary out to Owner's Equity and post the entry to the proper T-account.

4. Prepare a post-closing trial balance.

Problem 15

On September 1, 20X7, Casey Price opened Casey Catering. During that month, she completed the following transactions:

Sept. 1	Deposited $7,000 in a checking account the name of the business.
Sept. 2	Signed a lease for $400 per month for 1000 square feet of space. Paid the rent for September.
Sept. 3	Purchased $5,000 worth of equipment by paying $1,000 down and being extended credit on account by RE, Inc. for $4,000.
Sept. 4	Leased a delivery van for three years for $450 per month. Paid the rent for September.
Sept. 5	Purchased operating supplies costing $800. (Record as an asset)
Sept. 6	Paid the $6,000 premium on a one-year insurance policy covering September 1, 20X7, through August 31, 20X8.
Sept. 7	Purchased $400 of food for the first catered event on account from Food Supplies Co.
Sept. 8	Paid wages of $300 for assistance with the first catered event.
Sept. 9	Received $1,500 as revenue for the first event.
Sept. 10	Paid Food Supplies Co. $200 on account.
Sept. 11	Paid the Lansing State Journal $200 for advertising.
Sept. 15	Purchased $500 of food on account from Food Supplies Co.
Sept. 17	Catered a second event and paid wages of $400.
Sept. 18	Received $2,000 for catering sales.
Sept. 22	Paid Food Supplies Co. $200 on account.
Sept. 23	Catered the third event of the month. Purchased food costing $650 on account from Food Supplies Co., paid wages of $700, and received $2,500 for catering sales.
Sept. 28	Paid RE, Inc. $500 on account
Sept. 29	Withdrew $1,000 from the business for personal use.

Required:

1. Open the following T-accounts: Cash; Operating Supplies Inventory; Prepaid Insurance; Equipment; Accumulated Depreciation—Equipment; Accounts Payable—RE, Inc.; Accounts Payable—Food Supplies Co.; Casey Price, Capital; Casey Price, Withdrawals; Income Summary; Catering Sales; Food Expense; Wages Expense; Rent Expense—Building; Rent Expense—Van; Depreciation Expense; Operating Supplies Expense; Advertising Expense; and Insurance Expense.

2. Record entries in the T-accounts. Label the entries with the day paid such as "1" for the activity on September 1.

3. Prepare the trial balance of accounts in the trial balance columns of a worksheet.

4. Enter the adjustments on the worksheet adjustments columns for the following items:

   a. The inventory of operating supplies at the end of September showed $250 of remaining operating supplies

   b. One month's insurance has expired

   c. Estimated depreciation for September is $100

5. Complete the rest of the columns of the worksheet, including the:

   a. Adjusted trial balance.

   b. Income statement.

   c. Balance sheet.

6. Prepare a September income statement.

7. Prepare a September 30 balance sheet.

8. Post the adjusting entries to the T-accounts.

9. Prepare closing entries.

10. Prepare a post-closing trial balance.

Chapter 5 Outline

Major Elements of the Income Statement
Relationship with the Balance Sheet
Sales
Cost of Goods Sold
Expenses
Gains and Losses
Income Taxes
Extraordinary Items
Earnings per Share
Income Statements for Internal and
    External Users
Uniform System of Accounts
Internal Income Statements—A
    Contribution Approach
      Contents of the Summary Operating
        Statement
Departmental Statements
Uniform System of Accounts for
    Restaurants
Statement of Retained Earnings

Competencies

1. Identify the purpose of the income statement, its major elements, and its relationship to the balance sheet. (pp. 141–143)

2. Identify when a sale is recorded, describe how to account for allowances and returns, and describe how to account for the cost of goods sold. (pp. 143–146)

3. Identify some common operational expenses and explain how they are recorded, and describe how to calculate and account for gains and losses. (pp. 146–148)

4. Explain how earnings per share is calculated and reported, and describe how income statements for internal and external users differ. (pp. 149–152)

5. Explain the purposes of uniform systems of accounts and identify those systems that are relevant to the hospitality industry. (p. 152)

6. Outline the contents of the income statement and identify the purpose of departmental statements. (pp. 152–162)

7. Describe the purpose of and information reported on the statement of retained earnings. (pp. 162–163)

5

Income Statement

FINANCIAL STATEMENTS are the major result of the accounting cycle. Data is accumulated, analyzed, summarized, and reported in meaningful formats to users of financial statements. The financial statement used to convey operating performance is the **income statement**. Also called the *statement of operations*, the *profit and loss statement*, and various other titles, the income statement reports sales and expenses that ideally result in net income, but sometimes in a net loss for an accounting period. This information is provided in fairly abbreviated statements to outsiders such as bankers and suppliers and in considerable detail to internal users such as the property's general manager and various department heads.

In this chapter, we will focus on the income statement and discuss its major users and its major elements. We will also discuss earnings per share, external versus internal statements, and the various uniform systems of accounts.

Owners and potential owners, creditors such as suppliers and financial institutions, and managers are all users of financial information. In general, users are divided into two groups: internal and external users. **Internal users** are the managers of the business. **External users** include potential investors, creditors, and owners not active in managing the hospitality enterprise. The information needs of the two groups are generally quite different.

External users are given a statement that reflects only the basics, that is, sales and a few categories of expenses. More detailed information, such as breakdowns by department and comparisons to the operating budgets, is best kept within the particular operation lest it fall into the hands of competitors. This information is often provided in accordance with the uniform system of accounts for the appropriate segment of the hospitality industry.

Each user of financial information seeks operations information for his or her own reasons. Owners and potential owners are interested in profitability as an indicator of potential cash dividends and increases in market prices of publicly traded stocks. Creditors are interested in profitability as an indicator of the firm's ability to pay its bills, perhaps thinking, "Today's profits lead to tomorrow's cash for paying bills." Management wants the operating results to indicate the degree of its success in managing operations. In addition, management expects the operating results to reveal problem areas so it can ensure that the firm generates profits in accordance with the operating plans.

Major Elements of the Income Statement

With an accrual basis accounting system, revenues are recorded when they are earned. When a hotel guest is served a meal, the food sales have been earned.

The Annual Reports Library

Tip: Use Yahoo Finance to quickly locate company financial information online. Select "profile" for a company you are interested in - the "Investor Relations" link will usually contain annual reports, SEC filings etc.for public companies)

See: 10-K WIZARD for SEC filings

For Investors

Public Register's Annual Report Service - source for online and hardcopy reports
Tips for Reading an Annual Report - by Jim Milner
Silicon Investor - top 300 Technology Stocks
About Your Broker - from NASD
National Association of Investors (NAIC)
Securities Class Action Clearinghouse - at Stanford University

Annual Reports online:
IRIN - Annual Report Resource Center

Places to request free reports ...
PRARS - The Public Register's Annual Report Service
Annual Reports Service - from the Wall Street Journal
www.AnnualReports.com

For Producers of Annual Reports

Tips for creating a good Annual Report
National Investor Relations Institute (NIRI)

Non Profit - Charity

Notes about Non-profit, Charity and Other types of Annual Reports
The Foundation Center - gateway to online Philanthropy
GuideStar - reports on more than 700,000 U.S. nonprofit organizations.
Giving - A Special Report - links from the NY Times, Nov 20, 2000

Education

Money - from the Federal Consumer Information Center
Education Resources at SF Fed and Education at NY Fed
Money - Past, Present & Future

Fun

Templeton Investment Maxims
Trivia from the Annual Reports Library

Resources

Sid Cato's Official Annual Report Website
SEC.gov and FTC.gov

Links

Business Connections - at the *New York Times*
Annual Report Gallery - links to many annual reports online
InvestMove.com - online investment research
Related Links - the list of user contributed links

The Annual Report Library's Internet site (at www.zpub.com/sf/arl) gives users ways to look up companies' annual reports. (Courtesy of the Annual Reports Library)

When funds are invested in a certificate of deposit, revenue in the form of interest is earned over time. So, generally, with sales and interest, revenue is recorded before cash is received. When future lodging guests pay cash as a room deposit, the amount is initially recorded as a liability, then recognized later as revenue when services are provided to the guest. The revenues shown on an income statement generally are net revenues—that is, the amounts charged (gross sales) less any allowances granted after the sale.

Expenses recorded include outflows related to the accounting period *and* expenses that have been matched to revenues. Expenses related to the period are expenses incurred, even though revenues may not have been earned. For example, insurance on a building provides coverage regardless of the hospitality firm's level of sales. The prepaid insurance is reduced periodically to reflect the insurance expense based on time, not revenue. Many expenses, however, are incurred in direct relation to revenue, and adjusting entries at the end of the accounting period are recorded to match expense to revenue.

Relationship with the Balance Sheet

The income statement covers a period of time, while the balance sheet is prepared as of the last day of the accounting period. Thus, the income statement reflects operations of the hospitality property for the period between balance sheet dates, as shown below:

The result of operations, net income (net loss), for the period is added to (subtracted from) the proper owners' equity account and shown on the balance sheet at the end of the accounting period.

Sales

The sale of goods or services occurs between the seller (the lodging property) and the buyer (the lodging guest). The goods or services are provided by the seller in exchange for the guest's cash or promise to pay at a later date.

Services are recorded as sales as the services are provided. For example, when a lodging guest occupies a guestroom, a sale is recorded. Likewise, food or other merchandise sales are recorded at the time of the sale. The server's check is the source document for the sale of goods such as food and beverages. The revenue from the sale is recorded at the time of the sale for the following reasons:

1. Legal title to the goods (food and beverages) has passed from the seller to the buyer.

2. The selling price has been established.

3. The seller's obligation has been completed.

4. The goods have been exchanged for another asset, such as cash or accounts receivable.

Each time sales are made, the appropriate sales accounts are credited and Cash or Receivables is debited. Sales are recorded at the agreed-upon price. When the lodging guest is dissatisfied with the goods or services, an allowance may be made; that is, the guest may be given partial credit. For example, assume a guest is displeased with his or her room. Management may decide to give a $10 allowance. In this case, the account Room Sales Allowances is debited and the guest's Accounts Receivable is credited for the $10. In effect, room revenue is reduced by $10, since room sales allowances are offset against room revenue in determining net room revenue to be shown on the firm's income statements.

When a hospitality firm sells items not consumed on the premises, such as gift shop merchandise, there may be some returns. For example, the merchandise may have been damaged at the time of the sale. If the guest had charged the purchase from the gift shop to his or her room, the sales returned would be recorded as follows:

Gift Shop Sales Returns	$XXX	
Accounts Receivable		$XXX
To record a sales return by a hotel guest.		

If the hotel guest had paid cash for the merchandise, cash generally would be disbursed from the cash register, and the Cash account would be credited instead of Accounts Receivable.

Allowances and returns are recorded in contra-sales accounts to track the amount of such activities. Many firms use one account for both returns and allowances for a given department, such as Gift Shop Sales Returns and Allowances.

Cost of Goods Sold

The sales of food, beverages, and other merchandise require that the cost of the goods sold also be recorded. Generally, when goods are purchased for resale, they are recorded as inventory. When they are sold, the costs are transferred to a **cost of goods sold** account. The costs may be transferred at the time of sale, or they may be recorded at the end of the accounting period. At this point, for the sake of simplicity, we will assume that food, beverage, and other merchandise purchased are recorded in separate purchases accounts. For example, $100 of food purchased is recorded as follows:

Food Purchases	$100	
Cash		$100
To record food purchases.		

At the end of the accounting period, a physical inventory of food is taken and the cost of the food inventory is determined. Cost of food sold for the period is determined as follows:

Food inventory, beginning of period	$ XX
Plus: food purchases	XXX
Food available for sale	XXX
Less: food inventory, end of period	XX
Cost of food sold	$XXX

This assumes that no food was used for other purposes during the period. If food was used for other purposes, additional adjustments are required. Other uses could include employee meals provided free of charge, transfers to the beverage department, and food used for promotional purposes. If food is used for these purposes, the line "Cost of food sold" is changed to "Cost of food used," and adjustments are made as follows:

Cost of food used	$ XXX
Less: Cost of employee meals	XX
Less: Promotional meals	XX
Less: Transfers to beverage department	XX
Cost of food sold	$ XXX

For example, assume a hotel's food service department provides the following information at the end of its accounting period, December 31, 20X1:

Food inventory, beginning of month	$ 5,000
Food purchases (during December)	20,000
Food inventory, end of month	6,000
Cost of employee meals	300
Cost of promotional meals	200
Food transfers to beverage department	50

The cost of food sold to be reported on the income statement would be determined as follows:

Food inventory, December 1, 20X1	$ 5,000
Food purchases	20,000
Food available	25,000
Less: food inventory, December 31, 20X1	(6,000)
Cost of food *used*	19,000
Less: cost of employee meals	(300)
Less: cost of promotional meals	(200)
Less: transfers to beverage department	(50)
Cost of food sold	$18,450

The journal entry to record the cost of food sales and the ending inventory would be as follows:

Cost of Food Sold	$19,000	
Food Inventory	1,000	
Food Purchases		$20,000
To record cost of food sales and to adjust food		
inventory to its ending inventory.		

The debit to food inventory of $1,000 effectively increases the food inventory account to the physical inventory of $6,000, since $1,000 plus the food inventory account balance of $5,000 as of December 1, 20X1, equals $6,000. The $19,000 debit to Cost of Food Sold and the $1,000 debit to Food Inventory are offset by the $20,000 credit to Food Purchases. Remember, debits must equal credits. The credit of $20,000 reduces the Food Purchases account to a zero balance.

The journal entry to record the cost of employee meals, promotional meals, and transfers to the beverage department would be as follows:

Employee Meals (food department)	$300	
Promotional Meals (marketing department)	200	
Transfers to Beverage Department	50	
Cost of Food Sold		$550
To record food used in operations.		

This entry records the expense of using food in operations (employee meals and promotional meals) and transfers to the beverage department. In addition, the Cost of Food Sold account is credited to reflect the cost of food sold for the month as previously calculated, since $19,000 less $550 equals $18,450. This entry assumes all employee meals are consumed by food department employees. The Employee Meals (food department) account is an expense account in the food department. The Transfers to the Beverage Department account and the Beverage Purchases account are treated similarly when determining the cost of beverages sold for the period. The Promotional Meals account is an expense account of the marketing department.

Expenses

Expenses other than cost of goods sold include day-to-day operational expenses such as supplies and labor as well as depreciation, interest expense, and income taxes.

Expenses are generally recorded for each department. Labor costs related to the rooms department are recorded as expenses of that department, while labor costs of the food and marketing departments are recorded in their respective departments. Labor costs include the three major areas of (1) salaries and wages, (2) fringe benefits, and (3) payroll taxes.

Assume a hotel's payroll for the month included the following wages:

Rooms department employees		$10,000
Food department employees		5,000
General manager		2,000
	Total	$17,000

Further, assume the related payroll taxes were as follows:

Rooms department employees		$1,000
Food department employees		500
General manager		200
	Total	$1,700

Finally, assume the only fringe benefit is health insurance, which is assigned to departments based on coverage of their respective employees:

Rooms department employees		$2,500
Food department employees		1,400
General manager		300
	Total	$4,200

The total labor costs by department would be as follows:

	Rooms Dept.	Food Dept.	General Manager
Salaries/wages	$10,000	$5,000	$2,000
Payroll taxes	1,000	500	200
Fringe benefits	2,500	1,400	300
Totals	$13,500	$6,900	$2,500

A hospitality business normally has separate accounts for each major category by department.

Hospitality businesses record other expenses in selected accounts for each department. Departments that sell goods or services to guests, such as the rooms department, food department, and gift shop, are commonly called **profit centers**. Departments that provide services to profit centers, such as accounting and human resources (personnel), are called **service centers**. Each department has several accounts for recording its various other expenses. These classifications are typically based on the uniform system of accounts (discussed later in this chapter) and facilitate the preparation of the income statement. Several expenses are not directly related to any department and are simply recorded in separate (nondepartmental) accounts. These expenses usually relate to the operation as a whole rather than to individual parts, and include depreciation, interest, insurance, rent, and property taxes.

Gains and Losses

Gains are defined as increases in assets, reductions in liabilities, or a combination of both. Gains result from a hospitality operation's incidental transactions and from all other transactions and events affecting the operation during the period, except those that count as revenue or investments by owners. For example, there may be a gain on the sale of equipment. The business uses equipment to provide goods and services and, when that equipment is sold, only the excess proceeds over its net book value (purchase price less accumulated depreciation) is recognized as gain.

For example, assume a lodging business sold a van that it had used to transport guests to and from the airport for $6,000. Further, assume the van cost $15,000 when purchased and had accumulated depreciation of $10,000. Its net book value would be determined as follows:

Cost	$ 15,000
Accumulated depreciation	− 10,000
Net book value	$ 5,000

The gain on the sale is the result of the selling price exceeding the net book value as follows:

Selling price	$6,000
Net book value	− 5,000
Gain on sale	$1,000

Finally, **losses** are defined as decreases in assets, increases in liabilities, or a combination of both resulting from a hospitality operation's incidental transactions and from other transactions and events affecting the operation during a period, except those that count as expenses or distributions to owners. In the earlier equipment example, if the proceeds were less than the net book value, a loss would occur and would be recorded as "loss on sale of equipment." Another example would be a loss from an "act of nature," such as a tornado or hurricane. The loss reported is the reduction of assets less any insurance proceeds received.

In income statements for hospitality operations, revenues and gains are reported separately, and expenses are distinguished from losses. These distinctions are important in determining management's success in operating the hospitality property. Management is held accountable primarily for operations (revenues and expenses) and only secondarily (if at all) for gains and losses.

Income Taxes

The order of elements presented on the income statement is shown as follows:

  Revenue (sales)
  − Cost of goods sold
  − Labor expenses
  − Other expenses
  = Operating income
  + Gains
  − Losses
  = Income before taxes

Income tax expense shown on the income statement is based on relevant revenues and expenses on the income statement. Textbooks are written on the topic of income taxes; however, for our purposes it is sufficient to say that the income taxes shown on the income statement are seldom the same taxes shown on the firm's income tax return. The major reason for this is the difference between the accounting method used for financial statement purposes and that for income tax purposes.

For example, consider a hypothetical restaurant company that has $100,000 of pre-depreciation income. Assume that the only additional expense to be considered before the calculation of income taxes is depreciation. However, many companies use accelerated methods of calculating depreciation for tax purposes and the straight-line method for book purposes. Assume that this restaurant firm has $40,000 of depreciation for book purposes based on the straight-line method and $60,000 of depreciation for tax purposes. Then the income tax expense for books and taxes, assuming a tax rate of 25 percent, would be as follows:

	Books	Taxes
Pre-depreciation income	$100,000	$100,000
Depreciation expense	40,000	60,000
Taxable income	60,000	40,000
Tax rate	× .25	× .25
Taxes	$ 15,000	$ 10,000

This restaurant would show $15,000 as income taxes on its income statement and $10,000 due on its tax return. The journal entry to record income taxes would be as follows:

Income Tax Expense	$15,000	
Income Tax Payable		$10,000
Deferred Income Taxes		5,000
To record income taxes for the year.		

The Deferred Income Taxes account is a liability account and will be included on the firm's balance sheet.

Extraordinary Items

In addition to the preceding elements of an income statement, a hospitality firm may very infrequently report an **extraordinary item** on its income statement. Extraordinary items are reported at the bottom of the income statement after income taxes and just above the bottom line of net income.

To show an item as extraordinary, the event must meet two major criteria:

1. Unusual nature—the underlying event should possess a high degree of abnormality and be clearly unrelated to the ordinary and typical activities of the hospitality enterprise.

2. Infrequency of occurrence—the underlying event should not reasonably be expected to recur in the foreseeable future.

If an event does not meet both criteria, it is not reported as an extraordinary item. Of course, what is extraordinary for one firm may not be for another. A hotel in California suffering loss from an earthquake may not consider that loss extraordinary, while a Michigan hotel may have a casualty loss from an earthquake that would probably be considered extraordinary.

Extraordinary items are reported net of tax. That is, if an extraordinary loss results in taxes saved, the tax savings are offset against the loss in reporting the loss. For example, consider a hotel that has an extraordinary loss of $40,000 and a tax rate of 25 percent. Because of the $40,000 loss, $10,000 of taxes are saved. The extraordinary loss is shown on the income statement as $30,000.

Earnings per Share

Owners and potential investors of a hospitality enterprise are most interested in the bottom line of the income statement, that is, in net income. However, the net income amount by itself often lacks meaning. To provide a more meaningful number, accountants include **earnings per share**. Earnings per share (EPS) in its simplest form is determined with this equation:

$$\text{EPS} = \frac{\text{Net Income}}{\text{Common Shares Outstanding}}$$

EPS is calculated only for hospitality businesses organized as corporations or limited liability companies, since proprietorships and partnerships do not issue shares of stock. If a firm has types of stock other than common outstanding stock, net income is reduced by the amount of income that "belongs" to non-common stockholders. Further, EPS must be shown on the income statement before extraordinary items and net income.

Income Statements for Internal and External Users

Hospitality properties prepare income statements for both internal users and external users. These statements differ substantially. The income statements provided to external users are relatively brief, providing only summary detail about the results of operations. Exhibit 1 is the income statement presentation of Marriott International, Inc., from its Annual Report for 2005. Marriott's income statement shows the following:

- Revenues by segment

- Operating costs and expenses by segment

- Operating income

- Interest expense and income

- Other items before income taxes

- Provision for income taxes

- Minority interest

- Discontinued operations

Footnotes, which generally appear after the financial statements in the financial report (but are not included in Exhibit 1), are critical to interpreting the numbers reported on the income statement.

Although the amount of operating information shown in the income statement and accompanying footnotes may be adequate for external users, management requires considerably more information, on a more frequent basis, than outsiders do. In general, the more frequent the need to make decisions, the more frequent the need for financial information. Management's information needs are met, in part, by detailed monthly operating statements that reflect budget numbers and report performance for the most recent period, the same period a year ago, and year-to-date numbers for both the current and the past year.

Many firms in the hospitality industry revise their budgets and show the latest forecast of results if they expect a major difference between the year-to-date numbers and the originally budgeted numbers. Management can then compare actual results against the most recent forecasts. In addition to the monthly operating statement, a major report prepared more often for management is the daily report of operations.

Exhibit 1 Consolidated Statement of Income for Marriott International

(in millions, except per share amounts) Year Ended December 31,	2005	2004	2003
Revenues			
Base management fees[1]	$ 497	$ 435	$ 388
Franchise fees	329	296	245
Incentive management fees[1]	201	142	109
Owned, leased, corporate housing and other revenue[1]	944	730	633
Timeshare interval, fractional, and whole ownership			
sales and services	1,487	1,247	1,145
Cost reimbursements[1]	7,671	6,928	6,192
Synthetic fuel	421	321	302
	11,550	10,099	9,014
Operating Costs and Expenses			
Owned, Leased and corporate housing—direct	778	629	505
Timeshare—direct	1,228	1,039	1,011
Reimbursed costs[1]	7,671	6,928	6,192
General, administrative and other[1]	753	607	523
Synthetic fuel	565	419	406
	10,995	9,622	8,637
Operating Income	555	477	377
Gains and other income	181	164	106
Interest expense	(106)	(99)	(110)
Interest income[1]	79	146	129
(Provision for) reversal of provision for loan losses[1]	(28)	8	(7)
Equity in (losses) earnings			
Synthetic fuel[1]	—	(28)	10
Other[1]	36	(14)	(17)
Income from Continuing Operations before			
Income Taxes and Minority Interest	717	654	488
(Provision for) benefit from income taxes	(94)	(100)	43
Income from Continuing Operations before			
Minority Interest	623	554	531
Minority interest	45	40	(55)
Income from Continuing Operations	668	594	476
Discontinued operations	1	2	26
Net Income	$ 669	$ 596	$ 502
Earnings Per Share—Basic			
Earnings from continuing operations	$ 3.09	$ 2.62	$ 2.05
Earnings from discontinued operations	—	.01	.11
Earnings per share	$ 3.09	$ 2.63	$ 2.16
Earnings Per Share—Diluted			
Earnings from continuing operations	$ 2.89	$ 2.47	$ 1.94
Earnings from discontinued operations	—	.01	.11
Earnings per share	$ 2.89	$ 2.48	$ 2.05
Dividends Declared per share	$ 0.400	$ 0.330	$ 0.295

[1] See Footnote 21, "Related Party Transactions," of the Notes to Consolidated Financial Statements for Disclosure of related party amounts.

See notes to consolidated financial statements

Source: www.marriott.com

Accountants may meet management's need for financial information on a monthly basis, to a large degree, by using an income statement and accompanying departmental income statements as discussed in the various uniform systems of accounts.

Uniform System of Accounts

The **uniform systems of accounts** are standardized accounting systems prepared for various segments of the hospitality industry.[1] A uniform system of accounts provides a turnkey system for new entrants into the hospitality industry by offering detailed information about accounts, classifications, formats, and the different kinds, contents, and uses of financial statements and reports. For example, the *Uniform System of Accounts for the Lodging Industry (USALI)* contains not only the basic financial statements, but also more than 20 supplementary departmental operating statements and a section covering ratio analysis and statistics.

The uniform system of accounts also allows for a more reasonable comparison of the operational results of similar hospitality properties. As similar establishments follow a uniform system of accounts, the differences in accounting among these hospitality properties are minimized, thus ensuring comparability.

A uniform system of accounts is a time-tested system. The *Uniform System of Accounts for Hotels (USAH)* was first produced in 1925–26 by a designated group of accountants for the Hotel Association of New York City. Since then, the *USAH* has been revised many times by committees, in the beginning by New York City accountants and, most recently, by accountants from across the United States. The tenth revised edition of the *USALI* was prepared by the Financial Management Committee of the American Hotel & Lodging Association and Hospitality and Financial Technology Professionals.

Finally, the uniform system of accounts can be adapted for use by large and small hospitality operations. The tenth revised edition of the *USALI* illustrated in this chapter contains many more accounts and classifications than a single hotel or motel will generally use. Therefore, each facility simply selects the schedules and accounts that it requires and ignores the others.

The *USALI* is designed to be used at the property level rather than at the corporate level of a hotel. The format of the income statement is based on **responsibility accounting;** that is, the presentation is organized to focus attention on departmental results for such departments as rooms and food and beverage. The income statements prepared at the corporate level, where more than one lodging property is owned by the lodging corporation, would most likely be considerably different. They would likely include sale of properties, corporate overhead expenses, and other items that would not necessarily appear on an individual lodging property's income statement.

Internal Income Statements—A Contribution Approach

We will base our internal income statements on a modified version of the *USALI*'s summary operating statement. The summary operating statement format in the *USALI* approach consists of the following:

	Revenue
Less:	Direct operating expenses
Equals:	Total departmental income
Less:	Undistributed operating expenses
Equals:	Gross operating profit
Less:	Management fees
Less:	Fixed charges
Equals:	Net operating income
Less:	Replacement reserves
Equals:	Adjusted net operating income

Revenue less direct operating expenses equals **total departmental income,** which is the *contribution* by profit centers to both overhead expenses and net income. Total departmental income less undistributed operating expenses equals gross operating profit (GOP). GOP less management fees and fixed charges equals net operating income (NOI). NOI less replacement reserves equals adjusted NOI. **Direct operating expenses** include not only the cost of goods sold, but also the direct labor expense and other direct expenses of the profit centers. Direct labor expense is the expense of personnel working in the profit centers, such as the rooms, food, and beverage departments. Other direct expenses include supplies used by these revenue-producing departments.

Income statements based on the *USALI*'s summary operating statement provide separate line reporting by profit center. Sales and direct expenses are shown separately for the rooms and food and beverage departments, among others. In addition, the overhead expenses are divided among **undistributed operating expenses** and the group of management fees and **fixed charges**. The undistributed operating expenses are further detailed on the income statement by major service centers such as administrative and general and marketing. The detail provided by both profit centers and service centers reflects reporting by areas of responsibility and is commonly referred to as *responsibility accounting.*

Thus, the *USALI*–based income statement is useful to managers in the hospitality industry because it is designed to provide the information necessary to evaluate the performance of managers of the lodging facility by area of responsibility.

The *USALI*'s summary operating statement must be modified in order to reflect all expenses and to eliminate replacement reserves, which are not an expense, as follows:[2]

	Net operating income
−	Depreciation and amortization expense
−	Interest expense
=	Income before gains or losses on sale of property equipment
+ or −	Gains or losses on sale of property and equipment
=	Income before income taxes
−	Income taxes
=	Net income

154   *Chapter 5*

Exhibit 2   Summary Operating Statement per *USALI*

SUMMARY OPERATING STATEMENT[1]	CURRENT PERIOD						YEAR-TO-DATE					
	ACTUAL		FORECAST		PRIOR YEAR		ACTUAL		FORECAST		PRIOR YEAR	
	$	%	$	%	$	%	$	%	$	%	$	%
REVENUE Rooms, Food and Beverage, Other Operated Departments, Rentals and Other Income, **Total Revenue**												
DEPARTMENTAL EXPENSES[2] Rooms, Food and Beverage, Other Operated Departments, **Total Departmental Expenses**												
TOTAL DEPARTMENTAL INCOME												
UNDISTRIBUTED OPERATING EXPENSES Administrative and General, Sales and Marketing, Property Operations and Maintenance, Utilities, **Total Undistributed Expenses**												
GROSS OPERATING PROFIT												
MANAGEMENT FEES												
INCOME BEFORE FIXED CHARGES												
FIXED CHARGES Rent, Property Taxes, Insurance, **Total Fixed Charges**												
NET OPERATING INCOME												
LESS REPLACEMENT RESERVES												
ADJUSTED NET OPERATING INCOME												

1 For a complete Statement of Income, refer to page 19
2 Departmental Expenses is the sum of Cost of Sales (when applicable) and Total Expenses

Source: *Uniform System of Accounts for the Lodging Industry,* 10th Rev. Ed. (Lansing, Mich: Educational Institute of the American Hotel & Lodging Association, 2006). © Hotel Association of New York City.

Note that the amount for replacement reserves was not added back by this modification, as the adjustments started with NOI rather than adjusted NOI. Hereafter, the results of this modification will be referred to as the modified *USALI*.

Contents of the Summary Operating Statement

The summary operating statement per the *USALI* (illustrated in Exhibit 2) is divided into four major sections: Revenues, Departmental Expenses, Undistributed Operating Expenses, and a final part that includes management fees, fixed charges, and replacement reserves.

The first section, Revenues, reports net revenue by department for rooms, food and beverage combined, other operated departments, and, finally, rentals and other. According to the *USALI*, the telecommunications department is included in other operated departments, but many properties may still choose to list it as a separate line item. Net Revenue results when allowances are subtracted from related revenues. Allowances include reductions in price due to a service problem. For example, a hotel guest may have been charged $100 for his room, but because of poor service the charge is reduced to $80. The subsequent adjustment of $20 the following day is treated as an allowance. Revenues earned from investment activities are shown with rentals.

The second major section is Departmental Expenses and includes direct expenses of each department generating revenue. These expenses relate directly to the department incurring them and consist of three major categories: cost of sales, payroll and related expenses, and other expenses. They are shown as a single figure for each reported department on the summary operating statement. Though not shown separately, the cost of sales is normally determined as follows:

	Beginning inventory
Plus:	Inventory purchases
Equals:	Goods available for sale
Less:	Ending inventory
Equals:	Cost of goods consumed
Less:	Goods used internally
Equals:	Cost of goods sold

The second major direct expense category of operated departments is Payroll and Related Expenses. This category includes the salaries, wages, bonuses and incentives of employees working in the designated operated departments, such as servers in the food department. Salaries, wages, bonuses, incentives, and related expenses of departments that do not generate revenue but provide service, such as marketing, are recorded by service departments. The "Related Expenses" of "Payroll and Related Expenses" includes all payroll taxes and fringe benefits relating to employees of each operated department. For example, the front office manager's salary and related payroll taxes and fringe benefits would be included in the Payroll and Related Expenses of the rooms department.

The final major expense category for the operated departments is Other Expenses. This category includes only other direct expenses. For example, the 26 major other expense categories for the rooms department (per the *USALI*) include Cable/Satellite Television, Cleaning Supplies, Commissions and Rebates—Group, Complimentary Services and Gifts, Contract Services, Decorations, Equipment Rentals, Guest Relocation, and several others. Expenses such as Marketing and Administration are recorded as expenses of service departments. They benefit the rooms department and other profit centers but only on an indirect basis. Total revenue from the first section less total departmental expenses equals total departmental income.

The third major section of the income statement is Undistributed Operating Expenses. This section includes the four general categories of Administrative and General, Sales and Marketing, Property Operation and Maintenance, and Utility

Costs. These expense categories are related to the various service departments. A separate schedule supporting the total expense for each department should be prepared. The Administrative and General expense category includes service departments such as the general manager's office and the accounting office. In addition to salaries, wages, and related expenses of service department personnel covered by Administrative and General, other expenses include, but are not limited to, credit card commissions, professional fees, and provisions for doubtful accounts. The appendix at the end of this chapter includes the *USALI*'s recommended schedule for administrative and general expenses, which details the several expense categories for administrative and general expenses, as well as a complete set of other recommended schedules.

Sales and marketing expenses include costs relating to personnel working in marketing areas of sales, advertising, and promotion. In addition, marketing expenses include advertising and promotion expenses such as direct mail, in-house graphics, media, and e-commerce. Agency fees and other fees and commissions are also included as marketing expenses. Franchise fees are also part of the marketing expenses.

The third major category of undistributed operating expenses is Property Operation and Maintenance. Included in Property Operation and Maintenance are salaries and related payroll costs of the personnel responsible for property operation and maintenance, and the various supplies used to maintain the buildings, grounds, furniture, fixtures, and equipment.

The final category of undistributed operating expenses is Utility Costs. The recommended schedule includes separate listings of the various utilities, such as electricity and water. Sales by the hotel to tenants and charges to other departments are subtracted in determining net utility costs.

Subtracting the total undistributed operating expenses from total departmental income results in gross operating profits (GOP).

Operating management is considered fully responsible for all revenues and expenses reported to this point on the income statement, as they generally have the authority to exercise their judgment to affect all these items. However, the management fees and the fixed charges that follow in the next major section of the income statement are the responsibility primarily of the hospitality property's board of directors. The expenses listed on this part of the statement generally relate directly to decisions by the board, rather than to management decisions.

Management fees are the cost of using an independent management company to operate the hotel or motel. The fixed charges are also called *capacity costs,* since they relate to the physical plant or the capacity to provide goods and services to guests.

The fixed charges include rent, property taxes, and insurance according to the *USALI.* Rent includes the cost of renting real estate, computer equipment, and other major items that, had they been purchased instead, would have been recorded as fixed assets. Rental of miscellaneous equipment for specific functions such as banquets is shown as a direct expense of the food and beverage department.

Property taxes include real estate taxes, personal property taxes, business and transient occupation taxes, taxes assessed by utilities, and other taxes (but not income taxes and payroll taxes) that cannot be charged to guests.

Insurance includes the cost of insuring the building and its contents against damage from fire, weather, and similar agents. In addition, the general insurance costs for liability, fidelity, and theft are included in this category.

The summary operating statement at this point shows management fees and fixed charges subtracted from GOP to equal NOI. The cash that is set aside for replacement expenses is subtracted from NOI to equal adjusted NOI. Many lodging properties may desire to prepare their income statement to show all expenses in determining net income. The modified income statement continues from NOI as explained previously. Depreciation of fixed assets and amortization of other assets are shown after fixed charges on the modified income statement. The depreciation methods and useful lives of fixed assets are normally disclosed in footnotes.

Interest expense is the cost of borrowing money and is based on the amounts borrowed, the interest rate, and the length of time for which the funds are borrowed. Generally, loans are approved by the operation's board of directors, since most relate to the physical plant. Thus, interest expense is not under the direct control of operating management.

The modified *USALI* income statement shows gains or losses on the sale of property and equipment. A gain or loss on the sale of property and equipment results from a difference between the proceeds from the sale and the carrying value (net book value) of a fixed asset. The gain or loss is included on the modified *USALI* income statement just before income taxes. Gains are added while losses are subtracted in determining Income before Income Taxes. Finally, income taxes are subtracted from Income before Income Taxes to determine Net Income.

Departmental Statements

Departmental statements, which supplement the income statement and are called *schedules,* provide management with detailed information by operated department and service center. The classifications listed in the tenth revised edition of the *USALI* suggest up to 20 schedules and subschedules. Each of these schedules is included in the appendix at the end of this chapter.

Exhibit 3 illustrates an operated department schedule using the rooms department of the Honeymoon Inn. The operated department schedule reflects both revenue and direct expenses. Totals from the operated department schedules are reflected on the income statement. In the rooms department illustration, the following totals are carried from the departmental statement to the property's summary operating statement:

- Net Revenue $1,041,200
- Expenses $264,414

Exhibit 4 is the Honeymoon Inn's modified *USALI* income statement. The figures from the rooms department schedule are reflected in the first item under the revenues and departmental expense categories.

Exhibit 3   Rooms Department Schedule—Honeymoon Inn

Honeymoon Inn Rooms Department For the year ended December 31, 20X1	
Revenue	
Transient Rooms Revenue	$ 543,900
Group Rooms Revenue	450,000
Contract Rooms Revenue	48,000
Other	2,000
Less: Allowances	(2,700)
Net Revenue	1,041,200
Expenses	
Salaries, Wages, and Bonuses	
Salaries and Wages	159,304
Payroll Related Expenses	
Payroll Taxes	11,015
Employee Benefits	15,015
Total Payroll and Related Expenses	185,334
Other Expenses	
Cable/Satellite Television	4,900
Cleaning Supplies	3,200
Commissions	5,124
Contract Services	3,100
Guest Supplies	6,442
Laundry and Dry Cleaning	12,706
Linen	9,494
Miscellaneous	8,126
Operating Supplies	6,300
Reservations	9,288
Telecommunications	4,685
Training	4,315
Uniforms	1,400
Total Other Expenses	79,080
Total Expenses	264,414
Departmental Income	$ 776,786

In contrast to the profit center schedules prepared by the revenue-producing operated departments of a hospitality operation, a service center schedule reports only expenses by area of responsibility. Although these activity areas do not generate revenue, they do provide service to the operated departments and, in some cases, to other service centers. Exhibit 5 illustrates a service center departmental schedule by using the property operation and maintenance schedule of the Honeymoon Inn. The only number that is carried over to the Honeymoon Inn's

Exhibit 4   Modified *USALI* Income Statement—Honeymoon Inn

Honeymoon Inn For the year ended December 31, 20X1	
Revenue	
Rooms	$1,041,200
Food and Beverage	626,165
Telecommunications	52,028
Total Revenue	1,719,393
Departmental Expenses	
Rooms	264,414
Food and Beverage	493,493
Telecommunications	67,638
Total Departmental Expenses	825,545
Total Departmental Income	893,848
Undistributed Operating Expenses	
Administrative and General	152,423
Sales and Marketing	66,816
Property Operations and Maintenance	80,964
Utility Costs	88,782
Total Undistributed Expenses	388,985
Gross Operating Profit	504,863
Management Fees	60,000
Income before Fixed Charges	444,863
Fixed Charges	
Rent	20,861
Property and Other Taxes	69,888
Insurance	50,112
Total Fixed Charges	140,861
Net Operating Income	304,002
Depreciation and Amortization	115,860
Interest Expense	52,148
Income before Income Taxes	135,994
Income Taxes	48,707
Net Income	$ 87,287

modified income statement (Exhibit 4) for this department is total expense of $80,964.

The number and nature of the supporting schedules reported in a lodging facility depends on the size and organization of the establishment.

Exhibit 5   Property Operation and Maintenance Schedule—Honeymoon Inn

Honeymoon Inn
Property Operation and Maintenance
For the year ended December 31, 20X1

Expenses

Payroll and Related Expenses

Salaries, Wages, and Bonuses	$ 27,790
Payroll Related Expenses	
Payroll Taxes	2,102
Employee Benefits	1,760
Total Payroll and Related Expenses	31,652
Other Expenses	
Building	8,900
Contract Service	2,499
Electrical and Mechanical Equipment	8,761
Engineering Supplies	1,981
Furniture and Equipment	14,322
Grounds and Landscaping	6,241
Operating Supplies	2,651
Swimming Pool	2,624
Uniforms	652
Uniform Laundry	681
Total Other Expenses	49,312
Total Expenses	**$ 80,964**

Uniform System of Accounts for Restaurants

Operations of a commercial food service operation differ from operations of a lodging business or a club and, therefore, the financial information as presented in financial statements also differs. The income statement recommended for commercial food service operations is prescribed in the *Uniform System of Accounts for Restaurants (USAR)* published by the National Restaurant Association.

The benefits of the *USAR* are similar to those of the *USALI*. The *USAR*:

- Provides uniform classification and presentation of operating results.

- Allows easier comparisons to food service industry statistics.

- Provides a turnkey accounting system.

- Is a time-tested system prepared by some of the food service industry's best accounting minds.

Exhibit 6 is the statement of income for the hypothetical Steak-Plus Restaurant. As with the *USALI's* income statement, there are several recommended

Exhibit 6 *USAR* **Summary Statement of Income**

Summary Statement of Income
Steak-Plus Restaurant
For the year ended December 31, 20X1

	Exhibit	Amounts	Percentages
Sales:			
Food	D	$1,045,800	75.8%
Beverage	E	333,000	24.2
Total Sales		1,378,800	100.0
Cost of Sales:			
Food		448,000	32.5
Beverage		85,200	6.2
Total Cost of Sales		533,200	38.7
Gross Profit		845,600	61.3
Operating Expenses:			
Salaries and Wages	F	332,200	24.1
Employee Benefits	G	57,440	4.2
Direct Operating Expenses	H	88,400	6.4
Music and Entertainment	I	14,200	1.0
Marketing	J	30,000	2.2
Utility Services	K	37,560	2.7
General and Administrative Expenses	L	56,400	4.1
Repairs and Maintenance	M	28,600	2.1
Occupancy Costs	N	82,200	6.0
Depreciation	N	31,200	2.3
Other Income	O	(5,400)	(0.4)
Total Operating Expenses		752,800	54.6
Operating Income		92,800	6.7
Interest	P	21,600	1.6
Income before Income Taxes		71,200	5.2
Income Taxes		22,000	1.6
Net Income		$ 49,200	3.6%

subsidiary schedules to this statement of income. Although they are not shown here, they provide supplementary information, as do the subsidiary schedules for the *USALI*–based income statement.

The basic similarities and differences between the *USAR*'s and *USALI*'s income statement formats are as follows:

	USALI	*USAR*
Sales segmented	yes	yes
Cost of sales segmented	yes	yes
Payroll and related costs segmented	yes	no

Exhibit 7   Statement of Retained Earnings—Honeymoon Inn

Honeymoon Inn Statement of Retained Earnings For the year ended December 31, 20X1	
January 1, 20X1 balance	$285,000
Add: Net income for 20X1	87,287
Less: Dividends	25,000
Less: Adjustment for failure to record depreciation in prior year	2,000
December 31, 20X1 balance	$345,287

Direct costs segmented	yes	no
Controllable expenses separated from fixed charges	yes	yes
Fixed charges segmented	yes	yes

Statement of Retained Earnings

Most businesses include four financial statements in their annual reports: a balance sheet, an income statement, a statement of cash flows, and a statement of retained earnings.

Incorporated businesses typically provide a **statement of retained earnings**, while unincorporated businesses provide a statement of owners' equity.

The statement of retained earnings is a formal statement showing changes in retained earnings during the accounting period. Exhibit 7 shows the statement of retained earnings for the Honeymoon Inn.

Since the statement covers the accounting period of one year in this illustration, the retained earnings balance at the beginning of the period is the first line of the statement. Net income for the period is added; a net loss would be subtracted. Dividends declared during the year, regardless of when they are paid, are subtracted. Dividends become a legal liability of a corporation when they are declared by the corporation's board of directors. At that point, Retained Earnings is reduced (debited) and Dividends Payable is increased (credited). Later, when the dividends are paid, Cash is credited and Dividends Payable is debited.

The next item on the statement of retained earnings is called a **prior period adjustment**. The correction of an error in a financial statement of a prior period is shown on the statement of retained earnings rather than as part of operations for the current year. In our illustration, the Honeymoon Inn failed to record depreciation in the prior period for a piece of equipment it had purchased. The depreciation expense that should have been recorded was $2,000. Therefore, rather than reduce net income for 20X1 when the depreciation relates to the prior year, Retained Earnings is simply reduced. The journal entry to record this prior period adjustment would be as follows:

Exhibit 8   Statement of Stockholders' Equity—Marriott International, Inc.

Fiscal Years 2005, 2004, and 2003

(in millions, except per share amounts)

Common Shares Outstanding		Class A Common Stock	Additional Paid-in Capital	Deferred Compensation	Retained Earnings	Treasury Stock, at Cost	Accumulated Other Comprehensive (Loss) Income
235.9	Balance at fiscal year-end 2002	$ 3	$3,224	$ (43)	$1,126	$ (667)	$(70)
—	Net income	—	—	—	502	—	—
—	Dividends ($0.295 per share)	—	—	—	(68)	—	—
5.8	Employee stock plan issuance and other	—	93	(38)	(55)	182	29
(10.5)	Purchase of treasury stock	—	—	—	—	(380)	—
231.2	Balance at fiscal year-end 2003	3	3,317	(81)	1,505	(865)	(41)
—	Net income	—	—	—	596	—	—
—	Dividends ($0.330 per share)	—	—	—	(75)	—	—
8.6	Employee stock plan issuance and other	—	106	(27)	(75)	322	50
(14.0)	Purchase of treasury stock	—	—	—	—	(654)	—
225.8	Balance at fiscal year-end 2004	3	3,423	(108)	1,951	(1,197)	9
—	Net income	—	—	—	669	—	—
—	Dividends ($0.400 per share)	—	—	—	(87)	—	—
5.8	Employee stock plan issuance and other	—	141	(29)	(33)	180	(20)
(25.7)	Purchase of treasury stock	—	—	—	—	(1,650)	—
205.9	Balance at fiscal year-end 2005	$ 3	$3,564	$(137)	$2,500	$(2,667)	$(11)

See Notes to Consolidated Financial Statements

Courtesy of Marriott International, Inc.

Retained Earnings	$2,000
Accumulated Depreciation, Equipment	$2,000
To record depreciation on equipment for the prior year.	

Some corporations provide a statement of stockholders' equity that explains changes in retained earnings and the contributed capital accounts such as Capital Stock, Paid-In Capital in Excess of Par, and Treasury Stock. Exhibit 8 is a statement of stockholders' equity from Marriott International.

Summary

The income statement, complete with all departmental statements, is considered the most useful financial statement for management. It reports sales and expenses that ideally result in net income, but sometimes in a net loss, for the period. The income statement has different uses for different groups of people. External users such as creditors and potential investors need general information about profitability, sales, and some expenses. Internal users such as managers need detailed information so they can manage operations.

The income statement shows four major elements: revenues, expenses, gains, and losses. Revenues (increases in assets or decreases in liability accounts) and expenses (decreases in assets or increases in liability accounts) are directly related to operations while gains and losses result from transactions incidental to the property's major operations.

The original *Uniform System of Accounts for Hotels* was written in 1925–26 to standardize income statements within the hospitality industry. Changes and revisions have been made since then, the most recent being the tenth revised edition of the *Uniform System of Accounts for the Lodging Industry (USALI)*, published in 2006. A uniform system of accounts provides a turnkey accounting system for a complete and systematic accounting for the hotel's operations. The various uniform systems also facilitate comparison among large and small hospitality operations.

To enhance the usefulness of the income statement, the modified *USALI* format includes statements of departmental income showing the revenues produced by each profit center (operated department) and subtracting from each the corresponding direct operating expenses. Included in the direct operating expenses are the cost of goods sold, the direct payroll, and other direct expenses. Next, undistributed operating expenses, which consist of four major service center categories—Administrative and General Expenses, Marketing, Property Operation and Maintenance, and Utility Costs—must be subtracted to determine gross operating profit. This is followed by management fees and fixed charges (rent, property taxes, insurance) to determine net operating income. To determine the net income of an operation, depreciation and interest expense are subtracted prior to recognizing gains or losses from property and equipment. Gains (losses) on the sale of property and equipment are added (subtracted) to determine Income before Income Taxes. Finally, income taxes are subtracted, resulting in Net Income.

Departmental income statements supplement the income statement and are called *schedules*. They provide management with detailed information by operated department and service center. The number and nature of the supporting schedules that a firm uses depend on the size and organization of the firm.

The statement of retained earnings is a formal statement that shows the changes in owners' equity during the accounting period. It is through the retained earnings account that the impact of the income statement is shown on the balance sheet. This statement is prepared for companies that are incorporated, as opposed to proprietorships, which prepare a statement of owners' equity.

Endnotes

1. Uniform systems of accounts are available as follows:

    Uniform System of Accounts for the Lodging Industry, 10th Rev. Ed. (Lansing, Mich.: Educational Institute of the American Hotel & Lodging Association, 2006). © Hotel Association of New York City, Inc.

    Uniform System of Financial Reporting for Clubs, 6th Rev. Ed. (Washington, D.C.: Club Managers Association of America, 2003).

    Uniform System of Accounts for Restaurants, 7th Rev. Ed. (Washington, D.C.: National Restaurant Association, 1996).

2. Replacement reserves are not an expense. They represent a cash transfer for future use when replacing furniture, fixtures and equipment.

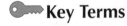 # Key Terms

cost of goods sold—The cost of the products that are sold in the operation of the business.

departmental statements—Supplements to the income statement that provide management with detailed financial information by operating department and service center; also referred to as *schedules*.

direct operating expenses—Expenses related directly to the department incurring them and consisting of cost of sales, payroll and related expenses, and other expenses.

earnings per share (EPS)—A ratio providing a general indicator of the profitability of a hospitality operation by comparing net income to the average common shares outstanding. If preferred stock has been issued, preferred dividends are subtracted from net income before calculating EPS.

external users of financial statements—Creditors, potential investors, and passive owners of a business who need general information regarding sales, expenses, assets, and liabilities.

extraordinary item—An item (usually a loss) reported at the end of the income statement that is both highly unusual and highly infrequent in occurrence.

fixed charges—A category of expenses reported on the income statement that relates to decisions outside the area of control of operating management and consists of rent, property taxes, insurance, interest, and depreciation and amortization.

gains—Increases in assets, reductions in liabilities, or a combination of both, resulting from a hospitality operation's incidental transactions and from all other transactions and events affecting the operation during the period, except those that count as revenues or investments by owners.

income statement—A report on the profitability of operations, including revenues earned and expenses incurred in generating the revenues for the period of time covered by the statement.

internal users of financial statements—The managers of the hospitality firm who need detailed information to most effectively run daily operations.

losses—Decreases in assets, increases in liabilities, or a combination of both, resulting from a hospitality operation's incidental transactions and from the other transactions and events affecting the operation during a period, except those that count as expenses or distributions to owners.

management fees—The cost of using an independent management company to manage the hospitality operation.

prior period adjustment—The correction of an error in a financial statement from a prior period, shown on the statement of retained earnings.

profit center—An operating department within a hospitality operation that generates revenues and incurs expenses.

responsibility accounting—The organization of accounting information (as on an income statement) that focuses attention on departmental results such as the rooms, food, and beverage departments.

service center—A department within a hospitality operation that is not directly involved in generating revenue but that provides supporting services to revenue-generating departments within the operation.

statement of retained earnings—A formal statement that is prepared for an incorporated business and that shows changes in retained earnings during the accounting period.

total departmental income—The difference between an operating department's revenue and direct expenses.

undistributed operating expenses—Expenses not directly related to income-generating departments and consisting of Administrative and General Expenses, Marketing, Property Operation and Maintenance, and Utility Costs.

uniform system of accounts—Standardized accounting systems prepared by various segments of the hospitality industry offering detailed information about accounts, classifications, formats, the different kinds, contents, and uses of financial statements and reports, and other useful information.

 **Review Questions**

1. Why are internal and external users interested in the income statement?

2. What is the relationship between the income statement and the balance sheet?

3. How do accountants treat employee meals, transfers, and promotional meals when determining cost of food sold?

4. What are three examples of departmental operating expenses for the rooms department?

5. Why are certain kinds of expenses classified as fixed?

6. What are the characteristics of direct expenses and undistributed operating expenses?

7. What are the advantages of a uniform system of accounts?

8. What is the purpose of separate departmental schedules or statements?

9. What is the difference between a profit center and a service center?

10. What are the rules for declaring an extraordinary item? How might the guidelines change for different hotels in different locations?

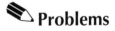 **Problems**

Problem 1

The following is information for the Texas Two-Step Bar and Grill.

Purchases	$57,900
Food Inventory Beginning of Year—20X3	1,160
Food Inventory End of Year—20X3	1,450

Transfers from Bar to Kitchen	95
Employee Meals	732
Transfers from Kitchen to Bar	50
Promotional Meals	432

Required:

Using the information provided, calculate the cost of food sold for 20X3.

Problem 2

Gene Washburn owns the GW Café and needs assistance in determining both cost of food used and cost of food sold for June 20X6. He provides information as follows:

Beginning food inventory	$10,500
Food purchases	24,000
Cost of employee meals	500
Cost of promotional meals	300
Transfers from the beverage department	100
Transfers to the beverage department	150
Physical food inventory, end of June 20X6	8,400

Required:

1. Determine the cost of food used.
2. Determine the cost of food sold.

Problem 3

The New York Strip Steak House is undergoing renovation. A consulting firm has recommended that the NYS Steak House replace its old ovens and grills with new ones that will make the kitchen more efficient.

The old equipment was purchased 10 years ago for $35,000. The annual depreciation was $2,500.

The consulting firm has found a buyer who is interested in the ovens and grills and who will pay $13,000 cash for them.

The new equipment will cost $75,000.

Required:

Using the information provided, determine the amount of gain or loss on the sale that will be incurred if the NYS Steak House takes the consulting firm's advice and replaces the ovens and grills.

Problem 4

A delivery van was purchased for $30,000 on July 1, 20X4. It was depreciated on a straight-line basis for 3½ years prior to being sold on December 31, 20X7, for $8,000. It has a salvage value of $3,000. Assume its life for depreciation purposes is five years.

Required:

1. What was the depreciation expense for 20X4?
2. What was the accumulated depreciation expense over the life of the van prior to the sale?
3. What was the gain or loss on the sale?

Problem 5

The Southwest Hotel issues a full set of financial statements annually to its stockholders. Buzz Barr, the chief accountant, has provided you with the following information:

Retained earnings account balances:

December 31, 20X1	$150,000
December 31, 20X2	$200,000

Sale of capital stock:

20X2	$10,000
20X3	$15,000

Dividends *declared*:

20X2	$20,000
20X3	$30,000

Dividends *paid*:

20X2	$15,000
20X3	$25,000

Operating results:

20X2 net income	$70,000
20X3 net loss	$10,000

Required:

Using the information provided, prepare statements of retained earnings for 20X2 and 20X3.

Problem 6

The Treetops Resort is incorporated and pays dividends each quarter. The balance of the retained earnings account at the beginning of 20X6 was $105,000. During 20X6, net income of $85,000 was earned. In each calendar quarter, a dividend of $1.00 per share of common stock was declared. The number of shares of common stock were as follows:

Quarter	
First	10,500
Second	12,000
Third	12,500
Fourth	14,000

Also during 20X6, a correction of $10,000 was made to correct the excessive deprecation expense shown on the 20X5 income statement.

Required:

Prepare the statement of retained earnings for the Treetops Resort for the year ended December 31, 20X6.

Problem 7

The Upper Room Inn (URI), an incorporated lodging operation, prepares its income tax return using the same information as it shows on its annual report to its owners with the exception of depreciation. The pre-depreciation income of the URI for 20X2 is $200,000. Assume that depreciation expenses for book and tax purposes are $50,000 and $100,000, respectively. Further assume the relevant tax rate is 25 percent.

Required:

Determine the amount of taxes (1) to be shown in its annual report, (2) to be shown on its tax return, and (3) to be recorded as deferred taxes.

Problem 8

Lisa Brandt is the owner of Brandt's Bed and Breakfast. Even though she runs a small operation, Lisa still likes to use the *USALI*. The following are some accounts pertaining to the rooms division of her business.

Salaries and Wages	$16,560
Operating Supplies	2,484
Linen	500
Sales	82,800
Laundry	5,500
Commissions	700
Dry Cleaning	120
Uniforms	200

In addition, Lisa's fringe benefits and payroll taxes are 30 percent of Salaries and Wages. She incurs other expenses of 2 percent of sales.

Required:

Prepare a rooms department schedule for Brandt's Bed and Breakfast according to the *USALI*.

Problem 9

The following are several accounts and balances from the general ledger of the Hilltop Motel.

Allowances—Rooms	$ 500
Commissions	1,000
Contract Cleaning	1,800
Dry Cleaning	1,200
Fringe Benefits	3,000

Laundry	3,000
Linen Expense	1,000
Operating Supplies	1,500
Other Expenses	1,800
Payroll Taxes	2,000
Salaries	10,000
Sales—Transient (Group)	50,000
Sales—Transient (Regular)	100,000
Uniforms	500
Wages	15,000

Required:

Prepare a rooms department schedule following the *USALI*.

Problem 10

The following are several accounts and balances from the general ledger of the Shifting Sands Casino and Hotel that pertain to property operation and maintenance.

Building Supplies	$ 1,125
Operating Supplies	11,250
Furniture	5,250
Uniforms	300
Employee Benefits	18,750
Grounds and Landscaping	6,750
Other	750
Engineering Supplies	4,050
Swimming Pool	4,725
Removal of Waste Matter	3,720
Salaries and Wages	75,000
Electrical and Mechanical Equipment	12,000

Required:

Prepare a property operation and maintenance schedule following the *USALI* for the month ended July 31, 20X4.

Problem 11

The account balances for the administrative and general schedule are as follows:

Salaries	$250,000
Wages	80,000
Fringe benefits	48,000
Payroll taxes	21,000
Bank charges	250
Credit card commissions	8,400

Contributions to charity	10,000
Dues—HFTP	250
Information systems	14,600
Miscellaneous	1,200
Operating supplies	1,300
Postage	650
Printing and stationary	850
Professional subscriptions	400
Provisions for bad debts	2,400
Telephone and fax	1,850
Travel	4,500

Required:

Prepare the administrative and general schedule following the schedule provided in the Appendix. Use the terminology of the *USALI.*

Challenge Problems

Problem 12

Goran Blomberg is interested in investing in a new rooms-only lodging property. He needs some financial projections for a single year for the proposed operations. He provides the following:

1. Room sales:
   a. Average room rate—$50
   b. Average daily occupancy—65%
   c. Available rooms per day—50

2. Administrative and general fixed labor—$12,000/month

3. Variable expenses (as a percentage of total room sales):
   a. Rooms labor—20%
   b. Rooms other expense—10%
   c. Administrative and general other—3%
   d. Marketing—5%
   e. Maintenance—5%

4. Other fixed expenses:
   a. Depreciation—$5,000/month
   b. Utilities—$3,000/month
   c. Insurance—$1,000/month
   d. Property taxes—$2,000 for the year
   e. Maintenance—$500/month

5. Income tax rate—20 percent (as a percentage of income before taxes).

6. Assume the property will be open 365 days of the year.

Required:

Prepare an income statement based on the *USALI* summary operating statement.

Problem 13

The Kaminski Motel (KM) has two major operated departments: rooms and food. The following information is supplied to you as of December 31, 20X2:

Account	Account Balance
Insurance (fire)	$?
Rooms Department—Salaries and Wages	90,000
Food Department—Salaries and Wages	60,000
Supplies and Other—Food Department	20,000
Food Purchases	65,000
Room Sales	550,000
Interest Income	?
Cost of Food Sold	?
Food Sales	250,000
Administrative and General—Salaries	60,000
Advertising	12,000
Maintenance—Contract	40,000
Depreciation	40,000
Electricity	15,000
Heating Oil	12,000
Amortization of Intangible Assets	5,000
Supplies and Other—Rooms Department	30,000
Property Taxes	15,000
Administrative and General—Other Expenses	15,000
Franchise Fees	?
Room—Allowances	1,000

Other information is as follows:

1. The KM invested $30,000 on July 1, 20X2, in Daytona Aircraft Bonds. The funds were invested at an annual interest rate of 12 percent.

2. The beginning and ending inventories of food were $5,000 and $4,000, respectively. Food consumed by the food and rooms department employees during the year (free of charge) totaled $500 and $300, respectively.

3. Fringe benefits and payroll taxes for all employees, inclusive of employee meals, are 20 percent of gross salaries and wages.

4. The KM pays an average of 30 percent of its pretax income to the various governmental units in the form of income taxes.

5. The management fee to be paid to the management company is 2 percent of net room sales and 6 percent of total income before management fees and fixed charges.

6. Fire insurance protection was secured on June 1, 20X1, for a two-year period of coverage from July 1, 20X1, through June 30, 20X3. The two-year premium was $36,000.

7. Franchise fees (a marketing expense) is paid to Best Eastern Corporation at a rate of 3 percent of net room sales and 2 percent of net food sales.

Required:

Prepare the modified income statement for 20X2. Use Exhibit 4 as a guide.

Problem 14

The general ledger of Ramsey's, a 100-seat restaurant, as of December 31, 20X3, includes revenue and expense accounts as follows:

Salaries	$ 150,000
Wages	280,000
Payroll Taxes	30,000
Fringe Benefits (excludes employee meals)	50,000
Employee Meals	5,000
Food Sales	1,200,000
Beverage Sales	500,000
Food Purchases	460,000
Beverage Purchases	130,000
Other Sales	20,000
Direct Operating Expenses	100,000
Music	20,000
Marketing	30,000
Heat, Light, and Power	35,000
Rent	152,000
Interest Expense	20,000
Depreciation	50,000
Repairs	30,000
Administrative and General	92,000

Other information is as follows:

Income tax rate—30 percent on pretax income

Inventories	1/1/X3	12/31/X3
Food	$20,000	$22,000
Beverage	15,000	17,000

Required:

Prepare Ramsey's income statement for 20X3 in accordance with the *USAR*.

Problem 15

The Wilson Motel has two major operated departments: rooms and food. The following information is supplied as of December 31, 20X6:

Account	Account Balance
Insurance (Fire)	$ 5,000
Rooms Department—Salaries and Wages	80,000
Food Department—Salaries and Wages	60,000
Other Expenses—Food Department	20,000
Food Purchases	55,000
Rooms Sales	380,000
Interest Income	1,000
Interest Expense	?
Cost of Food Sold	?
Food Sales	180,000
Administrative and General—Wages	50,000
Advertising	10,000
Maintenance—Expenses	30,000
Depreciation	50,000
Heat	15,000
Power and Lights	12,000
Amortization of Franchise Fee	2,000
Supplies and Other—Rooms Department	30,000
Property Taxes	12,000
Administrative and General—Other Expense	10,000

Other information is as follows:

1. The Wilson Motel borrowed $50,000 on January 1, 20X6, at 10 percent, and no payments were made during 20X6.
2. The beginning and ending inventories of food were $2,000 and $3,000, respectively. Food consumed by the Food and Rooms department employees during the year (free of charge) totaled $500 and $300, respectively.
3. Fringe benefits and payroll taxes for all employees, excluding free food, are 20 percent of gross salaries and wages.
4. The Wilson Motel's average income tax rate is 25 percent of pretax income.
5. The management fee to be paid to the management company is 3 percent of room sales and 10 percent of total income before management fees and fixed charges.

Required:

Prepare an income statement based on the *USALI* summary operating statement.

Chapter Appendix:

Departmental Schedules from the

Uniform System of Accounts for the Lodging Industry

Rooms Department—Schedule 1

	CURRENT MONTH						YEAR-TO-DATE					
	ACTUAL		FORECAST		PRIOR YEAR		ACTUAL		FORECAST		PRIOR YEAR	
	$	%	$	%	$	%	$	%	$	%	$	%
REVENUE												
Transient Rooms Revenue												
Group Rooms Revenue												
Contract Rooms Revenue												
Other Rooms Revenue												
Less: Allowances												
Total Rooms Revenue												
EXPENSES												
Payroll and Related Expenses												
Salaries, Wages, and Bonuses												
Salaries and Wages												
Bonuses and Incentives												
Total Salaries, Wages, and Bonuses												
Payroll Related Expenses												
Payroll Taxes												
Supplemental Pay												
Employee Benefits												
Total Payroll Related Expenses												
Total Payroll and Related Expenses												
Other Expenses												
Cable/Satellite Television												
Cleaning Supplies												
Commissions												
Commissions and Rebates—Group												
Complimentary Services and Gifts												
Contract Services												
Corporate Office Reimbursables												
Decorations												
Equipment Rental												
Guest Relocation												
Guest Supplies												
Guest Transportation												
Laundry and Dry Cleaning												
Licenses and Permits												
Linen												
Miscellaneous												
Operating Supplies												
Printing and Stationery												
Reservations												

(continued)

Rooms Department—Schedule 1 *(continued)*

	CURRENT MONTH						YEAR-TO-DATE					
	ACTUAL		FORECAST		PRIOR YEAR		ACTUAL		FORECAST		PRIOR YEAR	
	$	%	$	%	$	%	$	%	$	%	$	%
Royalty Fees												
Telecommunications												
Training												
Travel—Meals and Entertainment												
Travel—Other												
Uniforms												
Uniform Laundry												
Total Other Expenses												
TOTAL EXPENSES												
DEPARTMENTAL INCOME (LOSS)												

Food and Beverage Department—Schedule 2

	CURRENT MONTH						YEAR-TO-DATE					
	ACTUAL		FORECAST		PRIOR YEAR		ACTUAL		FORECAST		PRIOR YEAR	
	$	%	$	%	$	%	$	%	$	%	$	%
REVENUE												
Outlet Food Revenue												
Outlet Beverage Revenue												
In-Room Dining Food Revenue												
In-Room Dining Beverage Revenue												
Banquet/Catering Food Revenue												
Banquet/Catering Beverage Revenue												
Mini Bar Food Revenue												
Mini Bar Beverage Revenue												
Other Food Revenue												
Other Beverage Revenue												
Less: Allowances												
Total Food and Beverage Revenue												
OTHER REVENUE												
Audiovisual												
Public Room Rentals												
Cover Charges												
Service Charges												
Miscellaneous Other Revenue												
Less: Allowances												
Total Other Revenue												
TOTAL REVENUE												
COST OF FOOD AND BEVERAGE SALES												
Cost of Food Sales												
Cost of Beverage Sales												
Total Cost of Food and Beverage Sales												
COST OF OTHER REVENUE												
Audiovisual Cost												
Miscellaneous Cost												
Total Cost of Other Revenue												
TOTAL COST OF SALES AND OTHER REVENUE												
GROSS PROFIT (LOSS)												
EXPENSES												
Payroll and Related Expenses												
Salaries, Wages, and Bonuses												
Salaries and Wages												
Bonuses and Incentives												
Total Salaries, Wages, and Bonuses												
Payroll Related Expenses												
Payroll Taxes												
Supplemental Pay												
Employee Benefits												
Total Payroll Related Expenses												
Total Payroll and Related Expenses												

(continued)

Food and Beverage Department—Schedule 2 *(continued)*

	CURRENT MONTH						YEAR-TO-DATE					
	ACTUAL		FORECAST		PRIOR YEAR		ACTUAL		FORECAST		PRIOR YEAR	
	$	%	$	%	$	%	$	%	$	%	$	%
Other Expenses												
Banquet Expense												
China												
Cleaning Supplies												
Complimentary Services and Gifts												
Contract Services												
Corporate Office Reimbursables												
Decorations												
Dishwashing Supplies												
Equipment Rental												
Flatware												
Glassware												
Ice												
Kitchen Fuel												
Laundry and Dry Cleaning												
Licenses and Permits												
Linen												
Management Fees												
Menu and Beverage Lists												
Miscellaneous												
Music and Entertainment												
Operating Supplies												
Paper and Plastics												
Printing and Stationery												
Royalty Fees												
Telecommunications												
Training												
Travel—Meals and Entertainment												
Travel—Other												
Uniforms												
Uniform Laundry												
Utensils												
Total Other Expenses												
TOTAL EXPENSES												
DEPARTMENTAL INCOME (LOSS)												

Food Department—Subschedule 2-1

	CURRENT MONTH						YEAR-TO-DATE					
	ACTUAL		FORECAST		PRIOR YEAR		ACTUAL		FORECAST		PRIOR YEAR	
	$	%	$	%	$	%	$	%	$	%	$	%
REVENUE												
Outlet Food Revenue												
In-Room Dining Food Revenue												
Banquet/Catering Food Revenue												
Mini Bar Food Revenue												
Other Food Revenue												
Less: Allowances												
Total Food Revenue												
OTHER REVENUE												
Audiovisual												
Public Room Rentals												
Cover Charges												
Service Charges												
Miscellaneous Other Revenue												
Less: Allowances												
Total Other Revenue												
TOTAL REVENUE												
COST OF FOOD SALES												
COST OF OTHER REVENUE												
Audiovisual Cost												
Miscellaneous Cost												
Total Cost of Other Revenue												
TOTAL COST OF FOOD SALES AND OTHER REVENUE												
GROSS PROFIT (LOSS)												
EXPENSES												
Payroll and Related Expenses												
Salaries, Wages, and Bonuses												
Salaries and Wages												
Bonuses and Incentives												
Total Salaries, Wages, and Bonuses												
Payroll Related Expenses												
Payroll Taxes												
Supplemental Pay												
Employee Benefits												
Total Payroll Related Expenses												
Total Payroll and Related Expenses												
Other Expenses												
Banquet Expense												
China												
Cleaning Supplies												
Complimentary Services and Gifts												
Contract Services												
Corporate Office Reimbursables												
Decorations												
Dishwashing Supplies												
Equipment Rental												

(continued)

Food Department—Subschedule 2-1 *(continued)*

	CURRENT MONTH						YEAR-TO-DATE					
	ACTUAL		FORECAST		PRIOR YEAR		ACTUAL		FORECAST		PRIOR YEAR	
	$	%	$	%	$	%	$	%	$	%	$	%
Flatware												
Glassware												
Ice												
Kitchen Fuel												
Laundry and Dry Cleaning												
Licenses and Permits												
Linen												
Management Fees												
Menu and Beverage Lists												
Miscellaneous												
Music and Entertainment												
Operating Supplies												
Paper and Plastics												
Printing and Stationery												
Royalty Fees												
Telecommunications												
Training												
Travel—Meals and Entertainment												
Travel—Other												
Uniforms												
Uniform Laundry												
Utensils												
Total Other Expenses												
TOTAL EXPENSES												
DEPARTMENTAL INCOME (LOSS)												

Beverage Department—Subschedule 2-2

	CURRENT MONTH						YEAR-TO-DATE					
	ACTUAL		FORECAST		PRIOR YEAR		ACTUAL		FORECAST		PRIOR YEAR	
	$	%	$	%	$	%	$	%	$	%	$	%
REVENUE												
Outlet Beverage Revenue												
In-Room Dining Beverage Revenue												
Banquet/Catering Beverage Revenue												
Mini Bar Beverage Revenue												
Other Beverage Revenue												
Less: Allowances												
Total Beverage Revenue												
OTHER REVENUE												
Audiovisual												
Public Room Rentals												
Cover Charges												
Service Charges												
Miscellaneous Other Revenue												
Less: Allowances												
Total Other Revenue												
TOTAL REVENUE												
COST OF BEVERAGE SALES												
COST OF OTHER REVENUE												
Audiovisual Cost												
Miscellaneous Cost												
Total Cost of Other Revenue												
TOTAL COST OF BEVERAGE SALES AND OTHER REVENUE												
GROSS PROFIT (LOSS)												
EXPENSES												
Payroll and Related Expenses												
Salaries, Wages, and Bonuses												
Salaries and Wages												
Bonuses and Incentives												
Total Salaries, Wages, and Bonuses												
Payroll Related Expenses												
Payroll Taxes												
Supplemental Pay												
Employee Benefits												
Total Payroll Related Expenses												
Total Payroll and Related Expenses												
Other Expenses												
Banquet Expense												
China												
Cleaning Supplies												
Complimentary Services and Gifts												
Contract Services												
Corporate Office Reimbursables												
Decorations												
Dishwashing Supplies												

(continued)

Beverage Department—Subschedule 2-2 *(continued)*

	CURRENT MONTH						YEAR-TO-DATE					
	ACTUAL		FORECAST		PRIOR YEAR		ACTUAL		FORECAST		PRIOR YEAR	
	$	%	$	%	$	%	$	%	$	%	$	%
Equipment Rental												
Flatware												
Glassware												
Ice												
Kitchen Fuel												
Laundry and Dry Cleaning												
Licenses and Permits												
Linen												
Management Fees												
Menu and Beverage Lists												
Miscellaneous												
Music and Entertainment												
Operating Supplies												
Paper and Plastics												
Printing and Stationery												
Royalty Fees												
Telecommunications												
Training												
Travel—Meals and Entertainment												
Travel—Other												
Uniforms												
Uniform Laundry												
Utensils												
Total Other Expenses												
TOTAL EXPENSES												
DEPARTMENTAL INCOME (LOSS)												

Other Operated Departments—Schedule 3

	CURRENT MONTH						YEAR-TO-DATE					
	ACTUAL		FORECAST		PRIOR YEAR		ACTUAL		FORECAST		PRIOR YEAR	
	$	%	$	%	$	%	$	%	$	%	$	%
REVENUE												
Other Operated Department 1												
Other Operated Department 2												
...												
...												
Other Operated Department *x*												
Minor Operated Departments												
Total Revenue												
DEPARTMENTAL EXPENSES[1]												
Other Operated Department 1												
Other Operated Department 2												
...												
...												
Other Operated Department *x*												
Minor Operated Departments												
Total Departmental Expenses												
DEPARTMENTAL INCOME (LOSS)												
Other Operated Department 1												
Other Operated Department 2												
...												
Other Operated Department *x*												
Minor Operated Departments												
TOTAL OTHER DEPARTMENTAL INCOME (LOSS)												

1. Departmental Expenses is the sum of Cost of Sales (when applicable) and Total Expenses.

Telecommunications Department—Subschedule 3-1

	CURRENT MONTH						YEAR-TO-DATE					
	ACTUAL		FORECAST		PRIOR YEAR		ACTUAL		FORECAST		PRIOR YEAR	
	$	%	$	%	$	%	$	%	$	%	$	%
REVENUE												
Local Call Revenue												
Long Distance Revenue												
Internet Revenue												
Other Revenue												
Less: Allowances												
Total Telecommunications Revenue												
COST OF CALLS												
Cost of Local Calls												
Cost of Long Distance Calls												
Cost of Internet Service												
Other Cost												
Total Cost of Calls												
GROSS PROFIT (LOSS)												
EXPENSES												
Payroll and Related Expenses												
Salaries, Wages, and Bonuses												
Salaries and Wages												
Bonuses and Incentives												
Total Salaries, Wages, and Bonuses												
Payroll Related Expenses												
Payroll Taxes												
Supplemental Pay												
Employee Benefits												
Total Payroll Related Expenses												
Total Payroll and Related Expenses												
Other Expenses												
Contract Services												
Corporate Office Reimbursables												
Dues and Subscriptions												
Equipment Rental												
Miscellaneous												
Operating Supplies												
Printing and Stationery												
Professional Fees												
Telecommunications												
Training												
Travel—Meals and Entertainment												
Travel—Other												
Uniforms												
Uniform Laundry												
Total Other Expenses												
TOTAL EXPENSES												
DEPARTMENTAL INCOME (LOSS)												

Golf Course and Pro Shop—Subschedule 3-2

| | CURRENT MONTH | | | | | | YEAR-TO-DATE | | | | | |
| | ACTUAL | | FORECAST | | PRIOR YEAR | | ACTUAL | | FORECAST | | PRIOR YEAR | |
	$	%	$	%	$	%	$	%	$	%	$	%
REVENUE												
Greens Fee Revenue												
Tournament Fee Revenue												
Golf Cart Rental Revenue												
Golf Equipment Rental Revenue												
Practice Range Fee Revenue												
Lesson Fee Revenue												
Golf Club Maintenance Revenue												
Storage Fee Revenue												
Membership Fee Revenue												
Merchandise Revenue												
Clothing Revenue												
Other Revenue												
Less: Allowances												
Total Revenue												
COST OF SALES												
Cost of Merchandise Sold												
Cost of Clothing Sales												
Total Cost of Sales												
GROSS PROFIT (LOSS)												
EXPENSES												
Payroll and Related Expenses												
Salaries, Wages, and Bonuses												
Salaries and Wages												
Bonuses and Incentives												
Total Salaries, Wages, and Bonuses												
Payroll Related Expenses												
Payroll Taxes												
Supplemental Pay												
Employee Benefits												
Total Payroll Related Expenses												
Total Payroll and Related Expenses												
Other Expenses												
Cleaning Supplies												
Complimentary Services and Gifts												
Contract Services												
Corporate Office Reimbursables												
Decorations												
Dues and Subscriptions												
Equipment Rental												
Gasoline and Lubricants												
Golf Cart Batteries/Electricity												
Golf Cart Repairs and Maintenance												
Grounds Maintenance and Landscaping												
Irrigation												
Laundry and Dry Cleaning												
Licenses and Permits												
Linen												

(continued)

Golf Course and Pro Shop—Subschedule 3-2 *(continued)*

	CURRENT MONTH						YEAR-TO-DATE					
	ACTUAL		FORECAST		PRIOR YEAR		ACTUAL		FORECAST		PRIOR YEAR	
	$	%	$	%	$	%	$	%	$	%	$	%
Management Fees												
Miscellaneous												
Operating Supplies												
Printing and Stationery												
Professional Fees												
Royalty Fees												
Telecommunications												
Travel—Meals and Entertainment												
Training												
Travel—Other												
Uniforms												
Uniform Laundry												
Water												
Total Other Expenses												
TOTAL EXPENSES												
DEPARTMENTAL INCOME (LOSS)												

Health Club/Spa—Subschedule 3-3

	CURRENT MONTH						YEAR-TO-DATE					
	ACTUAL		FORECAST		PRIOR YEAR		ACTUAL		FORECAST		PRIOR YEAR	
	$	%	$	%	$	%	$	%	$	%	$	%
REVENUE												
Club Use Revenue												
Fitness Lessons Revenue												
Health/Wellness Services Revenue												
Massage Revenue												
Membership Fee Revenue												
Personal Training Revenue												
Spa Treatment Revenue												
Salon Treatment Revenue												
Merchandise Revenue												
Clothing Revenue												
Other Revenue												
Less: Allowances												
Total Revenue												
COST OF SALES												
Cost of Merchandise Sales												
Cost of Clothing Sales												
Total Cost of Sales												
GROSS PROFIT (LOSS)												
EXPENSES												
Payroll and Related Expenses												
Salaries, Wages, and Bonuses												
Salaries and Wages												
Bonuses and Incentives												
Total Salaries, Wages, and Bonuses												
Payroll Related Expenses												
Payroll Taxes												
Supplemental Pay												
Employee Benefits												
Total Payroll Related Expenses												
Total Payroll and Related Expenses												
Other Expenses												
Ambience												
Athletic Supplies												
Cleaning Supplies												
Complimentary Services and Gifts												
Contract Services												
Corporate Office Reimbursables												
Decorations												
Dues and Subscriptions												
Equipment Rental												
Health and Beauty Products												
Laundry and Dry Cleaning												
Licenses and Permits												
Linen												
Management Fees												
Miscellaneous												
Operating Supplies												

(continued)

Health Club/Spa—Subschedule 3-3 *(continued)*

	CURRENT MONTH						YEAR-TO-DATE					
	ACTUAL		FORECAST		PRIOR YEAR		ACTUAL		FORECAST		PRIOR YEAR	
	$	%	$	%	$	%	$	%	$	%	$	%
Printing and Stationery												
Professional Fees												
Royalty Fees												
Telecommunications												
Training												
Travel—Meals and Entertainment												
Travel—Other												
Uniforms												
Uniform Laundry												
Total Other Expenses												
TOTAL EXPENSES												
DEPARTMENTAL INCOME (LOSS)												

Parking Garage—Subschedule 3-4

	CURRENT MONTH						YEAR-TO-DATE					
	ACTUAL		FORECAST		PRIOR YEAR		ACTUAL		FORECAST		PRIOR YEAR	
	$	%	$	%	$	%	$	%	$	%	$	%
REVENUE												
Self Parking Revenue												
Valet Parking Revenue												
Other Revenue												
Less: Allowances												
Total Revenue												
COST OF SALES												
GROSS PROFIT (LOSS)												
EXPENSES												
Payroll and Related Expenses												
Salaries, Wages, and Bonuses												
Salaries and Wages												
Bonuses and Incentives												
Total Salaries, Wages, and Bonuses												
Payroll Related Expenses												
Payroll Taxes												
Supplemental Pay												
Employee Benefits												
Total Payroll Related Expenses												
Total Payroll and Related Expenses												
Other Expenses												
Cleaning Supplies												
Complimentary Services and Gifts												
Contract Services												
Corporate Office Reimbursables												
Decorations												
Dues and Subscriptions												
Equipment Rental												
Laundry and Dry Cleaning												
Licenses and Permits												
Management Fees												
Miscellaneous												
Operating Supplies												
Printing and Stationery												
Professional Fees												
Royalty Fees												
Telecommunications												
Training												
Travel—Meals and Entertainment												
Travel—Others												
Uniforms												
Uniform Laundry												
Total Other Expenses												
TOTAL EXPENSES												
DEPARTMENTAL INCOME (LOSS)												

Other Operated Departments—Subschedule 3-X

	CURRENT MONTH						YEAR-TO-DATE					
	ACTUAL		FORECAST		PRIOR YEAR		ACTUAL		FORECAST		PRIOR YEAR	
	$	%	$	%	$	%	$	%	$	%	$	%
REVENUE												
Revenue												
Less: Allowances												
Total Revenue												
COST OF SALES												
GROSS PROFIT (LOSS)												
EXPENSES												
Payroll and Related Expenses												
Salaries, Wages, and Bonuses												
Salaries and Wages												
Bonuses and Incentives												
Total Salaries, Wages, and Bonuses												
Payroll Related Expenses												
Payroll Taxes												
Supplemental Pay												
Employee Benefits												
Total Payroll Related Expenses												
Total Payroll and Related Expenses												
Other Expenses												
Cleaning Supplies												
Complimentary Services and Gifts												
Contract Services												
Corporate Office Reimbursables												
Decorations												
Dues and Subscriptions												
Equipment Rental												
Laundry and Dry Cleaning												
Licenses and Permits												
Management Fees												
Miscellaneous												
Operating Supplies												
Other Detailed Expenses (as warranted)												
Printing and Stationery												
Professional Fees												
Royalty Fees												
Telecommunications												
Training												
Travel—Meals and Entertainment												
Travel—Other												
Uniforms												
Uniform Laundry												
Total Other Expenses												
TOTAL EXPENSES												
DEPARTMENTAL INCOME (LOSS)												

Minor Operated Departments—Subschedule 3–XX

	CURRENT MONTH						YEAR-TO-DATE					
	ACTUAL		FORECAST		PRIOR YEAR		ACTUAL		FORECAST		PRIOR YEAR	
	$	%	$	%	$	%	$	%	$	%	$	%
REVENUE												
Minor Operated Department 1												
Minor Operated Department 2												
…												
…												
Minor Operated Department x												
Less: Allowances												
Total Revenue												
DEPARTMENTAL EXPENSES[1]												
Minor Operated Department 1												
Minor Operated Department 2												
…												
…												
Minor Operated Department x												
Total Minor Operated Departmental Expenses												
DEPARTMENTAL INCOME (LOSS)												
Minor Operated Department 1												
Minor Operated Department 2												
…												
Minor Operated Departments x												
TOTAL MINOR OPERATED DEPARTMENTAL INCOME (LOSS)												

1. Departmental Expenses is the sum of Cost of Sales (when applicable) and Total Expenses.

Rentals and Other Income—Schedule 4

	CURRENT MONTH						YEAR-TO-DATE					
	ACTUAL		FORECAST		PRIOR YEAR		ACTUAL		FORECAST		PRIOR YEAR	
	$	%	$	%	$	%	$	%	$	%	$	%
Space Rental and Concessions												
Commissions												
Cash Discounts Earned												
Cancellation Penalties												
Attrition Penalties												
Foreign Currency Transaction Gains (Losses)												
Guest Laundry and Dry Cleaning												
Interest Income												
Proceeds from Business Interruption Insurance												
Other												
TOTAL RENTALS AND OTHER INCOME												

Administrative and General—Schedule 5

	CURRENT MONTH						YEAR-TO-DATE					
	ACTUAL		FORECAST		PRIOR YEAR		ACTUAL		FORECAST		PRIOR YEAR	
	$	%	$	%	$	%	$	%	$	%	$	%
EXPENSES												
Payroll and Related Expenses												
Salaries, Wages, and Bonuses												
Salaries and Wages												
Bonuses and Incentives												
Total Salaries, Wages, and Bonuses												
Payroll Related Expenses												
Payroll Taxes												
Supplemental Pay												
Employee Benefits												
Total Payroll Related Expenses												
Total Payroll and Related Expenses												
Other Expenses												
Audit Charges												
Bank Charges												
Cash Overages and Shortages												
Centralized Accounting Charges												
Complimentary Services and Gifts												
Contract Services												
Corporate Office Reimbursables												
Credit and Collection												
Credit Card Commissions												
Decorations												
Donations												
Dues and Subscriptions												
Equipment Rental												
Human Resources												
Information Systems												
Laundry and Dry Cleaning												
Legal Services												
Licenses and Permits												
Loss and Damage												
Miscellaneous												
Operating Supplies												
Payroll Processing												
Postage and Overnight Delivery Charges												
Printing and Stationery												
Professional Fees												
Provision for Doubtful Accounts												
Security												
Settlement Costs												
Telecommunications												
Training												
Transportation												
Travel—Meals and Entertainment												
Travel—Other												
Uniforms												
Uniform Laundry												
Total Other Expenses												
TOTAL EXPENSES												

Sales and Marketing—Schedule 6

	CURRENT MONTH						YEAR-TO-DATE					
	ACTUAL		FORECAST		PRIOR YEAR		ACTUAL		FORECAST		PRIOR YEAR	
	$	%	$	%	$	%	$	%	$	%	$	%
EXPENSES												
Payroll and Related Expenses												
Salaries, Wages, and Bonuses												
Salaries and Wages												
Bonuses and Incentives												
Total Salaries, Wages, and Bonuses												
Payroll Related Expenses												
Payroll Taxes												
Supplemental Pay												
Employee Benefits												
Total Payroll Related Expenses												
Total Payroll and Related Expenses												
Other Expenses												
Sales Expenses												
Complimentary Services and Gifts												
Contract Services												
Corporate Office Reimbursables												
Decorations												
Dues and Subscriptions												
Equipment Rental												
Fam (Familiarization) Trips												
Miscellaneous												
Operating Supplies												
Outside Sales Representation												
Postage and Overnight Delivery Charges												
Printing and Stationery												
Promotion												
Telecommunications												
Trade Shows												
Training												
Travel—Meals and Entertainment												
Travel—Other												
Total Sales Expenses												
Marketing Expenses												
Agency Fees												
Collateral Material												
Contract Services												
Direct Mail												
E-Commerce												
Franchise and Affiliation Advertising												
Franchise Fees												
In-House Graphics												
Loyalty Programs and Affiliation Fees												
Media												
Miscellaneous												
Outdoor												
Outside Services												
Photography												
Total Marketing Expenses												
Total Other Expenses												
TOTAL EXPENSES												

Property Operation and Maintenance—Schedule 7

	CURRENT MONTH						YEAR-TO-DATE					
	ACTUAL		FORECAST		PRIOR YEAR		ACTUAL		FORECAST		PRIOR YEAR	
	$	%	$	%	$	%	$	%	$	%	$	%
EXPENSES												
Payroll and Related Expenses												
Salaries, Wages, and Bonuses												
Salaries and Wages												
Bonuses and Incentives												
Total Salaries, Wages, and Bonuses												
Payroll Related Expenses												
Payroll Taxes												
Supplemental Pay												
Employee Benefits												
Total Payroll Related Expenses												
Total Payroll and Related Expenses												
Other Expenses												
Building												
Complimentary Services and Gifts												
Contract Services												
Corporate Office Reimbursables												
Decorations												
Electrical and Mechanical Equipment												
Elevators and Escalators												
Engineering Supplies												
Equipment Rental												
Floor Covering												
Furniture and Equipment												
Grounds and Landscaping												
Heating, Ventilation, and Air Conditioning Equipment												
Kitchen Equipment												
Laundry Equipment												
Licenses and Permits												
Life Safety												
Light Bulbs												
Miscellaneous												
Operating Supplies												
Painting and Decorating												
Plumbing												
Swimming Pool												
Telecommunications												
Training												
Travel—Meals and Entertainment												
Travel—Other												
Uniforms												
Uniform Laundry												
Waste Removal												
Total Other Expenses												
TOTAL EXPENSES												

Utilities—Schedule 8

	CURRENT MONTH						YEAR-TO-DATE					
	ACTUAL		FORECAST		PRIOR YEAR		ACTUAL		FORECAST		PRIOR YEAR	
	$	%	$	%	$	%	$	%	$	%	$	%
UTILITY COSTS												
Electricity												
Gas												
Oil												
Steam												
Water												
Sewer												
Other Fuels												
Utility Taxes												
TOTAL UTILITY COSTS												

Management Fees—Schedule 9

	CURRENT MONTH						YEAR-TO-DATE					
	ACTUAL		FORECAST		PRIOR YEAR		ACTUAL		FORECAST		PRIOR YEAR	
	$	%	$	%	$	%	$	%	$	%	$	%
MANAGEMENT FEES												
Base Fee												
Incentive Fees												
TOTAL MANAGEMENT FEES												

Rent, Property and Other Taxes, and Insurance—Schedule 10

	CURRENT MONTH						YEAR-TO-DATE					
	ACTUAL		FORECAST		PRIOR YEAR		ACTUAL		FORECAST		PRIOR YEAR	
	$	%	$	%	$	%	$	%	$	%	$	%
RENT												
Land and Buildings												
Information Systems Equipment												
Telecommunications Equipment												
Other Property and Equipment												
Total Rent Expense												
PROPERTY AND OTHER TAXES												
Real Estate Tax												
Personal Property Taxes												
Business and Transient Occupation Taxes												
Other Taxes												
Total Property and Other Taxes Expense												
INSURANCE												
Building and Contents												
Liability												
Total Insurance Expense												
TOTAL RENT, PROPERTY AND OTHER TAXES, AND INSURANCE												

House Laundry—Schedule 11

	CURRENT MONTH						YEAR-TO-DATE					
	ACTUAL		FORECAST		PRIOR YEAR		ACTUAL		FORECAST		PRIOR YEAR	
	$	%	$	%	$	%	$	%	$	%	$	%
EXPENSES												
Payroll and Related Expenses												
Salaries, Wages, and Bonuses												
Salaries and Wages												
Bonuses and Incentives												
Total Salaries, Wages, and Bonuses												
Payroll Related Expenses												
Payroll Taxes												
Supplemental Pay												
Employee Benefits												
Total Payroll Related Expenses												
Total Payroll and Related Expenses												
Other Expenses												
Cleaning Supplies												
Complimentary Services and Gifts												
Contract Services												
Equipment Rental												
Laundry and Dry Cleaning												
Laundry Supplies												
Licenses and Permits												
Miscellaneous												
Operating Supplies												
Printing and Stationery												
Telecommunications												
Training												
Travel—Meals and Entertainment												
Travel—Other												
Uniforms												
Uniform Laundry												
Waste Removal												
Total Other Expenses												
TOTAL EXPENSES												
CREDITS												
Cost of Guest and Outside Laundry												
Concessionaires' Laundry												
COST OF HOUSE LAUNDRY												

Employee Cafeteria—Schedule 12

	CURRENT MONTH						YEAR-TO-DATE					
	ACTUAL		FORECAST		PRIOR YEAR		ACTUAL		FORECAST		PRIOR YEAR	
	$	%	$	%	$	%	$	%	$	%	$	%
NET REVENUE												
COST OF FOOD												
GROSS PROFIT (LOSS)												
EXPENSES												
Payroll and Related Expenses												
Salaries, Wages, and Bonuses												
Salaries and Wages												
Bonuses and Incentives												
Total Salaries, Wages, and Bonuses												
Payroll Related Expenses												
Payroll Taxes												
Supplemental Pay												
Employee Benefits												
Total Payroll Related Expenses												
Total Payroll and Related Expenses												
Other Expenses												
China, Glassware, Silver, and Linens												
Cleaning Supplies												
Contract Services												
Fuel												
Laundry and Dry Cleaning												
Licenses and Permits												
Miscellaneous												
Operating Supplies												
Paper and Plastics												
Printing and Stationery												
Telecommunications												
Training												
Travel—Meals and Entertainment												
Travel—Other												
Uniforms												
Uniform Laundry												
Utensils												
Total Other Expenses												
TOTAL EXPENSES												
DEPARTMENTAL INCOME (LOSS)												

Payroll Related Expenses—Schedule 13

	CURRENT MONTH			YEAR-TO-DATE		
	ACTUAL	FORECAST	PRIOR YEAR	ACTUAL	FORECAST	PRIOR YEAR
	$ | %	$ | %	$ | %	$ | %	$ | %	$ | %
PAYROLL TAXES						
Federal Retirement (FICA)						
Federal Unemployment (FUTA)						
Medicare Tax (FICA)						
State Disability						
State Unemployment						
Total Payroll Taxes						
EMPLOYEE BENEFITS						
Automobile Allowance						
Child Care						
Contributory Savings Plan [401(k)]						
Dental Insurance						
Disability Pay						
Group Life Insurance						
Health Insurance						
Housing and Educational Allowances						
Meals						
Miscellaneous						
Nonunion Insurance						
Nonunion Pension						
Profit Sharing						
Stock Benefits						
Stock Options						
Union Insurance						
Union Pension						
Workers' Compensation Insurance						
Total Employee Benefits						
TOTAL PAYROLL TAXES AND EMPLOYEE BENEFITS						

Chapter 6 Outline

Purposes of the Balance Sheet
Limitations of the Balance Sheet
Balance Sheet Formats
Content of the Balance Sheet
    Current Accounts
    Noncurrent Receivables
    Investments
    Property and Equipment
    Other Assets
    Long-Term Liabilities
    Owners' Equity
    Footnotes
    Consolidated Financial Statements

Competencies

1. Explain the purposes of the balance sheet. (pp. 201–203)

2. Identify the limitations of the balance sheet. (pp. 203–204)

3. Define the various elements of assets, liabilities, and owners' equity as presented on the balance sheet. (pp. 204–215)

4. Explain the use of footnotes in balance sheets, and describe the use of consolidated financial statements. (pp. 215–217)

6

Balance Sheet

THE BALANCE SHEET is a major financial statement prepared at the end of each accounting period. It reflects a balance between an organization's assets and the claims to its assets called *liabilities and owners' equity*. This statement is also called the *statement of financial position*.

The balance sheet answers many questions that managers, owners (investors), and creditors may ask, such as:

1. How much cash was on hand at the end of the period?

2. What was the total debt of the hospitality operation?

3. What was the mix of internal and external financing at the end of the period?

4. How much did guests owe to the hotel?

5. What amount of taxes did the operation owe to the various governmental tax agencies?

6. What is the operation's ability to pay its current debt?

7. What is the financial strength of the operation?

8. How much interest do stockholders have in the operation's assets?

In this chapter, we will address the purposes and limitations of the balance sheet. We will also consider the formats and contents of balance sheets, paying special attention to the suggested balance sheet from the *Uniform System of Accounts for the Lodging Industry (USALI)*. In addition, we will discuss the kinds and purposes of footnotes attached to financial statements. The appendix to this chapter includes the financial statements and the accompanying footnotes from the 2004 annual report of the Hilton Hotels Corporation.

Purposes of the Balance Sheet

Other major financial statements—the income statement, the statement of retained earnings, and the statement of cash flows—pertain to a period of time. The balance sheet reflects the financial position of the hospitality operation—its assets, liabilities, and owners' equity—at a given date.

The balance sheet was considered the major financial statement issued to investors in the early 1900s, since many firms did not issue income statements.

Management believed the income statement contained confidential information that, if issued to external users, would end up in the hands of competitors. After the stock market crash of 1929 and subsequent governmental regulation, the Securities and Exchange Commission required businesses under its regulation to issue income statements. In the past, so much emphasis was placed on earnings that investors largely ignored the balance sheet. However, in recent years, investors have shown much more interest in the balance sheet.

Management, although generally more interested in the income statement and related departmental operations statements, will find balance sheets useful for conveying financial information to creditors and investors. In addition, management must determine if the balance sheet accurately reflects the financial position of the hospitality operation. For example, many long-term loans specify a required **current ratio** (current assets divided by current liabilities). An operation's failure to meet this ratio requirement may result in all its long-term debt being reclassified as current and thus due immediately. If the firm were unable to raise large sums of cash quickly, it might go bankrupt. Therefore, management must carefully review the balance sheet to ensure that the operation is in compliance with its current ratio requirement. For example, assume that at December 31, 20X1 (year-end), a hotel has $500,000 of current assets and $260,000 of current liabilities. Further assume that the current ratio requirement in a bank's loan agreement with the hotel is 2 to 1. Based on these numbers, the hypothetical hotel's current ratio is less than 2 to 1. The required current ratio can be attained simply by taking the appropriate action. In this case, the payment of $20,000 of current liabilities with cash of $20,000 results in current assets of $480,000 and current liabilities of $240,000, resulting in a current ratio of 2 to 1.

Creditors are interested in the hospitality operation's ability to pay its current and future obligations. The operation's ability to pay its current obligations is shown, in part, by a comparison of current assets and current liabilities. The ability to pay future obligations depends, in part, on the relative amounts of long-term financing by owners and creditors. Everything else being the same, the greater the financing from investors, the higher the probability that long-term creditors will be paid and the lower the risk that these creditors take in "investing" in the enterprise.

Investors are most often interested in earnings that lead to dividends. To maximize earnings, an organization should have financial flexibility, which is the operation's ability to change its cash flows to meet unexpected needs and take advantage of opportunities. Everything else being the same, the greater the financial flexibility of the hospitality operation, the greater its opportunities to take advantage of new profitable investments, thus increasing net income and, ultimately, cash dividends for investors.

In addition, the balance sheet reveals the liquidity of the hospitality operation. **Liquidity** measures the operation's ability to convert assets to cash. Even though a property's past earnings may have been substantial, this does not in itself guarantee that the operation can meet its obligations as they become due. The hospitality operation should have sufficient liquidity not only to pay its bills, but also to provide its owners with adequate dividends.

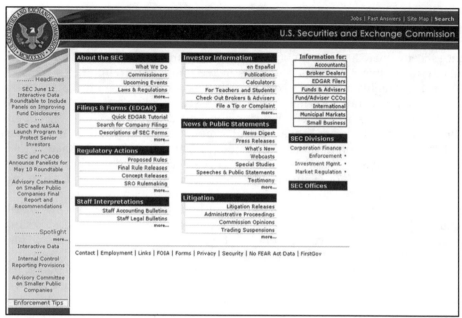

More information about the U.S. Securities and Exchange Commission is available on its Internet site (at www.sec.gov). Information about such commissions in other countries is available through the site of the International Organization of Securities Commissions (at www.iosco.org).

Analysis of balance sheets for several periods will yield trend information that is more valuable than single-period figures. In addition, comparison of balance sheet information with projected balance sheet numbers (when available) will reveal management's ability to meet various financial goals.

Limitations of the Balance Sheet

As useful as the balance sheet is, it is generally considered less useful than the income statement to investors, long-term creditors, and especially to management. Since the balance sheet is based on the cost principle, it often does not reflect current values of some assets, such as property and equipment. For hospitality operations whose assets are appreciating rather than depreciating, the difference between an asset's book value (shown on the balance sheet) and its current value can be significant. Hilton Hotels Corporation presents a good example of what this limitation of the balance sheet might lead to. In one annual report, the corporation revealed the current value of its assets (footnote disclosure only) to be $4,027,000,000, while its balance sheet showed the book value of its assets to be $1,892,500,000. The difference between current value and book value was $2,134,500,000. The assets reflected in the balance sheet for Hilton were only 47 percent of their current value.[1] This "understatement," if unknown to or ignored by management, investors, and creditors, could lead to less than optimal use of Hilton's assets and less borrowing potential.

Another limitation of balance sheets is that they fail to reflect many elements of value to hospitality operations. Most important to hotels, motels, restaurants, clubs, and other sectors of the hospitality industry are people. Nowhere in the balance sheet is there a reflection of the human resource investment. The major hospitality firms spend millions of dollars in recruiting and training to achieve an efficient and highly motivated work force, yet this essential ingredient for successful hospitality operations is not shown as an asset.

Balance sheets are limited by their static nature; that is, they reflect an operation's financial position only at a particular moment. Thereafter, they are less useful because they become outdated very quickly. Thus, the user of the balance sheet must be aware that the financial position reflected at year-end may be quite different one month later. For example, a hospitality operation with $1,000,000 in cash may appear financially strong at year-end. However, if it invests most of this cash in fixed assets two weeks later, its financial flexibility and liquidity are greatly reduced. The user of financial documents would generally know about this situation only if another balance sheet or other financial statements were available for a date after this investment had occurred.

Finally, the balance sheet, like much of accounting, is based on judgment; that is, it is *not* exact. Certainly, assets equal liabilities plus owners' equity. However, several balance sheet items are based on estimates. The amounts shown as accounts receivable (net) reflect the estimated amounts to be collected. The amounts shown as inventory reflect the *lower of cost or market* (that is, the lower of its original cost and its current replacement cost) of the items expected to be sold. The amount shown as property and equipment reflects the cost less estimated depreciation. In each case, accountants use estimates to arrive at "values." To the degree these estimates are in error, the balance sheet items will be wrong.

Balance Sheet Formats

The balance sheet can be arranged in either the account format or the report format. The **account format** lists asset accounts on the left side of the page and liability and owners' equity accounts on the right side. Exhibit 1 illustrates this arrangement.

The **report format** shows assets first, followed by liabilities and owners' equity. The group totals on the report form can show either that assets equal liabilities and owners' equity or that assets minus liabilities equal owners' equity. Exhibit 2 illustrates the report format.

Content of the Balance Sheet

The balance sheet consists of assets, liabilities, and owners' equity. Simply stated, assets are things owned by the firm, liabilities are claims of outsiders to assets, and owners' equity is claims of owners to assets. Think of the asset portion of the balance sheet as a "pool of valuable things" owned by the firm. The liability and equity portion is a pool of rights or claims to those valuable things. The two "pools" must be equal; assets must equal (balance) liabilities and owners' equity. Assets include accounts such as Cash, Inventory for Resale, Buildings, and

Exhibit 1   Balance Sheet Account Format

Morrison Motel
Balance Sheet
December 31, 20X1

ASSETS		LIABILITIES AND OWNERS' EQUITY	
Current Assets:		Current Liabilities:	
Cash	$ 2,500	Notes Payable	$ 23,700
Accounts Receivable	5,000	Accounts Payable	8,000
Cleaning Supplies	2,500	Wages Payable	300
Total	10,000	Total	32,000
Property & Equipment:		Long-Term Liabilities:	
Land	20,000	Mortgage Payable	120,000
Building	300,000	Total Liabilities	152,000
Furnishings and Equipment	50,000	Marvin Morrison, Capital at	
	370,000	January 1, 20X1	64,500
Less Accumulated		Net Income for 20X1	38,500
Depreciation	125,000	Marvin Morrison, Capital at	
Net Property &		December 31, 20X1	103,000
Equipment	245,000	**Total Liabilities**	
Total Assets	$ 255,000	**and Owners' Equity**	$ 255,000

Accounts Receivable. Liabilities include accounts such as Accounts Payable, Wages Payable, and Mortgage Payable. Owners' equity includes Capital Stock and Retained Earnings. These major elements are generally divided into various classes as shown in Exhibit 3. While balance sheets may be organized in different ways, most hospitality operations follow the order shown in Exhibit 3.

Current Accounts

The Assets section and the Liabilities section each include a current-accounts classification. **Current assets** normally refer to items that are to be converted to cash or used in operations within one year or within a normal operating cycle. **Current liabilities** are obligations that are expected to be satisfied either by using current assets or by creating other current liabilities within one year or a normal operating cycle.

Exhibit 4 reflects a normal operating cycle that includes (1) the purchase of inventory for resale and labor to produce goods and services, (2) the sale of goods and services, and (3) the collection of accounts receivable from the sale of goods and services.

A normal operating cycle may be as short as a few days, as is typical for many quick-service restaurants, or it may extend over several months for some hospitality operations. It is common in the hospitality industry to classify assets as current

Exhibit 2   Balance Sheet Report Format

Morrison Motel
Balance Sheet
December 31, 20X1

ASSETS

Current Assets:

Cash		$ 2,500
Accounts Receivable		5,000
Cleaning Supplies		2,500
Total Current Assets		10,000

Property and Equipment:

Land	$ 20,000	
Building	300,000	
Equipment	10,000	
Furnishings	40,000	
Less Accumulated Depreciation	125,000	
Net Property and Equipment		245,000
Total Assets		**$255,000**

LIABILITIES AND OWNER'S EQUITY

Current Liabilities:

Notes Payable	$ 23,700	
Accounts Payable	8,000	
Wages Payable	300	$ 32,000
Long-Term Liabilities:		
Mortgage Payable		120,000
Total Liabilities		152,000

Owner's Equity:

Marvin Morrison, Capital		103,000
Total Liabilities and Owner's Equity		**$255,000**

or noncurrent on the basis of one year rather than on the basis of the normal operating cycle.

Current Assets. Current assets, listed in the order of decreasing liquidity, generally consist of cash, short-term investments (also called marketable securities), receivables, inventories, amounts due to or from a management company, owner, or related entity, and prepaid expenses. Cash consists of cash in house banks, cash in checking and savings accounts, and certificates of deposit. The exception is cash

Exhibit 3   Order of Balance Sheet Elements

Assets	**Liabilities and Owners' Equity**
Current Assets	Current Liabilities
Noncurrent Assets:	Long-Term Liabilities
Noncurrent Receivables	Owners' Equity
Investments	
Property and Equipment	
Other Assets	

Exhibit 4   Normal Operating Cycle

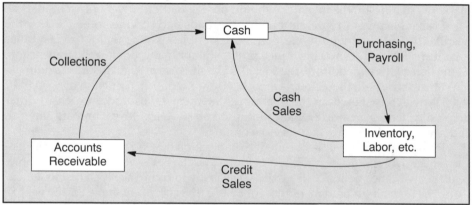

that is restricted for retiring long-term debt, which should be shown under Other Assets. If restricted cash is to pay debt due within 12 months of the balance sheet date, it should be shown separately as a current asset. Cash is shown on the balance sheet at its face value.

Short-term investments include investments in stocks and bonds of other entities. For example, a hotel company may own 100 shares of stock in General Motors Corporation. Short-term investments are shown as current assets when they are immediately salable at a quoted market price and expected to be converted to cash within a year of the balance sheet date. Short-term investments that are not available for conversion to cash are considered noncurrent investments. Generally, the critical factor in deciding whether an asset is current or noncurrent is management's intent. Short-term investments are usually shown on the balance sheet at their market value.

The Current Assets category of receivables consists of Accounts Receivable—Trade and Notes Receivable. Accounts Receivable—Trade includes open accounts carried by a hotel or motel on the guest, city, or rent ledgers. Notes receivable due within one year are also listed, except for notes from affiliated companies, which should be shown under Noncurrent Receivables. A note receivable is a promissory note held by the payee that states the amount due and the maturity date, and often states an interest rate, since interest is generally paid on notes receivable. Both accounts receivable and notes receivable should be stated at the amount estimated to be collectible. An allowance for doubtful accounts, the amount of receivables estimated to be uncollectible, should be subtracted from receivables to provide a net receivables amount.

Amounts due to or from a management company, owner, or related entity include balances due to or from a management company, the owner, or other related entities for loans, advances for capital improvements, management fees, and other expenses or advances provided to a property.

Inventories of a hospitality operation consist of merchandise held for resale and other items such as guestroom supplies. Inventories are generally an insignificant percentage of the total assets of a hospitality operation and may be valued at cost. If the amount of inventory is material and the difference between cost and market is significant, the inventory should be stated at the lower of cost or market.

Prepaid expenses represent purchased goods and services to be used by the hospitality operation within one year. For example, assume that a fire insurance premium of $6,000 affords insurance protection for one year after the transaction. At the date of the expenditure, the $6,000 is classified as prepaid insurance or unexpired insurance and, thereafter, is amortized by a monthly reduction of $500 ($\frac{1}{12}$ of $6,000), which is shown on the operating statement as insurance expense. Other prepaid expenses include prepaid rent, prepaid property taxes, prepaid interest, and prepaid maintenance and service contracts.

Prepaid expenses that will benefit the operation beyond one year from the balance sheet date should be classified as Other Assets. For example, assume a three-year fire insurance policy costs $18,000. The entry to record the cash disbursement would be to debit Prepaid Insurance for $6,000 (the cost of coverage for the next 12 months) and to debit Deferred Charges—Insurance for $12,000 (the cost of insurance coverage paid that benefits the operation for periods beyond 12 months from the balance sheet date). The entry would credit Cash for $18,000.

Current assets, according to the *USALI*, may also include deferred income taxes. Deferred Income Taxes—Current is a line that represents the tax effects of temporary differences between the bases of current assets and current liabilities for financial and income tax reporting purposes. For example, if the allowance for doubtful accounts is not deductible for tax purposes until such time as the debt is written off, the allowance for doubtful accounts will result in a current deferred tax asset. Current deferred income taxes are presented as net current assets or net current liabilities as circumstances dictate.

Other current assets include items not shown elsewhere that are reasonably expected to be realized in cash or otherwise used in the business within the next 12 months. The category Other under Current Assets is normally used to capture minor items that are not separately disclosed.

Current Liabilities. In order for an obligation to be classified as a current liability, the obligation must be due within one year and management must intend to use existing current assets or create other current liabilities to satisfy the debt. For example, the debt related to the purchase of food and beverages would be classified as a current liability since the amount due is expected to be paid in the near future. On the other hand, if a debt payment due in one month is to be paid with restricted cash funds (a noncurrent asset that will be discussed later), this obligation would be classified as a noncurrent liability.

Current liabilities generally consist of one of the four following types:

1. Payables resulting from the purchase of goods, services, labor, and the applicable payroll taxes

2. Amounts received in advance of the delivery of goods and services, such as advance deposits on rooms and banquet deposits

3. Obligations to be paid in the current period relating to fixed-asset purchases or to reclassification of long-term debt as current

4. Dividends payable and income taxes payable

The major classifications of current liabilities according to the *USALI* are Accounts Payable, Notes Payable, Current Maturities of Long-Term Debt, Income Taxes Payable, Deferred Income Taxes, Accrued Expenses, Advance Deposits, and Due to/from Owner, Management Company, or Related Entity. Notes payable include short-term notes that are due within 12 months. Current maturities of long-term debt include the principal payments of long-term debt such as notes and similar liabilities, sinking fund obligations, and the principal portions of capitalized leases due within 12 months. Accounts Payable include amounts due to creditors for merchandise, services, equipment, or other purchases. Deferred Income Taxes—Current includes amounts that represent the tax effects of timing differences attributable to current assets and current liabilities being accounted for differently for financial and income tax reporting purposes. (The concept of deferred income taxes is discussed in greater detail in the Long-Term Liabilities section of this chapter.) Accrued expenses, such as accrued payroll, are expenses incurred before but not due until after the balance sheet date. Advance deposits include amounts received for services that have not been provided as of the balance sheet date.

Due to/from Owner, Management Company, or Related Entity includes balances due to these parties for such things as advances for capital improvements that must be repaid in a year or unpaid management fees due to the management company.

Obligations to be paid with **restricted cash** (that is, cash that has been deposited in separate accounts, often for the purpose of retiring long-term debt) should be classified not as current, but rather as long-term.

Current liabilities are often compared with current assets in two ways. Current assets minus current liabilities is commonly called **net working capital**. Current assets divided by current liabilities is called the *current ratio*. Many hospitality properties operate successfully with a current ratio approximating 1 to 1, compared with a reasonable current ratio of 2 to 1 for many other industries. The major reason for this difference lies in the relatively low amount of inventories required and relatively high turnover of receivables by hospitality operations as compared with many other industries.

Noncurrent Receivables

Noncurrent receivables include both accounts receivable and notes receivable that are not expected to be collected within one year of the balance sheet date. If a hospitality organization is uncertain of its ability to collect noncurrent receivables, an allowance for doubtful noncurrent receivables should be used (similar to the allowance account for current receivables) and subtracted from total noncurrent receivables to provide net noncurrent receivables.

In the balance sheet based on the *USALI*, noncurrent receivables are divided between noncurrent receivables from "owners, officers, employees, and affiliated entities" and "others."

Investments

Investments consist of long-term investments that are to be held for more than one year. Included as investments are investments in securities (capital stock and debt instruments), cash advances to affiliated companies, and investments in property not currently used in operations. For example, a hotel company may have invested in center-city land with the expectation of constructing a hotel in the future. The land purchase should be shown as an investment and not listed under Property and Equipment on the balance sheet. Certain investments are generally stated on the balance sheet at cost, while others are stated at their market values.

For example, suppose a hotel corporation invests $10,000 in 100 shares of a large firm ($100 per share), intending to hold the shares for several years. At the balance sheet date, the market value per share is $85. The market value for the stock is $8,500, which should be reflected on the balance sheet.

Property and Equipment

Property and equipment consists of fixed assets including land, buildings, furnishings and equipment, construction in progress, leasehold improvements, and operating equipment. Operating Equipment includes china, glassware, silver, linens, and uniforms but many properties may choose to account for these on a separate line item. Property and equipment under capital leases should also be shown in this section of the balance sheet. With the exception of land, the cost of all property and equipment is written off to expense over time due to the matching principle. Depreciation methods used should be disclosed in a footnote to the balance sheet. The depreciation method used for financial reporting to outsiders and that used for tax purposes may differ, resulting in deferred income taxes. Deferred income taxes are generally a liability and will be discussed later in the chapter. On the balance sheet, fixed assets are shown at cost and are reduced by the related accumulated depreciation.

Other Assets

Other Assets consists of all assets not included in the aforementioned categories. The *USALI* identifies examples of Other Assets as follows:

1. Intangible assets include patents, trademarks, customer lists, and so on. Goodwill is also an intangible asset. **Purchased goodwill** represents the excess of the purchase price over the fair value of net assets acquired in the purchase of a business. Goodwill is evaluated periodically and impairment losses must be recognized.

2. The cash surrender value of life insurance is the amount of cash the lodging company would receive if it surrendered the life insurance policy it had on the lives of key individuals.

3. Deferred charges include financing costs related to long-term debt. Such costs are typically amortized over the life of the related financing.

4. Deferred Income Taxes—Noncurrent represents the tax effects of temporary differences between the bases of noncurrent assets and noncurrent liabilities for financial and income tax reporting purposes. For example, if a liability is accrued that will not be paid for an extended period of time and the expense is deductible only when paid for tax purposes, the accrual will result in a noncurrent deferred income tax asset.

Other assets also include the costs to organize the hospitality operation (organization costs), security deposits, and unamortized franchise costs. Organization costs consist of any cost of establishing a business, including incorporation costs, legal and accounting fees, promotional costs incidental to the sale of stock, printing of stock certificates, and so forth. Theoretically, organization costs benefit the business over its entire life; however, this asset is generally written off over a five-year period. Thus, the amount shown on a balance sheet for organization costs is the unamortized amount. Security deposits include funds deposited with public utility companies and similar types of deposits. The initial franchise fee paid by the franchisee should be recorded under Other Assets and amortized against revenue over the life of the franchise agreement.

Long-Term Liabilities

Long-term liabilities are obligations at the balance sheet date that are expected to be paid beyond the next 12 months or, if paid in the current year, will be paid from restricted funds. Common long-term liabilities consist of notes payable, mortgages payable, bonds payable, capitalized lease obligations, and deferred income taxes. Any long-term debt to be paid with current assets within the next year is reclassified as a current liability.

A long-term *note payable* is a formal promise to pay an amount at a date more than 12 months beyond the balance sheet date. A promissory note is signed and, generally, interest is paid on the note at the interest rate stated on the note. To the payee, the note is a note receivable, as discussed previously. Unpaid interest on notes payable at the balance sheet date should be accrued as Accrued Interest, a liability. If the accrued interest is to be paid within a 12-month period from the balance sheet date, it should be reported as a current liability; otherwise, as a long-term liability.

A *mortgage payable* is a debt that is secured by using real property, such as a building, as collateral. The amount due within 12 months or less of the balance sheet date is classified as a current liability.

Bonds payable are certificates of indebtedness that take on many forms. Bonds due within 12 months of the balance sheet date are reclassified as current, while other bonds are classified as long-term.

Lease obligations reported as long-term liabilities generally cover several years, while short-term leases are usually expensed when paid. *Deferred income taxes* result from timing differences in reporting for financial and income tax purposes—that is, the accounting treatment of an item for financial reporting purposes results in a different amount of expense (or revenue) from that taken for tax purposes. Generally, the most significant timing difference for hotels and motels relates to depreciation, since many operations use the straight-line method for financial reporting purposes and an accelerated method for income tax purposes.

For example, suppose a hotel decides to depreciate a fixed asset on a straight-line basis at $15,000 a year for reporting purposes, and depreciates the same asset $25,000 for the year using an accelerated method for tax purposes. If the firm's marginal tax rate is 30 percent, the difference in depreciation expense of $10,000 ($25,000 − $15,000) times 30 percent results in $3,000 cash saved and reported as a noncurrent liability. The book entry to record this savings is as follows:

Income Tax Expense	$3,000	
Deferred Income Taxes		$3,000

Owners' Equity

The Owners' Equity section of the balance sheet reflects the owners' interest in the operation's assets. The detail of the Owners' Equity section is a function of the organization of the business. The four major types of business organization are corporations, sole proprietorships, partnerships, and limited liability companies (LLCs). Exhibits 5 and 6 are the prescribed formats of the Assets section and the Liabilities and Owners' Equity section of the balance sheet from the *USALI.* Exhibit 7 is the equity section for a corporation from the *USALI.* The Owners' Equity section of a corporation includes capital stock, additional paid-in capital, retained earnings, accumulated other comprehensive income (loss) net of tax, and treasury stock. Capital stock for most hospitality operations is common stock; however, a few operations have also issued preferred stock. When more than one type of stock has been issued, each type should be reported separately. **Capital stock** is the product of the number of shares outstanding and the par value of the shares.

The **Additional Paid-In Capital** category consists of payments for capital stock in excess of the stated or par value of the capital stock. For example, cash of $50 received from the sale of common stock with a par value of $10 would be recorded as $10 to the common stock account and the remainder ($40) as Paid-In Capital in Excess of Par.

Exhibit 5   Assets Section of the *USALI* Balance Sheet

BALANCE SHEET
Assets

	Current Year	Prior Year
CURRENT ASSETS		
Cash		
House Banks	$	$
Demand Deposits		
Temporary Cash Investments		
Total Cash		
Short-Term Investments		
Receivables		
Accounts Receivable		
Notes Receivable		
Current Maturities of Noncurrent Receivables		
Other		
Total Receivables		
Less Allowance for Doubtful Accounts		
Net Receivables		
Due to/from Owner, Management		
Company, or Related Entity		
Inventories		
Operating Equipment		
Prepaid Expenses		
Deferred Income Taxes, Current		
Other		
Total Current Assets		
NONCURRENT RECEIVABLES, Net of Current Maturities		
INVESTMENTS		
PROPERTY AND EQUIPMENT		
Land		
Buildings		
Leaseholds and Leasehold Improvements		
Construction in Progress		
Furnishings and Equipment		
Less Accumulated Depreciation and Amortization		
Net Property and Equipment		
OTHER ASSETS		
Intangible Assets		
Cash Surrender Value of Life Insurance		
Deferred Charges		
Deferred Income Taxes—Noncurrent		
Operating Equipment		
Restricted Cash		
Other		
Total Other Assets		
TOTAL ASSETS	$	$

Source: *Uniform System of Accounts for the Lodging Industry,* 10th Rev. Ed. (Lansing, Mich.: Educational Institute of the American Hotel & Lodging Association, 2006). ©Hotel Association of New York City.

Exhibit 6   Liabilities and Owners' Equity Section of the *USALI* Balance Sheet

BALANCE SHEET
Liabilities and Owners' Equity

	Current Year	Prior Year
CURRENT LIABILITIES		
Notes Payable		
Banks	$	$
Others		
Total Notes Payable		
Due to/from Owner, Management Company, or Related Entity		
Accounts Payable		
Accrued Expenses		
Advance Deposits		
Income Taxes Payable		
Deferred Income Taxes—Current		
Current Maturities of Long-Term Debt		
Others		
Total Current Liabilities		
LONG-TERM DEBT, Net of Current Maturities		
Mortgage Notes, other notes, and similar liabilities		
Obligations under Capital Leases		
Total Long-Term Debt		
OTHER LONG-TERM LIABILITIES		
DEFERRED INCOME TAXES—Noncurrent		
OWNERS' EQUITY		
COMMITMENTS AND CONTINGENCIES		
TOTAL LIABILITIES AND OWNERS' EQUITY	$	$

Source: *Uniform System of Accounts for the Lodging Industry,* 10th Rev. Ed. (Lansing, Mich.: Educational Institute of the American Hotel & Lodging Association, 2006). ©Hotel Association of New York City.

Retained earnings reflect earnings generated but not distributed as dividends. Changes in this account during the year are commonly shown on a statement of retained earnings.

Treasury stock represents the property's own capital stock that it has repurchased but not retired. The cost of the treasury shares is shown as a reduction of owners' equity.

When a lodging operation is organized as a sole proprietorship, all the owners' equity is reflected in one account (Marvin Morrison, Capital), as illustrated in Exhibit 2. Marvin Morrison's $103,000 of capital would have been spread across at least two accounts, Capital Stock and Retained Earnings, if the Morrison Motel had been incorporated.

Exhibit 7   Stockholders' Equity Section of the *USALI* Balance Sheet

> **BALANCE SHEET**
> **Stockholders' Equity**
>
> | | Current Year | Prior Year |
> |---|---|---|
> | _____% Cumulative Preferred Stock, $_____ par value, authorized _____ shares; issued and outstanding _____ shares | $ | $ |
> | Common Stock, $ _____ par value, authorized _____ shares; issued and outstanding _____ shares | | |
> | Additional Paid-In Capital | | |
> | Retained Earnings | | |
> | Accumulated Other Comprehensive Income (Loss), Net of income tax | | |
> | Less: Treasury Stock, _____ shares of Common Stock, at cost | | |
> | Total Stockholders' Equity | $ | $ |

Source: *Uniform System of Accounts for the Lodging Industry*, 10th Rev. Ed. (Lansing, Mich.: Educational Institute of the American Hotel & Lodging Association, 2006). ©Hotel Association of New York City.

Many lodging businesses are organized as partnerships. The Owners' Equity section of a partnership should reflect each partner's equity. The balance sheet for a partnership with many partners simply refers to a supplementary schedule showing each partner's share. The Owners' Equity section of a business organized as a partnership by its three owners is illustrated as follows:

M. Kass, Capital	$ 50,000
J. Ninety, Capital	25,000
R. Chicklets, Capital	25,000
Total Owners' Equity	$100,000

Finally, when a lodging operation is organized as a limited liability company, the owners are called *members* and the Owners' Equity section is similar to that of a partnership.

Footnotes

The balance sheets of hospitality operations, although filled with considerable financial information, are not complete without the other financial statements and footnotes. The full disclosure principle requires that businesses supply sufficient financial information to inform the users—creditors, owners, and others. This can be accomplished only by providing footnote disclosure in addition to the financial statements. Thus, **footnotes** are an integral part of the financial statements of a hospitality operation. They contain additional information not presented in the body of the financial statements. They should not contradict or soften the disclosure of the financial statements, but should provide additional explanations. The financial statements of publicly held companies generally include the following footnotes:

- Description of business
- Earnings per share
- Stock-based compensation
- Basis of consolidation
- Use of estimates
- Cash and temporary cash investments
- Inventory methods and valuation
- Accounting for investments, including the valuation of marketable securities
- Depreciation and amortization policies
- Amortization—Goodwill
- Accounting for deferred charges
- Advertising costs
- Accounting for pensions
- Revenue recognition
- Accounting for income taxes
- Fair value of financial instruments
- Computation of net income (loss) per share (only public companies)
- Foreign currency translation
- Concentration of credit risk

Consolidated Financial Statements

Many major hospitality companies consist of several corporations. For example, the hypothetical XYZ Hotel Company consists of a parent corporation, XYZ Hotel Company, and three separately incorporated hotels—Hotel X, Hotel Y, and Hotel Z. The XYZ Hotel Company owns 100 percent of the capital stock of each of the three hotels. Each hotel has its own set of financial statements, but for purposes of financial reporting, they are combined with the parent's financial statements. The combined statements are referred to as **consolidated financial statements**. The first footnote usually includes a brief description of the principles of consolidation used to combine the statements of a parent corporation and its subsidiary corporations.

Hilton Hotels Corporation's financial statements in the appendix to this chapter are consolidated financial statements. The "Notes to Consolidated Financial Statements" cover the basis of presentation and principles of consolidation for the reports.

In effect, consolidated financial statements reflect a single economic unit rather than the legal separate entities resulting from separate corporations. Generally, more than 50 percent of the voting stock of a subsidiary should be owned by the holding company or by the same interests if the associated companies' financial statements are to be combined. Complex procedures involving consolidation are covered in advanced accounting textbooks.

Summary

Although the balance sheet may not play the vital role in management decision-making that other financial statements play, it is still an important tool. By examining it, managers, investors, and creditors may determine the financial position of the hospitality operation at a given point in time. It is used to help determine an operation's ability to pay its debts and purchase fixed assets.

The balance sheet is divided into three major categories: Assets, Liabilities, and Owners' Equity. Assets are the items owned by the operation, while liabilities and owners' equity represent claims to the operation's assets. Liabilities are amounts owed to creditors. Owners' equity represents the residual interest in assets for investors. Both assets and liabilities are divided into current and noncurrent sections. Current assets are cash and other assets that will be converted to cash or used on the property's operations within the next year. Current liabilities represent present obligations that will be paid within one year. The major categories of noncurrent assets include Noncurrent Receivables, Investments, Property and Equipment, and Other Assets. Long-term liabilities are present obligations expected to be paid beyond the next 12 months from the date of the balance sheet.

Owners' equity generally includes common stock, paid-in capital in excess of par, and retained earnings. Common stock is the product of the number of shares outstanding and the par value of the shares. Paid-in capital in excess of par is the amount over the par value paid by investors when they purchased the stock from the hospitality corporation. Retained earnings are the past earnings generated by the operation but not distributed to the stockholders in the form of dividends.

Since assets are the items owned by the property, and liabilities and owners' equity are claims to the assets, the relationship involving the three is stated as follows: Assets = Liabilities + Owners' Equity. The balance sheet is prepared either with assets on one side of the page and liabilities and owners' equity on the other (account format) or with the three sections in one column (report format).

Endnotes

1. *Hilton Hotels Corporation 1988 Annual Report* (Beverly Hills, Calif.: Hilton Hotels Corp., 1989), pp. 32–44.

Key Terms

account format—An arrangement of a balance sheet that lists the asset accounts on the left side of the page and the liability and owners' equity accounts on the right side. Compare *report format*.

additional paid-in capital—Payments for capital stock in excess of the stated or par value of the capital stock.

capital stock—Shares of ownership of a corporation.

consolidated financial statements—The combined financial statements of a parent corporation and its subsidiary corporations.

current assets—Resources of cash and items that will be converted to cash or used in generating income within one year or a normal operating cycle.

current liabilities—Obligations at the balance sheet date that are expected to be satisfied either by using current assets or by creating other current liabilities within one year or a normal operating cycle.

current ratio—Ratio of total current assets to total current liabilities expressed as a coverage of so many times; calculated by dividing Current Assets by Current Liabilities.

footnotes—Disclosures in the financial statements that contain additional information that is not presented in the body of the financial statements.

liquidity—The ability of a hospitality operation to meet its short-term (current) obligations by maintaining sufficient cash or short-term investments that are easily convertible to cash.

long-term liabilities—Obligations at the balance sheet date that are expected to be paid beyond the next 12 months or, if paid in the current year, they will be paid from restricted funds; also called *noncurrent liabilities.*

net working capital—Current Assets minus Current Liabilities.

noncurrent receivables—Accounts and notes receivable that are not expected to be collected within one year of the balance sheet date.

other assets—A category of the balance sheet that includes purchased goodwill, cash surrender value of life insurance policies, deferred charges, noncurrent deferred income taxes, security deposits, organization costs, and unamortized franchise costs.

property and equipment—A category of the balance sheet in which accountants record the values of fixed assets such as land, buildings, furniture, equipment, construction in progress, and leasehold improvements.

purchased goodwill—The excess of a hospitality operation's purchase price over the dollars assigned to its individual assets.

report format—An arrangement of a balance sheet that lists the assets first, followed by liabilities and owners' equity. Compare *account format.*

restricted cash—Cash that has been deposited in separate accounts, often for the purpose of retiring long-term debt.

retained earnings—An account for recording undistributed earnings of a corporation.

treasury stock—A corporation's own capital stock that the corporation has repurchased but not retired or reissued.

Review Questions

1. What is the importance of the balance sheet to management, investors, and creditors?

2. How do the three major parts of the balance sheet (Assets, Liabilities, and Owners' Equity) relate to each other?

3. Why is liquidity important to a hospitality firm?

4. What are some limitations of the balance sheet?

5. What is the difference between current and noncurrent assets?

6. Why are marketable securities shown before accounts receivable on the balance sheet?

7. What does the phrase *lower of cost or market* mean?

8. What is the difference between short-term and long-term debt?

9. When would a corporation have an Additional Paid-In Capital account?

10. What is the purpose of footnotes?

Problems

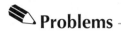

Problem 1

The following are accounts from the balance sheet of the Stewartville Hotel.

Building	Note Payable (2 Year)
Prepaid Insurance	Investment in GM Stock (100 shares)
House Banks	Organization Expenses
Obligations under Capital Leases	Construction in Progress
Common Stock, Par Value $150,000	Accounts Payable
Petty Cash	Additional Paid-In Capital
Accrued Payroll	Deferred Income Taxes (Long-Term)*
Retained Earnings	Treasury Stock
Supplies Inventory	Notes Payable (6 Months)
Advance Deposits	Security Deposits

* Relates to how businesses depreciate property and equipment.

Required:

Classify these accounts using the major classifications from the *USALI* balance sheet (see Exhibits 5 and 6).

Problem 2

The TexMex Café has recently purchased new office equipment. The owner, José Tex, wonders how the cost will be shown on the balance sheet and where the cost will be expressed.

Assume the equipment cost $20,000 and has a useful life of six years. Further assume that the estimated value of this equipment at the end of the six years is $2,000.

Required:

1. Using the straight-line method of depreciation, determine the amount of depreciation expense for years 1 through 6.

2. What net book value (cost-accumulated depreciation) will be shown on the balance sheet for the office equipment at the end of each year from years 1 through 6?

Problem 3

The Bravo has the following current balance sheet accounts:

Cash	$ 10,000
Accounts Receivable	200,000
Accounts Payable	50,000
Inventory	20,000
Income Taxes Payable	30,000
Prepaid Expenses	10,000
Accrued Expenses	40,000
Current Portion—Long-Term Debt	100,000
Wages Payable	30,000
Marketable Securities	25,000
Allowance for Doubtful Debts	5,000

Required:

1. Determine the Bravo's total current assets.
2. Determine the Bravo's total current liabilities.
3. Determine the Bravo's net working capital.
4. Determine the Bravo's current ratio.

Problem 4

A listing of selected accounts of Scotty's Café at the end of 20X6 are as follows:

Accounts Payable	$ 50,000
Accounts Receivable	30,000
Allowance for Doubtful Accounts	5,000
Cash	50,000
Food Inventory	20,000
Interest Payable	5,000

Notes Receivable (current)	12,000
Prepaid Insurance	2,000
Wages Payable	8,000

Required:

1. Determine the amount of current assets.
2. Determine the total of current liabilities.
3. Determine the net working capital.
4. If Scotty's must have twice the amount of current assets as it has current liabilities at the end of the year, what is the easiest thing management can do to achieve this?

Problem 5

The David Hotel took advantage of a major discount and paid a two-year premium of $24,000 for fire insurance on July 4, 20X6. The insurance coverage is for August 1, 20X6, through July 31, 20X8.

Required:

1. Provide the journal entry to record the payment of $24,000.
2. How much of the two year premium should be expensed by the end of 20X6?
3. How much is shown as prepaid insurance (current asset) at the end of 20X6?
4. How much is shown as deferred charges—insurance at the end of 20X6?

Problem 6

The Property and Equipment section of the Potterville Inn's balance sheet reflects the following after its first year of operation on December 31, 20X1:

Land	$ 200,000
Building	1,600,000
Equipment	600,000
Accumulated Deprecation	(110,000)
Net Property and Equipment	$ 2,290,000

During 20X2 the following transactions occurred:

a. Purchased equipment costing $50,000 on July 1, 20X2.

b. Sold equipment costing $20,000 on June 30, 20X2, that had been depreciated over 18 months. Cash received on the sale was $18,000.

c. Purchased additional land next to the inn on October 1, 20X2, for $100,000 for future expansion.

Assume the inn depreciates its building and equipment as follows:
Building—30 year life, $100,000 salvage value, straight-line depreciation
Equipment—10 year life, $0 salvage value, straight-line depreciation

Required:

1. Provide the journal entry to record the sale of equipment on June 30, 20X2.
2. Determine the amount of depreciation expense for 20X2.
3. Prepare the property and equipment section of the balance sheet as of December 31, 20X2.

Problem 7

The following are account balances from the trial balance of the Village Inn at October 31, 20X1 (the end of the Inn's fiscal year), arranged in alphabetical order.

	Debits	Credits
Accounts Payable		$ 77,000
Accounts Receivable	$ 96,900	
Accrued Liabilities		91,000
Accumulated Depreciation		338,400
Additional Paid-In Capital		25,000
Building	1,786,400	
Cash	47,800	
Common Stock		300,000
Current Portion—Long-Term Debt		14,000
Furniture and Fixtures	275,400	
Inventories	19,900	
Land	115,500	
Long-Term Debt		1,527,000
Other Assets	172,200	
Other Current Liabilities		40,800
Prepaid Expenses	2,400	
Retained Earnings		103,300

Required:

Prepare the balance sheet for the Village Inn according to the *USALI*.

Problem 8

Listed below are asset, liability, and owners' equity accounts for Sue & Jerry's Sleepy Hollow as of December 31, 20X7.

Common Stock	$144,600
Inventories	23,241
Treasury Stock	7,278
Land	111,158

House Banks	11,738
Deferred Income Taxes (Noncurrent/Credit Balance)	190,038
Paid-In Capital in Excess of Par	115,501
Notes Payable	42,611
Retained Earnings	327,137
Demand Deposits	8,803
Other Current Liabilities	21,246
Accounts Receivable	128,179
Accrued Salaries	78,293
Certificates of Deposit	2,934
Prepaid Expenses	13,499
Notes Receivable	22,420
Building	682,093
Marketable Securities	134,634
Long-Term Debt	262,930
Investments	30,049
Accounts Payable	58,690
Allowance for Doubtful Accounts	16,316
Deferred Charges	12,794
Advance Deposits—Banquets	14,203
Equipment	250,424
Current Maturities of Long-Term Debt	25,824
Security Deposits	8,569
Accumulated Depreciation, Equipment	150,424

Required:

Prepare the Assets section of the balance sheet for Sue & Jerry's Sleepy Hollow according to the *USALI.*

Problem 9

Using the account balances given in Problem 8, prepare the Liabilities and Owners' Equity sections of the balance sheet for Sue & Jerry's Sleepy Hollow according to the *USALI.*

Problem 10

The Wells Park Hotel's activities affecting retained earnings and other equity accounts during 20X2 were as follows:

1. 10,000 shares of common stock with a par value of $5.00 were sold for $15.00 per share.
2. Dividends declared in 20X1 of $60,000 were paid in 20X2.
3. Dividends declared in 20X2 and paid in 20X2 totaled $150,000.

4. Dividends declared in 20X2 to be paid during 20X3 totaled $50,000.
5. Net earnings for 20X2 equaled $300,000.

The balance of the retained earnings account was $200,000 at the beginning of 20X2.

Required:

Prepare the Statement of Retained Earnings for 20X2 for the Wells Park Hotel. (Assume the Wells Park Hotel's fiscal year ends on December 31, 20X2.)

Problem 11

Noreen Bayley, the owner/manager of Winkie's Motel, has come to you with some accounting questions. As a result of a fire at the motel, many of the records as of December 31, 20X2, were either burned or soaked by the sprinkler system.

Required:

You are to help Ms. Bayley determine the following balances:

1. In one report, the current ratio for the motel is 1.2 to 1. In addition, you have determined the amount of current liabilities (including $14,736 of current portion of long-term debt) to be $105,380 and long-term debt to be $60,000. What is the amount of current assets for Winkie's Motel?

2. Ms. Bayley has her December 31, 20X2, bank statement, which says she has $49,765 in her savings account and $36,072 in her checking account. She has a copy of the inventory sheet, which states total inventory on December 31, 20X2, of $15,491. Assuming that the only current assets are cash, inventory, and accounts receivable, what is the total accounts receivable owed to Ms. Bayley?

3. Ms. Bayley has a copy of the balance sheet from November 30, 20X2, which states that Current Assets was 30 percent of Total Assets. Assuming this relationship is the same at December 31, 20X2, what is the amount of total assets as of December 31, 20X2?

4. Based on the information in parts 1 through 3, what is the Owner's Equity as of December 31, 20X2?

Challenge Problems

Problem 12

The Spartan Inn, a sole proprietorship, has several accounts as follows:

Room Sales	$1,000,000
Land	80,000
Cash	5,000
Accounts Payable	20,000
Inventories	15,000
Accounts Receivable	80,000
Bonds Payable (Long-Term)	300,000

Jerry Spartan, Capital (1/1/20X3)	300,000
Accrued Expenses	10,000
Prepaid Expenses	8,000
Temporary Investments	25,000
Building	500,000
Equipment and Furnishings	200,000
Franchise Fees (Deferred)	15,000
Accumulated Depreciation	150,000
Income Tax Payable	10,000
Deferred Income Taxes (Long-Term Liability)	20,000

Other information is as follows:

The Spartan Inn's net income for 20X3 was $145,000, and Jerry Spartan withdrew $27,000 for personal use during 20X3.

Required:

Prepare a balance sheet for the Spartan Inn as of December 31, 20X3, in accordance with the *USALI*.

Problem 13

The balance sheet account balances of the Dominic Inn at the end of 20X3 are as follows:

Cash	$ 10,000
Accounts Receivable	150,000
Allowance for Doubtful Accounts	10,000
Food Inventory	50,000
Prepaid Insurance	12,000
Investments (long-term)	100,000
Land	300,000
Building	14,000,000
Equipment	850,000
Accumulated Depreciation—Building	2,500,000
Accumulated Depreciation—Equipment	200,000
Accounts Payable	50,000
Wages Payable	20,000
Income Taxes Payable	30,000
Current Maturities of Long-Term Debt	80,000
Long-Term Debt	9,870,000
Common Stock	650,000
Paid-in Capital in Excess of Par	1,000,000
Retained Earnings	1,062,000

Required:

Prepare the balance sheet in accordance with the *USALI*.

Problem 14

Julie Wayne is the new owner of the Moby Hotel in Washington, D.C. However, she has no experience in the hospitality industry and has hired you to help the newest employee, Carol Niks, computerize the back office operations. The first job you must tackle is teaching Carol about the balance sheet. The following is (1) a list of selected account balances in the general ledger on December 31, 20X1, and (2) some additional information.

Bank Balance	$ 141,022
Marketable Securities	550,000
Accounts Payable	1,530,761
Land	3,861,725
Retained Earnings	462,476
Current Portion—Long-Term Debt	392,000
Building	4,768,333
Accounts Receivable	1,843,999
Furniture & Equipment	2,000,741
Paid-In Capital in Excess of Par	1,795,463
Prepaid Insurance	??
Accumulated Depreciation	847,937
Long-Term Debt	??
Capital Stock	??

Additional information:

1. The market value of the marketable securities as of December 31, 20X1, is $532,000.

2. On January 1, 20X1, the previous owner purchased a two-year insurance policy for $40,000 to cover years 20X1 through 20X2.

3. On December 31, 20X1, there were 50,000 shares of stock issued and outstanding with a par value of $10 per share. The 50,000 shares were sold for $2,295,463.

4. Long-term debt can be calculated by subtracting owners' equity and all liabilities other than long-term debt from total assets.

Required:

Prepare the balance sheet in accordance with the *USALI.*

Problem 15

The trial balance of balance sheet accounts of Lancer's, a popular casual dining spot, as of December 31, 20X3, is as follows:

	Debits	Credits
Cash	$ 5,000	
Marketable Securities	10,000	
Accounts Receivable	100,000	
Allowance for Doubtful Accounts		$ 5,000
Food Inventory	15,000	
Prepaid Rent	5,000	

Prepaid Insurance	8,000	
Investments	50,000	
Land	80,000	
Building	420,000	
Equipment	100,000	
Accumulated Depreciation		100,000
Accounts Payable		15,000
Income Taxes Payable		–0–
Accrued Expenses		25,000
Dividends Payable		–0–
Long-Term Debt		300,000
Capital Stock		89,000
Paid-In Capital in Excess of Par		68,000
Retained Earnings (1/1/X3)		61,000

Additional information:

1. Dividends declared during 20X3 totaled $30,000. Only $20,000 of the dividends declared in 20X3 have been paid as of December 31, 20X3. The unpaid dividends have not been recorded.

2. Operations generated $800,000 of revenue for 20X3. Expenses recorded totaled $650,000. Additional adjustments required are as follows:

   a. The allowance for doubtful accounts should be adjusted to 10 percent of accounts receivable.

   b. Prepaid insurance of $8,000 is the premium paid for insurance coverage for July 1, 20X3, through June 30, 20X4.

   c. Unrecorded depreciation expense for 20X3 totals $41,000.

   d. Income taxes have not been recorded. Lancer's average rate is 20 percent.

3. The Long-Term Debt account includes $50,000 that must be paid on June 30, 20X4.

Required:

Prepare a balance sheet according to the *USALI.*

Appendix

Consolidated Statements of Income

(in millions, except per share amounts)	Year Ended December 31, 2002	2003	2004
Revenue			
Owned hotels	$2,100	2,031	2,062
Leased hotels	111	103	111
Management and franchise fees	329	337	384
Timeshare and other income	324	378	463
	2,864	2,849	3,020
Other revenue from managed and franchised properties	952	970	1,126
	3,816	3,819	4,146
Expenses			
Owned hotels	1,462	1,500	1,501
Leased hotels	101	96	101
Depreciation and amortization	348	334	330
Impairment loss and related costs	21	22	5
Other operating expenses	294	335	395
Corporate expense	66	81	85
	2,292	2,368	2,417
Other expenses from managed and franchised properties	952	970	1,120
	3,244	3,338	3,537
Operating income from unconsolidated affiliates	31	34	49
Operating Income	603	515	658
Interest and dividend income	43	29	26
Interest expense	(328)	(295)	(274)
Net interest from unconsolidated affiliates and non-controlled interests	(19)	(20)	(26)
Net loss on asset dispositions and other	(14)	(6)	(5)
Loss from non-operating affiliates	—	—	(6)
Income Before Taxes and Minority and Non-Controlled Interests	285	223	373
Provision for income taxes	(81)	(53)	(127)
Minority and non-controlled interests, net	(6)	(6)	(8)
Net Income	$ 198	164	238
Basic Earnings Per Share	$ .53	.43	.62
Diluted Earnings Per Share	$ .53	.43	.60

See notes to consolidated financial statements

Courtesy of Hilton Hotels Corporation.

Consolidated Balance Sheets

(in millions)	December 31, 2003	2004
ASSETS		
Current Assets		
Cash and equivalents	$ 9	303
Restricted cash	73	163
Accounts receivable, net	246	269
Inventories	193	144
Deferred income taxes.	78	85
Current portion of notes receivable, net	32	68
Receivable from Caesars Entertainment, Inc	325	—
Other current assets	64	74
Total current assets	1,020	1,106
Investments, Property and Other Assets		
Investments and notes receivable, net	558	635
Property and equipment, net	3,641	3,510
Management and franchise contracts, net	383	336
Leases, net	115	111
Brands	970	970
Goodwill	1,240	1,240
Other assets	256	334
Total investments, property and other assets	7,163	7,136
Total Assets	$ 8,183	8,242
LIABILITIES AND STOCKHOLDERS' EQUITY		
Current Liabilities		
Accounts payable and accrued expenses	$ 553	611
Current maturities of long-term debt	338	14
Income taxes payable	4	4
Total current liabilities	895	629
Long-term debt	3,801	3,633
Non-recourse debt of non-controlled entity	—	100
Deferred income taxes	775	781
Insurance reserves and other	473	531
Total liabilities	5,944	5,674
Commitments and Contingencies		
Stockholders' Equity		
Common Stock, 381 million and 389 million shares outstanding, respectively	971	997
Additional paid-in capital	970	1,086
Retained earnings	456	689
Accumulated other comprehensive loss	(1)	(3)
	2,396	2,769
Less treasury stock, at cost	(157)	(201)
Total stockholders' equity	2,239	2,568
Total Liabilities and Stockholders' Equity	$ 8,183	8,242

See notes to consolidated financial statements

Consolidated Statements of Cash Flow

(in millions)	Year Ended December 31, 2002	2003	2004
Operating Activities			
Net income	$ 198	164	238
Adjustments to reconcile net income to net cash provided by operating activities:			
Depreciation and amortization	348	334	330
Amortization of loan costs	9	13	9
Net loss on asset dispositions and other	14	6	5
Loss of non-operating affilates	—	—	6
Impairment loss and related costs	21	22	5
Change in working capital components:			
Inventories	13	(34)	45
Accounts receivable	12	37	(24)
Other current assets	55	2	(9)
Accounts payable and accrued expenses	26	(26)	59
Restricted cash	(15)	(39)	(90)
Change in deferred income taxes	(39)	(48)	27
Change in other liabilities	(22)	35	49
Unconsolidated affiliates' distributions in excess of earnings	19	17	20
Change in timeshare notes receivable	(36)	(73)	(105)
Other	21	(30)	(17)
Net cash provided by operating activities	624	380	548
Investing Activities			
Capital expenditures	(245)	(202)	(178)
Additional investments	(32)	(25)	(72)
Proceeds from asset dispositions	174	279	80
Payments received on notes and other	21	8	38
Acquisitions, net of cash acquired	(71)	—	—
Net cash (used in) provided by investing activities.	(153)	60	(132)
Financing Activities			
Change in revolving loans	(550)	(510)	(160)
Long-term borrowings	373	562	—
Reduction of long-term debt	(278)	(513)	(14)
Issuance of common stock	18	40	131
Repurchase of common stock	—	—	(48)
Cash dividends	(30)	(30)	(31)
Net cash used in financing activities	(467)	(451)	(122)
Increase (Decrease) in Cash and Equivalents	4	(11)	294
Cash and Equivalents at Beginning of Year	16	20	9
Cash and Equivalents at End of Year	$ 20	9	303

See notes to consolidated financial statements

Consolidated Statements of Stockholders' Equity

(in millions, except per share amounts) Year Ended December 31, 2002	2003	2004
COMMON STOCK		
Balance at beginning of year.	$ 948	962	971
Issuance of common stock	14	—	—
Exercise of stock options	—	9	26
Balance at end of year	$ 962	971	997
ADDITIONAL PAID-IN CAPITAL		
Balance at beginning of year.	$ 873	950	970
Issuance of common stock	70	1	(4)
Exercise of stock options	—	13	105
Deferred compensation.	7	6	15
Balance at end of year	$ 950	970	1,086
RETAINED EARNINGS		
Balance at beginning of year	$ 168	322	456
Net Income	198	164	238
Exercise of stock options	(14)	—	26
Common dividends($.08 per share)	(30)	(30)	(31)
Balance at end of year	$ 322	456	689
ACCUMULATED OTHER COMPREHENSIVE INCOME (LOSS)		
Balance at beginning of year	$ (5)	(11)	(1)
Cash flow hedge adjustment, net of deferred tax	(3)	5	7
Cumulative translation adjustment, net of deferred tax	1	1	—
Change in unrealized gain / loss on marketable securities,net of deferred tax	(4)	11	3
Minimum pension obligation adjustment, net of deferred tax	—	(7)	(12)
Balance at end of year	$ (11)	(1)	(3)
TREASURY STOCK, AT COST		
Balance at beginning of year	$ (201)	(170)	(157)
Issuance of common stock	1	1	4
Exercise of stock options	30	12	—
Repurchase of common stock	—	—	(48)
Balance at end of year	$ (170)	(157)	(201)
TOTAL STOCKHOLDERS' EQUITY		
Balance at beginning of year	$1,783	2,053	2,239
Net income	198	164	238
Cash flow hedge adjustment, net of deferred tax	(3)	5	7
Cumulative translation adjustment, net of deferred tax	1	1	—
Change in unrealized gain / loss on marketable securities, net of deferred tax	(4)	11	3

(continued)

Consolidated Statements of Stockholders' Equity *(continued)*

(in millions, except per share amounts)	Year Ended December 31, 2002	2003	2004
Minimum pension obligation adjustment, net of deferred tax	—	(7)	(12)
Comprehensive income	192	174	236
Issuance of common stock	85	2	—
Exercise of stock options	16	34	157
Repurchase of common stock	—	—	(48)
Deferred compensation	7	6	15
Common dividends ($.08 per share)	(30)	(30)	(31)
Balance at end of year	**$2,053**	**2,239**	**2,568**

See notes to consolidated financial statements

Notes

NOTES TO CONSOLIDATED FINANCIAL STATEMENTS

December 31, 2004

NOTE 1: BASIS OF PRESENTATION AND ORGANIZATION

Hilton Hotels Corporation is engaged in the ownership, management and development of hotels, resorts and timeshare properties and the franchising of lodging properties. We operate in select markets throughout the world, predominately in the United States. Revenue and income are derived from three reportable segments: Hotel Ownership, Managing and Franchising, and Timeshare.

NOTE 2: SUMMARY OF SIGNIFICANT ACCOUNTING POLICIES

Principles of Consolidation

The consolidated financial statements include the accounts of Hilton Hotels Corporation, our wholly owned subsidiaries, variable interest entities where we are the primary beneficiary and entities in which we have a controlling financial interest. The determination of controlling financial interest is based upon the terms of individual joint venture agreements, including evaluation of rights held by other ownership interests. Entities in which we have a controlling financial interest are generally comprised of majority owned joint ventures. All material intercompany transactions are eliminated and net earnings are reduced by the portion of earnings of affiliates applicable to other ownership interests.

Cash and Equivalents

Cash and equivalents include investments with initial maturities of three months or less.

Restricted Cash

Restricted cash includes cash related to certain consolidated hotels, the use of which is restricted for hotel purposes under the terms of collateralized borrowings; refundable deposits on the sale of timeshare intervals; and cash balances held by a consolidated non-controlled entity.

Accounts Receivable

Accounts receivable are reflected net of allowance for uncollectible accounts of $20 million and $27 million as of December 31, 2003 and 2004, respectively.

Investments

We maintain investments in unconsolidated affiliates, including hotel joint ventures as well as other entities that support the operations of our hotel properties. Investments are accounted for using the equity method when we exercise significant influence over the venture but lack a controlling financial interest, which is determined based upon the terms of individual joint venture agreements, including evaluation of rights held by other ownership interests. Generally, we account for investments using the equity method when we own more than a minimal investment but have no more than a 50% ownership interest. When we have a controlling financial interest in the venture, which is generally when our ownership exceeds 50%, the balance sheet and results of operations are consolidated, with net earnings reduced by the portion of earnings applicable to other ownership interests. All other investments in unconsolidated affiliates are generally accounted for under the cost method. The hotels in which we own a non-controlling financial interest are an integral component of our hotel ownership segment and are strategically and operationally important to that segment's results. Therefore, our operating income from unconsolidated affiliates is included as a component of consolidated operating income in the accompanying consolidated statements of income.

Currency Translation

Assets and liabilities denominated in most foreign currencies are translated into U.S. dollars at year-end exchange rates and related gains and losses, net of applicable deferred income taxes, are reflected in stockholders' equity. Gains and losses from foreign currency transactions are included in earnings.

Valuation of Long-Lived Assets

The carrying value of our long-lived assets are reviewed when events or changes in circumstances indicate that the carrying amount of an asset may not be recoverable. If it is determined that an impairment loss has occurred based on the lowest level of identifiable expected future cash flow, then a loss is recognized in the income statement using a fair value based model.

Property and Equipment

Property and equipment are stated at cost less accumulated depreciation. Interest incurred during construction of facilities is capitalized and depreciated over the life of the asset. Costs of improvements are capitalized. These capitalized costs may include structural costs, equipment, fixtures and floor and wall coverings. Costs of normal repairs and maintenance are charged to expense as incurred.

Depreciation is provided using the straight-line method over the estimated useful life of the assets. Leasehold improvements are depreciated over the shorter of the asset life or lease term. The estimated useful lives of assets are generally 40 years for buildings and three to eight years for building improvements and furniture and equipment. Depreciation expense for 2002, 2003 and 2004 was $283 million, $270 million and $271 million, respectively.

Management and Franchise Contracts

Management and franchise contracts acquired in acquisitions that were accounted for as purchases are recorded at the estimated present value of net cash flow expected to be received over the lives of the contracts. This value is amortized using the straight-line method over the remaining contract lives. Costs incurred to acquire individual management and franchise contracts are amortized using the straight-line method over the life of the respective contract. Accumulated amortization of management and franchise contracts totaled $185 million and $211 million at December 31, 2003 and 2004, respectively.

Leases

Leases acquired in acquisitions that were accounted for as purchases are recorded at the estimated present value of net cash flow expected to be received over the lives of the lease agreements. This value is amortized using the straight-line method over the remaining lease terms. Accumulated amortization of leases totaled $15 million and $19 million at December 31, 2003 and 2004, respectively.

Brands

The brand names of hotels acquired in acquisitions are assigned a fair market value. To arrive at a value for each brand name, an estimation is made of the amount of royalty income that could be generated from the brand name if it was licensed to an independent third-party owner. The resulting cash flow is discounted using the estimated weighted average cost of capital for each respective brand name. We account for brands in accordance with Statement of Financial Accounting Standard (FAS) 142, which requires that intangible assets with indefinite lives are not amortized, but are reviewed annually for impairment.

Goodwill

Goodwill represents the excess of the purchase price over the fair value of net assets of businesses acquired. We account for goodwill in accordance with FAS 142, which requires that goodwill is not amortized, but is reviewed annually for impairment.

Derivative Instruments

We have an outstanding swap agreement which qualifies for hedge accounting as a cash flow hedge of a foreign currency denominated liability. The gain or loss on the change in fair value of the derivative is included in earnings to the extent it offsets the earnings impact of changes in fair value of the hedged obligation. Any difference is deferred in accumulated other comprehensive income, a component of stockholders' equity.

We have an interest rate swap on certain fixed rate senior notes which qualifies as a fair value hedge. This derivative impacts earnings to the extent of increasing or decreasing actual interest expense on the hedged notes to simulate a floating interest rate. Changes in the fair value of the derivative are offset by an adjustment to the value of the hedged notes. We also have an interest rate swap on the floating rate mortgage of a consolidated joint venture which qualifies as a cash flow hedge. This derivative impacts earnings to the extent of increasing or decreasing actual interest expense on the hedged mortgage to simulate a fixed interest rate, with any incremental fair value change deferred in accumulated other comprehensive income.

We assess on a quarterly basis the effectiveness of our hedges in offsetting the variability in the cash flow or fair values of the hedged obligations. There were no amounts recognized or reclassified into earnings for the years ended December 31, 2002, 2003 or 2004 due to hedge ineffectiveness or due to excluding from the assessment of effectiveness any component of the derivatives.

Concurrent with our investment in a synthetic fuel facility in August 2004, we entered into a derivative contract covering 2.5 million barrels of oil, which is effective for the calendar year ending December 31, 2005. The derivative contract involves two call options that provide for net cash settlement at expiration based on the full year 2005 average trading price of oil in relation to the strike price of each option. If the average price of oil in 2005 is less than $55, the derivative will yield no payment. If the average price of oil exceeds $55, the derivative will yield a payment equal to the excess of the average price over $55 per barrel, multiplied by the number of barrels covered, up to a maximum price per barrel of $68. The purpose of the transaction is to provide economic protection against an increase in oil prices that could limit the amount of tax credits available under Section 29 of the Internal Revenue Code. The strike prices of the two call options are intended to approximate the price ranges under which the tax credit could be reduced or eliminated by an increase in oil prices. The cost of the derivative agreement totaled approximately $2.5 million. This agreement does not qualify for hedge accounting and, as a result, changes in the fair value of the derivative agreement are reflected in earnings.

Unamortized Loan Costs

Debt discount and issuance costs incurred in connection with the placement of long-term debt are capitalized and amortized to interest expense over the lives of the related debt. These balances are included in other assets in our consolidated balance sheets.

Self-Insurance

We are self-insured for various levels of general liability, workers' compensation and employee medical and dental insurance coverage at our owned locations.

Managed properties may be required to participate in certain of the programs where we are the employer of the employees at the hotel. Managed properties may also elect to participate in our self-insured liability insurance program. We purchase insurance coverage for claim amounts which exceed our self-insured retentions. Depending on the type of insurance, these self-insured retention amounts range from $250,000 to $500,000 per claim. Our self-insurance reserves are included in accounts payable and accrued expenses (current portion) and insurance reserves and other (long-term portion) in the accompanying consolidated balance sheets. The undiscounted amount of our self-insurance reserves totaled $141 million and $148 million at December 31, 2003 and 2004, respectively.

Our insurance reserves are accrued based on estimates of the present value of claims expected to occur during the covered period. These estimates are prepared with the assistance of outside actuaries and consultants. Our actuaries periodically review the volume and amount of claims activity, and based upon their findings, we adjust our insurance reserves accordingly. The ultimate cost of claims for a covered period may differ from our original estimates. General liability and workers compensation claim estimates are discounted to determine the present value of projected settlements; the discount rates used in the 2002 through 2004 program years were approximately 3.0% to 4.25%, which we considered reasonable based on claims settlement patterns. Since medical and dental claims are generally paid within several months, we do not discount the related insurance reserves.

Revenue Recognition

Revenue is generally recognized as services are performed. Owned and leased hotel revenue represents primarily room rentals and food and beverage sales from owned, majority owned and leased hotels.

Management fees represent fees earned from hotels managed by us, usually under long-term contracts with the hotel owner. Management fees include a base fee, which is generally a percentage of hotel revenue, and an incentive fee, which is generally based on the hotel's profitability. We recognize base fees as revenue when earned in accordance with the terms of the contract. In interim periods we recognize incentive fees that would be due if the contract were terminated at the end of the interim period.

Franchise fees represent fees received in connection with the franchise of our brand names, usually under long-term contracts with the hotel owner. Depending on the brand, we charge franchise royalty fees of up to five percent of rooms revenue. We recognize fee revenue as earned, in accordance with FAS 45, "Accounting for Franchise Fee Revenue."

Timeshare and other income primarily consists of earnings from our timeshare operations. Timeshare revenue is generated primarily from the sale and financing of timeshare intervals and operating timeshare resorts. We recognize revenue from deeded timeshare sales in accordance with FAS 66, "Accounting for Real Estate Sales." Sales are included in revenue when a minimum of a ten percent down payment has been received, certain minimum sales thresholds have been attained, the purchaser's period to cancel for a refund has expired and the related receivable is deemed to be collectable. We defer revenue recognition for sales that do not meet these criteria. During periods of construction, profits from timeshare sales are recognized under the percentage-of-completion method. Our Hilton City Club timeshare product is accounted for as a long-term lease with a reversionary interest rather than the sale of a deeded interest in real estate. Hilton City Club sales revenue is recognized over the term of the lease.

Timeshare and other income also includes revenue generated by the incidental support of hotel operations and the recognition of deferred gains on asset sales. We account for the sale of real estate in accordance with FAS 66. To the extent we realize gains from the sale of real estate and maintain significant continuing involvement in the form of a long-term management contract, the gain is deferred and recognized in earnings over the term of the contract. Results in 2002, 2003 and 2004 include the recognition of pre-tax deferred gains totaling $6 million, $10 million and $15 million, respectively. The deferral of gain recognition is dependent on the structure of individual sale transactions.

We incur certain reimbursable costs on behalf of managed hotel properties and franchisees. We report reimbursements from managed properties and franchisees as revenue and the related costs as expenses. These costs, which relate primarily to payroll costs at managed properties where we are the employer, are reflected in other revenue and expenses from managed and franchised properties in the consolidated statements of income. Since the reimbursements are made based upon the costs incurred with no added margin, the presentation of these reimbursable costs has no effect on our operating income, total or per share net income, cash flow or financial position.

Hilton HHonors

Hilton HHonors is a guest loyalty program operated by Hilton HHonors Worldwide (HHW), a joint venture 50% owned by us and 50% owned by Hilton Group plc. Hilton Group's wholly owned subsidiary, Hilton International Co., owns the rights to the Hilton brand name outside the United States. The HHonors program is operated for the benefit of the Hilton family of brands worldwide.

Members of the HHonors program earn points based on their spending at most of the hotel properties operated and franchised by us and Hilton Group. HHW accumulates and tracks points on the member's behalf and fulfills the awards upon request. Points can be redeemed for hotel stays at participating properties, and for a variety of other awards such as airline tickets, cruises and car rentals. As we exercise significant influence over the operation of HHW but lack a controlling financial interest, our investment in HHW is accounted for under the equity method.

HHonors is provided as a guest loyalty program to participating hotels. HHW charges the cost of operating the program, including the estimated fair value of award redemption, to participating hotels based on member's qualifying expenditures. The charges do not include a markup or profit element. We record our share of program costs, which we expense and pay to HHW based upon contractual amounts when qualified members stay at our hotels. When members redeem awards at our hotels, we receive contractual amounts from HHW.

Earnings Per Share (EPS)

Basic EPS is computed by dividing net income available to common stockholders by the weighted average number of common shares outstanding for the period. The weighted average number of common shares outstanding for 2002, 2003 and 2004 were 374 million, 378 million and 384 million, respectively. Diluted EPS reflects the potential dilution that could occur if securities or other contracts to issue common stock were exercised or converted. The dilutive effect of the assumed exercise of stock options and convertible securities increased the weighted average number of common shares by 27 million, 32 million and 34 million in 2002, 2003 and 2004, respectively. In addition, the increase to net income resulting from interest on convertible securities assumed to have not been paid was approximately $16 million in 2002, $14 million in 2003, and $12 million in 2004.

Stock-Based Compensation

We apply Accounting Principles Board (APB) Opinion 25 and related interpretations in accounting for our stock-based compensation plans. Prior to 2004, our stock-based compensation consisted primarily of stock options. No compensation cost is reflected in our net income related to our stock option awards for the periods presented, as all options had an exercise price greater than or equal to the market value of the underlying common stock on the date of grant.

We granted 7,469,400 options with a grant date fair value of approximately $4.37 per share in 2002 and we granted 7,144,775 options with a grant date fair value of approximately $4.00 per share in 2003. No options were granted in 2004. For disclosure purposes, we estimated the fair value of each option grant on the date of grant using the Black-Scholes option-pricing model with the following weighted average assumptions used for grants in 2002 and 2003 respectively: dividend yield of one percent for both years; expected volatility of 34 and 35 percent, respectively; risk-free interest rates of 4.6 and 3.0 percent, respectively, and expected lives of five years for both 2002 and 2003.

In the second quarter of 2004, we awarded restricted stock under the new 2004 Omnibus Equity Compensation Plan which includes two forms of restricted stock: time-based and performance-based. The time-based restricted stock awards vest annually in a straight-line manner generally over four years. The performance-based restricted stock awards vest in full at the end of a three-year period, with the shares to be issued subject to upward or downward revision based on the extent a pre-determined performance measure is achieved. In accordance with APB 25, compensation expense for the time-based awards is measured at the fair value of the underlying stock at the date of grant. Compensation expense associated with the performance-based awards is subject to adjustment for changes in the underlying stock price over the vesting period, as well as changes in estimates relating to whether the performance objective will be achieved. We granted 1,560,670 time-based units and 765,309 performance-based units in 2004, both with a grant date fair value of approximately $17.37 per share. No restricted stock units were awarded in 2002 or 2003. Compensation expense for both the time-based and performance-based awards is amortized over the respective vesting periods. Consolidated compensation expense under the 2004 plan was approximately $6 million in 2004.

We also provide supplemental retirement benefits to eligible senior officers in the form of fixed stock units that settle for shares of our common stock on a one-for-one basis. We granted 62,440 units with a grant date fair value of $11.85 per share in 2002 and we granted 8,425 units with a grant date fair value of $12.65 per share in 2003. No units were granted in 2004. The compensation expense associated with the benefits is expensed over a four year vesting period. The aggregate expense under these plans totaled $7 million, $6 million and $4 million in 2002, 2003 and 2004, respectively.

Had the expense for all forms of our stock-based compensation been determined using the fair value based method defined in FAS 123, "Accounting for Stock-Based Compensation," our net income and net income per share would have been reduced to the pro forma amounts indicated below. These pro forma results may not be indicative of the future results for the full fiscal year due to potential grants, vesting and other factors:

(in millions, except per share amounts)	2002	2003	2004
Net income:			
As reported	$ 198	164	238
Add back: Compensation expense			
included in reported net income,net of tax	4	4	6
Deduct: Fair-value compensation expense			
for all awards, net of tax	(24)	(21)	(18)
As adjusted	$ 178	147	226
Basic earnings per share:			
As reported	$ .53	.43	.62
As adjusted	$ .48	.39	.59
Diluted earnings per share:			
As reported	$ .53	.43	.60
As adjusted	$ .48	.39	.57

Use of Estimates

The preparation of financial statements in conformity with accounting principles generally accepted in the United States requires us to make estimates and assumptions that affect the reported amounts of assets and liabilities and disclosure of contingent assets and liabilities at the date of the financial statements and the reported amounts of revenue and expenses during the reporting period. Actual results could differ from our estimates and assumptions.

Reclassifications

Our consolidated statements of cash flow in 2002 and 2003 have been reclassified to present the net change in timeshare notes receivable in cash provided by operating activities. We previously reflected the issuance of timeshare notes and the related payments received within investing activities. This reclassification resulted in a decrease in cash provided by operating activities totaling $36 million and $73 million in 2002 and 2003, respectively, with a corresponding reduction in net cash used in investing activities. The reclassification has no impact on our previously reported consolidated statements of income or consolidated balance sheets. Certain other prior period amounts have been reclassified to conform with the current year presentation, primarily related to our separate presentation of restricted cash in the consolidated balance sheets and consolidated statements of cash flow.

New Accounting Standards

In January 2003, the Financial Accounting Standards Board (FASB) issued FASB Interpretation No. 46, "Consolidation of Variable Interest Entities" (FIN 46) to expand upon existing accounting guidance that addresses when a company should include in its financial statements the assets, liabilities and results of operations of another entity. Under previous accounting guidance, we generally have included another entity in our consolidated financial statements only if we have a controlling financial interest in the entity through voting or other interests. FIN 46 changed that guidance by requiring a variable interest entity (VIE), as defined, to be consolidated by the company that is subject to a majority of the risk of loss from the VIE's activities, or is entitled to receive a majority of the entity's residual returns, or both. The losses and residual returns are based on the potential variability from the anticipated cash flow of the VIE attributable to the holders of variable interests. FIN 46 also requires disclosure about VIEs that a company is not required to consolidate, but in which it has a significant variable interest.

Our evaluation of the provisions of FIN 46 as it relates to our various forms of arrangements has focused primarily on reviewing the key terms of our joint venture agreements, management contracts and franchise agreements against the criteria in FIN 46 to determine if any of these arrangements qualify as VIEs. In general, a VIE represents a structure used for business purposes that either does not have equity investors with voting rights or that has equity investors that do not provide sufficient financial resources for the entity to support its activities. However, other contractual arrangements could qualify an entity as a VIE and designate which party to the contract is the primary beneficiary.

In the first quarter of 2003, we adopted FIN 46 for VIEs created after January 31, 2003, which resulted in no impact to our consolidated financial statements. In December 2003, the FASB issued a revision to FIN 46 (FIN 46R) that replaced the original interpretation and codified proposed modifications and other decisions previously issued through certain FASB Staff Positions, including the deferral of the effective date of applying FIN 46R to certain variable interests created before February 1, 2003. We adopted FIN 46R in the first quarter of 2004. Except as described in the following paragraphs, our joint venture agreements, management contracts and franchise agreements are not variable interests, and therefore are not subject to the consolidation and disclosure provisions of FIN 46R.

Our evaluation of our joint venture agreements, management contracts and franchise agreements has identified two managed hotels in which we have variable interests, due to the terms of performance guarantees. The performance guarantee associated with one of the hotel management agreements does not expose us to the majority of expected cash flow variability and therefore this hotel is not consolidated. Our maximum exposure to loss on this contract consists of future management fees and our potential obligation to fund the performance guarantee which, as of December 31, 2004, totaled an aggregate amount of approximately $45 million through 2012.

The second of the two contracts contains provisions that expose us to the majority of expected cash flow variability. As a result, we are considered to be the primary beneficiary under FIN 46R and are required to consolidate the balance sheet and results of operations of the hotel. Therefore, this previously unconsolidated managed hotel has been consolidated as of January 1, 2004. Our consolidated balance sheet as of December 31, 2004 includes the assets and liabilities of this non-controlled hotel, including $9 million of cash and equivalents (reflected as restricted cash) and $100 million of debt which is non-recourse to us. The debt is secured by the fixed assets of the hotel with a historical cost of $84 million. The net equity of the hotel is a retained deficit of approximately $61 million as of December 31, 2004 and is reflected on our consolidated balance sheet in other assets. The revenue and operating expenses of this property are included in other revenue and expenses from managed and franchised properties in the consolidated statements of income. Our financial exposure to this property consists of the fees we earn under the management agreement and costs we may incur under the performance guarantee. The net effect of the other earnings of this property, which belong to the hotel owners, are reversed from our consolidated results through minority and non-controlled interests expense in the consolidated statements of income. As a result, the implementation of FIN 46R had no impact on reported net income or net income per share.

In September 2004, the Emerging Issues Task Force (EITF) of the FASB reached a consensus regarding accounting issues related to certain features of contingently convertible debt and the effect on diluted earnings per share (EITF Issue No. 04-8, "The Effect of Contingently Convertible Instruments on Diluted Earnings Per Share"). In November 2004, the EITF changed the transition provisions of the consensus to require that the guidance be applied to reporting periods ending after December 15, 2004. Under current interpretations of FAS 128, "Earnings per Share", issuers of contingently convertible debt exclude the potential common shares underlying the debt instrument from the calculation of diluted earnings per share until the contingency is met. The EITF consensus requires that potential shares underlying the debt instrument should be included in diluted earnings per share computations (if dilutive) regardless of whether the contingency has been met.

Our consolidated debt balance includes $575 million of contingently convertible debt, which was issued in the second quarter of 2003. Our calculation of diluted earnings per share for 2004 reflects the impact of the required implementation of EITF 04-8. As required, the consensus has been retroactively applied to all periods during which the instrument was outstanding. The retroactive application to 2003 did not result in a change to previously reported earnings per share for the year ended December 31, 2003.

In December 2004, the FASB issued FAS 123R, "Share-Based Payment," which eliminates the ability to account for share-based compensation transactions using

APB Opinion No. 25, "Accounting for Stock Issued to Employees," and generally requires instead that such transactions be accounted for using a fair-value-based method. Pro forma disclosure is no longer an alternative. FAS 123R also requires that the tax benefit associated with these share-based payments be classified as financing activities in the statement of cash flow rather than operating activities as currently permitted. FAS 123R must be adopted no later than July 1, 2005. Early adoption is permitted in periods in which financial statements have not yet been issued. FAS 123R offers alternative adoption methods. We have not yet determined which alternative method we will use.

As permitted by FAS 123, we currently account for share-based payments to employees using APB 25's intrinsic value method and, as such, generally recognize no compensation expense for employee stock options. The adoption of FAS 123R will result in increased compensation expense in our reported results. Had we adopted FAS 123R in prior periods, the impact of the standard would have approximated the impact of FAS 123 as described in the disclosure of pro forma net income and earnings per share in "Stock-Based Compensation" above.

In December 2004, the FASB issued FAS 152, "Accounting for Real Estate Time-Sharing Transactions." FAS 152 amends existing accounting guidance to reference the financial accounting and reporting guidance for real estate time-sharing transactions provided in AICPA Statement of Position 04-02, "Accounting for Real Estate Time-Sharing Transactions." FAS 152 is effective for our financial statements issued after January 1, 2006. The new accounting guidance requires, among other things, that costs incurred to sell timeshare units generally be charged to expense as incurred, including marketing expenses. This is consistent with our existing accounting treatment and is not expected to impact our reported results. The new standard will also require a change in the classification of certain items currently reported as expenses, requiring these items to be reflected as reductions of revenue. The impact to reported revenue is not expected to be significant, and time-share operating income will not be affected.

FAS 152 will also impact the timing of expense recognition when pre-sales of projects under construction occur and we use the percentage-of-completion method of accounting. We are currently allowed to defer sales and marketing expenses in the same proportion as the deferred revenue during construction. FAS 152 allows only the deferral of "direct" sales and marketing expenses. This will result in earlier recognition of sales and marketing expenses during the construction period, but will not impact the total sales and marketing expenses recognized. The impact of this change is dependent on the timing and duration of construction and the extent of pre-sales; however, it is not expected to affect reported results in 2006.

NOTE 3: ACQUISITIONS AND DISPOSITIONS

Acquisition of the Hilton Waikoloa Village

In May 2002, we purchased our partner's interest in the 1,240-room Hilton Waikoloa Village on Hawaii's Big Island, a property we manage and in which we previously had an ownership interest of approximately 13 percent. We acquired the remaining 87 percent interest for approximately $155 million, consisting of $75 million in cash and 5.2 million shares of our common stock.

Synthetic Fuel Investment

In August 2004, we acquired a 24 percent minority interest in a coal-based synthetic fuel facility for approximately $32 million. Our investment is accounted for using the equity method as we lack a controlling financial interest. The facility produced pre-tax operating losses, our proportionate share of which totaled approximately $6 million in 2004. This loss is reflected as loss from non-operating affiliates in the accompanying consolidated statements of income.

The synthetic fuel produced at this facility qualifies for tax credits based on Section 29 of the Internal Revenue Code, which reduce our provision for income taxes. The Section 29 credits are expected to continue to be available for fuel produced at the facility through 2007. The tax credits, combined with the tax benefit associated with the operating losses, totaled approximately $9 million in 2004. As a result, the benefit to our net income of the investment totaled approximately $3 million for the year ended December 31, 2004.

Asset Dispositions

In the 2004 first quarter, we sold the Doubletree La Posada Resort - Scottsdale in Arizona for total consideration of approximately $30 million, including approximately $6 million in cash and a note receivable for approximately $24 million. The note receivable is due to be repaid in the first quarter of 2005 and has been classified as a current asset on the December 31, 2004 consolidated balance sheet. No book gain or loss was realized on the sale; however, the transaction generated a capital gain for tax purposes, which enabled us to utilize existing capital loss tax carryforwards that had been fully reserved in prior periods. The transaction resulted in a net benefit to our income tax provision of approximately $2 million. We will continue to operate the hotel under a short-term management agreement that expires when the outstanding note is due.

In the second quarter of 2004, we sold the Doubletree Modesto and Doubletree Bakersfield, both in California. Total consideration from the sale of both hotels was approximately $40 million in cash. Gains of approximately $3 million on Modesto and approximately $2 million on Bakersfield were deferred due to our continuing involvement with each hotel and will be recognized over the life of the long-term management contract retained on each hotel. Both management contracts are for a term of ten years. The transaction also generated a capital gain for tax purposes, which enabled us to utilize existing capital loss tax carryforwards that had been fully reserved in prior periods. The transaction resulted in a net benefit to our income tax provision of approximately $4 million.

In the fourth quarter of 2004, we sold the Doubletree Jantzen Beach and the Doubletree Columbia River, both near Portland Oregon, for total consideration of approximately $29 million in cash. The sale resulted in a pre-tax loss of approximately $3 million. The $5 million pre-tax loss on asset dispositions and other in 2004 includes the $3 million loss on the sale of the two Doubletrees and a $5 million loss related to the write-off of values assigned to certain long-term management and franchise agreements that were terminated in 2004. These losses were partially offset by a $3 million gain from the sale of our investment in Travelweb.

In the 2003 first quarter, we sold four Homewood Suites by Hilton hotel properties in two separate transactions for approximately $40 million. We continue to operate three of the hotels under long-term management agreements and we have retained a long-term franchise contract on the fourth hotel. In the fourth quarter of 2003, an Embassy Suites hotel in which we held a 65% interest was sold, resulting in a pre-tax loss of approximately $4 million. We retained a long-term franchise contract on this hotel. Also in the 2003 fourth quarter, we sold certain marketable securities, which resulted in a pre-tax gain of approximately $2 million. In addition, we wrote off the value assigned to certain long-term management and franchise agreements that were terminated in 2003 totaling approximately $4 million. In the aggregate, these transactions resulted in a net $6 million pre-tax loss on asset dispositions and other in 2003.

In 2002, we entered into a $125 million facility with a wholly owned subsidiary of GE Capital for the sale of notes receivable originated by our timeshare business. During 2002, we completed two sales of notes receivable under the facility, totaling approximately $119 million. These transactions resulted in a gain of approximately $5 million. Also in 2002, we completed the sale of two owned, two leased and seven managed properties operating as Harrison Conference Centers for approximately $49 million. Under transition management and continuing services agreements, we provide certain services to the sold properties for terms ranging up to six years from the date of sale. We recorded a $16 million pre-tax book loss on the sale. However, the sale generated a capital gain for tax purposes, which enabled us to utilize existing capital loss tax carryforwards that had been fully reserved in prior periods. The transaction, including the impact of the reduction of the valuation allowance associated with the capital loss tax carryforwards, resulted in a $16 million book tax benefit. Thus, on an after-tax basis, the sale had no impact on reported net income. The total pre-tax loss on asset dispositions and other of $14 million in 2002 represents the $11 million net pre-tax loss on the aforementioned asset sales and a loss of approximately $3 million primarily as a result of writing off the value assigned to several long-term management and franchise agreements which were terminated during the year.

CNL Transactions

In the fourth quarter of 2002, we entered into a partnership with CNL Hospitality Corp. to acquire seven hotel properties. The partnership acquired the 500-room Doubletree at Lincoln Centre in Dallas, Texas and the 428-room Sheraton El Conquistador Resort and Country Club in Tucson, Arizona in December 2002. Both properties were converted to the Hilton brand. In connection with the formation of the joint venture, we contributed $11 million to the partnership in December 2002.

In the first quarter of 2003, we contributed the 437-room Hilton Rye Town in Rye Brook, New York and CNL contributed the 630-room Doubletree Crystal City in Arlington, Virginia to the partnership. The gain resulting from our contribution of the Hilton Rye Town totaling approximately $35 million has been deferred and will be recognized over the ten-year life of the long-term management contract retained on the property. Also in the first quarter of 2003, the partnership acquired the 257-suite Embassy Suites Santa Clara in Santa Clara, California, the 267-suite Embassy Suites Crystal City in Arlington, Virginia, and the 174-suite Embassy Suites Orlando Airport in Orlando, Florida. We operate all seven hotels under long-term management contracts and have a 25% ownership interest in the partnership.

In connection with the structuring of the CNL partnership, including our contribution of the Hilton Rye Town, we received a cash distribution totaling approximately $46 million in the 2003 first quarter. This distribution is reflected as proceeds from asset dispositions in the accompanying consolidated statements of cash flow. In addition, the tax gain resulting from the contribution of the Hilton Rye Town enabled us to utilize capital loss tax carryforwards, resulting in a reduction in our provision for income taxes totaling approximately $4 million.

In the fourth quarter of 2003, we entered into another partnership with CNL to own two hotel properties. We contributed the 544-room Capital Hilton in Washington, D.C. and the 394-room Hilton La Jolla Torrey Pines outside of San Diego, California to the partnership. The gain resulting from our contribution of the two hotels totaling approximately $57 million has been deferred and will be recognized over the ten-year life of the long-term management contracts retained on the properties. We have a 25% ownership interest in the partnership. In connection with this transaction, we received a distribution from the partnership of approximately $190 million. This distribution is reflected as proceeds from asset dispositions in the accompanying consolidated statements of cash flow. This transaction also resulted in tax gains that enabled us to utilize capital loss tax carryforwards, resulting in a reduction in our provision for income taxes totaling approximately $22 million.

NOTE 4: IMPAIRMENT LOSS AND RELATED COSTS

Results in 2004 include impairment loss and related costs totaling $5 million. This pre-tax charge is to reduce the value of an owned hotel to its estimated fair value and is included in Hotel Ownership segment results.

Results in 2003 include impairment loss and related costs totaling $22 million. These costs include a $17 million pre-tax charge related to the decline in value of certain equity securities held by us. The decline in value of the securities was deemed to be other-than-temporary in the 2003 first quarter, thus requiring an earnings charge, primarily based on the length of time the securities had traded below cost. The 2003 charge also includes a $5 million pre-tax charge to reduce the value of an owned hotel and a management contract to their respective fair values. The write-down of the hotel and management contract are included in Hotel Ownership and Managing and Franchising segment results, respectively, while the charge related to the marketable securities is included in corporate and other unallocated expenses in our reported segment results.

Results in 2002 include a charge of $21 million for mold remediation in certain areas of the Hilton Hawaiian Village. The charge includes approximately $17 million for remediation efforts at the property's Kalia Tower, which is included in our Hotel Ownership segment, and approximately $4 million for remediation efforts at the Lagoon Tower timeshare development.

NOTE 5: INVENTORIES

Included in inventories at December 31, 2003 and 2004 are unsold intervals at our vacation ownership properties of $180 million and $132 million, respectively. Inventories are valued at the lower of cost or estimated net realizable value.

NOTE 6: INVESTMENTS AND NOTES RECEIVABLE

Investments and notes receivable at December 31, 2003 and 2004 are as follows:

(in millions)	2003	2004
Equity investments		
Hotels	$ 274	276
Other	28	49
Timeshare notes receivable, with an average rate of 12.9%, due 2005 to 2014	165	262
Other notes receivable, with an average rate of 6.3%, due 2005 to 2015	71	88
Marketable securities	21	27
Other investments	31	1
	590	703
Less current portion of notes receivable	(32)	(68)
Total	558	635

Notes receivable are reflected net of allowances for uncollectible amounts of $11 million and $18 million as of December 31, 2003 and 2004, respectively.

Our investments in unconsolidated affiliates accounted for under the equity method totaled $302 million and $325 million at December 31, 2003 and 2004, respectively, representing approximately four percent of total assets at the end of 2003 and 2004. At December 31, 2004, our unconsolidated affiliates accounted for under the equity method had total assets of approximately $2.52 billion and total debt of approximately $1.34 billion. Of the $1.34 billion of total debt, $1.31 billion is secured solely by the affiliate's assets or is guaranteed by other partners without recourse to us. We are the creditor on $50 million of the $1.34 billion of debt.

NOTE 7: PROPERTY AND EQUIPMENT

Property and equipment at December 31, 2003 and 2004 are as follows:

(in millions)	2003	2004
Land	$ 535	513
Buildings and leasehold improvements	3,587	3,650
Furniture and equipment	846	829
Property held for sale or development	40	46
Construction in progress	14	20
	5,022	5,058
Less accumulated depreciation	(1,381)	(1,548)
Total	$3,641	3,510

NOTE 8: ACCOUNTS PAYABLE AND ACCRUED EXPENSES

Accounts payable and accrued expenses at December 31, 2003 and 2004 are as follows:

(in millions)	2003	2004
Accounts andnotes payable	$ 84	95
Accrued compensation and benefits	147	150
Deposits	21	42
Accrued property	29	28
Accrued interest	35	35
Insurance reserves	37	45
Other accrued expenses	200	216
Total	$ 553	611

NOTE 9: LONG-TERM DEBT

Long-term debt at December 31, 2003 and 2004 is as follows:

(in millions)	2003	2004
Industrial development revenue bonds at adjustable rates, due 2015	$ 82	82
Senior notes, with an average rate of 7.6%, due 2007 to 2031[1]	2,049	2,045
7% Senior notes, due 2004[2]	325	—
Mortgage notes, 4.8% to 8.6%, due 2006 to 2022[1]	348	341
7.95% Collateralized borrowings, due 2010	479	471
Chilean inflation-indexed note, effective rate of 7.65%, due 2009[1]	119	131
3.375% Contingently convertible senior notes due 2023	575	575
Revolving loans	160	—
Other	2	2
	4,139	3,647
Less current maturities of long-term debt	(338)	(14)
Net long-term debt	$3,801	3,633

(1) Interest rates include the impact of interest rate swaps.
(2) Represents balance assumed by Caesars Entertainment (formerly Park Place) in connection with the December 31, 1998 spin-off of our gaming business.

Interest paid, net of amounts capitalized, was $291 million, $261 million and $246 million in 2002, 2003 and 2004, respectively. Capitalized interest totaled $5 million, $7 million and $3 million in 2002, 2003 and 2004, respectively.
Debt maturities are as follows:

	(in millions)
2005	$ 14
2006	48
2007	449
2008	460
2009	346
Thereafter	2,330
Total	$3,647

In August 2003, we established a $1 billion five-year revolving credit facility, with an option to increase the size of the facility by an additional $250 million. Borrowings under this facility were completely repaid during the 2004 second quarter. The capacity under our revolver is also used to support certain outstanding letters of credit. Total revolving debt capacity of approximately $850 million was available to us at December 31, 2004.

In October 1997, we filed a shelf registration statement with the Securities and Exchange Commission registering up to $2.5 billion in debt or equity securities. At December 31, 2004, available financing under the shelf totaled $825 million. The terms of any additional securities offered under the shelf will be determined by market conditions at the time of issuance.

In connection with the spin-off in 1998 of our gaming business to a new corporation named Park Place Entertainment Corporation (subsequently renamed Caesars Entertainment, Inc.), Caesars assumed and agreed to pay 100% of the amount of each payment required to be made by us under the terms of the indentures governing our $325 million 7% Senior Notes due 2004. Caesars repaid these notes, as scheduled, in July 2004. Because these notes were our legal obligation, they are reported in our 2003 consolidated balance sheet as current maturities of long-term debt with the offsetting receivable classified in current assets.

In November 2002, we entered into a derivative contract which swaps the fixed interest payments on our $375 million 7.95% Senior Notes due 2007 to a floating interest rate equal to the six-month London Interbank Offered Rate plus 415 basis points. In connection with our $100 million 7.43% bonds due 2009 denominated in Chilean pesos, we have a derivative contract which swaps the principal payment to a fixed U.S. dollar amount of $100 million and fixed interest payments at 7.65% of that amount. We also have a derivative contract which swaps the floating rate mortgage of a majority owned hotel, with a principal balance of $34 million at December 31, 2004, to a fixed interest rate. As of December 31, 2004, approximately 13% of our long-term debt (including the impact of interest rate swaps) was floating rate debt.

Provisions under various loan agreements require us to comply with certain covenants which include limiting the amount of our outstanding indebtedness. Our revolving credit facilities contain two significant financial covenants: a leverage ratio and a debt service coverage ratio. We are in compliance with our loan covenants as of December 31, 2004.

Provisions of the financing agreement related to our 7.95% collateralized borrowings due 2010 require that certain cash reserves be maintained and also restrict the transfer of excess cash generated by the related properties to Hilton if net cash flow falls below a specified level (the cash trap). The cash trap became effective in 2003 due to reduced cash flow from the collateralized properties, primarily the Hilton San Francisco. As of December 31, 2004, cash restricted under the terms of the collateralized borrowings, including required reserves and the cash trap, totaled $97 million. The impact of the cash trap, which is expected to remain in effect throughout 2005, is not expected to have a material impact on our liquidity.

NOTE 10: FINANCIAL INSTRUMENTS

The estimated fair values of our financial instruments at December 31, 2003 and 2004 are as follows:

(in millions)	2003 Carrying Amount	2003 Fair Value	2004 Carrying Amount	2004 Fair Value
Cash and equivalents and long-term marketable securities	$ 30	30	330	330
Restricted cash	73	73	163	163
Timeshare notes receivable (including current portion)	165	169	262	265
Other notes receivable (including current portion)	71	70	88	89
Derivative assets	26	26	44	44
Long-term debt (including current maturities)	(4,139)	(4,464)	(3,647)	(4,088)
Derivative liabilities	(2)	(2)	(1)	(1)

Cash Equivalents, Long-Term Marketable Securities and Restricted Cash

The fair value of cash equivalents, long-term marketable securities and restricted cash is estimated based on the quoted market price of the investments.

Timeshare and Other Notes Receivable

The estimated fair value of timeshare and other notes receivable is based on recent market prices or the expected future cash flows discounted at risk adjusted rates.

Long-Term Debt

The estimated fair value of long-term debt is based on the quoted market prices for the same or similar issues or on the current rates offered to us for debt of the same remaining maturities.

Derivative Instruments

The fair value of derivative assets and liabilities is based on the present value of estimated future cash flow, including the use of foreign currency forward exchange rates, as appropriate.

NOTE 11: INCOME TAXES

The provision for income taxes for the three years ended December 31 are as follows:

(in millions)	2002	2003	2004
Current			
Federal	$ 129	77	114
State, foreign and local	20	16	25
	149	93	139
Deferred	(68)	(40)	(12)
Total	$ 81	53	127

During 2002, 2003 and 2004, we paid income taxes of $58 million, $44 million and $99 million, respectively, net of refunds received.

The income tax effects of temporary differences between financial and income tax reporting that gave rise to deferred income tax assets and liabilities at December 31, 2003 and 2004 are as follows:

(in millions)	2003	2004
Deferred tax assets		
Compensation	$ 75	96
Insurance	49	49
Franchise system funds	17	13
Reserves	20	23
NOL carryforwards, expiring 2005 to 2008	1	1
Capital loss carryforward, expiring 2006	14	6
Other	—	3
	176	191
Valuation allowance	(19)	(10)
	157	181
Deferred tax liabilities		
Basis difference	(187)	(168)
Property	(181)	(194)
Investments	(86)	(107)
Brand value	(378)	(378)
Deferred income	(4)	(1)
Accrued interest expense	(9)	(20)
Other	(9)	(9)
	(854)	(877)
Net deferred tax liability	$ (697)	(696)

The reconciliations of the Federal income tax rate to our effective tax rate for the three years ended December 31 are as follows:

	2002	2003	2004
Federal income tax rate	35.0%	35.0	35.0
Increase (reduction) in taxes			
State and local income taxes, net of Federal			
tax benefits	1.5	.8	4.7
Foreign taxes, net	2.0	2.3	1.3
Federal income tax credits	(2.9)	(3.8)	(4.3)
Change in deferred tax asset valuation allowance	(8.4)	(13.3)	(2.3)
Option exercises	—	4.4	—
Refund claim	—	(2.8)	—
Other	1.2	1.2	(.4)
Effective tax rate	28.4%	23.8	34.0

Capital loss tax carryforwards available to offset future capital gains are recorded as deferred tax assets and are fully reserved until evidence indicates it is more likely than not that the benefit will be realized. The deferred tax assets related to capital loss tax carryforwards are fully reserved at December 31, 2004.

Our tax provision, deferred taxes and effective rate in 2004 were impacted by a reduction in the valuation allowance for capital loss tax carryforwards, primarily as a result of the sale of three Doubletree properties and the sale of our interest in Travelweb. The 2004 effective rate also reflects the utilization of Section 29 synthetic fuel production credits. Excluding the impact of these items, our effective rate in 2004 was 38%.

Our tax provision, deferred taxes and effective rate in 2003 were impacted by a reduction in the valuation allowance for capital loss tax carryforwards, primarily as a result of the transactions with CNL. In addition, our tax provision, deferred taxes and effective rate were impacted by a reduction in the valuation allowance for capital loss tax carryforwards due to higher than expected utilization on our 2002 Federal tax return filed in 2003, as well as a settlement relating to a tax liability associated with a prior year tax return. These items resulted in a reduction of the tax provision and effective rate in 2003. These benefits were partially offset by the write-off of an unutilized deferred tax asset resulting from a stock option exercise. Excluding the impact of these items, our effective rate in 2003 was 35%.

Deferred taxes were also impacted in 2003 by the settlement and closure of certain tax audits and the adjustment of certain deferred tax balances, each related to our acquisition of Promus Hotel Corporation in 1999. In accordance with the provisions of FAS 109, these changes in estimates were reflected as an adjustment of goodwill related to the Promus acquisition and did not impact the tax provision in 2003. These adjustments resulted in a reduction of both goodwill and deferred income taxes and other liabilities totaling approximately $48 million.

Our tax provision, deferred taxes and effective rate in 2002 were impacted by asset sales, which generated capital gains for tax purposes, enabling us to utilize capital loss tax carryforwards generated by the Red Lion sale in 2001. The reduction of the valuation allowance for capital loss tax carryforwards resulted in a reduction of the tax provision and effective rate in 2002. Also in 2002, our tax provision, deferred taxes and effective rate were impacted by higher than expected utilization of capital loss tax carryforwards on our 2001 Federal tax return filed in 2002. This reduction in the valuation allowance for capital loss tax carryforwards also resulted in a reduction of the tax provision and effective rate for 2002. Excluding the impact of asset sales and the impact of the higher utilization of capital loss tax carryforwards on our 2001 Federal tax return, our effective rate in 2002 was 37%.

NOTE 12: STOCKHOLDERS' EQUITY

Five hundred million shares of common stock with a par value of $2.50 per share are authorized, of which 389 million and 399 million were issued at December 31, 2003 and 2004, respectively, including treasury shares of eight million in 2003 and ten million in 2004. We have 25 million shares of preferred stock with a par value of $1.00 per share authorized for issuance. No preferred shares were issued or outstanding at December 31, 2003 and 2004.

Our Board of Directors has approved our repurchase of up to 20 million shares of our common stock pursuant to a stock repurchase program. The timing of stock purchases are made at the discretion of management. An aggregate of 10.7 million shares had been repurchased under this program prior to 2004. During 2004, we repurchased approximately 2.3 million shares of our common stock for a total cost of approximately $48 million. No shares were repurchased during 2002 and 2003. As of December 31, 2004, approximately 7.0 million shares remained authorized for repurchase under this authority. In March 2005, we announced that our Board of Directors authorized the repurchase of up to an additional 50 million shares of common stock under the repurchase program.

We have a Preferred Share Purchase Rights Plan under which a right is attached to each share of our common stock. The rights may only become exercisable under certain circumstances involving actual or potential acquisitions of 20% or more of our common stock by certain people or groups. Depending on the circumstances, if the rights become exercisable, the holder may be entitled to purchase units of our junior participating preferred stock, shares of our common stock or shares of common stock of the acquiror. The rights remain in existence until November 2009 unless they are terminated, exercised or redeemed.

NOTE 13: STOCK PLANS

At December 31, 2004, 49 million shares of common stock were reserved for issuance under our stock incentive plans. We have three active stock plans with substantially identical terms that allow the grant of options plus the 2004 Omnibus Equity Compensation Plan, which was approved in 2004 and allows the grant of options, stock units, performance units, and other stock-based awards. No stock options were granted in 2004. See "Note 2: Summary of Significant Accounting Policies—Stock-Based Compensation" for discussion of restricted stock awards in 2004.

Options may be granted to salaried officers, directors and other key employees to purchase our common stock at not less than the fair market value at the date of grant. Generally, options vest over a four year period, contingent upon continued employment, and remain outstanding for ten years from the date of grant. Options may generally be exercised in installments commencing one year after the date of grant. At December 31, 2004, there were 28 million shares authorized for issuance under the 2004 plan and no authorized shares remaining available for grant under the other three stock plans.

A summary of the status of our stock option plans as of December 31, 2002, 2003 and 2004, and changes during the years ending on those dates, is presented below:

	Options Price Range (per share)	Weighted Average Price (per share)	Options Outstanding	Available for Grant
Balance at December 31, 2001	$ 6.66– 27.53	$ 13.44	32,531,136	24,287,594
Granted	11.85–13.95	11.86	7,469,400	(7,469,400)
Exercised	6.66–14.84	9.86	(1,455,096)	—
Cancelled	6.66–20.66	12.40	(1,654,675)	1,624,900
Balance at December 31, 2002	6.66–27.53	13.33	36,890,765	18,443,094
Granted	11.87–13.40	11.88	7,144,775	(7,144,775)
Exercised	6.66–16.23	11.46	(9,542,341)	—
Cancelled	6.66–19.65	13.27	(1,248,825)	1,209,025
Balance at December 31, 2003	6.66–27.53	13.56	33,244,374	12,507,344
Authorized			—	30,000,000
Granted			—	(2,325,979)
Exercised	6.66–19.65	12.68	(10,337,449)	—
Cancelled	6.66–20.66	12.12	(1,292,425)	(12,496,515)
Balance at December 31, 2004	6.66–27.53	14.06	21,614,500	27,684,850

The following table summarizes information about stock options outstanding at December 31, 2004:

	Options Outstanding			Options Exercisable	
Exercise Price	Number Outstanding	Weighted Average Remaining Contractual Life	Weighted Average Exercise Price	Number Exercisable	Weighted Average Exercise Price
$ 6.66–9.81	1,717,614	4.8	$9.16	1,717,614	$9.16
10.48–11.87	10,776,728	7.6	11.85	2,981,892	11.84
12.22–18.30	5,934,308	4.4	13.84	4,880,082	14.19
18.38–27.53	3,185,850	3.7	24.59	1,185,850	19.63
6.66–27.53	21,614,500	5.9	14.06	10,765,438	13.33

NOTE 14: EMPLOYEE BENEFIT PLANS

We have a noncontributory retirement plan (Basic Plan) which covers many of our non-union employees. Benefits are based upon years of service and compensation, as defined. The annual measurement date for the Basic Plan is December 31. Since December 31, 1996, employees have not accrued additional benefits under the Basic Plan. Therefore, the projected benefit obligation is equal to the accumulated benefit obligation, and both are referred to simply as the "benefit obligation" below. Plan assets will be used to pay benefits due employees for service through December 31, 1996. As employees have not accrued additional benefits since 1996, we do not utilize a rate of compensation increase assumption in calculating our benefit obligation. The assumptions used to determine our benefit obligations at December 31, 2003 and 2004 are as follows:

	2003	2004
Discount Rate	6.00%	5.50

The rollforwards of our benefit obligations and fair value of plan assets for the years ended December 31, 2003 and 2004 are as follows:

(in millions)	2003	2004
Benefit obligation at beginning of year	$ 257	297
Interest cost	18	18
Actuarial loss	39	27
Benefits paid	(17)	(18)
Benefit obligation at end of year	$ 297	324

(in millions)	2003	2004
Fair value of plan assets at beginning of year	$ 262	278
Actual return on plan assets	33	28
Benefits paid	(17)	(18)
Fair value of plan assets at end of year	$ 278	288

The investment objectives for the Basic Plan are preservation of capital, current income and long-term growth of capital. Substantially all plan assets are managed by outside investment managers. Asset allocations are reviewed quarterly. Equity securities are primarily S&P 500 and S&P 400 index funds. Equity securities include Hilton common stock in the amounts of $14 million and $10 million at December 31, 2003 and 2004, respectively, representing approximately 5% and 3% of total plan assets in each period. Debt securities are primarily U.S. Treasury and government agency debt securities. The expected long-term return on plan assets is based on the following assumed rates of return for the assets held: 4% to 7% for government debt securities and 8% to 10% for U.S. common stocks. The asset allocations for the Basic Plan, as a percentage of total plan assets at December 31, 2003 and 2004, are as follows:

(in millions)	2003	2004
Equity securities	50%	56
Debt securities	50	44
Total	100%	100

The following table provides a reconciliation between the funded status of the Basic Plan and the accrued benefit cost liability on the balance sheet for the years ended December 31, 2003 and 2004, as well as the other components recognized in our consolidated balance sheets:

(in millions)	2003	2004
Funded status	$ (19)	(36)
Unrecognized actuarial loss	12	32
Unamortized prior service cost	5	4
Accrued benefit cost	(2)	—
Intangible assets	5	4
Additional minimum liability	(16)	(36)
Accumulated other comprehensive loss, excluding tax impact	11	32
Net amount recognized	$ (2)	—

Comprehensive income includes net adjustments of $7 million and $13 million, reflecting increases of $11 million and $21 million related to the minimum pension liability, net of the deferred tax impact, for 2003 and 2004, respectively. There was no such adjustment in 2002.

As described above, employees have not accrued additional benefits under the Basic Plan since 1996. Therefore, we do not utilize a rate of compensation increase assumption in calculating the net periodic benefit cost. The key actuarial assumptions used to determine the annual benefit cost for the years ended December 31, 2002, 2003 and 2004 are as follows:

	2002	2003	2004
Discount Rate	7.00%	6.75	6.00
Expected long-term return on plan assets	7.25	7.25	7.25

Our annual benefit cost (income) for the years ended December 31, 2002, 2003 and 2004 consisted of the following:

	2002	2003	2004
Expected return on plan assets	$ 19	20	20
Interest cost	(16)	(18)	(18)
Amortization of prior service cost	(1)	(1)	(1)
Amortization of net gain	3	—	—
Net annual benefit income	$ 5	1	1

We do not expect to make any contribution to the Basic Plan in 2005. As of December 31, 2004, the benefits expected to be paid in the next five fiscal years and in the aggregate for the five fiscal years thereafter are as follows:

	(in millions)
2005	$ 17
2006	17
2007	18
2008	18
2009	18
2010–2014	96

We also have plans covering qualifying employees and non-officer directors (Supplemental Plans). Benefits for the Supplemental Plans are based upon years of service and compensation, as defined. Since December 31, 1996, employees and non-officer directors have not accrued additional benefits under the Supplemental Plans. These plans are self-funded by us and therefore have no plan assets isolated to pay benefits due employees. As of December 31, 2003 and 2004, these plans have benefit obligations of $9 million for both years, which are fully accrued in our consolidated balance sheets. Pension expense under the Supplemental Plans for the years ended December 31, 2002, 2003 and 2004 was not significant.

Certain employees are covered by union sponsored, collectively bargained multi-employer pension plans. We contributed and charged to expense $18 million per year for the years ended December 31, 2002 and 2003 and $19 million in 2004 for such plans. Information from the plans' administrators is not sufficient to permit us to determine our share, if any, of unfunded vested benefits.

We have various employee investment plans whereby we contribute certain percentages of employee contributions. The aggregate expense under these plans totaled $11 million in 2002 and $12 million in both 2003 and 2004.

NOTE 15: SEGMENT INFORMATION

Our operations consist of three reportable segments which are based on similar products or services: Hotel Ownership, Managing and Franchising, and Timeshare. The Hotel Ownership segment derives revenue primarily from owned, majority owned and leased hotel properties. The Managing and Franchising segment provides services including hotel management and licensing of our family of brands to franchisees. This segment generates its revenue from fees charged to hotel owners. The Timeshare segment consists of multi-unit timeshare resorts. This segment produces its results from the sale and financing of timeshare intervals and operating timeshare resorts. Segment results are presented net of consolidating eliminations for fee based services at the operating income level, without allocating corporate expenses, which is the basis used by management to evaluate segment performance.

Segment assets as of December 31 are as follows:

(in millions)	2003	2004
Assets		
Hotel Ownership	$5,001	4,825
Managing and Franchising	2,048	2,112
Timeshare	425	507
Corporate and other	709	798
Total assets	$8,183	8,242

Segment results for the three years ended December 31 are as follows:

	2002	2003	2004
Revenue			
Hotel Ownership	$2,239	2,167	2,215
Managing and Franchising	1,281	1,307	1,510
Timeshare	296	345	421
	$3,816	3,819	4,146
Operating income			
Hotel Ownership	$ 412	343	394
Managing and Franchising	278	284	343
Timeshare	73	82	99
Corporate and other unallocated expenses	(160)	(194)	(178)
Total operating income	603	515	658
Interest and dividend income	43	29	26
Interest expense	(328)	(295)	(274)
Net interest from unconsolidated affiliates and non-controlled interests	(19)	(20)	(26)
Net loss on asset dispositions and other	(14)	(6)	(5)
Loss from non-operating affiliates	—	—	(6)
Income before taxes and minority and non-controlled interests	285	223	373
Provision for income taxes	(81)	(53)	(127)
Minority and non-controlled interests, net	(6)	(6)	(8)
Net Income	$ 198	164	238

At December 31, 2004, the Hotel Ownership segment includes goodwill and brand values totaling $609 million and $98 million, respectively, and the Managing and Franchising segment includes goodwill and brand values totaling $631 million and $872 million, respectively.

NOTE 16: LEASES

We lease hotel properties and land under operating leases. As of December 31, 2004, we leased seven hotels. Our hotel leases require the payment of rent equal to the greater of a minimum rent or percentage rent based on a percentage of revenue or income, and expire through December 2020, with varying renewal options. Our land leases represent ground leases for certain owned hotels and, in addition to minimum rental payments, may require the payment of additional rents based on varying percentages of revenue or income. Total rent expense incurred under our leases was $55 million, $54 million and $57 million in 2002, 2003 and 2004, respectively, which included minimum rent payments of $37 million, $39 million and $41 million in 2002, 2003 and 2004, respectively.

Minimum lease commitments under non-cancelable operating leases are as follows:

(in millions)	
2005	$ 38
2006	35
2007	34
2008	31
2009	30
Thereafter	541
	$ 709

NOTE 17: COMMITMENTS AND CONTINGENCIES

We have established franchise financing programs with third party lenders to support the growth of our Hilton Garden Inn, Homewood Suites by Hilton, Hampton and Embassy Suites hotels. As of December 31, 2004, we have provided guarantees of $38 million on loans outstanding under the programs. In addition, we have guaranteed $37 million of debt and other obligations of unconsolidated affiliates and third parties, bringing our total guarantees to approximately $75 million. Our outstanding guarantees have terms of one to seven years. We also have commitments under letters of credit totaling $64 million as of December 31, 2004. In April 2004, we funded a loan guarantee of approximately $9 million and recorded a corresponding receivable from the party for which we funded the guarantee. Based on remedies available to us upon an event of default by the borrower, we believe that the receivable related to this funding should be fully realized. We believe it is unlikely that other material payments will be required under these agreements.

In addition, we remain a guarantor on 12 operating leases sold to WestCoast Hospitality Corporation as part of the sale of the Red Lion hotel chain in 2001. However, we have entered into an indemnification and reimbursement agreement with WestCoast, which requires WestCoast to reimburse us for any costs and expenses incurred in connection with the guarantee. The minimum lease commitment under these 12 operating leases totals approximately $5 million annually through 2020.

We have also provided performance guarantees to certain owners of hotels we operate under management contracts. Most of these guarantees allow us to terminate the contract rather than fund shortfalls if specified performance levels are not achieved. In limited cases, we are obligated to fund performance shortfalls. At December 31, 2004, we have two contracts containing performance guarantees with possible cash outlays totaling approximately $178 million through 2012. Funding under these performance guarantees totaled approximately $4 million in 2004, and is expected to total approximately $5 million in 2005. Funding under these guarantees in future periods is dependent on the operating performance levels of these hotels over the remaining term of the performance guarantee. Although we anticipate that the future operating performance levels of these hotels will be largely achieved, there can be no assurance that this will be the case. In addition, we do not anticipate losing a significant number of management contracts in 2005 pursuant to these guarantees.

Our consolidated financial statements at December 31, 2004 include liabilities of approximately $6 million for potential obligations under our outstanding guarantees. Under certain circumstances, we may be obligated to provide additional guarantees or letters of credit totaling $5 million at December 31, 2004.

At December 31, 2004, we had contractual commitments of approximately $76 million for construction and renovation projects at certain owned and majority owned properties, including timeshare.

We are subject to litigation in the ordinary course of our business. Management believes that resolution of pending litigation against us will not have a material adverse effect on our financial position or results of operations.

Chapter 7 Outline

Control Accounts and Subsidiary Ledgers
Specialized Journals
    Sales Journal
    Cash Receipts Journal
    Purchases Journal
    Cash Disbursements Journal
General Ledger
General Journal
Payroll Journal
Specialized Journals for Lodging
   Operations
Computerized Systems
    Hardware
    Software
    Hotel Computer Systems

Competencies

1. Define *control account* and *subsidiary ledger* and describe the relationship between them. (pp. 261–264)

2. Explain the functions of specialized journals, including sales journals, cash receipts journals, purchases journals, and cash disbursements journals. (pp. 264–274)

3. Describe the general ledger, the general journal, the payroll journal, and specialized journals for the lodging industry. (pp. 274–280)

4. Explain features and functions of computerized accounting systems and property management systems. (pp. 280–281)

7

Specialized Journals and Subsidiary Ledgers

THE MANUAL ACCOUNTING SYSTEM discussed in this chapter uses several specialized journals and subsidiary ledgers. The addition of these specialized journals and subsidiary ledgers to a manual system results in greater efficiency. In manual systems, each transaction is recorded in a general journal and posted individually to general ledger accounts. Specialized journals allow for vastly reduced postings, and specialized ledgers allow for a much smaller general ledger.

However, the complete manual accounting system we describe in this chapter is less efficient than an automatic system, so we will briefly discuss the highly computerized accounting systems prevalent in hospitality businesses today. Remember, though, that to thoroughly understand a fully automated accounting system, one must first understand the basics of a manual system.

We will use the Sample Restaurant to illustrate a complete manual accounting system that uses special journals and subsidiary ledgers. This food service facility has 50 seats and is open six days of the week. Some customers choose to pay cash for food, while others pay with credit cards.

Control Accounts and Subsidiary Ledgers

When a hospitality business has only a few guests and suppliers, it can establish separate accounts for each in its general ledger. However, as a business grows and its number of guests and suppliers increases, the business operates more efficiently if it sets up **control accounts** in its general ledger for accounts receivable and accounts payable. That is, all transactions affecting guest accounts are debited or credited to a single control account, Accounts Receivable, in the general ledger. A hospitality business can also establish a **subsidiary ledger** of accounts receivable to account for the activities of each guest. Likewise, the hospitality business can establish a single control account, Accounts Payable, for recording all transactions with suppliers, as well as a subsidiary ledger of accounts payable to account for business activities with each individual supplier.

Thus, the balance of the Accounts Receivable control account in the general ledger *must* equal the sum of the balances of individual guest accounts in the **accounts receivable subsidiary ledger**. Likewise, the balance of the Accounts Payable control account in the general ledger *must* equal the sum of the supplier accounts in the **accounts payable subsidiary ledger**.

The subsidiary ledger accounts provide the detail for each account. For example, assume Mary Jones, a previous guest, charged three nights' stay at $40 per night on April 30. The accounts receivable subsidiary ledger would contain an account for Mary Jones reflecting the $120 charge for the three days of her stay (April 27–29). The $120 charge would be included in the total of the Accounts Receivable account in the general ledger along with amounts due from other current and past guests.

Further assume in our example that this motel had four other outstanding accounts receivable. The T-accounts for the guests from the subsidiary ledger and the accounts receivable from the general ledger would look like this:

Control Ledger
General Ledger

Accounts Receivable—Trade

20X1	
Apr. 30 (balance)	600

Accounts Receivable Subsidiary Ledger

Bill Adams

20X1	
Apr. 30 (balance)	160

Fred Dills

20X1	
Apr. 30 (balance)	80

Mary Jones

20X1	
Apr. 30 (balance)	120

Walter Miller

20X1	
Apr. 30 (balance)	160

Barb Smith		
20X1		
Apr. 30 (balance)	80	

The sum of the balances of the accounts receivable accounts for guests in the accounts receivable subsidiary ledger equals the $600 balance of the Accounts Receivable—Trade control account, as shown below:

Bill Adams	$160
Fred Dills	80
Mary Jones	120
Walter Miller	160
Barb Smith	80
Total	$600

Any time a transaction affects a control account, it also affects an account in a subsidiary ledger. When the transaction is journalized, the recording must indicate which account in the subsidiary ledger is affected. Posting will be made to both the control account and the account in the subsidiary ledger. For example, assume a hotel purchases food worth $300 on account from General Foods, Inc., and records the transaction as follows:

		Post. Ref.	Debit	Credit
July 1	Food Purchases	401	$300	
	Accounts Payable—General Foods, Inc.	201/✓		$300

The food purchase amount is posted as a debit to Food Purchases (account #401) in the general ledger. Accounts Payable (account #201) in the general ledger is credited for $300, and the General Foods, Inc. account in the accounts payable subsidiary ledger is also credited for $300. The posting to the account in the accounts payable subsidiary ledger is indicated with a check mark (✓), while postings to general ledger accounts are indicated with the account number of the appropriate general ledger accounts as shown above in the Post. Ref. (posting reference) column.

The number of control accounts and subsidiary ledgers maintained by a hospitality business depends on the business's information needs. When detailed information for similar types of accounts should be maintained, a control account and related subsidiary ledger should also be established. The most common control accounts and subsidiary ledgers are for accounts receivable and accounts payable.

In the lodging segment of the hospitality industry, Accounts Receivable—Trade consists of accounts receivable for current guests and nonguests. These accounts are generally kept in two separate ledgers. The related subsidiary ledgers are typically called the *guest ledger* and the *city ledger.*

The **guest ledger** consists of accounts for guests currently staying in the lodging facility, while the **city ledger** consists of accounts for noncurrent guests and local businesses. The guest ledger is maintained in the front office and the accounts are maintained in guestroom order to facilitate posting various charges to the guest accounts. The city ledger is generally maintained in the accounting office for posting cash received on account. These separate ledgers result in greater efficiency in processing accounting transactions than a single accounts receivable subsidiary ledger would afford.

In addition to control accounts and subsidiary ledgers, hospitality firms use specialized journals. Each specialized journal is used for recording transactions of a particular nature.

Specialized Journals

The use of only the general journal to record transactions is adequate for the very smallest businesses. However, accounting systems in larger businesses are more efficient if the firms use a special journal for each type of transaction. For example, a firm might use a different specialized journal to record each type of activity, such as cash disbursements, purchases, and sales.

Several advantages of using specialized journals include increased efficiency and improvements in internal control. Increased efficiencies include:

1. Time saved in recording transactions. Just one line is used in the journal, since debits and credits are recorded in the appropriate columns and no explanation is required.

2. Time saved in posting to the ledger accounts. Transactions recorded in the general journal are posted individually to general ledger accounts. With specialized journals, column *totals*—not individual transactions—are posted to the appropriate general ledger accounts.

Specialized journals provide several safeguards that improve internal control. They reduce the potential for errors in the following ways:

1. The division of duties prevents one employee from handling any single transaction from beginning to end. For example, one employee records a meal charged in the hotel's restaurant and another posts the amount to the guest's account while a third, the cashier, collects the amount due when the guest checks out of the hotel.

2. Since the general ledger accounts have significantly fewer entries, the potential for errors in posting is greatly reduced.

Several journals are designed to systematically record the major recurring types of transactions. The following specialized journals, illustrated in this section of the chapter, pertain to the Sample Restaurant:

1. **Sales journal,** used to record sales of food on account

2. **Cash receipts journal**, used to record all cash received by the business, including cash sales, collection of accounts, and other cash inflows

3. **Purchases journal**, used to record all purchases of food on account

4. **Cash disbursements journal**, used to record all checks written by the Sample Restaurant

In addition, the Sample Restaurant uses a general journal to record transactions and activities that are not recorded in one of the specialized journals. The Sample Restaurant uses the general journal to record adjusting and closing entries.

The various ledger account pages contain a posting reference column. The accounting employee records the sources of the postings in this column. For example, the employee writes an *S* in this column if the transaction was originally recorded in the sales journal. Businesses commonly use the following abbreviations in the posting reference column for the five journals:

Journal	Abbreviation
Sales journal	S
Cash receipts journal	CR
Purchases journal	P
Cash disbursements journal	CD
General journal	GJ

Each entry in these specialized journals must be supported by evidence that proves that the transaction did occur. For example, each charge sale must be supported by a server check that indicates the date, the amount of the sale, the food sold to the customer, and the customer's signature acknowledging the purchase. Required documentation might also include a supplier invoice to support each cash disbursement. The supplier invoice would reveal the date of the purchase, the invoice number, the items purchased, and the amount of the purchase.

Sales Journal

Sales in most hospitality businesses may be either cash or *charge* (also known as *credit*) sales. The sales journal is used to record the charge sales, while cash sales are recorded in the cash receipts journal (discussed in the next section of this chapter). The sales journal of the Sample Restaurant has the following column headings:

Date	Customer	Server Check No.	Accts. Rec. Dr. 105 Sales Cr. 301	
			Amount	✓

The date of the sale is recorded in the Date column. The customer's name is recorded to show which accounts receivable subsidiary ledger account is to be debited by the amount of the sales transaction. The number of the server check that documents the sale is recorded in the Server Check Number column. The Accounts Receivable and Sales column is for recording the amount due the Sample

Restaurant and the amount of the sale. A check mark is placed in the "✓" column when the amount is posted to the customer's account in the subsidiary ledger.

Exhibit 1 shows the Sample Restaurant's sales journal for May. Remember, only charge sales are recorded in this journal, while cash sales are recorded in the cash receipts journal. The sales journal shows that only five charge sales were made during May. The name of each customer making a food purchase was recorded in the sales journal, along with the server check number and the amount. (Other server checks were used in cash sales.) A check was placed in the "✓" column as each amount was posted to the customer's account. To ensure that customers' accounts are updated, amounts are posted daily to them. The posting reference of *S1* (*sales* journal, page 1) is entered by each posting in the customer's account and also by the totals posted to general ledger accounts. The total of $219.57 for the month was posted at the end of May to the general ledger accounts—as a debit to Accounts Receivable (account #105) and as a credit to Sales (account #301). These two account numbers are written in the sales journal under the total amount of $219.57 to reflect the completed posting to the general ledger accounts.

As discussed previously, the total of the accounts receivable subsidiary accounts must equal the balance of the control account, Accounts Receivable. The sum of the accounts in the accounts receivable subsidiary ledger of $33.28 + $43.19 + $29.22 + $67.08 + $46.80 equals $219.57, the balance of the accounts receivable control account in the general ledger.

Cash Receipts Journal

A hospitality business uses a cash receipts journal to record all its cash inflows. The major column headings in the cash receipts journal reflect the most frequent cash transactions. Less frequent sources of cash are usually recorded in the Other Accounts columns of the cash receipts journal. The following are the Sample Restaurant's cash receipts journal column headings:

Date	Description	Cash Dr. 101	Accounts Rec. Cr. 105		Sales Cr. 301	Other Accounts Cr.			
			Amount	✓		Acct. Title	Acct. #	Amount	✓

The Date column is for recording the date of the cash receipt. The Description column allows a brief description of the activity, such as "cash sales" or "sale of capital stock." Each transaction recorded in the cash receipts journal involves cash; therefore, a cash amount will be recorded in the Cash column for each activity. The Accounts Receivable columns are for recording the amount of the cash received on account from customers and also for entering a check in the "✓" column when the amounts are posted to the customers' accounts in the accounts receivable subsidiary ledger. Customers' accounts should be posted daily to maintain current account balances. When a customer pays on account, the bookkeeper should indicate the customer's name in the Description column, such as "payment on account—Fred Weeks." The Sales column is used to record cash sales, while the Other Accounts columns are used to record all cash activities

Exhibit 1 Sales Journal

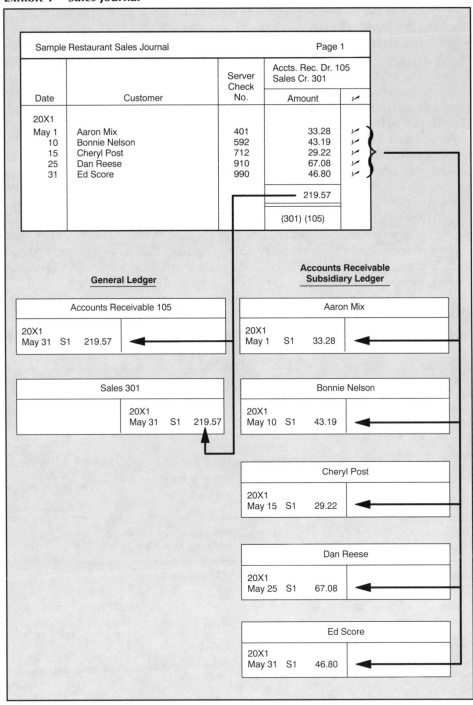

Sample Restaurant Sales Journal			Page 1		
		Server Check No.	Accts. Rec. Dr. 105 Sales Cr. 301		
Date	Customer		Amount	✔	
20X1					
May 1	Aaron Mix	401	33.28	✔	
10	Bonnie Nelson	592	43.19	✔	
15	Cheryl Post	712	29.22	✔	
25	Dan Reese	910	67.08	✔	
31	Ed Score	990	46.80	✔	
			219.57		
			(301) (105)		

General Ledger

Accounts Receivable 105	
20X1 May 31 S1 219.57	

Sales 301	
	20X1 May 31 S1 219.57

Accounts Receivable Subsidiary Ledger

Aaron Mix	
20X1 May 1 S1 33.28	

Bonnie Nelson	
20X1 May 10 S1 43.19	

Cheryl Post	
20X1 May 15 S1 29.22	

Dan Reese	
20X1 May 25 S1 67.08	

Ed Score	
20X1 May 31 S1 46.80	

other than those just described. For example, in a sale of capital stock for $1,000, Cash would be debited for $1,000, while the Capital Stock account (account #257) would be credited for $1,000.

Exhibit 2 is the Sample Restaurant's cash receipts journal for May 20X1, which shows detail only for May 1–4 and May 31. All cash receipts are recorded in this journal. The totals of the Cash, Accounts Receivable, and Sales columns are posted to the respective general ledger accounts at the end of the month. Amounts are posted to accounts in the accounts receivable subsidiary ledger on a daily basis. A check is placed in the "✓" column next to the amount in the journal when the posting is completed. Each item in the Other Accounts columns is posted individually to the appropriate general ledger account. During May, the Capital Stock account was affected when the Sample Restaurant sold 100 shares of stock for $10 each for a total of $1,000. The *total* of this column is not posted to any account, since each amount in the column is posted individually, and so indicated with a check mark.

In each ledger account, the source of the posting CR1 (for *cash receipts* journal, page *1*) is shown alongside the amount and the date. As we noted with the sales journal postings to the accounts receivable subsidiary ledger, the amounts posted to the individual accounts of $20.00 + $43.19 must equal the total of $63.19 posted to the control account in the general ledger.

The Accounts Receivable control account in the general ledger reflects a balance of $156.38 after it receives postings from the sales journal and the cash receipts journal at the end of May:

Accounts Receivable 105

20X1			20X1		
May 31	S1	219.57	May 31	CR1	63.19
May 31	(balance)	156.38			

The accounts in the Sample Restaurant's accounts receivable subsidiary ledger after postings from the sales and cash receipts journals would be as follows:

Aaron Mix

20X1			20X1		
May 1	S1	33.28	May 4	CR1	20.00
May 31	(balance)	13.28			

Bonnie Nelson

20X1			20X1		
May 10	S1	43.19	May 31	CR1	43.19
May 31	(balance)	–0–			

Exhibit 2   Cash Receipts Journal

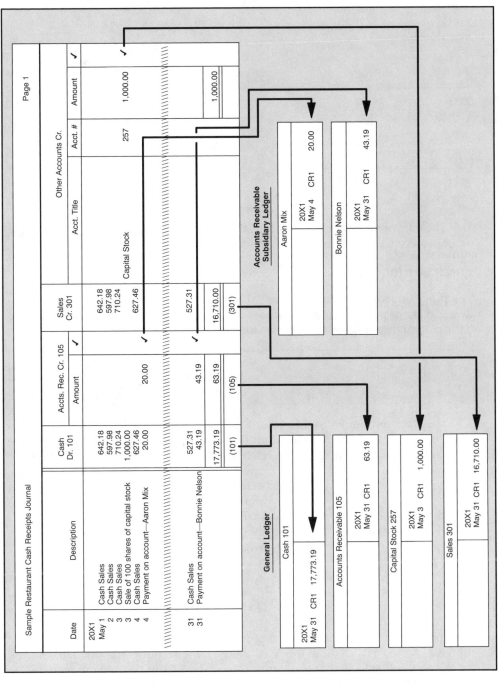

Sample Restaurant Cash Receipts Journal   Page 1

Date	Description	Cash Dr. 101	Accts. Rec. Cr. 105 Amount	✓	Sales Cr. 301	Other Accounts Cr. Acct. Title	Acct. #	Amount	✓
20X1									
May 1	Cash Sales	642.18			642.18				
2	Cash Sales	597.98			597.98				
3	Cash Sales	710.24			710.24				
3	Sale of 100 shares of capital stock	1,000.00				Capital Stock	257	1,000.00	✓
4	Cash Sales	627.46			627.46				
4	Payment on account—Aaron Mix	20.00	20.00	✓					
31	Cash Sales	527.31			527.31				
31	Payment on account—Bonnie Nelson	43.19	43.19	✓					
		17,773.19	63.19		16,710.00			1,000.00	
		(101)	(105)		(301)				

Accounts Receivable Subsidiary Ledger

Aaron Mix

20X1		
May 4	CR1	20.00

Bonnie Nelson

20X1		
May 31	CR1	43.19

General Ledger

Cash 101

20X1		
May 31	CR1	17,773.19

Accounts Receivable 105

20X1		
May 31	CR1	63.19

Capital Stock 257

20X1		
May 3	CR1	1,000.00

Sales 301

20X1		
May 31	CR1	16,710.00

	Cheryl Post	
20X1 May 15 S1	29.22	

	Dan Reese	
20X1 May 25 S1	67.08	

	Ed Score	
20X1 May 31 S1	46.80	

The total of these accounts of $156.38 is and must be equal to the balance of the accounts receivable control account in the general ledger.

Purchases Journal

The purchases journal is used to record all purchases on account. For the Sample Restaurant, the purchases on account are food items for resale. The following are the basic column headings in a purchases journal:

Date	Supplier	Invoice No.	Accts. Pay. Cr. 201 Food Purch. Dr. 401	
			Amount	✓

The Date column is used to record the date of the purchase. The supplier is listed by name, and the number from the supporting invoice is recorded in the Invoice Number column for future reference. A single column is provided for the amount since Accounts Payable is credited and Food Purchases is debited by the same amount for each transaction. Checks in the check column indicate the posting of the amount to the appropriate accounts payable account in the accounts payable subsidiary ledger. Just as the individual accounts receivable accounts are posted daily, so the individual accounts payable accounts should be posted daily to maintain up-to-date records of amounts owed. A hospitality business that purchases goods other than food for resale would use additional columns, and the Food Purchases column would be separate from accounts payable. For example, such a firm would record beverage, food, and gift shop items for resale in separate accounts, and separate columns would be used in the purchases journal.

Exhibit 3 shows the Sample Restaurant's purchases journal for May 20X1. Food purchases on account totaled $4,686.34 for May. The total of the Amount column was posted as a credit to the Accounts Payable account (account #201) and as a debit to the Food Purchases account (account #401) in the general ledger. The cross-reference noted in the ledger accounts is *P1* (for *purchases* journal, page *1*). The account numbers for these two accounts, 401 and 201, are noted under the total

Exhibit 3 Purchases Journal

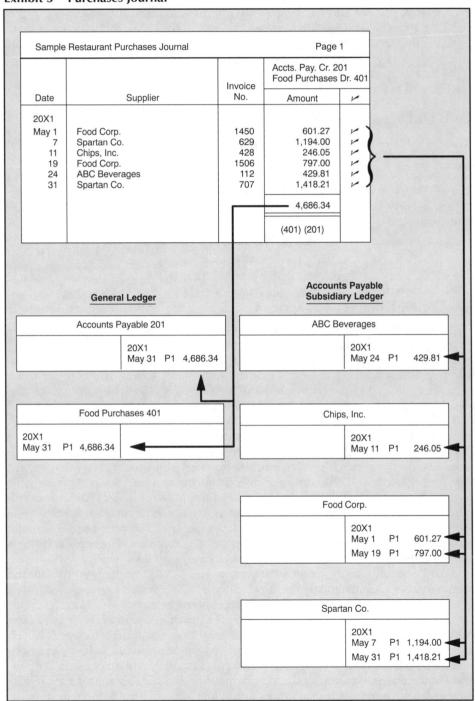

of the Amount column in the purchases journal to indicate posting of the totals. Each transaction amount has been posted to an account in the accounts payable subsidiary journal and so indicated with a check in the "✓" column of the journal. Each posting in the accounts payable subsidiary ledger account reveals the date and the source, which in this example is P1 for each amount.

The total postings to the accounts payable subsidiary ledger must equal the total posted to the Accounts Payable control account in the general ledger.

Cash Disbursements Journal

Accountants use the cash disbursements journal to record all transactions involving the payment of cash. Most hospitality businesses pay their bills by check, since this provides greater control over cash. The columns of a cash disbursement journal will vary by the business, depending on the purposes of the disbursements. A fairly simple cash disbursements journal would have the following column headings:

Date	Payee/ Description	Check No.	Cash Cr. 101	Accounts Pay. Dr. 201		Payroll Exp. Dr. 501	Other Accounts Dr.			
				Amount	✓		Acct. Title	Acct. #	Amount	✓

The Date column is for recording the date of the cash disbursement. The Payee/Description column is used for recording to whom the check is written and an explanation. For example, a payment to XYZ Corporation for its invoice #500 might be shown as "XYZ Corp., invoice #500." The Check No. column is for recording the numbers of the company's checks. (For control purposes checks should be used in numerical order. The employee writing the checks should void any unusable checks by writing *VOID* across the face of the check.) The first amount column is for cash since each transaction will involve cash. The Accounts Payable column is further divided into an amount column and a check (✓) column. The check column is used to indicate posting to the accounts payable subsidiary ledger account. In this particular journal form, a column is provided for payroll expense to record the amounts paid to employees. Finally, the last four columns pertain to accounts that will be debited. Examples of such accounts include Rent Expense, Supplies Expense, and Utilities Expense. For each transaction, the account title, account number, and amount must be recorded. The check column is used to indicate the posting to each account in the general ledger.

Exhibit 4 contains the Sample Restaurant's cash disbursements journal for the month of May. Disbursements for May totaled $11,257.56; this amount was posted as a credit to the Cash account in the general ledger. Three charge bills from suppliers of food, which were recorded earlier in the purchases journal, were paid. The Accounts Payable control account in the general ledger was debited for $2,041.32, and the individual accounts in the accounts payable subsidiary ledger were debited the day of payment so that they were kept current. Payroll Expense in the general ledger was posted for total amounts paid to Sample Restaurant employees. Businesses often maintain a separate payroll journal. Since the Sample Restaurant

Exhibit 4 Cash Disbursements Journal

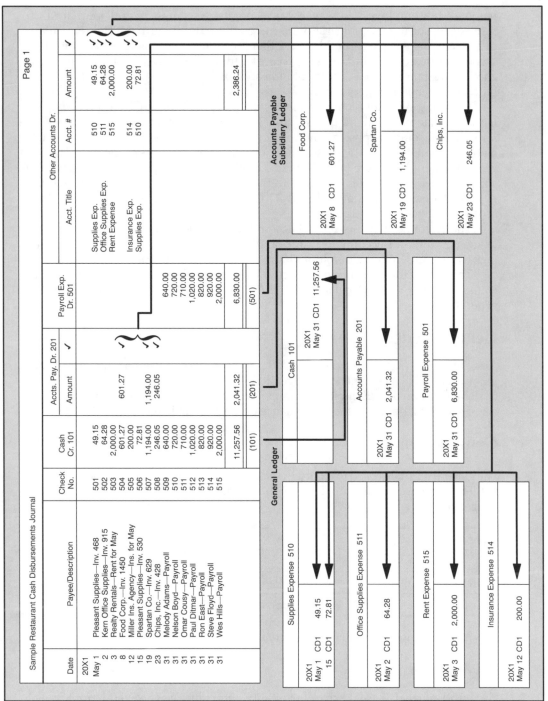

has just a few employees, however, it does not use a separate payroll journal. (The next section of the chapter briefly discusses the payroll journal.) The remaining disbursements were recorded in the Other Accounts columns. The account title, account number, and amount were recorded for each transaction. Furthermore, a check in the journal by each amount indicates that the amounts were posted to the individual general ledger accounts.

Each posting to an account indicates the date; the source, *CD1* (*cash disbursements* journal, page 1); and the amount. The total of each amount column except for Other Accounts is posted, and the account number is written below the total amount to indicate that the posting has occurred. The amounts of the three checks written to suppliers were posted to the supplier accounts in the accounts payable subsidiary ledger. The total postings to these three accounts ($601.27 + $1,194.00 + $246.05) equal the total of $2,041.32 posted to the Accounts Payable control account in the general ledger.

The Accounts Payable control account and the accounts payable subsidiary ledger accounts in T-account form appear in Exhibit 5 as they would look after postings were made from the purchases journal and the cash disbursements journal.

The sum of the accounts in the accounts payable subsidiary ledger of $2,645.02 equals the May 31, 20X1 balance of the Accounts Payable control account in the general ledger.

General Ledger

After amounts from the specialized ledgers have been posted at the end of the month, a trial balance of general ledger accounts is prepared to prove the equality of debits and credits. Exhibit 6 contains the Sample Restaurant's general ledger accounts, and Exhibit 7 is the trial balance of the general ledger accounts.

General Journal

The general journal is used to record transactions that do not fit in a specialized journal. The purchase of land with a hospitality company's stock would be recorded in the general journal as follows:

Land (Acct. #150)	$10,000	
Common Stock (Acct. #250)		$10,000
To record acquisition of land with 1,000		
shares of the company's common stock.		

All adjusting and closing entries are recorded in the general journal.

Payroll Journal

A **payroll journal** is used when hospitality companies have several employees. The column headings of a payroll journal may look like this:

Exhibit 5   Accounts Payable Control and Detailed Accounts

General Ledger

Accounts Payable Subsidiary Ledger

Accounts Payable 201	
20X1 May 31 CD1 2,041.32	20X1 May 31 P1 4,686.34
	Balance 2,645.02

ABC Beverages	
	20X1 May 24 P1 429.81
	Balance 429.81

Chips, Inc.	
20X1 May 23 CD1 246.05	20X1 May 11 P1 246.05
	Balance 0.00

Food Corp.	
20X1 May 8 CD1 601.27	20X1 May 1 P1 601.27 May 19 P1 797.00
	Balance 797.00

Spartan Co.	
20X1 May 19 CD1 1,194.00	20X1 May 7 P1 1,194.00 May 31 P1 1,418.21
	Balance 1,418.21

Date	Employee	Check No.	Salary Expense Dr. 501	Deductions			Net Pay
				Fed. Inc. Taxes Payable Cr. 207	FICA Taxes Payable Cr. 208	St. Inc. Taxes Payable Cr. 209	Payroll Cash Cr. 102

The Date column is used to record the date of each check. The employee's name is recorded in the Employee column, and the check number is recorded in the Check No. column. The gross amount of the check is recorded under Salary Expense, while deductions (for taxes due) are recorded in three columns: Federal Income Taxes Payable, FICA Taxes Payable, and State Income Taxes Payable. The

Exhibit 6 Sample Restaurant General Ledger

Account Title __Cash__   Account No. __101__

Date		Accounts/Explanation	Post. Ref.	Debit	Credit	Balance
20X1						
May	31	Cash receipts for May	CR 1	1 7 7 7 3 19		1 7 7 7 3 19
	31	Cash disbursements for May	CD 1		1 1 2 5 7 56	6 5 1 5 63

Account Title __Accounts Receivable__   Account No. __105__

Date		Accounts/Explanation	Post. Ref.	Debit	Credit	Balance
20X1						
May	31	Sales on account	S 1	2 1 9 57		2 1 9 57
	31	Collections during May	CR 1		6 3 19	1 5 6 38

Account Title __Accounts Payable__   Account No. __201__

Date		Accounts/Explanation	Post. Ref.	Debit	Credit	Balance
20X1						
May	31	Purchases on account for May	P 1		4 6 8 6 34	4 6 8 6 34
	31	Payments on account for May	CD 1	2 0 4 1 32		2 6 4 5 02

Account Title __Capital Stock__   Account No. __257__

Date		Accounts/Explanation	Post. Ref.	Debit	Credit	Balance
20X1						
May	3	Sale of 100 shares	CR 1		1 0 0 0 00	1 0 0 0 00

Account Title __Sales__   Account No. __301__

Date		Accounts/Explanation	Post. Ref.	Debit	Credit	Balance
20X1						
May	31	Sales on account	S 1		2 1 9 57	2 1 9 57
May	31	Cash sales	CR 1		1 6 7 1 0 00	1 6 9 2 9 57

Exhibit 6 *(continued)*

Account Title	Food Purchases		Account No.	401		
Date		**Accounts/Explanation**	**Post. Ref.**	**Debit**	**Credit**	**Balance**
20X1						
May	31	Purchases during May	P 1	4 6 8 6 34		4 6 8 6 34

Account Title	Payroll Expense		Account No.	501		
Date		**Accounts/Explanation**	**Post. Ref.**	**Debit**	**Credit**	**Balance**
20X1						
May	31	Payroll expense for May	CD 1	6 8 3 0 00		6 8 3 0 00

Account Title	Supplies Expense		Account No.	510		
Date		**Accounts/Explanation**	**Post. Ref.**	**Debit**	**Credit**	**Balance**
20X1						
May	1	Purchased supplies	CD 1	4 9 15		4 9 15
	15	Purchased supplies	CD 1	7 2 81		1 2 1 96

Account Title	Office Supplies Expense		Account No.	511		
Date		**Accounts/Explanation**	**Post. Ref.**	**Debit**	**Credit**	**Balance**
20X1						
May	2	Purchased office supplies	CD 1	6 4 28		6 4 28

Account Title	Insurance Expense		Account No.	514		
Date		**Accounts/Explanation**	**Post. Ref.**	**Debit**	**Credit**	**Balance**
20X1						
May	12	Insurance expense for May	CD 1	2 0 0 00		2 0 0 00

Account Title	Rent Expense		Account No.	515		
Date		**Accounts/Explanation**	**Post. Ref.**	**Debit**	**Credit**	**Balance**
20X1						
May	3	Rent expense for May	CD 1	2 0 0 0 00		2 0 0 0 00

Exhibit 7   Trial Balance

	Trial Balance		
	Sample Restaurant		
Account Title	Account Number	Debits	Credits
Cash	101	$ 6,515.63	
Accounts Receivable	105	156.38	
Accounts Payable	201		$ 2,645.02
Capital Stock	257		1,000.00
Sales	301		16,929.57
Food Purchases	401	4,686.34	
Payroll Expense	501	6,830.00	
Supplies Expense	510	121.96	
Office Supplies Expense	511	64.28	
Insurance Expense	514	200.00	
Rent Expense	515	2,000.00	
		$ 20,574.59	$ 20,574.59

difference between salary expense and the deductions is net pay, which is the amount of each check. The net pay amount is recorded in the Payroll Cash column. The only expense account shown in this payroll journal is Salary Expense, while the three liability accounts are used to record payroll tax amounts due to various governmental agencies. Payroll Cash is a checking account used only for payroll purposes. There may be many more deductions, such as those for other taxes and for life insurance, health insurance, and savings bonds. The process remains the same: salary expense less deductions equals net pay.

Specialized Journals for Lodging Operations

In lodging operations, certain specialized journals are maintained in the front office for recording transactions involving guests. The three journals we'll discuss are the front office cash receipts and disbursements journal, the allowance journal, and the transfer journal.

The **front office cash receipts and disbursements journal** is used for recording cash transactions involving lodging guests. The column headings of this journal are as follows:

Room No.	Guest	✓	Cash Receipts			Cash Disbursements		
			Cash Debit	Credits		Cash Credit	Debit	
				Guest	City		Guest	City

The room number pertains to the lodging guest's room number, while the guest's name is recorded to show which guest account in one of the subsidiary ledgers should be debited or credited for the activity. The posting reference column indicates that the amount has been posted to the guest account in the subsidiary ledger. Cash receipts received from current or former guests are recorded in the Cash column. The credit is recorded under either the guest or city columns, depending on where the guest's ledger account is located. Cash disbursements for specific guests, such as payments for packages received COD, are also recorded in this journal. The amount expended is debited to the guest's account and recorded in the appropriate column (Guest or City, depending on the location of the guest's ledger account), and the Cash account is credited.

Amounts recorded in the front office cash receipts and disbursements journal should be posted as soon as possible to guests' ledger accounts to avoid unposted charges when guests check out of the lodging facility.

Allowance vouchers are recorded in the **allowance journal**. The following are the column headings of this journal:

Date	Voucher No.	Guest	Room No.	✓	Guest Cr.	City Cr.	Room Sales Allow. Dr.	Food Sales Allow. Dr.	Telephone Sales Allow. Dr.	Other Accounts Dr.			
										Acct. Title	Acct. #	Amount	✓

The Date column is used to record the date of the voucher. The allowance voucher number is recorded in the Voucher No. column. Guests' names are recorded in the Guest column, while current guests' room numbers are recorded in the Room No. column. The posting reference column indicates that the amount has been posted to the guest's ledger account. Since allowances are issued to reduce charges, a credit results in a reduction to the guest's account. The amount is recorded in the Guest or City column, depending on the location of the guest's account. The amount is also debited to a sales allowance account. This particular allowance journal form allows for debits to Room Sales Allowances, Food Sales Allowances, or Telecommunications Sales Allowances. If other accounts were to be debited, such as Beverage Sales Allowance, the amount and account number would be recorded in the two columns on the right side of this journal. The monthly totals are posted to the proper general ledger accounts.

The **transfer journal** records the transfer of one person's account to another in the same ledger or to another ledger. For example, suppose a guest checks out of the hotel and is to be billed direct. Since the individual is no longer a hotel guest, his or her account would be transferred from the guest ledger to the city ledger.

The column headings of a transfer journal would look like this:

Date	Guest	Room No.	Guest Ledger				City Ledger			
			Debit	✓	Credit	✓	Debit	✓	Credit	✓

The Date column records the date of the transfer. The guest's name and room number are recorded in the Guest and Room No. columns, respectively. The Guest Ledger Debit column is used to record transfers to an account in the guest ledger, while the Guest Ledger Credit column records transfers from an account in the guest ledger. The City Ledger columns relate to similar transfers involving accounts in the city ledger. All posting reference columns are for indicating that the amount has been recorded in the ledger account.

Computerized Systems

The accounting system described in this chapter is a manual system that uses physical journals and ledgers. In practice, however, only the smallest hospitality organizations still use such manual systems.

Instead of manual accounting systems, many hospitality organizations use fully integrated computerized systems. The major advantages of computerized accounting systems are their speed, accuracy, and efficiency. Hospitality businesses have become so large and complex that they can provide the highest possible level of services only by using computers.

Technological advances have made computers affordable for smaller hospitality businesses. Computers, commonly used for reservations and front office accounting, are now used by many accounting operations in small and medium-sized lodging and food service establishments.

Many computer systems perform real-time processing, an operating feature that processes input very quickly, updates files, and makes output immediately available on a current basis. A system of this kind is invaluable to a hotel, which may conduct business 24 hours a day, 365 days a year.

Computer systems possess two major components: hardware and software. *Hardware* is the equipment that makes up a computer system: keyboards, monitors, printers, disk drives, tape drives, and other input/output devices. *Software* refers to the instructions and programs that direct computer operations.

Hardware

The major hardware components of a microcomputer system are a central processing unit (CPU), a display screen, a keyboard, and disk drives.

The CPU is the control center of a computer system. Inside are the circuits and mechanisms that process and store information and send instructions to the other components of the system. The same physical frame that houses the CPU may also include the disk drives.

Information can be entered into or retrieved from the CPU using a keyboard similar to a typewriter keyboard. Data can be entered, updated, and recalled at will using the keyboard, a mouse, a touch-sensitive screen, or other devices.

The information requested through keyboard commands may be printed on paper by means of a printer or displayed on a *screen,* which is also called a *monitor* or *video display terminal.*

Volumes of data can be stored (filed) on storage devices such as magnetic tape units or magnetic disk units. Data stored on tape units must be in a sequential arrangement; the updating or retrieval of information on these units is time-consuming because of this sequential operation. Magnetic disks store data in an arrangement that allows random access. Magnetic disk storage units allow almost immediate posting and quick access to any record.

Software

Software programs tell the computer what to do, how to do it, and when to do it. *Applications software* refers to sets of computer programs that are designed for specific uses such as word processing, electronic spreadsheet analysis, and database management.

Today's computer systems and software programs are designed to be user-friendly—easier to operate and more efficient. Many programs have built-in options through which operators can request help from the computer itself. Computer suppliers may assist their customers by providing computer installation and employee training.

Hotel Computer Systems

Computer systems for hotel property management are as varied as the hotels they serve. They are available for both small and large hotels. Some systems are modular and can be expanded to fit the needs of the hotel and its management. A computer-based property management system (PMS) offers opportunities for improved guest services, increased employee productivity, and greater management efficiency.

Property management systems are designed to give hotel employees access to the hotel's electronic information system. Various types of computer terminals allow direct access and communication within the hotel using this information system. Users at remote locations can instantly update the hotel's accounts. Terminals are usually equipped with keyboards and display screens (and sometimes printers) and are located in vital areas of the hotel. Computer systems can be interfaced with telephone call accounting systems, point-of-sale systems, and in-house entertainment systems.

PMS applications can be divided into two broad functional areas: front office and back office applications. PMS front office applications integrate such functions as reservations, rooms management, and guest accounting within a hotel's information network. PMS back office applications typically include such functions as accounts receivable, accounts payable, payroll accounting, fixed asset accounting, financial reporting, and the general ledger.

Summary

All accounting transactions could be recorded in a general journal and posted to general ledger accounts that might include separate accounts for each guest and supplier. However, hospitality businesses are more efficient when they use specialized journals and ledgers. Businesses use a ledger of accounts for customers, generally referred to as a *subsidiary accounts receivable ledger,* for tracking charges and payments from each customer. The total of these accounts equals the total in the control account Accounts Receivable in the general ledger. Likewise, the accounts payable subsidiary ledger consists of an account for each supplier; the total of the accounts in this ledger equals the balance of the control account Accounts Payable.

Specialized journals are established to record sales, cash disbursements, cash receipts, and purchases. These journals greatly reduce the number of postings to general ledger accounts. And, as different personnel are assigned to maintaining the ledgers and journals, more effective internal control is achieved.

A hotel operation has specialized journals maintained in the front office to account for hotel guest activities. Three major specialized journals are the front office cash receipts and disbursements journal, the allowance journal, and the transfer journal.

Most of the chapter focuses on manual accounting systems. However, many of today's hospitality firms use some computerization, which makes a firm's accounting operations more efficient.

Key Terms

accounts payable subsidiary ledger—A subsidiary ledger that holds the accounts of those suppliers from which the hospitality firm purchases items on account.

accounts receivable subsidiary ledger—A subsidiary ledger that holds the accounts of those guests of the hospitality firm who purchase things on account.

allowance journal—A journal used to record allowance vouchers when a sale is discounted.

cash disbursements journal—A journal used to record all transactions involving the payment of cash.

cash receipts journal—A journal used to record all cash inflows into a hospitality firm, including cash sales and cash collections.

city ledger—A subsidiary ledger with an alphabetical listing of accounts receivable from guests who have already checked out of the hotel, and any other receivables.

control accounts—Accounts used to summarize all similar transactions that occur in a hospitality firm, such as all accounts receivable transactions.

front office cash receipts and disbursements journal—A journal used to record cash receipts and disbursements involving lodging guests.

guest ledger—A subsidiary ledger that lists the accounts receivable of guests currently staying in the hotel.

payroll journal—A journal containing a record of each payroll check issued, along with the corresponding gross pay and various deductions for federal tax, state tax, city tax, FICA, employee health care contributions, and miscellaneous contributions such as union dues.

purchases journal—A journal used to record all purchases made on account.

sales journal—A journal used for posting all sales transactions on account.

subsidiary ledger—A special ledger that provides more detailed information about an account, is controlled by the general ledger, and is used when there are several accounts with a common characteristic.

transfer journal—A journal used to record the transfer of one person's account to another in the same ledger or to another ledger.

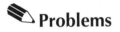

Review Questions

1. What is a *control account?*
2. When should control accounts be established?
3. What are *subsidiary ledgers?*
4. How do businesses record purchases on account?
5. Why do businesses use specialized journals?
6. When are column totals of specialized journals posted, and why then?
7. How do hospitality firms record payroll accruals at the end of the accounting period?
8. What journals are maintained in the front office of a lodging property?
9. What disbursements are recorded in the front office cash receipts and disbursements journal?
10. When should activities of hotel guests be posted to the subsidiary ledger accounts, and why then?

Problems

Problem 1

Identify the journal in which each of the following transactions would be recorded. Assume the business uses the specialized journals discussed in this chapter, as well as a general journal.

1. Cash beverage sales are for $1,500.
2. Beverages purchased on account totaled $800.
3. An adjusting entry to recognize bad debt expenses of $500.
4. Charge food sales total $2,000.
5. Wages of $500 for James Haslett, an employee, for the pay period.
6. A payment to a beverage supplier of $500 on account.
7. A payment from a restaurant patron of $150 on his account.
8. A utility bill payment of $200.

Problem 2

The Stockbridge Inn has incurred several transactions as follows:

1. Paid employee wages of $1,400.
2. Paid the IRS payroll taxes of $300.

3. Paid Health Central $2,000 for healthcare premiums.
4. Purchased $800 of food on account from F.D. Foods, Inc.
5. Sold 50 rooms on account to guests at an average price of $80.
6. Received $2,500 from former guests for payments on account.
7. Paid Stilles Linen $300 on account.
8. Purchased cleaning supplies costing $350 on account.

The Stockbridge Inn uses several specialized journals, including a rooms sales journal, cash receipts journal, purchase journal, payroll journal, and check register.

Required:

Indicate the journal used to record each transaction.

Problem 3

The Dansville Café uses the following journals:

- Sales journal
- Cash receipts journal
- Purchases journal
- Cash disbursements journal
- Payroll journal
- General journal

Several business transactions and activities of the Dansville Café are as follows:

1. Lunch sales for cash totaled $454.48 on May 31.
2. Lunch sales on account totaled $128.14 on May 31.
3. Food purchased on account from Food Corp. costs $647.
4. Fresh fruit purchased with cash (check no. 1897) costs $147.
5. Consumers Electric Co. was paid $647 for electricity used during April.
6. Jack Jones, the café manager, was paid a salary of $2,400 for May.
7. The federal income taxes total of $648, withheld from employee checks during May, was deposited with Bank One.
8. The account receivable of James Nopay, for $58, was deemed uncollectible and written off on May 31.
9. Wages of $1,254 were accrued at the end of May.
10. Frost Pak, Inc., a supplier, was paid $300 on account.

Required:

Indicate the journal used to record each transaction or activity.

Problem 4

Carson City Catering's cash receipts journal for June 15, 20X7, is shown below:

Cash Receipts Journal								
Date	Customer/Other	Cash Dr. 101	Accounts Receivable Cr. 105		Sales Cr. 301	Other Accounts Cr.		
			Amount	✓		Acct. Title	Acct. #	Amount	✓
20X7								
June 1	Bob Woods	200.11	200.11	✓				
2	James Party	1,200.00			1,200.00			
4	Bank One	10,000.00				Note Payable	206	10,000.00	✓
5	Larry Smith	1,000.00				Common Stock	280	1,000.00	✓
10	Bush Event	2,451.00			2,451.00			
12	Terry Wright	652.00	652.00	✓				
15	Gore Celebration	742.18			742.18			

Required:

1. Describe each transaction recorded in the cash receipts journal.
2. What does a "✓" indicate?

Problem 5

The Haslett Diner allows selected customers to charge meals. The sales on account and cash payments from Gregory Case were as follows for April 20X1:

April	Sales	Cash Payment
1	$14.72	—
2	12.47	—
7	—	$20.00
10	6.50	—
15	7.28	—
22	14.15	—
29	13.12	—
30	—	30.00

The balance of Case's account at the beginning of April 20X1 was $50.00.

Required:

Determine the balance of Case's account at the end of April 20X1.

Problem 6

The Fowlerville Café needs to record the following business activities and required adjustments:

1. Cash lunch sales totaled $502.15 on June 30.
2. Lunch sales on account totaled $256.00 on June 30.
3. Food purchased from Howell Supply on account totaled $846.15 on June 30.

4. Electricity costs for June based on reading the electric meter and the cost per kwh total $231.00. (No bill has been received.)
5. Depreciation expense is $235.00 for June.
6. Wages accrued at the end of June total $452.00.
7. Elroy Jones is paid $562.00 on June 30 for his work as an employee.
8. Ernst & Jones Accounting Consultants has billed the Café $500.00 for its services through June 25.
9. On June 30 Rob Wells, a customer, paid $200.00 on his account.
10. Howell Supply is paid $300 on account at the end of June.

Assume the Fowlerville Café has journals as follows: cash receipts, cash disbursements, general, sales, payroll, and purchases.

Required:
Indicate the journal used to record each of the above items.

Problem 7

The Brighton Motel allows selected guests to charge their stays on account. The sales to and cash payments from Greg Kasavana were as follows for November 20X4:

November	Sales	Cash Payments
1	$ 97.15	—
5	—	$100.00
9	62.14	—
12	—	100.00
18	126.72	—
22	115.19	—
24	—	100.00
29	132.20	—
30	76.14	100.00

The balance of Kasavana's account on October 31, 20X4, was $152.15.

Required:
Determine the balance of Kasavana's account on November 30, 20X4.

Problem 8

The Leslie Grill purchased food on account from several suppliers during June as follows:

June	Supplier	Amount
4	Bates Meats	$847.15
6	Lash Dairy	148.71
7	Aguiler Supply	749.92
12	Jake's Frozen Foods	652.66
15	Lash Dairy	129.46
18	Spartan Foods	597.77
21	Bates Meats	668.88
22	Minoso's Foods	372.22

25	Lash Dairy	$172.71
27	Aguiler Supply	497.73
30	Jake's Frozen Foods	455.54

Required:

1. Post the above amounts to T-accounts in the accounts payable subsidiary ledger. Assume the above transactions were recorded on page 5 of the purchases journal.
2. Assume the accounts payable control account had a $–0– balance on May 31. What is the balance of the accounts payable control account after posting the total from the purchases journal to the accounts payable control account?

Problem 9

The Howell Hotel (HH) purchases its produce from Mellon Farms on account and pays the purveyor twice a month. On April 30, 20X1, HH owed Mellon Farms $215.45. Purchases on account and cash payments to Mellon Farms for May 20X1 were as follows:

May	Purchase	Cash Payment
2	$115.42	—
5	—	$215.45
7	89.15	—
11	136.42	—
15	79.36	—
19	47.15	—
20	—	204.57
24	78.15	—
29	123.41	—

Required:

Determine the amount owed to Mellon Farms at the end of May 20X1.

Problem 10

The Leslie Grill has made the following payments on account during June:

June	Check No.	Supplier	Amount
8	9894	Bates Meats	$300.00
10	9903	Lash Dairy	148.71
14	9943	Bates Meats	300.00
18	9987	Aguiler Supply	749.92
23	10014	Bates Meats	300.00
27	10029	Jake's Frozen Foods	600.66
30	10051	Lash Dairy	129.46

In addition, spoiled food costing $52.00 was returned to Jake's Frozen Foods on June 27 and credit was issued to the Leslie Grill.

Required:

1. Based on the above information and the purchases on account from Problem 8, prepare T-accounts and determine how much the Leslie Grill owes each of its suppliers at the

end of June. Assume that all payments were recorded on page 8 of the cash disbursements journal.

2.   What is the total amount the Leslie Grill owes to all suppliers at the end of June?

Challenge Problems

Problem 11

The North Woods Motel (NWM), a 20-room lodging facility, generally does not extend credit to its guests beyond check-out. However, a few extremely loyal guests have been extended credit. The balances of their accounts as of January 31, 20X3, are as follows: M. Terrace $194.28; J. K. Weed $275.29; F. M. Fordham $84.21; Martin Block $64.28; Mary Cervantes $124.91. The balance of the city ledger control account (acct. #112) is $742.97.

The following transactions during February 20X3 involve these five customers:

Feb. 3   M. Terrace stayed at the NWM for two nights and $75.26 was charged to his account.

   5   A check for $275.29 was received from J. K. Weed for payment on account.

   7   F. M. Fordham charged $275.20 for dinner for a small group to her account.

   11   Martin Block checked out of the NWM and charged $59.42 to his account.

   13   Mary Cervantes paid $100.00 on her account.

   14   J. K. Weed checked out of the motel and charged $85.22 to her account.

   17   Martin Block paid $50.00 on his account.

   19   M. Terrace stayed one night at the NWM and charged $41.40 to his account.

   22   F. M. Fordham paid $200.00 on her account.

   23   A check for $200.00 was received from M. Terrace on his account.

   28   Mary Cervantes charged $94.20 to her account after staying for two nights at the NWM.

Required:

Prepare a sales journal (see Exhibit 1), a cash receipts journal (see Exhibit 2), and T-accounts for each of the five guests who are extended credit. Also, prepare a T-account for the city ledger control account. When preparing the T-accounts, include the balance as of January 31, 20X3.

1.   Record each sales transaction in the sales journal (assume all sales were for rooms and are recorded on page 10).

2.   Record each cash transaction in the cash receipts journal on page 12.

3.   Post all charges to the guest accounts. Then post all amounts received from guests to their accounts. Post totals from the two journals to the city ledger control account.

4.   Prepare a schedule of receivables and compare it to the balance of the city ledger control account at the end of February 20X3.

Problem 12

The Okemos Café made the following food purchases and cash disbursements during September 20X4:

1. On September 2, $452.00 of meat was purchased from Borden Meats on account (invoice 1349).

2. Food supplies costing $337.42 were purchased from Givens Foods on account on September 4 (invoice 15872).

3. Check 475 for $550.00 was written to Ganakas Beverages on September 6 as payment on account.

4. Beverages costing $185.21 were purchased on account from Ganakas Beverages on September 7 (invoice K-4871).

5. On September 8, food costing $687.09 was purchased on account from Spartan Enterprises (invoice 9876).

6. Borden Meats delivered $398.15 of meat on account on September 10 (invoice 1398).

7. Check 476 for $452.00 was written to Borden Meats on September 12.

8. Additional checks written on September 12 were as follows:

Check #	Payee	Amount	Acct. #	Account Title
477	Givens Foods	$337.42	201	Accounts Payable
478	Richard Smith	480.00	501	Payroll Expense
479	Sandy Rhodes	420.00	501	Payroll Expense
480	Twyla Miller	380.00	501	Payroll Expense
481	Rose Aquaro	400.00	501	Payroll Expense
482	William Jones	390.40	501	Payroll Expense
483	R. J. Realty	800.00	520	Rent Expense
484	Okemos Power	450.29	510	Utilities Expense
485	Motor Repair Inc.	227.94	508	Repair Expense

9. On September 15, meat costing $567.50 was purchased on account from Borden Meats (invoice 1420).

10. Food costing $695.00 was purchased on account from Spartan Enterprises on September 17 (invoice 9902).

11. Beverages costing $345.00 were purchased on account from Ganakas Beverages on September 21 (invoice K-4997).

12. Check 486 was written for $687.09 to Spartan Enterprises on September 24 for payment on account.

13. Checks written on September 26 were as follows:

Check #	Payee	Amount	Acct. #	Account Title
487	Richard Smith	$480.00	501	Payroll Expense
488	Sandy Rhodes	425.00	501	Payroll Expense
489	Twyla Miller	385.00	501	Payroll Expense
490	Rose Aquaro	398.00	501	Payroll Expense
491	William Jones	405.00	501	Payroll Expense
492	*Ingham Newspaper*	85.00	506	Advertising
493	Bank One	290.00	502	Employee Benefits
494	Blue Cross	875.50	502	Employee Benefits

14. On September 29, meat costing $627.91 was purchased on account from Borden Meats (invoice 1435).

Required:

1. Prepare a cash disbursements journal (see Exhibit 4) and a purchases journal (see Exhibit 3). Record all disbursements for payroll in the cash disbursements journal. These transactions are recorded on page 18 of each journal.

2. Record all of the above transactions in the two journals and total the columns of each journal.

Problem 13

The Lowell Lounge (LL) purchases food on account from five suppliers. During October 20X4, the LL made purchases on account and payments as follows:

	Purchases			Payments	
October	Supplier	Amount		Supplier	Amount
1	Alpha Foods	$352.14		—	—
2	Delco Produce	132.18		Delco Produce	$200.00
4	Smith Dairy	96.12		Vermil Meats	500.00
7	Ceru Drinks	215.31		—	—
10	Vermil Meats	375.00		—	—
11	—	—		Alpha Foods	400.00
12	—	—		Smith Dairy	300.00
15	Alpha Foods	692.15		—	—
20	Delco Produce	194.21		Ceru Drinks	200.00
21	Smith Dairy	127.62		—	—
22	Ceru Drinks	153.14		—	—
23	—	—		Alpha Foods	500.00
27	Alpha Foods	651.86		—	—
28	Vermil Meats	415.00		—	—
30	Smith Dairy	142.18		—	—
31	Delco Produce	215.46		—	—

The balances owed to the five suppliers at the end of September were as follows:

Alpha Foods	$497.18
Delco Produce	218.73
Smith Dairy	49.18
Ceru Drinks	350.47
Vermil Meats	628.19

Required:

1. Determine the balance owed to each supplier at the end of October.

2. Determine the total accounts payable on October 31, 20X4. Assume accounts payable consists of only these five suppliers.

Problem 14

Use information provided in Problem 12 to solve this problem.

Required:

1. Make T-accounts for each of the following general ledger accounts:

Account Title	Acct. #	Account Balance September 1, 20X4
Cash	101	$9,521.00
Accounts Payable	201	2,678.20
Food Purchases	401	—
Payroll Expense	501	—
Employee Benefits	502	—
Advertising Expense	506	—
Repair Expense	508	—
Utilities Expense	510	—
Rent Expense	520	—

2. Make T-accounts for the accounts payable subsidiary ledger as follows:

Supplier	September 1, 20X4 Balance
Borden Meats	$697.45
Givens Foods	846.92
Ganakas Beverages	650.00
Spartan Enterprises	483.83

3. Post the totals from the cash disbursements and purchases journals (solution to Problem 12) to the general ledger and subsidiary ledger accounts.

4. Post the amounts pertaining to suppliers to the proper accounts in the accounts payable subsidiary ledger.

5. Prepare a list of accounts payable accounts and compare the total to the Accounts Payable control account.

Problem 15

The Mason Dairy Cream is preparing to open on June 7, 20X8. It will maintain three specialized journals: a cash receipts journal, a purchases journal, and a cash disbursements journal. It will also use a general journal. Its general ledger will consist of the following:

Account Title	Acct. #	Account Title	Acct. #
Cash	101	Food Purchases	401
Equipment	150	Payroll Expense	501
Accumulated Depreciation	151	Utilities Expense	503
Accounts Payable	201	Supplies Expense	505
E. Mason, Capital	250	Advertising Expense	507
Sales	301	Rent Expense	509
		Depreciation Expense	511

Transactions for June 20X8 are as follows:

June 1 E. Mason invests $15,000 in the business.

2 $500 rent for June is paid (check 101).

3 Equipment costing $8,000 is purchased with cash (check 102).

4 Food costing $850 is purchased on account from Supplies, Inc. (invoice 1872).

5   *Webberville Times* is paid $200 for advertising (check 103).

6   $180 in supplies are purchased (check 104).

7   Cash sales total $750.50.

10–15   Cash sales total $2,810.

19   Food is purchased on account from Ice Cream, Inc., for $690 (invoice 4897).

20   *Webberville Times* is paid $250 for advertising (check 105).

21   Three employees are paid wages:

Aaron Dakan	$150.00	check 106
Laurie Golden	140.50	check 107
Marla Maps	162.00	check 108

22   $625 in food is purchased on account from Supplies, Inc. (invoice 1926).

22   Ice Cream, Inc., is paid $500 on account (check 109).

19–23   Cash sales total $2,545.

26   Supplies, Inc., is paid $850 on account (check 110).

27   Food costing $590 is purchased from Springtime Co. on account (invoice F-3941).

28   The utility bill for the first 20 days of June of $350.50 is paid (check 111).

26–30   Cash sales total $2,458.

The depreciation on the equipment for June totals $200.

Required:

1. Record transactions for June 20X8 in the proper journals. All journal pages should be numbered page 1.
2. Establish T-accounts for each general ledger account and post entries to them.
3. Establish T-accounts for each food supplier and post all appropriate activity to these accounts.
4. Record the depreciation expense in the general journal and post the amounts to the proper accounts.
5. Prepare a trial balance of general ledger accounts.

Chapter 8 Outline

Internal Control of Cash
Voucher System
    Preparation of a Voucher
Petty Cash
Bank Reconciliation
    Preparing a Bank Reconciliation
    Illustration of a Bank Reconciliation
Gross Method of Recording Purchases
Net Method of Recording Purchases
Credit Card Sales
Integrated Cash Management for Multi-
    Unit Operations

Competencies

1. Describe assets that accountants represent as Cash or Cash Equivalents, and describe procedures that help ensure internal control of a firm's cash. (pp. 295–297)

2. Explain the purpose of a voucher system and how it works. (pp. 297–299)

3. Describe the petty cash fund and the accounting procedures related to it. (pp. 299–301)

4. Explain the purpose of performing bank reconciliations, and demonstrate how to prepare a bank reconciliation. (pp. 301–305)

5. Compare and demonstrate the gross and net methods of recording purchases. (pp. 305–307)

6. Distinguish between the two types of credit cards, and demonstrate how to account for sales that involve each type. (pp. 307–308)

7. Describe an integrated cash management system. (p. 308)

8

Cash

ASSETS AND LIABILITIES are listed on the balance sheet in order of liquidity. Liquidity measures an operation's ability to convert assets to cash. This chapter discusses **cash**, the most liquid current asset.

Cash is a very critical asset for hospitality businesses. The amount of cash a firm holds may not be related to the amount of income it generates. Certainly investors and managers are concerned that the firm generates an adequate profit, but cash is more critical on a day-to-day basis. It is cash, not income, that pays employee wages and the firm's sales taxes, vendors' bills, rent, utilities expenses, and so forth. Although adequate income ensures the long-run survival of the firm, cash keeps the operation running smoothly.

Cash refers not only to the currency and coins that a hospitality firm holds, but also to **time deposits**, demand deposits, money orders, certificates of deposit, and credit card slips signed by the firm's customers. Cash that is formally restricted for a long-term purpose such as for equipment replacement should be listed under Noncurrent Assets.

It is not uncommon for a business to list Cash and Equivalents in place of Cash on the balance sheet. **Cash equivalents** would include very liquid short-term investments held by the firm, such as commercial paper, treasury bills, or certificates of deposit.

Internal Control of Cash

Cash is the most vulnerable of all assets because of its "portability." It is therefore essential to have an effective system of internal control over cash in all phases of the operation. The theft of cash is always possible. The following is a list of general procedures that help ensure that cash is adequately controlled:

1. Cash-handling duties should be segregated.

2. Bookkeeping and cash-handling duties should be separated.

3. All expenditures should be paid by check.

4. Mechanical devices should be used to help safeguard cash.

5. Servers and cashiers should use prenumbered sales tickets.

6. Cash should be deposited daily.

7. Employees should be bonded.

8. Internal and external audits should be performed periodically.

9. A voucher system should be implemented.

Each of these procedures is discussed in this section.

Segregation of Duties. The responsibility for handling cash transactions should be divided among two or more individuals. The segregation of cash-handling duties does not guarantee that fraud will not be perpetrated; it simply makes fraud more difficult because it makes collusion necessary for fraud to occur.

The following example involving the deposit of cash illustrates the advantages of segregating duties. Any cash or checks mailed to the firm should be recorded by the employee who opens the mail. This employee should forward the cash and checks to another employee, who will prepare the bank deposit. The employee opening the mail should also prepare a list of the day's receipts and send a copy of it to the controller. The person preparing the bank deposit should forward a duplicate deposit ticket to the controller. The controller can then compare the list of cash receipts with the day's deposit ticket to look for any discrepancies.

Separate Bookkeeping and Cash-Handling Duties. Employees who have access to cash should not have access to accounting records such as the cash receipts or cash disbursements journals. Similarly, employees who have access to the accounting records should not have access to cash. Separating the bookkeeping and cash-handling duties can be a very challenging chore in small operations with limited personnel available.

Pay for All Expenditures by Check. All disbursements should be made by check or by **electronic funds transfer (EFT)** after proper authorization procedures are completed. Checks written for more than a certain amount should require two signatures. The only exception to paying by check or EFT should be the small business transactions that invariably occur, such as postage stamp purchases or small freight charges. Such small expenditures should be paid out of a petty cash fund, which will be discussed in more detail later in this chapter. As the name indicates, EFT is a method of distributing cash electronically, without sending a hard copy of a check through the banking system's check-clearing process. Due to its convenience and lower cost, EFT is growing more popular. EFT is commonly used to pay for rent, mortgage, utility, insurance, and payroll costs.

Use of Mechanical Devices. Whenever feasible, mechanical devices should be integrated into the hospitality operation to assist in safeguarding cash. Cash registers, time clocks, and check protectors are examples of such devices. The cash register, for example, should record all transactions on a two-ply tape that is locked inside the register and inaccessible to the employee operating the machine. At the end of a shift, the employee operating the cash register should count the cash and transfer it to the cashier's office where the cash receipts will be listed on a deposit slip. A third employee from the accounting department should remove the tape from the machine, compare the total to the cash amount listed by the cashier, and record the cash sales in the appropriate journal.

Use of Prenumbered Sales Tickets. All restaurant servers should be given prenumbered sets of sales slips that they must account for at the end of each shift. To prevent fraudulent use of sales slips by servers, some food service operations charge a fixed amount of money for each sales slip that is unaccounted for at the end of a shift. However, managers must ensure that such charges do not put an employee below the minimum wage for the pay period. Another useful control device increasingly used by restaurant servers is the hand-held electronic ordering unit. This device is connected to the operation's electronic information system and helps reduce the amount of unrecorded sales.

Daily Deposits of Cash. All of the operation's cash receipts should be deposited daily and intact in the bank. All checks received from guests should immediately be restrictively endorsed with the words *for deposit only*. Miscellaneous small expenditures should never be paid for out of the day's receipts; instead, they should be paid for through the petty cash fund.

Employee Bonding. Key employees who handle cash should be bonded by an insurance company. Bonds of this type are commonly referred to as fidelity bonds.

Audit Procedures. Periodic reviews of the internal control system policies and procedures that safeguard cash should be performed internally by the company's auditors and externally by independent Certified Public Accountants.

In the last decade, there have been serious abuses in the area of financial reporting by companies. The abuses involving WorldCom and Enron led to the demise of the once-prestigious Arthur Andersen, LLP, which had issued clean opinions on both companies. One of the results of these abuses is the Sarbanes-Oxley Act of 2002. This act created the Accounting Oversight Board to oversee the work done by auditors on public companies. The act requires the financial offices of publicly traded companies to file quarterly statements swearing that their company's financial statements are complete and accurate. In addition, public companies must file annual internal control reports and auditors must evaluate the internal controls of their clients.

Voucher System. A voucher system should be implemented to control cash disbursements. The next section of this chapter discusses the workings of a voucher system.

Voucher System

A **voucher** is a business's written authorization to make a cash payment. Firms use the voucher system to provide better control over cash disbursements. Use of the voucher system ensures that, before a firm makes any cash payment, transactions are verified, approved in writing, and recorded by the firm's employees. Whenever an obligation to pay cash is incurred, a numerically sequenced voucher is attached to the invoice supporting the obligation.

A sample of a voucher is shown in Exhibit 1. Notice that space is provided for the payee's name and address, the date the voucher originates, and the date the

Exhibit 1   Sample Voucher

Voucher
Leisure Time Hotel
Miami, Florida
Voucher #1563

Date of Voucher   /   /
Due Date of Payment   /   /
Invoice Date   /   /   Invoice Number   #_____
Invoice Amount $_____   Terms of Sale   _____
Discount Available $_____
Net Amount of Invoice $_____

Verification and Approval

	Individual	Date
Quantities Compared with Receiving Report	_____	____
Prices Compared with Purchase Order	_____	____
Credit Terms Checked with Purchase Order	_____	____
Footings and Extensions Checked	_____	____
Ledger Accounts Identified and Approved	_____	____
Payment Authorized	_____	____

Voucher   #1563 Invoice Amount $_____   Date of Voucher   /   /
                  Discount Available $_____   Payment Due Date   /   /
                  Net Amount of Invoice $_____

Payee Name _____   Date Check Drawn   /   /
Address   _____   Check Number   #_____
            _____   Amount of Check $_____
                                    Recorded in Voucher Register—Initial _____

Ledger Account Identification

<u>Account Debited</u>   <u>Account Credited</u>

Wages Expense   Vouchers Payable
Administrative Salaries
Purchases
Utilities
Marketing
Property Operation & Maintenance
Rent
Insurance
Administrative & General
Other

payment is due. Also provided are blanks for the invoice date and number, the credit terms, and the amount of the invoice.

Accounting employees fill in the second section of the voucher to indicate verification and approval. This section provides spaces for approval dates and for the initials of employees responsible for checking extensions and footings on the invoice, or of the employee who checks to see if the quantities originally ordered match those on the receiving report.

The final section of the voucher lists names of accounts that may be debited or credited with the amount of the transaction. The list of accounts helps the accounting department to journalize the transaction correctly.

Preparation of a Voucher

An accounting department employee initiates the voucher process when the firm receives an invoice from a supplier of goods or services. The employee enters the dates, the invoice number, and the amounts and terms of sale in the appropriate places on the voucher. Then he or she attaches the invoice to the voucher and sends both documents to another employee, who will check extensions and verify prices and quantities.

After completing the checking and verification procedures, the second employee initials and dates the voucher and forwards it to a third employee, who indicates which accounts are to be debited and credited. The debit will frequently be to an expense account, but sometimes will be to an asset or liability account. The credit will be to a short-term liability account called Vouchers Payable. The balance sheet will not normally list Vouchers Payable among the liabilities; instead, it includes the amount of the outstanding vouchers in Accounts Payable.

The voucher is then entered in a voucher register and is placed in a tickler file. The tickler file could be housed in an accordion folder that has a pocket for each of the 31 days in a month. If a particular bill is due on the 15th of the month, it is placed in the 15 pocket of the folder. The tickler file is checked every day for bills that are due to ensure that bills are paid when due but not before. The unpaid voucher file in essence becomes the accounts payable subsidiary ledger.

When a bill is due to be paid, an employee in the accounting department removes the voucher from the file and prepares a check for the treasurer (who is in the finance department) to sign. In an ideal system of internal control, no single person or department should prepare a check *and* sign it. At this time, the voucher amount is recorded in the check register. The journal entry for this transaction would be:

Vouchers Payable	$XXX	
Cash		$XXX

Once the check is prepared, it is forwarded along with the supporting documentation to the treasurer for an authorized signature. At this time, the treasurer reviews the voucher, signs the check, and perforates the voucher with a stamp that reads *PAID*, and the voucher is sent back to the accounting department to be filed. Finally, the check is mailed directly to the billing firm by the treasurer.

A voucher system, with its requirements for written approval, provides a trail of documentation that is referred to as an "audit trail."

Petty Cash

Although a hospitality business would prefer to have all purchases paid for by check using the voucher system, that is not always possible. For instance, a small

COD package may arrive or a small purchase of postage stamps or office supplies may be necessary. Such miscellaneous expenditures are paid out of a small fund of cash called the **petty cash** fund.

A business starts a petty cash fund by cashing a check for an amount that it considers adequate to cover small, miscellaneous transactions. A person designated as the custodian of the fund keeps the cash under his or her control in an envelope, a cardboard box, or a drawer.

The entry to start a petty cash fund for $100 would be:

Petty Cash	$100	
Cash		$100

Note that the total amount of cash held by the company has not changed as a result of this entry. Rather, the composition of cash has changed. There is now $100 more in actual cash in the firm and $100 less in **demand deposits**. Petty Cash is not listed separately on the balance sheet; instead, it is included in the Cash amount.

Disbursements from the petty cash fund should be supported by receipts such as cash register tapes, invoices, or other documents. At any given time, the total of the cash and receipt amounts should equal the amount of the fund; in this case, the cash and receipt amounts should total $100.

When the cash in the fund is reduced to a level considered inadequate to cover likely expenditures, the fund is said to need reimbursing or replenishing. A check is drawn and cashed for an amount that will replenish the fund (that is, bring it back to its original level).

To illustrate the reimbursement of a petty cash fund, assume that an examination of the fund for the Chippewa Motel reveals $18 in cash and the following receipts: postage, $38; freight charges, $27; and office supplies, $17. Based on this information, the entry to reimburse the fund would be:

Postage Expense	$38	
Freight Expense	27	
Office Supplies	17	
Cash		$82

If the original amount of the petty cash fund proves to be too low and must be increased by $50, the following entry would be made:

Petty Cash	$50	
Cash		$50

Note that the most common entry involving the petty cash fund is the entry to reimburse the fund. This particular journal entry does not involve the Petty Cash account.

Occasionally an employee, when reimbursing the petty cash fund, will find that the receipts and remaining cash do not equal the amount of the fund. For example, a $100 fund may contain $12 and the following receipts: spare parts, $23; shop supplies, $18; freight charges, $32; and postage, $13. If the credit to Cash was entered as simply the total of the debits to the expense accounts, the fund would not be properly reimbursed. Remember, reimbursing means bringing the fund back to its original balance. In this case, there is a $2 shortage unaccounted for in the fund.

To avoid underfunding or overfunding the petty cash fund, businesses follow this three-step procedure to reimburse it:

1. Debit the expense accounts relating to the receipts in the fund.

2. Subtract the amount of the remaining cash from the amount of the fund, and credit Cash for that amount.

3. If the credit entry does not equal the debit entries, use the Cash Short and Over account to balance the entry.

For the example just given, this procedure would result in the following journal entry:

Spare Parts	$23	
Shop Supplies	18	
Freight Expense	32	
Postage Expense	13	
Cash Short and Over	2	
Cash		$88

Cash Short and Over is a miscellaneous expense or revenue account, depending on its balance at the end of the year. A debit balance indicates expense, while a credit balance indicates revenue. At the end of the fiscal period, it is closed into the Income Summary account just as the other nominal accounts are.

Bank Reconciliation

A **bank reconciliation** is a monthly procedure that provides additional control over cash. The bank reconciliation explains any differences between the bank's cash balance and the cash balance in the company's books. A company starts its bank reconciliation when it receives a statement from the bank.

The bank statement provides a list of the deposits made by the company, the company's checks that have cleared the bank during the month, and other miscellaneous debits and credits to the bank balance. Included with the bank statement are the company's canceled checks that have cleared the bank.

Any differences in the bank and book balances of cash may be due to any of the following five possible reasons:

1. Deposits in transit

2. Outstanding checks

3. NSF checks

4. Bank service charges

5. Credits for interest earned or receivables collected

The following section describes each of these in more detail.

Deposits in transit are deposits made by the company at the end of the month but not included on the bank statement. For example, a restaurant may drop a deposit in the bank's night depository on June 30. The bank would probably then record it as a July 1 deposit and include it on the July bank statement.

Outstanding checks are checks written by the hospitality firm to third parties who have not yet presented them to the bank for collection.

NSF checks are checks that the bank returned to the hospitality business because the customer writing the check did not have enough funds to cover it. *NSF* stands for *Not Sufficient Funds*. NSF checks are often called *bounced checks*.

Bank service charges are charges for services provided by the bank, such as fees for new checks or fees charged to the bank customer for collecting notes receivable. Another common charge would be the monthly bank fee for processing bank credit card slips that the firm has deposited.

Credits for interest earned or receivables collected. If the checking account earned interest on the average balance held in the account, a credit would appear on the bank statement for this amount. Occasionally a hospitality firm will leave a note receivable with the bank for collection, such as when both the maker of the note and the payee do business at the same bank. When the receivable is collected by the bank, the credit appears on the current bank statement.

Preparing a Bank Reconciliation

Although there are several ways to proceed when preparing a bank reconciliation, we recommend the following steps:

1. Compare the deposits listed on the bank statement with the deposits listed in the company's records. Any deposit not listed on the bank statement represents a deposit in transit and should be added to the balance listed on the bank statement.

2. Put the canceled checks in numerical order. Compare the amounts on the bank statement with the amounts on the checks and investigate any discrepancies. Compile a list of checks that have been written but not returned with the bank statement. The sum of check amounts from this list, which is called an *outstanding check list*, should be subtracted from the *balance per bank* (that is, the balance listed on the bank statement). The outstanding check list from the previous month's bank reconciliation should be examined and any canceled checks received with the current statement should be checked off that list. Any checks still not returned should be included on the current month's outstanding check list.

3. Add any credit memoranda listed on the bank statement to the *balance per books* (that is, the balance listed in the company's books). These credit memoranda could include such items as interest earned or notes receivable collected.

4. Deduct from the balance per books any debit memoranda on the bank statement, such as bank service charges, credit card fees, or NSF checks.

5. Make any necessary corrections resulting from errors made by either the bank or the company. For example, perhaps the company entered a $56 amount in the check register when the check was actually written for $65. This would necessitate a reduction in the balance per books of $9.

6. After making all necessary adjustments to both the bank and book balances, verify that the adjusted balances are equal.

7. Make any necessary adjusting entries to the books. Note that items requiring adjusting entries will appear in the portion of the bank reconciliation dealing with the adjusted *book* balance.

Illustration of a Bank Reconciliation

Assume that the Bayview Hotel received the bank statement shown in Exhibit 2. Furthermore, assume that the balance per books is currently $5,265.10. The following checks were written in June but not returned with the bank statement:

Check #	Amount
1194	$ 75.00
1198	23.82
1200	146.58
1202	12.90

An examination of the deposits on the bank statement reveals that a deposit the hotel made on June 30 for $400.00 is not included on the statement. The credit memo for $500.00 on June 20 represents the collection of a note receivable by the bank. The current cash balance on the bank statement is $5,578.63.

Suppose that check #1197 for $45.00 for office supplies was incorrectly recorded on the books as $54.00. Using this information along with the bank statement, the bank reconciliation at June 30 would appear as follows:

Bayview Hotel
Bank Reconciliation
June 30, 20X4

Balance per bank statement, June 30, 20X4		$5,578.63
Add: Deposit in transit: June 30		400.00
Deduct: Outstanding checks:		
#1194	$ 75.00	
#1198	23.82	
#1200	146.58	
#1202	12.90	(258.30)
Adjusted bank balance:		$5,720.33

Exhibit 2   Bank Statement

Bank Statement
First National City Bank of Mt. Pleasant, MI

Customer: Bayview Hotel
Account #:   408576
Address: 22900 Dock Street, Clinton, MI 49068

Previous statement balance:	$ 324.81
5 credits totaling	7,490.00
12 debits totaling	2,182.41
NSF check	50.00
Bankcard draft fees	8.00
Interest @ 5.25%	4.23
Current statement balance	5,578.63
Average collected balance	932.29

Deposits and Other Credits

Date	Amount	
6/3	$1,500.00	regular deposit
6/8	500.00	regular deposit
6/18	1,090.00	regular deposit
6/20	500.00	credit memo
6/25	3,900.00	regular deposit

Checks

Date	Check #	Amount	Date	Check #	Amount
6/2	1188	$247.72	6/17	1195	$163.09
6/5	1189	264.88	6/19	1196	120.75
6/8	1190	334.98	6/20	1197	45.00
6/10	1191	554.43	6/24	1199	31.50
6/12	1192	50.11	6/25	1201	258.24
6/15	1193	81.87	6/30	1203	29.84

Balance per books, June 30, 20X4		5,265.10
Add: Note receivable collected by bank	$500.00	
Interest earned during June	4.23	
Error in recording check #1197	9.00	513.23
Deduct: NSF check	$ 50.00	
Bankcard draft processing fees	8.00	(58.00)
Adjusted book balance:		$5,720.33

The bank reconciliation for the Bayview Hotel indicates that the correct cash balance at June 30 is $5,720.33. Remember, the books currently have a cash balance of $5,265.10. The important last step in the reconciliation process is to make the necessary journal entries to adjust the cash balance. For this example, the entries would be as follows:

Cash	$513.23	
Notes Receivable		$500.00
Interest Income		4.23
Office Supplies		9.00

Accounts Receivable	$50.00	
Bank Service Charges	8.00	
Cash		58.00

Gross Method of Recording Purchases

An additional control procedure over cash disbursements involves accounting for purchases of inventory on account. To understand the gross method of recording purchases, assume that a hospitality firm receives an invoice for a $1,000 inventory purchase. The invoice is dated March 1 with terms of 2/10, *n*/30. The "2/10" means that the buyer may take a 2 percent discount if the invoice is paid within 10 days of the invoice date. The "*n*/30" means that if the discounted invoice is not paid within 10 days of the invoice date, the entire amount (net) is due within 30 days of the invoice date. The $1,000 purchase of inventory on account would be recorded as follows under the **gross recording method:**

Purchases	$1,000	
Accounts Payable		$1,000

This entry reflects the total invoice price.

The subsequent payment within the discount period (by March 11) would be recorded this way:

Accounts Payable	$1,000	
Cash		$980
Purchase Discounts		20

Note that Purchase Discounts is reduced by the discounted portion (2% × $1,000).

If the 2 percent discount on this invoice is not taken, the entry on the payment date would be as follows:

Accounts Payable	$1,000	
Cash		$1,000

Net Method of Recording Purchases

A major disadvantage of the gross method is that it does not reveal discounts that are lost. In addition, recording invoices at their gross billing inflates accounts payable if a company customarily takes most or all discounts in its normal accounts payable cycle. The net method of recording purchases uses the invoice amount *minus* any potential cash discount. With the **net recording method,** cash discounts are recorded upon receipt of an invoice, enabling an operation to measure purchasing and payment efficiency.

Under the net method of recording purchases, the discount is anticipated and the purchases and accounts payable are recorded at net price (invoice price less the cash discount). Upon payment, any discounts lost are recorded in an expense account called Discounts Lost.

Assume that a firm makes an inventory purchase for $1,000 dated March 1 with terms of 2/10, *n*/30. Under the net method, the entry to record the invoice is:

Purchases	$980	
Accounts Payable		$980

In this case, the entry reflects the net invoice price.

If the invoice is paid within the discount period, the entry would be:

Accounts Payable	$980	
Cash		$980

However, if the invoice is not paid within the discount period, the discount is lost and the invoice is due in full. The entry upon payment would be:

Accounts Payable	$980	
Discounts Lost	20	
Cash		$1,000

The Discounts Lost account is listed separately on the income statement as an additional operating expense. Like other expense accounts, it is closed into the Income Summary account at the end of the fiscal period.

The gross method of recording purchases provides a record of the discounts taken in the Purchase Discounts account, while the net method provides a record of the discounts lost in an expense account called Discounts Lost. Since they are mutually exclusive methods and most managers would prefer to have a record of the discounts lost, the net method is generally preferred. Exhibit 3 summarizes the gross and net methods of recording purchases.

Exhibit 3   Gross and Net Methods of Recording Purchases of Inventory

GROSS METHOD		NET METHOD	
Purchase of Inventory:		**Purchase of Inventory:**	
Inventory	$1,000	Inventory	$980
Accounts Payable	$1,000	Accounts Payable	$980
Payment within Discount Period:		**Payment within Discount Period:**	
Accounts Payable	$1,000	Accounts Payable	$980
Cash	$980	Cash	$980
Purchase Discount	20		
Payment after Discount Period:		**Payment after Discount Period:**	
Accounts Payable	$1,000	Accounts Payable	$980
Cash	$1,000	Discounts Lost	20
		Cash	$1,000

Credit Card Sales

Guests use credit cards extensively to pay for goods and services in most areas of the hospitality industry. When a guest pays a bill with a credit card, the hospitality firm keeps a copy of the credit slip, which is essentially a check drawn on the credit card company. The firm should process signed credit card slips into its bank account as promptly as possible.

There are basically two types of credit cards: bankcards and nonbankcards. Visa and MasterCard are examples of bankcards. When hospitality firms deposit signed Visa or MasterCard drafts given to them by guests, the bank accepts them for immediate deposit.

The journal entry for the deposit of $800 worth of bankcard drafts is recorded in the same way a cash sale is. The entry in this instance would be:

Cash	$800	
Sales		$800

Usually once a month the bank will charge the hospitality firm 1.5 to 3.5 percent for processing the bankcard drafts. The charge will appear on the firm's monthly bank statement as a service charge and will be deducted from the firm's cash balance. Most firms consider this monthly charge a very reasonable one since it allows the firm to avoid the costs of credit investigation and collection on those particular accounts.

Examples of nonbankcards are Diners Club, Carte Blanche, and American Express. Hospitality firms cannot deposit the drafts from these credit cards directly into their bank accounts. Instead, they are required to mail the drafts directly to the credit card companies. Consequently, when guests use nonbankcards, hospitality firms must wait for the credit card companies to reimburse them for the guests' purchases. The following entry would be made on the books if guests signed $600 worth of drafts using American Express cards:

Accounts Receivable—American Express	$600	
Sales		$600

Between six and ten days later, after American Express received the signed slips, it would remit to the firm the amount of the slips less a fee of 3 to 5 percent. On the day that the firm received the cash, the firm would make the following entry, assuming a 4 percent American Express fee:

Cash	$576	
Credit Card Expense	24	
Accounts Receivable—American Express		$600

Credit Card Expense would be included among the other selling expenses on the income statement, which include such accounts as Sales Salaries and Advertising.

Integrated Cash Management for Multi-Unit Operations

More and more restaurants and hotels are expanding into multi-unit operations. As a company progresses from a single-unit operation to one with several units, it should adopt an integrated cash management system. Such a system centralizes the collection and disbursement of cash at the corporate level under the responsibility of the corporate treasurer. Cash received at the unit level is quickly transferred to corporate headquarters. Similarly, cash disbursements for the individual units are also made at the corporate level.

The integrated cash management system represents an attempt to provide better internal control over cash. By consolidating cash at the corporate level, a properly installed system will reduce the overall cash balances that the firm holds.

Another important aspect of this type of system involves cash forecasting. Under this system, both the individual units and the corporation prepare integrated cash budgets for the short term and the long term. Cash forecasting indicates when the corporation will need to borrow money and also allows management to consider how to invest excess cash when it accumulates.

Summary

The asset *cash* is critical to the day-to-day operations of hospitality firms. *Cash* refers not only to currency and coins, but also to time deposits, demand deposits, money orders, certificates of deposit, and signed credit card slips. Since cash is both highly desirable and mobile, it is essential that management safeguard it with an effective system of internal control.

This internal control system should include the segregation of duties, the separation of bookkeeping and cash-handling duties, payment of expenditures by check using a voucher system, use of mechanical devices to help safeguard and control cash, use of prenumbered sales tickets, daily deposits of cash, bonding of employees, and periodic internal and external audits. There should be an adequate petty cash procedure in place to take care of small cash expenditures.

Not only is it necessary to carefully monitor cash as it flows through the company, it is also necessary to verify that all transactions involving the bank are compared to the bank statement. This is accomplished through a procedure known as the *bank reconciliation.*

Other control procedures over cash transactions include using the *net method* of recording purchases (rather than the *gross method*), monitoring credit card sales, and installing an integrated system for multi-unit operations.

Key Terms

bank reconciliation—A monthly procedure that provides additional control over cash by explaining any differences between the bank's cash balance and the book's cash balance. A firm starts the bank reconciliation procedure when it receives a bank statement from the bank. The statement provides a list of the deposits made by the company, the checks that have cleared the bank during the month, and miscellaneous debits and credits to the bank balance.

cash—A category of current assets consisting of cash in house banks, cash in checking and savings accounts, and certificates of deposit. Cash is shown on the balance sheet at its stated value.

cash equivalents—Short-term, highly liquid investments such as treasury bills and money market accounts.

demand deposit—A checking account with a commercial bank.

electronic funds transfer (EFT)—An electronic system for paying bills that does not make use of a hard-copy check.

gross recording method—A method of recording cash discounts that uses the full invoice amount as the basis of a journal entry. If the discount is realized, it may be treated as a reduction of the account originally debited (nonrevenue treatment) or as other income (revenue treatment).

NSF check—A check for which there are "Not Sufficient Funds" in the bank to cover payment; also known as a *bounced check.*

net recording method—A method of recording cash discounts that uses the invoice amount minus any potential cash discount as the basis of a journal entry. If the anticipated discount is realized, then no later adjustment is required. If the anticipated discount is not realized, it may be recorded to an expense account called Discounts Lost.

petty cash—A small amount of cash set aside to be used when items must be purchased on the spur of the moment or when it isn't feasible to go through the normal voucher and check procedure to buy an item.

time deposit—A savings account with a commercial bank.

voucher—A business's written authorization to make a cash payment; also, a written document used for posting a transaction to a guest account.

 Review Questions ——————————————————————————————

1. What items other than coins or currency might be included in the balance sheet account Cash?

2. What major procedures did the chapter recommend for providing internal control over cash?

3. How does the voucher system help establish control over disbursements? Where is the Vouchers Payable account found on the balance sheet?

4. What is the three-step procedure for making the journal entry to replenish the petty cash fund?

5. What are the journal entries for the establishment of a petty cash fund for $100, increasing the fund by $50, and decreasing the fund by $25?

6. What is the account classification (i.e., asset, liability, etc.) of the account Cash Short and Over? How is it disposed of at the end of the fiscal period?

7. What is the purpose of a bank reconciliation? What is the chapter's recommended procedure for completing a bank reconciliation?

8. What kinds of transactions require additions to book balances? subtractions from book balances? What kinds of transactions require additions to bank balances? subtractions from bank balances?

9. How does the net method of recording purchases differ from the gross method? How would firms that use each method make journal entries for a $1,000 invoice with a 2 percent discount?

10. What is the purpose of establishing an integrated cash management system in a multi-unit operation?

 **Problems** ————————————————————————————————————

Problem 1

Using the following information, calculate the amount that would be included in Cash and Cash Equivalents on the Waywest Hotel balance sheet at December 31, 20X4.

Signed credit card slips—Diners Club	$ 250
Time deposits	3,256
Money orders	350
Receivable from Bob Golden	200
Petty cash	100

Signed credit card slips—Visa	480
Shares of stock in Motors International	1,000
Certificates of deposit	2,000

Problem 2

Explain the mechanics of the voucher system and include explanations of the following terms: voucher, voucher register, check register, vouchers payable, and tickler file.

Problem 3

Journalize the following transactions involving the petty cash fund for the Sunshine Motel:

1. Establish a petty cash fund on February 1, 20X4, for $150.
2. Increase the fund to $200 on March 1, 20X4.
3. Eliminate the petty cash fund on November 15, 20X4.

Problem 4

The custodian of the petty cash fund for the Wade Inn examined the $100 fund and found $10 cash and the following receipts:

Taxi fare, $15; postage, $29; office supplies, $18; parking receipts, $20; and freight charges, $12.

Required:

Make the journal entry for the replenishment of the fund.

Problem 5

This chapter provides a list of general procedures that help ensure that cash is adequately controlled. Indicate which item on the list relates to the following statements:

1. The person who counts cash is not the one who deposits the cash.
2. Disbursements that exceed a certain amount should not be paid out of petty cash.
3. Cash registers, time clocks, and check protectors are good ways to protect cash.
4. Cash-handling employees should be bonded by an insurance company.
5. Internal auditors and external CPAs should conduct periodic reviews.
6. Hospitality companies should have a written system to control cash disbursements.

Problem 6

Explain the purpose of a bank reconciliation. List three possible reasons for differences in the bank and book cash balances and briefly explain each one.

Problem 7

Journalize the following transactions involving petty cash for the Kent Estates:

1. Establish a petty cash fund on May 1, 20X8, for $50.
2. Record entries for $20 in travel expense and $15 in office supplies, and reimburse the petty cash fund on May 3, 20X8.

3. Increase the fund to $100 on May 15, 20X8.

Problem 8

Lakeside Restaurant purchased inventory from Valley Packing, receiving an invoice dated February 3, 20X4, for $2,000 with terms 2/10, *n*/30.

Required:

Using the net method of recording purchases, complete the following:

1. Record the purchase of the inventory.
2. Record the payment of the invoice within the discount period.
3. Record the payment of the invoice after the discount period.

Problem 9

The Oyster Restaurant has deposited $1,200 in bankcard drafts in its local bank on June 15, 20X4. On June 17, 20X4, the restaurant is paid $2,000 for a banquet, receiving a credit card draft on American Express (a nonbankcard). On June 22, 20X4, American Express remits to Oyster a check for the June 17, 20X4, draft less a 3 percent fee.

Required:

1. Record the journal entries for June 15.
2. Record the journal entries for June 17.
3. Record the journal entries for June 22.

Challenge Problems

Problem 10

The following information relates to the Clearwater Lake Restaurant checking account for the month of April:

Balance of cash per books, 4/30/20X4	$3,735
Balance of cash per bank, 4/30/20X4	3,528
Outstanding checks as of 4/30/20X4	256
Bank service charges for April	12
Deposit in transit at 4/30/20X4	422
NSF check returned with statement	38
Error in recording check #1568—	
(Office Supplies) recorded as	98
should be	89

Required:

Prepare a bank reconciliation for the restaurant for April 30, 20X4.

Problem 11

Chippewa Golf Club purchased merchandise on the following dates:

Date	Vendor	Amount	Terms
April 5	Golf Unlimited	$30,000	2/10, *n*/60
April 12	Pro Line Sports	$20,000	1/10, *n*/30

Required:

1. Using the *gross* method of recording purchases, complete the following:

   a. Record the purchases of April 5 and April 12.

   b. Record the payment of the April 5 invoice as if it had been paid on April 15 and the payment of the April 12 invoice as if it had been paid on April 20.

   c. Record the payment of the April 5 invoice as if it had been paid on April 17 and the payment of the April 12 invoice as if it had been paid on April 24.

2. Record all of the above transactions under the *net* method.

Problem 12

During July, several events occurred at the Flamingo Resort.

a. On July 1, a Petty Cash Fund was established in the amount of $100.

b. On July 15, the fund was replenished, since it had a balance of $4 with the following receipts:

Postage	$30
Office Supplies	$25
Shipping Charges to UPS	$40

c. On July 16, the fund was increased to $200.

d. On July 31, the fund was replenished, since it had a balance of $12 with the following receipts:

Spare Parts	$35
Stamps	$28
Shop Supplies	$27
Inventory	$100

Required:

Journalize all of the necessary transactions for July in chronological order.

Problem 13

PlaidLad Furniture Co. sold ten table/chair sets to HatsOff Restaurant on January 1, 20X8 for $10,000 with terms 2/10; *n*/30. HatsOff also purchased dishware from Venice Depot on January 15, 20X8 for $5,000 with terms 2/10; *n*/30. HatsOff paid PlaidLad on January 6, 20X8 and Venice Depot on January 26, 20X8.

Required:

1. Record the transactions for HatsOff Restaurant using the gross method.

2. Record the transactions for HatsOff Restaurant using the net method.

Problem 14

The National Bank has a balance of $1,253.86 for Heathrow Corp. on December 31, 20X8. Heathrow's books have a balance of $1,725.53. The following items were brought to the attention of Heathrow's treasurer:

1. A deposit for $1,050.00 was made on December 31, 20X8, but was recorded by the bank on January 3, 20X9.
2. The bank charged Heathrow a $25 fee for a canceled check.
3. Checks #256 and #258 were not cashed as of December 31. Each check was written for $200.00.
4. Interest collected from Heathrow by the bank on a note receivable was $203.33 during the year.

<u>Required:</u>

Reconcile the bank and book balances as of December 31.

Problem 15

N 2 Surfing Resort's June bank statement showed the following deposits and checks:

<table>
<tr><td colspan="5" align="center">**N 2 Surfing Resort**
Bank Statement</td></tr>
<tr><td colspan="2" align="center">**Deposits**</td><td></td><td colspan="2" align="center">**Checks**</td></tr>
<tr><td>**Date**</td><td>**Amount**</td><td></td><td>**Date**</td><td>**Number**</td><td>**Amount**</td></tr>
</table>

Date	Amount		Date	Number	Amount
06/01	$2,205.60		06/01	652	$1,261.50
06/05	$3,872.42		06/03	654	$1,000.00
06/17	$5,105.18		06/08	655	$1,250.00
06/22	$2,764.87		06/12	656	$800.00
06/30	$1,835.92		06/16	657	$627.31
			06/18	659	$250.00
			06/25	660	$861.12
			06/30	662	$500.00

The cash records per books for June showed the following:

Cash Receipts Journal			Cash Payments Journal		
Date	**Amount**		**Date**	**Number**	**Amount**
06/04	$3,872.42		06/01	654	$1,000.00
06/16	$5,105.18		06/03	655	$1,250.00
06/21	$2,764.87		06/09	656	$800.00
06/29	$1,853.92		06/10	657	$672.31
06/30	$1,386.45		06/11	658	$300.00
			06/12	659	$250.00
			06/20	660	$861.12
			06/22	661	$387.50
			06/28	662	$500.00
			06/29	663	$500.00

The bank statement for June 30 showed a cash balance of $12,458.27; the cash balance per books on that date was $12,174.62. The outstanding checks list for May included the following:

Number	Amount
648	$328.05
649	$150.00
652	$1,261.50

There was a debit memo of $22.00 for bank service charges that was included with the bank statement. The bank made no errors, while the company made two errors.

Required:

Prepare a bank reconciliation for the company as of June 30.

Chapter 9 Outline

Uncollectible Accounts Expense (Bad Debts)
   Direct Write-Off Method
   Allowance Method
Using Debit and Credit Cards to Manage
   Receivables and Credit
Notes Receivable
   Interest-Bearing Notes
Notes Payable
   Non-Interest-Bearing Notes

Competencies

1. Define terms associated with receivables and payables, and outline ways to avoid bad debt losses. (pp. 317–318)

2. Describe and demonstrate the direct write-off method of accounting for bad debt expense, and identify its major flaw. (pp. 318–319)

3. Describe and demonstrate the allowance method of accounting for bad debt expense. (pp. 319–320)

4. Describe and demonstrate the aging of accounts receivable method of estimating bad debt expense. (pp. 320–321)

5. Describe and demonstrate the percentage of sales method of estimating bad debt expense. (p. 322)

6. Describe notes receivable, demonstrate how to account for honored and dishonored notes receivable, and demonstrate how to change an account receivable to a note receivable. (pp. 323–326)

7. Demonstrate how to account for interest-bearing and non-interest-bearing notes payable. (pp. 326–329)

9

Receivables and Payables

THIS CHAPTER discusses accounts receivable and notes receivable, which are both current assets. It also addresses short-term notes payable and accounts payable. The term **creditor** refers to the company that has either an account receivable or a note receivable on its books, while the term **debtor** refers to the company with an account payable or a note payable on its books.

Accounts receivable are very liquid current assets that a company expects to convert into cash generally within 30 to 60 days. These assets are typically listed after "Cash" or "Cash and Equivalents" on the balance sheet.

Hotels generally keep accounts receivable in two subsidiary ledgers. The accounts receivable pertaining to guests currently staying in the hotel are kept in a *guest ledger*. The second ledger, called a *city ledger*, is an alphabetical file of accounts receivable pertaining to guests who have checked out of the hotel. It also contains accounts of any other receivables.

It is important that the sales personnel of any hospitality firm understand that a credit sales transaction is not completed until the cash from the sale is collected. It is relatively easy to sell goods and services on credit but often more difficult to collect the cash from the sales. To avoid uncollectible account losses, or what are often called *bad debt losses*, companies should establish proper credit-checking procedures before extending credit.

It is fairly easy to avoid bad debt losses when accepting credit cards. Before accepting a signed credit card draft in payment of a sale, the seller should request an authorization code from the appropriate credit card company when the dollar amount of the sale exceeds a certain figure. Once the authorization code is granted, the credit card company cannot return to the seller for payment if the owner of the credit card fails to pay for the purchase.

The firm must also have a formal set of credit-checking procedures in place when dealing with open account credit. The payment histories and current statuses of the accounts of existing guests would normally determine whether additional credit should be extended.

A credit check should always be completed for a new guest. This involves investigating the guest's references, examining the guest's financial statements when available, and checking with local credit bureaus or a national credit-checking firm such as Dun & Bradstreet, Inc.

No matter how efficient a credit investigation may be, some accounts receivable will still not be paid when due. Therefore, hospitality companies should establish policies for dealing with past-due accounts. The following is an example of such a policy:

Exhibit 1   Methods Used to Account for Bad Debts

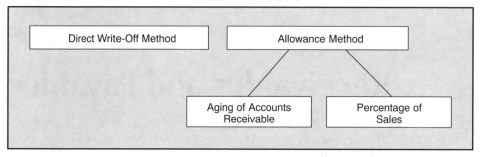

1. Send a courteous reminder letter to the guest when the account becomes past due.

2. If there is no response to the first letter, send a second letter with a sterner tone.

3. If the client doesn't respond to the second letter, follow it up with a phone call from the credit manager.

4. If the first three steps don't succeed, the firm's attorney should write a letter to the guest.

5. If the first four steps fail, the account should be turned over to a collection agency. If the account is small, the guest should be taken to small-claims court.

This is just one of several sets of procedures for handling past-due accounts. The key is to establish a well-considered set of procedures before an account becomes past due.

Uncollectible Accounts Expense (Bad Debts)

Any firm that extends credit will eventually experience bad debt losses regardless of the effectiveness of its system of credit investigation. Bad debts can be accounted for in one of two basic ways: the direct write-off method or the allowance method. Exhibit 1 shows these basic methods of handling bad debts expense.

Direct Write-Off Method

Under the **direct write-off method,** an account receivable is written off at the time that it is determined to be uncollectible. Assume that the $150 account receivable of a former guest, I. Leftown, is determined to be uncollectible. Using the direct write-off method, the journal entry in this instance would be:

Provision for Doubtful Accounts	$150	
Accounts Receivable/I. Leftown		$150

This expense account, Provision for Doubtful Accounts, would be closed along with the other expense accounts at the end of the fiscal period and listed under Administrative and General Expenses on the income statement.

If the $150 were eventually collected from I. Leftown, the following journal entries would be made:

Accounts Receivable/I. Leftown	$150	
Provision for Doubtful Accounts		$150

Cash	$150	
Accounts Receivable/I. Leftown		$150

Notice that it is necessary to make two entries when such an account is paid. The first entry reestablishes the account receivable on the books and reduces the expense account. If the second entry were the only entry made, I. Leftown's account would have a credit balance, which in the case of a receivable is actually a liability.

The direct write-off method is only occasionally used in business because it has a major flaw. Assume, in the example discussing I. Leftown, that the account receivable was journalized in December 20X3 and the account was written off in June 20X4. In this example, the revenue from the sale would be reported in the 20X3 income statement, while the expense relating to the revenue (i.e., the bad debt) would be reflected in the 20X4 income statement. The obvious flaw in the direct write-off method is that it violates the matching principle. Businesses could use the direct write-off method, however, when the amount of the mismatch of revenues and expenses is immaterial.

Allowance Method

Most accountants prefer the **allowance method** of accounting for bad debts to the direct write-off method because it better matches expenses with revenues. It makes use of a contra-asset account called Allowance for Doubtful Accounts. Accountants using the allowance method estimate bad debts expense at the end of each accounting period. For example, a hospitality firm with $30,000 in accounts receivable on December 31, 20X3, may be unable, at that time, to identify which receivables will prove uncollectible in the future. From experience, however, it can estimate the dollar amount of the receivables that will be written off. Once the estimate is made, the following journal entry is entered on the books:

Provision for Doubtful Accounts	$XXX	
Allowance for Doubtful Accounts		$XXX

If a hospitality firm had cash of $18,500, accounts receivable of $30,000, and a balance in the Allowance for Doubtful Accounts account of $3,000, the Current Assets section of the balance sheet would be as follows:

Current Assets		
Cash & Equivalents		$18,500
Accounts Receivable	$30,000	
Less: Allowance for Doubtful Accounts	3,000	27,000

Exhibit 2   Sample Aging of Accounts Receivable Schedule

Guest	Amount	Current	1–30	30–60	60–90	Over 90
		December 31, 20X3				
Darryl Brile	$ 250		$ 250			
Scott Miller	300	$ 300				
June Stephens	700			$ 700		
Mike Toddard	500					$ 500
Sarah Wynn	250				$ 250	
(Others)	28,000	23,000	1,900	1,200	1,400	500
	$30,000	$23,300	$2,150	$1,900	$1,650	$1,000

Once a specific account is determined to be uncollectible as in the following example involving a $300 receivable, the account is written off against the Allowance account as follows:

Allowance for Doubtful Accounts	$300	
Accounts Receivable/XYZ		$300

The following illustration involving the write-off of a $300 receivable shows that the entry has no effect on the carrying value of Accounts Receivable:

Before write-off:		
Accounts Receivable	$30,000	
Less: Allowance for Doubtful Accounts	3,000	27,000
After write-off:		
Accounts Receivable	$29,700	
Less: Allowance for Doubtful Accounts	2,700	27,000

The term *carrying value* refers to the balance in the asset account Accounts Receivable less the balance in the related contra-asset account Allowance for Doubtful Accounts.

Under the allowance method, two different approaches may be used to estimate uncollectibles: the aging of accounts receivable method (the balance sheet approach) and the percentage of sales method (the income statement approach).

Aging of Accounts Receivable Method. Under this allowance method, an **aging of accounts receivable** schedule is compiled, as illustrated in Exhibit 2.

Once the columns of the aging schedule are totaled, historical percentages are applied to the totals to determine the balance in the allowance account. Assume that a firm expects, from experience, to lose the following percentages of bad debts:

Days Past Due	Percentage Considered Uncollectible
0 (Current)	1
1–30	2
30–60	3
60–90	4
over 90	32.55

Using these percentages, the Sleeptite Motel would estimate bad debts as follows:

Days Past Due	Accounts Receivable Amount	Percentage Considered Uncollectible	Estimated Uncollectible Accounts
Current	$23,300	1	$233.00
1–30	2,150	2	43.00
30–60	1,900	3	57.00
60–90	1,650	5	82.50
over 90	1,000	32.55	325.50
	$30,000		$741.00

It is important to note that this analysis indicates that the correct balance in the Allowance for Doubtful Accounts account should be $741. We now need to examine the existing balance in the account before making the journal entry. If the Allowance account shows a credit balance of $34, the entry should be as follows:

Provision for Doubtful Accounts	$707	
Allowance for Doubtful Accounts		$707

This T-account shows the status of the Allowance account before and after the journal entry:

Allowance for Doubtful Accounts

		34
		707
	Balance	741

If the Allowance account had a debit balance of $34 before the adjusting entry, the journal entry would change as illustrated below:

Provision for Doubtful Accounts	$775	
Allowance for Doubtful Accounts		$775

The following T-account shows the status of the Allowance account before and after this journal entry:

Allowance for Doubtful Accounts

34		775
	Balance	741

Percentage of Sales Method. Whereas the aging of accounts receivable method focuses on the balance sheet, the **percentage of sales method** focuses on the income statement. Under the percentage of sales method, the firm looks at the historical amount of bad debts as a percentage of net credit sales. For example, the Sleeptite Motel may have found that bad debts averaged 2 percent of net credit sales over the last five years.

To estimate this year's bad debts, the firm simply applies 2 percent to the amount of net credit sales for the year. If for Sleeptite the net credit sales amount was $35,000 for 20X3, the bad debts would be computed as $35,000 × .02 = $700. Based on this calculation, the journal entry would be:

Provision for Doubtful Accounts	$700	
Allowance for Doubtful Accounts		$700

It is very important to note that once the amount of bad debts is estimated under this method, the existing balance in the Allowance for Doubtful Accounts account is ignored when constructing the journal entry. This is in direct contrast to the aging technique. Assuming that the balance in the Allowance account was a credit of $34 before the entry, the account would change, as illustrated below:

Allowance for Doubtful Accounts

	34
	700
Balance	734

Using Debit and Credit Cards to Manage Receivables and Credit

For hospitality operations that extend credit to their customers, credit and debit cards are an excellent way to manage credit and receivables.

A debit card is a credit card that, when used by a purchaser, reduces the purchaser's cash balance at a particular card company (usually a bank). The balance in the purchaser's cash account is a liability to the card company. Hence, when the debit card is used by the purchaser, the card company debits the account for the purchase amount. The use of debit cards is reducing the number of checks used in the U.S. economy.

Credit cards represent an authorization by a credit card company to extend a line of credit to a given purchaser. The card is called a credit card because the card company extends credit to a customer with predetermined payment terms.

Some credit card companies are national, such as Visa, MasterCard, Discover, American Express, and Diner's Club. Hospitality firms that accept these national credit cards are in essence selling their accounts receivable. This is sometimes referred to as factoring of accounts receivable.

The major advantages of accepting national credit cards include:

1. Elimination of credit checking on credit card transactions.

Exhibit 3   Interest-Bearing Note

$2,000	Topeka, Kansas	June 15, 20X3

Sixty days after date I promise to pay to the order of Oakbrook

Motel - - - - - - Two thousand and no/100 - - - - - - dollars payable at

First City Bank of Topeka with an interest at 12 percent.

Charles White

2. Reduction of effort in managing receivables.

3. Reduction of bad debt losses.

4. Speedier collection of receivables.

Notes Receivable

While accounts receivable represent verbal promises to receive cash, notes receivable are written promises to receive cash in the future. The individual or company promising to pay is called the **maker** of the note, while the individual expecting to be paid is called the **payee**. Exhibit 3 is an example of a promissory note for $2,000.

Interest-Bearing Notes

An interest-bearing note is a note on which interest accrues over the life of the note. In the promissory note shown in Exhibit 3, Charles White, the maker, has signed an interest-bearing note and agreed to pay the payee, Oakbrook Motel, $2,000 plus interest at 12 percent per annum over the life of the note. The principal and interest due at maturity are referred to as the **maturity value**. The basic formula for calculating simple interest on a note is Interest = Principal × Rate × Time. The interest on the note shown in Exhibit 3 would be calculated as follows:

$$
\begin{aligned}
\text{Interest} &= \text{Principal} \times \text{Rate} \times \text{Time} \\
&= \$2,000 \times .12 \times \tfrac{60}{360} \\
&= \$40
\end{aligned}
$$

For the sake of simplicity, we will assume that there are 360 days in a year.

The maturity value on the note would be:

$$
\begin{aligned}
\text{Maturity Value} &= \text{Principal} + \text{Interest} \\
&= \$2,000 + \$40 \\
&= \$2,040
\end{aligned}
$$

Accounting for Notes Receivable. Now let us examine the journal entries used in accounting for notes receivable. Assuming that the Oakbrook Motel received the note in exchange for renting a large block of rooms, the entry on the date of the sale would be:

Notes Receivable	$2,000	
Rooms Revenue		$2,000

On the maturity date of the note, the entry to record the receipt of the cash would be:

Cash	$2,040	
Notes Receivable		$2,000
Interest Income		40

Calculating Maturity Dates. The actual maturity date of the note would be August 14, calculated as follows:

Days remaining in June (June 16–30)	15
Days in July	31
Days needed in August	14
Total days of note	60

Note: When calculating the maturity date for this type of note, accountants do not count the date that the note is issued. For example, the maturity date for Charles White's note was calculated from June 16, the day *after* he took out the note.

Sometimes, however, the time period of a note is stated in months rather than days. For notes of this type, the maturity date falls on the same date of the month on which the note was written. For example, if a three-month note is written on August 4, its maturity date is November 4.

Exchange of Account Receivable for Note Receivable. Occasionally a company may purchase goods or services from a hospitality firm, fully intending to pay the account receivable according to the regular terms. If, for some reason, payment is not made at the end of the credit period, the seller may allow the purchaser to sign a note receivable. The exchange of the account receivable for the note receivable in the amount of $10,000 would be journalized as follows:

Notes Receivable	$10,000	
Accounts Receivable		$10,000

Dishonored Notes. However, if the maker fails to pay a note receivable when due, the note is said to be **dishonored**. If the $2,000 note to the Oakbrook Motel were dishonored on the due date, the following entry would be made:

Exhibit 4   Discount Period for a Note

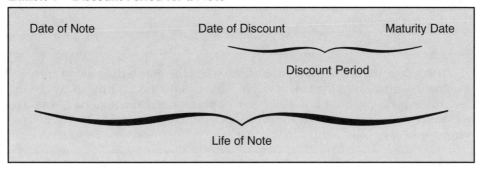

Accounts Receivable	$2,040	
Notes Receivable		$2,000
Interest Income		40

Notice that the note is written off the books, the interest is recorded and the total is debited to Accounts Receivable.

Discounting a Note Receivable. Occasionally the payee of a note receivable is unable to wait until the maturity date of the note to receive payment. If the maker of the note has a good credit rating, the payee could take the note to a bank and discount it before maturity. *Discounting* simply means cashing a note in before it is due and receiving less than the maturity value in the process.

Assume that 30 days after the Oakbrook Motel accepted the note from Charles White, the treasurer takes the note to the local bank, which discounts it at a rate of 14 percent. In this case, the cash that Oakbrook would receive, usually called the *proceeds*, would be calculated using the same formula used to calculate simple interest (Interest = Principal × Rate × Time), but substituting Discount in place of Interest, Maturity Value in place of Principal, Discount Rate in place of Rate, and Discount Period in place of Time.

$$
\begin{aligned}
\text{Discount} &= \text{Maturity Value} \times \text{Discount Rate} \times \text{Discount Period} \\
&= \$2,040 \times .14 \times \tfrac{30}{360} \\
&= \$24
\end{aligned}
$$

$$
\begin{aligned}
\text{Proceeds} &= \text{Maturity Value} - \text{Discount} \\
&= \$2,040 - \$24 \\
&= \$2,016
\end{aligned}
$$

Observe that the bank discount rate can be different from the rate on the note. In this case, the bank discount rate is 14 percent while the note rate is 12 percent. Also notice that the discount period consists of the time that elapses between the discount date and the due date, as illustrated in Exhibit 4. The journal entry to record the proceeds on the discount date for the note would be:

Cash	$2,016	
Notes Receivable		$2,000
Interest Income		16

In this case, the actual proceeds realized when the note is discounted are more than the face amount of the note payable. This will not necessarily always be the case. If the bank discount rate had been 20 percent and the note had been discounted 20 days after issuance, the proceeds would have been $1,995. The journal entry would have been written in this way:

Cash	$1,995	
Interest Expense	5	
Notes Receivable		$2,000

The Oakbrook Motel has a **contingent liability** to the bank for the note once it is discounted and until it is finally paid by the maker. Assume in the case of its $2,000 note that the maker does not pay on the maturity date. Oakbrook would have to pay the bank the maturity value of the note and would make the following journal entry:

Accounts Receivable	$2,040	
Cash		$2,040

Note Receivable Spanning Two Fiscal Periods. Sometimes the receipt and collection of a note span two fiscal periods. Consider a $3,000, two-month, 12 percent note received on December 1, 20X3. The journal entry on December 31, 20X3, to record the accrued interest on the note would be:

Interest Receivable	$30	
Interest Income		$30

On February 1, 20X4, the due date of the note, the following entry would be made:

Cash	$3,060	
Interest Receivable		$ 30
Interest Income		30
Notes Receivable		3,000

Notes Payable

The average hospitality firm has several short-term liabilities or payables on its books, including wages payable, taxes payable, accounts payable, and notes payable. The topic of notes payable so closely parallels the topic of notes receivable that we will briefly discuss notes payable here.

A note payable could simply result when a company borrows money on a short-term basis from a bank. For example, assume that on October 1, 20X3, the Bayshore Country Club borrows $12,000 for 120 days at 10 percent from the Kentfield Bank. The journal entry for this transaction would be:

Cash	$12,000	
Notes Payable		$12,000

On December 31, 20X3, the Bayshore would make the following entry for the interest accrued to date on the note:

Interest Expense	$300	
Interest Payable		$300

The journal entry required on the payment date of the note, February 1, 20X4, would be:

Notes Payable	$12,000	
Interest Payable	300	
Interest Expense	100	
Cash		$12,400

Occasionally a firm has an account payable that it is unable to pay when due, and consequently signs a note payable for the amount of the account payable, agreeing to pay the principal and interest at a later date. If a $5,000 account payable were replaced by a note payable, the journal entry recording it would be:

Accounts Payable	$5,000	
Notes Payable		$5,000

Non-Interest-Bearing Notes

A **non-interest-bearing note** is one that includes the interest in the face value of the note. For example, assume that on October 1, the Bayshore Country Club borrowed $12,000 from the Kentfield bank for 120 days with an interest rate of 10 percent. The bank could simply compute the interest to maturity and include it in the face amount of the note as follows:

$$
\begin{aligned}
\text{Interest} &= \text{Principal} \times \text{Rate} \times \text{Time} \\
&= 12{,}000 \times .1 \times \tfrac{120}{360} \\
&= 400
\end{aligned}
$$

Exhibit 5   Note with Interest Included in Face Value

October 1, 20X3

One hundred and twenty days after the date of this note, Bayshore
Country Club promises to pay the Kentfield Bank $12,400.

Signed   *Robert Stevens*

Title   *Vice-President—Finance*

Maturity Value = Principal + Interest
= 12,000 + 400
= 12,400

The bank could simply write the note as shown in Exhibit 5. Notice that, despite the fact that this type of note is referred to as a *non-interest-bearing note,* interest is still paid at maturity.

The accounting for non-interest-bearing notes differs from that for interest-bearing notes. In the case of a non-interest-bearing note, at the time the note was borrowed, Bayshore would make the following entry:

Cash	$12,000	
Discount on Notes Payable	400	
Notes Payable		$12,400

The Discount on Notes Payable account is a contra-liability account and will normally carry a debit balance. Over the life of the note, the $400 balance in the account is reduced, and the Interest Expense account is gradually increased by the $400.

For example, an adjusting entry would be made at December 31, 20X3, to accrue interest on the note as shown below:

Interest Expense	$300	
Discount on Notes Payable		$300

The balance sheet at December 31, 20X3, would show the carrying value of the note as $12,300, as illustrated below:

Current Liabilities:
Notes Payable $12,400
Less: Discount on Notes Payable   100   12,300

Exhibit 6   Comparison of Interest-Bearing and Non-Interest-Bearing Notes

Event/Date	Journal Entry for Interest-Bearing Notes		Journal Entry for Non-Interest-Bearing Notes	

Cash Borrowed, October 1	Cash $12,000
	    Notes Payable
		$12,000	Cash $12,000
			 Discount on Notes Payable 400
			    Notes Payable
				$12,400

Adjusting Entry December 31	Interest Expense $ 300
	    Interest Payable
		$ 300	Interest Expense $ 300
			    Discount on Notes Payable
				$ 300

Payment Date January 29	Notes Payable $12,000
	 Interest Expense 100
	 Interest Payable 300
	    Cash
		
		$12,400
			Notes Payable $12,400
			 Interest Expense 100
			    Discount on Notes Payable
			    Cash
				
				$ 100
				12,400

The journal entry on the maturity date of the note would be:

Notes Payable	$12,400	
Interest Expense	100	
Cash		$12,400
Discount on Notes Payable		100

A key point to remember is that the Notes Payable account is always credited for the face value of the note, whether it is interest-bearing or not. Exhibit 6 compares the journal entries for interest-bearing and non-interest-bearing notes.

Summary

The assets Accounts Receivable and Notes Receivable, as well as the liabilities Accounts Payable and Notes Payable, all play a very big role in a company's actual and potential cash flow. (Of course, a company wishes to collect receivables as soon after a sale as possible, and delay the payment of payables as long as possible, provided there are no adverse consequences such as loss of discounts for timely payment.)

To help avoid nonpayment problems, a hospitality business should follow a set of credit-checking procedures before issuing credit to a new guest. Even with a proper credit check, some guests will pay late. Therefore, it is wise to establish procedures for following up on late accounts and for dealing with uncollectible accounts. Two such procedures used when dealing with uncollectible accounts are the direct write-off method and the allowance method. Under the allowance method, there are two ways to determine the amount of bad debts to be written off: the aging of accounts receivable method and the percentage of sales method.

The chapter also shows how interest is computed and what entries are used in accounting for it.

🔑 Key Terms

aging of accounts receivable method—A method of accounting for bad debts expense in which the aging of accounts receivable schedule (a list of accounts receivable according to length of time outstanding) is used to estimate the total amount of bad debts.

allowance method—A method of accounting for bad debts expense in which accountants set up a contra-asset account called Allowance for Doubtful Accounts at the beginning of a fiscal year, give it a balance equal to the sum of accounts expected to be uncollectible in the coming year, then write off uncollectible accounts against this account; includes *aging of accounts receivable* method and *percentage of sales* method.

contingent liability—A liability that is based on a future event that may or may not take place; it is not yet an actual liability and therefore should not be included in the Liabilities section of the balance sheet. Instead, it should be included in footnotes to the financial statements.

creditor—A company with either an account receivable or a note receivable on its books.

debtor—A company with either an account payable or a note payable on its books.

direct write-off method—A method of accounting for bad debts expense in which an account receivable is written off at the time that it is determined to be uncollectible; does not match expenses with revenues.

dishonored note—A note payable that the maker fails to pay.

maker—The individual or company promising to pay the amount of a note.

maturity value—The principal and interest due at the maturity date of a note.

non-interest-bearing note—A note payable that has the interest included in its face value.

payee—The individual expecting to be paid by the maker of a note.

percentage of sales method—A method of accounting for bad debts expense in which the total amount of bad debts is calculated as a percentage of net credit sales.

❓ Review Questions

1. How does a hotel's guest ledger differ from its city ledger? How do these ledgers relate to a subsidiary ledger?

2. What is a major disadvantage of the direct write-off method of accounting for bad debts?

3. What is the ledger account classification for Allowance for Doubtful Accounts? What is its normal balance?

4. If the allowance method of accounting for bad debts indicates a debit balance at the end of the year, were bad debts underestimated or overestimated for the year?

5. What accounts are debited and credited when a specific account is written off during the year under the allowance method of accounting for bad debts?

6. How does the aging of accounts receivable method differ from the percentage of sales method in accounting for bad debts?

7. How is the maturity value of a note calculated?

8. What is the difference between an interest-bearing note and a non-interest-bearing note?

9. What is the account classification for Discount on Notes Payable? What is its normal balance?

10. Does the year-end adjusted entry for accruing the interest of a non-interest-bearing note increase or decrease the carrying value of the note?

 **Problems** ───────────────────────────────────

Problem 1

On June 15, the Pines Restaurant decided to write off the account of Thomas Sunbart in the amount of $350. The restaurant uses the direct write-off method of accounting for bad debts.

Required:
1. Make the necessary journal entry for June 15.
2. On August 10, the restaurant receives a check in the amount of $350 from Sunbart. Make the necessary entry or entries for this date.

Problem 2

The FireSun Resort decided to write off the account of Debra Threloff for $500.00 on August 3. FireSun uses the direct write-off method of accounting for bad debts.

Required:
1. Make the necessary journal entry for August 3.
2. On November 15, Debra Threloff paid FireSun Resort $500.00. Make the necessary journal entry or entries to reinstate Debra's account and record the collection.

Problem 3

The Downtown Restaurant uses the percentage of sales method of estimating bad debts.

Required:

Using the following information, journalize the necessary entry on December 31, 20X3:

Cash Sales	$200,000
Credit Sales	300,000
Total Sales	$500,000
Expected Bad Debts Percentage	1.5
Current credit balance in the allowance account:	$ 1,500

Problem 4

The Goal Post Inn has the following notes receivable:

Customer	Date of Note	Terms	Amount
Jarvis Advertising	January 8, 20X3	60 days	$10,000
Methods Inc.	March 12, 20X3	2 months	$8,000
Salvos Engineering	May 22, 20X3	90 days	$4,000
Raphael Corporation	August 15, 20X3	3 months	$6,000
Valspar Technology	October 6, 20X3	180 days	$2,000
Valvomatics	November 1, 20X3	6 months	$12,000

Required:

Determine the maturity dates for the notes. Assume 20X3 was a leap year.

Problem 5

The following information relates to the Broadway Suites on December 31, 20X8:

Sales	$305,000
Accounts Receivable	27,500

Required:

If bad debts are calculated to be 2 percent of sales, create the journal enry to record the allowance for doubtful accounts.

Problem 6

Write a memo to Mr. Sanders, the president of the lodging operation where you work, explaining the difference between credit cards and debit cards. Also discuss the major advantages of accepting national credit cards in place of extending your company's credit to your customers.

Problem 7

The Home Run Sports Bar has the following notes receivable:

	Customer	Date of Note	Date of Maturity	Principal	Rate
1.	Tino's Supplies	Jan. 4	Feb. 4	$2,000	12%
2.	Marchus Ins.	Jan. 20	April 20	10,000	10%

3.	Beams Lighting	March 7	May 7	3,000	12%
4	Benson's	June 3	Dec. 3	5,000	10%
5.	Renaissance Ads.	July 5	Nov. 5	7,000	12%

Required:

Determine the interest at maturity for the above notes.

Problem 8

In 20X8 and 20X9, Dorothy's Restaurant made the following transactions:

1. On July 1, 2008, Dorothy's restaurant borrowed $20,000 from the Kansas Bank at 12 percent interest for nine months.
2. On December 31, 2008, it accrued interest on the note
3. On April 1, 2009, it repaid the loan to Kansas Bank, including interest.

Required:

Journalize the transactions for this note payable.

Problem 9

Following are the terms for a discounted note:

Date of note	June 1
Life of note	90 days
Maturity date of note	?
Discount date of note	July 31
Amount of note	$20,000
Interest rate on note	8%
Discount rate on note	9%

Required:

Calculate the proceeds on the discounted note. Assume 360 days in a year.

Problem 10

The Carolina House Restaurant borrowed $30,000 at 14 percent from its bank for three months on December 1, 20X3.

Required:

1. Prepare the journal entry for December 1, 20X3.
2. Prepare the adjusting entry for December 31, 20X3.
3. Prepare the entry for the payment of the principal and interest on the note for March 1, 20X4.

Problem 11

Use all of the information given in Problem 10 to solve this problem. However, assume that the note in Problem 11 is a *non-interest-bearing note*.

Required:

1. Prepare the journal entry for December 1, 20X3.
2. Prepare the adjusting entry for December 31, 20X3.
3. Prepare the entry for the payment of the principal and interest on March 1, 20X4.

Challenge Problems

Problem 12

The Pacific Hotel uses the aging of accounts receivable method of accounting for uncollectible accounts. The current aging of receivables schedule indicates the allowance for bad debts to be $2,500.

Required:

1. Prepare an adjusting entry for December 31, 20X3, assuming a credit balance of $200 in the allowance account.
2. Prepare an adjusting entry for December 31, 20X3, assuming a debit balance of $200 in the allowance account.
3. The $300 balance in Mary Lewis's account is written off the books on January 31, 20X4. Prepare the journal entry.
4. Mary Lewis sends a check for $300 in payment of her account, which was previously written off. Prepare the necessary entry or entries on October 15, 20X4.

Problem 13

The 12/31/X3 accounts receivable of the Cabana Resort Inn are represented by the following:

Guest	Date of Invoice	Terms of Sale	Amount
Lou Shields	Oct. 12	*n*/30	$ 500
Paul Martin	Sept. 6	*n*/60	800
John Anthony	Aug. 9	*n*/30	300
Chris Silas	Dec. 22	*n*/30	600
Rick Switzer	Nov. 15	*n*/30	1,500
Bob Sheldon	Sept. 10	*n*/60	700
Dave Rice	Dec. 19	*n*/30	300

The firm expects to lose the following percentages of bad debts:

Days Past Due	Percentage Considered Uncollectible
0 (Current)	1
1 – 30	3

31 – 60	4
61 – 90	10
Over 90	20

Required:

1. Prepare an aging of accounts receivable schedule.
2. Prepare the journal entry to allow for bad debts for 12/31/X3, assuming the current balance in the allowance account is $94.

Problem 14

The Southbreeze Hotel uses the aging of accounts receivable method of estimating bad debts. As of December 31, 20X3, the summarized aging schedule and expected loss percentages are as follows:

Aging of Accounts Receivable

	Current	0–30	30–60	60–90	Over 90
Amount	$18,000	$2,200	$1,800	$1,000	$750
Loss % expected	1%	2%	4%	10%	30%

Required:

1. Assuming a zero balance in the allowance account, make the necessary journal entry on December 31, 20X3.
2. Assuming a $150 debit balance in the allowance account, make the necessary journal entry on December 31, 20X3.

Problem 15

The Conway Hotel accepts a 120-day, $15,000, 10 percent note from a client on April 1, 20X3, in exchange for conference services.

Required:

1. Prepare the journal entry required on April 1, 20X3.
2. The Conway Hotel decides to discount the note at the local bank on May 1, 20X3, at a rate of 12 percent. Prepare the entry for the discounting of the note.
3. Prepare the necessary journal entry on August 1, 20X3, assuming that the note is dishonored.

Chapter 10 Outline

Periodic versus Perpetual Inventory
   Systems
     Taking a Physical Inventory
     Consigned Goods
     Transportation Costs
Inventory Valuation Methods
     Comparison and Evaluation of
       Inventory Valuation Methods
Estimating Ending Inventory and Cost of
   Goods Sold
     The Retail Method
     The Gross Profit Method
Lower of Cost or Market (LCM)
Perpetual Inventory System

Competencies

1. Identify broad guidelines for controlling inventory, and explain the role of inventory in the calculation of profit. (pp. 337–339)

2. Explain procedures for taking a physical inventory, and describe the roles of transportation costs, consigned goods, and terms of sale in recording inventory. (pp. 339–341)

3. Demonstrate and compare the four basic methods of valuing ending inventory. (pp. 341–343)

4. Demonstrate and distinguish between the retail and gross profit methods of estimating ending inventory. (pp. 343–345)

5. Perform the lower of cost or market (LCM) computation and outline situations in which it is used. (p. 345)

6. Distinguish the perpetual inventory system from the periodic inventory system. (pp. 345–346)

10

Inventory

MERCHANDISE INVENTORY represents the goods that a hospitality firm holds for resale to its guests. In the case of a restaurant, the food and beverages stocked constitute the operation's merchandise inventory. **Merchandise inventory** is normally expected to be sold within a year. Therefore, it is considered a current asset.

Inventory as a percentage of total assets is relatively low for the average hospitality firm. However, because of its impact on profit, it is important to control and account for inventory carefully. In addition to merchandise inventory, hospitality firms have supplies inventory. A hotel's housekeeping department would keep an inventory of such supplies as brooms, waxes, and mops. Other supplies inventory categories include guestroom amenities and office stocks of stationery. Supplies inventory is considered a current asset on the balance sheet, and is usually listed after cash and receivables.

Inventory is a very portable asset in a hospitality firm and consequently should be maintained under an adequate system of internal control. The following are some of the broad guidelines that should be followed in controlling inventory:

1. There should be a separation between custody of the inventory records and custody of the inventory. The custodian of the inventory should not have access to the inventory records. Conversely, the accountant who maintains the inventory records should not have access to the inventory itself.

2. A physical inventory should be taken periodically using preprinted inventory control forms.

3. Any significant underage or overage of inventory should be reported to the controller when it is discovered.

4. A daily inventory of high-priced items should be taken.

5. The storeroom where the inventory is kept should be secured, and access should be limited to authorized personnel.

Periodic versus Perpetual Inventory Systems

The two basic types of inventory systems are the periodic and the perpetual systems. Except for a brief discussion of the perpetual inventory system at the end of this chapter, the following concepts assume the use of a **periodic inventory system**. Under the periodic inventory system, no continuous record of the inventory items is kept. After the beginning of a fiscal period, one can only estimate the inventory value. When items are purchased, the Purchases account is debited and

Cash or Accounts Payable is credited. When items are sold, the Sales account is credited for the retail value, Cash or Accounts Receivable is debited, and no deduction is made from the Inventory account.

Under the periodic inventory system, the exact dollar amount of the inventory is not known until the next physical inventory is taken. The perpetual inventory system, however, keeps continuous track of inventory as it is purchased as well as when it is sold. At any given time, one can look at the books and know exactly what the value of inventory is.

A firm starts an accounting period with beginning inventory, which is the inventory that remains from the previous period. Purchases made during the current period represent goods bought for resale. Inventory purchases include the purchase cost of goods for sale plus the related shipping cost. *Beginning inventory* and *purchases* added together are referred to as the *cost of goods available for sale*. *Ending inventory* is the inventory left at the end of an accounting period.

Inventory is a unique accounting item. Although Inventory is a balance sheet account, it is also included on the income statement. This is because accountants use Inventory when calculating cost of goods sold for the firm. Cost of goods sold is traditionally computed as follows:

	Beginning inventory
Plus:	Inventory purchases
Equals:	Cost of goods available for sale
Less:	Ending inventory
Equals:	Cost of goods consumed
Less:	Goods used internally (such as Employee Meals—Food & Beverage Department)
Equals:	Cost of goods sold

An important but relatively small category of direct expenses is "Goods used internally." An example of this would be food provided free of charge to employees (Employee Meals—Rooms Department). Many hospitality operations provide free meals to employees as part of their benefits package. Cost of employee meals for the rooms department is subtracted to determine cost of food sold. The cost of employee meals for rooms department employees is shown as an expense in the rooms department.

Cost of goods sold is then subtracted from sales to obtain the gross profit for the operation. An error in either the counting or the valuation of inventory will cause an error in reported income. Exhibit 1 illustrates the effects that an error in ending inventory can have on profit.

When ending inventory is understated, profit is understated. When ending inventory is overstated, profit is overstated. An error in beginning inventory has the opposite effect on profit. An understatement of beginning inventory causes an overstatement of profit. This is shown in Exhibit 2. If, on the other hand, beginning inventory is overstated, profits are understated. The effects of errors in beginning and ending inventory are summarized in Exhibit 3.

Note that, since the ending inventory of one accounting period is the beginning inventory of the next period, the effect of an error in the first period will likewise cause an error in profit in the subsequent period. Although total profits for

Exhibit 1   Effects of Error in Ending Inventory on Profit

Correct Ending Inventory			Incorrect Ending Inventory		
Sales		$100,000	Sales		$100,000
Cost of Goods Sold:			Cost of Goods Sold:		
Beginning Inventory	$ 30,000		Beginning Inventory	$ 30,000	
Purchases	90,000		Purchases	90,000	
Cost of Goods Available	120,000		Cost of Goods Available	120,000	
Ending Inventory	− 40,000		Ending Inventory	− 35,000	
Cost of Goods Sold		80,000	Cost of Goods Sold		85,000
Gross Profit		$ 20,000	Gross Profit		$ 15,000

Exhibit 2   Effects of Error in Beginning Inventory on Profit

Correct Beginning Inventory			Incorrect Beginning Inventory		
Sales		$100,000	Sales		$100,000
Cost of Goods Sold:			Cost of Goods Sold:		
Beginning Inventory	$ 30,000		Beginning Inventory	$ 25,000	
Purchases	90,000		Purchases	90,000	
Cost of Goods Available	120,000		Cost of Goods Available	115,000	
Ending Inventory	− 40,000		Ending Inventory	− 40,000	
Cost of Goods Sold		80,000	Cost of Goods Sold		75,000
Gross Profit		$ 20,000	Gross Profit		$ 25,000

Exhibit 3   Effects of Error in Inventory on Profit

Error in Inventory	Effect on Profit
Beginning Inventory Understated	Overstated
Beginning Inventory Overstated	Understated
Ending Inventory Understated	Understated
Ending Inventory Overstated	Overstated

the two periods will be correct, the individual profit figure for each period will be incorrect. Owners' equity will be incorrect for the first period but will be correct by the end of the second period.

Taking a Physical Inventory

Since an accurate inventory amount is essential to the computation of net income, it is important that the procedures for taking a physical inventory be followed carefully. A physical inventory involves two basic steps. Step one constitutes the actual counting of the inventory items. Care must be taken both in counting the individual items and in recording the cost of each particular item. Employees taking a physical inventory should work in pairs; one employee should count the items while the other writes down the amounts and individual costs of the items. Step two involves the *footing of the inventory*. This means multiplying the items by their costs and adding together the costs of all items of inventory.

It is important to ensure that there is a proper cutoff in taking inventory at the end of the physical inventory period. This means that any items physically in the storeroom but already sold to customers *should not be* included in inventory. In addition, items that are part of an inventory but not physically in the storeroom *should be* included in the ending inventory.

Consigned Goods

Consigned goods can create an additional challenge in taking a physical inventory. Occasionally a gift shop in a hotel may stock consigned merchandise. Consigned goods represent inventory that is shelved with the inventory of a business but is not owned by the business. Consigned goods are shipped to a business, but are not paid for until they are sold. Consigned goods are therefore never owned by the business that carries the goods.

Since consigned goods are in stock but never owned, it is important that they are not included in the inventory of the hospitality firm.

Transportation Costs

Dollar amounts used to record inventory and cost of sales should reflect the total purchase cost involved in obtaining a shipment of goods. The total purchase cost should, therefore, include not only the cost of the merchandise but also the cost of getting the merchandise to the place of business. This cost is variously called *shipping, transportation,* or *freight.*

Some suppliers absorb the expenses involved in transporting goods to the buyer. Other suppliers who deliver will charge the buyer for freight costs. In freight terminology, *FOB* means *free on board.* However, it does not necessarily mean *free freight. FOB* is only one part of the terms of freight. Either the point of origin or the point of destination must be specified to determine whether the buyer or seller pays the additional freight charges required to complete delivery. Two common freight terms are *FOB destination* and *FOB shipping point.*

FOB destination means that the seller will deliver the product free of any freight charges to the destination specified by the buyer. By contrast, *FOB shipping point* indicates point of origin. It basically means that the buyer must pay transportation charges to have the merchandise transported to a specified location.

Items that are in transit at the end of an accounting period must be carefully scrutinized through an examination of the terms of sale. If the seller ships merchandise with terms *FOB destination,* title does not pass to the purchaser until the goods reach the purchaser. Merchandise shipped FOB destination should be included on the seller's books at the end of this particular accounting period. If, on the other hand, the seller ships the goods with the terms *FOB shipping point,* the shipped goods are no longer considered part of the seller's inventory.

Items purchased on terms *FOB destination* should not be included on the books of the purchaser until they arrive, while goods purchased on terms *FOB shipping point* should be included on the purchaser's books at the end of the period even if they have not yet arrived.

Inventory Valuation Methods

The four basic methods for valuing ending inventory are specific identification; weighted average; first-in, first-out (FIFO); and last-in, first-out (LIFO). It is important to understand that these four inventory valuation techniques are simply methods of valuing the ending inventory on the books. *The method of inventory valuation a business uses does not usually parallel the physical flow of merchandise through the storeroom.*

Using the data listed in the following table, we will illustrate the four inventory valuation methods:

	Number of Units	Cost per Unit	Total Cost
Beginning inventory	25	$10.00	$ 250.00
February 15 purchase	30	11.00	330.00
May 6 purchase	20	13.00	260.00
August 22 purchase	35	14.00	490.00
October 10 purchase	40	15.00	600.00
December 2 purchase	25	16.00	400.00
Available for sale	175		$2,330.00
Units sold	145		
Ending inventory	30		

Notice that there were 175 units available for sale, 145 units sold, and 30 units remaining in ending inventory. In this section, we will use each of the four techniques to value the same 30 units of ending inventory.

The **specific identification method** is used for valuing big-ticket items. Hotel accountants typically use this method to value certain food and beverage items, such as cases of expensive wine. Under this method, the amounts actually paid for individual items determine their value at the end of the period. Food and beverage items are physically marked at their cost when they are received. These costs are used to value the inventory.

Assuming that the ending inventory of 30 units consisted of 20 units at $16 (December 2 purchase), 2 units at $15 (October 10 purchase), and 8 units at $10 (beginning inventory), the ending inventory under the specific identification method would be valued at $430.

Under the **weighted average method**, the total number of units available for sale is divided into the total cost of the units available for sale. In our example, a unit of ending inventory would be valued at $13.314 per unit, as shown below:

$$\frac{\text{Cost of units available for sale}}{\text{Divided by units available}} \quad \frac{\$2,330.00}{175} = \$13.314$$

Exhibit 4   Summary of Inventory Valuation Methods

	Specific ID	Weighted Average	FIFO	LIFO
Sales	$6,000	$6,000	$6,000	$6,000
Cost of Goods Sold:				
Beginning Inventory	250	250	250	250
Purchases	2,080	2,080	2,080	2,080
Cost of Goods Available	2,330	2,330	2,330	2,330
Ending Inventory	380	399	475	305
Cost of Goods Sold	1,950	1,931	1,855	2,025
Gross Profit	$4,050	$4,069	$4,145	$3,975

Under this method, the ending inventory would be valued at $399.42, calculated as follows:

30 units @ $13.314 = $399.42 (or $399, rounded)

The **first-in, first-out (FIFO) method** assumes that the first units into inventory are the first units out of inventory. The ending inventory therefore consists of the latest purchases, while the cost of goods sold consists of the earliest purchases. The 30 units of ending inventory would be valued as follows under FIFO:

25 units from December 2 purchase @ $16.00 = $400.00
5 units from October 10 purchase @ $15.00 = 75.00
Ending inventory value of 30 units, FIFO $475.00

The 30 units of inventory under FIFO are valued at $475.00, whereas under the weighted average method they were valued at $399.

The **last-in, first-out (LIFO) method** of valuing inventories assumes that the first units in are the last units out of inventory and that the ending inventory consists of the earliest purchases. The value of the ending inventory would be calculated as follows under LIFO:

25 units of beginning inventory @ $10.00 = $250.00
5 units from February 15 purchase @ $11.00 = 55.00
Ending inventory value of 30 units, LIFO $305.00

Comparison and Evaluation of Inventory Valuation Methods

The four inventory methods assign different values to the same 30 units of inventory. Exhibit 4 summarizes these four methods and illustrates their effects on income, assuming that sales are $6,000 for the period.

Notice that the information provided in the table indicated a period of rising prices. That is, every time merchandise was ordered, it cost more than it had before. Because of this inflationary climate, FIFO results in the highest value for ending inventory, and LIFO results in the lowest. This occurs because, under FIFO, the latest (higher) costs are assigned to the ending inventory. Under LIFO, the earliest (lowest) costs are assigned to ending inventory. The weighted average method results in a value for the ending inventory somewhere between those for FIFO and LIFO, since it averages all the costs of inventory for the period.

Since FIFO results in the highest value for the ending inventory, it also results in the lowest value for the cost of goods sold for the period and the highest gross profit for the period. On the other hand, since LIFO has the lowest value for the ending inventory, it results in the highest cost of goods sold figure and the lowest gross profit amount. Since LIFO provides the lowest reported income figure, most companies prefer to use it when reporting to the Internal Revenue Service (IRS).

An inventory valuation computation involving a period of falling prices would produce the opposite effect on profits. Under deflationary conditions, FIFO would result in a lower value for the ending inventory and a higher cost of goods sold than LIFO. FIFO would also result in lower reported income than LIFO.

The consistency principle dictates that once a business selects an inventory valuation method, it should use that method in subsequent years. If the business adheres to this generally accepted accounting principle, its reported profit will be more consistent from year to year. However, this does not mean that once an inventory valuation method is selected, a firm may never change methods. If the firm has a valid reason for changing inventory valuation methods, it may do so. Such a change must be disclosed in the notes to the financial statements.

Estimating Ending Inventory and Cost of Goods Sold

Hospitality firms always take a physical inventory at the end of each fiscal year, whether they use the periodic or the perpetual inventory method. They do this to accurately compile financial statements and to comply with IRS regulations. On a monthly basis, however, it may be too costly or inconvenient to take a physical inventory. Sometimes it may be impossible to do so, such as when a business is destroyed by a fire or flood. However, companies still need to produce financial statements. In lieu of taking a physical inventory, businesses can use one of two methods to estimate ending inventory. They are the retail method and the gross profit method.

The Retail Method

Although the **retail method of inventory valuation** is used primarily by department stores, hospitality firms can also use it effectively. To implement this method, a firm must maintain records at both cost and retail for beginning inventory and purchases. The retail price is the amount at which the item is priced for sale.

Since an accountant would have a record of both beginning inventory and purchases, he or she should therefore know the cost of goods available for sale at both cost and retail. Recall that at the end of a fiscal period, the items included in cost of goods available must either have been sold or be in ending inventory. With that information and a record of sales for the period, the accountant can subtract cost of goods available at retail from sales at retail and end up with ending inventory at retail.

The books list ending inventory at cost, not retail, so there is one more step in the computation. It involves finding the percentage relationship between cost and retail for the business. This is accomplished by simply dividing *the cost of goods available for sale at cost* by *the cost of goods available for sale at retail*. The resulting percentage is then multiplied by the ending inventory at retail. The result is ending inventory at cost.

The following illustration shows the estimate of ending inventory at July 31, 20X3, for a hypothetical firm. Assume the following:

Beginning inventory at cost	$ 12,376
Beginning inventory at retail:	$ 22,277
Purchases at cost:	$ 76,840
Purchases at retail:	$138,312
Net sales at retail:	$132,068

Using these balances, an estimate of ending inventory would be computed as follows:

	Cost Price	Retail Selling Price
Beginning Inventory	$12,376	$ 22,277
Purchases	+ 76,840	+ 138,312
Cost of Goods Available	89,216	160,589

Cost Percentage: $\dfrac{\$89,216}{\$160,589} = 56\%$

Subtract Net Sales at Retail		− 132,068
Ending Inventory at Retail		$ 28,521
Ending Inventory at Cost:		
$28,521 × .56	$15,972	

The Gross Profit Method

The basic assumption under the **gross profit method of inventory valuation** is that the gross profit percentage for the firm is fairly constant from period to period. Therefore, if a restaurant's gross profit percentage was 60 percent over the past five years, it can assume that the current period's gross profit percentage is also 60 percent. Recall the relationship between the gross profit percentage and the cost of goods sold percentage: added together, they must equal 100 percent.

Once the accountant obtains the gross profit percentage, he or she goes to the general ledger and adds beginning inventory and purchases to get cost of goods available for sale. Next, the accountant estimates cost of goods sold by multiplying sales by the gross profit percentage. Finally, the accountant determines ending inventory by subtracting cost of goods sold from cost of goods available for sale.

We will use the following example to illustrate the gross profit method:

Beginning inventory, August 1, 20X3	$16,586
Purchases in August	48,522
Sales in August	93,407
Gross profit percentage	53%

Exhibit 5   Computation of Lower of Cost or Market

Inventory Item	Number of Units	Cost/ Unit	Current Market Value/Unit	1 Cost	2 Market	3 LCM
A	20	$12	$11	$ 240	$ 220	$ 220
B	15	11	10	165	150	150
C	12	16	17	192	204	192
D	30	14	13	420	390	390
E	18	17	17	306	306	306
				$1,323	$1,270	$1,258

Using these account balances and the gross profit ratio of 53 percent, the ending inventory would be $21,207, computed as follows:

Beginning inventory, August 1, 20X3		$16,586
Purchases in August		48,522
Cost of goods available for sale		65,108
Subtract estimated cost of goods sold:		
Sales in August	$93,407	
Cost of goods sold % (1 − .53) × .47		43,901
Estimated ending inventory, August 31, 20X3		$21,207

Lower of Cost or Market (LCM)

Obsolescence, deterioration, or a drop in the current market prices of inventory may cause a firm to lower the value of inventory on its books. The generally accepted accounting principle of conservatism states that inventory should be carried at the lower of cost (on the purchase date) or the market value of the inventory as of the balance sheet date. (This is true for both the periodic and perpetual inventory systems.)

The **lower of cost or market (LCM)** computation can be done either on an item-by-item basis or by comparing total cost with total market value. Exhibit 5 illustrates the lower of cost or market computation. The columns numbered 1 and 2 show the computation on the basis of the lower of total cost or market, while column 3 provides an amount for inventory on an item-by-item basis.

Applying the lower of cost or market value on an item-by-item basis would result in an ending inventory value of $1,258; applying the lower of cost or market to the total of the entire inventory would result in a value of $1,270.

Perpetual Inventory System

Until this point, the chapter discussion has for the most part revolved around periodic inventory systems. The **perpetual inventory system** continuously updates the Merchandise Inventory account. Every time merchandise is purchased for resale, the inventory account is increased. Every time merchandise is sold, the inventory account is decreased.

Exhibit 6   Periodic versus Perpetual Inventory Systems

Event	Periodic		Perpetual	
Purchased 48 bottles of wine @ $8/bottle	Purchases $384		Merchandise Inventory $384	
	Accounts Payable	$384	Accounts Payable	$384
Sold 10 bottles of wine @ $15/bottle for cash	Cash $150		Cash $150	
	Sales	$150	Sales	$150
			Cost of Goods Sold $ 80	
			Merchandise Inventory	$80

Under this system, it is not necessary to estimate the ending inventory for interim statement purposes. Rather, one can simply look at the Inventory account to ascertain the inventory's value. A physical inventory is taken at the end of the year to prove that the book inventory matches the actual inventory.

Under the perpetual system, the Purchases account is not used when merchandise is purchased. Instead, the Merchandise Inventory account is debited, as shown below when $2,000 worth of inventory is purchased on account.

Merchandise Inventory	$2,000	
Accounts Payable		$2,000

Two entries are required under this system when merchandise is sold. The following entries illustrate the cash sale of $4,000 worth of merchandise that has a cost of $1,800.

Cash	$4,000	
Sales		$4,000

Cost of Goods Sold	$1,800	
Merchandise Inventory		$1,800

From these two entries, one can conclude that the gross profit on the sale was $2,200, since Sales minus Cost of Goods Sold equals Gross Profit. Exhibit 6 compares the journal entries that would be made under the periodic and perpetual inventory systems.

Summary

Although inventory as a percentage of total assets is relatively low for most hospitality firms, its impact on profits can be great. Therefore, inventory must be accounted for and controlled carefully. The two primary types of inventory systems are the periodic and the perpetual systems.

Four basic methods for valuing ending inventory are specific identification; weighted average; first-in, first-out (FIFO); and last-in, first-out (LIFO). Each of these methods provides a slightly different valuation of inventory. Therefore, for the sake of consistency, the firm should use the same method each period, unless it has a valid reason for changing it.

Sometimes it may be necessary to estimate the value of inventory, such as when a fire destroys the inventory and its value must be estimated for insurance purposes, or when a physical inventory would be inconvenient or too costly. Two methods used to estimate the value of inventory are the retail method and the gross profit method.

Occasionally, obsolescence, deterioration, or a drop in the current market prices of inventory may cause a firm to lower the value of inventory on its books to comply with the accounting principle of conservatism.

With the growth of technology, many firms are switching to a perpetual inventory system wherein the value of inventory on hand is updated continuously through the firm's computer systems. Of course, even a perpetual inventory system doesn't entirely eliminate the need to perform physical inventory counts.

Key Terms

consigned goods—Goods that have been shipped to a company but do not have to be paid for until they are sold.

first-in, first-out (FIFO) method of inventory valuation—A method of valuing inventory in which the first units into inventory are considered sold first; hence, ending inventory consists of the latest purchases.

gross profit method of inventory valuation—A method of estimating ending inventory based on a historical gross profit percentage for the firm.

last-in, first-out (LIFO) method of inventory valuation—A method of valuing inventory in which the last units into inventory are considered sold first; hence, ending inventory consists of the earliest purchases.

lower of cost or market (LCM)—An accounting procedure for valuing ending inventory based on the generally accepted accounting principle of conservatism.

merchandise inventory—Goods that a hospitality firm holds for resale to guests.

periodic inventory system—A system of accounting for inventory under which cost of goods sold must be computed. There are no continuous inventory records kept, so a physical count of the storeroom is required to determine the inventory on hand.

perpetual inventory system—A system of accounting for inventory that records receipts and issues and provides a continuous record of the quantity and cost of merchandise in inventory.

retail method of inventory valuation—A method of estimating ending inventory based on the relationship between cost and retail price.

specific identification method of inventory valuation—A method of valuing inventory by identifying the actual costs of the purchased and issued units.

weighted average method of inventory valuation—A method of valuing inventory in which the value is determined by averaging the cost of items in the beginning inventory with the cost of items purchased during the period.

 **Review Questions**

1. What major guidelines should a hospitality business follow to control inventory?

2. What are the differences between the periodic and perpetual inventory systems?

3. How is cost of goods sold calculated? How is it related to gross profit?

4. Does an overstatement of ending inventory overstate or understate cost of goods sold for the period? What is the effect of the error on net income for the period?

5. How do the terms under which a supplier ships goods affect inventory valuation and accounting for inventory?

6. How do the LIFO and FIFO methods of inventory valuation differ?

7. How can an area's economic environment affect managers' choices of inventory valuation methods?

8. What special records must be maintained to implement the retail method of estimating inventory?

9. What is the gross profit method of estimating inventory? When would it be necessary to use this method?

10. How is inventory accounted for differently under the perpetual inventory method as opposed to the periodic method?

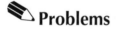 **Problems**

Problem 1

Based on the following transactions and shipping terms between Coldpac Distributors and Marco's Pizzeria, determine who should include the inventory in question on their 12/31/20X8 balance sheet.

1. Marco's received $4,000 worth of inventory on January 3 that was shipped FOB destination by Coldpac on December 28.
2. Marco's received $5,000 worth of inventory on January 2 that was shipped FOB shipping point on December 24.

Problem 2

On July 6, 20X3, the Pro Shop at the Hilton Lagoons Hotel ordered golf clubs and clothing that together cost $8,000, which managers charged to the hotel's account. On July 15, 20X3, the shop sold $2,500 worth of merchandise, which cost $1,400.

Required:

Journalize the entries for July 6 and July 15, assuming:

1. The Pro Shop uses the periodic inventory system.
2. The Pro Shop uses the perpetual inventory system.

Problem 3

The following data is for the month of May 20X8 for the Signature Café:

Purchases	$ 32,400
Ending Inventory	59,000
Cost of Food Sold	29,676

Employee meals are 10 percent of monthly purchases.

Required:

Calculate inventory at May 1, 20X8.

Problem 4

Determine whether the following statements regarding inventory guidelines are true or false.

1. Expensive items should be inventoried daily.
2. Inventory should be kept in a locked storeroom, and every employee should have a key to access it.
3. Inventory control forms should be made ahead of time so that when the inventory is checked periodically, the process will go smoothly.
4. Inventory records should be kept by an accountant who does not have access to the physical inventory.
5. The controller should be notified if there is a significant underage or overage in the inventory.
6. The custodian of the inventory should have access to the inventory records so he or she can be sure that the actual inventory matches the records.

Problem 5

The following data is for the month of June 20X3 for the Fairbanks Hotel:

Beginning Inventory	$ 28,300
Purchases	16,200
Ending Inventory	29,500
Employee Meals—Rooms Department	300
Employee Meals—Food & Beverage Department	500

Required:

Calculate the cost of food used and the cost of food sold for the Fairbanks Hotel for the month of June.

Problem 6

The following data is presented for Tessoff's Restaurant for the month of April:

Beginning inventory, April 1	$ 15,240
Purchases	60,500
Sales	107,020
Gross Profit Percentage	48%

Required:

Find the ending inventory for April using the gross profit method.

Problem 7

Indicate the effects of the following errors on cost of goods sold and net income.

1. Beginning inventory is understated by $10,000.
2. Ending inventory is overstated by $25,000.
3. Beginning inventory is overstated by $30,000 and ending inventory is understated by $10,000.
4. Ending inventory is understated by $5,000 and beginning inventory is understated by $5,000.

Problem 8

The following inventory purchases are made for the Grille:

Date	Units	Price
May 1	30	$6.00
May 8	35	6.50
May 15	32	6.75
May 31	35	6.85

Required:

1. If ending inventory is 40 units, calculate its value using FIFO.
2. If ending inventory is 40 units, calculate its value using LIFO.

Problem 9

The following information relates to the merchandise of the Pro Shop of the Lagoons Resort through May 31, 20X4.

	# of Sets of Golf Clubs	Cost/Set	Total Cost
Beginning Inventory	5	$ 250.00	$ 1,250.00
January 8 purchase	12	265.00	3,180.00
February 12 purchase	20	270.00	5,400.00
March 20 purchase	20	280.00	5,600.00
April 5 purchase	20	290.00	5,800.00
May 18 purchase	10	300.00	3,000.00
Available for sale	87		$ 24,230.00
Sets sold	57		
Ending Inventory	30		

Required:

Journalize the purchase of April 5 and sale of those 20 sets of golf clubs, assuming that each set sells for $495 and that:

1. The Pro Shop uses the periodic inventory system.
2. The Pro Shop uses the perpetual inventory system.

Problem 10

Indicate the effects of the following errors on cost of goods sold and net income:

Error	Amount
1. Ending inventory understated	$ 50,000
2. Beginning inventory overstated	$ 20,000
3. Ending inventory overstated	$ 30,000
4. Beginning inventory understated	$ 12,000

Problem 11

La Boca Restaurant made the following purchases of chardonnay wine:

	# of Cases	Price/Case	Total Cost
Beginning Inventory Jan. 1:	20	$60	$ 1,200
March 10	25	61	1,525
June 20	30	63	1,890
Aug. 29	27	64	1,728
Oct. 10	35	67	2,345
Dec. 1	20	68	1,360
Available for sale	157		10,048

On December 31, La Boca had an inventory of 25 cases of chardonnay wine.

Required:

Calculate the value of the ending inventory of 25 cases under weighted average, LIFO, and FIFO.

Challenge Problems

Problem 12

Using the information provided in Problem 9, complete the following:

Required:

1. Assume that all sets of golf clubs were sold for $495 each, and that the remaining sets consisted of the following:

    > 8 sets from the May 18 purchase
    >
    > 18 sets from the April 5 purchase
    >
    > 4 sets from Beginning Inventory

    Calculate gross profit through May 31 for the Pro Shop.

2. Assume the same selling price for the golf clubs ($495 each). Using the weighted average method of inventory valuation, calculate gross profit through May 31 for the Pro Shop.

Problem 13

Using the information provided in Problem 9, calculate gross profit through May 31 for the Pro Shop, assuming that:

a. The business uses the FIFO inventory valuation.

b. The business uses the LIFO inventory valuation.

Problem 14

The following data pertaining to the Stellar Cellars Restaurant shows both cost and current market value for five items of inventory.

Inventory Item	# of Units	Cost	Market Value
1	25	$12.60	$12.80
2	20	14.25	13.75
3	15	18.30	18.60
4	18	16.40	15.90
5	32	11.20	11.20

Required:

Calculate the value of the inventory using lower of cost or market (LCM) on both a unit basis and a total basis.

Problem 15

The Pro Shop at the Hilton Lagoons Hotel and Golf Club is compiling its July income statement. It is the middle of the busy season and the manager decides not to take the time to do a physical inventory. Instead, she chooses the retail method of estimating inventory.

Beginning inventory was $18,000 at cost and $35,500 at retail. Purchases for the month amounted to $12,000 at cost and $23,600 at retail. Sales for the month were $26,800.

<u>Required:</u>

Estimate ending inventory using the retail method of inventory valuation.

Chapter 11 Outline

Property and Equipment
    Lump Sum Purchase
    Depreciation of Property and
      Equipment
Intangible Assets
Other Assets

Competencies

1. Identify and describe assets that are classified as Property and Equipment on the balance sheet, demonstrate how to account for them, and distinguish between revenue expenditures and capital expenditures. (pp. 355–358)

2. Explain and demonstrate the straight-line method of depreciation. (pp. 358–359)

3. Explain and demonstrate the units of production method of depreciation. (p. 359)

4. Explain and demonstrate the sum-of-the-years' digits method of depreciation. (p. 359)

5. Explain and demonstrate the double declining balance method of depreciation. (p. 360)

6. Explain and demonstrate how to account for china, glassware, silver, linens, and uniforms. (p. 361)

7. Explain and demonstrate how to account for revisions of useful lives of assets and the sale, disposal, or exchange of property and equipment. (pp. 362–364)

8. Describe assets that typically are listed as Intangible Assets or Other Assets on the balance sheet, and demonstrate and explain how to account for them. (pp. 364–365)

11

Property, Equipment, and Other Assets

THE ASSETS of a hospitality firm are typically organized into two main categories: Current Assets and Noncurrent Assets. Current assets are those that are expected to be converted into cash within a year, such as inventory or receivables. Noncurrent assets are expected to have a life of greater than a year.

The four major categories of noncurrent assets include Property and Equipment, Investments, Noncurrent Receivables, and Other Assets. Noncurrent receivables are simply amounts owed to the firm (by owners and officers) that are not due within 12 months. Only the Property and Equipment and Other Assets categories are discussed in this chapter.

Property and Equipment

The Property and Equipment group includes those assets that are depreciated, such as buildings and equipment, and those that are not depreciated, namely land. The Property and Equipment assets were formerly called Fixed Assets. Today, the term *fixed asset* is rarely found on a company's financial statements. The percentage of total assets that are in the Property and Equipment group for a hospitality firm is substantially greater than that for a manufacturing firm. Property and Equipment assets constitute 55 to 85 percent of the total assets of a hospitality firm; this group of assets generally represents only about 30 percent of the assets of a manufacturing firm. Exhibit 1 shows property and equipment assets as a percentage of total assets for several hospitality firms.

The *Uniform System of Accounts for the Lodging Industry,* Tenth Revised Edition, uses the following classifications for the Property and Equipment group of assets: Land, Buildings, Furnishings and Equipment, Leaseholds, and Leasehold Improvements. Similar assets held under capital leases, if material, should be separately presented on the balance sheet or in notes to the financial statements.

Expenditures for Property and Equipment assets are capital expenditures, as opposed to revenue expenditures. **Revenue expenditures** are those expenditures a hospitality firm makes for which the benefits are expected to be received within a year. Examples of revenue expenditures include wages expense and utilities expense. **Capital expenditures**, on the other hand, are expenditures for which the benefits are expected to be received over a period greater than one year. For example, when a hotel is built, its owners expect to realize its benefits over many years, not just one. It is important that capital expenditures be recorded as capital

Exhibit 1   Property, Plant, and Equipment as a Percentage of Total Assets

Company	Percentage
Hilton	43%
InterContinental Hotels Group	63%
Marriott	28%
McDonald's	74%
Wendy's	74%

expenditures rather than as revenue expenditures because of the impact these entries have on the income statement. If a capital expenditure with a life of ten years is recorded as a revenue expenditure, all of the expense will be recorded in one year instead of spread over ten years, which would distort the income statements for all ten years. In this case, net income for year 1 would be understated, whereas net income for years 2 through 10 would be overstated. For example, WorldCom capitalized about $7 billion in maintenance costs that should have been expensed. This serious accounting fraud caused a gross overstatement of income and led to WorldCom's bankruptcy.

Occasionally a company may purchase an item that is technically a capital expenditure, but treat it as a revenue expenditure because the amount is immaterial. An example of this would be the purchase of a $20 calculator.

Property and equipment should be recorded at cost when purchased. The costs of these assets should include all reasonable and necessary expenditures required to get the asset in operating condition. Examples of expenditures that ought to be included in the cost of Property and Equipment are such items as freight charges, sales tax on the purchase, and installation charges. Charges that would not be considered reasonable and necessary include repairs due to damages in handling or a traffic ticket incurred by the truck driver during delivery.

The following will illustrate the recording of an asset's purchase. Assume that the Oakdale Inn has just purchased some exercise equipment from a supplier. The list price of the equipment is $40,000 with terms of 2/10, $n/60$. Under these terms, the Inn receives a 2 percent discount for paying within 10 days; otherwise, the full amount is due in 60 days. The Inn, in this case, is able to pay within the cash discount period. Also assume that sales tax of $1,568 must be paid. Freight charges of $650 and installation costs of $290 are to be paid by the Inn. The Inn also purchases a two-year maintenance contract on the equipment at a total cost of $1,000. Based on this information, the cost to be recorded for the asset is determined as follows:

List price of equipment	$40,000
Less 2% cash discount	800
Net price	39,200
Sales tax	1,568
Freight charges	650
Installation charges	290
Cost of equipment	$41,708

Notice that the maintenance contract is not added to the cost of the equipment and depreciated over the asset's life. Instead, the $1,000 would be recorded as a prepaid asset and expensed over the two years of the contract's life.

When land is purchased, all of the reasonable and necessary expenditures to buy the land are included in the purchase price. These expenditures include property taxes paid, title opinions, surveying costs, brokerage commissions, and any excavating expenses required to get the land into proper condition.

Occasionally a hospitality firm will lease an asset under an agreement requiring the firm to record the lease as a **capital lease**. When this occurs, the leased asset is recorded as an asset on the lessee's books and is included under Property and Equipment as "Leased Asset under Capital Lease."

When a business leases a building, it often finds it necessary to make extensive improvements before opening. Such improvements made to walls, carpeting, ceiling, and lighting are called **Leasehold Improvements,** an asset that is to be amortized over the remaining life of the lease or the life of the improvement, whichever is shorter. For example, assume that the Surfside Restaurant leased a building for ten years and immediately spent $50,000 on improvements that had a life of five years. The restaurant would amortize $10,000 of the cost of the improvements each year with the following entry:

Amortization of Leasehold Improvements	$10,000
Leasehold Improvements	$10,000

Construction in Progress is another asset commonly found in the Property and Equipment section of a hospitality firm's balance sheet. Construction in progress represents all labor, materials, advances on contracts, and interest on construction loans that are incurred in the current construction of property and equipment.

China, Glassware, Silver, Linen, and Uniforms are listed as operating equipment on hospitality firm balance sheets. This asset is an important asset for hospitality firms to control. If silverware is carelessly thrown away with the garbage, for example, there will be an increase in expenses and a corresponding decrease in net income. These assets will be discussed in detail later in this chapter.

Lump Sum Purchase

Occasionally the purchase of two or more assets is made for one price. This is referred to as a **lump sum** (or basket) **purchase**. Sometimes this will include a building, which is depreciable, and land, which is nondepreciable. In this case, the procedure for placing individual assets on the books is as follows. Both assets should be appraised at their current market values. The values of the individual assets are then added up, and each asset is expressed as a percentage of the total appraised value. Next, those respective percentages are multiplied by the total purchase price of the combined assets, and the individual assets are then recorded at their respective amounts.

Assume that a restaurant business makes a lump sum purchase of land, building, and equipment for $500,000. The individual asset accounts would be debited for amounts based on the following computations:

ASSET	APPRAISED VALUE	PERCENTAGE OF TOTAL	APPORTIONMENT OF COST
Land	$300,000	50%	$250,000
Building	240,000	40%	200,000
Equipment	60,000	10%	50,000
	$600,000	100%	$500,000

Depreciation of Property and Equipment

The process by which property or equipment is expensed over its life is called **depreciation**. The total amount of depreciation that can be taken over the life of an asset is equal to the cost of the asset less its salvage value. Through the matching process, every year in the life of an asset, an amount is placed in a contra-asset account called Accumulated Depreciation and the carrying value of the asset is reduced by the same amount. It is important to realize that no one writes a check for depreciation. Depreciation is different from most other expenses in that it is a noncash expense. Depreciation is also not a fund of cash set aside by a company. However, depreciation does save cash in this way: it provides a tax shelter for the firm, since it, like other expenses, reduces taxable income. Property and Equipment assets are typically shown on the books at their book values or at what are sometimes called *carrying values. Book value* (also called *net book value*) is determined when the accumulated depreciation on the asset to date is subtracted from the cost of the asset. Accumulated Depreciation is a contra-asset account and carries a credit balance.

Methods of Depreciation. The four basic methods used to depreciate assets are straight-line, sum-of-the-years' digits, double declining balance, and units of production. Sum-of-the-years' digits and double declining balance are called **accelerated methods of depreciation** because they result in the highest charges in the first year, with lower and lower charges in successive years. These accelerated methods allocate the largest portion of an asset's depreciation costs to the early years of the asset's estimated useful life.

An important concept relating to depreciation is the **salvage value** or residual value of the asset. This value is sometimes referred to as the scrap value of the asset. This is the estimated value of the asset at the end of its useful life. Most of the depreciation methods take salvage value into consideration; the double declining balance method does not.

Straight-line depreciation is the simplest of the four methods. Under this technique, the same amount of depreciation is taken on the asset in each year of its life. To compute the annual depreciation under straight-line, one simply takes the cost of the asset less its salvage value and divides that figure by the estimated life of the asset. For example, assume that a delivery truck costs the firm $34,000, and has a salvage value of $4,000 and a life of five years. As shown in the following illustration, the annual depreciation under straight-line would be $6,000 per year:

Cost of truck	$34,000	
Less salvage value	4,000	
Depreciable cost	$30,000	÷ 5 Yrs. = $6,000 annual depreciation

Total depreciation over life: $6,000 × 5 = $30,000

Under the **units of production depreciation** method, depreciation taken is based on the usage of the asset. In the preceding example of the $34,000 delivery truck with a $4,000 salvage value, the depreciation would be computed in the following way: First, the truck's useful miles would be estimated. Assume that this figure is 100,000. We would divide this into the cost less salvage value of $30,000. This would give a depreciation rate of $.30 per mile. If, in the first year of its use, the truck had been driven 12,000 miles, the depreciation taken for the first year would be 12,000 miles times $.30, or $3,600.

Under the **sum-of-the-years' digits depreciation** method, the years of the asset's life are added together; the resulting total becomes the denominator in a fraction used to calculate each year's depreciation. For instance, using the truck example once again, we would sum the years of its life in this way:

$$5 + 4 + 3 + 2 + 1 = 15$$

The following is a quick formula for figuring this:

$$\frac{n(n + 1)}{2}$$

$$\text{where, if } n = 5, \quad \frac{5(6)}{2} \quad = \quad 15$$

The first year we would take $\frac{5}{15}$ of the difference between the cost and the salvage value, a difference of $30,000, and get $10,000 depreciation. Depreciation for the other years is shown in the following table:

Table I

			$34,000
Cost of truck			$34,000
Less salvage value			4,000
Depreciable cost			$30,000
YEAR	RATE	DEPRECIABLE COST	ANNUAL DEPRECIATION
1	5/15	$30,000	$10,000
2	4/15	30,000	8,000
3	3/15	30,000	6,000
4	2/15	30,000	4,000
5	1/15	30,000	2,000
Total Depreciation			$30,000

The **double declining balance depreciation** method ignores salvage value while computing annual depreciation. Under this method, the straight-line rate of depreciation is calculated first with the division of the life of the asset into 100 percent. In the example of the $34,000 truck, we would divide 5 (years) into 100 (percent) and get 20 percent per year. Then the straight-line rate of 20 percent would be multiplied by two to get the double declining rate, which would be 40 percent. Thus, in the first year of depreciation for the truck, the depreciation would be $34,000 times 40 percent, or $13,600. In the second year, the $34,000 cost minus the first year's depreciation of $13,600 would yield $20,400, which would be multiplied by 40 percent to get the second year's depreciation of $8,160. The remaining years' depreciation is illustrated in the following table. Notice that although the salvage value is not used in the computation of the annual depreciation under this method, one must be careful not to depreciate the asset below the salvage value in the later years. Also notice that the depreciation in year 5 is limited to $406 rather than 40 percent of $4,406 so that the asset is not depreciated below its $4,000 salvage value.

Table II

Cost of truck			$34,000
YEAR	RATE	DECLINING BALANCE	ANNUAL DEPRECIATION
1	40%	$34,000	$13,600
2	40%	20,400	8,160
3	40%	12,240	4,896
4	40%	7,344	2,938
5	40%	4,406	406
	Total Depreciation		$30,000

Depreciation for Fractional Periods. If the $34,000 truck had been purchased on September 1, 20X3, the depreciation taken in 20X3 under the straight-line method would have been $2,000 for the four months it was owned, as follows:

$$\text{Depreciable cost of } \$30,000 \div 5 \text{ Years} = \$6,000$$

$$\text{Depreciation for September–December 20X3} = \$6,000 \times \frac{4}{12} = \underline{\$2,000}$$

Calculation of the depreciation for the truck for September through December of 20X3 and full-year 20X4 under the sum-of-the-years' digits method would be as follows:

$$\text{Year 20X3}$$

$$\text{Depreciable cost of } \$30,000 \times \frac{5}{15} \times \frac{4}{12} = \$3,333$$

Year 20X4

Depreciable cost of $30,000 $\times \frac{5}{15} \times \frac{8}{12}$ = $6,667

+ $30,000 $\times \frac{4}{15} \times \frac{4}{12}$ = $\underline{2,667}$

Total Depreciation $\underline{\underline{\$9,334}}$

If the truck were being depreciated under the double declining balance method, the depreciation for 20X3 and 20X4 would be $4,533 and $11,787, respectively, as illustrated:

Year 20X3

Cost = $34,000 $\times$ 40% $\times \frac{4}{12}$ = $4,533

Year 20X4

Declining balance of $34,000 − 4,533 = $29,467 $\times$ 40% = $11,787

China, Glassware, Silver, Linen, and Uniforms. Properties use a variety of methods to charge the cost of china, glassware, silver, linen, and uniforms to operations. Listed below are examples of these methods:

1. Consider these items part of inventory and physically count and reflect the aggregate cost of the items on hand.

2. Capitalize the base stock of these items and then expense the cost of the items subsequently bought and placed in service.

3. Initially capitalize the base stock and then depreciate that amount to 50 percent of the cost over a reasonably short period. Properties that use this method take no further depreciation and expense the cost of items subsequently bought and placed in service.

Each of these methods has conceptual merit; however, in order to foster uniformity, the tenth edition of the *USALI* suggests a new approach. If china, linen, glassware, silver, or uniforms are purchased and determined to have a useful life of less than one year, they should be recorded as current assets and expensed when they are replaced. If any of these items are determined to have a useful life of more than one year, they should be recorded as long–term assets. Once they are placed in service, these long–term assets should be expensed ratably to the appropriate expense account over their estimated useful life.[1]

Financial versus Tax Reporting. Any of the depreciation methods discussed here can be used for financial reporting purposes. Tax legislation in 1981 and 1982 liberalized tax depreciation rules with the enactment of an Accelerated Cost Recovery System (ACRS), which provided for faster recovery (depreciation) of capital expenditures. For tax reporting purposes, all assets acquired after 1981 must be depreciated with either straight-line depreciation or ACRS. Under ACRS, assets are arbitrarily placed into one of six property class lives. Predetermined rates are then applied to the asset's cost with salvage value ignored. The Tax Reform Act of

1986 created the Modified Accelerated Cost Recovery System (MACRS), which provided for eight classes of property and lengthened the recovery periods. In financial accounting, a building may be depreciated over 30 years or more. MACRS currently allows, for tax purposes, recovery over 39 years. Similarly, furnishings and equipment may be depreciated over seven to ten years (or more) for financial accounting purposes, while the same items are depreciated for tax purposes over five years under MACRS. Thus, the timing of reported net income for financial purposes can be significantly different from that for taxable income.

In the later years of an asset's life, the deduction for depreciation, especially that for furnishings and equipment, will be greater for financial accounting than for tax accounting. At the end of the asset's life, the deduction for depreciation will be the same in total for both financial reporting and tax accounting. The difference is in the timing of the deduction. Firms may now choose to use optional straight-line depreciation with half-year convention instead of MACRS. (*Half-year convention* means that, regardless of the month of the year when an asset is purchased, one-half of a year's depreciation is taken in the year of purchase.)

Revision of Useful Lives of Assets. Occasionally during the life of a depreciable asset, the asset's useful life is revised. In this situation, the remaining depreciable cost of the asset is simply spread over its remaining life. Assume in the case of the $34,000 delivery truck that, after three years of its life, managers determined that its total life was eight years instead of five years. The depreciation for year 4 would be computed as follows:

Depreciable cost	$30,000
Depreciation for years 1, 2, & 3	18,000
Remaining depreciable cost	12,000
Remaining life: 5 years	
Depreciation for year 4: $12,000 ÷ 5 = $2,400	

Disposal of Property and Equipment. Occasionally a firm will take a Property and Equipment asset off the books because the asset is being scrapped, sold, or traded in. If an asset is scrapped and has been fully depreciated, it is necessary to remove both the asset and related accumulated depreciation from the books. Assume that a truck with a cost of $34,000 and a salvage value of zero was fully depreciated. In this case, the following entry would be made:

Accumulated Depreciation—Truck	$34,000	
Truck		$34,000

If the same asset is scrapped before it is fully depreciated, a different entry is made. Assume that the same truck costing $34,000 has been depreciated in the amount of $28,000. In this case, the journal entry would be:

Accumulated Depreciation—Truck	$28,000	
Loss on Disposal of Asset	6,000	
Truck		$34,000

The loss on the disposal of this asset would be closed into the Income Summary account at the end of the next fiscal period.

Sometimes Property and Equipment assets are disposed of through a sale that results in a gain or loss. Suppose the same truck had a book value of $6,000, based on a cost of $34,000 and an accumulated depreciation balance of $28,000. If this truck were sold for $8,000, the following journal entry would be made:

Cash	$ 8,000	
Accumulated Depreciation—Truck	28,000	
Truck		$34,000
Gain on Disposal of Asset		2,000

The gain of $2,000 is simply the difference between the selling price of $8,000 and the book value of $6,000.

Assume the same facts concerning the $34,000 truck, except that it is sold for $4,000. Since it had a book value of $6,000 and was sold for $4,000, a loss of $2,000 would result. The journal entry to record this transaction would be as follows:

Cash	$ 4,000	
Accumulated Depreciation—Truck	28,000	
Loss on Disposal of Asset	2,000	
Truck		$34,000

Exchange of Property and Equipment Assets. Property and Equipment assets, such as the truck, are commonly exchanged or traded in for similar assets. Assume that the $34,000 truck is exchanged along with $36,000 cash for a new truck that has a list price of $38,000. At the time of the exchange, the old $34,000 truck has accumulated depreciation of $28,000; hence, it has a book value of $6,000. Notice that, although the book value is $6,000, the firm is getting only $2,000 on the trade-in. Therefore, there is a loss of $4,000. The entry to record the exchange is:

Truck—New	$38,000	
Accumulated Depreciation—Old Truck	28,000	
Loss on Disposal of Asset	4,000	
Cash		$36,000
Truck—Old		34,000

Notice how this entry would change if, instead, the hospitality firm were given $7,000 on the trade-in and consequently had to pay only $31,000 for the new truck. In this case, the journal entry would be:

Truck—New	$37,000	
Accumulated Depreciation—Old Truck	28,000	
Cash		$31,000
Truck—Old		34,000

The Financial Accounting Standards Board (FASB) has stated that no gains are to be recorded on exchanges. Instead, the gain is to be reflected in the value of the asset acquired. Two points should be noted concerning these two entries:

1. The generally accepted accounting principle of conservatism states that losses should be recorded, but not gains.

2. Tax reporting rules differ from financial reporting rules. In reporting for tax purposes, neither gains nor losses are recorded on exchanges of similar assets.

Intangible Assets

Intangible assets are assets that have long lives but no physical substance. Common intangible assets are franchises, trademarks, patents, goodwill, copyrights, leaseholds, and leasehold improvements.

The **franchise** is a very common intangible asset in the hospitality business. It is the right to do a certain business in a given geographical area for a certain period of time. Days Inns Worldwide and Taco Bell are examples of companies that grant franchises around the world.

A **trademark** is defined as a name, mark, or character given legal protection. McDonald's Golden Arches is an example of a trademark.

A **patent** is an exclusive right given by the federal government for use and sale of a product. Patent protection is granted for a period of 17 years. The recipe for Coca-Cola is an example of a patent.

Goodwill is the excess of purchase price over the appraised value of assets. Goodwill exists when the expected future earnings are greater than the normal rate for the industry. However, goodwill is put on the books only when it is purchased by a company.

A **copyright** is an exclusive right over a literary or artistic work. Copyrights are granted to the creator and extend for the life of the creator plus 50 years. Copyrights should be amortized over their lives or over the years in which revenue from the work is expected, whichever is shorter. Operating manuals are an example of the kind of item that should be copyrighted.

A **leasehold** is a right to lease a given property for a fixed number of years. A leasehold could be put on the books if a lease requires the lessee to pay the last year's rent in advance. The advance payment is debited to Leaseholds; in the last year of the lease, the advance payment is transferred to Rent Expense.

Leasehold improvements (mentioned earlier in the chapter) should be amortized over the life of the improvements or the life of the lease, whichever is shorter.

Intangible assets, when purchased, are placed in an asset account, as illustrated below in the case of a franchise being purchased for $100,000:

Franchise Fee	$100,000	
Cash		$100,000

Intangible assets are amortized under a straight-line technique over a period of up to 40 years. **Amortization** is a process similar to depreciation. For example, assume that a hospitality firm purchases a franchise granting it rights for a period of up to 20 years in exchange for $50,000. Every year the firm would make a journal entry debiting Amortization Expense for $2,500 and crediting Franchise Fee for $2,500. The Amortization Expense account would be closed to the Income Summary account at the end of each fiscal period.

Other Assets

The Other Assets category on the balance sheet typically includes these four areas:

- Security Deposits
- Deferred Charges
- Deferred Income Taxes
- Other

Security deposits include funds deposited to secure occupancy or utility services (such as telecommunications, water, electricity, and gas) and any similar types of deposits.

Deferred charges, also called *deferred assets* or *deferred expenses*, are expenses that are prepaid yet are noncurrent. They are distinguished from Prepaid Expenses that would show up in the Current Assets section of the balance sheet. Since they are noncurrent, they benefit future periods. An example of a deferred charge would be financing costs related to long-term debt.

Deferred income taxes result from the tax effects of temporary differences between the bases of noncurrent assets and noncurrent liabilities for financial and income tax reporting purposes.

Other is a miscellaneous category for items that do not fit neatly into the other three categories. Items included here are the cash surrender value of life insurance on the officers of the company, organization costs such as legal fees, and any intangible assets carried on the books.

The *USALI* requires that **preopening expenses** be expensed when incurred. Hospitality firms outside the United States may be allowed to amortize preopening expenses, depending on local conventions and laws.

Summary

Property and Equipment, Intangible Assets, and Other Assets are assets that have a life of greater than one year. Assets in the Property and Equipment group are depreciated over their lives. It is important to include all reasonable and necessary expenditures in the cost of an asset.

The commonly used depreciation methods are straight-line, units of production, sum-of-the-years' digits, and double declining balance. The latter two are called *accelerated methods of depreciation* because they take more depreciation in the early years of the asset's life and less depreciation in the later years. Salvage value or residual value is the value of the depreciable asset at the end of its useful life. An asset cannot be depreciated below salvage value. When a depreciable asset is purchased during a fiscal year, it is necessary to calculate the depreciation for only part of the year. Occasionally a revision is made in the life of a depreciable asset. In this event, the remaining depreciable cost is spread over the remaining useful life of the asset.

When Property and Equipment assets are disposed of, it is necessary to calculate the gain or loss on the sale. In the case of exchanges of property assets, losses are recognized but gains are not. Financial and tax rules differ in the case of gains or losses on exchange of similar assets.

The Other Assets category includes items such as security deposits, deferred charges, deferred income taxes, and intangible assets, such as goodwill and unamortized franchise fees.

Endnotes

1. This section is based on the discussion of China, Glassware, Silver, Linen, and Uniforms in *Uniform System of Accounts for the Lodging Industry*, 10th rev. ed. (Lansing, Mich.: Educational Institute of the American Hotel & Lodging Association, 2006; © Hotel Association of New York City).

 # Key Terms

accelerated methods of depreciation—Methods of depreciation that result in higher depreciation charges in the first year; charges gradually decline in amount over the lives of fixed assets. Sum-of-the-years' digits and double declining balance are accelerated methods of depreciation.

amortization—The systematic transfer of the partial cost of an intangible long-lived asset (such as purchased goodwill, franchise rights, and trademarks) to an expense called Amortization. The asset cost is generally reduced and shown at its remaining cost to be amortized.

capital expenditure—An expenditure for which the benefits are expected to be received over a period of greater than one year. It is recorded to an asset account and not directly to expense.

capital lease—A classification of lease agreements that are of relatively long duration, are generally noncancellable, and in which the lessee assumes responsibility for executory costs. For accounting purposes, capital leases are capitalized in a way similar to that for the purchase of a fixed asset (i.e., recorded as an asset with recognition of a liability).

China, glassware, silver, linen, and uniforms—Assets included under Operating Equipment on a hospitality firm's balance sheet.

Construction in Progress—An asset commonly found in the Property and Equipment section of a hospitality firm's balance sheet. It represents all labor, materials, advances on contracts, and interest on construction loans that are incurred in the current construction of property and equipment.

copyright—An exclusive right over a literary or artistic work granted by the federal government to the creator and extended for the life of the creator plus 50 years. Copyrights should be amortized over their lives or over the years in which revenue from the work is expected, whichever is shorter.

deferred charges—Expenses that are prepaid yet are noncurrent. Since they are noncurrent, they benefit future periods. They are distinguished from prepaid expenses that would show up in the Current Assets section of the balance sheet. Deferred charges are typically associated with financing costs related to long-term debt. Also called *deferred assets* or *deferred expenses.*

deferred income taxes—When the income taxes on the statement of income exceed the amount of liability to government tax agencies for the year, the business records the excess as deferred income taxes. This excess generally represents timing differences with respect to payment dates of taxes.

depreciation—The systematic transfer of part of a tangible long-lived asset's cost to an expense called Depreciation. The asset cost is generally not reduced, but is offset by an entry to the Accumulated Depreciation account, which represents the depreciation recorded on an asset from the point at which it was acquired. Depreciation is usually associated with assets classified as Property and Equipment, but not with land.

double declining balance depreciation—An accelerated method of depreciation that ignores salvage value in the computation of annual depreciation. Although the salvage value is ignored, one must be careful not to depreciate the asset below its salvage value in the later years.

franchise—A common intangible asset found in the hospitality business. It is the right to do a certain business in a given geographical area for a certain period of time.

goodwill—An intangible asset that is the excess of the purchase price over the appraised value of a company's assets. Goodwill exists when the expected future earnings of an operation are greater than the normal rate for the industry. Goodwill is put on the books, however, only when it is purchased by a company.

intangible assets—Noncurrent assets that do not have physical substance; their value is derived from rights or benefits associated with their ownership. Examples include franchises, leaseholds, goodwill, patents, copyrights, and trademarks. When intangible assets are purchased, they are placed in an asset account and amortized under a straight-line technique over a period of up to 40 years.

leasehold—The right to use property or equipment by virtue of a lease for a fixed number of years. It could be put on the books if a lease requires the lessee to pay the last year's rent in advance.

leasehold improvements—Renovations or remodeling performed on leased buildings or space prior to the commencement of operations. For accounting purposes, all leasehold improvements are capitalized (i.e., recorded as an asset with recognition of a liability). This asset is to be amortized over the remaining life of the lease or the life of the improvement, whichever is shorter.

lump sum purchase—The purchase of two or more assets made for one price. Sometimes this will include a building, which is depreciable, and land, which is nondepreciable.

patent—An exclusive right granted by the federal government to use, manufacture, sell, or lease a product or design. The right is granted for 17 years.

preopening expense—Costs associated with certain business activities that occur before a company is operational. They include amounts spent for employee training, salaries, and wages; and advertising and promotional expenses.

revenue expenditure—An expenditure a hospitality firm makes for which the benefits are expected to be received within a year. Examples include wages expense and utilities expense.

salvage value—Estimated market value of an asset at the time it is to be retired from use. Also called *residual value* or *scrap value.*

security deposits—Funds deposited to secure occupancy or utility services (such as telecommunications, water, electricity, and gas) and any similar types of deposits.

straight-line depreciation—A method of distributing depreciation expense evenly throughout the estimated life of an asset (that is, the same amount of depreciation is taken on the asset in each year of its life).

sum-of-the-years' digits depreciation—A method that uses a fraction in computing depreciation expense. The numerator of the fraction is the remaining years of the asset's estimated useful life. This figure changes with each year's computation of depreciation. The denominator of the fraction is the sum of the digits of the asset's useful life. This figure remains constant with each year's computation of depreciation. Each year's depreciation expense is determined by multiplying this fraction by the asset's cost less its salvage value. This method is an accelerated method of depreciation and hence assigns more depreciation in the early years and less in the later years.

trademark—A name, mark, or character given legal protection. It is an intangible asset.

units of production depreciation—A method of depreciation in which depreciation is taken based on the usage of the asset.

Review Questions

1. How does a revenue expenditure differ from a capital expenditure? What are some examples of each?

2. What are some common expenditures included in the cost of a Property and Equipment asset?

3. How are the values of individual assets determined in the case of a lump-sum or basket purchase?

4. How valid are the following two statements about depreciation?

    a. Depreciation represents a fund of cash set aside for the replacement of an asset.

    b. Depreciation has no effect on the taxes an organization pays.

5. What does *accelerated depreciation* mean? Which depreciation methods are considered accelerated?

6. What is *salvage value* or *residual value?* Which depreciation methods take the salvage value into account when the annual depreciation is calculated?

7. What is the preferred procedure used to account for china, glassware, silver, linen, and uniforms?

8. What are the differences between financial and tax reporting of gains or losses on the exchange of a Property and Equipment asset?

9. How is the gain or loss on the sale of a Property and Equipment asset calculated?

10. What four specific items could be included in the Other Assets section of the balance sheet?

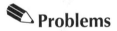 Problems ─────────────────────────────────

Problem 1

For each of the following purchases, does the purchase represent a capital or a revenue expenditure?

a. Complete remodeling of a restaurant dining room at a cost of $80,000.

b. Repainting the exterior of a delivery truck at a cost of $500.

c. Purchase of a pizza oven at a cost of $18,000.

d. Purchase of a dozen pencil sharpeners with a life of ten years at a total cost of $65.

e. Overhaul of the engine on a tour bus at a cost of $5,000, extending the life of the bus by five years.

f. Purchase of a computer system at a cost of $35,000.

Problem 2

Indicate whether the assets below should be listed on the balance sheet under Current Assets or Property and Equipment:

Inventory	Prepaid Expenses
Land	Notes Receivable
Accounts Receivable	Furnishings and Equipment
Leaseholds	Building
Construction in Progress	Short-Term Investments

Problem 3

Windswept Inns recently leased a building for 10 years. Before opening the building for business, Windswept made $40,000 worth of improvements to the walls, ceilings and carpeting. The life of the improvements is expected to be eight years.

Required:

Record the annual journal entry for the amortization of the improvements.

Problem 4

The Bay View Restaurant has purchased a new dishwasher for its own use.

Required:

Using the following information, determine the proper amount to be capitalized in the asset account Equipment.

Invoice price of equipment	$8,000
Cash discount allowed: 2% of invoice	160
Freight-in paid	300
Speeding ticket given to our truck driver while the driver was delivering equipment	25
Installation costs	150
Sales tax on purchase	308
Repair of damages due to equipment being dropped off truck	200

Problem 5

Festive Properties has just purchased a parcel of land for a hotel. The following expenditures are related to this land purchase:

Cost of land	$400,000
Property taxes	6,000
Title opinion	800
Surveying costs	3,000
Brokerage commission paid	10,000
Cost of demolition of existing building	5,000

Required:

Determine the amount that should be capitalized in the land account for this purchase.

Problem 6

Premier Properties purchased equipment costing $60,000 in 20X4. The equipment has no salvage value and had been depreciated in 20X4 and 20X5 using straight–line depreciation based on a six–year life. At the beginning of 20X6, Premier revised the estimated life of the equipment to a total life of eight years.

Required:

Calculate the annual depreciation for 20X6.

Problem 7

Wanda's Pantry has purchased $45,000 worth of equipment, which has a four–year life and a salvage value of $5,000.

Required:

Calculate the annual depreciation over the life of the equipment using double declining balance depreciation.

Problem 8

Hospitality Services Corporation has purchased a new delivery vehicle. The cost is $30,000 with an estimated life of five years and a $2,500 residual value.

Required:

Calculate the depreciation for years one and five under the straight–line and the double declining balance methods of depreciation.

Problem 9

The Tree Line Inn has purchased a shuttle bus to transport guests to and from a local ski lodge. The cost of the bus is $40,000; its salvage value is $4,000; and its life is five years with expected usable mileage of 100,000.

Required:

Calculate the first year's depreciation under each of the following methods:

1. Straight-line.
2. Units of production, assuming the bus traveled 15,000 miles in year 1.
3. Sum-of-the-years' digits.
4. Double declining balance.

Problem 10

Blue Lake Inn purchased an ice machine with a ten-year life on January 6, 20X3. The $3,500 purchase was recorded as a debit to Equipment Expense and a credit to Cash.

Required:

This capital expenditure was recorded as a revenue expenditure. Determine the effect of this error on the following (assume straight-line depreciation and no salvage value):

1. The amount of understatement or overstatement of Operating Income in 20X3 and 20X4.

2. The amount of understatement or overstatement of Property and Equipment in 20X3 and 20X4.

Problem 11

Empire Hotels recently purchased a parcel of land, a building, and some furnishings for $1,200,000 cash. The land was appraised $400,000, the building at $1,400,000, and the furnishings at $200,000.

Required:

Journalize the entry to record this lump sum purchase.

Challenge Problems

Problem 12

Deli Catering is trading in its old delivery truck for a new model with a list price of $24,000. The old truck cost $18,000 and has accumulated depreciation of $15,000.

Required:

1. Record the exchange, assuming the additional cash paid is $20,000.
2. Record the exchange, assuming the additional cash paid is $22,000.
3. Explain how the recognition of the gains or losses would differ under tax reporting rules.

Problem 13

Star Resorts plans to depreciate $50,000 worth of equipment over eight years. The equipment has a salvage value of $5,000.

Required:

Calculate the annual depreciation over the life of the equipment under straight-line and double declining balance methods.

Problem 14

For the year 20X1, the Landmark Restaurant had sales of $800,000 and expenses of $700,000 excluding depreciation. The building is being leased and the only depreciable asset is equipment in the amount of $100,000. The equipment has a life of 10 years with zero salvage value. Calculate the earnings before tax for 20X1 if:

1. The equipment is depreciated under straight-line depreciation.
2. The equipment is depreciated under double declining balance depreciation.

Problem 15

The Valley Hotel is remodeling its fitness center and disposing of exercise equipment that cost $20,000 and has accumulated depreciation of $18,000.

Required:

Record the disposal under each of the following conditions:

1. The equipment is scrapped.
2. The equipment is sold for $4,000.
3. The equipment is sold for $1,000.

Chapter 12 Outline

Notes Payable
Accounting for Payroll-Related Liabilities
    Payroll Records
    Regular Pay and Overtime Pay
    Payroll Journal Entries
    Reporting Tips
Other Current Liabilities
    Property Taxes

Competencies

1. Identify and describe current liabilities that hospitality firms commonly carry. (p. 375)

2. Distinguish between notes payable and accounts payable, and demonstrate how to account for notes payable. (pp. 376–378)

3. Describe payroll systems, internal control policies and procedures that are appropriate for them, and some of the forms, records, and procedures required in payroll systems. (pp. 378–381)

4. Demonstrate how to calculate regular and overtime pay and describe the circumstances under which each is due to staff. (pp. 381–383)

5. Demonstrate how to make payroll journal entries, and describe the payroll taxes imposed on U.S. employers and the related forms and procedures. (pp. 383–389)

6. Describe payroll accounting for tipped employees with respect to employee tip reporting, minimum wage, tip credit, net pay, and overtime pay. (pp. 389–391)

7. Demonstrate how to account for property taxes. (pp. 391–392)

12

Current Liabilities and Payroll

THIS CHAPTER covers the major current liabilities of the hospitality firm, with an emphasis on payroll liabilities. Liabilities are debts of the organization that are typically classified on the basis of their maturity. Long-term liabilities are expected to be paid off over a period of greater than a year; they include bonds payable and mortgages payable. Current liabilities are expected to be paid off within a year. Current liabilities include accounts payable, notes payable, and wages payable.

The amounts of most current liabilities are exact and known to exist for the firm. For example, if the company purchases $15,000 worth of merchandise from a supplier, the liability is recorded at $15,000. A company may know of the existence of certain other liabilities, but may be uncertain of their amounts. These liabilities are referred to as *estimated liabilities*. Examples include liabilities for product warranty and liability for income tax. If a firm expects to have a liability resulting from product warranty, it would estimate that amount and record the liability accordingly. In the case of a $50,000 estimated liability for product warranty, the journal entry would be:

Warranty Expense	$50,000	
Liability for Warranty		$50,000

When a company estimates its income taxes and determines them to be approximately $80,000, it makes the following journal entry:

Income Tax Expense	$80,000	
Income Tax Payable		$80,000

The term **loss contingency** refers to situations in which a liability is reasonably estimable; while it is not certain in nature, it is rather probable. An example of a loss contingency would be a pending lawsuit. In this case, the liability should be put on the books at its estimated amount.

A **contingent liability**, on the other hand, is a liability that is based on some future event. A common contingent liability is a debt guarantee that a company has agreed to. For example, a parent company might agree to guarantee the debt of a subsidiary should the subsidiary fail to pay the debt. It is important to realize that contingent liabilities are not real liabilities and therefore should not be included in the Liabilities section of the balance sheet. Instead, they should be included as footnotes to the financial statements.

Notes Payable

Accounts payable are the most common current liability on the books of hospitality firms. They represent amounts owed to suppliers of goods or services due in one year or less. Typically these liabilities have maturities of 30, 60, or 90 days.

Like accounts payable, notes payable are current liabilities, but they differ in this way: a note payable is a written promise to pay an amount in the future, whereas an account payable is an oral promise to pay. A note payable, because it is in writing, represents a more stringent claim on the debtor. A firm might sign a note payable in the following situation. Suppose the firm owed a supplier an amount on open account represented by an account payable, and was unable to pay at the maturity date. In this case, the supplier could require the debtor to sign a note to promise to pay the principal with interest at some future date.

Assume that a company exchanged an account payable for a note payable in the amount of $10,000 with interest at 12 percent due in 90 days. It would make the following journal entry:

Accounts Payable	$10,000	
Notes Payable		$10,000

In 90 days, at the maturity date of the note, the following journal entry would be made when payment is made on the note:

Notes Payable	$10,000	
Interest Expense	300	
Cash		$10,300

The interest is calculated based on the basic formula Interest = Principal × Rate × Time, or $10,000 × .12 × $\frac{90}{360}$. (To simplify matters, we are assuming that there are 360 days in a year rather than 365.)

Alternatively, a company could sign a note payable simply upon borrowing cash from a bank. Assume that the Alpine Company borrowed $15,000 from the Commercial Bank on November 1, 20X1, agreeing to pay principal and interest at 8 percent in six months. On November 1, 20X1, the journal entry for borrowing the money at the bank would be:

Cash	$15,000	
Notes Payable		$15,000

Assuming that financial statements were not prepared at the end of November, the Alpine Company would make the following adjusting entry on December 31, 20X1, to accrue the interest on the note for November and December:

Interest Expense	$200	
Interest Payable		$200

Tax and Accounting Sites Directory

Tax			
Tax Topics	Federal Tax Law	State & Local Tax	Internat'l Tax
Tax Forms & Pubs	Tax Software	Guides-Tips-Help	IRS Links
Rates & Tables	News & Updates	Tax Associations	Policy & Reform
Finance & Investing	Publishers & CPE	Tax Discussions	Academia
Tax & Acctg Jobs	Firms & Careers	Tax Bookstore	

Accounting			
Financial Reporting	Auditing & Fraud	Managerial	Gov. & NFP
International	Information Systems	Software	AICPA Links
On-Line News	Regulatory Bodies	Associations	Certification
Firms & Careers	Government & Data	Publishers & CPE	Academia
Discussions	General Law	Web Services	Web Search

Payroll / HR			
Federal Topics	State Topics	Human Resources	APA Links
Forms & Pubs	Payroll Services	Benefit Admin.	IRS Links
Payroll Software	Govt & Regulation	Retirement Plans	Associations
	Tax & Compliance	Discussions	

| Home | Search | Add URL | About | Awards | Legal Disclaimer | Privacy Policy |

Taxsites.com provides links to many Internet sites that relate to accounting or taxes. (Courtesy of Schmidt Enterprises, LLC, 2 November 1998) © 1995–2005 Accountants World, LLC/ E-mail: webmaster@taxsites.com

The amount of interest ($200) was determined as follows:

$$\text{Interest} = \text{Principal} \times \text{Rate} \times \text{Time}$$
$$= \$15,000 \times .08 \times \frac{60}{360}$$

On the maturity date of the note, it is important that the firm recall the entry it made on December 31, 20X1, because that entry affects the entry made on the payment date. On May 1, 20X2, the payment date of this note, the following journal entry would be made:

Notes Payable	$15,000	
Interest Expense	400	
Interest Payable	200	
Cash		$15,600

The $15,600 represents the total principal of $15,000 plus the interest of $600 on the note.

Our discussion so far has assumed that the note payable was written for the principal only. Sometimes, however, the interest is included in the face amount of the note. For example, in the case of the preceding $15,000 note, the bank could add the $600 interest to the principal and make the note for $15,600. The November 1, 20X1, journal entry in this case would be:

Cash	$15,000	
Discount on Notes Payable	600	
Notes Payable		$15,600

It would be incorrect on November 1 to debit Interest Expense for the difference between the cash received and the amount of the note payable. This is because the $600 difference is not yet interest expense; rather, it will accrue as interest expense over the life of the note. Since it is not yet interest expense, the proper account to use is Discount on Notes Payable, which is a contra-liability account with a debit balance. This note would require the following journal entry on December 31, 20X1, to accrue interest:

Interest Expense	$200	
Discount on Notes Payable		$200

Finally, in this case, the following journal entry would be made on May 1, 20X2, the maturity date of the note:

Notes Payable	$15,600	
Interest Expense	400	
Discount on Notes Payable		$ 400
Cash		15,600

Accounting for Payroll-Related Liabilities

Payroll represents a very large expense for hospitality operations. It usually represents the greatest expense for the club and lodging industries; in the restaurant industry, payroll expense runs closely behind the cost of food and beverage sold. Our discussion of payroll begins with the following list of the most important control features that should be in place for this major liability:

1. Payroll functions should be segregated wherever possible. As in all accounting procedures, there should be an attempt to segregate by function; the area of payroll is certainly no exception. This can be a problem in small operations that don't have many employees. However, the following functions should be performed by separate individuals where possible:

    *   Authorization of employment and establishment of wage rates for employees.

    *   Reporting of hours worked by employees.

- Actual preparation of the payroll.

- Signing of the payroll checks.

- Distribution of checks to employees. Checks should be distributed to employees by individuals independent of the payroll department. Some larger companies with hundreds or even thousands of employees will use what is called the *payoff test;* that is, they will require a periodic "shaking of hands" of employees receiving the checks to make certain the individuals actually exist.

- Reconciliation of payroll bank accounts by an independent party.

2. The human resources (personnel) department should be the only department allowed to add individuals to or delete them from the labor force. In addition, this department should be the only one that provides the payroll department with employees' wage rates.

3. Proper procedures should be in place for recording time worked, including the use of time clocks where possible.

4. Employees should be paid by check only, not in cash. In addition, a special **imprest payroll account** should be used. An imprest payroll account is one into which only the exact amount of a given payroll period is deposited. Payroll checks totaling that deposit are then written on that account. Once all of the checks clear the bank, there is nothing left in the account.

5. Payroll sheets and employee paychecks should be independently checked.

6. Any unclaimed payroll checks should be immediately returned to the controller who will hold them until the employees return to work and pick up their checks directly from the controller.

Payroll Records

The Fair Labor Standards Act (FLSA), commonly known as the *federal wage and hour law,* covers such things as equal pay for equal work, recordkeeping requirements, minimum wage rates, and overtime pay. Hospitality firms, except for certain small operations, are subject to this act.

To comply with the FLSA, employers must keep records of the time worked by hourly employees. Time cards or time sheets are generally used to satisfy this requirement. The time cards or sheets can be administered manually or through an electronic time clock. An example of an employee time card is shown in Exhibit 1.

Companies will typically keep a **master payroll file** of records that include important information on employees. The information in the file would include employee names, addresses, Social Security numbers, and wage rates, as well as deduction information for the employees.

An important form filled out by the employee and given to the employer is Internal Revenue Service (IRS) form W-4, which helps the employer calculate the amount of taxes withheld from the individual employee's payroll check. The front

Exhibit 1   Sample Employee Time Card

| WEEK ENDING _____ 20 _____ |
| Form No. 1212 |

No.

NAME

DAY	MORNING IN	NOON OUT	NOON IN	NIGHT OUT	EXTRA IN	EXTRA OUT	TOTAL

TOTAL TIME _____ HRS.

RATE _____

TOTAL WAGES FOR WEEK $ _____

of a W-4 form is shown in Exhibit 2. W-4 forms are also completed for state and city income tax withholdings. Another payroll record is the **payroll journal** shown in Exhibit 3. This lists a record of each payroll check issued by the company along with the corresponding gross pay and various deductions for federal, state, city, and Social Security taxes; employee health care contributions; and miscellaneous contributions such as union dues. IRS form W-2, which employers must provide to employees annually, is shown in Exhibit 4. A file called an **employee's earnings record** is also kept for each individual employee of the operation. An example of this file is shown in Exhibit 5. This record is used to compile information for government reporting of employees' wages. Some taxes apply to earnings up to a certain dollar amount only; this record is used to make sure that those caps are not exceeded.

Exhibit 2   IRS Form W-4—Employee's Withholding Allowance Certificate

Form **W-4**	**Employee's Withholding Allowance Certificate**	OMB No. 1545-0010
Department of the Treasury Internal Revenue Service	► Whether you are entitled to claim a certain number of allowances or exemption from withholding is subject to review by the IRS. Your employer may be required to send a copy of this form to the IRS.	2005

1 Type or print your first name and middle initial	Last name		2 Your social security number
Home address (number and street or rural route)		3 ☐ Single ☐ Married ☐ Married, but withhold at higher Single rate. Note. If married, but legally separated, or spouse is a nonresident alien, check the "Single" box.	
City or town, state, and ZIP code		4 **If your last name differs from that shown on your social security card, check here. You must call 1-800-772-1213 for a new card.** ► ☐	

5 Total number of allowances you are claiming (from line **H** above **or** from the applicable worksheet on page 2)	**5**	
6 Additional amount, if any, you want withheld from each paycheck	**6** $	
7 I claim exemption from withholding for 2005, and I certify that I meet **both** of the following conditions for exemption. • Last year I had a right to a refund of **all** federal income tax withheld because I had **no** tax liability **and** • This year I expect a refund of **all** federal income tax withheld because I expect to have **no** tax liability. If you meet both conditions, write "Exempt" here . . . . ►	**7**	

Under penalties of perjury, I declare that I have examined this certificate and to the best of my knowledge and belief, it is true, correct, and complete.

Employee's signature
(Form is not valid
unless you sign it.) ►   **Date** ►

8 Employer's name and address (Employer: Complete lines 8 and 10 only If sending to the IRS.)	9 Office code (optional)	10 Employer identification number (EIN)

For Privacy Act and Paperwork Reduction Act Notice, see page 2.   Cat. No. 10220Q   Form **W-4** (2005)

Exhibit 3   Payroll Journal

Payroll Journal

			TAXES PAYABLE AND ACCRUED			ACCOUNTS PAYABLE			NET PAY CASH IN BANK CREDIT	CHECK NUMBER
NAME	PAY PERIOD ENDING		F.I.C.A.	ST. INCOME WH	TOTAL CREDIT	RET. CONT.	HEALTH INS.	TOTAL CREDIT		

Regular Pay and Overtime Pay

According to the FLSA, regular pay for an employee is based on a 40-hour work-week. *Regular hourly rate* refers to the rate per hour that is used to compute regular pay. The FLSA also requires that overtime pay be given for any hours worked in excess of 40 hours in a week. *Overtime hourly rate* refers to the rate per hour used to compute overtime pay. The FLSA requires that overtime be paid at the rate of 1.5 times the employee's regular hourly rate.

To calculate the overtime pay for some employees, it may be necessary to convert a weekly wage into an hourly rate. For example, assume that an employee is hired at a weekly wage of $218 for a 40-hour workweek. The regular hourly rate for this employee would be $5.45, calculated as follows:

Exhibit 4   IRS Form W-2—Wage and Tax Statement

a Control number		22222		OMB No. 1545-0008		
b Employer identification number (EIN)				1 Wages, tips, other compensation	2 Federal income tax withheld	
c Employer's name, address, and ZIP code				3 Social security wages	4 Social security tax withheld	
				5 Medicare wages and tips	6 Medicare tax withheld	
				7 Social security tips	8 Allocated tips	
d Employee's social security number				9 Advance EIC payment	10 Dependent care benefits	
e Employee's first name and initial Last name				11 Nonqualified plans	12a	
				13 Statutory employee Retirement plan Third-party sick pay	12b	
				14 Other	12c	
					12d	
f Employee's address and ZIP code						
15 State Employer's state ID number	16 State wages, tips, etc.	17 State income tax	18 Local wages, tips, etc.	19 Local income tax	20 Locality name

Form **W-2** Wage and Tax Statement   **2005**   Department of the Treasury—Internal Revenue Service
Copy 1—For State, City, or Local Tax Department

Exhibit 5   Sample Employee's Earnings Record

Pay Period Ending	EARNINGS				Wages for WH	Meals & Lodging	Wages for F.I.C.A.	DEDUCTIONS						NET PAY
	Regular	Overtime	Gross	Tips				F.I.C.A.	Fed. Income WH	St. Income WH	Ret. Cont.	Health Ins.		

NAME:
ADDRESS:
SOCIAL SECURITY NUMBER:

$$\text{Regular Hourly Rate} = \frac{\text{Weekly Wage}}{\text{Number of Hours in Regular Workweek}}$$

$$= \frac{\$218}{40}$$

$$= \$5.45$$

Now that the regular hourly rate has been calculated, the overtime rate can easily be determined. Since the FLSA requires the overtime rate to be 1.5 times the regular hourly rate, this employee would have an hourly overtime rate of $8.175, calculated as follows:

$$\text{Overtime Hourly Rate} = \text{Regular Hourly Rate} \times 1.5$$
$$= \$5.45 \times 1.5$$
$$= \$8.175$$

Payroll Journal Entries

There are two major journal entries involving payroll. These two separate and distinct entries are referred to as *the entry to record the payroll* and *the entry to record the payroll taxes.*

The Entry to Record Payroll. It may be useful to think of the payroll entry as a "check stub" entry, because if we had only one employee and that employee's check stub were in front of us, we could use the stub's information to journalize the entry. The following items would be included in the payroll entry:

1. *Gross Pay.* Gross pay is calculated by multiplying the hours the employee worked for the pay period by the hourly rate, including any overtime premium. In the case of salaried employees, gross pay for a month, for example, would be $\frac{1}{12}$ of their annual salaries.

2. *Federal Income Tax (FIT).* Exhibit 6 is an example of withholding tables employers refer to for this deduction. The withholding amounts for federal income tax vary depending on marital status. Exhibit 6 shows an excerpt from the table that applies to a married individual who is paid biweekly and who files jointly with his or her spouse. Recent actual rates for a married person filing jointly are shown in the following table:

INCOME	TAX RATE
$0–$14,600	10%
$14,600–$59,400	$1,460 + 15% of excess
$59,400–$119,950	$8,180 + 25% of excess
$119,950–182,800	$23,317.50 + 28% of excess
$182,800–326,450	$40,915.50 + 33% of excess
$326,450 and up	$88,320 + 35% of excess

Suppose a married individual files a joint return and has a taxable income of $65,000. Based on the rates in the above table, the federal tax liability for this individual would be $9,580, determined as follows:

$$\text{Tax Liability} = \$8,180 + 25\% \text{ of Excess } (\$65,000 - \$59,400)$$
$$= \$8,180 + 25\% \text{ of } \$5,600$$
$$= \$9,580$$

Exhibit 6   Excerpt from Federal Withholding Tax Table

FEDERAL WITHHOLDING TAX TABLE FOR WAGES PAID JANUARY 1, 2006 AND AFTER

BI-WEEKLY PAYROLL PERIOD					MONTHLY PAYROLL PERIOD				
SINGLE PERSONS					SINGLE PERSONS				
IF THE TAXABLE INCOME IS...		COMPUTED TAX IS...			IF THE TAXABLE INCOME IS...		COMPUTED TAX IS...		
OVER	BUT NOT OVER	The total of this column PLUS »	The % In this column TIMES »	The amount over (Taxable income less the amount in this column)	OVER	BUT NOT OVER	The total of this column PLUS »	The % In this column TIMES »	The amount over (Taxable income less the amount in this column)
0	102	NO TAX WITHHELD			0	221	NO TAX WITHHELD		
102	385	0	10%	102	221	833	0	10%	221
385	1,240	28.30	15%	385	833	2,687	61.20	15%	833
1,240	2,817	156.55	25%	1,240	2,687	6,104	339.30	25%	2,687
2,817	6,025	550.80	28%	2,817	6,104	13,054	1,193.55	28%	6,104
6,025	13,015	1,449.04	33%	6,025	13,054	28,200	3,139.55	33%	13,054
13,015	OVER	3,755.74	35%	13,015	28,200	OVER	8,137.73	35%	28,200
MARRIED PERSONS					MARRIED PERSONS				
IF THE TAXABLE INCOME IS...		COMPUTED TAX IS...			IF THE TAXABLE INCOME IS...		COMPUTED TAX IS...		
OVER	BUT NOT OVER	The total of this column PLUS »	The % In this column TIMES »	The amount over (Taxable income less the amount in this column)	OVER	BUT NOT OVER	The total of this column PLUS »	The % In this column TIMES »	The amount over (Taxable income less the amount in this column)
0	308	NO TAX WITHHELD			0	667	NO TAX WITHHELD		
308	881	0	10%	308	667	1,908	0	10%	667
881	2,617	57.30	15%	881	1,908	5,5670	124.10	15%	1,908
2,617	4,881	317.70	25%	2,617	5,670	10,575	688.40	25%	5,670
4,881	7,517	883.70	28%	4,881	10,575	16,288	1,914.65	28%	10,575
7,517	13,213	1,621.78	33%	7,517	16,288	28,629	3,514.29	33%	16,288
13,213	OVER	3,501.46	35%	13,213	28,629	OVER	7,586.82	35%	28,629

Source: www.payroll.ucla.edu/charts/taxfdcur.htm.

3. *Social Security Taxes.* Social Security taxes result from the **Federal Insurance Contributions Act (FICA)**. The 2005 rate for FICA taxes was 7.65 percent. This rate is actually a combination of two rates: 6.2 percent on the first $90,000 of income (for old age, survivors', and disability insurance), plus 1.45 percent on all income for Medicare.

4. *State Income Tax (SIT).* States vary widely in the amount of state income tax assessed, ranging from zero percent in several states to Vermont's rate of about 9.5 percent.

5. *Miscellaneous deductions.* Other deductions from an individual's pay might include local income tax, the employee's contribution to health care benefits, union dues taken by the employer and later remitted to the union, or a payroll deduction for items such as charitable contributions.

All of these current liabilities, such as FIT, SIT, FICA, and miscellaneous deductions, are eventually remitted to the respective agencies. From the time period in which they are deducted from employee wages until they are remitted to the agencies, they are considered current liabilities for the hospitality firm.

6. *The amount of the employee's net pay.* Net pay, of course, is simply gross pay minus the various deductions. It is the amount the payroll check is written for.

Let us assume for a given pay period that a hotel had sales salaries and administrative salaries of $30,000 and $19,000, respectively. Let us also assume that the total federal income tax withheld for this pay period was $13,720, the state income tax withheld was $2,254, the FICA deduction was $3,749, and the health insurance deduction $980, making the net pay $28,297. The entry to record this transaction would be as follows:

Sales Salaries	$30,000	
Administrative Salaries	19,000	
FIT Payable		$13,720
SIT Payable		2,254
FICA		3,749
Health Insurance Payable		980
Salaries Payable		28,297

This entry would be made on the date the payroll was computed. On the date the payroll was actually paid to the employees and the amount of net pay transferred into the payroll imprest fund, the journal entry would be:

Salaries Payable	$28,297	
Cash		$28,297

Note the large difference in this case between the gross payroll of $49,000 and the net pay to the employees of $28,297.

The Entry to Record Payroll Taxes. The second major entry involving payroll is the one recording the employer's payroll taxes. **Payroll taxes** represent additional taxes paid by the employer based on employee wages. The three major elements of payroll taxes are the employer's FICA tax contribution and its contributions under the **Federal Unemployment Tax Act (FUTA)** and the **State Unemployment Tax Act (SUTA)**.

We have already discussed FICA taxes in relation to the first payroll entry. The Federal Insurance Contribution Act also states that the employer must match the amounts withheld from employees' pay for Social Security taxes. As a result, the dollar amount of the credit to FICA Tax Payable in the first journal entry (that is, the entry to record the payroll) will be the same dollar amount in this second journal entry. Employers are required to report the amounts of FICA taxes for employees on Federal Form 941, which is filed quarterly. The first page of Federal Form 941 is shown in Exhibit 7.

The Federal Unemployment Tax Act (FUTA) establishes a tax that pays unemployment wages to people who have lost their jobs. This fund is financed through taxes levied on employer payrolls. The 1997 federal unemployment tax was 6.2 percent on employee's wages up to $7,000. This tax is no longer levied on an employee's wages after the first $7,000.

States must contribute dollars into the federal unemployment fund. To do so, they levy their own state unemployment tax rates. These rates vary by state, but, whatever that rate is, employers are allowed to use the state tax rate as a credit against the federal rate. For example, assume that a state levied a 5.4 percent state unemployment tax while the federal rate was 6.2 percent. This would result in a federal unemployment tax rate of only .8 percent, calculated as follows:

$$6.2\% - 5.4\% = .8\%$$

With the information given in the earlier example for the payroll of the hotel, and using a federal unemployment rate of 6.2 percent and a state rate of 5.4 percent, the hotel would make the following journal entry (assuming no employee had earned $7,000 yet) to record its payroll taxes:

Payroll Tax Expense	$6,787	
FICA Tax Payable		$3,749
Federal Unemployment Tax Payable		
($49,000 × .8%)		392
State Unemployment Tax Payable		
($49,000 × 5.4%)		2,646

The debit to Payroll Tax Expense is simply the total of the three credits to the liability accounts. (The annual unemployment tax return for reporting federal taxes is Form 940; the form is shown in Exhibit 8.)

Once again, let us point out that these are two separate and distinct entries: One records the payroll and the other records the payroll tax expense. The only connection between the two entries is the FICA Tax Payable credit amount, which should be the same in both journal entries. Note the cost of employees to the employer; that is, in this example, it costs the employer the gross wages of $49,000 plus the payroll taxes of $6,787. This represents a total cost to the employer of $55,787.

Employees often do not realize what the costs of their employment actually are to the employer. In this case, there is a 14 percent difference between the gross wages of the employees and the total payroll cost to the employer (and this does not include the cost of any additional benefits the employer provides to its

Exhibit 7   IRS Form 941—Employer's Quarterly Federal Tax Return

Form **941** (Rev. January 2004) Department of the Treasury Internal Revenue Service (99)	**Employer's Quarterly Federal Tax Return** ▶ **See separate instructions revised January 2004 for information on completing this return.** **Please type or print.**	

Enter state code for state in which deposits were made **only** if different from state in address to the right ▶ [ ] (see page 2 of separate instructions).	Name (as distinguished from trade name)	Date quarter ended	OMB No. 1545-0029
			T
	Trade name, if any	Employer identification number	FF
			FD
	Address (number and street)	City, state, and ZIP code	FP
			I
			T

| If address is different from prior return, check here ▶ [ ] | **IRS Use** | 1 1 1 1 1 1 1 1 1 1   2   3 3 3 3 3 3 3   4 4   5 5 5 |
| | | 6   7   8 8 8 8 8 8 8   9 9 9 9   10 10 10 10 10 10 10 10 10 10 |

A   If you **do not have to file** returns in the future, check here ▶ [ ] and enter date final wages paid ▶
B   If you are a seasonal employer, see **Seasonal employers** on page 1 of the instructions and check here ▶ [ ]

1	Number of employees in the pay period that includes March 12th . ▶	1	
2	Total wages and tips, plus other compensation (see separate instructions)		**2**
3	Total income tax withheld from wages, tips, and sick pay		**3**
4	Adjustment of withheld income tax for preceding quarters of **this calendar year** . . .		**4**
5	Adjusted total of income tax withheld (line 3 as adjusted by line 4)		**5**
6	Taxable social security wages	**6a**	× 12.4% (.124) =	**6b**
	Taxable social security tips	**6c**	× 12.4% (.124) =	**6d**
7	Taxable Medicare wages and tips . . .	**7a**	× 2.9% (.029) =	**7b**
8	Total social security and Medicare taxes (add lines 6b, 6d, and 7b). **Check here if wages are not subject to social security and/or Medicare tax** . . . . ▶ [ ]		**8**
9	Adjustment of social security and Medicare taxes (see instructions for required explanation) Sick Pay $ _____ ± Fractions of Cents $ _____ ± Other $ _____ =		**9**
10	Adjusted total of social security and Medicare taxes (line 8 as adjusted by line 9)		**10**
11	**Total taxes** (add lines 5 and 10)		**11**
12	Advance earned income credit (EIC) payments made to employees (see instructions) . . .		**12**
13	Net taxes (subtract line 12 from line 11). **If $2,500 or more, this must equal line 17, column (d) below (or line D of Schedule B (Form 941))**		**13**
14	Total deposits for quarter, including overpayment applied from a prior quarter		**14**
15	**Balance due** (subtract line 14 from line 13). See instructions		**15**
16	**Overpayment.** If line 14 is more than line 13, enter excess here ▶ $ _____ and check if to be: [ ] Applied to next return **or** [ ] Refunded.		

● **All filers:** If line 13 is less than $2,500, **do not** complete line 17 or Schedule B (Form 941).
● **Semiweekly schedule depositors:** Complete Schedule B (Form 941) and check here . . . . ▶ [ ]
● **Monthly schedule depositors:** Complete line 17, columns (a) through (d), and check here. . . . . ▶ [ ]

17	Monthly Summary of Federal Tax Liability. (Complete **Schedule B (Form 941)** instead, if you were a semiweekly schedule depositor.)			
	(a) First month liability	(b) Second month liability	(c) Third month liability	(d) Total liability for quarter

Third Party Designee	Do you want to allow another person to discuss this return with the IRS (see separate instructions)? [ ] **Yes.** Complete the following. [ ] **No**		
	Designee's name ▶	Phone no. ▶ ( )	Personal identification number (PIN) ▶ [ ][ ][ ][ ][ ]

Sign Here   Under penalties of perjury, I declare that I have examined this return, including accompanying schedules and statements, and to the best of my knowledge and belief, it is true, correct, and complete.

Signature ▶ _____   Print Your Name and Title ▶ _____   Date ▶ _____

For Privacy Act and Paperwork Reduction Act Notice, see back of Payment Voucher.   Cat. No. 17001Z   Form **941** (Rev. 1-2004)

Exhibit 8   IRS Form 940—Employer's FUTA Tax Return

Form **940**	**Employer's Annual Federal Unemployment (FUTA) Tax Return**	OMB No. 1545-0028
Department of the Treasury Internal Revenue Service (99)	▶ See the separate Instructions for Form 940 for information on completing this form.	**2005**

You must complete this section. ▶

Name (as distinguished from trade name)	Calendar year	T
		FF
Trade name, if any	Employer identification number (EIN)	FD
		FP
Address (number and street)	City, state, and ZIP code	I
		T

A Are you required to pay unemployment contributions to only one state? (If "No," skip questions B and C.)   ☐ Yes   ☐ No

B Did you pay all state unemployment contributions by January 31, 2006? ((1) If you deposited your total FUTA tax when due, check "Yes" if you paid all state unemployment contributions by February 10, 2006. (2) If a 0% experience rate is granted, check "Yes." (3) If "No," skip question C.)   . . . .   ☐ Yes   ☐ No

C Were all wages that were taxable for FUTA tax also taxable for your state's unemployment tax? . . . .   ☐ Yes   ☐ No

D **Did you pay any wages in New York?** . . . .   ☐ Yes   ☐ No

If you answered "No" to questions A, B, or C, or "Yes" to question D, you must file Form 940. If you answered "Yes" to questions A-C and "No" to question D you may file Form 940-EZ, which is a simplified version of Form 940. (Successor employers, see **Special credit for successor employers** in the separate instructions.) You can get Form 940-EZ by calling 1-800-TAX-FORM (1-800-829-3676) or from the IRS website at **www.irs.gov.**

If you will not have to file returns in the future, check here (see **Who Must File** in the separate instructions) **and complete and sign the return** . . . . ▶ ☐

If this is an Amended Return, check here (see **Amended Returns** in the separate instructions) . . . . ▶ ☐

Part I Computation of Taxable Wages		
1 Total payments (including payments shown on lines 2 and 3) during the calendar year for services of employees	**1**	
2 Exempt payments. (Explain all exempt payments, attaching additional sheets if necessary.) ▶ ------------------------------	**2**	
3 Payments of more than $7,000 for services. Enter only amounts over the first $7,000 paid to each employee (see separate instructions). Do not include any exempt payments from line 2. The $7,000 amount is the federal wage base. Your state wage base may be different. **Do not use your state wage limitation**	**3**	
4 Add lines 2 and 3	**4**	
5 **Total taxable wages** (subtract line 4 from line 1) . . . . ▶	**5**	
6 Credit reduction for unpaid advances to the states listed. Enter the wages **included on line 5** above for each state and multiply by the rate shown. (See separate Instructions for Form 940.) **(a)** NY_____ x .006 =_____ **(b)** XX _____ x .nnn =_____ **(c)** XX _____ x .nnn =_____		
7 Add credit reduction amounts from lines 6(a) through 6(c) and enter the total here and in Part II, line 5. ▶	**7**	

Be sure to complete both sides of this form, and sign in the space provided on the back.

For Privacy Act and Paperwork Reduction Act Notice, see separate instructions.   ▼ **DETACH HERE** ▼   Cat. No. 11234O   Form **940** (2005)

Form **940-V**	**Payment Voucher**	OMB No. 1545-0028
Department of the Treasury Internal Revenue Service	Use this voucher only when making a payment with your return.	**2005**

Complete boxes 1, 2, and 3. Do not send cash, and do not staple your payment to this voucher. Make your check or money order payable to the "United States Treasury." Be sure to enter your employer identification number (EIN), "Form 940," and "2005" on your payment.

1 Enter your employer identification number (EIN).	**2**		Dollars	Cents
	Enter the amount of your payment. ▶			
	3 Enter your business name (individual name for sole proprietors).			
	Enter your address.			
	Enter your city, state, and ZIP code.			

Exhibit 8 *(continued)*

Form 940 (2005)   Page **2**

Name   Employer identification number (EIN)

Part II   **Tax Due or Refund**

1   Gross FUTA tax. (Multiply the wages from Part I, line 5, by .062) **1**
2   Maximum credit. (Multiply the wages from Part I, line 5, by .054) . . **2**
3   Computation of tentative credit (**Note:** *All taxpayers must complete the applicable columns.*)

(a) Name of state	(b) State reporting number(s) as shown on employer's state contribution returns	(c) Taxable payroll (as defined in state act)	(d) State experience rate period From	To	(e) State experience rate	(f) Contributions if rate had been 5.4% (col. (c) x .054)	(g) Contributions payable at experience rate (col. (c) x col. (e))	(h) Additional credit (col. (f) minus col.(g)) If 0 or less, enter -0-.	(i) Contributions paid to state by 940 due date.

3a   Totals . . . ▶

3b   **Total tentative credit** (add line 3a, columns (h) and (i) only—for late payments, also see the instructions for Part II, line 4) . . . . ▶ **3b**

4   **Credit:** Enter the smaller of the amount from Part II, line 2 or line 3b; or the amount from the worksheet on page 7 of the separate instructions **4**

5   Enter the amount from Part I, line 7 . . . . **5**

6   **Credit allowable** (subtract line 5 from line 4). If zero or less, enter "-0-" **6**

7   **Total FUTA tax** (subtract line 6 from line 1). If the result is over $500, also complete Part III . . **7**

8   Total FUTA tax deposited for the year, including any overpayment applied from a prior year . . **8**

9   **Balance due** (subtract line 8 from line 7). Pay to the "United States Treasury." If you owe more than $500, see **Depositing FUTA Tax** on page 3 of the separate instructions . . . . . ▶ **9**

10   **Overpayment** (subtract line 7 from line 8). Check if it is to be: ☐ **Applied to next return** or ☐ **Refunded** . . . . ▶ **10**

Part III   **Record of Quarterly Federal Unemployment Tax Liability** (Do not include state liability.) **Complete only if line 7 is over $500.** See page 7 of the separate instructions.

Quarter	First (Jan. 1–Mar. 31)	Second (Apr. 1–June 30)	Third (July 1–Sept. 30)	Fourth (Oct. 1–Dec. 31)	Total for year
Liability for quarter					

Third-Party Designee   Do you want to allow another person to discuss this return with the IRS (see separate instructions)? ☐ **Yes.** Complete the following.   ☐ **No**

Designee's name ▶   Phone no. ▶ ( )   Personal identification number (PIN) ▶ ☐☐☐☐☐

Under penalties of perjury, I declare that I have examined this return, including accompanying schedules and statements, and, to the best of my knowledge and belief, it is true, correct, and complete, and that no part of any payment made to a state unemployment fund claimed as a credit was, or is to be, deducted from the payments to employees.

Signature ▶   Title (Owner, etc.) ▶   Date ▶

Form **940** (2005)

employees). Since fringe benefits and payroll taxes can be costly, hospitality firms may hire independent contractors rather than employees to perform certain services. Suppose that an independent contractor could provide a service such as accounting, data processing, or repair work for the hotel. If the employer hired this independent contractor, the employer would not have to pay payroll taxes. The IRS rules for determination of employee status versus independent contractor status are detailed and very strict, and are beyond our scope.

Reporting Tips

Certain employees in the hospitality industry, such as table servers, commonly receive tips from customers. There are both federal and state regulations on tip reporting, and the calculation of tip reporting can be complex. The form that the

Exhibit 9   IRS Form 4070—Employee's Report of Tips to Employer

Form **4070** (Rev. August 2005) Department of the Treasury Internal Revenue Service	**Employee's Report of Tips to Employer**	OMB No. 1545-0074
Employee's name and address		Social security number
Employer's name and address (include establishment name, if different)		1 Cash tips received
		2 Credit and debit card tips received
		3 Tips paid out
Month or shorter period in which tips were received from , , to ,		4 Net tips (lines **1** + **2** - **3**)
Signature		Date
For Paperwork Reduction Act Notice, see the instructions on the back of this form.	Cat. No. 41320P	Form **4070** (Rev. 8-2005)

government provides for reporting tips, Form 4070 (shown in Exhibit 9), is the employee's report of tips to the employer.

Certain provisions of state and federal laws allow employers to apply a tip credit against the minimum wage of tipped employees. In this way, the employer can reduce the amount of gross wages paid to those employees. Assume, for example, that the minimum wage is $5.15 per hour and that the state allows a 40 percent maximum tip credit. Under these conditions, the employer could apply a credit of $2.06 (40% of $5.15) toward the hourly wage of tipped employees as long as the actual tips received by the employees were not less than the maximum allowable tip credit. In this case, the employer would comply with the law by paying employees $3.09 per hour ($5.15 − $2.06).

The next illustration shows how the gross wages payable to an employee are calculated when the actual tips received by the employee are greater than the maximum tip credit. Assume that an employee who worked 40 hours reports tips of $90, and is paid a minimum wage of $5.15 per hour. Also assume that the employer applies a maximum tip credit of $2.06. The gross wages payable to this employee would be calculated as follows:

Gross Wages: 40 hours at $5.15/hour		$206.00
Less lower of:		
Maximum FLSA tip credit (40 hours at $2.06)	$82.40	
Actual tips received	90.00	
Allowable tip credit		− 82.40
Gross wages payable by employer		$123.60

If the actual tips received by the employee were less than the maximum allowed tip credit, the *tips received* would be subtracted from the gross wages of $206 to determine the actual gross wages payable by the employer.

It is important to note that the gross taxable earnings of a tipped employee include both the gross wages payable by the employer and the actual tips received by the employee.

The Tax Equity and Fiscal Responsibility Act of 1982 (TEFRA) established regulations that govern tip-reporting requirements for food and beverage operations. The regulations state that the tips reported by hospitality establishments should be at least 8 percent of the qualified gross receipts of the business. Receipts from banquets, for which gratuities and service charges are often charged automatically, do not qualify. If the tips reported do not meet this 8 percent requirement, the deficiency is called a *tip shortfall*. When there is a shortfall, the employer must provide each directly tipped employee with an information sheet showing the tips reported by the employee and the tips that should have been reported.

The 8 percent tip regulation does not apply to all food and beverage operations. Cafeteria and fast-food operations, for example, are exempt from the regulation.

Other Current Liabilities

Accounts payable, notes payable, wages payable, and taxes payable resulting from payroll are the major current liabilities in hospitality operations. A review of the balance sheets of restaurant and lodging operations would also disclose other liabilities, such as unearned revenue, the current portion of long-term debt, income taxes payable, advance deposits, and other accrued items. A current liability that warrants discussion is property taxes.

Property Taxes

Property taxes are taxes on real estate and personal property (such as restaurant equipment and fixtures) levied by local taxing entities such as townships, cities, or counties. These property taxes are *ad valorem* **taxes**; that is, they are based on the assessed value of the asset itself. Once that value is determined by an authorized assessor of the taxing entity, the voted millage rate is applied to the value of the asset. A **mill** is a tax dollar per $1,000 of valuation. Assume, for example, that a restaurant is assessed at a value of $300,000 with a tax rate of 45 mills. The property taxes would amount to $13,500, shown in this calculation:

$$\$300,000 \div \$1,000 = 300 \times 45 \text{ mills} = \$13,500$$

The bill for $13,500 would not normally be received until December. In actual practice, most businesses receive two tax bills, one for summer and one for winter taxes; in this case, an adjustment would be made twice a year.

Normally, the hospitality firm would estimate the annual property taxes and accrue a portion of that amount every month, and adjust to the actual tax rate when it receives the bill. For example, assume that the estimated tax on the restaurant was $12,000 for the year, or $1,000 per month. The monthly journal entry would be as follows:

Property Tax Expense	$1,000	
Property Tax Payable		$1,000

Next, assume that the bill for $13,500 was received on December 1, 20X1, and was payable on February 14, 20X2. The entry on December 31, 20X1, would adjust the estimated tax to the actual tax:

Property Tax Expense	$2,500	
Property Tax Payable		$2,500

The entry on February 14, 20X2, the day on which the taxes are due, would be as follows:

Property Tax Payable	$13,500	
Cash		$13,500

Summary

Current liabilities are those liabilities that are expected to be paid off within one year. Examples include accounts payable, notes payable, and wages payable. Most current liabilities are known and exact in amount; a few are known, but the amount must be estimated; and a very few are not only unknown in amount, but are not even certain to arise (such as a potential lawsuit judgment against the firm). Nevertheless, they must be recorded on the company's books.

Payroll, along with all of its related tax liabilities, represents one of the largest current liabilities for the hospitality firm, if not the largest. As such, payroll requires a good system of controls. One of the primary means of control is the segregation of the various payroll-related duties.

Other current liabilities are property taxes on real estate and personal property (such as restaurant equipment and fixtures) levied by local taxing authorities such as townships, cities, or counties. Tax bills are generally received twice a year, but are reflected in monthly journal entries to more closely match expenses with revenues for the period.

Key Terms

ad valorem **tax**—A tax based on the assessed value of the asset itself, usually a fixed percentage of the value.

contingent liability—A liability that is based on a future event that may or may not take place; it is not yet an actual liability and therefore should not be included in the Liabilities section of the balance sheet. Instead, it should be included in footnotes to the financial statements.

employee's earnings record—A record for each employee of the operation, used to record gross pay, taxes withheld, deductions, and net pay; used to compile information for reporting employee wages to governments.

Federal Insurance Contributions Act (FICA)—The federal law governing the national Social Security system, which imposes a payroll tax on the employee and the employer.

Federal Unemployment Tax Act (FUTA)—A federal law imposing a payroll tax on the employer for the purpose of funding national and state unemployment programs.

imprest payroll account—A control account into which only the exact amount of payroll funds for a given payroll period is deposited. Payroll checks totaling that deposit are then written on that account. Once all of the checks clear the bank, there is nothing left in the account.

loss contingency—A situation in which a liability is reasonably estimable, though uncertain but still rather probable in nature. An example would be a pending lawsuit against the company that the company's counsel expected to lose. Such a liability should be put on the books at its estimated amount.

master payroll file—A file containing information, including employee names, addresses, Social Security numbers, wage rates, and payroll deduction information.

mill—A tax dollar per $1,000 of valuation.

payroll journal—A journal containing a record of each payroll check issued, along with the corresponding gross pay and various deductions for federal tax, state tax, city tax, FICA, employee health care contributions, and miscellaneous contributions such as union dues.

payroll taxes—Additional taxes paid by the employer based on employee wages. The three major elements of payroll taxes are the employer's Federal Insurance Contributions Act (FICA) tax contribution, Federal Unemployment Tax Act (FUTA) tax contribution, and State Unemployment Tax Act (SUTA) tax contribution.

State Unemployment Tax Act (SUTA)—An unemployment tax rate levied by individual states. States must contribute dollars into the federal unemployment fund; to do this, they levy their own state unemployment tax rates. The tax rates vary by state, but whatever the state's rate is, employers are allowed to use the state tax rate as a credit against the federal rate.

Review Questions

1. What is the difference between a current liability and a long-term liability?

2. What are the differences between estimated liabilities, contingent liabilities, and loss contingencies?

3. What type of note payable results in the use of a Discount on Notes Payable account? What type of account is Discount on Notes Payable? What is the account's normal balance?

4. What six major control features can a firm use to safeguard payroll?

5. What basic items should be included in a master payroll file?

6. What information is provided in a payroll journal? What information is provided by an employee earnings record?

7. What are the differences between the entry to record *payroll* and the entry to record *payroll taxes*?

8. What does the acronym *FICA* stand for? Is a FICA tax an employer tax or an employee tax?

9. What do the acronyms *FUTA* and *SUTA* represent? Are FUTA and SUTA taxes paid by the employer, the employee, or both?

10. What do the terms *ad valorem* and *mill* mean?

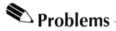 # Problems

Problem 1

Longview Hotels operates ten properties in the Midwest. The company employs the following procedures to control payroll:

a. Tom Johnson, the human resources manager, carefully interviews all prospective employees, authorizes their hiring, prepares the payroll, and distributes the checks.

b. Donna Miller, the front desk manager, deletes individuals from her department's labor force and provides payroll employees with front desk employees' wage rates.

c. At the end of each shift, hotel dining room employees write down their hours on a blank sheet of paper and place it on the desk of the food and beverage manager.

d. All employees are paid by checks drawn on the general bank account of the company.

e. All individual paychecks are kept in the respective departments until they are claimed by employees.

Required:
Draft a memo suggesting changes that the operation should make to better control payroll.

Problem 2

Indicate whether the following statements are true or false and explain why:

a. If a company is a mom and pop operation, it would be acceptable under current tax laws to pay employees in cash with no withholding.

b. An employee's immediate supervisor should hold a check for the employee if he or she is taking a leave of absence.

c. Duties regarding the payroll process should be segregated to ensure that proper payroll procedures are followed.

   d. The labor force master list should be under the control of the human resources department.

   e. Time clocks are a great way to ensure the proper recording of time worked.

   f. Employees' wage rates are provided to payroll by the marketing department.

Problem 3

Explain the difference between accounts payable and notes payable and determine whether the following items are accounts payable or notes payable:

   a. An amount owed to a supplier for a purchase.

   b. A written promise to pay $1,000 within 90 days.

   c. A debt witnessed contractual agreement.

Problem 4

Indicate which of the following items should appear in the financial statements of Holen Hotel and where they would appear.

   a. A $100,000 lawsuit pending against the hotel that the hotel's attorney believes the hotel will probably lose.

   b. FICA taxes payable.

   c. Estimated property taxes.

   d. A commitment to pay a certain entertainer $30,000 if he performs at the hotel in six months.

   e. Estimated income taxes.

   f. The guarantee of $250,000 worth of a subsidiary's debt.

Problem 5

Indicate whether each of the following items is a real liability, loss contingency, or contingent liability:

   a. Debt guarantee of a subsidiary's loan

   b. Note payable due in 90 days

   c. Liability for income tax

   d. Salaries payable

   e. Liability due to a pending lawsuit

   f. Liability for product warranty

   g. Accounts payable

Problem 6

Koles, Inc. has purchased supplies in exchange for a $6,000 note payable with Guthrey Corp. on April 1, 20X8. The note is to be paid in 90 days with interest of 10 percent. Assume a 360-day year.

Required:

Record the journal entries for April 1, 20X8, and June 30, 20X8.

Problem 7

Lakeside Restaurant, Inc., borrowed $40,000 from Empire Savings on November 1, 20X1. The note was written for $40,000 at 12 percent interest for 90 days and was due on February 1, 20X2.

Required:

Create the journal entries needed for Lakeside for November 1, 20X1; December 31, 20X1; and February 1, 20X2.

Problem 8

The Eastbay Restaurant had the following transactions related to its property taxes:

a. An estimated tax of $2,500 for the month of January.

b. An adjustment on December 31 for an actual tax bill of $38,000 for the year.

c. Payment of the bill on February 15 of the following year.

Required:

Record the journal entries for these transactions.

Problem 9

One of the key control features for payroll involves the separation of payroll functions.

Required:

1. List three functions that should be performed by separate individuals where possible.

2. List three other control features that should be in place for payroll.

Problem 10

You have been asked to prepare the entry to record the payroll on February 15, 20X1, for Hotel Properties, Inc. The gross wages are $8,000 for administrative salaries and $6,000 for sales salaries. The federal income tax rate is 28 percent, the state income tax rate is 4.6 percent, and the FICA rate is 7.65 percent for all employees. All wages are subject to these taxes. In addition to taxes withheld, the employer has withheld $128 for the employees' contribution to a health insurance plan.

Required:

1. Prepare the necessary journal entry to record the payroll of Hotel Properties, Inc., on February 15, 20X1.

2. Prepare the journal entry that would be made on the date the payroll was actually paid.

Problem 11

Using the information given in Problem 10 and the following additional information, make the journal entry necessary to record Hotel Properties, Inc., *payroll taxes* on February 15, 20X1:

- Federal unemployment tax rate (FUTA) is 6.2 percent.
- State unemployment tax rate (SUTA) is 4.2 percent. (The full 4.2 percent state rate can be used as a credit against the federal rate.)
- All employees' wages are subject to federal and state unemployment taxes.

Problem 12

Calculate the accrued interest expense on the following notes on December 31, 20X8 (assume a 360-day year):

	Date Issued	Rate	Principal	Maturity Date
a.	Jan. 1, 20X8	12%	$25,000	Dec. 31, 20X8
b.	March 31, 20X8	11%	16,000	March 30, 20X9
c.	June 30, 20X8	14%	80,000	Dec. 31, 20X9
d.	Aug. 1, 20X8	10%	10,000	Dec. 31, 20X8
e.	Oct. 31, 20X8	14%	9,000	Oct. 31, 20X9

Challenge Problems

Problem 13

The payroll journal for Northport Enterprises, Inc., is shown. Using the information provided in the following journal, construct the entry to record the payroll for the company. Brown and Pung are administrative personnel, while the other employees are sales personnel.

Payroll Journal								
Name	Pay Period Ending	Gross Wages	FICA	Federal Inc. Tax	State Inc. Tax	Health Ins.	Net Pay	Check #
Brown, J.	2/12/X1	$800	$50.00	$224.00	$38.40	$18.00	$469.60	4265
Smith, T.	"	750	46.87	210.00	36.00	–0–	457.13	4266
Woods, L.	"	725	45.31	203.00	34.80	18.00	423.89	4267
Pung, A.	"	825	51.56	231.00	39.60	20.00	482.84	4268
Jones, B.	"	600	37.50	168.00	28.80	9.00	356.70	4269

Problem 14

Ralph Jenkins is the assistant manager of the Hemlock Hotel. Tom Patterson, the owner of the hotel, has asked you to compute the hotel's total cost of employing Jenkins.

<u>Required:</u>

1. Using the following information, compute the total annual expense that Jenkins represents for the hotel.

Jenkins's gross salary	$32,000
FICA tax rate	7.65% on earnings up to $72,600
SUTA	5.20% on earnings up to $7,000
FUTA	6.20% on earnings up to $7,000
Federal Income Tax Rate	28% on all earnings
State Income Tax Rate	5.4% on all earnings

2. Compare the cost to the hotel of employing Jenkins with the amount Jenkins sees in his check.

Problem 15

The payroll journal for the SeaGate Hotel on the June 30 payday shows the following:

Employee	Gross Wages	Federal Income Tax	FICA	State Income Tax	Health Insurance	Union Dues	Net Pay
M. Cleaves	$400	$112	$25	$19	$ 9	$10	$225
A. Hutson	375	105	23	18	8	10	$211
T. Peterson	360	100	22	17	–	–	$221
J. Klein	410	116	26	20	12	12	$224

Assume that SeaGate's FUTA rate is 5.8 percent, that its SUTA rate is 4.8 percent, and that the full state rate can be used as a credit against the federal rate. Also assume that all wages are subject to federal and state unemployment taxes and that all wages are subject to FICA taxes. Round to the nearest dollar.

<u>Required:</u>

1. Record the entry for SeaGate's payroll on June 30.
2. Record the entry for SeaGate's payroll tax expense on June 30.

Chapter 13 Outline

Advantages of Partnerships
    Ease of Formation
    No Partnership Taxes
    Synergy
Disadvantages of Partnerships
    Limited Life
    Mutual Agency
    Unlimited Liability
General versus Limited Partnerships
Partners' Capital and Drawing Accounts
Formation of a Partnership
    Division of Income
Admission of a New Partner
Withdrawal of a Partner
Liquidation of a Partnership

Competencies

1. Outline characteristics of business partnerships and their advantages and disadvantages. (pp. 401–402)

2. Distinguish between a general partnership and a limited partnership. (pp. 402–403)

3. Describe partners' drawing and capital accounts, how partnerships are formed, and common ways to divide partnership income. (pp. 403–406)

4. Explain and demonstrate how to account for the admission of a new partner, the withdrawal of a partner, and the liquidation of a partnership. (pp. 406–412)

13

Partnerships

T HE FOUR FORMS of business organization are the sole proprietorship, the partnership, the limited liability company, and the corporation. This chapter covers basic accounting principles for the second form of business, the partnership. Accounting for assets and liabilities in a partnership is basically the same as it is for a sole proprietorship; however, there are a few changes in the equity section of the balance sheet.

First we will discuss what a business partnership is all about: two or more individuals engaged in some economic activity. The partners co-own all the assets and liabilities of the entity and share, in some manner, in its profits or losses. Although some partnership agreements are oral, most are written, and should include at least the following important details:

1. The names of the partners

2. The amount of the investments of each individual partner

3. The profit-sharing arrangement

4. The buy/sell agreement of the partnership

Advantages of Partnerships

Compared to a corporation, a partnership has three major advantages. These are ease of formation, lack of partnership taxes, and synergy.

Ease of Formation

It is relatively easy to form a partnership. Partners get together, decide on the amounts of their investments and their profit sharing, and start the business. The process is much different from the process of forming a corporation, where articles of incorporation, as well as other important documents, must be drawn up.

No Partnership Taxes

Unlike the corporation, the partnership itself pays no taxes on its profits. However, the partnership must file a partnership tax return. This may seem confusing, but the partnership return is simply an informational return. The partnership is a form of business organization through which profits flow to the individual tax returns of the partners. The individual partners pay taxes on their shares of the profits.

Synergy

In its basic form, **synergy** means that the total effect of something is greater than the sum of its individual effects. For example, suppose an individual owns a restaurant and is extremely good at dealing with customers and promoting the business, but poorly manages the accounting work, the ordering, and various other duties. Let's further suppose that there is a second individual who owns a restaurant on the other side of town. This person is very detail-oriented, and very effectively keeps the books, works behind the scenes, plans the menu, and so forth, but does not work very well with the public. Each of these two individuals may adequately manage his or her own restaurant and make a reasonable profit. However, if the two people formed a partnership and each specialized in their respective areas of expertise, the resulting restaurant probably would make more total profit than the individual restaurants did on their own.

Disadvantages of Partnerships

The partnership form of business organization also has a few disadvantages, including limited life, mutual agency, and unlimited liability.

Limited Life

A partnership is like a sole proprietorship in that the life of the business is contingent on the owners. If a partner were to leave the partnership, or if a partner died, a whole new partnership would have to be drawn up for the remaining partners or any new partners joining the partnership. In other words, the partnership itself has a life limited to the lives of the individual partners.

Mutual Agency

The term **mutual agency** refers to the fact that partners are responsible for their partners' individual business actions. For example, suppose that a partnership is owned by Partners A, B, and C. If Partner A decided to increase the inventory by 50 percent and to purchase that inventory on open account, Partners B and C would be just as liable for the purchase as Partner A. Mutual agency pertains only to actions that relate to the partnership, not to any partner's personal debts or actions.

Unlimited Liability

Like the owner of a sole proprietorship, partners have **unlimited liability** with regard to the business. This means that if the business should fail, the business's creditors could seize the partners' personal assets. (This is not the case in the corporate form of business organization, where the owners have limited liability, or in limited liability companies.)

General versus Limited Partnerships

The partnerships described so far are called **general partnerships**, in which all of the partners are called *general partners* and have unlimited liability. Partners can avoid unlimited liability if they form a **limited partnership**. This is a partnership in which one or more of the partners have limited liability; that is, their liability is limited to the amount of their investment in the partnership, and their personal assets are not vulnerable to their business's creditors. Every partnership must have at least one general partner; several criteria must be met in the case of a limited partnership. These criteria are covered in advanced textbooks.

Partners' Capital and Drawing Accounts

In a sole proprietorship, the owner has a capital and a drawing account in the equity section of the general ledger accounts. In the case of a partnership, the equity accounts are expanded so that each partner has both a capital account and a drawing account. The following partial balance sheet shows the Owners' Equity section for the Jenkins and Phillips partnership.

Partial Balance Sheet		
Owners' Equity Section		
Ralph Jenkins, Capital	$150,000	
Betty Phillips, Capital	$175,000	
Total Capital		$325,000

Assume that during the fiscal year 20X1 Jenkins drew $50,000 out of the partnership, while Phillips drew $60,000 out. The journal entries to close those drawing accounts into the partners' capital accounts would be as follows:

Ralph Jenkins, Capital	$50,000	
Ralph Jenkins, Drawing		$50,000

Betty Phillips, Capital	$60,000	
Betty Phillips, Drawing		$60,000

Formation of a Partnership

Now we will examine how a partnership begins and how the accounting entries are journalized in the early stages. Often the partners coming together bring personal assets from a previous business. Sometimes these assets are worth substantially more than the books of the individual sole proprietorships show they are worth. As a result, when assets are brought into a partnership, they are recorded on the books at fair market value rather than at cost at the time the partnership is formed.

Let's assume that George Clark and John Barry are going to pool their assets and liabilities to form a partnership in the restaurant business. Clark will bring in land that cost him $30,000 but now has a fair market value of $80,000, and a building that cost him $50,000 and now has a fair market value of $150,000. In addition, Clark will bring inventory that is on the books at $10,000 and a note payable in the amount of $25,000. Barry, on the other hand, will bring to the partnership $150,000 in cash and equipment that has a fair market value of $80,000. The assets and liabilities of this partnership will be at their stated amounts, except for the land and building, which will be brought on at $80,000 and $150,000, respectively, their fair market values.

The journal entries for the formation of this partnership would be as follows:

Land	$ 80,000	
Building	150,000	
Inventory	10,000	
Notes Payable		$ 25,000
George Clark, Capital		215,000

Cash	$150,000	
Equipment	80,000	
John Barry, Capital		$230,000

The balance sheet of the partnership after these entries were made would appear as illustrated below:

Balance Sheet
Clark & Barry Restaurant
January 1, 20X1

Cash	$150,000	Notes Payable	$ 25,000
Inventory	10,000	George Clark, Capital	215,000
Equipment	80,000	John Barry, Capital	230,000
Building	150,000		
Land	80,000		
		Total Liability and	
Total Assets	$470,000	Equity	$470,000

Division of Income

There are many possible ways to divide income, but we will limit our discussion to three common methods:

- Division of income in a fixed ratio, the simplest method.

- Division of income with salary distributed first, followed by remaining income in a fixed ratio.

- Division of income with salary distributed first, followed by a percentage of the partners' beginning capital balances, concluded by a division of the remaining income in some fixed ratio. This is the most complex profit-sharing arrangement.

Division of Income—Fixed Ratio. The simplest way for two partners to divide income is to use a 50-50 ratio. However, they don't always do so. Partners may decide, for various reasons, to divide income on a 60-40 basis, a 70-30 basis, or even a 90-10 basis. Assume that two partners, Robbins and Byrd, form a partnership with Robbins contributing $80,000 and Byrd, $100,000. Assume also that the two partners agree to share profits in the ratio of 60 percent for Robbins to 40 percent for Byrd. At the end of 20X1, profits of $80,000 would be divided as shown below:

Robbins	Byrd	Income $80,000
$48,000	$32,000	$80,000

This format would result in Robbins receiving $48,000 and Byrd $32,000 of the $80,000 profit for the year. The schedule shows that the full $80,000 is distributed and that the partners' profit-sharing amounts equal the $80,000 balance.

Division of Income with Salary and Fixed Ratio. Next, assume that Robbins and Byrd form a partnership with the same capital contributions as in the previous example, and agree to pay Robbins a $30,000 salary and Byrd a $20,000 salary. After the salary is distributed, the remaining profits will be divided in the same 60-40 ratio. If in 20X1 the partnership earned $80,000, the division of profits under this profit-sharing arrangement would appear as follows:

	Robbins	Byrd	Income $80,000
Salary	$30,000	$20,000	$50,000
Profits	18,000	12,000	30,000
Total	$48,000	$32,000	$80,000

The illustration shows that under these circumstances Robbins would receive $48,000 and Byrd $32,000 for a total of $80,000.

Division of Income with Salary, Interest on Beginning Capital Balances, and the Remainder in a Fixed Ratio. Assume that Robbins and Byrd form the same partnership with the same capital contributions as in the previous examples, but agree to share profits as follows:

1. Salary of $30,000 to Robbins, $20,000 to Byrd,
2. Interest at 10 percent on beginning capital balances for both partners, and
3. The remainder in a 60-40 ratio.

If profits for 20X1 were again $80,000, the division of profits would appear as follows:

	Robbins	Byrd	Income $80,000
Salary	$30,000	$20,000	$50,000
Interest (10% of beginning capital balance)	8,000	10,000	18,000
Profits (remainder)	7,200	4,800	12,000
Total	$45,200	$34,800	$80,000

Under this profit-sharing arrangement, Robbins would end up with $45,200 while Byrd would receive $34,800, once again totaling the $80,000 annual profit.

Occasionally, a partnership does not earn enough profit to meet all of the provisions of the profit-sharing agreement. Suppose that a partnership has the same profit-sharing agreement mentioned in the previous example. Also suppose that the partnership profit amounted to only $60,000. Under these circumstances, the division of profits would appear as shown in this table:

	Robbins	Byrd	Income $60,000
Salary	$30,000	$20,000	$50,000
Interest (10% of beginning capital balance)	8,000	10,000	18,000
Loss	(4,800)	(3,200)	(8,000)
Total	$33,200	$26,800	$60,000

Under this profit-sharing arrangement, Robbins would receive $33,200 and Byrd $26,800 for a total of $60,000. Notice that even though there was a "loss" in the middle of the computations, we still continued the computations as if there were enough profit.

Admission of a New Partner

Admission of a new partner into a partnership can be accomplished in one of two distinct ways: An individual can buy an existing partner's entire interest from that partner or he or she can invest cash or other assets in the partnership for an equity interest. The journal entries for these two situations are very different.

It is very simple to account for the first situation. Assume, for instance, that Wood and Conrad have a partnership with $60,000 in each partnership equity account and that they share profits equally. Next assume that Hale buys Conrad's entire equity interest by paying Conrad $80,000. The journal entry for this transaction on the partnership books would appear as follows:

Conrad, Capital	$60,000
Hale, Capital	$60,000

The amount that Hale pays for Conrad's interest is irrelevant to this journal entry in the partnership books. Conrad is leaving the partnership; therefore, her total equity is removed from the books and replaced by Hale's interest. In this instance, no cash entered or exited the partnership.

Now we will consider the admission of a new partner into the partnership by way of an investment of cash in the partnership. Assume the same facts exist for the partners mentioned previously; that is, Wood's capital is $60,000 and Conrad's capital is $60,000. Wood and Conrad agree to admit Hale into the partnership for a $\frac{1}{3}$ interest in exchange for an investment of $60,000. The journal entry in this case would be:

Cash	$60,000
Hale, Capital	$60,000

The partners' equity accounts on the balance sheet after this transaction would appear as follows:

Owners' Equity Section of the Balance Sheet	
Wood, Capital	$ 60,000
Conrad, Capital	60,000
Hale, Capital	60,000
Total Capital	$180,000

Now consider the original partnership of Wood and Conrad, but with these differences: they agree to admit Hale for a $\frac{1}{3}$ interest based on an investment of $90,000 in the partnership. Notice that Hale is paying $90,000 cash for an equity interest of $70,000. This $20,000 difference could be due to undervaluation of assets that have been on the partnership books for many years. The $70,000 equity interest is computed as follows:

Equity in the partnership before new partner	$120,000
+ New equity brought in by the new partner	90,000
Total Equity after admission of new partner	$210,000
$\frac{1}{3}$ of $210,000 = Equity interest of new partner	$ 70,000

The journal entry to record the admission of Hale under these circumstances would be as follows:

Cash	$90,000	
Hale, Capital		$70,000
Wood, Capital		10,000
Conrad, Capital		10,000

Since Hale is paying $90,000 for an equity interest of $70,000, the $20,000 difference represents a bonus to the original partners, who divide it between them on the basis of their 50-50 profit-sharing arrangement. After this journal entry, the partners' capital accounts would have been as follows:

Hale, Capital	$ 70,000
Wood, Capital	70,000
Conrad, Capital	70,000
Total Capital	$210,000

Occasionally, an existing partnership may be so eager to admit a new partner (either because of the incoming partner's assets or expertise) that it does so for less than the value of the equity interest. If, for example, Wood and Conrad had agreed to admit Hale for a $\frac{1}{3}$ interest in the partnership based on an investment of $30,000, the computation of Hale's equity interest would have been as follows:

Equity of the old partnership	$120,000
+ New equity coming into the partnership	30,000
Total Equity after admission of new partner	$150,000
Total Equity divided by 3 = Capital per partner	$ 50,000

The journal entry to record this would be as follows:

Cash	$30,000	
Wood, Capital	10,000	
Conrad, Capital	10,000	
Hale, Capital		$50,000

After this journal entry, the partnership capital accounts would be as follows:

Wood, Capital	$50,000
Conrad, Capital	$50,000
Hale, Capital	$50,000

The $20,000 difference between the cash invested in the partnership and the new partner's equity interest represents a bonus to the new partner that comes out of the capital accounts of the old partners.

Withdrawal of a Partner

The withdrawal of a partner can result either when a partner dies or simply when a partner wishes to leave the partnership. The withdrawal of a partner, like the admission of a partner, could occur in one of two ways. First, if a partner withdraws by receiving a cash settlement from an outside individual, the entry is very simple. The outgoing partner's capital account is debited for the amount that was in the account, and the incoming partner's capital account is credited for the amount of the outgoing partner's capital regardless of the amount paid for the interest. The transaction is handled this way because the cash paid for the partnership interest goes directly to the outgoing partner and not into the partnership. In the second way of leaving a partnership, the outgoing partner receives cash from the partnership equal to the value of his or her interest. The entry for this is also simple: the outgoing partner's Capital account is debited and Cash is credited for the amount of the settlement. On the other hand, if the outgoing partner receives an amount for his or her interest that is more or less than the book value of the interest, a bonus would be paid either to the outgoing partner or to the remaining partners. The entries would be similar to those entries for the admission of a partner, only in reverse.

Liquidation of a Partnership

The last event to occur chronologically in the life of a partnership is its liquidation. At the time of liquidation, the assets are converted to cash, the debts are paid, and the balance is distributed to the partners based on the balances in their capital accounts. Notice the important last step in the liquidation—that is, that the liquidating cash dividend (the final distribution paid to the partners based on their capital accounts) paid to the partners is not distributed according to their profit-sharing agreement; rather, it is based on their final equity balances.

To illustrate a simple liquidation of a partnership, assume that Field, Stream, and Woods, who share profits equally, produce the following balance sheet on June 30, 20X1.

Field, Stream, and Woods Balance Sheet June 30, 20X1			
Assets		**Liabilities & Owners' Equity**	
Cash	$ 50,000	Notes Payable	$ 40,000
Equipment	130,000	Field, Capital	50,000
		Stream, Capital	70,000
		Woods, Capital	20,000
Total Assets	$180,000	Total Liabilities	
		& OE	$180,000

If the equipment were sold for $100,000, the first journal entry would be:

Cash	$100,000	
Loss on Disposal of Equipment	30,000	
Equipment		$130,000

Next, the loss would be distributed to the partners by means of the following journal entry:

Field, Capital	$10,000	
Stream, Capital	10,000	
Woods, Capital	10,000	
Loss on Disposal of Equipment		$30,000

At this point, the capital balances of the partners would be $40,000, $60,000, and $10,000 for Field, Stream, and Woods, respectively. The next entry would occur when the note payable was paid off, and would simply be:

Notes Payable	$40,000	
Cash		$40,000

At this point, the balance sheet of the partnership would appear as follows:

Balance Sheet			
Cash	$110,000	Field, Capital	$ 40,000
		Stream, Capital	60,000
		Woods, Capital	10,000
Total Assets	$110,000	Total Owners' Equity	$110,000

The final entry for the liquidation of this partnership would be:

Field, Capital	$40,000	
Stream, Capital	60,000	
Woods, Capital	10,000	
Cash		$110,000

Once again, notice that when the liquidating dividend is paid, the profit-sharing agreement is disregarded and the cash is distributed based on the final capital balances in the partners' accounts.

In this next illustration, we will assume the same facts that we did before, except that the equipment in this case sells for $55,000 rather than $130,000. In this case, the journal entry for the disposal of the equipment would be:

Cash	$55,000	
Loss on Disposal of Equipment	75,000	
Equipment		$130,000

The loss would then be distributed to the partners by means of the following journal entry:

Field, Capital	$25,000	
Stream, Capital	25,000	
Woods, Capital	25,000	
Loss on Disposal of Equipment		$75,000

At this point, the partners' balances in their capital accounts would be $25,000, $45,000, and ($5,000) respectively for Field, Stream, and Woods. The note payable would be disposed of as it was before, with a debit to Notes Payable and a credit to Cash of $40,000. At this point, the partnership's balance sheet would appear as follows:

Balance Sheet			
Cash	$65,000	Field, Capital	$25,000
		Stream, Capital	45,000
		Woods, Capital	(5,000)
Total Assets	$65,000	Total Owners' Equity	$65,000

At this point, Field and Stream would ask Woods to pay the $5,000 deficit in her partnership account. If Woods was able to pay the $5,000, the entry would be:

Cash	$5,000	
Woods, Capital		$5,000

This would produce a zero balance in Woods's capital account.

The final journal entry for the liquidation of this partnership would be as follows:

Field, Capital	$25,000	
Stream, Capital	45,000	
Cash		$70,000

If, however, Field and Stream asked Woods to pay the $5,000 and she could not, the $5,000 deficit in her account would be distributed to the remaining partners based on their profit-sharing arrangement, which at this point would be 50-50. The journal entry to record this would be:

Field, Capital	$2,500	
Stream, Capital	$2,500	
Woods, Capital		$5,000

The final entry for this partnership liquidation would be:

Field, Capital	$22,500	
Stream, Capital	42,500	
Cash		$65,000

Summary

A business partnership is an entity made up of two or more individuals engaged in some economic activity. The partners co-own all the assets and liabilities of the entity and also share in some manner in the profits or losses of the enterprise. Although some partnership agreements are oral, most are written and should include at least the names of the partners, the amounts of the investments of each individual partner, the profit-sharing arrangement, and the buy/sell agreement of the partnership.

Some of the advantages of a partnership are:

- Its ease of formation.

- The fact that there are no partnership taxes to be paid.

- The potential for synergy.

Some disadvantages of the partnership form of business organization are:

- Its limited life.

- Mutual agency.

- Unlimited liability.

The rest of the chapter discussed the differences between general and limited partnerships; the partners' capital and drawing accounts; the formation of a partnership; the division of the income produced by the partnership; the admission of a new partner; the withdrawal of a partner; and, finally, the steps necessary for the liquidation of a partnership.

Key Terms

general partnership—A form of business organization in which all of the partners are called *general partners* and have unlimited liability for the debts of the partnership.

limited partnership—A partnership in which one or more of the partners have limited liability. That is, their liability is limited to the amounts of their investment in the partnership and their personal assets are not vulnerable to their business's creditors. Every partnership must have at least one general partner, and there are several criteria that must be met in the case of a limited partnership.

mutual agency—The responsibility of partners in a partnership for their partners' individual business actions. Mutual agency pertains only to actions that relate to the partnership, not to any partner's personal debts or actions.

synergy—The interaction of two or more separate individuals or agencies to achieve an effect of which each is individually incapable; more commonly, "the whole is greater than the sum of its parts."

unlimited liability—The type of liability experienced by a sole proprietorship or a partnership. The liability of sole proprietors or partners extends beyond their investments in the business to their personal assets.

Review Questions

1. What are the disadvantages of the partnership form of business organization?

2. What is the difference between a general partnership and a limited partnership?

3. Discuss the validity of the following three statements:

   a. Partnerships pay no taxes.

   b. Partnerships file no tax returns.

   c. Partners pay no tax on partnership profits.

4. Duke and Earl form a partnership to start a fine dining restaurant. What is Duke's liability for Earl's actions in each of the following situations?

   a. Earl orders $25,000 worth of food and beverages from American Foods, Inc., for use in the restaurant.

   b. Earl purchases a personal automobile for driving to and from the restaurant, and signs a note for $18,000.

   c. Earl signs a lease on a building for the restaurant, agreeing to pay $3,000 per month.

   d. Earl signs a home improvement loan in the amount of $8,000 for an addition to his home.

5. How does the balance sheet of a partnership differ from that of a sole proprietorship?

6. What are the major items that ought to be included in a partnership agreement?

7. What are the three common profit-sharing agreements discussed in the chapter, and what are their characteristics?

8. Dewey, Cheatum, and Howe share partnership profits in a $\frac{1}{4}$, $\frac{1}{2}$, and $\frac{1}{4}$ ratio, respectively. If Howe were paid a $30,000 bonus to leave the partnership, how would the bonus affect the capital accounts of Dewey and Cheatum?

9. Land and See, who share profits in a $\frac{2}{3}\frac{1}{3}$ ratio respectively, are liquidating their partnership. After the assets have been converted to cash and the liabilities have been paid, the accounts have the following balances: Cash, $30,000; Land, Capital $18,000; and See, Capital $12,000. What would be the final closing entry for the partnership?

10. In what two different ways can a new partner be admitted to a partnership?

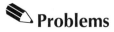 Problems ───────────────────────────────────────

Problem 1

Cook and Sell are forming a partnership to start a catering business. Cook's contribution will be cash of $20,000, equipment that cost $8,000 and has a fair market value of $10,000, and inventory worth $10,000. Sell's contribution includes land that cost $15,000 and is now worth $40,000, a building with a fair market value of $80,000 and a mortgage of $60,000, and equipment worth $5,000.

Required:

Determine the capital balances for the two partners at the date of the partnership's formation.

Problem 2

Griffin and Hall are partners in the motel business. On January 1, 20X1, their capital balances were $50,000 and $40,000 respectively. During 20X1 Griffin drew $25,000 and Hall drew $30,000 out of the partnership. The profit for 20X1 was $60,000 and is to be divided in the ratio of 40 percent for Griffin to 60 percent for Hall.

Required:

Determine the capital balances of Griffin and Hall for December 31, 20X1.

Problem 3

Reed, Dolan, and Gates are partners in a ski resort and have agreed to share profits in the following way: salaries of $25,000 to Reed, $35,000 to Dolan, and $40,000 to Gates. The remaining profit will be distributed as follows: 30 percent to Reed, 20 percent to Dolan, and 50 percent to Gates.

Required:

Assuming the partnership earned a profit of $150,000 in 20X1, compute the amount that each partner would earn in 20X1.

Problem 4

Powers and Hall have a partnership agreement that calls for the following annual distribution:

 a. Salaries of $50,000 to Powers and $60,000 to Hall.

 b. Remaining profit to be shared—60 percent to Powers and 40 percent to Hall.

The profit for 20X7 was $300,000.

Required:

Determine the division of profit for 20X7.

Problem 5

Spruce and Willow have a partnership and are about to admit Oak as a new partner. Spruce and Willow each currently have partnership capital balances of $70,000. Spruce and Willow have agreed to admit Oak into the partnership, granting her a one–third interest in exchange for a $100,000 investment of cash in the partnership.

Required:

Journalize the entry to admit Oak into the partnership.

Problem 6

Wilson and Byrne have decided to form a partnership and call their new venture The Firefly. You have been provided with the following information about Wilson and Byrne's assets on December 31, 20X7:

	Wilson	Byrne
Cash	$55,000	$45,000
Inventory	5,000	2,000
Equipment at cost	20,000	15,000
Equipment at market value	25,000	20,000
Land	150,000	0
Notes payable	50,000	0

Required:

Compile the balance sheet as of December 31, 20X7, for The Firefly.

Problem 7

Haul and Oates start a partnership with the following assets:

			Original Asset Owned by	
Asset	Market Value	Cost	Haul	Oates
Cash	$ 50,000	$ 50,000	X	
Building	100,000	75,000		X
Inventory	30,000	40,000	X	
Equipment	60,000	80,000		X
Supplies	10,000	10,000	X	
Land	200,000	100,000		X

Required:

1. What is the amount of Haul's capital in the partnership?
2. What is the amount of Oates's capital in the partnership?

Problem 8

Street has $80,000 in capital and Barnes has $60,000 in capital in a restaurant partnership. They have agreed that Street will sell her entire interest to Townes for $80,000 in cash.

Required:

1. Write the journal entry for this sale.
2. Write the journal entry if the sale is made for $90,000.

Problem 9

Gold, Silver and Bronze are partners in a lodging venture. They have agreed to salaries as follows: Gold, $60,000; Silver, $70,000; and Bronze, $80,000. After salaries, they distribute income at the rate of 8 percent interest on their capital balances. Lastly, they divide the remaining income equally. Their current capital balances are:

Gold	$150,000
Silver	200,000
Bronze	250,000

Required:
Determine the proper division of this year's income of $408,000.

Problem 10

Siggy, Babbs, and Emily are partners in a small contract food service business. The equity in the partnership accounts is $20,000 each.

Required:
Construct the journal entry for the withdrawal of Emily under each of the following two sets of circumstances:

1. The partnership pays Emily $20,000 for her entire interest.
2. Sarah pays Emily $25,000 for her interest and is admitted to the partnership for a $\frac{1}{3}$ interest.

Problem 11

Fox and Wolfe are partners in a destination resort operation with capital balances of $120,000 each. They share profits equally. They are badly in need of cash and have agreed to admit Lyon for $90,000 in exchange for a $\frac{1}{3}$ equity interest in the partnership.

Required:

1. Journalize the entry for the admission of Lyon.
2. Illustrate the Owners' Equity section of the balance sheet after the admission of Lyon.

Challenge Problems

Problem 12

Cleaves, Klein, and Hunter form a partnership with the following assets:

Partner	Asset	Cost Basis of Asset	Market Value of Asset
Cleaves	Cash	$100,000	
Klein	Building	80,000	$160,000
	Equipment	60,000	40,000
Hunter	Cash	50,000	
	Inventory	60,000	50,000

The partnership agreement calls for profit sharing in the following way:
Salaries of $40,000 to Cleaves
                   $50,000 to Klein
                   $30,000 to Hunter
Interest of 10 percent on beginning of year capital balances.
Remaining profits distributed as follows:
        40 percent to Cleaves
        30 percent to Klein
        30 percent to Hunter

Required:

Assume the profit before wages and interest for Year 1 was $200,000.

1. Prepare a balance sheet for the starting date of the partnership.
2. Determine the division of profits for the partners in Year 1.

Problem 13

At 12/31/20X1, Smith's and Wesson's drawing and capital accounts are as follows:

Partner	Balance
Smith, Capital	$50,000
Smith, Drawing	70,000
Wesson, Capital	80,000
Wesson, Drawing	30,000

The profit-sharing agreement is as follows:

a. Salary of $30,000 to Smith and $20,000 to Wesson.
b. Divide the remaining profit or loss in a 60-40 ratio with 60 percent to Smith and 40 percent to Wesson.

Required:

Based on the existing account balances and profit sharing agreement, determine the ending balances in the partners' accounts if the business had a $50,000 loss in this year.

Problem 14

Smith and Wesson have decided to liquidate their partnership at August 31, 20X7. Their balance sheet appears below:

Smith and Wesson
Balance Sheet
August 31, 20X7

Assets:		Liabilities:	
Cash	$ 100,000	Notes Payable	$ 75,000
Inventory	4,000	Capital:	
Equipment	42,000	Smith, Capital	36,000
		Wesson, Capital	35,000
Total Assets	$ 146,000	Total Liabilities and Capital	$ 146,000

Required:

Assuming the equipment is sold for $30,000 and the inventory is sold for $4,000, journalize the entries for the liquidation of the partnership. Also assume that the partners share profits and losses equally.

Problem 15

Hill and Dale are partners in a successful resort called the Timberline Inn. The general ledger accounts of the partnership appear as follows:

Cash	$ 20,000
Accounts Receivable	45,000
Inventory	23,000
Equipment	23,000
Land	180,000
Buildings	450,000
Accounts Payable	16,000
Mortgage Payable	325,000
Hill, Capital	220,000
Dale, Capital	180,000

Hill and Dale have agreed to admit Valley on December 31, 20X1, for $200,000 cash to a $\frac{1}{3}$ interest in the partnership.

Required:

1. Journalize the entry to admit Valley.
2. Compile the balance sheet for the partnership at December 31, 20X1, after the admission of Valley.

Chapter 14 Outline

Financial Statements
Advantages and Disadvantages of the
    Corporation
Taxes
Organizational Structure
Forming a Corporation
Common Stock
Dividends
Retained Earnings
Stock Subscription Plan
Preferred Stock
Cash Dividends Compared to Stock
    Dividends
Stock Splits
Treasury Stock
Book Value per Share of Common Stock
      Book Value versus Market Value per
        Share

Competencies

1. Identify unique features of corporate financial statements, and outline advantages and disadvantages of the corporate form of business. (pp. 421–422)

2. Explain how corporations' taxes are accounted for and how corporations are structured and formed. (pp. 422–423)

3. Describe common stock and cash dividends and demonstrate how to account for them. (pp. 423–425)

4. Demonstrate how to prepare a statement of retained earnings and how to account for a stock subscription plan. (pp. 425–427)

5. Distinguish between common and preferred stock, and describe preferred stock. (pp. 427–428)

6. Describe stock dividends and stock splits and demonstrate how to account for them. (pp. 428–429)

7. Describe treasury stock and demonstrate how to account for it. (pp. 429–430)

8. Demonstrate how to calculate book value per share of stock, and explain why this figure and the market value per share interest shareholders. (pp. 430–431)

14

Corporate Accounting

THERE ARE FOUR basic forms of business organization: the sole proprietorship, the partnership, the limited liability company, and the corporation. Corporation accounting is by far the most difficult of the four forms in terms of its accounting requirements.

Financial Statements

The financial statements produced for corporations are basically the same as the statements produced for the sole proprietorship, partnership, or LLC—in most areas. There are very few, if any, changes in the Assets and Liabilities sections. However, there are major changes in the equity section of the balance sheet. The Stockholders' Equity section of the balance sheet can be very complex compared to the equity section of a balance sheet produced for the other three business forms.

The Stockholders' Equity section of the balance sheet includes two major sections: Paid-In Capital and Earned Capital. The Paid-In Capital section includes the amounts of capital paid into the corporation over its life. Typical paid-in capital accounts include Common Stock, Preferred Stock, Additional Paid-In Capital, and Common Stock Subscribed.

Earned Capital represents the capital that the corporation has earned through profits over its life that has not been paid out in dividends. These accumulated earnings are recorded in an account called Retained Earnings. All of these capital accounts will be discussed in detail in this chapter.

A corporation is very different from the other forms of organization. A corporation is a legal entity in itself, given a life in the state in which it is incorporated. Since the corporation has a life, it can be taken to court and can enter into long-term contracts, which is not possible to do in the case of partnerships and sole proprietorships.

Advantages and Disadvantages of the Corporation

There are advantages and disadvantages of the corporate form of organization. The advantages of incorporation include limited liability. This is very important because it limits the potential losses of the owners to the amount of their original investments. (This is not true of the sole proprietorship or partnership, where the owners can lose amounts beyond their original investment.) Another advantage of the corporation is that it has unlimited life. The life of a sole proprietorship or partnership is limited to the lives of the owners. However, a corporation continues regardless of any changes in ownership. Another advantage of the corporate form of organization is its ease in acquiring capital. Corporations can acquire large amounts of capital with relatively little difficulty compared to partnerships or sole proprietorships. In addition, shares of ownership in a corporation are easily transferable. It could take many months for a sole proprietor to turn over the business to another individual. However, in the case of a huge corporation, thousands of shares of stock can change hands as the result of a simple phone call. The corporation also benefits from professional management. The corporation is organized differently from the sole proprietorship or partnership in that a professional management team runs it and its owners are usually uninvolved in day-to-day management.

Disadvantages of the corporate form of business include **double taxation**, which can be a severe disadvantage. Since corporations are legal entities, they are required to pay taxes on their profits. Later, when the profits are distributed to the owners as dividends, the owners must pay taxes again. The issue of taxation is a complex one; further discussion of it is beyond our scope.

Regulation is another disadvantage of the corporate form of business. Federal and state government agencies require many more reports of corporations than they require of other business forms.

Taxes

The corporation is the only form of business that pays taxes on profits. In sole proprietorships, partnerships, and LLCs, the owners pay taxes only on their personal tax returns.

In the case of the corporation, income taxes are estimated quarterly. The following accounting entry would be made in the event of a $25,000 tax liability:

Income Tax Expense	$25,000	
Income Tax Payable		$25,000

The liability will appear in the Current Liabilities section of the balance sheet, while Income Tax Expense will appear at the bottom of the income statement just before Net Income.

Organizational Structure

The organizational structure of the corporation is different from the other forms of business. The owners of a corporation vote for members of the corporation's board of directors, which is responsible for setting broad policy guidelines for the operations of the business and is not involved in its daily management. The board's responsibilities include hiring individuals to manage the company's day-to-day activities.

Forming a Corporation

To form a corporation, individuals must apply to a state for organization within that state. After the necessary paperwork is submitted and approved, the state allows a corporation to begin operating its business. There are many costs involved in forming a corporation. These costs include legal fees, promoter's fees, and fees paid to the state for incorporating. Corporations may account for **organization costs** by placing them in an intangible-asset account called Organization Costs and writing them off over a number of years. Organization costs should not be written off over a period of greater than 40 years. Federal tax law states that organization costs for tax purposes may be written off over a shorter period of time, but no less than five years.

Common Stock

The basic unit of ownership in a corporation is a share of stock. The term **capital stock** refers broadly to ownership in a corporation. When a corporation applies to a state for a charter, it is required to ask for a certain authorized number of shares of stock. The *authorized number of shares of stock* represents the maximum amount of shares that the company can eventually issue to the public. *Issued shares of stock*, on the other hand, refers to the number of shares of stock that the company has sold to the public. *Outstanding shares of stock* equals issued shares of stock less *treasury stock* (to be discussed later in the chapter). For example, a company that has issued 40,000 shares of stock and purchased back 5,000 shares of treasury stock has 35,000 shares of stock outstanding.

Shares of stock must have either a **par value** or a stated value. Par value or stated value represents the legal capital of the corporation. Although technically there are differences between par value and stated value, we will assume they are similar. Understand that the par value of a stock has no relation to the market value of the stock. Companies will usually set the par value of a stock very low. Let's assume that a certain corporation decided to issue 20,000 shares of par value stock that have a par value of $2 a share, for $10 a share. The journal entry would be as follows:

Cash	$200,000	
Common Stock		$ 40,000
Additional Paid-In Capital in Excess of Par		160,000

Amounts are always entered in the Common Stock account at par value. The excess of the selling price over the par value is credited to an account called Additional Paid-In Capital in Excess of Par. This is an equity account that normally carries a credit balance. The $40,000 common stock and $160,000 paid-in capital represent the legal capital of the firm.

The owners of these shares of stock expect two things in return for the money they gave the corporation for the stock. First, they hope that the shares of stock increase in value. Second, they expect to receive a return of the company's profits every year. Profits returned to the stockholders are referred to as **dividends**.

Dividends

Dividends are paid out of the company's accumulated earnings and are available to stockholders only when dividends are declared by the board of directors. There are four important dividend dates relating to cash dividends. They are the date of declaration, the date of record, the ex-dividend date, and the date of payment.

1. *The date of declaration.* This is the date on which the board of directors announces a future dividend. At this time, the board of directors will state when the payment date will be and what the amount of the dividend will be.

2. *The date of record.* This is the date on which a list of the holders of the shares of stock is compiled so that the dividend checks can be mailed to them.

3. *The ex-dividend date.* On this date, the stock sells without the dividend; that is, even though a dividend will be paid soon on the stock, the new purchaser will not receive the dividend. The ex-dividend date normally precedes the date of record by three days. The purpose of setting an ex-dividend date is to allow the paperwork on exchanges of ownership of shares of stock to be cleared up before the date of record.

4. *The date of payment.* This is the date on which the actual dividend is paid.

Assume that a company declares a $.30 dividend on 50,000 shares of outstanding stock. The journal entry to record the declaration of the dividend would be:

| Retained Earnings | $15,000 | |
| Dividends Payable | | $15,000 |

Rather than debit Retained Earnings when a dividend is declared, some corporations will debit an account called Dividends or Dividends Declared. This account will then be closed into Retained Earnings at the end of the fiscal period.

Note that once a dividend is declared by the board of directors, the company must pay the dividend. On the dividend payment date, the following entry would be made in the case of the $.30 dividend just mentioned:

| Dividends Payable | $15,000 | |
| Cash | | $15,000 |

Once the dividend is declared, it will be paid shortly thereafter; hence, it is classified as a current liability. No accounting entries are made on either the date of record or the ex-dividend date.

Normally a corporation itself will not handle the payment of a dividend. Rather, it will use a transfer agent and registrar to keep track of the corporation's shareholders and to issue the dividend checks. The transfer agent or registrar is typically a large bank or a trust company.

Shares of stock of large corporations like Marriot International are traded in securities markets. A line from the financial pages of the *Wall Street Journal* is included below. It shows the 52-week high and low price for Marriot International, the annual cash dividend of 42 cents per share, the yield of .6 percent, the day's volume of shares of 876,000, its closing price of $66.59/share, and the change in its market price from the preceding day.

52 week								
HI	LO		DIV	Yield%	PE	VOL100s	CLOSE	NET CHANGE
70.78	58.01	MARRIOT INT	.42	.6	25	8,767	66.59	0.01

Retained Earnings

Retained Earnings is an equity account that appears only on the books of a corporation. Whereas partnerships and sole proprietorships close their Income Summary accounts into the owners' capital accounts at the end of a fiscal period, corporations close their Income Summary accounts into Retained Earnings.

Retained Earnings represents the amount of a company's earnings to date that have not been paid out in dividends. Retained earnings is *not* the same as cash for a given corporation. A corporation can have a large amount of cash and no retained earnings or a large amount of retained earnings and no cash. There is not necessarily a relationship between the amounts in these two accounts. One prerequisite for paying a dividend is that the company must have retained earnings. A second prerequisite is that the company also must have the cash on hand to pay the dividend. The third prerequisite is that the dividend must be declared by the board of directors.

The following is a statement of retained earnings for United Hotels.

United Hotels Statement of Retained Earnings For Year Ended December 31, 20X1	
Retained Earnings, January 1, 20X1	$150,000
Net Income for 20X1	48,000
Subtotal	$198,000
Dividends Declared during 20X1	24,000
Retained Earnings, December 31, 20X1	$174,000

On rare occasions a firm may discover an error in the income reported in a prior year. Since the net income of that year has already been closed into Retained Earnings, the correction is logically made to the Retained Earnings account. This correction is called a *prior period adjustment*. The correction should be made to the beginning balance of Retained Earnings, as shown in the following statement:

United Hotels Statement of Retained Earnings For Year Ended December 31, 20X1	
Retained Earnings, January 1, 20X1	$150,000
Add: Error of prior period: Recorded purchase of Equipment as an expense rather than an asset (net of taxes)	25,000
Adjusted Retained Earnings	175,000
Net Income for 20X1	48,000
Subtotal	223,000
Dividends Declared during 20X1	24,000
Retained Earnings, December 31, 20X1	$199,000

It is not uncommon for a hospitality firm to operate at a loss in the first years of its existence. When those losses are closed into Retained Earnings, a debit balance is created in that account. This debit balance in Retained Earnings is referred to as a *deficit*. The deficit is subtracted from the rest of the owners' equity, as shown in this illustration:

Stockholders' Equity	
Preferred Stock	$150,000
Common Stock	200,000
Additional Paid-In Capital	600,000
Subtotal	$950,000
Less Deficit	50,000
Total Stockholders' Equity	$900,000

Stock Subscription Plan

Occasionally, a company will offer new shares of stock through what is called a **stock subscription plan**. In this case, individuals choosing to buy new shares of stock in the corporation complete a subscription form, agreeing to buy the stock at a certain price. Assume that a certain corporation receives subscriptions to 5,000 shares of $10 par value stock at a price of $30 a share. The entry to record the subscription of these 5,000 shares of stock would be as follows:

Stock Subscriptions Receivable	$150,000	
Common Stock Subscribed		$ 50,000
Additional Paid-In Capital in Excess of Par		100,000

The Stock Subscriptions Receivable account appears in the Current Assets section of the balance sheet.

Assume that later in the month cash is paid for 3,000 shares of the subscribed stock. In this case, the following two entries would be made:

Cash	$90,000	
Stock Subscriptions Receivable		$90,000

Common Stock Subscribed	$30,000	
Common Stock		$30,000

If a balance sheet were drawn up for the company between the subscription date and the date the new stock is actually issued, the Common Stock Subscribed account would appear on the balance sheet in the equity section. The following is an example of a Stockholders' Equity section of the balance sheet, including Common Stock Subscribed:

Stockholders' Equity	
Common Stock	$1,000,000
Common Stock Subscribed	20,000
Paid-In Capital in Excess of Par	100,000
Retained Earnings	250,000
Total Stockholders' Equity	$1,370,000

Preferred Stock

So far we have discussed one type of stock, **common stock,** which is the most popular form of stock issued by corporations. Another type of stock occasionally found on the books of hospitality firms is called **preferred stock.** Preferred stock has many characteristics that common stock does not have. First, as its name implies, it is preferred in terms of dividend payment. Any given corporation will pay dividends to its preferred stockholders before it pays any dividends to common stockholders. Second, preferred dividends are preferred in the event of the liquidation of the company. If the company should decide to liquidate its assets after paying off its liabilities, preferred stockholders would be paid before common stockholders. Third, preferred stock is generally **cumulative** in nature. This means that if a dividend is not paid in one year, before anything can be paid to the common stockholders in a subsequent year, the past preferred dividend and the current year's dividend must be paid. Most preferred stocks are cumulative; however, a few preferred stocks are noncumulative.

Fourth, preferred stock is **callable.** This means that the corporation has the option of paying the preferred stockholders the par value of the stock (or some other predetermined value above par) in return for the stock certificates. Fifth, preferred stock, unlike common stock, normally gives holders no voting rights. Sixth, some preferred stock is convertible into common stock of the corporation. Seventh, some preferred stock is *participating preferred*. This means that in years when excess profits are earned, preferred stockholders participate with the common stockholders in additional dividend payments.

The journal entries recording the issuance of preferred stock are similar to those used to record common stock.

Cash Dividends Compared to Stock Dividends

People often confuse stock dividends and cash dividends. *Cash dividends* are cash payments to owners of shares of stock that come out of the company's income. **Stock dividends**, on the other hand, are additional shares of stock in the company granted to existing shareholders.

What is the benefit of receiving a stock dividend? If, for instance, a stockholder receives additional stock dividends in the amount of 10 percent of the stock he or she owns and every other stockholder also receives 10 percent more stock than he or she currently owns, is any stockholder really in any better position after the stock dividend than before the stock dividend? Stockholders *may* be in a better position after a stock dividend in two instances. First, if the company keeps the same cash dividend per share after distributing the stock dividend, stockholders are better off, because they receive the same dividend per share times the greater number of shares—a greater overall dividend amount. Second, when a stock dividend is declared, the company's stock will usually drop in value, often making it more attractive to potential investors and thus providing some appreciation potential for the stockholders in the future.

Assume that Hercules Properties Corporation has 200,000 shares of $5 par value stock authorized and 150,000 shares issued and outstanding. Hercules declares a 5 percent stock dividend when the market price of the stock is $20 per share. The journal entry to record this declaration of the stock dividend is:

Retained Earnings	$150,000	
Stock Dividend to Be Distributed		$ 37,500
Additional Paid-In Capital: Stock Dividend		112,500

The $150,000 debit to Retained Earnings is equal to 150,000 shares × 5% × $20/share. The $37,500 credit to Stock Dividend to Be Distributed is equal to 7,500 shares × $5/share. Additional Paid-In Capital is credited for $20 − $5 = $15 × 7,500 shares, or $112,500.

Later, when the stock dividend was actually distributed, the journal entry would be:

Stock Dividend to Be Distributed	$37,500	
Common Stock		$37,500

Notice that in the case of this small stock dividend, Retained Earnings is decreased by the number of shares in the dividend times the current market price of the stock (7,500 shares × $20 = $150,000). The Common Stock account, of course, is increased by the par value of the stock in the second journal entry.

We described this entry as a *small stock dividend* because the dividend amounted to less than 20 to 25 percent of the shares of stock outstanding at the date of the dividend. In the case of a *large stock dividend*, which is defined as a dividend that is greater than 20 to 25 percent of the stock outstanding, the same accounts would be used in the journal entry on the date of declaration, except that Retained Earnings would be debited for the par value of the stock and not the market price of the stock.

Stock Splits

Corporations may want to increase the number of shares of their stock outstanding for various reasons or may want to see the stock price reduced in the marketplace. Both scenarios can be accomplished through the use of a **stock split**. In the case of a two-for-one stock split, a corporation would grant two shares for every one share currently held by the owners. For example, assume that Hercules Property Corporation has 50,000 shares of common stock outstanding at a par value of $10 for $500,000 worth. After a two-for-one stock split, the company would have 100,000 shares of stock at $5 par value, again yielding $500,000. Note that there is no change in the total assets, no change in total liabilities, and no change in total stockholders' equity. Thus, no journal entry is made in the case of a stock split; instead, a memo is made in the general journal.

Treasury Stock

Treasury stock is common stock that was once issued by a corporation and later repurchased by the same corporation. A company that has treasury stock will show a difference between the number of shares of stock issued and the number of shares outstanding, since treasury stock is not currently outstanding even though it has been issued. There are two basic ways to account for treasury stock. These are the *par method* and the *cost method*. Here, we will discuss only the cost method of accounting for treasury stock.

First, it is important to note that treasury stock is not an asset. Also, since treasury stock is stock that is not outstanding, no dividends are paid on it. Treasury stock shows up in the Stockholders' Equity section of the balance sheet as a reduction to Total Stockholders' Equity. Assume that Pristine Hotels reacquires 5,000 shares of its own stock at a market price of $30 per share. Recording this purchase at cost, the journal entry would be as follows:

Treasury Stock	$150,000	
Cash		$150,000

If later on that treasury stock were sold at cost, the company would merely reverse the preceding entry. However, if 3,000 shares of treasury stock that had been purchased at $30 per share were later sold back to the public at $40 per share, the following entry would be made:

Cash	$120,000	
Treasury Stock		$90,000
Additional Paid-In Capital from Treasury Stock		30,000

If, following that resale, 1,000 shares of treasury stock were resold to the public at $20 per share, the following entry would be made:

Cash	$20,000	
Additional Paid-In Capital from Treasury Stock	10,000	
Treasury Stock		$30,000

Notice that no gains or losses are recorded on the sale of treasury stock. In the second case, in which the treasury stock was resold at a price below its cost, the difference between cost and selling price is debited to the Additional Paid-In Capital account. If there had been no additional paid-in capital, rather than giving Paid-In Capital a debit balance, accountants would have debited Retained Earnings for $10,000.

Book Value per Share of Common Stock

Common stockholders closely watch the market price of their stock as listed on the organized stock exchanges or the over-the-counter markets. Although of lesser interest to stockholders, book value per share is also a concern to owners.

Book value per share of stock refers to the per-share value of the company's net assets (assets minus liabilities). For a corporation offering only common stock, book value per share of stock is computed by dividing Total Stockholders' Equity by the number of common shares outstanding. For example, assume that Greenwood Hotels, Inc., had the following Stockholders' Equity section:

Common Stock, $5 par (10,000 shares outstanding)	$ 50,000
Additional Paid-In Capital	150,000
Retained Earnings	80,000
Total Stockholders' Equity	$280,000

The book value per share would be $28.00, determined as follows:

Total Stockholders' Equity	$280,000
÷ Common Shares Outstanding	10,000
= Book Value per Share	$ 28

The calculation of book value per share is complicated when the corporation has preferred stock outstanding. First, the preferred stock must be deducted at its call price from the value of the net assets. Second, any dividends in arrears on the preferred stock must be deducted also. The remaining value of the net assets is then divided by the number of common shares outstanding.

For example, assume that Greenwood Hotels, Inc., had 500 shares of $100 par, 8 percent preferred, callable at $105, with $20,000 dividends in arrears. Under these circumstances, book value per share of common stock would be calculated as follows:

Preferred Stock, $100 par, 8%, callable at $105, 500 shares outstanding		$ 50,000
Common Stock, $5 par, 10,000 shares outstanding		50,000
Additional Paid-In Capital		150,000
Retained Earnings		80,000
Total Stockholders' Equity		$330,000
Total Stockholders' Equity		$330,000
Less Call Value of Preferred Stock		(52,500)
Less Preferred Dividends in Arrears		(20,000)
Equity of Common Stockholders		$257,500
Divided by Common Shares Outstanding	÷	10,000
Equals Book Value per Share of Common Stock	=	$ 25.75

Book Value versus Market Value per Share

Book value per share is based on historical cost figures for the items on the balance sheet. For example, land that was purchased for $500,000 ten years ago has a book value of $500,000, even though it may now be worth $10,000,000. Book value is generally lower than market value for a given company. If a stock happened to be selling at a market price below book value, it could be of interest to potential stockholders, since the sale of the assets at book value would yield enough to pay the debts and leave more dollars per share than the stock was currently selling for in the market.

Summary

Accounting for the corporate form of business organization is more complex than accounting for the sole proprietorship, the partnership, or the limited liability company.

Advantages of the corporate form of business organization include limited liability, unlimited life, ease of acquiring capital, easily transferable shares of ownership, and professional management. Some disadvantages of the corporate form are double taxation (that is, taxes are paid on the profits of the corporation and also on the dividends distributed to the shareholders) and regulation by local, state, and federal governments.

The remainder of the chapter discusses the types of stock issued by a corporation and the accounting procedures associated with them for dividend determination and payment. Also noted are stock splits, treasury stock, book value per share of common stock, market value per share, and the differences between cash dividends and stock dividends.

Key Terms

callable—Subject to a demand for presentation for payment.

capital stock—Shares of ownership of a corporation; general term that covers all classes of common and preferred stock.

common stock—Capital stock of a corporation; stockholders who own common stock generally have voting rights.

cumulative—Refers to the fact that if a dividend is not paid in one year, the past preferred dividend and the current year's dividend must be paid before anything can be paid to the common stockholders in a subsequent year.

dividend—A distribution of earnings to owners of a corporation's stock.

double taxation—This occurs when both corporate profits and dividends paid to stockholders are taxed.

organization costs—Costs incurred before a business is incorporated. They include such things as legal fees, promoter's fees, and fees paid to the state for incorporating.

par value—An arbitrarily selected amount associated with authorized shares of stock; it is also referred to as *legal value*.

preferred stock—Corporate stock that entitles the holder to preferential treatment on dividends, but may not give the holder voting rights.

stock dividend—The payment by a corporation of a dividend in the form of shares of its own stock without change in par value.

stock split—A division of corporate stock by the issuance to existing stockholders of a specified number of new shares with a corresponding lowering of par value for each outstanding share. In the case of a two-for-one stock split, the corporation would grant two shares for every one share previously held by the owners.

stock subscription plan—A stock purchase plan in which individuals choosing to buy new shares of stock in the corporation complete a subscription form, agreeing to buy the stock at a certain price.

treasury stock—A corporation's own capital stock that the corporation has repurchased but not retired or reissued.

Review Questions

1. What are the major advantages and disadvantages of the corporate form of business?

2. What do common stockholders expect to receive in return for their investment?

3. What is the significance of the par value of a common stock? What is the relationship between par value and market value?

4. What are the four dividend dates? What is the significance of each?

5. Where are the accounts Stock Subscriptions Receivable and Common Stock Subscribed located on the balance sheet?

6. What are the main characteristics of preferred stock?

7. What are the differences between a cash dividend and a stock dividend?

8. How does accounting for a stock dividend differ from accounting for a stock split?

9. How does a firm acquire treasury stock? Where does it appear on the balance sheet?

10. How would the journal entry for a small stock dividend differ from the journal entry for a large stock dividend?

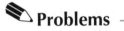 **Problems** _____

Problem 1

The following data about McDonald's was included in the financial section of the *Wall Street Journal*:

52 week			DIV	Yield%	PE	VOL100s	CLOSE	NET CHANGE
HI	LO							
35.91	27.36	MCDONALDS	.67	1.9	19	68,782	35.71	–.15

Required:
Explain the meaning of each item on this stock quote.

Problem 2

Condor Hotels, Inc., currently has common stock of $200,000, additional paid-in capital of $800,000, and retained earnings of $75,000. On December 15, 20X1, it issues 10,000 shares of $5 par common stock at $20 per share.

Required:

1. Write the journal entry for December 15, 20X1.

2. Prepare, in good form, the Stockholders' Equity section of the balance sheet after the issuance of the additional shares.

Problem 3

The following data is from a balance sheet of McDonald's Corporation on December 31, 20X4:

Common Stock	$ 16,600
Treasury Stock	(9,756,900)
Retained Earnings	21,755,800
Total Liabilities	13,636,000
Paid-in Capital	2,186,000

Required:

1. Calculate the total stockholder's equity on December 31, 20X4.
2. Calculate the total amount of assets on December 31, 20X4.

Problem 4

Based on the following information, compile the statement of retained earnings for Top Flight Hotels, Inc., for the year ended December 31, 20X1.

Net income for the year	$ 92,000
Retained earnings as of January 1, 20X1	125,000
Dividends declared during 20X1	46,000
Error of prior period: add $50,000 net of taxes	50,000

Problem 5

The accounts for the Lighthouse Hotel Corporation are given below:

Common Stock	Land
Bonds Payable	Equipment
Accounts Receivable	Treasury Stock
Additional Paid-In Capital—Common Stock	Common Stock Subscribed
Buildings	Accounts Payable
Retained Earnings	Stock Dividend to Be Distributed
Wages Payable	Preferred Stock

Required:

Classify the above accounts as assets, liabilities, or equity, and indicate the normal balance (debit or credit) for each.

Problem 6

Journalize the following transactions for Blue Water Resorts, Inc.

1. Purchased 10,000 shares of its own stock at a price of $20 per share on May 6, 20X1.
2. Resold 4,000 shares of Treasury Stock at $30 per share.
3. Resold 4,000 shares of Treasury Stock at $15 per share.

Problem 7

Vacationland Properties declares a $.70 per share dividend on April 1, 20X1. On that date, the corporation has 15,000 shares of stock issued and 12,000 shares outstanding. The date of record is May 1, 20X1, and the ex-dividend date is April 28, 20X1. The dividend is to be paid on May 15, 20X1.

Required:

Write the necessary journal entries for April 1, April 28, May 1, and May 15.

Problem 8

1. Record the journal entries for Allied Hotels, Inc., for the following transactions:

   a. Received subscriptions for 10,000 shares of $5 par value common stock at a price of $15 per share on August 5, 20X1.

   b. Received a check for payment of 6,000 shares of stock and issued the common stock on August 28, 20X1.

2. Before the stock subscription, the company had $300,000 in common stock, $650,000 in additional paid-in capital, and $95,000 in retained earnings. Prepare a Stockholders' Equity section for August 31, 20X1.

Problem 9

The following is the balance sheet of Treadway Inns, Inc.:

Stockholders' Equity:

6% Preferred Stock, $50 par, callable at $55, 60,000 shares authorized, 30,000 shares issued	$ 1,500,000
Common Stock, $5 par value, 1,000,000 shares authorized, 500,000 shares issued	?
Additional Paid-In Capital—Common Stock	10,000,000
Retained Earnings	8,000,000

Required:

Using the information provided in the partial balance sheet, answer the following questions:

1. What is the dollar amount in the Common Stock account?
2. What is the total dollar amount of stockholders' equity?
3. What is the total amount of legal capital?
4. What is the book value per share of the common stock?
5. What is the average issuance price of the common stock?

Challenge Problems

Problem 10

The Royce Karlton Hotel Corporation had the following transactions for April 20X1:

Date   Transaction
4/01   Sold 1,000 shares of common stock, $20 par, for $25 per share.
4/05   Sold 500 shares of 8% preferred stock, $100 par, for $105 per share.

4/08   Declared a 10% common stock dividend on 10,000 common shares when the market price of the stock was $40.
4/15   Declared a dividend of $.20 per share on 10,000 shares of common stock.
4/16   Declared a dividend of $2.00 per share on 2,000 shares of preferred stock.
4/25   Paid the preferred and common stock dividends.
4/27   Distributed the common stock dividend.
4/30   Closed the April income of $200,000 into retained earnings.

Required:

Record the journal entries for the above transactions for April.

Problem 11

Brownstone Corporation issued 10,000 shares of $1 par value stock for $20/share on January 15. On April 15, Brownstone estimated its tax liability to be $35,000. On May 30, Brownstone declared a cash dividend of $10,000 that was paid on June 15.

Required:

Journalize the transactions for the Brownstone Corporation for January 15, April 15, May 30, and June 15.

Problem 12

Evergreen Resorts, Inc., has 400,000 shares of $2 par value common stock authorized and 200,000 shares issued and outstanding.

Required (all of the following are independent cases):

1.   Record the journal entries for the declaration of a 10 percent stock dividend on June 1, 20X1, and the subsequent distribution of the dividend on July 1, 20X1. The market price of the stock on June 1 is $40 and on July 1 is $50.

2.   Record the journal entries for the declaration of a 30 percent stock dividend on August 1, 20X1, and subsequent distribution of the dividend on September 1, 20X1. The market price of the stock on August 1 is $55, and on September 1 is $60.

3.   A two-for-one stock split is declared on October 1, when the stock price is $65. Record the appropriate entries for this event.

Problem 13

Compile the equity section of the Balance Sheet for the Sea-Witch Restaurant Company at 12/31/XX based on the following incomplete data:

Additional Paid-In Capital—Common Stock	$860,000
8% Preferred Stock, $100 par, callable at $110, cumulative, 10,000 shares authorized, 6,000 shares issued and outstanding	?
Treasury Stock, 10,000 shares purchased at $8 per share	?
Additional Paid-In Capital—Preferred Stock	30,000

Common Stock, no par, $5 stated value, 500,000 shares authorized,
400,000 shares issued, and 390,000 shares outstanding ?

Deficit	40,000
Common Stock Subscription Receivable	50,000
Common Stock Subscribed	50,000

Problem 14

Bushwood Hotels has 1,000 shares of $100 par 8 percent preferred stock, callable at $106, with $16,000 dividends in arrears. It has 25,000 shares of $10 par common stock outstanding. It also has additional paid-in capital of $200,000 and retained earnings of $175,000.

Required:

Calculate the book value per share for the common stock.

Problem 15

The following transactions occurred for the Carter Corporation:

May 15	Purchased 5,000 shares of its own stock at $25/share
June 30	Resold 2,000 shares of treasury stock at $35/share
July 10	Declared a dividend of $.30/share on 15,000 shares of common stock
July 30	Paid the July 10 common stock dividend
Aug. 15	Issued 5,000 shares of $2 par value common stock at $40/share
Sep. 15	Estimated income taxes to be $15,000
Sep. 30	Paid its September 15 tax liability

Required:

Journalize the above transactions for the Carter Corporation.

Chapter 15 Outline

Disadvantages and Advantages of Bond
    Financing
        Disadvantages of Bond Financing
        Advantages of Bond Financing
Classifying Bonds
Other Features of Bonds
Journal Entries for Issuance of Bonds
    Bonds Sold between Interest Payment
    Dates
Market Value versus Face Value
    Bonds Issued at a Discount
    Bonds Issued at a Premium
Year-End Adjusting Entries for Bonds
    Payable
Effective Interest Rate Method of Bond
    Amortization
Bond Sinking Fund
Convertible Bonds
Retirement of Bonds
Leases
Pensions
Mortgages Payable

Competencies

1. Describe bonds, the advantages and
   disadvantages of bond financing, and
   the types of bonds. (pp. 439–443)

2. Demonstrate and explain how to
   account for bond issues and for bond
   sales between interest payment dates.
   (pp. 443–444)

3. Demonstrate and explain how to
   account for bonds sold at a premium
   or at a discount. (pp. 444–446)

4. Demonstrate and explain how to make
   year-end adjusting entries for bonds
   payable. (pp. 446–447)

5. Describe the effective interest rate
   method of bond amortization, and
   explain how to account for bond
   sinking funds, convertible bonds, and
   the retirement of bonds. (pp. 447–449)

6. Describe leases, pensions, and
   mortgages payable, and explain how
   to account for each. (pp. 449–451)

15

Bonds, Leases, and Mortgages Payable

BONDS PAYABLE are long-term liabilities that the issuing company plans to pay off over a period greater than one year. The holders of the bonds are creditors of the corporation, not owners. In exchange for providing funds to the hospitality firm, the bondholders are paid interest on the bonds, usually semiannually. The bonds are generally sold through an **underwriting firm**.

The underwriting firm is a very important institution in U.S. financial markets. The underwriting firm, or a syndicate of several underwriting firms, will buy the entire bond issue from the corporation that is issuing the bonds. The underwriting firm will then resell the bonds to the public. These bonds can be sold at their face value, at a price above face value (at a *premium*), or at a price below face value (at a *discount*). Premiums and discounts on bonds will be discussed in detail later in this chapter.

The holders of the bonds can keep the bonds until maturity or sell them in what are called the secondary securities markets. Bonds of large corporations are readily marketable with prices quoted daily in the financial pages of the newspapers. The following Walt Disney Co. example from the *Wall Street Journal* shows a typical listing of a bond in the financial pages.

Bonds	Coupon	Cur Yld	Mat	Vol–000s	Last Price
Walt Disney Co.	6.375	5.272	3/1/12	38,432	105.668

Bonds normally have a face value of $1,000 and are quoted as a percentage of face value. This listing shows that the Walt Disney Co. bonds quoted at 105.668 are actually selling at $1,056.68 per bond. The listing also reveals that Walt Disney Co.'s 6.375 percent bonds due on 3/1/12 are yielding 5.272 percent. On this particular day, $38,432,000 worth of bonds were traded.

The company that issues bonds typically must adhere to many contractual provisions. Technically, the bond contract exists between the firm issuing the bonds and an institution called the *trustee*. The trustee in most cases is a commercial bank. For all practical purposes, however, the agreement is between the bondholders and the corporation issuing the bonds. This agreement is called the **bond indenture** and lists in detail the contractual provisions of the bond. The items listed in the indenture include the interest payment dates and the interest rate on the bond. Any specific collateral on the bonds is also listed in the bond indenture. The *maturity date* (the date the bond is to be paid off) is included in the bond indenture along with any call provisions on the bonds or any convertible provisions. All of these contractual provisions will be discussed later in the chapter.

Disadvantages and Advantages of Bond Financing

Hospitality firms issue bonds to raise large amounts of capital. A hospitality firm needing capital may choose among several alternatives, including bonds, preferred stock, or common stock financing. To decide which method of financing to use, the hospitality firm must consider the advantages and disadvantages of bond financing.

Disadvantages of Bond Financing

First, since the bond indenture includes many contractual provisions that the corporation must comply with, the corporation can find the indenture very restricting. For example, if the corporation earns no profit in a given year, it does not have to pay any dividends on preferred or common stock. However, even in loss years, the bond interest still must be paid on outstanding bonds payable.

A second disadvantage of bond financing over preferred or common stock financing involves the maturity date of the bonds. Preferred and common stock have no maturity date; that is, when these stocks are issued to the public, the public never expects to be paid off by the corporation. If a holder of preferred or common stock decides to sell the stock, he or she sells it in the secondary markets. Such a sale has very little effect on the corporation itself. Bonds, on the other hand, always have a maturity date, thus forcing the firm to plan ahead to accumulate the funds necessary to pay the bond issue off at some future date, or sell another bond issue to pay off the maturing bonds.

A third disadvantage of bond financing concerns the fact that the interest represents a fixed charge. That is, when a bond is issued, both the corporation and the bondholder know exactly the rate that must be paid on the bond until maturity. The same fixed rate is paid on the bonds in good and bad economic times, regardless of the company's profitability. If a bond is issued when the rates are high, the company has to pay those high rates or pay the bond off before its maturity date, which is called *retiring* the bond.

Advantages of Bond Financing

The fixed rates just mentioned as a disadvantage could also be considered an advantage of bond financing. If market rates of interest go up after a company has issued bonds at a low interest rate, the company continues to pay the lower contractual rate.

In addition, since bondholders are paid interest before preferred or common stockholders are paid dividends, bondholders take less risk. As a result, due to the risk/return trade-off pervasive in the financial markets, we expect bonds to yield a lower rate than preferred or common stock.

A third advantage of bond financing is that bondholders have no control over the activities of the corporation, unlike common stockholders. As long as the interest is paid on the bonds and the provisions of the indenture are complied

Exhibit 1   Tax Deductibility of Interest

	Bond Financing	Stock Financing
Earnings before Interest and Taxes	$4,000,000	$4,000,000
Interest	200,000	-0-
Earnings before Tax	3,800,000	4,000,000
Tax (30%)	1,140,000	1,200,000
Net Income after Tax	2,660,000	2,800,000
Dividends	-0-	200,000
Net Income after Tax and Dividends	$2,660,000	$2,600,000

with, bondholders have no say in the operation of the business. In contrast, common stockholders can attend a company's annual stockholders' meeting and vote on the board of directors as well as other major issues involving the corporation.

The last major advantage of bond financing is the tax advantage. Stockholders receive dividends on their investments, whereas bondholders receive interest on their investments. The corporation cannot deduct dividends, whether on preferred stock or common stock, for tax purposes. Instead, corporations must pay dividends out of after-tax earnings. However, bond interest, like all other legitimate expenses, serves to reduce the corporation's taxable income. This tax advantage of bond financing is shown in Exhibit 1.

Classifying Bonds

Bond issues can be classified according to the procedure used to pay them off. **Term bonds** are bonds that will be paid off in one lump sum at some future date. Companies must accumulate the large sum of money needed for this payoff, and usually do so through an arrangement called a *sinking fund*. (Sinking funds will be discussed later in this chapter.)

A bond issue can also be paid off through equal installments over its life. This type of bond is called a **serial bond**. The bonds that are to be paid off each year are usually determined through a random selection process. For example, if a bond issue had a 10-year life, 10 percent of the bonds would be randomly selected for retirement each year. With a serial bond, the portion of the long-term bond that comes due within one year or less should be reclassified from the Long-Term Liabilities section to the Current Liabilities section of the balance sheet.

Bonds can also be classified according to the collateral behind the bonds. Secured bonds, sometimes called **mortgage bonds**, are bonds that have some *specific* collateral behind them. For example, a company might issue a mortgage bond with the company's building pledged as specific collateral should the company default on the bond. Bonds that have no specific collateral behind them are called **debenture bonds**. It is important to note that debenture bonds, although they do not have any specific collateral pledged as security, are secured by the company's

The Bond Market Association's Internet site (www.bondmarkets.com) can help readers keep up-to-date on bond financing in hospitality and other industries. (Courtesy of The Bond Market Association)

assets in general. If a company were to go out of business, the mortgage bondholders would seize the asset pledged as specific collateral on that bond and collect those funds gained from the sale of the seized asset. Next, the debenture bondholders and other unsecured creditors would be paid off from the sale of the rest of the assets. Certain bonds are called **subordinated bonds.** Subordinated bonds are bonds whose rights to interest payments are ranked after those of other secured groups of creditors. Only after all of the secured and unsecured creditors were paid would the stockholders receive some type of liquidating dividend.

Bonds may be classified according to the procedure used to pay interest on them. In the case of **registered bonds**, the bondholders' names are recorded with the corporation or its transfer agent. The transfer agent is usually a bank chosen by the corporation to facilitate the actual payment of the interest for the corporation. When interest payment dates arrive, interest checks are mailed to the registered bondholders.

Coupon bonds, sometimes called *bearer bonds,* are not registered with the corporation that issued them or with its trustee. When an interest payment date for a coupon bond arrives, the bondholder merely detaches a coupon from the bond and presents it at a bank for payment. The bank then forwards the coupon to the corporation's bank for reimbursement for the interest. Most bonds today are registered bonds rather than coupon bonds. Currently, all municipal bonds must be registered bonds; they cannot be coupon bonds.

Other Features of Bonds

Sometimes bond issues are convertible. Convertible bonds can be exchanged at the will of the holder for shares of the corporation's common stock. (Convertible bonds and the entries involving them will be discussed later in this chapter.)

Some bonds also have a call feature. **Callable bonds** can be paid off before maturity at the company's option. Companies issuing callable bonds usually provide some call protection to the bondholders. Call protection ensures that the company issuing the bonds contractually agrees not to call the bonds until a certain number of years have passed after the issuance date. When the bonds are called, the bondholder typically receives a premium on the call date. The premium is a dollar amount above the face value of the bond; it compensates the bondholders for having to reinvest their funds.

Journal Entries for Issuance of Bonds

We will begin our discussion of the issuance of bonds with a very simple example of bonds issued at their face value. Assume that on January 2, 200X, the Alpine Hotel issued $500,000 worth of 8 percent, 10-year bonds, with interest payable on July 2 and January 2. The entry to record this sale follows:

Cash	$500,000	
Bonds Payable		$500,000

The next relevant date involving these bonds would be the first semiannual interest date, July 2. At that time, the company would pay one-half of the annual interest on the bonds and make the following journal entry:

Interest Expense	$20,000	
Cash		$20,000

The interest is calculated using the formula Interest = Principal × Rate × Time. In this example, the formula results in interest of $20,000:

$$\begin{aligned} \text{Interest} &= \text{Principal} \times \text{Rate} \times \text{Time} \\ &= \$500,000 \times .08 \times \tfrac{1}{2} \\ &= \$20,000 \end{aligned}$$

This same entry would be made every six months over the life of the bond. Following the bond over the rest of its life, the last entry would be for the retirement of the bonds at maturity. This entry, which would be written on January 2, 201X, follows:

Bonds Payable	$500,000	
Cash		$500,000

Bonds Sold between Interest Payment Dates

The entry for the issuance of bonds is complicated when the bond issue is sold between interest payment dates. Issuers of bonds traditionally pay the full amount of interest on each semiannual payment date regardless of how long the bond is held. For example, if the bond in the previous example were dated January 2 and not sold until April 1, the company would still pay the full six months' interest on the first payment date. The firm would, however, require the purchaser of the bond on April 1 to pay the first three months' interest—that is, the interest from January 2 to April 1—in addition to the face value of the bond.

Again, assume that the Alpine Hotel issued $500,000 worth of 8 percent, ten-year bonds. Based on this information and the fact that the bonds were sold on April 1, the journal entry on April 1 for the sale of the bonds would be as follows:

Cash	$510,000	
Bond Interest Payable		$ 10,000
Bonds Payable		500,000

The liability Bond Interest Payable credited in this entry would be listed in the Current Liabilities section of the balance sheet.

The next relevant date for this bond issue would be the first semiannual interest payment date, July 2. On this date, the following entry would be made:

Bond Interest Expense	$10,000	
Bond Interest Payable	10,000	
Cash		$20,000

This entry eliminates the liability of $10,000 that was set up on the date the bonds were sold and records the interest expense of $10,000 for the period of April, May, and June.

Market Value versus Face Value

Until this point in the chapter, we have assumed that bonds have sold at their face value, but in reality, this is not usually the case. Bonds usually sell at a price above or below their face value, resulting in an associated premium or discount. When a firm decides to sell a bond issue in the financial markets, the firm must make a decision regarding the rate investors expect to earn on the bond, based on current and future interest rates. Remember, no matter what the $1,000, 8 percent bond sells for, the holder will receive $80 per year (8% of $1,000) in interest. If potential investors think that the 8 percent coupon rate (sometimes called the *stated rate* or *contract rate*) is too low, the price of the bond will fall in order to raise the market rate of interest on the bond, resulting in the sale of the bond at a discount from face value. On the other hand, if investors believe the 8 percent bond is a good buy, they will bid its market price up, resulting in the sale of the bond at a premium over stated value. As you can see, bond prices and bond yields are inversely related.

The higher the market price of a bond, the lower the yield, and the lower the market price of a bond, the higher the yield.

Bonds Issued at a Discount

Assume that the bond issue in the previous example sold for $450,000 on January 2 instead of the face value of $500,000. The journal entry to record the sale of this bond follows:

Cash	$450,000	
Discount on Bonds Payable	50,000	
Bonds Payable		$500,000

Bonds Payable is always credited for the face value of the bond issue regardless of the selling price. The Discount on Bonds Payable account is a contra-liability account that carries a debit balance and is offset against Bonds Payable on the balance sheet, as shown here:

Bonds Payable	$500,000	
Less: Discount on Bonds Payable	50,000	$450,000

Although the bond was sold for $450,000, the bondholders expect to receive not $450,000 but rather the face value of $500,000 on the maturity date ten years later. The difference between the selling price and the face value represents additional interest expense to the firm. Rather than calling the $50,000 difference additional interest in the year the bond matures, the matching principle dictates that the $50,000 difference be spread over the life of the bond.

In the case of this discounted bond, on July 2, the first semiannual interest payment date, the following two entries would be made:

Bond Interest Expense	$20,000	
Cash		$20,000

Bond Interest Expense	$2,500	
Discount on Bonds Payable		$2,500

The $2,500 amortization of the discount is $\frac{1}{20}$ of the total of $50,000, determined as follows:

$$\$50,000 \div 20 \text{ six-month periods over bond's life} = \$2,500$$

The first entry records the cash interest paid; the second entry records the semiannual amortization of the discount. Traditionally, these two entries are combined into one entry:

Bond Interest Expense	$22,500	
Cash		$20,000
Discount on Bonds Payable		2,500

Bonds Issued at a Premium

Assume that the bonds issued by the Alpine Hotel were sold at a price of $540,000 rather than the face value of $500,000 on January 2. In this case, the journal entry to record the sale of the bonds would be as follows:

Cash	$540,000	
Bonds Payable		$500,000
Premium on Bonds Payable		40,000

The Premium on Bonds Payable account will carry a credit balance and will be added to the amount of the Bonds Payable account on the balance sheet:

Bonds Payable	$500,000	
Premium on Bonds Payable	40,000	$540,000

Since this bond sold at a premium, the bondholders are paying $540,000 for the bond and at maturity will receive only the face value of $500,000. In this case, the difference of $40,000 should be considered a reduction of interest. Again, rather than being recorded as an offset against revenue in one year, the premium should be amortized over the life of the bond. On July 2, the first interest payment date, the following two entries should be made:

Bond Interest Expense	$20,000	
Cash		$20,000

Premium on Bonds Payable	$2,000	
Bond Interest Expense		$2,000

These two entries could be combined into a compound entry:

Bond Interest Expense	$18,000	
Premium on Bonds Payable	2,000	
Cash		$20,000

Year-End Adjusting Entries for Bonds Payable

Now we will examine the adjusting entry necessary at year-end that results from having a bond issue outstanding. Assume, once again, the same facts concerning the bond selling at a discount. Also assume that the firm's fiscal year ends on September 30. The adjusting entry at September 30 in the first year the bond was issued would be as follows:

Bond Interest Expense	$11,250	
Interest Payable		$10,000
Discount on Bonds Payable		1,250

The $1,250 amortization of the bond discount represents three months' interest (July, August, and September), calculated as follows:

$$\text{\$50,000 total discount to be amortized (over the 120 months of the bond's life)} \times \frac{3}{120} = \$1,250$$

This compound entry combines the following two entries:

Bond Interest Expense	$10,000	
Bond Interest Payable		$10,000

Bond Interest Expense	$1,250	
Discount on Bonds Payable		$1,250

In the case of the preceding bond that sold at a premium, the journal entry at year-end (on September 30) would be a little different. The year-end adjusting entry would be:

Bond Interest Expense	$9,000	
Premium on Bonds Payable	1,000	
Bond Interest Payable		$10,000

This compound entry combines the following two entries:

Bond Interest Expense	$10,000	
Bond Interest Payable		$10,000

Premium on Bonds Payable	$1,000	
Bond Interest Expense		$1,000

Effective Interest Rate Method of Bond Amortization

Until this point, we have amortized the premium or discount on the bond issue by using the straight-line method of amortization. The straight-line method can create confusion among investors, since the annual percentage return would appear to vary over the life of the bond. Recall that bonds pay a fixed return, yet the carrying value is obviously changing over its life, increasing when a bond sells at a discount and decreasing when a bond sells at a premium. Bondholders who expect to receive a fixed return when buying a bond can sometimes be confused by this changing annual effective interest rate.

To avoid this theoretical shortcoming of the straight-line method of amortization, another method can be used instead. It is called the *effective interest rate method.* It is more complicated and will not be discussed in detail. We will state, however, that the effective interest rate method results in the amortization of the discount or premium in a manner that makes the annual yield on the bond the same rate every year over its life.

Bond Sinking Fund

If a bond issue is to be paid off in a lump sum, companies issuing those bonds will usually make annual cash payments into a **bond sinking fund** in order to accumulate the amount due at maturity. Any income from a bond sinking fund is recorded as Other Revenue on the income statement. The fund of cash that is accumulating to pay off the bond is included under the Long-Term Investments category on the balance sheet.

Convertible Bonds

Corporations may issue bonds that can be converted into the company's common stock. Since many investors consider **convertible bonds** more attractive than non-convertible bonds, the issuing corporation can usually sell them at lower rates. While convertible bonds are outstanding, they are like regular bonds in that the holders are paid semiannual interest at a fixed rate. However, the bonds may be converted into the company's common stock when the common stock reaches a certain dollar price. The number of shares the bonds are convertible into is determined through use of the **conversion ratio**.

For example, a $1,000 bond may be converted into 20 shares of the company's common stock when the common stock reaches a price of $50 per share. The $50 stock price in this example is referred to as the **conversion parity price** of the bond. The convertible bond is good for the company due to the lower interest rate, but it is also good for the bondholder. The convertible bondholder has the best of both worlds in enjoying the security of a fixed investment and also the upside potential of the company's common stock. The upside potential results from the fact that since the bond is convertible into stock in a fixed ratio, as the stock goes up in price, the bond also increases in value. For example, if the company's stock goes from $50 to $70 per share, the bond, being convertible into 20 shares of stock, should sell for $1,400 (20 shares × $70/share).

Assume that the Merriway Hotel Corporation has an $800,000 convertible bond issue outstanding. Assume also that the conversion ratio is 20 shares per $1,000 bond, and that the conversion parity price of the common stock is $50 per share for the $5 par value stock. The journal entry to record the entire conversion of this bond issue into common stock would be as follows:

Convertible Bonds Payable	$800,000	
Common Stock		$ 80,000
Additional Paid-In Capital		720,000

The $800,000 debited to Convertible Bonds Payable represents 800 $1,000 bonds. 800 × 20 shares = 16,000 shares; 16,000 shares × $5 par value = $80,000 credited to the Common Stock account. Additional Paid-In Capital is credited for the difference between $800,000 and $80,000.

Retirement of Bonds

A corporation with a bond issue outstanding may decide to **retire** it (that is, pay it off before maturity). This is usually accomplished by purchasing the bonds in the open market. The retirement of the bond issue may result in a gain or loss to the corporation depending on the price paid for the bonds. The gain or loss on retirement is the difference between the purchase price of the bond at its current market value and the carrying value of the bond on the retirement date. In most cases, the gain or loss on the bond would be reported as an ordinary item on the income statement.

Assume that the Deli-Delite Corporation retired a $1,000,000 bond issue with an unamortized discount of $40,000 by purchasing it for $990 per bond. The journal entry to record the retirement would be:

Bonds Payable	$1,000,000	
Loss on Retirement of Bonds	30,000	
Discount on Bonds Payable		$ 40,000
Cash		990,000

The credit to Cash is for the amount paid for the bond. The credit to Discount on Bonds Payable is the amount of the unamortized discount at the retirement date. The debit to Bonds Payable is for the face value of the bonds. The Loss on Retirement of Bonds is determined by computing the difference between the carrying value of the bond and the purchase price of the bond. The loss of $30,000 would be determined by subtracting the book value of the bond issue of $960,000 ($1,000,000 less the unamortized discount of $40,000) from the $990,000 purchase price of the bond issue.

Leases

The topic of leases is presented in this chapter because certain leases result in long-term liabilities. The two basic types of leases are operating leases and capital leases.

You are probably familiar with operating leases, since leases covering the rental of a telephone, an apartment, or a dorm room are operating leases. Under an **operating lease**, the **lessor** (owner) allows the **lessee** to use the asset in exchange for a fixed periodic rental payment; there is no intent on the lessor's part to sell the asset to the lessee. The journal entry for this type of lease is very simple, as this illustration for the rental payment of $1,000 indicates:

Rental Expense	$1,000	
Cash		$1,000

Operating leases are sometimes referred to as *off balance sheet financing*, since the company leasing the asset (the lessee) has all of the uses of the asset yet does not have to put the liability of future payments on its books.

The **capital lease** results in a closer relationship between the lessor and the lessee. The Financial Accounting Standards Board (FASB) has set four criteria for determining whether a lease is a capital lease. If any—not all—of these criteria are met, the lease must be treated as a capital lease:

1. The lease provides for the transferability of ownership to the lessee at some point during the life of the lease.

2. There is a bargain purchase option in the lease. This means that the purchase price at the end of the lease period is substantially less than the leased property's expected market value at the date the option is to be exercised. The bargain price is generally considered substantially less than the market value only if the difference, for all practical purposes, ensures that the bargain purchase option will be exercised.

3. The life of the lease is greater than 75 percent of the economic life of the asset. The term *economic life* refers to the useful life of the leased property.

4. The present value of the minimum lease payments equals 90 percent or more of the property's market value.

If a lease were determined to be a capital lease, such as when equipment worth $50,000 was leased, the following journal entry would be made:

Leased Equipment	$50,000	
Obligations under Capital Lease		$50,000

In this case, Leased Equipment would appear as a long-term asset under Property and Equipment on the balance sheet, and Lease Liability would appear under Long-Term Liabilities on the balance sheet.

Pensions

Accounting for pensions can be very complex, usually requiring the services of an **actuary**. Pensions are typically covered in great detail in intermediate accounting texts. Only a limited discussion of pensions will be presented in this chapter since pensions result in large long-term liabilities for corporations. There are basically two types of pensions: defined contribution pensions and defined benefit pensions.

In the case of **defined contribution pensions**, employers or employees contribute fixed amounts per year into the pension fund. The benefits that individuals receive from the pension are based on the pension's accumulated amount at some future date. The entry to record payment into a pension involves a debit to Pension Fund and a credit to Cash.

The **defined benefit pension** is more complex. In this case, the amount of the benefit is based on some future amount. For example, this future amount may be

75 percent of the average of an employee's salary during the last three years of employment. In this type of pension, an evaluation must be made each year of the accumulated benefits versus the accumulated obligations. This analysis results every year in either a long-term asset or a long-term liability on the corporation's books.

Mortgages Payable

A *mortgage* is another long-term liability. Home mortgages are similar to mortgages on commercial buildings. A fixed monthly payment is made, part of which is interest on the outstanding balance of the mortgage. The rest of the payment reduces the principal on the mortgage.

Let's assume that a building was purchased for $100,000 with a 30-year, 9 percent mortgage, and that the company buying the building agrees to make a monthly payment of $900. The principal, the interest, and the ending balance on the mortgage for the first two months are shown in the following table:

Month	Beginning Balance	Total Payment	Interest	Principal	Ending Balance
1st	$100,000	$900	$750	$150	$99,850
2nd	99,850	900	749	151	99,699

The $750 interest for the first month is determined by multiplying $100,000 by 9 percent and dividing by 12 months. The $900 total payment less the $750 interest equals the principal amount of $150, which reduces the mortgage to $99,850. The journal entry to record the first payment on this mortgage is:

Mortgage Payable	$150	
Interest Expense	750	
Cash		$900

This example involves a fixed monthly payment with increasing amounts applied to the principal over the life of the mortgage. There are instances in which a fixed amount of principal is applied to a mortgage every month, thus varying the payment. This, however, is less common. Mortgage interest is included on the income statement and is closed to the Income Summary account at the end of the fiscal period. The **Mortgage Payable** liability is listed in the Long-Term Liabilities section of the balance sheet except for the portion due within a year. That portion is listed as a current liability.

Summary

Bonds payable represent a long-term liability for a hospitality firm. Bondholders are creditors of the firm, not owners. The following are some disadvantages of issuing bonds to raise capital:

- The bond's contractual provisions can be very restrictive to the corporation.

- Bonds eventually mature and must be paid off, whereas stock does not.

- Interest rates on bonds are fixed and must be paid until the bond issue is retired, even if interest rates in the broader market fall.

Some advantages of issuing bonds follow:

- Those same fixed interest rates may be a good deal for the firm in times of increasing interest rates.

- Since bonds usually represent a lesser degree of risk to the bondholder than common stock, bonds can offer a lower rate of return to the investor and hence a lower cost to the firm.

- Bond interest is paid out of pretax earnings and therefore is not taxed.

Bond issues can be classified according to the procedure used to pay them off. They can be term bonds, which require the firm to establish a bond sinking fund to enable it to pay off the bond issue on the designated date, or serial bonds, which are paid off in installments. Bonds can also be classified by the type of collateral behind them. Secured bonds have specific assets pledged as collateral. Debenture bonds have no specific collateral pledged, but rather have the general assets of the firm pledged as collateral. Bonds can also be classified as registered bonds, coupon bonds, convertible bonds, or callable bonds.

This chapter also discusses the accounting procedures required for the issuance of bonds, the sale of bonds between interest payment dates, determining the market value and the face value of bonds, the issuance of bonds at a discount and at a premium, year-end adjusting entries for bonds payable, the effective interest rate method of bond amortization, and, finally, the retirement of bonds.

Also discussed are operating leases, capital leases, pensions, and mortgages.

🔑 Key Terms ───────────────────────────────

actuary—Someone who calculates insurance and annuity premiums, reserves, and dividends.

bond indenture—Written agreement that details the contractual provisions of a bond.

bond sinking fund—A fund established by a company in which it will accumulate annual cash payments toward the amount it must pay in a lump sum at the maturity of a bond issue. Any income from a bond sinking fund is recorded as Other Revenue on the income statement. The fund is included under the Long-Term Investments category on the balance sheet.

callable bond—A bond that, at the company's option, can be paid off before maturity. Companies issuing callable bonds will usually provide some call protection to the bondholders. This means that the company contractually agrees not to call the bonds until a certain number of years have passed after the issuance date and agrees to pay the bondholder a premium on the call date.

capital lease—A classification of lease agreements that are of relatively long duration and are generally noncancelable and in which the lessee assumes responsibility for executory costs. For accounting purposes, capital leases are capitalized in a way similar to that for the purchase of a fixed asset (i.e., recorded as an asset with recognition of a liability).

conversion parity price—The per-share common stock price at which a convertible bond can be converted into shares of the company's common stock; calculated by dividing the value of one bond by the number of shares into which the bond may be converted. A $1,000 bond that could be converted into 20 shares of the company's common stock would have a conversion parity price of $50.

conversion ratio—A ratio that determines the number of shares of common stock into which a convertible bond can be converted. For example, a $1,000 bond may be converted into 20 shares of common stock when the common stock reaches a price of $50 per share.

convertible bond—A bond that can be exchanged at the option of the holder for shares of the corporation's common stock once the common stock reaches a certain price.

coupon bond—A bond with a coupon attached that the holder detaches and presents for payment when the interest payment date arrives. Also called a *bearer bond*.

debenture bond—A bond backed by the general credit of the issuer rather than a specific lien on particular assets.

defined benefit pension—A pension plan wherein the amount of the benefit is based on some future amount. For example, the amount could be 75 percent of the average of an employee's salary during the last three years of employment.

defined contribution pension—A pension plan wherein the employers or employees contribute fixed amounts per year to the pension fund. The benefits that individuals receive from the pension are based on the accumulated amount of the pension at some future date.

lessee—The person or company that makes periodic cash payments called *rent* to a lessor in exchange for the right to use the property.

lessor—The person or company that leases property or equipment to the lessee in exchange for a fixed periodic rental payment.

mortgage bonds—Secured bonds that have some specific collateral behind them.

mortgage payable—A liability listed in the Long-Term Liabilities section of the balance sheet except for the portion due within a year, which is listed as a current liability.

operating lease—A lease similar to a rental agreement without any appearance of present or future ownership of the leased property by the lessee.

registered bond—A bond for which the bondholders' names are recorded with the corporation or its transfer agent.

retire—To retire a bond is to pay it off before its maturity date.

serial bond—A bond issue paid off through equal installments over its life.

subordinated bond—A bond whose rights to interest payments are ranked after those of other creditors.

term bond—A bond that is to be paid off in one lump sum at some future date.

underwriting firm—A firm, or a syndicate of several firms, that buys an entire bond issue from the corporation issuing the bonds; the underwriting firm buys these for resale to the public.

Review Questions

1. What are the major advantages and disadvantages of bond financing?
2. What is the difference between a registered bond and a coupon bond? How does a term bond differ from a serial bond?
3. How does a debenture bond differ from a mortgage bond? What is a *bond indenture?* What is the role of the underwriter in bond financing?
4. What is the difference between the stated rate on a bond and the effective rate?
5. If a bond sells at a discount, is the stated rate greater than or less than the effective rate?
6. What is the nature of a bond sinking fund? Where is it listed on the balance sheet?
7. What is the *conversion ratio* of a bond? What is the *conversion parity price?*
8. How is the gain or loss on the retirement of a bond calculated?
9. How does a capital lease differ from an operating lease? What are the four FASB criteria for a capital lease?
10. What is the difference between a defined benefit pension plan and a defined contribution plan?

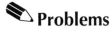 Problems

Problem 1

Record the following journal entries involving the bond transactions for Timber Ridge Hotels:

1. On July 1, 2001, sold $800,000, 8 percent, bonds dated June 1, 2001, at face value.
2. Paid semiannual interest on November 30, 2001.
3. Paid off bond issue on May 31, 2011.

Problem 2

Slide Inns owes $187,000 on a 10 percent long-term mortgage dated April 1, 20X1, which requires a total monthly payment of $1,800.

Required:

Journalize the entry necessary for the May 1, 20X1, monthly payment.

Problem 3

Provide an explanation for all of the numbers below in the Boyd Gaming Company bond listing:

Bonds	Coupon	Cur Yld	Mat	Vol–000s	Last Price
BYD	4.700	5.591	8/1/13	60,340	94.602

Problem 4

Harbor View Resorts retired a $2,000,000 bond issue with an unamortized discount of $70,000 by purchasing it for $980 per bond.

Required:

1. Journalize the entry for the retirement of the bond.
2. Indicate whether the gain or loss on the bond should be listed as an "ordinary" or "extraordinary" item on the income statement.

Problem 5

Heaven's Inn Corp. issued $500,000 of 5 percent bonds at $480,000 on March 1, 20X6. The semiannual interest payment dates are March 1 and September 1. The bonds have a ten-year life.

Required:

Journalize the necessary entries for March 1, 20X6, and September 1, 20X6.

Problem 6

Empire Corporation issued $1,000,000 of 6 percent ten–year bonds on May 1, 20X5 for $1,080,000.

Required:

Calculate the carrying value of the bonds on May 1, 20X9.

Problem 7

On April 1, 20X1, American Clubs, Inc., sold a 12 percent bond issue of $700,000 dated March 1, 20X1, at face value.

Required:

1. Journalize the entry necessary on the date of the sale.
2. Record the entry for the payment of semiannual interest on September 1, 20X1.

Problem 8

Hightower Hotels is retiring a bond issue that has a face value of $1 million and a carrying value of $1,050,000. The bonds will be retired at a price of $1,060 per bond.

Required:

Journalize the entry necessary for the retirement of the bond.

Problem 9

North Peaks, Inc., is entering into a lease on June 15, 20X1, for snow-making machines that have a market value of $150,000. The lease payment will be $2,000 per month with the first payment due on July 15, 20X1.

Required:

1. Record the journal entry necessary on June 15, 20X1, if the lease contains a bargain purchase option.
2. Record the journal entry necessary on July 15, 20X1, if the lease is an operating lease.

Problem 10

Fairview Hotels mortgaged a building on June 1, 20X6, for $250,000 with interest at 6 percent. It is expected to make monthly payments of $1,800.

Required:

Create a table showing the principal, interest, and ending balance on the mortgage for the first four months.

Problem 11

Carolina Hotels sold a 6 percent $10,000,000 bond on October 1, 20X6. The bond was dated August 1, 20X6. The bond issue sold for $10,060,000, has semiannual interest payment dates of August 1 and February 1, and has a ten–year life.

Required:

Journalize the necessary entries for August 1, 20X6, and October 1, 20X7.

Challenge Problems

Problem 12

Resort Hotels, Inc., is starting operations by raising $30 million. Earnings before Interest and Taxes are expected to be $20 million this year. The company has a 30 percent tax rate.

Required:

Calculate Earnings after Tax and Dividends under each of the following two financing options:

1. Bond financing: $20 million at 7 percent interest
2. Stock financing: $20 million with 8 percent annual dividend

Problem 13

On October 1, 20X1, Mayfair Hotels, Inc., issued ten-year, 10 percent debenture bonds with $50 million in total face value and with interest payable on April 1 and October 1. The company's year-end is December 31.

Required:

1. Construct the necessary entries for December 31, 20X1, and the journal entry to record payment of bond interest on April 1, 20X2, under each of the following assumptions:

    a. The bonds were issued at 97.
    b. The bonds were issued at 103.

2. What is the carrying value of the bonds at December 31, 20X1, under each of the previous two assumptions?

Problem 14

Apex Resorts Corporation has $500,000 of 9.5 percent convertible bonds outstanding that are convertible into 40 shares of the company's common stock. The bonds currently have an unamortized discount of $20,000. The par value of the company's stock is $10 per share.

Required:

Record the entry necessary for the conversion of half of the bond issue.

Problem 15

Garden Restaurant Corporation issued $12 million of 7 percent, 10-year bonds on April 1, 20X8. The bonds were dated March 1, 20X8, and were sold for $960 apiece. The semiannual interest payment dates are March 1 and September 1.

Required:

1. Journalize the following entries:

    a. Sale of bonds on April 1, 20X8.
    b. Payment of interest and amortization of discount on September 1, 20X8.
    c. Accrual of interest and amortization of discount on December 31, 20X8.
    d. Payment of interest and amortization of discount on March 1, 20X9.

2. Show how the bond would appear on the balance sheet on December 31, 20X8.

Chapter 16 Outline

Accounting for Investments
    Investments in Debt Securities
    Short-Term Equity Investments
    Long-Term Equity Investments
Valuation of Investments
    Held-to-Maturity Securities
    Trading Securities
    Available-for-Sale Securities

Competencies

1. Explain and demonstrate how to account for investments in debt securities (bonds). (p. 460)

2. Explain and demonstrate how to account for investments in equity securities (stocks). (pp. 460–461)

3. Explain and demonstrate the cost, equity, and consolidated statement methods of accounting for investments. (pp. 461–465)

4. Explain and demonstrate the approach to valuation of investments that is recommended by Financial Accounting Standards Board Statement 115. (pp. 465–468)

16

Investments in Corporate Securities

ACCORDING TO the *Uniform System of Accounts for the Lodging Industry (USALI)*, Tenth Revised Edition, there are two types of investments in securities: short-term and long-term. Short-term investments are readily marketable and are intended to be converted into cash within a year. Long-term investments in corporate securities are those held for more than one year and are included in the Investments category on the balance sheet. The Investments category includes three types of investments:

1. Cash advances to affiliated companies

2. Investments in property or equipment that is not currently used in the business or land held for speculation

3. Equity and debt investments (stocks and bonds) purchased by the company that are not short-term in nature

Accounting for the first two items is simple. The assets are recorded at cost and taken off the books or reclassified when necessary. Accounting for the third item—equity and debt securities—is complex. This chapter discusses equity and debt investments.

Accounting for Investments

Hospitality firms invest in the securities of other companies for one of two reasons:

1. To earn a good return on excess cash held for the short term

2. To exercise influence or control

If the securities are purchased for the short term to obtain a favorable return on excess cash, they are *not* listed under Investments. Instead, a current asset account, Short-Term Investments, is debited for the purchase price. The investments must be immediately convertible at the market price of the securities to be included in the Short-Term Investments account. The method of accounting used for the current asset Short-Term Investments depends on whether a debt or equity security is involved.

Investments in Debt Securities

The accounting for short-term and long-term debt securities is basically the same. When a hospitality firm invests in bonds, it expects to receive interest semiannually on its investment. To understand the investment in **marketable debt securities**, assume that Balboa Hotels purchased bonds on August 1, 20X4, for 97 percent of par. The bonds have a total face value of $100,000 and pay installments of the annual 9 percent interest on May 1 and November 1. Balboa Hotels pays a brokerage commission of $500, plus accrued interest, at the time of purchase. Based on this information, the journal entry on August 1, 20X4, would be:

Debt Investments	$97,500	
Bond Interest Receivable	2,250	
Cash		$99,750

The $97,500 debit to Debt Investments is the cost of the bonds plus the commission. The $2,250 debit to Bond Interest Receivable represents the interest accrued on the bonds from May 1 to August 1 ($100,000 $\times$ 9% $\times$ $\frac{3}{12}$).

The next relevant entry would be on November 1, 20X4, to record the receipt of six months' worth of interest:

Cash	$4,500	
Bond Interest Receivable		$2,250
Bond Interest Income		2,250

Although the company receives a check for a full six months' worth of interest, recall that it paid for three months' interest in advance on August 1. At the end of the calendar year, another entry would be made to accrue the interest on the bonds. The entry on December 31, 20X4, would be as follows:

Bond Interest Receivable	$1,500	
Bond Interest Income		$1,500

Short-Term Equity Investments

Accounting for **short-term equity investments** (stocks) is simpler than accounting for short-term debt investments (bonds). Recall that investments in stocks yield dividends rather than interest. Dividends are typically paid quarterly. Companies that have investments in the stocks of other companies do not accrue the dividends. Instead, dividend income is recorded when received. The following is the entry for the receipt of $3,000 worth of dividends:

Cash	$3,000	
Dividend Income		$3,000

Realized Gains or Losses from the Sale of Short-Term Equity Investments.
When these securities are sold, the cost of the securities should be written off the
books and the gain or loss on the sale recognized. The gain or loss should be closed
into the Income Summary account at the end of the fiscal period. Assume that
Greatway Hotels sold its holdings in other companies' stocks that had cost $99,000
for $97,000, less a $500 commission. Thus, Greatway received $96,500 from the sale.
The journal entry would be recorded as follows:

Cash	$96,500	
Loss on Sale of Short-Term Investments	2,500	
Short-Term Investments		$99,000

The $2,500 loss is the difference between the net selling price of $96,500 and the
cost of $99,000.

Long-Term Equity Investments

The following section focuses on accounting for long-term equity investments.
The cost method, the equity method, and the consolidated statement method are
discussed.

When the investment in the stock of another company is less than 20 percent
of the investee's stock, the **cost method** is used to account for the investment.
Under the cost method, long-term investments are put on the books at cost, gains
or losses are recognized as of the sale date, and income is recorded when received.

Sometimes the purchaser (the **investor**) purchases such a large percentage of
stock that it can have significant influence or even control over the **investee**. When
significant influence or control exists, the methods used to account for these investments include the equity method and the consolidated statement method. The percentage of ownership determines which of the methods is used. If the company
owns 20 to 50 percent of the investee, the equity method is used. However, if the
investor owns more than 50 percent of the investee, the consolidated statement
approach is used.

The Equity Method. Under the **equity method of accounting for investments,**
the investor records the original investment at cost, then adjusts the value of the
investment over time. The investor increases the value of the investment as the
investee generates income and decreases the value of the investment if the investee loses money. When the investee pays the investor dividends, the value of the
investment decreases, and the investor records the decrease as dividends. For
example, assume that Harris buys 25 percent, or $50,000 worth, of Tweed stock on
November 1, 20X4. On December 31, Tweed reports income of $20,000, and
on January 6 pays a dividend of $10,000. The entries under the equity method are
as follows:

Nov. 1	Investment in Tweed	$50,000	
	Cash		$50,000

Dec. 31	Investment in Tweed	$5,000	
	Income from Investment		$5,000

Jan. 6	Cash	$2,500	
	Investment in Tweed		$2,500

Based on these entries, the value of the investment in Tweed on January 6 would be $52,500, as shown:

Original Investment	$50,000
Plus: Share of Investee's Income	+ 5,000
Less: Dividends Paid	− 2,500
Equals: Investment in Tweed	$52,500

Notice that under the equity method, when the dividends are paid to the investor, the value of the investment drops to reflect the fact that part of the investment has been converted into cash. The income from the investee is reported on the investor's income statement.

The Consolidated Statement Method. If one company owns more than 50 percent of a second company, the first company is said to control the second; the purchaser is called the **parent company** and the purchased company is called the **subsidiary company**. When this occurs, **consolidated financial statements** *normally* are prepared for the one entity. The word *normally* is emphasized because the Financial Accounting Standards Board has stated that when two dissimilar companies, such as a bank and a hotel, are in a parent-subsidiary relationship, it would not be useful to combine the statements.

Although the parent and the subsidiary keep separate books during the year, at year-end they report as one consolidated entity. When the parent and the subsidiary combine items for the consolidated balance sheet, they cannot simply add all items for the companies together. If they were to do so, some items, such as a parent's loan of money to its subsidiary, would be counted twice. Therefore, when a parent and subsidiary prepare consolidated financial statements, they must also prepare some intercompany **eliminating entries**. Consolidated financial statements can be very complex for some companies. (A detailed discussion of complex consolidated financial statements is presented in more advanced accounting texts.)

This chapter will discuss three simple examples:

1. The purchase of 100 percent of a subsidiary at book value

2. The purchase of 100 percent of a subsidiary at a price above book value

3. The purchase of less than 100 percent of a subsidiary at book value

Purchase of 100 percent of a subsidiary at book value. A worksheet for a consolidated balance sheet of a parent company, Parentis Hotel, and its subsidiary, Subside Motel, is shown in Exhibit 1. Notice the two eliminating entries marked (a) and (b) on the worksheet. First, the parent company's Notes Receivable and the

Exhibit 1   Worksheet for Consolidated Balance Sheet

Parentis Hotel and Subside Motel
Worksheet for Consolidated Balance Sheet
January 1, 20X4

	Parentis	Subside	Eliminating Entries Debit	Eliminating Entries Credit	Consolidated Balance Sheet
Cash	$ 10,000	$ 55,000			$ 65,000
Accounts Receivable	20,000	15,000			35,000
Notes Receivable	25,000	—		(a) $ 25,000	—
Inventory	50,000	40,000			90,000
Investment in Subsidiary	140,000	—		(b) 140,000	—
Property & Equipment	105,000	80,000			185,000
Totals	$350,000	$190,000			$375,000
Accounts Payable	$ 40,000	$ 25,000			$ 65,000
Notes Payable	—	25,000	(a) $ 25,000		—
Common Stock	245,000	100,000	(b) 100,000		245,000
Retained Earnings	65,000	40,000	(b) 40,000		65,000
Totals	$350,000	$190,000	$165,000	$165,000	$375,000

subsidiary company's Notes Payable are both eliminated with eliminating entry (a). The $25,000 in this case involves the parent's loan to the subsidiary. This transfer of dollars within the consolidated entity is merely that: a transfer of money within the entity itself. In a sense, the company owes the money to itself; consequently, to avoid double counting, both affected accounts are eliminated.

Eliminating entry (b) involves the Investment in Subsidiary account on the parent's books, which is eliminated against the subsidiary's equity. The Investment in Subsidiary account of $140,000 on the parent's books represents the subsidiary's entire equity. Since the subsidiary's equity or its net assets are represented by the asset account Investment in Subsidiary on the parent's books, double counting would occur if eliminating entries were not made. Note that these eliminating entries are made only on the worksheet and not on each individual company's books—a very important point. The last column of the consolidated worksheet (labeled "Consolidated Balance Sheet") shows the items used to compile the entity's formal consolidated balance sheet.

Purchase of 100 percent of a subsidiary at a price above book value. A parent company could buy a subsidiary for above or below book value. (The discussion of a purchase for an amount below book value is deferred to advanced accounting courses.) A purchase above book value is more likely than a purchase below book value. There are two reasons for this; the first reason involves undervaluation of assets. Because of the cost principle, the subsidiary's assets could have been put on the books at cost and, despite appreciation over the years, would remain on the books at cost. The second reason involves future excess earning power. If the parent

Exhibit 2   Worksheet for Consolidated Balance Sheet with Goodwill

Parentis Hotel and Subside Motel
Worksheet for Consolidated Balance Sheet

	Parentis	Subside	Eliminating Entries Debit	Eliminating Entries Credit	Consolidated Balance Sheet
Cash	$ 10,000	$ 55,000			$ 65,000
Accounts Receivable	20,000	15,000			35,000
Notes Receivable	25,000	—		(a) $ 25,000	—
Inventory	50,000	40,000			90,000
Investment in Subsidiary	165,000	—		(b) 165,000	—
Property & Equipment	105,000	80,000			185,000
Goodwill	-0-		(b) $ 25,000		25,000
Totals	$375,000	$190,000			$400,000
Accounts Payable	$ 40,000	$ 25,000			$ 65,000
Notes Payable	—	25,000	(a) 25,000		—
Common Stock	270,000	100,000	(b) 100,000		270,000
Retained Earnings	65,000	40,000	(b) 40,000		65,000
Totals	$375,000	$190,000	$190,000	$190,000	$400,000

company anticipates that the earnings of the subsidiary will be above normal for the industry, it might pay a premium above book value. If the parent company makes the purchase above book value because some of the subsidiary's assets were under-valued on the subsidiary's books, the entity will attempt to raise the value of these particular assets on the books of the consolidated entity.

If the parent purchases the subsidiary above book value because of the subsidiary's excess earning power, a new account called Goodwill should be put on the consolidated entity's books. If this occurred in the case of the Parentis and Subside companies, the consolidated balance sheet would be compiled as shown in Exhibit 2. In this instance, the parent paid $165,000 for the subsidiary's net assets, which have a book value of only $140,000.

Once again, the note receivable on the parent's books and the note payable on the subsidiary's books are eliminated. In addition, the subsidiary's equity is elimi-nated as well as the investment on the parent's books. In this case, $25,000 of Good-will is put on the consolidated entity's balance sheet.

Purchase of less than 100 percent of a subsidiary at book value. Now we con-sider a situation in which the parent purchases less than 100 percent of the subsid-iary's stock at a price equal to book value. This situation gives rise to a new item on the consolidated balance sheet called **minority interest.** This item represents the equity interest in the subsidiary that is not owned by the parent, or the portion of the subsidiary's net assets owned by outsiders other than the parent. Assuming that Parentis Company purchased 70 percent of Subside's net assets, the consolidated balance sheet would be compiled as shown in Exhibit 3.

Eliminating entry (a), which eliminates Notes Receivable and Notes Payable in Exhibit 3, is the same as eliminating entry (a) in the consolidated worksheets

Exhibit 3   Worksheet for Consolidated Balance Sheet with Minority Interest

Parentis Hotel and Subside Motel
Worksheet for Consolidated Balance Sheet

	Parentis	Subside	Eliminating Entries Debit	Eliminating Entries Credit	Consolidated Balance Sheet
Cash	$ 10,000	$ 55,000			$ 65,000
Accounts Receivable	20,000	15,000			35,000
Notes Receivable	25,000	—		(a) $ 25,000	—
Inventory	50,000	40,000			90,000
Investment in Subsidiary	98,000	—		(b) 98,000	—
Property & Equipment	105,000	80,000			185,000
Totals	$308,000	$ 190,000			$375,000
Accounts Payable	$ 40,000	$ 25,000			$ 65,000
Notes Payable	—	25,000	(a) $ 25,000		—
Common Stock	203,000	100,000	(b) 100,000		203,000
Retained Earnings	65,000	40,000	(b) 40,000		65,000
Minority Interest				(b) 42,000	42,000
Totals	$308,000	$ 190,000	$165,000	$165,000	$375,000

shown in Exhibits 1 and 2. Eliminating entry (b) eliminates all of the subsidiary's equity and all of the investment that appears on the parent's books. In addition, eliminating entry (b) sets up the account Minority Interest. Note that the minority interest is in the amount of $42,000 and represents 30 percent of the subsidiary's equity, as shown here:

Common Stock of Subsidiary	$100,000
Retained Earnings of Subsidiary	+ 40,000
Total Equity of Subsidiary	140,000
Times 30%	× .30
Equals Minority Interest	$ 42,000

This chapter has focused on the balance sheet in its discussion of consolidated financial statements. Companies would, of course, have to compile consolidated income statements and other financial statements as well. Discussion of these consolidated statements is usually presented in advanced accounting courses.

Valuation of Investments

Both debt and equity investments can vary significantly over the time that they are held by an investor. Generally, the proper accounting treatment for these investments is to place them on the balance sheet at fair market value on a given balance sheet date.

Automating information for FASB Statement no. 115.

Taking Stock On The Internet

By *Terry J. Ward* and *Jon Woodroof*

Terry J. Ward, is an associate professor of accounting at Middle Tennessee State University in Murfreesboro, Tennessee. Jon Woodroof, CPA, PhD, is an assistant professor of accounting at the same university.

EXECUTIVE SUMMARY

- COMPANIES THAT MUST apply Financial Accounting Standards Board Statement no. 115, *Accounting for Certain Investments in Debt and Equity Securities,* can use the Internet and spreadsheet software to do the job most efficiently.
- AN INTERNET WEB PAGE offers, at no charge, up-to-the-minute prices of securities in customized portfolios. That information, when imported into a spreadsheet template, can generate the accounting information that complies with Statement no. 115.
- TWO WORKSHEET TEMPLATES are used: One is for the formulas and the other is a parsing sheet, into which you paste market information copied from the Internet.
- TO GET THE LATEST market information, tap into the Internet and go to http://www.imet.com/ pages/login.htp. Users are allowed a maximum of 15 stocks and 15 mutual funds for each login name. Companies can track additional stocks and mutual funds simply by registering under different login/password combinations.
- THE INTERNET IS beginning to revolutionize the way organizations conduct business and the way accountants perform their professional work. CPAs should be prepared to take full advantage of the Internet—for both their own work and for both their clients and employers.

If your company or client is required to track the current market value of securities it owns, then you know what an irksome, time-consuming task that can be. But now, with the help of the Internet, the task can be accomplished almost automatically.

Under Financial Accounting Standards Board Statement no. 115, *Accounting for Certain Investments in Debt and Equity Securities,* businesses must account for the securities in their financial statements. Using two computer tools—the Internet and spreadsheet software—you can do the job with little more than a few mouse clicks.

Terry J. Ward and Jon Woodroof tout the use of the Internet for valuing investments in this January 1997 article from the *Journal of Accountancy Online* (vol. 183, no. 1; see www.aicpa.org/pubs/jofa/index.htm for more information). The parent site for this publication is that of the American Institute of Certified Public Accountants (www.aicpa.org), which has more resources for aspiring accounting professionals.

According to FASB's Statement 115, *Accounting for Certain Investments in Debt and Equity Securities,* these investments should be grouped into the following three categories:

1. Held-to-maturity securities

2. Trading securities

3. Available-for-sale securities

Held-to-Maturity Securities

Since equity securities have no maturity date, only debt securities fall into this category. These securities should be accounted for at amortized cost, not fair value. The valuation for **held-to-maturity securities** is complex and is generally discussed in intermediate accounting courses.

Trading Securities

Trading securities involve frequent purchase and sale. These securities are purchased with the intention of selling them in a short period of time, generally within three months of purchase. These securities are reported on the balance sheet at fair market value, with the difference between cost and fair market value reported as unrealized gain or loss and included in the income statement of the current year.

In order to illustrate these concepts, consider the trading security portfolio of the Fairview Hotel Company as of December 31, 20XX:

Investment	Cost	Fair Value	Unrealized Gain (Loss)
Agresso Stock	$ 12,000	$ 14,000	$ 2,000
Conservo Corp. Bonds	50,000	49,000	(1,000)
Reservo Corp. Stock	80,000	85,000	5,000
	$142,000	$148,000	$ 6,000

Both the unrealized gain and the increase in the value of the investment portfolio are recorded by the following entry:

Investment Securities Adjustment—Trading	$6,000	
Unrealized Gain on Securities—Income		$6,000

If the value of the portfolio had decreased over the accounting period, an unrealized-loss account would have been debited and the Investment Securities account would have been credited. Any unrealized gains or losses are closed to Income Summary and included on the income statement for the current period.

Available-for-Sale Securities

Available-for-sale securities are purchased with the intention of selling them sometime in the future. If the intent is to sell them within a year, they should be recorded as short-term investments. If the intent is to sell them more than 12 months from the purchase date, they should be classified as long-term investments.

Assuming that the investments of the Golden Corporation below are long-term investments, they should be reported at fair market value. The procedure for determining the unrealized gain or loss is the same as that for the case of trading securities, but the journal entry differs. Assume that the Golden Corporation has the following available-for-sale securities at 6/30/XX:

Investment	Cost	Fair Value	Unrealized Gain (Loss)
Conservo Bonds	$ 60,000	$ 61,000	$ 1,000
Retracto Stock	40,000	38,000	(2,000)
	$100,000	$ 99,000	$ (1,000)

The journal entry on 6/30/XX would be as follows:

Unrealized Loss—Equity	$1,000	
Investment Securities Adjustment—Available-for-Sale		$1,000

Since these securities are not expected to be sold soon, there is a good chance that there could be further unrealized gains or losses before their sale. Therefore, the unrealized gain or loss is not reported on the income statement but rather as a separate item on the Stockholders' Equity section of the balance sheet.

Summary

The asset account Investments includes cash advances to affiliated companies, property and equipment not currently used in the business, long-term debt, and equity investments. Not all debt and equity investments are put in this asset account. Short-term investments appear in their own Current Assets account, Short-Term Investments.

Three ways of accounting for long-term investments in equity securities are the cost method, the equity method, and the consolidated financial statements method. Under the cost method, investments are put on the books at cost, gains or losses are recognized when sold, and income is recorded when received. Under the equity method, investments are recorded at cost, and their value adjusted as earnings are reported by the subsidiary and dividends are paid.

If an investor owns more than 50 percent of a company, the investor is said to control the subsidiary and is called a *parent company*. In this case, the financial statements of the two entities are combined into a consolidated format.

Key Terms

available-for-sale securities—Debt and equity securities purchased with the intention of selling them sometime in the future. Available-for-sale securities are reported at fair value, with unrealized gains and losses excluded from the income statement's earnings and reported in a separate component of Stockholders' Equity on the balance sheet.

consolidated financial statements—The combined financial statements of a parent corporation and its subsidiary corporations. Parent companies must use the consolidated statement method to account for investments in subsidiaries.

cost method—A method of accounting for investments in which long-term investments are put on the books at cost, gains or losses are recognized as of the sale date, and income is recorded when received.

eliminating entries—Entries used in preparing consolidated financial statements for a parent-subsidiary entity to avoid double counting. For example, a parent's loan of money to its subsidiary would be "eliminated" from (not counted in) the consolidated financial statements, since in effect the entity owes money to itself.

equity method—A method of accounting for an investment in which the investor records the original investment at cost, then adjusts the value of the investment over time. A company owning more than 20 percent but less than 50 percent of the investee uses this method.

held-to-maturity securities—Debt securities that the enterprise has the positive intent and ability to hold to maturity. Held-to-maturity securities are reported at amortized cost.

investee—A company whose stock is purchased.

investor—A company or individual who buys stock in a company.

marketable debt securities—Bonds.

minority interest—The equity interest in a subsidiary that is not owned by the parent, or the portion of a subsidiary's net assets owned by outsiders other than the parent.

parent company—A company that owns greater than 50 percent of another company and is said to control that company.

short-term equity investments—Stocks intended to be converted to cash within one year.

subsidiary company—A company that has been purchased by a parent company, which owns greater than 50 percent of the subsidiary and controls it. See *parent company.*

trading securities—Debt and equity securities that are bought and held principally for the purpose of selling them in the near term (usually within three months of purchase). Trading securities are reported on the balance sheet at fair value, with unrealized gains and losses included in earnings on the income statement.

Review Questions

1. Cash Advances to Affiliated Companies is an example of an item listed in the Investments category on the balance sheet. What are the other two items found in this category?

2. When a hospitality firm purchases bonds of another firm with the intent of holding them for a long time, what accounts are involved in the purchase's journal entry if the bonds are bought between interest payment dates?

3. What determines whether an investment is classified in the Short-Term Investments account or the Investments account?

4. What are the differences between the cost method and the equity method of accounting for an investment?

5. What percentage of a company's stock must be held before there is significant influence or control? What is the nature of the account Minority Interest on the books of a consolidated entity? Where does Minority Interest appear on a consolidated balance sheet?

6. When the parent pays more than the book value for a subsidiary, how is the difference between book value and purchase price recorded on the books of the consolidated entity?

7. What are the common eliminating entries on the worksheet of a consolidated entity?

8. Based on the following information, what would be the eliminating entry on the worksheet of the consolidated entity? (Assume that the parent company bought the subsidiary because of the subsidiary's excess earning power.)

Subsidiary's common stock	$100,000
Retained earnings of subsidiary	50,000
Parent's investment	180,000

9. Where do short-term and long-term investments appear on a company's balance sheet?

10. How are marketable equity securities valued at year-end?

Problems

Problem 1

In the left column of the following table is a list of individual balance sheet items.

Required:
In the right column of the table, write the subclassification under which each of the individual balance sheet items would be found.

Balance Sheet Items	Balance Sheet Subclassifications
Minority Interest	
Marketable Securities	
Land Held for Future Use	
Goodwill	
Cash Advances to Affiliated Companies	
Allowance for Marketable Equity Securities	

Problem 2

Based on FASB 115, write a memo explaining the differences among held-to-maturity securities, trading securities, and available-for-sale securities.

Problem 3

The Brownstone Hotel had several marketable debt securities transactions in the month of May.

Required:

Make the relevant journal entries for the following transactions:

1. Brownstone purchased $100,000 worth of 9 percent bonds at 98 percent of par plus a $600 commission and accrued interest on May 1, 20X4. Interest payment dates are April 1 and October 1.
2. The hotel received a check for six months' interest on October 1, 20X4.
3. The hotel accrued interest income on December 31, 20X4.

Problem 4

Write a brief memo explaining how to account for long-term equity investments if the investment in the stock of the other company is:

a. Less than 20 percent.
b. Between 20 percent and 50 percent.
c. More than 50 percent.

Problem 5

Listed below is the trading security portfolio of the Grandview Hotel Corporation as of December 31, 20X6.

Investment	Cost	Fair Value	Unrealized Gain (Loss)
Billups Stock	$ 15,000	$ 18,000	$ 3,000
Wallace Stock	45,000	49,000	4,000
Hamilton Bonds	12,000	6,000	(6,000)
Saunders Stock	18,000	17,000	(1,000)
McDyess Bonds	62,000	68,000	6,000
	$152,000	$158,000	$ 6,000

Required:

1. Record the adjusting entry necessary for December 31, 20X6.
2. Record the adjusting entry necessary for December 31, 20X6, assuming the investment portfolio had an unrealized loss of $6,000.

Problem 6

When a parent company buys 100 percent of a subsidiary, it is usually at price above book value. Write a memo explaining the two reasons why the purchase price is usually above rather than below book value.

Problem 7

Pleasuredine Restaurants, Inc., purchased 3,000 of the 10,000 shares of Telecom Company for $15 per share on November 6, 20X4. On December 31, 20X4, Telecom reports income of $40,000 and, on January 15, 20X5, pays a dividend of $.30 per share.

Required:

1. Record the journal entries for Pleasuredine on November 6, 20X4.
2. Record the journal entries for Pleasuredine on December 31, 20X4.
3. Record the journal entries for Pleasuredine on January 15, 20X5.
4. Determine the value of Pleasuredine's investment in Telecom as of January 15, 20X5.

Problem 8

Skyway Corporation is treating the following securities as trading securities. The cost and fair market value as of December 31, 20XX, for their portfolio are listed below. Record the adjusting entry necessary for December 31, 20XX.

Investment	Cost	Fair Value	Unrealized Gain (Loss)
Bluesky Corp. Stock	25,000	$26,000	$ 1,000
Good Earth Corp. Bonds	12,000	10,000	(2,000)
	$ 37,000	$36,000	$(1,000)

Problem 9

Keystone Corporation accounts for the following securities as available-for-sale investments:

Investment	Cost	Fair Value as of 9/30/XX
GreenCo Inc. Stock	$15,000	$18,000
Whitefield Co. Bonds	$16,000	$15,000
Maroontide Co. Bonds	$18,000	$17,000
Golden Co. Stock	$12,000	$18,000

Required:

Journalize the appropriate adjusting entry for 9/30/XX.

Problem 10

Chippewa Hotels Corporation purchased some marketable debt securities on September 1, 20X6. The bonds were purchased at 106 percent of par and had a face value of $200,000 with 6 percent semiannual interest paid on July 1 and January 1. Chippewa Hotels paid a brokerage commission of $1,000 plus accrued interest.

Required:

Record the necessary journal entries for September 1, 20X6, and January 1, 20X7.

Problem 11

Jersey Hotels Corporation has a short-term equity investment in Holland Catering Corporation. On May 1, 20X6, Jersey Hotels received $6,000 worth of dividends from Holland Catering Corporation. On July 15, 20X6, Jersey Hotels Corporation sold its stock in Holland Catering for $125,000. The stock was purchased on January 15, 20X6, for $120,000.

Required:

Journalize the necessary entries for Jersey Hotels for May 1, 20X6, and July 5, 20X6.

Problem 12

Pizza Prince Company purchased 2,000 shares of Empire Corporation on August 15, 20X4, at $45 per share plus a brokerage commission of $300. Quarterly dividend dates are September 15, December 15, March 15, and June 15. The current dividend is $2.70 per share.

Required:

Record any necessary journal entries on the dates shown.

1. August 15, 20X4
2. September 15, 20X4
3. December 15, 20X4
4. December 31, 20X4

Challenge Problems

Problem 13

The information provided in the following table pertains to Cajun Carl's Restaurant and its subsidiary, Louisiana Lil's, as of December 31, 20X4:

	Parent Cajun Carl's	Subsidiary Louisiana Lil's
Cash	$ 18,000	$ 6,000
Accounts Receivable	14,000	2,500
Rent Receivable	15,000	–0–
Inventory	6,000	1,500
Investments	32,000	–0–
Property & Equipment	55,000	40,000
Total Assets	$ 140,000	$ 50,000
Accounts Payable	$ 9,000	$ 3,000
Rent Payable	–0–	15,000
Mortgage Payable	26,000	–0–
Common Stock	47,000	20,000
Retained Earnings	58,000	12,000
Total Liabilities and Owners' Equity	$ 140,000	$ 50,000

Additional information:

1.   The Rent Receivable of $15,000 on the parent's books is the $15,000 Rent Payable on the subsidiary's books.

2.   Cajun Carl's owns 100 percent of the subsidiary.

Required:

Compile the consolidated balance sheet for Cajun Carl's as of December 31, 20X4, based on the information provided.

Problem 14

Buffy's Hotels buys and sells marketable securities when excess cash is available. All of its marketable securities are classified as current assets.

Required:

Write the necessary journal entry for each of the following transactions.

1.   On October 6, purchased 100 shares of Allison Labs common stock at $51\frac{1}{4}$ per share plus brokerage commissions of $280.

2.   On October 15, purchased $60,000 worth of 9 percent face value bonds from McGuire International at 97 percent of par plus accrued interest of $2,250 and commission of $300.

3.   On November 15, received semiannual interest on McGuire International bonds.

4.   On November 28, purchased 200 shares of Farley Industries common stock at $26\frac{1}{2}$ per share plus brokerage commission of $175.

5.   On December 1, received quarterly dividend of $.75 per share on Allison Labs stock.

6.   At December 31, 20X4, the market price of Allison Labs stock was $49 per share, while the market price of Farley Industries stock was $27. Make any necessary adjusting entries.

7.   On January 25, sold 100 shares of Allison Labs for $49\frac{1}{4}$ per share less commission of $280.

Problem 15

Based on the account balances below, compile the consolidated balance sheet of the Webb Corporation for December 31, 20XX. (Hint: Some of the accounts below may not be needed.)

Account	Balance
Land	$60,000
Unrealized Gain on Available-for-Sale Securities—Equity	5,000
Cash	10,000
Unrealized Loss on Trading Securities—Income	3,000
Minority Interest	50,000
Retained Earnings	?
Building	75,000
Short-Term Investments	20,000

Accounts Receivable	20,000
Accounts Payable	12,000
Common Stock	60,000
Long-Term Investments	18,000
Inventory	25,000
Goodwill	40,000
Notes Payable	10,000
Mortgage Payable	60,000

Chapter 17 Outline

The Purpose of the Statement of Cash Flows
Classification of Cash Flows
Conversion of Accrual Income to Net Cash
    Flows from Operations
        Direct and Indirect Methods
Preparing the SCF
        Step 1: Determining Net Cash Flows
           from Operating Activities
        Step 2: Determining Net Cash Flows
           from Investing Activities
        Step 3: Determining Net Cash Flows
           from Financing Activities
        Step 4: Presenting Cash Flows by
           Activity on the SCF
        Interpreting the Results
Accounting for Other Transactions

Competencies

1. Explain the purpose and use of the statement of cash flows. (pp. 477–479)

2. Identify the general format for a statement of cash flows, and classify transactions as operating, investing, or financing activities. (pp. 479–481)

3. Explain the direct and indirect methods of reporting cash flows from operations. (pp. 482–484)

4. Explain the preparation of the Operating Activities section of a statement of cash flows. (pp. 484–489)

5. Explain the preparation of the Investing Activities section of a statement of cash flows. (pp. 489–490)

6. Explain the preparation of the Financing Activities section of a statement of cash flows. (pp. 490–492)

7. Describe special situations that may need to be accounted for in preparing a statement of cash flows. (pp. 493–495)

17

Statement of Cash Flows

TRADITIONALLY, the principal financial statements used by hospitality operations have been the income statement and the balance sheet. The balance sheet shows the financial position of the business at the end of the accounting period. The income statement reflects the results of operations for the accounting period. Although these statements provide extensive financial information, they do not provide answers to such questions as:

1. How much cash was provided by operations?

2. What amount of property and equipment was purchased during the year?

3. How much long-term debt was borrowed during the year?

4. What amount of funds was raised through the sale of capital stock?

5. What amount of dividends was paid during the year?

6. How much was invested in long-term investments during the year?

The **statement of cash flows (SCF)** is designed to answer these questions and many more as it shows the sources and uses of cash for the accounting period.

Our discussion will address the definition of *cash,* the relationship of the SCF to other financial statements, the purposes and uses of the SCF, a classification of cash flows, alternative formats that may be used for the SCF, a four-step approach for preparing the SCF, an illustration of the preparation of the SCF using the Sample Inn, and accounting for other transactions.

The Purpose of the Statement of Cash Flows

The statement of cash flows shows the effects on cash of a business's operating, investing, and financing activities for the accounting period. It explains the change in Cash for the accounting period; that is, if Cash decreases by $3,000 from January 1, 20X1 (the beginning of the accounting period), to December 31, 20X1 (the end of the accounting period), the SCF will reflect the decrease in the sum of cash from the firm's various activities.

For purposes of this statement, *cash* is defined to include both cash and cash equivalents. Cash equivalents are short-term, highly liquid investments such as U.S. Treasury bills and money market accounts. Firms use cash equivalents for investing funds that are temporarily not needed for operating purposes. Generally, these short-term investments are made for 90 days or less. Since cash and cash

equivalents are considered the same, transfers between Cash and Cash Equivalents are not considered cash receipts or cash disbursements for SCF purposes.

The major purpose of the SCF is to provide information regarding the cash
receipts and disbursements of a business that will help users (investors, creditors,
managers, and others) to:

1. Assess the organization's ability to generate positive future net cash flows.
   Although users of financial statements are less interested in the past than in
   the future, many users, especially external users, must rely on historical financial information to assess an operation's future abilities. Thus, the investor
   interested in future cash dividends will review the SCF to determine past
   sources and uses of cash to evaluate the firm's ability to pay future dividends.

2. Assess the firm's ability to meet its obligations. Users of financial statements
   want to determine the firm's ability to pay its bills as they come due. If a firm
   has little likelihood of being able to pay its bills, then suppliers will most likely
   not be interested in selling the firm their goods and services.

3. Assess the difference between the enterprise's net income and cash receipts
   and disbursements. The SCF allows a user to quickly determine the major net
   sources of cash and how much relates to the enterprise's operations. Investors,
   creditors, and other users generally prefer enterprises that are able to generate
   cash from operations (that is, from their primary purpose for being in business), as opposed to those generating cash solely from financing and investing
   activities (that is, activities which are incidental to the primary purpose).

4. Assess the effect of both cash and noncash investing and financing during the
   accounting period. Investing activities relate to the acquisition and disposition
   of noncurrent assets, such as property and equipment. Financing activities
   relate to the borrowing and payment of long-term debt and sale and purchase
   of capital stock. Noncash activities (that is, transactions involving no cash)
   include such transactions as the acquisition of a hotel in exchange for stock or
   long-term debt.

The three major user groups of the SCF are management (internal) and investors and creditors (external). Management may use the SCF to (1) assess the firm's
liquidity, (2) assess its financial flexibility, (3) determine its dividend policy, and (4)
plan investing and financing needs. Investors and creditors will most likely use the
SCF to assess the firm's (1) ability to pay its bills as they come due, (2) ability to pay
dividends, and (3) need for additional financing, including borrowing debt and
selling capital stock.

The relationship of the SCF to other financial statements is shown in Exhibit
1. The statement of retained earnings, mentioned in Exhibit 1, reflects results of
operations and dividends declared, and reconciles the Retained Earnings
accounts of two successive balance sheets. Net Income from the income statement
is transferred to the Retained Earnings account when the temporary accounts
(revenues and expenses) are closed at the end of the accounting period. In addition, Net Income is shown on the SCF when the SCF is prepared using the indirect
approach (discussed later in this chapter). Finally, the SCF indirectly reconciles

Exhibit 1   Relationship of SCF to Other Financial Statements

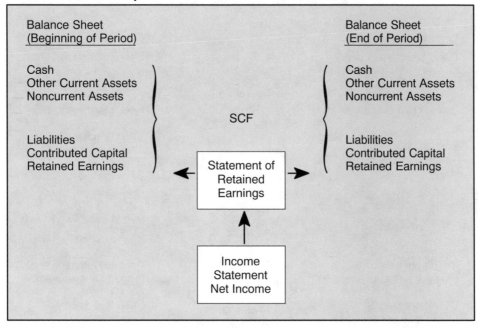

Balance Sheet
(Beginning of Period)

Cash
Other Current Assets
Noncurrent Assets

Liabilities
Contributed Capital
Retained Earnings

SCF

Statement of
Retained
Earnings

Income
Statement
Net Income

Balance Sheet
(End of Period)

Cash
Other Current Assets
Noncurrent Assets

Liabilities
Contributed Capital
Retained Earnings

most accounts on the balance sheet other than Cash by showing the sources and uses of cash.

Classification of Cash Flows

The SCF classifies cash receipts and disbursements as operating, investing, and financing activities. Both **cash inflows** and **cash outflows** are included within each category. Exhibit 2 presents classifications of cash flows under the various activities, which are further described below:

- **Operating Activities:** This category includes cash transactions related to revenues and expenses. Revenues (cash inflows) include sales of food, beverages, and other goods and services to lodging guests, as well as interest and dividend income. Expenses (cash outflows) are for operational cash expenditures, including payments for salaries, wages, taxes, supplies, and so forth. Interest expense is also included as an operations cash outflow.

- **Investing Activities:** These activities relate primarily to cash flows from the acquisition and disposal of all noncurrent assets, especially property, equipment, and investments. Also included are cash flows from the purchase and disposal of short-term investments (marketable securities).

- **Financing Activities:** These activities relate to cash flows from the issuance and retirement of debt and the issuance and repurchase of capital stock. Cash

Exhibit 2   Classification of Cash Flows

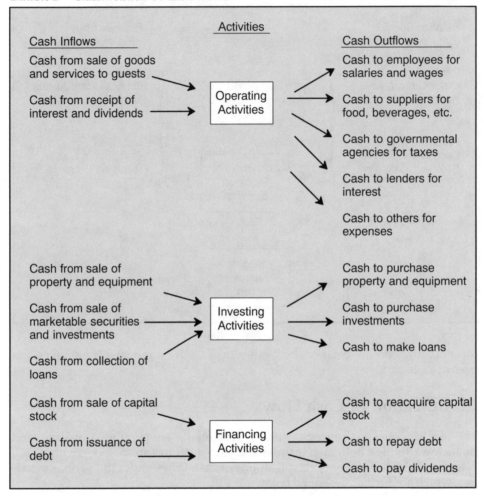

inflows include cash received from issues of stock and both short-term and long-term borrowing. Cash outflows include repayments of loans (although paying the interest expense portion of the debt is an operating activity) and payments to owners for both dividends and any repurchase of stocks. Payments of accounts payable, taxes payable, and the various accrued expenses, such as wages payable, are not payments of loans under financing activities, but they are classified as cash outflows under Operating Activities.

Finally, hospitality enterprises engage in noncash investing and financing activities, such as the exchange of capital stock for a hotel building. Since this represents only an exchange, no cash transaction has occurred. Therefore, these noncash activities are not shown on the SCF. However, since a major purpose of the

Exhibit 3   Schedule of Noncash Investing and Financing Activities—Gateway Inn

Common stock exchanged for long-term debt	$100,000
Capital lease obligations incurred for use of equipment	50,000
Total	$150,000

Exhibit 4   Basic Format of the SCF

Cash Flows from Operating Activities [direct or indirect approaches may be used]	$XX
Cash Flows from Investing Activities [list cash inflows and outflows]	XX
Cash Flows from Financing Activities [list cash inflows and outflows]	XX
Net Increase (Decrease) in Cash	XX
Cash at the Beginning of the Period	XX
Cash at the End of the Period	$XX
Schedule of Noncash Investing and Financing Transactions [list individual transactions]	$XX

SCF is to include financing and investing activities, and since these activities will affect future cash flows, they must be disclosed on a separate schedule of the SCF. Thus, the user of financial information is provided with a complete presentation of investing and financing activities. Exhibit 3 is an example of a supplementary schedule of noncash investing and financing activities of the Gateway Inn.

The basic format of the SCF is shown in Exhibit 4. Generally, cash flows from operating activities are shown first. The indirect or direct approaches (to be discussed later) may be used to show cash flows from operating activities. Cash flows from investing and financing activities follow. Individual cash outflows and inflows are shown in each section. For example, Long-Term Debt may increase by $100,000 due to payment of $50,000 and subsequent borrowing of $150,000. Each cash flow should be shown rather than netting the two flows. Finally, as stated above, a supplementary schedule of noncash investing and financing activities to the SCF must be included.

Conversion of Accrual Income to Net Cash Flows from Operations

A major purpose of the SCF is to show net cash flows from operations. The income statement is prepared on an **accrual basis;** that is, revenues are recorded when they are earned, not when cash is received from guests, and expenses are recorded when incurred, not necessarily when cash is disbursed. Consequently, there may be little correlation between net income and cash flow. Consider the hypothetical Wales Inn, which had $2,000,000 in sales for 20X1. Its accounts receivable (AR) from guests totaled $100,000 at the beginning of the year and $110,000 at the end of the year. The cash received from sales during 20X1 is determined as follows:

$$\begin{aligned}
\text{Cash receipts for sales} \quad &= \quad \text{Sales} - \text{increase in AR} \\
&\qquad or + \text{decrease in AR} \\
&= \quad \$2,000,000 - \$10,000 \\
&= \quad \underline{\underline{\$1,990,000}}
\end{aligned}$$

Thus, even though the Wales Inn had sales of $2,000,000 as reported on its income statement, it would show cash receipts from sales on its SCF as $1,990,000.

Direct and Indirect Methods

There are two methods of reporting cash flows from operations: the direct and the indirect methods. The **direct method** shows cash receipts from sales and cash disbursements for expenses. This method requires that each item on the income statement be converted from an accrual basis to a cash basis, as were the sales of the Wales Inn above. Another example of this conversion process for the Wales Inn is Payroll Expense. Assume that the Wales Inn reported $700,000 as Payroll Expense for 20X1, and its balance sheet's Accrued Payroll account at the beginning of the year showed $15,000 and at the end of the year showed $20,000. Its cash disbursement for payroll for 20X1 would be determined as follows:

$$\begin{aligned}
\text{Cash Disbursement for Payroll Expense} \quad &= \quad \text{Payroll Expense} - \text{increase in Accrued Payroll} \\
&\qquad or + \text{decrease in Accrued Payroll} \\
&= \quad \$700,000 - \$5,000 \\
&= \quad \underline{\underline{\$695,000}}
\end{aligned}$$

So even though payroll expense for the year totaled $700,000 as shown on the income statement, only $695,000 was disbursed during the year.

Some expenses shown on the income statement do not involve any direct cash disbursement and are simply ignored when the direct method is used. For example, depreciation expense is only an adjustment to help match expenses to revenues. Depreciation does not entail any cash, so it is ignored when the direct

Exhibit 5   Basic Formats of the Net Cash Flow from Operating Activities Section

Operating Activities		
<u>Direct Method</u>		
Cash Flows from Operating Activities:		
Cash Receipts from Sales		$ XXX
Interest and Dividends Received		<u>XXX</u>
Total		XXX
Cash Disbursements for:		
Payroll	$ XXX	
Purchases of Inventory	XXX	
Other Expenses	XXX	
Interest Expense	XXX	
Income Taxes	<u>XXX</u>	<u>XXX</u>
Net Cash Flows from Operating Activities		$ XXX
<u>Indirect Method</u>		
Cash Flows from Operating Activities:		
Net Income		$ XXX
Adjustments to Reconcile Net Income to Net Cash		
Flows from Operating Activities:		
Depreciation Expense	$ XXX	
Gain on Sale of Property	(XXX)	
Loss on Sale of Investments	XXX	
Increase in Accounts Receivable	(XXX)	
Decrease in Inventories	XXX	
•		
•		
•		
Increase in Accrued Payroll	<u>XXX</u>	<u>XXX</u>
Net Cash Flows from Operating Activities		$ <u>XXX</u>

method is used. The same approach is taken for amortization expense and gains and losses on the sale of property and equipment. The basic formats of cash flows from the Operating Activities section of the SCF for both the direct and indirect methods are shown in Exhibit 5.

Most hospitality businesses use the indirect method because the information needed to prepare it is more readily available than that needed for using the direct method. For that reason, the major focus in this chapter will be on the indirect method.

The **indirect method** for determining net cash flows from operations starts with net income. Net income is then adjusted for noncash items included on the income statement. The most common noncash expense deducted to determine net income is depreciation. Therefore, since depreciation is subtracted to compute net income on the income statement, it is added back to net income to compute net cash flows from operating activities. Other items on the income statement that must be added or subtracted include amortization expense and gains and losses on the sale of noncurrent assets and marketable securities.

To illustrate the addback of a loss on the sale of investments, assume that in 20X1 the Wales Inn sold for $200,000 a parcel of underdeveloped land (an investment) that originally cost $250,000. The journal entry to record the sale was as follows:

Cash	$200,000	
Loss on Sale of Investments	50,000	
Investment in Land		$250,000

The $200,000 of cash inflow will be shown as an investing activity on the SCF; however, the loss on sale of investments of $50,000 was included on the income statement in determining net income. Since it was subtracted in determining the Wales Inn's net income and it did not use cash, it must be added back to net income to determine the net cash flows from operating activities for the SCF.

In addition, to determine the net cash flows from operating activities while using the indirect method, the Wales Inn's net income must be adjusted for sales that were recorded but not paid during 20X1. This adjustment is accomplished by subtracting the increase in Accounts Receivable of $10,000 from net income on the SCF. Several similar adjustments must be made using the indirect method. These will be discussed in detail and illustrated in the next section of this chapter.

Regardless of the method used, the result will show the same amount of net cash provided by operating activities. The Financial Accounting Standards Board requires that firms using the indirect method report the amount of interest expense and taxes paid in separate disclosures.

Preparing the SCF

The principal sources of information needed for preparing the SCF are the income statement, the statement of retained earnings, and two successive balance sheets from the beginning and end of the accounting period. In addition, details of transactions affecting any change in noncurrent balance sheet accounts must be reviewed. For example, if a comparison of two successive balance sheets shows the Building account has increased by $5,000,000, the account must be analyzed to determine the reason(s) for the changes. Simply reflecting the net change of $5,000,000 on the SCF is generally not acceptable.

A four-step approach for preparing the SCF is as follows:

1. Determine the net cash flows from operating activities.

2. Determine the net cash flows from investing activities.

3. Determine the net cash flows from financing activities.

4. Present the cash flows by activity on the SCF.

Exhibits 6 and 7 contain balance sheets and a condensed income statement and statement of retained earnings for the Sample Inn. These will be used to illustrate this four-step approach. The preparation of the SCF is illustrated using the indirect method for showing net cash flows from operating activities.

Exhibit 6   Balance Sheets for the Sample Inn

Sample Inn
Balance Sheets
December 31, 20X1 and 20X2

		20X1	20X2
Assets			
Current Assets:			
Cash		$ 5,000	$ 10,000
Accounts Receivable		30,000	26,000
Inventory		10,000	12,000
	Total	45,000	48,000
Investments		50,000	300,000
Property and Equipment:			
Land		200,000	200,000
Building		10,000,000	10,000,000
Equipment		1,000,000	1,100,000
Less: Accumulated Depreciation		(5,000,000)	(5,500,000)
	Total	6,200,000	5,800,000
Total Assets		$ 6,295,000	$ 6,148,000
Liabilities and Owners' Equity			
Current Liabilities:			
Accounts Payable		$ 6,000	$ 6,500
Accrued Payroll		4,000	4,500
Income Taxes Payable		7,000	6,000
Dividends Payable		10,000	15,000
	Total	27,000	32,000
Long-Term Debt		4,500,000	3,750,000
Owners' Equity:			
Capital Stock		1,000,000	1,250,000
Retained Earnings		768,000	1,116,000
	Total	1,768,000	2,366,000
Total Liabilities and Owners' Equity		$ 6,295,000	$ 6,148,000

Step 1: Determining Net Cash Flows from Operating Activities

To determine the net cash flows from operating activities by using the indirect method, we focus first on the income statement by starting with net income of $500,000. Next, we need to adjust net income for items on the income statement that did not provide or use cash. In particular, depreciation expense and the gain on the sale of the investments are considered. Since depreciation was subtracted on the income statement to determine net income, it must be added to net income on the SCF to determine net cash flow from operating activities. Since the gain on the sale of investments is not a cash flow (the proceeds from the sale of investments of $150,000 are an investing activity on the SCF and will be discussed later), the gain of $100,000 must be subtracted from net income on the SCF. Thus, the net cash flows from operating activities are determined at this point as follows:

Exhibit 7   Income Statement and Statement of Retained Earnings for the Sample Inn

Sample Inn
Condensed Income Statement and Statement of Retained Earnings
For the Year Ended December 31, 20X2

Sales	$7,000,000
Cost of Goods Sold	1,000,000
Payroll Expenses	2,450,000
Other Operating Expenses	2,400,000
Income Taxes	250,000
Depreciation Expense	500,000
Gain on the Sale of Investments	100,000
Net Income	500,000
Retained Earnings—12/31/X1	768,000
Dividends Declared	152,000
Retained Earnings—12/31/X2	$1,116,000

Other Information:

1. No property and equipment were disposed of during 20X2.

2. Investment and equipment purchases during 20X2 were made with cash. No funds were borrowed.

3. Investments costing $50,000 were sold for $150,000, resulting in a $100,000 gain on the sale of investments during 20X2.

4. Long-term debt of $250,000 was converted to capital stock in a noncash transaction during 20X2. No other capital stock was issued, and there were no repurchases of capital stock.

5. Interest expense paid during the year totaled $400,000.

Net Cash Flows from Operating Activities:		
Net Income		$500,000
Adjustments to Reconcile Net Income to		
Net Cash Flows from Operating Activities:		
Depreciation Expense	$500,000	
Gain on Sale of Investments	(100,000)	400,000
Partial Net Cash Flows from Operating Activities		$900,000

The second type of adjustment includes changes in current accounts from the balance sheet. The Cash account is not considered, since we are essentially looking at all other balance sheet accounts to determine what caused the change in Cash for purposes of the SCF. In addition, the current liability account Dividends Payable is not considered in determining cash flows from operating activities, as dividends payable relate to financing activities and will be considered later. The changes in the remaining five current accounts and noncash current accounts are fully considered as follows:

Account	Balances—December 31		Change in Account Balance
	20X1	20X2	
Current Assets:			
Accounts Receivable	$30,000	$26,000	$4,000 (dec.)
Inventory	$10,000	$12,000	$2,000 (inc.)
Current Liabilities:			
Accounts Payable	$ 6,000	$ 6,500	$ 500 (inc.)
Accrued Payroll	$ 4,000	$ 4,500	$ 500 (inc.)
Income Taxes Payable	$ 7,000	$ 6,000	$1,000 (dec.)

A brief explanation follows for each of the above current accounts, including how the change affects net cash flows from operating activities.

Accounts receivable relate directly to sales, which were $7,000,000 for the Sample Inn for 20X2. Sales on account result in cash inflows when the hotel guests pay their bills. However, under accrual accounting, the sale is recorded when services are provided. Most of the sales during 20X2 resulted in cash as the guests paid their accounts, but at year-end, the Accounts Receivable account balance was $26,000. Analysis of the account will reveal how much cash resulted from sales as follows:

Accounts Receivable

12/31/X1 Balance	30,000	Cash Received	7,004,000
Sales to Hotel Guests	7,000,000		
12/31/X2 Balance	26,000		

Alternatively, the cash receipts from hotel guests could be determined as follows:

$$\text{Cash Receipts from Hotel Guests} = \text{AR Beginning Balance} + \text{Sales} - \text{AR Ending Balance}$$

$$= \$30,000 + \$7,000,000 - \$26,000$$

$$= \$7,004,000$$

In preparing the SCF, we need to show a decrease in Accounts Receivable of $4,000, which is added to Net Income as an increase in cash to determine net cash flows from operating activities.

The change in the balances of the Inventory account is an increase of $2,000. Inventory relates to the Purchases and Cost of Goods Sold (food and beverages) accounts. Remember, Cost of Goods Sold is the cost of food and beverage inventory sold, not the cash disbursed for purchases. Therefore, we need to determine the purchases for the year as follows:

	Ending inventory	$ 12,000
+	Cost of goods sold	1,000,000
	Goods available for sale	1,012,000
−	Beginning inventory	10,000
	Purchases	$1,002,000

The $2,000 increase in Inventory causes the accrual basis Cost of Goods Sold to be $2,000 less than Purchases. By assuming that Purchases is the cash amount paid for purchases, we must show a decrease in cash flows from operating activities of $2,000.

However, not all purchases were made for cash. The $500 increase in Accounts Payable represents the difference between purchases on account and cash paid to suppliers during 20X2. An increase in Accounts Payable means the amount of cash paid was less than the amount of purchases. Thus, the $500 increase in Accounts Payable must be added back to the accrual basis net income to determine net cash flows from operating activities. An analysis of the Accounts Payable account shows this as follows:

Accounts Payable

		1/1/X2 Balance	6,000
Payments to Suppliers	1,001,500	Purchases	1,002,000
		12/31/X2 Balance	6,500

The increase in the Accrued Payroll account of $500 represents the difference between the accrual basis payroll costs of $2,450,000 and the cash payments to personnel of $2,449,500. This determination is apparent in the analysis of the Accrued Payroll account as follows:

Accrued Payroll

		12/31/X1 Balance	4,000
Payments for Payroll	2,449,500	Payroll Expense	2,450,000
		12/31/X2 Balance	4,500

Since the payroll payments were $500 less than the payroll expense, the $500 increase in Accrued Payroll is added back to the accrual basis net income to determine net cash flows from operations.

Finally, the decrease of $1,000 in Income Taxes Payable represents the difference between the accrual basis income taxes of $250,000, shown on the condensed income statement of the Sample Inn, and the $251,000 paid, as determined by the analysis of the Income Taxes Payable account as follows:

Income Taxes Payable

		12/31/X1 Balance	7,000
Income Taxes Paid	251,000	Income Tax Expense	250,000
		12/31/X2 Balance	6,000

In reality, the $7,000 of income taxes due at the beginning of 20X1 were paid along with $244,000 of income taxes for 20X2. The remaining $6,000 of taxes for 20X2 will be paid in early 20X3. However, since income taxes paid during 20X2 exceed income tax expenses for 20X2 by $1,000, the $1,000 must be subtracted from the accrual basis net income to determine the net cash flows from operations.

In addition to differences from year to year in the payment of income taxes, a hospitality enterprise may have deferred income taxes over several years. The details of the account for deferred income taxes are beyond our scope.

The Sample Inn's SCF's net cash flows from operating activities based on the above would reflect the following:

Net Cash Flows from Operating Activities:		
Net Income		$500,000
Adjustments to Reconcile Net Income to Net		
Cash Flows from Operating Activities:		
Depreciation Expense	$500,000	
Gain on Sale of Investments	(100,000)	
Decrease in Accounts Receivable	4,000	
Increase in Inventory	(2,000)	
Increase in Accounts Payable	500	
Increase in Accrued Payroll	500	
Decrease in Income Taxes Payable	(1,000)	402,000
Net Cash Flows from Operating Activities		$902,000

In general, the rules for accounting for changes in current accounts in determining net cash flows provided by operating activities are as follows:

- A decrease in a current asset is added to Net Income.

- An increase in a current asset is deducted from Net Income.

- A decrease in a current liability is deducted from Net Income.

- An increase in a current liability is added to Net Income.

Step 2: Determining Net Cash Flows from Investing Activities

Step 2 of the four-step approach to preparing an SCF focuses on investing activities. In general, attention must be directed to noncurrent assets of the Sample Inn.

The investment account increased by $250,000. Further analysis of this account is as follows:

Investments			
12/31/X1 Balance	50,000	Sale of Investments	50,000
Purchase of Investments	300,000		
12/31/X2 Balance	300,000		

The analysis reveals both a sale of investments of $50,000 and a purchase of investments of $300,000. Thus, $300,000 of cash was used to purchase investments, which is a use of cash in the investing activities section of the SCF. However, further analysis of the sale of investments shows the journal entry to record this transaction as follows:

Cash	$150,000	
Investments		$ 50,000
Gain on Sale of Investments		100,000

The entry clearly shows a cash inflow of $150,000. Thus, this source of cash should be shown as an investing activity. Notice that the cost of investments sold ($50,000) and the gain on the sale of investments ($100,000) have no impact on net cash flow from investing activities.

There were no changes in the Land and Building accounts, as no purchases or sales were made during 20X2. Therefore, cash was not affected.

We will look next at the Equipment account. According to note 1 under Other Information, no equipment was disposed of during 20X2. Thus, the $100,000 difference must be due to purchases of equipment. The $100,000 of equipment is shown as a use of cash in determining net cash flows from investing activities.

The Sample Inn's final noncurrent account is Accumulated Depreciation, which increased by $500,000, the exact amount of depreciation expense for the year. Because depreciation does not affect cash, under the indirect method the $500,000 is added back to the accrual basis net income as discussed under Step 1. The change in no way affects investing activities of the Sample Inn.

Now that the noncurrent asset accounts of the Sample Inn have been analyzed, the Investing Activities section of the SCF reflects the following:

Net Cash Flows from Investing Activities:	
Proceeds from Sale of Investments	$ 150,000
Purchase of Investments	(300,000)
Purchase of Equipment	(100,000)
Net Cash Flows from Investing Activities	$(250,000)

Step 3: Determining Net Cash Flows from Financing Activities

To determine the net cash flows from financing activities, we must turn our attention to the noncurrent liabilities and owners' equity accounts. First, the change in the Long-Term Debt account is a decrease of $750,000. The analysis of the Long-Term Debt account is as follows:

Long-Term Debt (LTD)

		12/31/X1 Balance	4,500,000
Conversion to Common Stock	250,000		
Payment of LTD	500,000		
		12/31/X2 Balance	3,750,000

The above analysis is based on notes 2 and 4 under Other Information. Note 4 reveals that $250,000 of LTD was converted to capital stock. This is a noncash transaction and will be shown only in a supplementary schedule to the SCF. Note 2 indicates no funds were borrowed; therefore, the remaining $500,000 reduction in LTD had to be due to payment of LTD. The $500,000 payment is a cash outflow from financing activities.

The next account to be analyzed is Capital Stock. The increase for 20X2 is $250,000, which is due to the exchange of capital stock for LTD, as discussed above. According to note 4 under Other Information, there were no other Capital Stock transactions. Since this change in Capital Stock did not involve cash, it is not shown on the SCF. However, since it is a financing activity, it is shown on a supplementary schedule as mentioned previously.

The final account to be analyzed is Retained Earnings. The statement of retained earnings at the bottom of the income statement reflects the detailed changes in this account as follows:

Retained Earnings

		12/31/X1 Balance	768,000
Dividends Declared	152,000	Net Income	500,000
		12/31/X2 Balance	1,116,000

The net income has already been accounted for in the SCF as an operating activity. The declaration of $152,000 of dividends is not a cash activity by itself. For the SCF, the focus is on dividend payments, not dividend declaration. When dividends are declared, they are recorded as a reduction in Retained Earnings and as an increase in Dividends Payable, a current liability account. Therefore, to determine the amount of dividends paid during 20X2, we analyze the Dividends Payable account as follows:

Dividends Payable

		12/31/X1 Balance	10,000
Dividends Paid	147,000	Dividends Declared	152,000
		12/31/X2 Balance	15,000

Effectively, the $5,000 increase in the Dividends Payable account results in Dividends Declared during 20X2 exceeding Dividends Paid by $5,000. The $147,000 of dividends paid is shown in the SCF as a financing activity.

The Sample Inn's SCF Financing Activities section would show the following:

Net Cash Flows from Financing Activities:	
Payment of Long-Term Debt	$(500,000)
Payment of Cash Dividends	(147,000)
Net Cash Flows from Financing Activities	$(647,000)

Exhibit 8   SCF for the Sample Inn

Sample Inn		
Statement of Cash Flows		
For the Year Ended December 31, 20X2		
Net Cash Flows from Operating Activities:		
Net Income		$ 500,000
Adjustments to Reconcile Net Income to Net Cash Flows from		
Operating Activities:		
Depreciation	$ 500,000	
Gain on Sale of Investments	(100,000)	
Decrease in Accounts Receivable	4,000	
Increase in Inventory	(2,000)	
Increase in Accounts Payable	500	
Increase in Accrued Payroll	500	
Decrease in Income Taxes Payable	(1,000)	402,000
Net Cash Flows from Operating Activities		902,000
Net Cash Flows from Investing Activities:		
Sale of Investments	$ 150,000	
Purchase of Investments	(300,000)	
Purchase of Equipment	(100,000)	
Net Cash Flows from Investing Activities		(250,000)
Net Cash Flows from Financing Activities:		
Payment of Long-Term Debt	$(500,000)	
Dividends Paid	(147,000)	
Net Cash Flows from Financing Activities		(647,000)
Net Increase in Cash during 20X2		5,000
Cash at the Beginning of 20X2		5,000
Cash at the End of 20X2		$ 10,000
Supplementary Schedule of Noncash Financing and Investing Activities		
Exchange of capital stock for long-term debt		$ 250,000
Supplementary Disclosure of Cash Flow Information:		
Cash paid during the year for:		
Interest	$ 400,000	
Income taxes	$ 251,000	

Step 4: Presenting Cash Flows by Activity on the SCF

We now are ready to prepare the SCF based on the analysis in Steps 1 through 3.
The SCF for the Sample Inn is shown in Exhibit 8. The three activities show cash
flows as follows:

Operating activities provided cash	$ 902,000
Investing activities used cash	(250,000)
Financing activities used cash	(647,000)
Total	$ 5,000

The result is a bottom line of $5,000 cash inflow. The Sample Inn's operating activi-
ties provided large enough cash inflows to cover the outflows for investing
and financing.

In the preparation of the SCF, the net increase in cash of the Sample Inn per the SCF is added to the Sample Inn's Cash account at the beginning of 20X2 to equal the Cash account at the end of 20X2. The $5,000 net increase in the Cash account per the SCF equals the $5,000 increase in cash per the Sample Inn's successive balance sheets (Exhibit 6). This does not *prove* that the SCF is prepared correctly; however, if the $5,000 increase per the SCF had *not* been equal to the change per the successive balance sheets, we would know that we had improperly prepared the SCF. We would then need to locate our mistake and make the correction. Thus, this is at least a partial check on the SCF's accuracy.

Further, notice the supplementary schedule to the SCF, which shows the non-cash exchange of capital stock of $250,000 for long-term debt and the supplementary disclosure of the amounts of interest and income taxes paid during 20X2.

Interpreting the Results

The Sample Inn's SCF lends insight to the user as follows:

- While net income increased by $500,000, cash flows from operations increased by $902,000. The major differences are Depreciation Expense of $500,000 and the Gain on Sale of Investments of $100,000.

- Cash flows from operations were sufficient to allow the Sample Inn to (1) pay off LTD of $500,000, (2) pay dividends of $147,000, and (3) use $250,000 for investing purposes.

- Together with the supplementary schedule, the SCF reflects that $750,000 of debt was retired and that no additional funds were borrowed on a long-term basis.

Accounting for Other Transactions

The preparation of the SCF using the Sample Inn was reasonably straightforward. Now we turn our attention to additional situations that may be encountered and that would have to be considered in preparing the SCF.

First, consider the sale of investments for $150,000 that originally cost $200,000. The result is a $50,000 loss on the sale. On the SCF, the $50,000 loss would be added into the Cash Flows from Operating Activities section, as the $50,000 loss on sale of investments would have been subtracted on the income statement to determine net income. Also, the proceeds of $150,000 received from the sale would be reported as sale of investments of $150,000 in the Investing Activities section of the SCF.

Second, consider the current asset account Marketable Securities. This account is used for investments with an expected life of less than one year. Still, the account reflects investments, and accounting for changes in this account would be the same as that for the Investment account. Proceeds from the sale of marketable securities or the cost of the purchase of marketable securities would be reported on the Investing Activities section of the SCF. Any gain or loss on the sale of marketable securities would be included in the Operating Activities section of the SCF.

Third, consider amortization expense. Amortization expense is the write-off of an intangible asset such as franchise costs or goodwill. Like depreciation, amortization is a noncash expense subtracted to determine net income; therefore, it must be added to net income to determine the net cash flows provided by operating activities.

Fourth, consider the sale of property and equipment. Assume a hospitality firm sells a range for $500 and that the range originally cost $1,500 but had been depreciated over the years by $1,300. The gain on the sale would be $300, which is the difference between the proceeds of $500 and the net book value of $200. The gain on the sale would be reported on the income statement as an addition to income, yet the gain is *not* cash, and neither is the sale part of operations. Therefore, the gain on the sale must be subtracted from net income in the Operating Activities section of the SCF. In addition, the proceeds of $500 is an increase in cash that is included in the Investing Activities section of the SCF. If the range had been sold for only $100, a loss on the sale of $100 would have occurred. In this case, the loss on the sale of $100 would be added to net income in the Operating Activities section of the SCF and the proceeds of $100 reported in the Investing Activities section of the SCF.

Fifth, consider a firm's purchase of its own capital stock. Assume a hotel company pays $10,000 to purchase 1,000 shares of its common stock on the market. If the shares are retired, the Capital Stock account is debited. If the stock is held for future reissue, the Treasury Stock account is charged. Either way, the $10,000 expenditure would be included in the Financing Activities section of the SCF.

Sixth, consider the sale of stock. Assume a hotel sells 300 shares of $10 par value common stock for $30 per share. Both the Common Stock and Paid-In Surplus accounts will be credited. The entire proceeds received should be reported in the Financing Activities section of the SCF as "Proceeds from sale of common stock."

Finally, consider the borrowing of funds from a financial institution. Cash is received and a liability is incurred. The entire amount of cash borrowed would be shown as "Proceeds from loan" in the Financing Activities section of the SCF. As the loan was paid off, the amount paid, excluding interest expense, would be reported in the Financing Activities section. Generally, amounts due within one year of the balance sheet date are reported on the balance sheet as "Current maturities of long-term debt." This reclassification of long-term debt does *not* affect cash. Only the payment of the debt affects the cash flows. However, consider a hotel's comparative balance sheet at December 31, 20X2, which reflects the following:

	Dec. 31	
	20X1	20X2
Current Maturities of Long-Term Debt	$ 20,000	$ 20,000
Long-Term Debt (LTD)	$800,000	$900,000

The Current Maturities account is a current liability, while the LTD account is a noncurrent liability account. By definition, the amount of a current liability as of December 31, 20X1, must be paid during 20X2. If you had the above comparative information and nothing more, the analysis would reflect the payment of LTD of $20,000 and funds borrowed of $120,000 as follows:

Current Maturities—LTD		
	12/31/X1 Balance	20,000
Payment 20,000		
		–0–
	Reclassification	20,000
		20,000

LTD		
	12/31/X1 Balance	800,000
Reclassification 20,000		
		780,000
	Borrowed	120,000
		900,000

The rationale is as follows: The current maturities of LTD of $20,000 as of December 31, 20X1, *was paid* in 20X2. Remember, this was a current liability as of December 31, 20X1. Therefore, the $20,000 balance in current maturities of LTD as of December 31, 20X2, had to be a reclassification of LTD of $20,000 during 20X2. Finally, since the LTD account was reduced by $20,000 during 20X2, and the December 31, 20X2, balance was $900,000, we would assume the difference of $120,000 had to be due to the borrowing of funds on a long-term basis.

Summary

The SCF is an FASB–mandated financial statement that must be issued with other financial statements released to external users. It reflects the inflow and outflow of cash for a period of time.

The SCF must show operating, investing, and financing activities. Operating activities reflect cash flows as they relate to revenues and expenses. Investing activities relate to changes in marketable securities and noncurrent asset accounts. Commonly included in these activities are the purchase and sale of property and equipment. Financing activities relate to payments of dividends payable and long-term debt, borrowing of long-term debt, and sale of capital stock. The net sum of the three activities shown on the SCF must equal the change in the cash amount shown on the two successive balance sheets.

There are two basic approaches to preparing the SCF—the direct and indirect methods. The difference between the two approaches is reflected only in the

Operating Activities section of the SCF. The direct approach shows the direct sources of cash, such as cash receipts from sales, and direct uses of cash, such as disbursements for payroll. The indirect approach starts with net income and adjusts it to account for noncash transactions. Other adjustments for the indirect approach are the changes in current accounts related to operations. Most hospitality firms use the indirect approach because it is easier to prepare.

Key Terms

accrual basis accounting—System of reporting revenues and expenses in the period in which they are considered to have been earned or incurred, regardless of the actual time of collection or payment.

cash equivalents—Short-term, highly liquid investments such as U.S. Treasury Bills and money market accounts.

cash inflows—Cash received by the hospitality organization during the accounting period.

cash outflows—Cash disbursed by the hospitality organization during the accounting period.

direct method—With regard to the statement of cash flows, one of two methods for converting net income to net cash flow from operations. This method shows cash receipts from sales and cash disbursements for expenses and requires that each item on the income statement be converted from an accrual basis to a cash basis.

indirect method—With regard to the statement of cash flows, one of two methods for converting net income to net cash flow from operations. This method starts with net income and then adjusts for noncash items included on the income statement.

statement of cash flows (SCF)—A statement that reflects the cash inflows and outflows of a business for a period of time. It explains the change in Cash by showing the effects on cash of a business's operating, investing, and financing activities for the accounting period.

Review Questions

1. What is the major purpose of the SCF?
2. How do different users of the SCF use this statement?
3. What are the three major classifications of cash flows in the SCF?
4. What are the two alternative approaches to preparing the SCF?
5. How do the two methods of preparing the SCF differ?
6. What supplementary information must be provided when the indirect approach is used in preparing the SCF?
7. How are changes in the various current balance sheet accounts shown on an SCF that was prepared using the indirect approach?

8. Where is a $10,000 loss on the sale of an investment shown on an SCF that is prepared using the indirect approach?

9. How does the sum of the cash flows from the three major classifications on the SCF relate to the change in balance sheet accounts from two successive balance sheets?

10. How is the exchange of common stock for long-term debt shown on the SCF?

Problems ──────────────────────────────────────

Problem 1

The Westside Deli has engaged in several transactions during the year as follows:

1. Purchased a delivery van for $15,000 and paid cash.
2. Sold 100 shares of capital stock with a $5 par value per share for $10 per share.
3. Borrowed $15,000 from the local savings and loan institution on a long-term basis.
4. Paid dividends of $10,000 during the year.
5. Sold investments, with book value of $8,000, for $6,000.
6. Purchased short-term investments (stock in a Fortune 500 company) for $4,500.
7. Repurchased 50 shares of its own capital stock for $300. Stock is to be held for possible resale.
8. Paid $5,600 of long-term debt.
9. Exchanged 100 shares of capital stock for $1,000 of long-term debt owed to First Bank.
10. Purchased vacant land for $10,000 for potential expansion two years hence.

Required:
Identify how each transaction would be classified for the purpose of creating a statement of cash flows.

Problem 2

The Dobson Place purchased and sold the following pieces of equipment during 20X3:

Date	Activity	Cost	Acc. Depr.	Selling Price
Jan. 20	Purchased range	$10,000	–	–
Mar. 14	Sold delivery van	25,000	$20,000	$3,000
Jun. 6	Purchased computer	8,500	–	–
Oct. 1	Sold copier	6,000	5,500	1,000

Assume all sales and purchases involved cash.

Required:

1. Determine "gains" on the two items sold.
2. Assume these activities constitute the investing activities of the Dobson Place for 20X3. Prepare the cash flow from investing activities section of its statement of cash flows.

Problem 3

The Westland Inn had net earnings of $65,000 during 20X5. Included on its income statement for 20X5 were depreciation and amortization expenses of $150,000 and $5,000, respectively. Its current accounts on its comparative balance sheet showed the following:

	December 31	
	20X4	20X5
Cash	$10,000	$12,000
Marketable Securities	25,000	27,000
Accounts Receivable	45,000	40,000
Inventory	15,000	17,000
Prepaid Expense	10,000	8,000
Accounts Payable	25,000	30,000
Accrued Payroll	8,000	10,000
Income Taxes Payable	10,000	8,000
Current Maturities of Long-Term Debt	15,000	18,000
Dividends Payable	5,000	8,000

In addition, sales of equipment, marketable securities, and investments during 20X5 were as follows:

1. Equipment that cost $20,000 with accumulated depreciation of $12,000 was sold for $5,000.

2. Investments that cost $20,000 were sold for $25,000.

3. Marketable securities that cost $10,000 were sold for $8,000.

Required:

Prepare a schedule of cash flows from operating activities for 20X4.

Problem 4

The Staurt House (SH) has the following current accounts on its balance sheet at the end of the last two years.

	20X1	20X2
Cash	$ 60,000	$ 65,000
Accounts Receivable	120,000	100,000
Food Inventory	30,000	32,000
Total Current Assets	$210,000	$197,000
Accounts Payable	$ 40,000	$ 45,000
Accrual Wages	10,000	12,000
Total Current Liabilities	$ 50,000	$ 57,000

In addition, SH had $55,000 of net earnings for 20X2 after subtracting depreciation expense of $85,000.

Required:

Construct the cash flow from operating activities section of SH's statement of cash flows.

Problem 5

The Byrnes Chain (TBC) has undertaken a major expansion during 20X4 that will be financed with new debt and equity issues. During June 20X4, TBC sold 800,000 shares of common stock at $20 per share (net of commissions).

This sale resulted in 2,000,000 shares of common stock outstanding. A 10–year note for $5 million was signed in October 20X4 with Lansing Bank. The new cash was used to fund expansion and pay off $1.5 million on an old loan. At the end of 20X4, stockholders were paid a dividend of $.50 per share. Finally, at the end of December, Lansing Bank was paid $200,000, which included $50,000 of interest.

Required:

Prepare the cash flows from financing activities section of the firm's statement of cash flows.

Problem 6

Determine the indicated cash flows for the Broad Inn in each of the following situations:

1. During 20X3, the Broad Inn had cash sales of $800,000 and sales on account of $2,540,000. During the same year, Accounts Receivable—Hotel Guests increased by $10,000. Determine the cash received from hotel guests during 20X3.

2. During 20X3, the Broad Inn's board of directors declared cash dividends of $120,000. The Dividends Payable account was $10,000 at the beginning of the year and $15,000 at the end of the year. Determine the dividends paid by the Broad Inn during 20X3.

3. During 20X3, the Broad Inn had cost of food used of $400,000. During the year, Food Inventory increased by $8,000 and the related Suppliers Payable accounts decreased by $5,000. Determine the cash payments for food purchases during 20X3.

4. During the year, the Broad Inn's long-term debt of $1,000,000 as of January 1, 20X3, increased by $500,000 to $1,500,000 as of December 31, 20X3. Also during 20X3, $200,000 of long-term debt was converted to common stock, and $50,000 of long-term debt was reclassified as current debt. Determine the amount of cash that was borrowed and recorded as long-term debt during 20X3.

5. The Broad Inn's Income Tax Expense of 20X3 was $25,000. Its Income Taxes Payable account on the balance sheet was $4,000 at the beginning of the year and $5,000 at the end of the year. Determine the amount of income taxes paid during 20X3.

6. The Broad Inn's balance sheet at the beginning of 20X3 showed Accumulated Depreciation of $500,000 and at the end of the year the Accumulated Depreciation account totaled $600,000. During 20X3, a range that cost $10,000 was sold for $5,000, resulting in a $2,000 gain. The only other journal entry affecting the Accumulated Depreciation account was one for Depreciation Expense. Determine the amount of Depreciation Expense for 20X3.

Problem 7

The Spring Valley Resort had several transactions as shown below. In the columns to the right, describe the type of activity for each transaction and what amount (if any) would be shown on the SCF prepared according to the indirect method. (For example, the payment of utilities is not shown on the SCF because it is subtracted from sales to determine net income, which is shown on the SCF.)

Transaction				Type of Activity	Amount Shown on SCF
1.	Cash	$125,000			
	Common Stock		$100,000		
	Paid-In Capital in Excess of Par		25,000	_____	_____
2.	Cash	$ 25,000			
	Accumulated Depreciation	60,000			
	Equipment		$ 80,000		
	Gain on Sale of Equipment		5,000	_____	_____
3.	Cash	$125,000			
	Treasury Stock		$100,000		
	Paid-In Capital in Excess of Par		25,000	_____	_____
4.	Notes Payable	$ 75,000			
	Common Stock		$ 60,000		
	Paid-In Capital in Excess of Par		15,000	_____	_____
5.	Notes Payable	$100,000			
	Interest Expense	20,000			
	Cash		$120,000	_____	_____
6.	Cash	$ 10,000			
	Accounts Receivable	30,000			
	Sales		$ 40,000	_____	_____
7.	Salaries and Wages	$ 20,000			
	Cash		$ 20,000	_____	_____
8.	Cash	$ 5,000			
	Dividend Income		$ 5,000	_____	_____
9.	Cash	$ 40,000			
	Loss on Sale of Investments	$ 10,000			
	Investments		$ 50,000	_____	_____
10.	Equipment	$ 15,000			
	Notes Payable		$ 15,000	_____	_____

Problem 8

The Golden Gopher Corporation has engaged in various activities listed below:

1. Sold food on account

2. Received dividend income
3. Purchased undeveloped land
4. Opened a payroll checking account
5. Declared a cash dividend
6. Purchased food on account
7. Paid income taxes
8. Exchanged 2,000 shares of common stock for a long–term note
9. Reclassified long–term debt as current debt
10. Collected cash on a current note receivable
11. Recorded depreciation
12. Sold equipment at a gain
13. Sold common stock
14. Paid linen supplier
15. Paid interest on long–term debt

Required:

Identify each activity for SCF purposes as (1) an operating activity, (2) an investing activity, (3) a financing activity, (4) a noncash transaction, or (5) none of the above.

Problem 9

You have been hired by Lisa Idaho, a successful entrepreneur, to prepare a statement of cash flows for her two-year-old hotel, the Minney Motel. The following are copies of the condensed balance sheets and the income statement of the Minney Motel.

Minney Motel
Condensed Balance Sheets
December 31, 20X1 and 20X2

	20X1	20X2
Cash	$ 30,000	$ 40,000
Accounts Receivable	190,000	225,000
Inventory	30,000	35,000
Property and Equipment (net)	1,400,000	1,500,000
Other Assets (Preopening Expenses)	200,000	100,000
Total Assets	$1,850,000	$1,900,000
Accounts Payable	$ 140,000	$ 185,000
Wages Payable	10,000	15,000
Current Maturities—LTD	50,000	50,000
Long-Term Debt	1,000,000	950,000
Total Liabilities	1,200,000	1,200,000
Owners' Equity	650,000	700,000
Total Liabilities and Owners' Equity	$1,850,000	$1,900,000

Minney Motel
Condensed Income Statement
For the Year Ended December 31, 20X2

Sales	$2,000,000
Cost of Goods Sold	300,000
Contribution Margin	1,700,000
Undistributed Operating Expenses	1,050,000
Income before Fixed Charges	650,000
Depreciation Expense	300,000
Amortization of Preopening Expenses	100,000
Income before Tax	250,000
Income Tax	50,000
Net Income	$ 200,000

Additional information:

1. Equipment was purchased for $400,000.

2. Dividends of $150,000 were declared and paid during 20X2.

3. Long-term debt of $50,000 was paid during 20X2 and $50,000 of long-term debt was reclassified as current at the end of 20X2.

Required:

Prepare the SCF for the Minney Motel using the indirect method.

Problem 10

The condensed balance sheets and income statement of the Spartan Inn are as follows:

Spartan Inn
Condensed Balance Sheets
December 31, 20X1 and 20X2

Assets	20X1	20X2
Current Assets:		
Cash	$ 30,000	$ 40,000
Short-Term Investments	50,000	50,000
Accounts Receivable	100,000	95,000
Inventory	20,000	25,000
Total Current Assets	200,000	210,000
Investments	100,000	60,000
Property and Equipment:		
Land	500,000	500,000
Building	5,000,000	6,000,000
Equipment	1,000,000	1,000,000
Accumulated Depreciation	(1,600,000)	(2,000,000)
Net Property and Equipment	4,900,000	5,500,000
Total Assets	$ 5,200,000	$ 5,770,000

Liabilities and Owners' Equity

Current Liabilities:

Accounts Payable	$	60,000	$ 70,000
Dividends Payable		30,000	50,000
Current Portion of LTD		100,000	130,000
Total Current Liabilities		190,000	250,000
Long-Term Debt		4,200,000	4,470,000
Capital Stock		500,000	500,000
Retained Earnings		310,000	550,000
Total Liabilities and Owners' Equity		$ 5,200,000	$ 5,770,000

Condensed Income Statement
For the Year Ended December 31, 20X2

Sales	$ 6,000,000
Cost of Sales	1,000,000
Gross Profit	5,000,000
Depreciation	400,000
Other Expenses (Except Depreciation)	4,500,000
Net Operating Income	100,000
Gain on Sales of Investments	300,000
Income Taxes	110,000
Net Income	$ 290,000

Additional information:

1. Dividends declared during 20X2 totaled $50,000.

2. No investments were purchased during 20X2.

3. The current portion of long-term debt at the end of 20X2 was reclassified from non-current during 20X2.

4. No equipment or buildings were sold during 20X2.

5. Long-term debt was borrowed to partially finance the building purchase.

Required:

Prepare the Spartan Inn's SCF for 20X2 using the indirect method.

Problem 11

The operations of The McKenzie, a small lodging operation, are becoming more complex. Ms. Jo McKenzie, the owner, has asked for your help in preparing her statement of cash flows. She is able to present you with condensed balance sheets and some additional information.

The McKenzie
Condensed Balance Sheets
December 31, 20X3 and 20X4

	20X3	20X4
Cash	$ 10,000	$ 6,000
Accounts Receivable	26,500	25,500
Investments	10,000	5,000
Equipment	200,000	325,000
Accumulated Depreciation	(20,000)	(40,000)
Total Assets	$ 226,500	$ 321,500
Current Liabilities:		
Accounts Payable	$ 18,000	$ 21,000
Mortgage Payable (Current)	5,000	5,000
Dividends Payable	5,000	5,000
Noncurrent Liabilities:		
Mortgage Payable	75,000	70,000
Notes Payable	–0–	40,000
Common Stock	50,000	100,000
Retained Earnings	73,500	80,500
Total Liabilities and Owners' Equity	$ 226,500	$ 321,500

Additional information for 20X4:

1. Equipment that cost $20,000 depreciated to its salvage value of $2,000 and was sold for $8,000.
2. Common stock, purchased as a long-term investment for $5,000, was sold for $15,000.
3. Dividends declared totaled $15,000.
4. Equipment was purchased for $145,000.
5. Depreciation expense totaled $38,000.
6. Long-term debt of $5,000 was reclassified as current and $5,000 of long-term debt was paid.
7. Common stock of $50,000 was sold and long-term debt of $40,000 (note payable) was borrowed.
8. The McKenzie generated net income of $22,000.

Required:

Prepare the SCF as requested by Ms. McKenzie using the indirect method.

Challenge Problems

Problem 12

The Lakeside Hotel's sales for 20X1 totaled $5,000,000, of which 70 percent were on account. The remainder of the sales were for cash. All sales on account are recorded by debiting

Accounts Receivable and crediting the appropriate sales account. Assume that the balance of Accounts Receivable totaled $100,000 and $120,000 at the beginning and end of the year, respectively.

Required:

1. What was the total amount of cash sales?
2. What was the total amount of cash received from guests who charged their purchases during 20X1?
3. What was the total amount of cash received during 20X1 related to charge sales, regardless of when the sale occurred?

Problem 13

The Megan Café
Condensed Balance Sheets
December 31, 20X1 and 20X2

	20X1	20X2
Cash	$ 15,000	$ 20,000
Accounts Receivable	39,000	35,000
Inventory	20,000	24,000
Equipment	310,000	315,000
Accumulated Depreciation	(150,000)	(160,000)
Total Assets	$ 234,000	$ 234,000
Current Liabilities:		
Accounts Payable	$ 15,000	$ 17,000
Dividends Payable	23,000	12,000
Noncurrent Liabilities:		
Note Payable	80,000	80,000
Common Stock	100,000	110,000
Retained Earnings	16,000	15,000
Total Liabilities & Owners' Equity	$ 234,000	$ 234,000

Additional information about activities in 20X2:

1. Dividends declared during 20X2 totaled $30,000
2. The café's van, which cost $20,000, was sold at a gain of $5,000. Its net book value on the date of sale was $5,000.
3. Assume current liabilities are paid on a timely basis.
4. Net income earned totaled $29,000 for 20X2.
5. Depreciation expense for 20X2 totaled $25,000.

Required:

Prepare the statement of cash flows for 20X2.

Problem 14

The Oceanview Inn's comparative long-term debt for 20X1 and 20X2 was shown on its balance sheet as follows:

	December 31	
	20X1	20X2
Current Liabilities		
Current Portion—Mortgage Payable	$ 20,000	$ 25,000
Long-Term Liabilities		
Mortgage Payable	$1,000,000	$1,200,000
Bonds Payable	–0–	$ 500,000

Assume current liabilities are paid on a timely basis.

Required:

1. What amount of mortgage debt was paid during 20X2?
2. How much was borrowed on a long-term basis during 20X2?

Problem 15

The Valley Café's comparative balance sheet for December 31, 20X1 and 20X2 reflects both Dividends Payable and Retained Earnings. The only entries to the Retained Earnings account are net income and dividends declared. Assume the Valley Café's bills (dividends payable) are paid on a timely basis and that Dividends Payable is a current liability on its balance sheet. The comparative balance sheet shows the following:

	20X1	20X2
Dividends Payable	$10,000	$15,000
Retained Earnings	$50,000	$55,000

Required:

Determine the amount of dividends paid during 20X2 for each of the three independent situations:

1. Net income for 20X2 totaled $20,000.
2. Net income for 20X2 totaled $25,000.
3. Net income for 20X2 totaled $30,000.

Chapter 18 Outline

Analysis of Financial Statements
Horizontal Analysis
Vertical Analysis
Trend Analysis
Ratio Analysis
    Ratio Standards
    Purposes of Ratio Analysis
    Average versus Ending Value
    Classes of Ratios
Liquidity Ratios
    Current Ratio
    Acid-Test Ratio
    Operating Cash Flows to Current
        Liabilities Ratio
    Accounts Receivable Turnover
    Average Collection Period
Solvency Ratios
    Debt-Equity Ratio
    Long-Term Debt to Total Capitalization
        Ratio
    Number of Times Interest Earned Ratio
    Fixed Charge Coverage Ratio
    Operating Cash Flows to Total
        Liabilities Ratio
Activity Ratios
    Inventory Turnover
    Property and Equipment Turnover
    Asset Turnover
    Paid Occupancy Percentage and Seat
        Turnover
    Complimentary Occupancy
    Occupancy Percentage
    Average Occupancy per Room
    Multiple Occupancy
Profitability Ratios
    Profit Margin
    Operating Efficiency Ratio
    Return on Assets
    Return on Owners' Equity
    Earnings per Share
    Price Earnings Ratio
    Viewpoints Regarding Profitability
        Ratios
Operating Ratios
    Mix of Sales
    Average Daily Rate
    Revenue per Available Room
    Gross Operating Profit per Available
        Room
    Average Food Service Check
    Food Cost Percentage
    Beverage Cost Percentage
    Labor Cost Percentage
    Limitations of Ratio Analysis

Competencies

1. Describe types of numbers used in financial analysis, and distinguish between the types of financial analysis. (pp. 509–512)

2. Perform horizontal and vertical analyses of comparative balance sheets and comparative income statements. (pp. 512–515)

3. Demonstrate how to calculate trend percentages, and describe the advantages and limitations of trend analysis. (pp. 515–517)

4. Describe standards used in ratio analysis, the purposes of ratio analysis, and common classes of ratios and the general purpose of each class. (pp. 517–520)

5. Calculate common liquidity ratios and describe how creditors, owners, and managers view them. (pp. 520–524)

6. Calculate common solvency ratios and describe how creditors, owners, and managers view them. (pp. 525–528)

7. Calculate common activity ratios and describe how creditors, owners, and managers view them. (pp. 528–535)

8. Calculate common profitability ratios and describe how creditors, owners, and managers view them. (pp. 535–541)

9. Calculate common operating ratios and explain how managers use them to evaluate operational results. (pp. 541–547)

18

Analysis and Interpretation of Financial Statements

THE FINANCIAL STATEMENTS issued by hospitality establishments contain a lot of information. A good understanding of this information requires more than simply reading the reported facts. Users of financial statements must interpret the reported facts to discover aspects of the hospitality firm's financial situation that could otherwise go unnoticed. This is accomplished through various types of analysis that make significant comparisons between related facts reported on financial statements. Analysis makes the figures reported in a financial statement more meaningful, informative, and useful. In particular, analysis generates indicators for evaluating various aspects of a financial situation.

Analysis can provide users of financial statements with answers to such questions as:

1. Is there sufficient cash to meet the establishment's obligations for a given time period?

2. Are the profits of the hospitality operation reasonable?

3. Is the level of debt acceptable in comparison with the stockholders' investment?

4. Is the inventory usage adequate?

5. How do the operation's earnings compare with the market price of its stock?

6. Is the total of accounts receivable reasonable in light of credit sales?

7. Is the hospitality establishment able to service its debt?

In this chapter, we first explain the purposes of financial analysis. Then we will discuss the kinds of analysis, including vertical, horizontal, trend, and ratio analysis. The hypothetical Wonderland Lodge is used to illustrate the concepts discussed. Ratio standards are presented as well as limitations to ratio analysis.

Analysis of Financial Statements

Several types of analysis can be conducted on a company's financial statements. All of these analyses rely on comparisons to enhance the value of the accounting information. For example, suppose a company's net income for 20X3 was $300,000.

By itself, this information is not very useful. However, comparing this amount to Net Income of $250,000 for 20X2, Total Assets of $2,000,000, Total Owners' Equity of $1,000,000, and the Planned Net Income of $275,000 for 20X3 results in much more useful information.

Financial analysis may be expressed as:

1. Absolute changes of an item.

2. Relative changes of an item.

3. Trend percentages.

4. Percentages of single items to a total.

5. Ratios.

The absolute change in an item may be either an increase or a decrease and simply reflects the dollar change. For example, if a hotel has $10,000 in cash at the end of 20X1 and $15,000 in cash at the end of 20X2, the absolute change is simply $5,000. Absolute changes are reflected on **comparative financial statements** such as that shown in Exhibit 1.

The relative change in an item may also be either an increase or a decrease and simply reflects the percentage change in an item. Expressed another way, the relative change is the absolute change divided by the base of comparison. Using the cash example from above, we determine the relative change as follows:

$$\text{Relative Change} = \frac{\text{Absolute Change}}{\text{Base Amount}}$$

$$= \frac{\$5,000}{\$10,000}$$

$$= .5 \text{ or } 50\%$$

A relative change is always shown as a percentage and is often referred to as a *percentage change*. Relative changes are also reflected on comparative financial statements such as that shown in Exhibit 1. The calculation of absolute or relative changes in comparative financial statements is known as **horizontal analysis.**

Trend percentages are similar to relative changes except that accountants compare several periods to the base period. Using the cash example, assume that Cash at the end of 20X3, 20X4, and 20X5 was $18,000, $20,000, and $25,000, respectively. The trend percentages would be as follows:

20X1	100%
20X2	150%
20X3	180%
20X4	200%
20X5	250%

Trend percentages are useful, as they reflect changes over time. Many hospitality companies provide ten years of summary statistics to allow analysts to compute trends.

Exhibit 1   Comparative Balance Sheets

The Wonderland Lodge
Comparative Balance Sheets
December 31, 20X4 and 20X5

Assets	(1) 20X5	(2) 20X4	(3) Dollars	(4) Percent	(5) 20X5	(6) 20X4
		December 31	Change 20X5 over 20X4		Percent of Total Assets—Dec. 31	
Current Assets:						
Cash	$ 22,500	$ 10,000	$ 12,500	125.00%	1.01%	0.46%
Marketable Securities	25,000	20,000	5,000	25.00%	1.13%	0.91%
Accounts Receivable	110,000	100,000	10,000	10.00%	4.96%	4.56%
Inventories	12,500	9,000	3,500	38.89%	0.56%	0.41%
Prepaid Expenses	8,500	10,000	(1,500)	−15.00%	0.38%	0.46%
Total Current Assets	178,500	149,000	29,500	19.80%	8.05%	6.80%
Property and Equipment:						
Land	200,000	200,000	0	0.00%	9.02%	9.13%
Buildings	1,500,000	1,500,000	0	0.00%	67.61%	68.46%
Furnishings and Equipment	800,000	600,000	200,000	33.33%	36.06%	27.38%
Less: Accumulated Depreciation	500,000	300,000	200,000	66.67%	22.54%	13.69%
Total Property and Equipment	2,000,000	2,000,000	0	0.00%	90.15%	91.28%
Other Assets	40,000	42,000	(2,000)	−4.76%	1.80%	1.92%
Total Assets	$ 2,218,500	$2,191,000	$ 27,500	1.26%	100.00%	100.00%
Liabilities and Owners' Equity						
Current Liabilities:						
Accounts Payable	$ 65,000	$ 60,000	$ 5,000	8.33%	2.93%	2.74%
Current Maturities of						
Long-Term Debt	80,000	60,000	20,000	33.33%	3.61%	2.74%
Accrued Expenses	7,000	6,000	1,000	16.67%	0.32%	0.27%
Income Tax Payable	5,000	4,500	500	11.11%	0.23%	0.21%
Total Current Liabilities	157,000	130,500	26,500	20.31%	7.08%	5.96%
Long-Term Liabilities:						
Mortgage Payable	1,300,000	1,380,000	(80,000)	−5.80%	58.60%	62.98%
Total Liabilities	1,457,000	1,510,500	(53,500)	−3.54%	65.68%	68.94%
Owners' Equity:						
Common Stock	500,000	500,000	0	0.00%	22.54%	22.82%
Retained Earnings	261,500	180,500	81,000	44.88%	11.79%	8.24%
Total Owners' Equity	761,500	680,500	81,000	11.90%	34.32%	31.06%
Total Liabilities and						
Owners' Equity	$ 2,218,500	$2,191,000	$ 27,500	1.26%	100.00%	100.00%

Financial analysis also includes the comparison of a single item to a total. For example, the comparison of each asset to Total Assets is quite useful. The comparison of each expense to Total Sales provides real insight into a company's operations. Financial statements reduced to percentages are referred to as **common-size statements,** since every element is computed as a percentage of a base. This type of analysis is called **vertical analysis.**

Finally, financial ratios are expressions of logical relationships between certain items in the financial statements. Financial ratios are computed based on items in one or two financial statements. For example, the *current ratio* compares Total Current Assets and Total Current Liabilities from a single financial statement (the balance sheet), while *accounts receivable turnover* compares Average Accounts Receivable (from the balance sheet) to Total Sales (from the income statement).

Exhibits 1 and 2 contain the comparative balance sheets and income statements for 20X4 and 20X5 for the hypothetical Wonderland Lodge, which will be used throughout this chapter to illustrate financial statement analysis. The Wonderland Lodge is a 150-room lodging enterprise with food and beverage facilities. Additional information regarding the property's operations will be provided as we progress through this chapter.

Horizontal Analysis

Horizontal analysis consists of calculating the dollar change and the relative change for two accounting periods. Exhibits 1 and 2 show these calculations in columns 3 and 4.

The dollar change is simply the difference between the 20X5 and 20X4 amounts (columns 1 and 2). When the amount for 20X5 is greater than the amount for 20X4, the dollar difference is positive; when the amount for 20X5 is less than the amount for 20X4, the dollar difference is negative. For example, in Exhibit 1, Cash was $10,000 at the end of 20X4 and $22,500 at the end of 20X5. In other words, there was a positive change of $12,500. On the other hand, Prepaid Expenses decreased by $1,500 from the end of 20X4 to the end of 20X5; the change is therefore a negative number.

In reviewing the balance sheets by focusing on columns 1 through 4, we observe the following:

1. Total Current Assets increased by $29,500 from the end of 20X4 to the end of 20X5. Column 4 reflects the relative increase of 19.8 percent. The largest changes were increases in Cash and Accounts Receivable of $12,500 and $10,000, respectively. Although these amounts are not very different in absolute terms, they constitute a 125 percent relative change in Cash but only a 10 percent relative change in Accounts Receivable. Thus, the relative change provides additional insight to these changes.

2. Total Property and Equipment did not increase, as the total at the end of each year (20X5 and 20X4) was $2,000,000. However, Furnishings and Equipment increased by $200,000 or 33.33 percent, while Accumulated Depreciation increased by $200,000 or 66.67 percent.

3. Total Current Liabilities increased by $26,500 or 20.31 percent from the end of 20X4 to the end of 20X5. The major cause was the increase of $20,000 or 33.33 percent in Current Maturities of Long-Term Debt. Even though the percentage increase in Total Current Liabilities is greater than the percentage increase in Total Current Assets, the dollar change is greater for current assets than for

Exhibit 2 Comparative Income Statements

The Wonderland Lodge
Comparative Income Statements
for the years of 20X5 and 20X4

	December 31		Change 20X5 over 20X4		Percent of Total Revenue—Dec. 31	
	(1) 20X5	(2) 20X4	(3) Dollars	(4) Percent	(5) 20X5	(6) 20X4
Total Revenue	$3,135,000	$2,900,000	$ 235,000	8.10%	100.00%	100.00%
Rooms—Revenue	$2,400,000	$2,200,000	$ 200,000	9.09%	76.56%	75.86%
Payroll & Related Expense	360,000	330,000	30,000	9.09%	11.48%	11.38%
Other Expense	192,000	176,000	16,000	9.09%	6.12%	6.07%
Department Income	1,848,000	1,694,000	154,000	9.09%	58.95%	58.41%
Food & Beverage—Revenue	630,000	600,000	30,000	5.00%	20.10%	20.69%
Cost of Sales	220,500	210,000	10,500	5.00%	7.03%	7.24%
Payroll & Related Expense	189,000	180,000	9,000	5.00%	6.03%	6.21%
Other Expense	126,000	120,000	6,000	5.00%	4.02%	4.14%
Department Income	94,500	90,000	4,500	5.00%	3.01%	3.10%
Telecommunications—Revenue	105,000	100,000	5,000	5.00%	3.35%	3.45%
Cost of Sales	63,000	60,000	3,000	5.00%	2.01%	2.07%
Payroll & Related Expense	25,000	25,000	–0–	0.00%	0.80%	0.86%
Other Expense	10,000	10,000	–0–	0.00%	0.32%	0.34%
Department Income	7,000	5,000	2,000	40.00%	0.22%	0.17%
Total Operated Department Income	1,949,500	1,789,000	160,500	8.97%	62.19%	61.69%
Undistributed Operating Expenses						
Administrative and General	240,000	232,000	8,000	3.45%	7.66%	8.00%
Marketing	130,000	116,000	14,000	12.07%	4.15%	4.00%
Property Operation and Maintenance	312,000	290,000	22,000	7.59%	9.95%	10.00%
Energy Costs	155,000	145,000	10,000	6.90%	4.94%	5.00%
Total Undistributed Operating Expenses	837,000	783,000	54,000	6.90%	26.70%	27.00%
Gross Operating Profit	1,112,500	1,006,000	106,500	10.59%	35.49%	34.69%
Rent, Property Taxes, and Insurance	210,000	180,000	30,000	16.67%	6.70%	6.21%
Interest	190,000	200,000	(10,000)	–5.00%	6.06%	6.90%
Depreciation and Amortization	202,000	202,000	–0–	0.00%	6.44%	6.97%
Income before Income Taxes	510,500	424,000	86,500	20.40%	16.28%	14.62%
Income Taxes	153,150	127,200	25,950	20.40%	4.89%	4.39%
Net Income	$ 357,350	$ 296,800	$ 60,550	20.40%	11.40%	10.23%

Note: Food and Beverage are shown together because a single manager is often responsible for both.

current liabilities. This suggests that the firm probably has the ability to pay its bills as they come due.

4. Long-term debt had decreased by $80,000 by the end of 20X5. Although this may seem like a large sum, it is only a 5.8 percent decrease, since the decrease is compared to a relatively large amount of outstanding long-term debt at the end of 20X4.

5. Finally, Total Owners' Equity increased by $81,000 or 11.9 percent, due solely to the increase in Retained Earnings. Together, both Total Assets and Total Liabilities and Owners' Equity increased by 1.26 percent. We know these increases must be the same, as Assets always must equal Liabilities plus Owners' Equity on a balance sheet.

Horizontal analysis of the Wonderland Lodge's comparative income statements is shown in columns 1 through 4 of Exhibit 2. A few comments are as follows:

1. Total Revenue increased by $235,000 or 8.1 percent from 20X4 to 20X5. Total Revenue consists of revenue from rooms, food and beverage, and telecommunications. The largest increase was $200,000 or 9.09 percent for the rooms department.

2. The operated department income increase of $160,500 is 8.97 percent above the $1,789,000 for 20X4. The largest increase in dollars was from the rooms department with $154,000 or 9.09 percent. However, the $2,000 increase for the telecommunications department was a 40 percent increase over the telecommunications department income of $5,000 for 20X4.

3. Total Undistributed Operating Expenses increased by $54,000 or 6.9 percent. The major increases were in Marketing and Property Operation and Maintenance, which were $14,000 (12.07 percent) and $22,000 (7.59 percent), respectively.

4. The major increase in fixed charges was in Rent, Property Taxes, and Insurance of $30,000 or 16.67 percent. Income before Income Taxes increased by $86,500 or 20.4 percent over the 20X4 amount.

5. Finally, Net Income increased by $60,550 or 20.4 percent. Thus, an 8.10 percent increase in Total Revenue resulted in a 20.4 percent increase in Net Income for the Wonderland Lodge during 20X5.

Vertical Analysis

Vertical analysis consists of reducing the balance sheets and income statements to percentages. Exhibits 1 and 2 for the Wonderland Lodge reflect these percentages in columns 5 and 6. For the balance sheet, Total Assets (and, of course, Total Liabilities and Owners' Equity) equals 100 percent, and each asset line item is computed as a percentage of Total Assets. Each line item of liabilities and owners' equity is computed as a percentage of Total Liabilities and Owners' Equity. For the income statement, Total Revenue is 100 percent, and each line item is computed as a percentage thereof.

Vertical analysis allows an analyst to see the change in the composition of assets, liabilities, and owners' equity on the balance sheet from year to year. Looking at Exhibit 1, we can note the following:

1. Total Current Assets increased from 6.80 to 8.05 percent of Total Assets, while Total Property and Equipment decreased from 91.28 to 90.15 percent. Since Total Assets equals 100 percent for each year, an increase in one or more categories from year to year must be offset by decreases in one or more categories. It is interesting to note that Total Property and Equipment remained constant at $2,000,000 but decreased as a percentage of Total Assets, since Total Assets increased during 20X5.

2. Total Current Liabilities increased as a percentage of Total Liabilities and Owners' Equity from 5.96 percent at the end of 20X4 to 7.08 percent at the end of 20X5. Total Liabilities decreased from 68.94 to 65.68 percent, while Total Owners' Equity increased from 31.06 to 34.32 percent.

Vertical analysis of the Wonderland Lodge's comparative income statements is shown in columns 5 and 6 of Exhibit 2. Total Revenue for each year is set at 100 percent, and each line item is calculated as a percentage thereof. Thus, even though Total Revenue increased in 20X5 by $235,000 (8.1 percent), the percentages in columns 5 and 6 are both 100 percent. That is, the percentages in columns 5 and 6 for the individual line items reflect changes as they relate to total revenues for their respective years. Note the following:

1. Rooms revenue as a percentage of Total Revenue increased only slightly, from 75.86 percent in 20X4 to 76.56 percent, even though the dollar change was $200,000.

2. Total Operated Department Income increased by $160,500, but this was only a 0.5 percent increase in comparison to Total Revenue.

3. Income before Income Taxes was 16.28 percent and 14.62 percent as a percentage of Total Revenue for 20X5 and 20X4, respectively. Net Income as a percentage of Total Revenue increased from 10.23 percent for 20X4 to 11.4 percent for 20X5.

Trend Analysis

Trend analyses are useful in analyzing financial information over several accounting periods, generally years. Trend percentages, which are used for trend analyses, are calculated as follows:

1. Select several periods of financial information.

2. Assign 100 percent to each amount for the earliest (base) period.

3. Divide the corresponding amounts for later periods for each item by the amount for the base period.

Exhibit 3   Trend Analysis

The Wonderland Lodge
Condensed Income Statements
for the years of 20X1–20X5

	20X1	20X2	20X3	20X4	20X5
Total Revenue	$ 2,000,000	$ 2,350,000	$ 2,650,000	$ 2,900,000	$ 3,135,000
Room Department—Income	$ 1,200,000	$ 1,400,000	$ 1,560,000	$ 1,694,000	$ 1,848,000
Food & Beverage Department— Income	67,000	74,000	80,000	90,000	94,500
Telecommunications Department—Income	3,500	4,000	4,500	5,000	7,000
Total Operated Department Income	1,270,500	1,478,000	1,644,500	1,789,000	1,949,500
Undistributed Operating Expenses	560,000	648,600	725,000	783,000	837,000
Fixed Charges	587,000	597,000	592,000	582,000	602,000
Income before Income Taxes	123,500	232,400	327,500	424,000	510,500
Income Taxes	30,875	65,072	98,250	127,200	153,150
Net Income	$ 92,625	$ 167,328	$ 229,250	$ 296,800	$ 357,350

Trend Percentages
for the years of 20X1–20X5

	20X1	20X2	20X3	20X4	20X5
Total Revenue	100%	118%	133%	145%	157%
Room Department—Income	100%	117%	130%	141%	154%
Food & Beverage Department— Income	100%	110%	119%	134%	141%
Telecommunications Department—Income	100%	114%	129%	143%	200%
Total Operated Department Income	100%	116%	129%	141%	153%
Undistributed Operating Expenses	100%	116%	129%	140%	149%
Fixed Charges	100%	102%	101%	99%	103%
Income before Income Taxes	100%	188%	265%	343%	413%
Income Taxes	100%	211%	318%	412%	496%
Net Income	100%	181%	248%	320%	386%

4. Generally, the result in step 3 is multiplied by 100 to yield an index number.

To illustrate the use of trend percentages in trend analysis, we will use financial information from the Wonderland Lodge's condensed income statements for the years of 20X1 through 20X5 (shown in Exhibit 3). The base year is 20X1; Total Revenue and the other nine line items for 20X1 are set at 100 percent. Total Revenue rises a little every year from 100 percent in 20X1 to 157 percent in 20X5. Since Total Operated Department Income increases a little every year to 153 percent in 20X5 and Undistributed Operating Expenses and Fixed Charges each increase to less than 153 percent, we expect Income before Income Taxes to increase. In fact, it increases significantly each year to 413 percent for 20X5. This *appears* to be due primarily to the relative constancy of fixed charges over the five-year period (reflected in trend percentages varying between 99 and 103 percent for the five-year period). Finally, Net Income increased to 386 percent by 20X5. This is a fairly dramatic increase but appears to be due primarily to the constancy of fixed charges during a time of sizable increases in several other items.

Trends are useful for analyzing financial information over several accounting periods, especially years. However, one must remember the drawbacks in calculating trends. When the base period numbers are zero or negative, the result is not meaningful. An increase in net income to $10,000 in 20X2 from $0 in 20X1 yields a result of infinity, which is not meaningful. In addition, unusually small numbers in the base year will yield large and perhaps somewhat less useful results. For example, assume a firm has net income of $10, $10,000, $12,000, and $15,000 over a four-year period. Since the first year's net income of $10 is the base figure, the percentages for 20X2 through 20X4 would be 100,000 percent, 120,000 percent, and 150,000 percent.

Ratio Analysis

As stated earlier, financial ratios are expressions of logical relationships between certain items in one or two financial statements. **Ratio analysis** is used to evaluate the favorableness or unfavorableness of various financial conditions.

However, a computed ratio is not inherently good or bad, acceptable or unacceptable, reasonable or unreasonable. By itself, a ratio is neutral and simply expresses numerical relationships between related figures. To be useful as indicators or measurements of the success or well-being of a hospitality operation, the computed ratios must be compared with some standard. Only then will the ratios become meaningful and provide users of financial statements with a basis for evaluating the financial conditions.

Ratio Standards

There are basically three different standards that are used to evaluate the ratios computed for a given operation for a given period. Many ratios can be compared to corresponding ratios calculated for the prior period in order to discover any significant changes. For example, the occupancy percentage (discussed later in this chapter) for the current year may be compared to the occupancy percentage of the prior year in order to determine whether the lodging operation is selling more of its available rooms this year. This comparison may be useful in evaluating the effectiveness of the firm's current marketing plans.

Industry averages provide another useful standard against which to evaluate ratios. After calculating the return on investment (discussed later in this chapter) for a given firm, investors may want to compare this with the average return for similar firms in their particular industry segment. This may give investors an indication of the ability of the firm's management to effectively use resources to generate profits for the owners in comparison to other operations in the industry. In addition, managers may want to compare the occupancy percentage or food cost percentage for their own operation to industry averages in order to evaluate their abilities to compete with other operations in their industry segment. Published sources of average industry ratios are readily available.

While ratios can be compared to results of a prior period and also to industry averages, ratios are best compared against planned ratio goals. For example, to control the cost of labor more effectively, management may project a goal for the current year's labor cost percentage (discussed later in this chapter) that is slightly lower than the previous year's levels. The expectation of a lower labor cost percentage may reflect management's efforts to improve scheduling procedures and other factors related to the cost of labor. By comparing the actual labor cost percentage with the planned goal, management is able to assess the success of its efforts to control labor cost.

Different evaluations may result from comparing ratios to these different standards. For example, a food cost of 33 percent for the current period may compare favorably with the prior year's ratio of 34 percent and with an industry average of 36 percent, but may compare unfavorably to the operation's planned goal of 32 percent. Therefore, care must be taken when evaluating the results of operations with ratio analysis.

Purposes of Ratio Analysis

Managers, creditors (including lenders), and investors often have different purposes in using ratio analysis to evaluate the information reported in financial statements.

Ratios help managers monitor the operating performance of their operations and help them evaluate their success in meeting a variety of goals. By tracking a limited number of ratios, hospitality managers are able to maintain a fairly accurate perception of the effectiveness and efficiency of their operations. In a food service operation, most managers compute food cost percentage and labor cost percentage in order to monitor the two largest expenses of their operations. In lodging operations, occupancy percentage is one of the key ratios that managers use on a daily basis. Hospitality establishments often use ratios to express operational goals. For example, management may establish ratio goals as follows:

- Maintain a 1.25 to 1 current ratio.
- Do not exceed a debt-equity ratio of 1 to 1.
- Maintain return on owner's equity of 15 percent.
- Maintain fixed asset turnover of 1.2.

These ratios and many more will be fully explained later in this chapter. The point here is to note that ratios are particularly useful to managers as indicators of how well goals are being achieved. When actual results fall short of goals, ratios help indicate where a problem may be. In the food cost percentage example presented earlier (in which an actual ratio of 33 percent compared unfavorably with the planned 32 percent), additional research would be required to determine the cause(s) of the 1 percent variation. This 1 percent difference may be due to cost differences, sales mix differences, or a combination of the two. Only additional analysis will determine the actual cause(s). Ratio analysis can contribute significant information to such an investigation.

Creditors use ratio analysis to evaluate the solvency of hospitality operations and to assess the riskiness of future loans. For example, the relationship of Current Assets to Current Liabilities, referred to as the *current ratio* (discussed later in this chapter), may indicate an establishment's ability to pay its upcoming bills. In addition, creditors sometimes use ratios to express requirements for hospitality operations as part of the conditions set forth for certain financial arrangements. For example, as a condition of a loan, a creditor may require an operation to maintain a current ratio of 2 to 1.

Investors and potential investors use ratios to evaluate the performance of a hospitality operation as they consider their investment options. For example, the dividend payout ratio (dividends paid divided by earnings) indicates the percentage of earnings paid out by the establishment. Potential investors primarily interested in stock growth may shy away from investing in properties that pay out large dividends.

Ratios are used to communicate financial performance. Different ratios communicate different results. Individually, ratios reveal only part of the overall financial condition of an operation. However, collectively, ratios are able to communicate a great deal of information that may not be immediately apparent from simply reading the figures reported in financial statements.

Average versus Ending Value

When computing financial ratios for the Wonderland Lodge, figures will be used from the balance sheet, the income statement, and the statement of cash flows. Recall that the balance sheet is a stock statement and reflects figures at a point in time, while the other two statements are flow statements showing activity over a period of time.

There can be significant differences between balance sheet figures from year to year; therefore, a ratio that draws figures from both the balance sheet and one of the two flow statements must include an average for the figures from the balance sheet. For example, return on assets (ROA) is computed as follows:

$$\text{ROA} = \frac{\text{Net Income}}{\textit{Average Total Assets}}$$

When the current ratio is computed, the result is meant to reflect a point in time, so the relevant figures would be the numbers for the balance sheet at the end of the year as follows:

$$\text{Current Ratio} = \frac{\text{Current Assets}}{\text{Current Liabilities}}$$

In this case, both numbers were taken from the balance sheet.

If companies are relatively stable, meaning that account balances are barely changing, the difference between average and ending values is probably insignificant. Using averages as discussed above will result in "correct" answers and therefore the significance of the numbers need not be questioned.

Classes of Ratios

Ratios are generally classified by the type of information which they provide. Five common ratio groupings are as follows:

1. Liquidity

2. Solvency

3. Activity

4. Profitability

5. Operating

Liquidity ratios reveal the ability of a hospitality establishment to meet its short-term obligations. **Solvency ratios**, on the other hand, measure the extent to which the enterprise has been financed by debt and is able to meet its long-term obligations. **Activity ratios** reflect management's ability to use the firm's assets, while several **profitability ratios** show management's overall effectiveness as measured by returns on sales and investments. Finally, **operating ratios** assist in the analysis of hospitality establishment operations.

Knowing the meaning of a ratio and how it is used is always more important than knowing its classification. We will now turn to an in-depth discussion of individual ratios. For each ratio discussed, we will consider its purpose, the formula by which it is calculated, and the sources of data needed for the ratio's calculation. Exhibits 1 and 2 will be used throughout our discussion of individual ratios.

Liquidity Ratios ——————————————————————————

The ability of a hospitality establishment to meet its current obligations is important in evaluating its financial position. For example, can the Wonderland Lodge meet its current debt of $157,000 as it becomes due? Several ratios can be computed that suggest answers to this question.

Current Ratio

The most common liquidity ratio is the **current ratio**, which is the ratio of Total Current Assets to Total Current Liabilities and is expressed as a coverage of so many times. Using figures from Exhibit 1, we calculate the 20X5 current ratio for the Wonderland Lodge as follows:

$$\text{Current Ratio} = \frac{\text{Current Assets}}{\text{Current Liabilities}}$$

$$= \frac{\$178,500}{\$157,000}$$

$$= 1.14 \text{ times or } 1.14 \text{ to } 1$$

This result shows that for every $1 of current liabilities, the Wonderland Lodge has $1.14 of current assets. Thus, there is a cushion of $.14 for every dollar of current debt. Some shrinkage of inventory and receivables could occur before the Wonderland Lodge would be unable to pay its current obligations with cash from its current assets. The 20X4 current ratio for the Wonderland Lodge was also 1.14 times. Would a current ratio of 1.14 times please all interested parties?

Owners/stockholders normally prefer a low current ratio to a high one, because stockholders view investments in most current assets as less productive than investments in noncurrent assets. Since stockholders are primarily concerned with profits, they prefer a relatively low current ratio.

Creditors normally prefer a relatively high current ratio, as this provides assurance that they will receive timely payments. A subset of creditors, lenders of funds, believe adequate liquidity is so important that they often incorporate a minimum working capital requirement or a minimum current ratio into loan agreements. Violation of this loan provision could result in the lender demanding full payment of the loan.

Management is caught in the middle, trying to satisfy both owners and creditors while maintaining adequate working capital and sufficient liquidity to ensure the smooth operations of the hospitality establishment.

An extremely high current ratio may mean that Accounts Receivable is too high because of liberal credit policies or slow collections, or it may indicate that Inventory is excessive. Since ratios are indicators, management must follow through by analyzing possible contributing factors.

Acid-Test Ratio

A more stringent test of liquidity is the **acid-test ratio.** The acid-test ratio measures liquidity by considering only "quick assets"—cash and near-cash assets. Inventories and prepaid expenses are excluded from Current Assets in determining the total quick assets. In many industries, inventories are significant and their conversion to cash may take several months. The extremes appear evident in the hospitality industry. Some hospitality operations, especially quick-service restaurants, may entirely replenish their food inventory twice a week. On the other hand, some operations may replace the stock of certain alcoholic beverages only once in three months.

The difference between the current ratio and the acid-test ratio is a function of the amounts of inventory and prepaid expenses relative to Current Assets. In some operations, the difference between the current ratio and the acid-test ratio will be minor, while in others, it will be significant. Based on the relevant figures from Exhibit 1, the 20X5 acid-test ratio for the Wonderland Lodge is computed as follows:

$$\text{Acid-Test Ratio} \ = \ \frac{\text{Cash, Marketable Securities, and Accounts Receivable}}{\text{Current Liabilities}}$$

$$= \ \frac{\$157,500}{\$157,000}$$

$$= \ \underline{\underline{1.00}} \text{ times}$$

The 20X5 acid-test ratio reveals quick assets of $1.00 for every $1.00 of current liabilities. The acid-test ratio is also 1.0 for 20X4. Although the acid-test ratio was 1.0 for 20X4 and 20X5, the Wonderland Lodge was not in extremely difficult financial straits. Many hospitality establishments are able to operate efficiently and effectively with an acid-test ratio of 1.0 or less, for they have minimal amounts of both inventory and accounts receivable.

Operating Cash Flows to Current Liabilities Ratio

A fairly new ratio made possible by the statement of cash flows is the **operating cash flows to current liabilities ratio.** The operating cash flows are taken from the statement of cash flows, while Current Liabilities comes from the balance sheet. This measure of liquidity compares the cash flow from the firm's operating activities to its obligations at the balance sheet date that must be paid within twelve months. Using the relevant figures from Exhibits 1 and 4, we calculate the 20X5 operating cash flows to current liabilities ratio as follows:

$$\text{Operating Cash Flows to Current Liabilities Ratio} = \frac{\text{Operating Cash Flows}}{\text{Average Current Liabilities}}$$

$$= \frac{\$553,850}{.5(\$157,000 + \$130,500)}$$

$$= \underline{3.853} \text{ or } \underline{385.3\%}$$

The 20X5 ratio of 385.3 percent shows that the Wonderland Lodge provided $3.85 of cash flow from operations during 20X5 for each $1.00 of current debt at the end of 20X5.

Accounts Receivable Turnover

In hospitality operations that extend credit to guests, Accounts Receivable is generally the largest current asset. Therefore, in an examination of a firm's liquidity, the "quality" of its accounts receivable must be considered. The **accounts receivable turnover** measures the speed of the conversion of receivables to cash. The faster the accounts receivable are turned over, the more credibility the current and acid-test ratios have in financial analysis.

This ratio is determined by dividing Total Revenue by Average Accounts Receivable. A refinement of this ratio uses only charge sales in the numerator; however, quite often charge sales figures are unavailable to outsiders (stockholders, potential stockholders, and creditors). Regardless of whether Revenue or Charge Sales is used as the numerator, the calculation should be consistent from period to period. Average Accounts Receivable is the result of dividing the sum of the beginning-of-the-period and end-of-the-period Accounts Receivable by two. Using the relevant figures from Exhibits 1 and 2, we calculate the accounts receivable turnover of the Wonderland Lodge for 20X5 as follows:

Exhibit 4   Statement of Cash Flows

The Wonderland Lodge Statement of Cash Flows for the year of 20X5		
Net Cash Flows from Operating Activities:		
Net Income		$ 357,350
Adjustments to Reconcile Net Income to Net		
Cash Flows from Operating Activities:		
Depreciation and amortization	$ 202,000	
Increase in accounts receivable	(10,000)	
Increase in inventories	(3,500)	
Decrease in prepaid expenses	1,500	
Increase in accounts payable	5,000	
Increase in accrued expenses	1,000	
Increase in income taxes payable	500	196,500
Net Cash Flows from Operating Activities		553,850
Net Cash Flows from Investing Activities:		
Purchase of Furnishings and Equipment	$ (200,000)	
Purchase of Marketable Securities	(5,000)	
Net Cash Flows from Investing Activities		(205,000)
Net Cash Flows from Financing Activities:		
Payment of Long-Term Debt	(60,000)	
Payment of Dividends	(276,350)	
Net Cash Flows from Financing Activities		(336,350)
Net Increase in Cash during 20X5		12,500
Cash at January 1, 20X5		10,000
Cash at December 31, 20X5		$ 22,500

$$\text{Accounts Receivable Turnover} = \frac{\text{Total Revenue}}{\text{Average Accounts Receivable*}}$$

$$= \frac{\$3,135,000}{\$105,000}$$

$$= \underline{29.86 \text{ times}}$$

$$\text{*Average Accounts Receivable} = \frac{\text{Accounts Receivable at}}{\text{Beginning and End of Year}}{2}$$

$$= \frac{\$100,000 + \$110,000}{2}$$

$$= \underline{\$105,000}$$

The accounts receivable turnover of 29.86 times indicates that the total revenue for 20X5 is 29.86 times the average receivables. The accounts receivable turnover should be compared with the targeted turnover, and management would generally investigate any difference. An investigation might reveal that changes in the credit policy or collection procedures significantly contributed to the difference.

Although the accounts receivable turnover measures the overall rapidity of collections, it fails to address individual accounts. This matter is resolved by preparing an aging of accounts receivable, which reflects the status of each account. In an aging schedule, each account is broken down to the period when the charges originated. Like credit sales, this information is generally available only to management.

Average Collection Period

A variation of the accounts receivable turnover is the **average collection period,** which is calculated by dividing the accounts receivable turnover into 365 (the number of days in a year). This conversion simply translates the turnover into a more understandable result. For the Wonderland Lodge, the average collection period for 20X5 is as follows:

$$\text{Average Collection Period} = \frac{365}{\text{Accounts Receivable Turnover}}$$

$$= \frac{365}{29.86}$$

$$= \underline{\underline{12}} \text{ days}$$

This means that the Wonderland Lodge was collecting all its accounts receivable on an average of every 12 days throughout 20X5.

Generally, the time allowed for average payments should not exceed the terms of sale by more than 7 to 10 days. Therefore, if the terms of sale are $n/30$ (entire amount is due in 30 days), the maximum allowable average collection period is 37 to 40 days.

The above discussion assumes that all sales are credit sales. However, many hospitality operations have both cash and credit sales. Therefore, the mix of cash and credit sales must be considered when the accounts receivable turnover ratio uses revenue rather than credit sales in the numerator. This is accomplished by allowing for cash sales. For example, if sales are 50 percent cash and 50 percent credit, then the maximum allowable average collection period should be adjusted. An adjusted maximum allowable average collection period is calculated by multiplying the maximum allowable average collection period by credit sales as a percentage of total sales.

In the previous example of a maximum allowable collection period of 37 to 40 days and 50 percent credit sales, the adjusted maximum allowable average collection period is 18.5 to 20 days (37 to 40 days × 5). Generally, only management can make this adjustment because other interested parties do not know the mix of sales.

Exhibit 5   Return on Equity

	High Debt/ Low Equity	High Equity/ Low Debt
Debt	$80	$20
Equity	$20	$80
EBIT	$50	$50
Interest—15%	− 12*	− 3**
Income before Taxes	38	47
Income Taxes	− 15.20	− 18.80
Net Income	$22.80	$28.20

Return per $1 of equity:

$$\frac{\text{Net Income}}{\text{Equity}} = \frac{22.80}{20} = \$1.14 \qquad \frac{28.20}{80} = \$.35$$

*Debt × Interest Rate = Interest Expense
 $80 × .15 = $12
**$20 × .15 = $3

Solvency Ratios

Solvency ratios measure the degree of debt financing used by a hospitality enterprise and are partial indicators of the establishment's ability to meet its long-term debt obligations. These ratios reveal the equity cushion that is available to absorb any operating losses. Primary users of these ratios are outsiders, especially lenders, who generally prefer less risk to more risk. High solvency ratios show an operation's financial ability to weather financial storms.

Owners like to use debt to increase their **leverage,** which is the use of debt in place of equity dollars to increase the return on the equity dollars already invested. Leverage is used when the return on the investment exceeds the cost of the debt used to finance the investment. When using debt to increase their leverage, owners are, in essence, transferring part of their risk to creditors.

As a further explanation of the concept of leverage, let us consider the following example. Assume that Total Assets of a certain lodging facility is $100, Earnings before Interest and Taxes (EBIT) is $50, and Interest is 15 percent of debt. Further assume that two possible combinations of debt and equity are $80 of debt and $20 of equity, and the reverse ($80 of equity and $20 of debt). Also assume a tax rate of 40 percent. The return on equity for each of the two combinations is calculated in Exhibit 5.

The calculations in Exhibit 5 reveal that each $1 invested by stockholders in the high debt/low equity combination earns $1.14, while every $1 invested by stockholders in the low debt/high equity combination earns only $.35.

This class of ratios includes three groups—those based on balance sheet information, those based on income statement information, and one based on information on the balance sheet and the SCF.

Debt-Equity Ratio

The **debt-equity ratio,** one of the most common solvency ratios, compares the hospitality firm's debt to its net worth (owners' equity). The debt-equity ratio indicates the establishment's ability to withstand adversity and meet its long-term debt obligations. Figures from Exhibit 1 can be used to calculate the Wonderland Lodge's debt-equity ratio for 20X5:

$$\text{Debt-Equity Ratio} = \frac{\text{Total Liabilities}}{\text{Total Owners' Equity}}$$

$$= \frac{\$1,457,000}{\$761,500}$$

$$= \underline{\underline{1.91 \text{ to } 1}}$$

The Wonderland Lodge's debt-equity ratio of 1.91 to 1 at the end of 20X5 indicates that for each $1 of owners' net worth, the Wonderland Lodge owed creditors $1.91.

Long-Term Debt to Total Capitalization Ratio

Another solvency ratio is the calculation of Long-Term Debt as a percentage of the sum of Long-Term Debt and Owners' Equity, commonly called *total capitalization.* This ratio is similar to the debt-equity ratio except that current liabilities are excluded from the numerator, and long-term debt is added to the denominator of the debt-equity ratio. Current liabilities are excluded because current assets are normally adequate to cover them, which means they are not a long-term concern. Figures from Exhibit 1 can be used to calculate the 20X5 **long-term debt to total capitalization ratio** for the Wonderland Lodge:

$$\frac{\text{Long-Term Debt to Total}}{\text{Capitalization Ratio}} = \frac{\text{Long-Term Debt}}{\text{Long-Term Debt and Owners' Equity}}$$

$$= \frac{\$1,300,000}{\$2,061,500}$$

$$= \underline{\underline{63.06\%}}$$

Long-Term Debt of the Wonderland Lodge at the end of 20X5 is 63.06 percent of its total capitalization.

Number of Times Interest Earned Ratio

The **number of times interest earned ratio** is based on financial figures from the income statement and expresses the number of times interest expense can be covered. The greater the number of times interest is earned, the greater the safety afforded the creditors. Since interest is subtracted to determine Taxable Income, Income Taxes is added to Net Income and Interest Expense to yield Earnings before Interest and Taxes (EBIT), the numerator of the ratio, while Interest Expense is the denominator. Figures from Exhibit 2 can be used to calculate the 20X5 number of times interest earned ratio for the Wonderland Lodge:

$$\text{Number of Times Interest Earned Ratio} = \frac{\text{EBIT}}{\text{Interest Expense}}$$

$$= \frac{\$700,500}{\$190,000}$$

$$= 3.69 \text{ times}$$

The result of 3.69 times shows that the Wonderland Lodge could cover its interest expense by over three times. In general, a number of times interest earned ratio of greater than four reflects a sufficient amount of earnings for a hospitality enterprise to cover the interest expense of its existing debt. Thus, Wonderland Lodge's management may desire to give some attention to this area.

The number of times interest earned ratio fails to consider fixed obligations other than interest expense. Many hospitality firms have long-term leases that require periodic payments similar to interest. This limitation of the number of times interest earned ratio is overcome by the fixed charge coverage ratio.

Fixed Charge Coverage Ratio

The **fixed charge coverage ratio** is a variation of the number of times interest earned ratio and considers leases as well as interest expense. Hospitality establishments that have obtained the use of property and equipment through leases may find the fixed charge coverage ratio to be more useful than the number of times interest earned ratio. This ratio is calculated the same as the number of times interest earned ratio except that Lease Expense (Rent Expense) is added to both the numerator and the denominator of the equation.

Using figures from Exhibit 2 and assuming that Rent Expense for 20X5 is $50,000, we can calculate the 20X5 fixed charge coverage ratio for the Wonderland Lodge as follows:

$$\text{Fixed Charge Coverage Ratio} = \frac{\text{EBIT} + \text{Lease Expense}}{\text{Interest Expense and Lease Expense}}$$

$$= \frac{\$700,500 + \$50,000}{\$190,000 + \$50,000}$$

$$= 3.13 \text{ times}$$

The result indicates that earnings prior to lease expense, interest expense, and income taxes cover lease and interest expense 3.13 times.

Operating Cash Flows to Total Liabilities Ratio

The final solvency ratio presented here uses figures from both the statement of cash flows and the balance sheet by comparing operating cash flows to average total liabilities. Both the debt-equity and long-term debt to total capitalization ratios are based on static numbers from the balance sheet. The **operating cash flows to total liabilities ratio** overcomes the deficiency of using debt at a point in time by considering cash flow for a period of time.

Figures from Exhibits 1 and 4 are used to calculate the 20X5 operating cash flows to total liabilities ratio for the Wonderland Lodge as follows:

$$\begin{array}{ll} \text{Operating Cash Flows to} \\ \text{Total Liabilities Ratio} \end{array} = \frac{\text{Operating Cash Flows}}{\text{Average Total Liabilities}}$$

$$= \frac{\$553,850}{.5(\$1,457,000\ +\ \$1,510,500)}$$

$$= \underline{\underline{.373}}\ \text{or}\ \underline{\underline{37.3\%}}$$

This means the Wonderland Lodge's operating cash flows for 20X5 were $.373 for each $1 of debt at the end of 20X5.

Activity Ratios

Activity ratios measure management's effectiveness in using its resources. Management is entrusted with inventory and fixed assets (and other resources) to generate earnings for owners while providing products and services to guests. Since the fixed assets of most lodging facilities constitute a large portion of the operation's total assets, it is essential to use these resources effectively. Although Inventory is generally not a significant portion of Total Assets, management must adequately control it in order to minimize the cost of sales.

Inventory Turnover

The **inventory turnover** shows how quickly the inventory is being used. All things being the same, generally the quicker the inventory turnover the better, because inventory can be expensive to maintain. Maintenance costs include those for storage space, freezers, insurance, personnel expense, recordkeeping, and, of course, the opportunity cost of the funds invested in inventory. Inventories held by hospitality operations are highly susceptible to theft and must be carefully controlled.

Inventory turnovers should generally be calculated separately for food supplies and for beverages. Some food service operations will calculate several beverage turnovers based on the types of beverages available.

Exhibit 6 Condensed Food and Beverage Department Statement

Condensed Food and Beverage Department Statement
The Wonderland Lodge
for the year of 20X5

	Food	Beverage
Revenue	$450,000	$180,000
Cost of Sales:		
Beginning Inventory	6,000	3,000
Purchases	180,000	46,000
Less: Ending Inventory	8,500	4,000
Cost of Goods Used	177,500	45,000
Less: Employee Meals	2,000	–0–
Cost of Goods Sold	175,500	45,000
Gross Profit	274,500	135,000
Payroll and Related Expenses	144,000	45,000
Other Expenses	85,000	41,000
Total Expenses	229,000	86,000
Department Income	$ 45,500	$ 49,000

Exhibit 6 is a condensed food and beverage department statement of the Wonderland Lodge with food and beverage operations for 20X5 shown separately. Figures from this statement will be used to illustrate the food and beverage turnover ratios.

The 20X5 food inventory turnover ratio for the Wonderland Lodge is calculated as follows:

$$\text{Food Inventory Turnover} = \frac{\text{Cost of Food Used}}{\text{Average Food Inventory*}}$$

$$= \frac{\$177,500}{\$7,250}$$

$$= 24.5 \text{ times}$$

$$\text{*Average Food Inventory} = \frac{\text{Beginning and Ending Inventories}}{2}$$

$$= \frac{\$6,000 + \$8,500}{2}$$

$$= \$7,250$$

The food inventory turned over 24.5 times during 20X5, or approximately twice per month. The speed of food inventory turnover generally depends on the type of food service operation. A quick-service restaurant generally has a much faster food turnover (possibly more than 200 times a year) than does a fine dining establishment. A norm used in the hotel industry for hotels that may have several different types of restaurants and banquets calls for food inventory to turn over four times per month.

Although a high food inventory turnover is desired because it means that the establishment is able to operate with a relatively small investment in inventory, too high a turnover may indicate possible stockout problems. Failure to provide desired food items to guests may result not only in disappointed guests, but also negative goodwill if this problem persists. Too low an inventory turnover suggests that food is overstocked. In addition to the costs to maintain inventory previously mentioned, the cost of spoilage may become a problem.

Another way to view inventory is to calculate the **inventory holding period.** This is accomplished by dividing the days in the year (365) by the inventory turnover. The food inventory holding period for the Wonderland Lodge is 14.9 days:

$$\text{Food Inventory Holding Period} = \frac{365}{24.5}$$

$$= \underline{\underline{14.9}} \text{ days}$$

Using figures from Exhibit 6, we can calculate the 20X5 beverage turnover ratio for the Wonderland Lodge as follows:

$$\text{Beverage Turnover Ratio} = \frac{\text{Cost of Beverages Used}}{\text{Average Beverage Inventory*}}$$

$$= \frac{\$45,000}{\$3,500}$$

$$= \underline{\underline{12.86}} \text{ times}$$

$$\text{*Average Beverage Inventory} = \frac{\text{Beginning and Ending Inventories}}{2}$$

$$= \frac{\$3,000 + \$4,000}{2}$$

$$= \underline{\underline{\$3,500}}$$

The beverage turnover of 12.86 times means that the average beverage inventory of $3,500 required restocking approximately every 28 days (365 days/year ÷ 12.86). Not all beverage items are sold evenly, so some items would have to be restocked more frequently. A norm used in the hotel industry for hotels that have several different types of lounges and banquets calls for beverage inventory to turn over 1.25 times per month or 15 times per year.

Property and Equipment Turnover

The **property and equipment turnover** is determined by dividing the average total of Property and Equipment into Total Revenue for the period. A more precise measurement would be to use only revenues related to property and equipment usage in the numerator. However, revenue by source is not available to many financial analysts, so Total Revenue is generally used.

This ratio measures management's effectiveness in using property and equipment. A high turnover suggests the hospitality enterprise is using its property and equipment effectively to generate revenue, while a low turnover ratio suggests the establishment is not making effective use of its property and equipment and should consider disposing of part of them.

A limitation of this ratio is that it places a premium on using older (depreciated) property and equipment, since their book value is low. Furthermore, this ratio is affected by the depreciation method employed by the hospitality operation. For example, an operation using an accelerated method of depreciation will show a higher turnover than an operation using the straight-line depreciation method, all other factors being the same.

Using figures from Exhibits 1 and 2, we calculate the 20X5 property and equipment turnover ratio for the Wonderland Lodge as follows:

$$\text{Property and Equipment Turnover} = \frac{\text{Total Revenue}}{\text{Average Property and Equipment}^*}$$

$$= \frac{\$3,135,000}{\$2,000,000}$$

$$= \underline{\underline{1.57 \text{ times}}}$$

$$^*\text{Average Property and Equipment} = \frac{\text{Total Property and Equipment at Beginning and End of Year}}{2}$$

$$= \frac{\$2,000,000 \ + \ \$2,000,000}{2}$$

$$= \underline{\underline{\$2,000,000}}$$

The property and equipment turnover of 1.57 times reveals that Total Revenue was 1.57 times the average total property and equipment.

Asset Turnover

Another ratio to measure the efficiency of management's use of assets is the **asset turnover.** It is calculated by dividing Total Revenue by Average Total Assets. The two previous ratios presented, inventory turnover and property and equipment turnover, concerned a large percentage of the total assets. The asset turnover examines the use of total assets in relation to Total Revenues. Limitations of the property and equipment ratio are also inherent in this ratio to the extent that property and equipment make up Total Assets. For most hospitality establishments, especially lodging businesses, property and equipment constitute the majority of the operation's total assets.

Using figures from Exhibits 1 and 2, we can calculate the 20X5 asset turnover for the Wonderland Lodge as follows:

$$\text{Asset Turnover Ratio} = \frac{\text{Total Revenues}}{\text{Average Total Assets}^*}$$

$$= \frac{\$3,135,000}{\$2,204,750}$$

$$= \underline{\underline{1.42 \text{ times}}}$$

$$^*\text{Average Total Assets} = \frac{\text{Total Assets at Beginning and End of Year}}{2}$$

$$= \frac{\$2,218,500 + \$2,191,000}{2}$$

$$= \underline{\underline{\$2,204,750}}$$

The asset turnover of 1.42 times indicates that each $1 of assets generated $1.42 of revenue in 20X5.

Both the property and equipment turnover and the asset turnover ratios are relatively low for most hospitality segments, especially for hotels and motels. The relatively low ratio is due to the hospitality industry's high dependence on property and equipment and its inability to quickly increase output to meet maximum demand. It is common for many hotels and motels to turn away customers four nights a week due to excessive demand, and operate at an extremely low level of output (less than 50 percent) the three remaining nights.

Four additional measures of management's ability to use available assets efficiently are paid occupancy percentage (or seat turnover), complimentary occupancy, average occupancy per room, and multiple occupancy percentage. Although these ratios are not based on financial information, they are viewed as excellent measures of management's effectiveness in selling space, whether it be rooms in a lodging facility or seats in a food service establishment.

Paid Occupancy Percentage and Seat Turnover

Paid occupancy percentage is a major indicator of management's success in selling its "product." It refers to the percentage of rooms sold in relation to the number of rooms available for sale in hotels and motels. In food service operations, it is commonly referred to as **seat turnover** and is calculated by dividing the number of people served by the number of seats available. Seat turnover is commonly

Exhibit 7 Statement of Retained Earnings and Other Information

Statement of Retained Earnings
The Wonderland Lodge
for the year of 20X5

Retained Earnings—Beginning of Year	$ 180,500
Net Income	357,350
Dividends Declared	(276,500)
Retained Earnings—End of Year	$ 261,350

Other Information

Rooms Sold	43,800
Paid Guests	61,320
Rooms Occupied by Two or More People	15,400
Complimentary Rooms	200*
Average Shares of Common Stock Outstanding	100,000
Food Covers	65,000

*Assume one guest per complimentary room.

calculated by meal period. Most food service facilities experience different seat turnovers for different dining periods. The occupancy percentage for lodging facilities and the seat turnovers for food service facilities are key measures of facility utilization.

Using the "Other Information" listed in Exhibit 7, the annual paid occupancy of the Wonderland Lodge can be determined by dividing total Paid Rooms Occupied by Available Rooms for sale. If the Wonderland Lodge has 150 rooms available for sale each day, its paid occupancy percentage for 20X5 is calculated as follows:

$$\text{Paid Occupancy Percentage} = \frac{\text{Paid Rooms Occupied}}{\text{Available Rooms}^*}$$

$$= \frac{43,800}{54,750}$$

$$= \underline{\underline{80\%}}$$

$$\text{*Available Rooms} = \text{Rooms Available per Day} \times 365 \text{ Days}$$

$$= 150 \times 365$$

$$= \underline{\underline{54,750}}$$

The Wonderland Lodge's 20X5 annual paid occupancy percentage is 80 percent. This percentage does not mean that every day 80 percent of the available rooms were sold, but rather that on the average 80 percent were sold. For example, a hotel experiencing 100 percent paid occupancy Monday through Thursday and 33 percent paid occupancy Friday through Sunday would end up with a combined result of 71.29 percent.

Many factors affect paid occupancy rates in the lodging industry, such as location within an area, geographic location, seasonal factors (both weekly and yearly), rate structure, and type of lodging facility, to mention a few.

Complimentary Occupancy

Complimentary occupancy, as stated in the *USALI*, is determined by dividing the number of complimentary rooms for a period by the number of rooms available. Using figures from the "Other Information" section of Exhibit 7, we can calculate the 20X5 complimentary occupancy for the Wonderland Lodge as follows:

$$\text{Complimentary Occupancy} = \frac{\text{Complimentary Rooms}}{\text{Rooms Available}}$$

$$= \frac{200}{54,750}$$

$$= \underline{\underline{0.37\%}}$$

Occupancy Percentage

In the tenth edition of the *USALI*, **occupancy percentage** is defined as rooms occupied as a percentage of rooms available. In essence, this combines the paid occupancy and complimentary occupancy percentages.

$$\text{Occupancy Percentage} = \frac{\text{Rooms Occupied}}{\text{Rooms Available}}$$

The Wonderland Lodge's 20X5 occupancy percentage is determined as follows:

$$\text{Occupancy Percentage} = \frac{44,000}{54,750}$$

$$= \underline{\underline{80.37\%}}$$

Given the paid occupancy and complimentary occupancy discussed above, the same result could have been achieved by adding the two percentages of 80 percent and 0.37 percent to equal 80.37 percent.

Average Occupancy per Room

Another ratio to measure management's ability to use lodging facilities is the **average occupancy per room.** This ratio is the result of dividing the number of guests by the number of rooms occupied. Generally, as the average occupancy per room increases, the room rate also increases.

Using figures from the "Other Information" section of Exhibit 7, the 20X5 average occupancy per room for the Wonderland Lodge can be calculated as follows:

$$\text{Average Occupancy per Room} = \frac{\text{Number of Guests}}{\text{Number of Rooms Occupied by Guests}}$$

$$= \frac{61,320}{44,000}$$

$$= \underline{\underline{1.39}} \text{ guests}$$

The Wonderland Lodge's 20X5 average occupancy per room was 1.39 guests. The average occupancy per room is generally highest for resort properties, where it can reach levels in excess of two guests per room, and lowest for transient lodging facilities.

Multiple Occupancy

Another ratio used to measure multiple occupancy of rooms is **multiple occupancy,** sometimes less accurately called **double occupancy.** This ratio is similar to the average occupancy per room and is determined by dividing the number of rooms occupied by more than one guest by the number of rooms occupied by guests.

Using figures from the "Other Information" section of Exhibit 7, we calculate the multiple occupancy of the Wonderland Lodge for 20X5 as follows:

$$\text{Multiple Occupancy} = \frac{\text{Rooms Occupied by Two or More People}}{\text{Rooms Occupied by Guests}}$$

$$= \frac{15,400}{44,000}$$

$$= \underline{\underline{35\%}}$$

The multiple occupancy ratio for the Wonderland Lodge during 20X5 indicates that 35 percent of the rooms sold were occupied by more than one guest.

Profitability Ratios

Profitability ratios reflect the results of all areas of management's responsibilities. All information conveyed by liquidity, solvency, and activity ratios affect the profitability of the hospitality enterprise. The primary purpose of most hospitality operations is the generation of profit. Owners invest for the purpose of increasing their wealth through dividends and through increases in the price of capital stock. Both dividends and stock price are highly dependent upon the profits generated by the operation. Creditors, especially lenders, provide resources for hospitality enterprises to use in the provision of services. Generally, future profits are required

Company Info

Company Name:

Industries:

| All |
| Agriculture |
| Apparel |
| Banking |
| Broadcasting |

(To select multiple industries, hold down the CTRL key)

Price Data

	Minimum	Maximum
Price		
Price 12 Month Low		
Price 12 Month High		
Percent Below 12 Month High		
Price 4 Week Change %		
Price 13 Week Change %		
Price 26 Week Change %		
Price 52 Week Change %		

Risk Data

	Minimum	Maximum
Beta		
Current Ratio		
Debt to Equity Ratio		
Short Interest Ratio		
Insider Shares Purchased		
% Insider Ownership		
% Institutional Ownership		

Many of the ratios discussed in this chapter can help hospitality executives choose investment vehicles. Stockfinder Pro (by Stockpoint.com at www.stockpoint.com/ neuralsearch.asp) allows Internet users to search for stocks that fit the hospitality firm's ratio criteria for investment. (Courtesy of Stockpoint.com)

to repay these lenders. Managers are also extremely interested in profits because their performance is, to a large degree, measured by the operation's bottom line. Excellent services breed goodwill, repeat customers, and other benefits that ultimately increase the operation's profitability.

The profitability ratios we are about to consider measure management's overall effectiveness as shown by return on sales (profit margin and operating efficiency ratio), return on assets, return on owners' equity, and the relationship between net income and the market price of the hospitality firm's stock (price earnings ratio).

Profit Margin

Hospitality enterprises are often evaluated in terms of their ability to generate profits on sales. **Profit margin,** a key ratio, is determined by dividing Net Income by Total Revenue. It is an overall measurement of management's ability to generate sales and control expenses, thus yielding the bottom line. Net Income is the income remaining after all expenses have been deducted, both those controllable by management and those directly related to decisions made by owner(s) or the board of directors.

Based on figures in Exhibit 2, the 20X5 profit margin of the Wonderland Lodge can be determined as follows:

$$\text{Profit Margin} = \frac{\text{Net Income}}{\text{Total Revenue}}$$

$$= \frac{\$357,350}{\$3,135,000}$$

$$= 11.4\%$$

The Wonderland Lodge's 20X5 profit margin of 11.4 percent is an increase over the profit margin of 10.2 percent of the prior year.

If the profit margin is lower than expected, then expenses and other areas should be reviewed. Poor pricing and low sales volume could be contributing to the low ratio. To identify the problem area, management should analyze both the overall profit margin and the operated departmental margins. If the operated departmental margins are satisfactory, the problem would appear to be with overhead expense.

Operating Efficiency Ratio

The **operating efficiency ratio** is a better measure of management's performance than the profit margin. This ratio is the result of dividing Gross Operating Profit by Total Revenue. Income after Undistributed Operating Expenses is the result of subtracting expenses generally controllable by management from Total Revenue. The remaining fixed charges are expenses relating to the capacity of the hospitality firm, including rent, property taxes, insurance, depreciation, and interest expense. Although these expenses are the results of decisions made by owners or boards of directors and thus are beyond the direct control of active management, management can and should review tax assessments and insurance policies and quotations and make recommendations to the owners or board of directors that can affect the facility's total profitability. In calculating the operating efficiency ratio, income taxes are also excluded, since fixed charges directly affect income taxes.

Using figures from Exhibit 2, we can calculate the 20X5 operating efficiency ratio of the Wonderland Lodge as follows:

$$\text{Operating Efficiency Ratio} = \frac{\text{Gross Operating Profit}}{\text{Total Revenue}}$$

$$= \frac{\$1,112,500}{\$3,135,000}$$

$$= \underline{\underline{35.49\%}}$$

The operating efficiency ratio shows that over $.35 of each $1 of revenue is available for fixed charges, income taxes, and profits.

The next group of profitability ratios compares profits to amounts of either assets or owners' equity. The result in each case is a percentage and is commonly called a *return.*

Return on Assets

The **return on assets (ROA)** ratio is a general indicator of the profitability of an enterprise's assets. Unlike the two preceding profitability ratios drawn only from income statement data, this ratio compares bottom-line profits to the total investment, that is, to Total Assets (listed on the balance sheet). This ratio, or a variation of it, is used by several large conglomerates to measure the performances of their subsidiary corporations operating in the hospitality industry.

Using figures from Exhibits 1 and 2, we can calculate the Wonderland Lodge's 20X5 ROA as follows:

$$\text{Return on Assets} = \frac{\text{Net Income}}{\text{Average Total Assets*}}$$

$$= \frac{\$357,350}{\$2,204,750}$$

$$= \underline{\underline{16.21\%}}$$

$$\text{*Average Total Assets} = \frac{\text{Total Assets at Beginning and End of Year}}{2}$$

$$= \frac{\$2,218,500 + \$2,191,000}{2}$$

$$= \underline{\underline{\$2,204,750}}$$

This result means that 16.21 cents of profit were generated for every $1 of Average Total Assets.

A very low ROA may result from inadequate profits or excessive assets. A very high ROA may suggest that older assets will require replacement in the near future, or that additional assets are needed to support growth in revenues. The determination of whether an ROA is low or high is usually based on industry averages and the hospitality establishment's own ROA profile that is developed over time.

ROA may also be evaluated by reviewing profit margin and asset turnovers, because when these ratios are multiplied by each other, they yield ROA:

$$\text{Profit Margin} \quad \times \quad \text{Asset Turnover} \quad = \quad \text{ROA}$$

$$\frac{\text{Net Income}}{\text{Total Revenue}} \quad \times \quad \frac{\text{Total Revenue}}{\text{Average Total Assets}} \quad = \quad \frac{\text{Net Income}}{\text{Average Total Assets}}$$

Return on Owners' Equity

A key profitability ratio is the **return on owners' equity (ROE).** The ROE ratio compares the profits of the hospitality enterprise to the owners' investment. Included in the denominator are all capital stock and retained earnings.

Using relevant figures from Exhibits 1 and 2, we calculate the 20X5 ROE for the Wonderland Lodge as follows:

$$\text{Return on Owners' Equity} = \frac{\text{Net Income}}{\text{Average Owners' Equity*}}$$

$$= \frac{\$357,350}{\$721,000}$$

$$= 49.56\%$$

$$\text{*Average Owners' Equity} = \frac{\text{Owners' Equity at Beginning and End of Year}}{2}$$

$$= \frac{\$761,500 + \$680,500}{2}$$

$$= \$721,000$$

In 20X5, for every $1 of owners' equity, 49.56 cents was earned.

To the owner, this ratio represents the end result of all management's efforts. The ROE reflects management's ability to produce for the owners.

Earnings per Share

A common profitability ratio shown on hospitality establishments' income statements issued to external users is **earnings per share (EPS).** The EPS calculation is a function of the firm's capital structure. If only common stock has been issued (that is, there is no preferred stock or convertible debt or similar dilutive securities), then EPS is determined by dividing Net Income by Average Common Shares Outstanding. When preferred stock has been issued, Preferred Dividends are first subtracted from Net Income; the result is then divided by the average number of common shares outstanding. If any dilutive securities have been issued, the EPS calculation is considerably more difficult and is beyond our scope.[1]

Based on figures from Exhibits 2 and 7, the 20X5 EPS for the Wonderland Lodge can be calculated as follows:

$$\text{Earnings per Share} = \frac{\text{Net Income}}{\text{Average Common Shares Outstanding}}$$

$$= \frac{\$357,350}{\$100,000}$$

$$= \$3.57$$

Simply stated, in 20X5 the Wonderland Lodge earned $3.57 per common share.

Increases in EPS must be viewed cautiously. For example, all other things being equal, the EPS will rise when an issuing establishment reduces the amount of common stock outstanding by purchasing its own stock (treasury stock). Further, EPS should be expected to increase as a hospitality enterprise reinvests earnings in its operations, because a larger profit can then be generated without a corresponding increase in shares outstanding.

Price Earnings Ratio

Financial analysts often use the **price earnings (PE) ratio** in presenting investment possibilities in hospitality enterprises. It is shown daily in the *Wall Street Journal* for all stocks listed on the New York and American stock exchanges. The PE ratio is computed by dividing the market price per share by the EPS.

Assume that the market price per share of the Wonderland Lodge is $20.00 at the end of 20X5. The PE ratio for the Wonderland Lodge at the end of 20X5 is calculated as follows:

$$\text{Price Earnings Ratio} = \frac{\text{Market Price per Share}}{\text{Earnings per Share}}$$

$$= \frac{\$20}{\$3.57}$$

$$= 5.60$$

The PE ratio of 5.60 indicates that if the 20X5 EPS ratio were maintained, it would take 5.60 years for earnings to equal the market price per share at the end of 20X5.

The PE ratio may vary significantly from one hospitality firm to another. Factors affecting these differences include relative risk, stability of earnings, perceived earnings trend, and perceived growth potential of the stock.

Viewpoints Regarding Profitability Ratios

Owners, creditors, and management obviously prefer high profitability ratios. Owners prefer high profitability ratios because they indicate the return the owners are receiving from their investments. Owners will be most concerned about ROE (return on common stockholders' equity if preferred stock has been issued), because ROE measures the precise return on their investments. Although other profitability measures are important to the owner, the ROE is the "bottom line" to him or her. Other profitability ratios may be relatively low and the ROE may still be excellent. For example, the profit margin could be only 2 percent, but the ROE could be 20 percent, based on the following:

Sales	$100
Net Income	$2
Owners' Equity	$10
Profit Margin	2%
ROE	20%

If the profitability ratios are not as high as other available investments with similar risks, stockholders may become dissatisfied and eventually move their funds to other investments. This move, if not checked, will result in lower stock prices and may make it more difficult for the enterprise to raise funds externally.

Creditors also prefer high, stable, or even growing profitability ratios. Although they desire stockholders to receive an excellent return (as measured by ROE), they will look more to the ROA ratio, because this ratio considers all assets, not simply claims to a portion of the assets, as does ROE. A high and growing ROA represents financial safety and indicates competent management. A high ROA also generally means high profits and cash flow, which suggests safety to the creditor and low risk to the lender.

Managers must keep both creditors and owners happy. Therefore, all profitability ratios are especially important to them. Everything else being the same, the higher the profitability ratios, the better. High ratios indicate that management is performing effectively and efficiently.

Operating Ratios

Operating ratios help management analyze the operations of a hospitality establishment. Detailed information necessary for computing these ratios is normally not available to creditors or even owners who are not actively involved in management. These ratios reflect the actual mix of sales (revenue) and make possible comparisons to sales mix objectives. Further, operating ratios relate expenses to revenues and are useful for control purposes. For example, food cost percentage is calculated and compared to the budgeted food cost percentage to evaluate the

Exhibit 8   Sales Mix

Departments	Sales	Percentage of Total
Rooms	$2,400,000	76.6%
Food	450,000	14.4
Beverage	180,000	5.7
Telecommunications	105,000	3.3
Totals	$3,135,000	100.0%

overall control of food costs. Any significant deviation is investigated to determine the cause(s) for the variation between actual results and planned goals.

There are literally hundreds of operating ratios that could be calculated. Consider the following examples:

• Departmental revenues as a percentage of Total Revenue (sales mix)

• Expenses as a percentage of Total Revenue

• Departmental expenses as a percentage of departmental revenues

• Revenues per room occupied, meal sold, and so forth

• Annual expenses per room

This section will consider only some of the most critical ratios, several relating to revenues and several relating to expenses. The revenue ratios include the mix of sales, average daily rate, revenue per available room, and average food service check. The expense ratios include food cost percentage, beverage cost percentage, and labor cost percentage.

Mix of Sales

Hospitality firms, like firms in other industries, try to generate sales as a means of producing profits. In the lodging segment of the hospitality industry, sales by the rooms department contribute more toward overhead costs and profits than the same amount of sales in other departments. In a food service operation, a given sales total can yield different contributions toward overhead and profits, depending on the sales mix. Therefore, it is essential for management to obtain the desired sales mix. To determine the sales mix, departmental revenues are totaled and percentages of the total revenue are calculated for each operated department.

Using figures from Exhibits 2 and 6, Exhibit 8 calculates the 20X5 sales mix for the Wonderland Lodge. The sales mix of a hospitality operation is best compared to the establishment's objectives as revealed in its budget. A second standard of comparison is the previous period's results. A third involves a comparison to industry averages.

An evaluation of revenue by department is accomplished by determining the amount of each department's average sale. For the rooms department, the amount of the average sale is the average room rate; for the food service department, it is the average food service check.

Average Daily Rate

A key rooms department ratio is the average room rate, usually referred to as **average daily rate (ADR).** Most hotel and motel managers calculate the ADR even though rates within a property may vary significantly from single rooms to suites, from individual guests to groups and conventions, from weekdays to weekends, and from busy seasons to slack seasons.

Using figures from Exhibits 2 and 7, we calculate the 20X5 average room rate for the Wonderland Lodge as follows:

$$\text{Average Daily Rate} = \frac{\text{Room Revenue}}{\text{Number of Rooms Sold}}$$

$$= \frac{\$2,400,000}{43,800}$$

$$= \$54.79$$

The best standard of comparison to use in evaluating an actual average room rate is the rate budgeted as the goal during the period. This average rate should also be calculated individually for each market segment (business groups, tourists, airline crews, and other segments) or by room type.

Revenue per Available Room

Paid occupancy percentage and ADR can be combined into a single ratio called **revenue per available room** or **RevPAR.**

Traditionally, many hoteliers have placed heavy reliance on paid occupancy percentage as a quick indicator of activity and possibly performance. Others have looked at the ADR as an indication of the quality their operations. However, paid occupancy percentage and average room rate by themselves are somewhat meaningless. One hotel may have a room occupancy of 80 percent and an ADR of $40, while a close competitor has a paid occupancy of 70 percent and an ADR of $60. Which hotel is in the preferable condition? RevPAR provides an answer to this question. It is calculated as follows:

$$\text{RevPAR} = \frac{\text{Room Revenue}}{\text{Available Rooms}}$$

or

$$\text{RevPAR} = \text{Paid Occupancy Percentage} \times \text{ADR}$$

Using the above example, the hotel with the 80 percent paid occupancy and the $40 ADR has a RevPAR of $32, while its competitor has a RevPAR of 70% ×

$60, or $42. Everything else being the same, hoteliers, creditors, and investors obviously prefer the hotel with the higher RevPAR. In this example, the RevPAR leads us to choose the hotel with the higher ADR, but this will not always be the case. Suppose, for example, that the second hotel in the above example had a paid occupancy of 50 percent instead of 70 percent; its RevPAR would then be $30 ($60 × 50%) and the RevPAR ratio would then favor the hotel with the higher occupancy percentage.

Based on the paid occupancy percentage and the ADR calculated earlier in this chapter, the Wonderland Lodge's RevPAR for 20X5 can be determined as follows:

$$
\begin{aligned}
\text{RevPAR} &= \$54.79 \times 80\% \\
&= \underline{\underline{\$43.83}}
\end{aligned}
$$

Alternatively, using information from Exhibit 2, we can determine RevPAR as follows:

$$
\begin{aligned}
\text{RevPAR} &= \frac{\text{Room Revenue}}{\text{Available Rooms}} \\
&= \frac{\$2,400,000}{150 \times 365} \\
&= \underline{\underline{\$43.83}}
\end{aligned}
$$

Evaluating RevPAR is an improvement over simply looking at occupancy percentage or ADR separately. Many industry executives prefer this combined statistic.

Gross Operating Profit per Available Room

Gross operating profit per available room (GOPAR) measures management's ability to produce profits by generating sales and controlling the operating expenses over which they have the most direct control. GOPAR is calculated by dividing Gross Operating Profit by the rooms available in the hotel. GOPAR is somewhat useful in relating gross operating profits, on a proportional basis, across properties in a competitive set or comparable property groups. Because GOPAR is calculated before any deduction for management fees, this ratio can be used to compare similar properties that are operated by a third-party management company with owner-operated properties. GOPAR can be calculated for the Wonderland Lodge as follows:

$$
\begin{aligned}
\text{GOPAR} &= \frac{\text{Gross Operating Profit}}{\text{Rooms Available}} \\
&= \frac{\$1,112,500}{54,750} \\
&= \underline{\underline{\$20.32}}
\end{aligned}
$$

Average Food Service Check

A key food service ratio is the **average food service check.** The ratio is determined by dividing Total Food Revenue by the number of food covers sold during the period.

Using figures from Exhibits 6 and 7, we can calculate the average food service check for 20X5 for the Wonderland Lodge as follows:

$$\text{Average Food Service Check} = \frac{\text{Total Food Revenue}}{\text{Number of Food Covers}}$$

$$= \frac{\$450,000}{65,000}$$

$$= \$6.92$$

The average food service check is best compared to the budgeted amount for 20X5. It can also be compared to industry averages.

Additional average checks should be calculated separately for beverages. Management may even desire to calculate the average check by dining area or by meal period.

Food Cost Percentage

The **food cost percentage** is a key food service ratio that compares the cost of food sold to Food Sales. Most food service managers rely heavily on this ratio for determining whether food costs are reasonable.

Based on figures from Exhibit 6, the 20X5 food cost percentage for the Wonderland Lodge is determined as follows:

$$\text{Food Cost Percentage} = \frac{\text{Cost of Food Sold}}{\text{Food Sales}}$$

$$= \frac{\$175,500}{\$450,000}$$

$$= 39\%$$

In other words, of every $1 of food sales, $.39 goes toward the cost of food sold. This is best compared to the budgeted percentage for the period. A significant difference in either direction should be investigated by management. Management should be just as concerned about a food cost percentage that is significantly lower than the budgeted goal as it is about a food cost percentage that exceeds budgeted standards. A lower food cost percentage may indicate that the quality of food served is lower than desired, or that smaller portions are being served than are specified by the standard recipes. A food cost percentage in excess of the objective may be due to poor portion control, excessive food costs, theft, waste, spoilage, and so on.

Beverage Cost Percentage

A key ratio for beverage operations is the **beverage cost percentage.** This ratio results from dividing the cost of beverages sold by Beverage Sales.

Based on figures from Exhibit 6, the 20X5 beverage cost percentage for the Wonderland Lodge is calculated as follows:

$$\text{Beverage Cost Percentage} \quad = \quad \frac{\text{Cost of Beverages Sold}}{\text{Beverage Sales}}$$

$$= \quad \frac{\$45,000}{\$180,000}$$

$$= \quad \underline{\underline{25\%}}$$

That is, for each $1 of beverage sales, $.25 is spent on the cost of beverages served. As with the food cost percentage, this ratio is best compared by management to the goal set for that period. Likewise, any significant variances must be investigated to determine the cause(s). Refinements of this ratio include beverage cost percentages by type of beverage sold and by beverage outlet.

Labor Cost Percentage

The largest expense in hotels, motels, clubs, and many restaurants is labor. Labor expense includes salaries, wages, bonuses, payroll taxes, and benefits. A general **labor cost percentage** is determined by dividing Total Labor Costs by Total Revenue. This general labor cost percentage is simply a benchmark for making broad comparisons. For control purposes, labor costs must be analyzed by department. The rooms department labor cost percentage is determined by dividing Rooms Department Labor Cost by Rooms Revenue. The food and beverage department labor cost percentage is determined by dividing Food and Beverage Department Labor Cost by Food and Beverage Revenue. Other operated department labor cost percentages are similarly determined.

Exhibit 9 uses figures from Exhibits 2 and 6 to calculate the 20X5 operated department labor cost percentages for the Wonderland Lodge. The food and beverage departments have the highest labor cost percentages at 32 percent and 25 percent, respectively. In most lodging firms, this is usually the case. The standards for these ratios are the budgeted percentages. Since labor costs are generally the largest expense, they must be tightly controlled. Management must carefully investigate any significant differences between actual and budgeted labor cost percentages.

Ratios for other expenses are usually computed as a percentage of revenue. If the expenses are operated department expenses, then the ratio is computed with the operated department revenues in the denominator and the expense in the numerator. An overhead expense ratio will consist of the overhead expense being divided by Total Revenue. For example, marketing expense percentage is determined by dividing the marketing expense by Total Revenue. Using figures for the Wonderland Lodge in 20X5 found in Exhibit 2, the marketing expense percentage

Exhibit 9   Operated Department Labor Cost Percentages

$$\text{Labor Cost Percentage} = \frac{\text{Labor Cost by Departments}}{\text{Department Revenues}}$$

Department	Total Labor Cost ÷	Total Revenue =	Labor Cost Percentage
Rooms	$ 360,000	$2,400,000	15.00%
Food	$ 144,000	$ 450,000	32.00%
Beverage	$ 45,000	$ 180,000	25.00%
Telecommunications	$ 25,000	$ 105,000	23.81%

can be calculated as 4.15 percent (marketing expense of $130,000 divided by total revenues of $3,135,000).

Limitations of Ratio Analysis

Ratios are extremely useful to owners, creditors, and management in evaluating the financial conditions and operations of hospitality establishments. However, ratios are only indicators. They do not resolve problems or even reveal exactly what the problem is. At best, when they vary significantly from budgeted standards, industry averages, or ratios for past periods, ratios only indicate that there *may be* a problem. Considerably more analysis and investigation are required.

Ratios are meaningful when they result from comparing two related numbers. Food cost percentage is meaningful because of the direct relationship between food costs and food sales. A goodwill/cash ratio is probably meaningless due to the lack of any meaningful relationship between goodwill and cash.

Ratios are most useful when compared to a standard. A food cost percentage of 32 percent is of little use until it is compared to a standard such as past performance, industry averages, or the budgeted percentages.

Ratios are often used to compare different hospitality establishments. However, many such comparisons (especially those using operating ratios) will not be meaningful if the two firms are in completely different segments of the industry. For example, comparing ratios for a luxury hotel to ratios for a quick-service restaurant would seldom serve a meaningful purpose.

In addition, if the accounting procedures used by two separate hospitality establishments differ in several areas, then a comparison of their ratios will likely show differences related to accounting procedures rather than to financial positions or operations.

Even though these limitations are present, a careful use of ratios that acknowledges their shortcomings will result in an enhanced understanding of the financial position and operations of various hospitality establishments.

Summary

Financial analysis permits investors, creditors, and operators to receive more valuable information from the financial statements than they could receive from reviewing the absolute numbers reported in the documents. Vital relationships can be monitored to determine solvency and risk, performance in comparison with other periods, and dividend payout ratios.

This chapter looked at four types of financial analysis: horizontal, vertical, trend, and ratio analyses. Horizontal analysis consists of calculating the absolute (dollar) change and the relative (percentage) change in line items for two accounting periods. Vertical analysis consists of reducing financial statement information to percentages of a whole for a given year in order to see the composition of the whole. Trend analysis is similar to horizontal analysis, except that it involves comparing several accounting periods to a single base period. Ratio analysis involves comparing related figures from one or two financial statements and expressing the relationship numerically. Most of this chapter focused on ratio analysis.

There are five major classifications of ratios: liquidity, solvency, activity, profitability, and operating. Although there is some overlap among these categories, each has a special area of concern. Exhibit 10 lists the 32 ratios presented in this chapter and the formulas for each. It is important to be familiar with the types of ratios in each category, to know what each ratio measures, and to be aware of the targets or standards against which they are compared.

For example, a number of liquidity ratios focus on the hospitality establishment's ability to cover its short-term debts. However, each person examining the establishment's financial position will have a desired performance in mind. Creditors desire high liquidity ratios because they indicate that loans will probably be repaid. Investors, on the other hand, like lower liquidity ratios, since current assets are not as profitable as long-term assets. Management reacts to these pressures by trying to please both groups.

The five ratio classifications vary in importance among the three major users of ratios. Creditors focus on solvency, profitability, and liquidity; investors and owners consider these ratios, but highlight the profitability ratios. Managers use all types of ratios, but are especially concerned with operating and activity ratios, which can be used in evaluating the results of operations.

It is important to realize that a percentage by itself is not meaningful. It is only useful when it is compared with a standard: an industry average, a ratio from a past period, or a budgeted ratio. It is the comparison with budgeted ratios that is the most useful for management. Any significant difference should be analyzed to determine its probable cause(s). Once management has fully investigated areas of concern revealed by the ratios, then corrective action can be taken to rectify any problems.

Endnotes

1. The interested student is referred to intermediate accounting texts, most of which contain a full discussion of EPS calculations in various situations.

Exhibit 10   List of Ratios

Ratio	Formula
Liquidity Ratios:	
1. Current ratio	Current Assets ÷ Current Liabilities
2. Acid-test ratio	(Cash + Marketable Securities + Notes + Accounts Receivable) ÷ Current Liabilities
3. Operating cash flows to current liabilities ratio	Operating Cash Flows ÷ Average Current Liabilities
4. Accounts receivable turnover	Revenue ÷ Average Accounts Receivable
5. Average collection period	365 ÷ Accounts Receivable Turnover
Solvency Ratios:	
6. Debt-equity ratio	Total Liabilities ÷ Total Owners' Equity
7. Long-term debt to total capitalization ratio	Long-Term Debt ÷ (Long-Term Debt + Owners Equity)
8. Number of times interest earned ratio	EBIT ÷ Interest Expense
9. Fixed charge coverage ratio	(EBIT + Lease Expense) ÷ (Interest Expense + Lease Expense)
10. Operating cash flows to total liabilities ratio	Operating Cash Flows ÷ Average Total Liabilities
Activity Ratios:	
11. Inventory turnover:	
Food inventory turnover	Cost of Food Used ÷ Average Food Inventory
Beverage inventory turnover	Cost of Beverages Used ÷ Average Beverage Inventory
12. Property and equipment turnover	Total Revenue ÷ Average Property and Equipment
13. Asset turnover ratio	Total Revenue ÷ Average Total Assets
14. Paid occupancy percentage	Paid Rooms Occupied ÷ Available Rooms
15. Complimentary occupancy percentage	Complimentary Rooms ÷ Available Rooms
16. Occupancy percentage	Rooms Occupied ÷ Available Rooms
17. Average occupancy per room	Number of Room Guests ÷ Number of Rooms Occupied
18. Multiple occupancy percentage	Rooms Occupied by More than One Person ÷ Number of Rooms Occupied

(continued)

Exhibit 10   *(continued)*

Ratio	Formula
Profitability Ratios:	
19. Profit margin	Net Income ÷ Total Revenue
20. Operating efficiency ratio	Gross Operating Profit ÷ Total Revenue
21. Return on assets	Net Income ÷ Average Total Assets
22. Return on owners' equity	Net Income ÷ Average Owners' Equity
23. Earnings per share	Net Income ÷ Average Common Shares Outstanding
24. Price earnings ratio	Market Price per Share ÷ Earnings per Share
Operating Ratios:	
25. Mix of sales	[Departmental revenues are totaled; percentages of Total Revenue are calculated for each]
26. Average daily rate	Rooms Revenue ÷ Number of Rooms Sold
27. Revenue per available room (RevPAR)	Paid Occupancy Percentage × Average Daily Rate
28. Gross operating profit per available room (GOPAR)	Gross Operating Profit ÷ Rooms Available
29. Average food service check	Total Food and Beverage Revenue ÷ Number of Food Covers
30. Food cost percentage	Cost of Food Sold ÷ Food Sales
31. Beverage cost percentage	Cost of Beverages Sold ÷ Beverage Sales
32. Labor cost percentage	Labor Cost by Department ÷ Department Revenue

Key Terms

accounts receivable turnover—A measure of the rapidity of conversion of accounts receivable into cash; revenue divided by average accounts receivable.

acid-test ratio—Ratio of total cash and near-cash current assets to total current liabilities.

activity ratios—A group of ratios that reflect management's ability to use the property's assets and resources.

asset turnover—An activity ratio; total revenues divided by average total assets.

average collection period—The average number of days it takes a hospitality operation to collect all its accounts receivable; calculated by dividing the accounts receivable turnover into 365 (days in a year).

average daily rate (ADR)—A key rooms department operating ratio; rooms revenue divided by number of rooms sold. Also called *average room rate.*

average food service check—Total food revenue divided by the number of covers for a period.

average occupancy per room—An activity ratio measuring management's ability to use lodging facilities; the number of guests divided by the number of rooms occupied.

beverage cost percentage—A ratio comparing the cost of beverages sold to beverage sales; calculated by dividing the cost of beverages sold by beverage sales.

common-size statements—Financial statements used in vertical analysis whose information has been reduced to percentages to facilitate comparisons.

comparative financial statements—The horizontal analysis of financial statements from the current and previous periods in terms of both absolute and relative variances for each line item.

complimentary occupancy—The number of complimentary rooms for a period divided by the number of rooms available.

current ratio—Ratio of total current assets to total current liabilities expressed as a coverage of so many times; calculated by dividing current assets by current liabilities.

debt-equity ratio—Compares the debt of a hospitality operation to its net worth (owners' equity) and indicates the operation's ability to withstand adversity and meet its long-term obligations; calculated by dividing total liabilities by total owners' equity.

double occupancy—The number of rooms occupied by more than one guest divided by the number of rooms occupied by guests. Sometimes called *multiple occupancy.*

earnings per share (EPS)—A ratio providing a general indicator of the profitability of a hospitality operation by comparing net income to the average number of common shares outstanding. If preferred stock has been issued, preferred dividends are subtracted from net income before calculating EPS.

fixed charge coverage ratio—A variation of the number of times interest earned ratio that considers leases as well as interest expense; the sum of lease expense and earnings before both interest and income taxes divided by the sum of interest expense and lease expense.

food cost percentage—A ratio comparing the cost of food sold to food sales; calculated by dividing the wholesale dollar amount of total sales by the retail dollar amount of total sales.

gross operating profit per available room (GOPAR)—A measurement of management's ability to produce profits; calculated by dividing gross operating profit by the number of rooms available.

horizontal analysis—Comparing financial statements for two or more accounting periods in terms of both absolute and relative variances for each line item.

inventory turnover—A ratio showing how quickly a hospitality operation's inventory is moving from storage to productive use; calculated by dividing the cost of products (e.g., food or beverages) used by the average product (e.g., food or beverages) inventory value.

inventory holding period—The number of days in the year divided by inventory turnover.

labor cost percentage—A ratio comparing the labor expense for each department to the total revenue generated by the department; total labor cost by department divided by department revenues.

leverage—The use of debt in place of equity dollars to finance operations and increase the return on the equity dollars already invested.

liquidity ratios—A group of ratios that reveal the ability of a hospitality establishment to meet its short-term obligations.

long-term debt to total capitalization ratio—A solvency ratio showing long-term debt as a percentage of the sum of long-term debt and owners' equity; long-term debt divided by the sum of long-term debt and owners' equity.

multiple occupancy—The number of rooms occupied by more than one guest divided by the number of rooms occupied by guests. Sometimes called *double occupancy.*

number of times interest earned ratio—A solvency ratio expressing the number of times interest expense can be covered; earnings before both interest and taxes divided by interest expense.

occupancy percentage—The number of rooms occupied as a percentage of rooms available.

operating cash flows to current liabilities ratio—A liquidity ratio that compares the cash flow from the firm's operating activities to its obligations at the balance sheet date that must be paid within 12 months; operating cash flows divided by average current liabilities.

operating cash flows to total liabilities ratio—A solvency ratio; operating cash flows divided by average total liabilities.

operating efficiency ratio—A measure of management's ability to generate sales and control expenses; calculated by dividing Income after Undistributed Operating Expenses by total revenue.

operating ratios—A group of ratios that assist in the analysis of hospitality establishment operations.

paid occupancy percentage—A measure of management's ability to efficiently use available assets; the number of rooms sold divided by the number of rooms available for sale.

price earnings (PE) ratio—A profitability ratio used by financial analysts when presenting investment possibilities; the market price per share divided by the earnings per share.

profit margin—An overall measure of management's ability to generate sales and control expenses; calculated by dividing net income by total revenue.

profitability ratios—A group of ratios that reflect the results of all areas of management's responsibility.

property and equipment turnover—A ratio measuring management's effectiveness in using property and equipment to generate revenue; calculated by dividing average total property and equipment into total revenue generated for the period.

ratio analysis—Comparing financial ratios in a business with standards, such as prior performance, industry averages, or planned goals, as a way of evaluating the performance and financial condition of the business.

return on assets (ROA)—A ratio providing a general indicator of the profitability of a hospitality operation by comparing net income to total investment; calculated by dividing net income by average total assets.

return on owners' equity (ROE)—A ratio providing a general indicator of the profitability of a hospitality operation by comparing net income to the owners' investment; calculated by dividing net income by average owners' equity.

revenue per available room (RevPAR)—A combination of paid occupancy percentage and average daily rate; room revenues divided by the number of available rooms or, alternatively, paid occupancy percentage times average daily rate.

seat turnover—An activity ratio measuring the rate at which people are served; the number of people served divided by the number of seats available.

solvency ratios—A group of ratios that measure the extent to which an enterprise has been financed by debt and is able to meet its long-term obligations.

trend analysis—A method of analyzing ratios over more than two time periods. Trend analysis allows management to identify and deal with emerging trends.

trend percentage—Expression of a given period's figure as a percentage of the base period's figure; used for several years' or financial periods' data in *trend analysis.*

vertical analysis—Analyzing individual financial statements by reducing financial information to percentages of a whole; that is, income statement line items are expressed as percentages of total revenue; balance sheet assets are expressed as percentages of total assets.

Review Questions

1. How does ratio analysis benefit creditors?
2. If you were investing in a hotel, which ratios would be most useful? Why?
3. How do the three user groups of ratio analysis react to the solvency ratios?

4. What is *leverage,* and why may owners want to increase it?
5. What do activity ratios highlight?
6. How is the profit margin calculated? How is it used?
7. Which standard is the most effective for comparison with ratios?
8. Of what value is the ratio of Food Sales to Total Sales to the manager of a hotel? To a creditor?
9. What is *RevPAR*? What is the reason for its increased use by managers?
10. What are the limitations of ratio analysis?

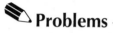 Problems

Problem 1

Steve Rannels, the founder of the Houston Hotel, wants to analyze 20X2's operations by comparing them with the 20X1 results. To help him, prepare a comparative income statement using the 20X1 and 20X2 information available.

Houston Hotel
Income Statements
For the years ending December 31, 20X1 and 20X2

	20X1	20X2
Revenues		
Rooms	$ 976,000	$ 1,041,000
Food and Beverage	604,000	626,000
Telephone	50,000	52,000
Total	1,630,000	1,719,000
Direct Expenses		
Rooms	250,000	264,000
Food and Beverage	476,000	507,000
Telephone	68,000	68,000
Total Operational Departmental Income	836,000	880,000
Undistributed Operating Expenses		
Administrative and General	195,000	206,000
Marketing	65,000	68,000
Property Operation and Maintenance	69,000	68,000
Energy Costs	101,000	102,000
Income after Undistributed Operating Expenses	406,000	436,000
Rent, Property Taxes and Insurance	200,000	201,000
Interest	55,000	52,000
Depreciation and Amortization	116,000	116,000
Income before Income Taxes	35,000	67,000
Income Taxes	7,000	17,000
Net Income	$ 28,000	$ 50,000

Note: Rearrange the income statement to conform to the *USALI* format; that is, subtract direct expenses from revenues of operated departments to show departmental incomes.

Problem 2

The Springs Hotel (TSH) has a 20 percent market share in a tri-county area of Western Colorado. Simplified income statements for TSH and the lodging industry for the tri-county area are as follows:

	000s	
	TSH	Industry
Sales	$50,000	$200,000
Cost of sales	5,000	25,000
Labor costs	15,000	64,000
Other operating costs	10,000	30,000
Fixed charges	15,000	50,000
Income before income taxes	5,000	31,000
Income taxes	1,000	6,000
Net income	$ 4,000	$ 25,000

Required:

1. Prepare common-sized income statements for both TSH and the lodging industry.
2. What areas appear to require the attention of TSH's management?

Problem 3

The following information is the Mobile Inn's balance sheet account balances as of December 31, 20X1 and 20X2. You have been hired by the owner to prepare a financial package for a bank loan, and the package is to include comparative balance sheets.

Assets	20X1	20X2
Cash	$ 16,634	$ 20,768
Accounts Receivable	16,105	11,618
Marketable Securities	10,396	10,496
Inventories	14,554	18,554
Prepaid Expenses	4,158	3,874
Land	116,435	116,435
Building	1,007,090	1,007,090
China, Glass, etc.	269,255	284,934
Accumulated Depreciation	453,263	537,849
Organization Costs	10,000	8,000
Liabilities & Owners' Equity		
Accounts Payable	23,265	20,945
Accrued Expenses	2,047	1,039
Deferred Income Taxes	8,163	7,927
Current Portion of Long-Term Debt	20,407	20,060
Long-Term Debt	553,429	533,369

Retained Earnings	192,853	149,380
Common Stock	261,200	261,200
Treasury Stock	50,000	50,000

Required:

Prepare comparative balance sheets for December 31, 20X1 and 20X2, in accordance with, USALI. Reflect both percentage and dollar differences between the two years.

Problem 4

Indicate the effects of the transactions listed below on each of the following: total current assets, working capital (current assets minus current liabilities), and current ratio. Indicate increase with "+", indicate decrease with "–", and indicate no effect or effect cannot be determined with "0." Assume an initial current ratio of greater than 1.0.

	Total Current Assets	Working Capital	Current Ratio
1. Food is sold for cash. (Assume a food cost of 40 percent.)	_____	_____	_____
2. Equipment is sold at less than its net book value.	_____	_____	_____
3. Food is sold on account. (Assume a food cost of 100 percent.)	_____	_____	_____
4. A cash dividend is paid.	_____	_____	_____
5. Accrued payroll is paid.	_____	_____	_____
6. Common stock is sold.	_____	_____	_____
7. A fully depreciated fixed asset is retired.	_____	_____	_____
8. Land is purchased with long-term notes.	_____	_____	_____
9. Utility expenses are paid (they were not previously accrued).	_____	_____	_____
10. Food is purchased on account.	_____	_____	_____

Problem 5

The Colorado Café has annual sales of $1.2 million. Its food cost percentage is 30 percent, and the average collection period is 30 days (assume a 360 day year.) Its current ratio is 1.2 and its inventory turnover ratio, based on cost of food sold, is 12.

Required:

Complete the current section of its balance sheet.

Cash	$_____	Accounts Payable	$_____
Accounts Receivable	$_____	Wages Payable	30,000
Food Inventory	$_____		
Current Assets	$_____	Current Liabilities	$200,000

Problem 6

Below is selected information from the comparative and common-size asset portion of balance sheets for the LA Grill.

	December 31 20X1	December 31 20X2	Dollar Difference	Common-Size (Dec. 31, 20X2)
Current Assets				
Cash				
House Bank	$_____	$_____	$ (10)	_____%
Demand Deposit	_____	60	_____	.6
Total Cash	_____	_____	(10)	1.0
Accounts Receivable	$ 1,241	_____	_____	14.0
Inventories	_____	_____	_____	_____
Total Current Assets	_____	1,620	201	_____
Investments	_____	_____	25	2.0
Property & Equipment (net)				
Land	957	1,030	_____	_____
Building	4,350	_____	_____	_____
Furniture	_____	_____	(75)	25.0
Other Assets	49	_____	_____	.5
Total Assets	$_____	$_____	$_____	_____%

Required:

Fill in the blanks above. Round all amounts to the nearest dollar.

Problem 7

The Rocky Mountain Inn's summarized income statement (in millions) for years 20X1–20X5 are as follows:

	20X1	20X2	20X3	20X4	20X5
Sales	$15.4	$18.0	$21.0	$22.0	$25.0
Direct labor	5.0	6.5	7.0	7.0	8.0
Operating supplies	1.0	1.2	1.4	1.3	1.5
Administrative	1.2	1.3	1.4	1.3	1.5
Marketing	0.8	0.9	1.2	1.3	2.0
Maintenance	2.1	2.3	2.5	3.1	3.0
Utilities	1.3	1.2	1.5	1.5	2.0
Fixed charges	2.0	1.9	1.8	1.7	1.5
Income taxes	.4	1.0	1.2	1.8	1.5
Net income	$ 1.6	$ 1.7	$ 3.0	$ 3.0	$ 4.0

Required:

1. Prepare trend percentages for years 20X1–20X5. See Exhibit 3 in chapter 18 for guidance.
2. What significant trends require management's attention?

Problem 8

The Western Café's planning includes targeting levels of various ratios. Information provided for the Western Café is as follows:

Projected sales:	$5,000,000
Cash:	$100,000
Wages payable:	$50,000
Food cost percentage:	35%
Average collection period:	18 days
Food inventory turnover:	15 times
Total asset turnover:	1.5
Current ratio:	1.4
Long-term debt to equity ratio:	1.1

Required:

Complete Western's balance sheet. Assume a 360-day year.

Assets		Liabilities & Equity	
Cash	$_____	Accounts Payable	$_____
Accounts Receivable	_____	Wages Payable	_____
Inventory	_____	Current Liabilities	_____
Current Assets	_____	Long-Term Debt	_____
Fixed Assets (net)	_____	Owners' Equity	_____
Total Assets	$_____	Total Liabilities & Equity	$_____

Challenge Problems

Problem 9

The Louis V Hotel is a 250-room facility with several profit centers. The hotel is open throughout the year, and generally about 2 percent of the rooms are being repaired or renovated at all times; therefore, assume that these rooms are unavailable for sale. During 20X1, the hotel sold 76,400 rooms and experienced an average occupancy per room of 1.42 people. The accounting department has supplied the following information concerning the food department:

Ending Inventory	$ 35,000
Consumption by Employees (free of charge)	5,000
Cost of Food Sales	312,000
Food Cost Percentage	35%
Food Inventory Turnover	12 times

Required:

Determine the following:

1. Paid occupancy percentage for 20X1

2. Number of paid guests of 20X1

3. Beginning inventory of food

4. Food sales

5. Multiple occupancy percentage (Assume that no more than two persons occupied a double room.)

Problem 10

The Tahoe Hotel's current assets and current liabilities from the past three years' balance sheets are as follows:

	20X1	20X2	20X3
Current Assets:			
Cash	$ 15,000	$ 20,000	$ 30,000
Marketable Securities	30,000	25,000	20,000
Accounts Receivable (Net)	70,000	85,000	95,000
Inventory—Food	20,000	22,000	25,000
Prepaid Expenses	10,000	12,000	15,000
Total	$ 145,000	$ 164,000	$ 185,000

	20X1	20X2	20X3
Current Liabilities:			
Accounts Payable	$ 60,000	$ 62,000	$ 65,000
Notes Payable	30,000	30,000	30,000
Wages Payable	20,000	22,000	25,000
Taxes Payable	10,000	11,000	12,000
Total	$ 120,000	$ 125,000	$ 132,000

Selected Operations Data:			
Sales (Total)	$1,000,000	$1,100,000	$1,200,000
Cost of Food Sold	150,000	160,000	168,000
Free Meals—Employees and Others	3,000	3,200	3,400

Required:

1. Compute the following for each year (except as noted):
    a. Current ratio
    b. Acid-test ratio
    c. Accounts receivable turnover (20X2 and 20X3 only)
    d. Inventory turnover (20X2 and 20X3 only)
    e. Working capital
2. Based on the above analysis, comment on the liquidity trend of the Tahoe Hotel.

Problem 11

The financial statements of The 10,000 Lakes Café are as follows:

The 10,000 Lakes Café
Income Statement
For the year ended December 31, 20X5

Revenue	
Food Sales	$1,800,000
Allowances	10,000
Net Revenue	1,790,000
Cost of Food Sold	500,000
Gross Profit	1,290,000

Operating Expenses

Payroll	600,000
Payroll Taxes and Employee Benefits	80,000
Laundry and Dry Cleaning	21,000
Operating Supplies	50,000
Advertising	20,000
Utilities	38,000
Repairs and Maintenance	19,000
Other Operating Expenses	40,000
Total Operating Expenses	868,000
Income after Undistributed Operating Expenses	422,000

Fixed Charges

Rent	20,000
Property Taxes	10,000
Insurance	5,000
Interest	80,000
Depreciation	20,000
Total Fixed Charges	135,000
Income Before Income Taxes	287,000
Income Taxes	101,000
Net Income	$ 186,000

Balance Sheets
December 31, 20X5 and December 31, 20X4

Assets

Current Assets		20X4		20X5
Cash	$	36,500	$	34,000
Accounts Receivable		3,400		4,000
Food Inventory		5,000		5,500
Prepaid Expenses		2,600		2,000
Total Current Assets		47,500		45,500
Property and Equipment				
Land	$	30,000	$	30,000
Building		960,000		960,000
Furniture and Equipment		248,000		262,000
Less Accumulated Depreciation		35,000		40,000
China, Glassware and Silver		18,000		19,000
Net Property and Equipment		$1,221,000		$1,231,000
Total Assets		$1,268,500		$1,276,500

Liabilities

Current Liabilities		20X4		20X5
Accounts Payable	$	25,000	$	21,000
Accrued Expenses		7,000		9,000
Current Portion of Long-Term Debt		16,000		16,000
Total Current Liabilities		48,000		46,000

Long-Term Liabilities		
Mortgage Payable, Net of		
Current Portion	940,000	934,000

Owners' Equity

Paid-In Capital:		
Common Stock	150,000	150,000
Additional Paid-In Capital	15,000	15,000
Retained Earnings	115,500	131,500
Total Liabilities and		
Shareholders' Equity	$1,268,500	$1,276,500

Required:

Compute the following ratios for The 10,000 Lakes Café for both 20X4 and 20X5 except as noted:

1. Current ratio
2. Acid-test ratio
3. Debt-equity ratio
4. Food inventory turnover for 20X5 only
5. Accounts receivable turnover for 20X5 only
6. Average collection period for 20X5 only
7. Long-term debt to total capitalization ratio
8. Asset turnover ratio for 20X5 only
9. Return on assets for 20X5 only
10. Return on owners' equity for 20X5 only

Problem 12

Using the information provided in Problem 11, compute the following ratios for The 10,000 Lakes Café for 20X5:

1. Number of times interest earned ratio
2. Fixed charge coverage ratio
3. Profit margin
4. Earnings per share (Assume 25,000 shares were outstanding.)
5. Average food service check (Assume 164,000 meals were served.)
6. Food cost percentage
7. Labor cost percentage
8. Operating cash flows to current liabilities ratio (Assume operating cash flows were $203,500 for 20X5.)
9. Operating cash flows to total liabilities ratio

Problem 13

The Dallas Budget Inn condensed income statements for the months of July and August 20X1 are as follows:

	July	August
Room Sales	$110,000	$112,000
Labor Expense	50,000	52,000
Laundry Expense	5,000	4,800
Utility Expense	6,500	6,700
Insurance Expense	1,500	1,500
Property Tax Expense	2,100	2,100
Interest Expense	8,000	8,000
Depreciation Expense	15,000	15,000
Income Tax	7,000	7,500
Net Income	$ 14,900	$ 14,400

Required:

Convert the two income statements to common-size income statements.

Problem 14

Using the condensed income statements for July and August for the Dallas Budget Inn, prepare comparative income statements. Show both dollar and percentage differences.

Problem 15

Selected information from the Assets sections of the comparative and common-size balance sheets of December 31, 20X1 and 20X2, of the Boloski Lodge is as follows:

	December 31 20X1	20X2	Dollar Difference	Common Size 12/31/20X2
Current Assets				
Cash				
Accounts Receivable	$ 150,000	$	$ 1,000	1.0%
Inventory		25,000	5,000	
Prepaid Expenses	10,000			
Total		200,000	10,000	10.0
Investments			(10,000)	10.0%

Property & Equipment

Land	_____	_____	–0–	20.0%
Building	_____	_____	50,000	%
Equipment	_____	_____	–0–	%
Accumulated Depreciation	_____	_____	_____	(10.0)%
Total	_____	_____	_____	%
Total Assets	$_____	$_____	$50,000	%

Required:

Fill in the blanks in the previous table. Round all percentages to the nearest 0.1 percent.

Index

A

accounting
  accrual, 22–23, 80–81
  adjustments, 79–95
  branches of, 4–6
  cash, 22–23, 80–81
  cost, 5
  cycle, 107–125
  defined, 3–4
  department organization,
    10–13
  department
    responsibilities, 10–13
  double-entry, 45
  financial, 5
  fundamental equation,
    23–27
  managerial, 5
  organizations, 6–7
  principles, 13–19
  systems, 5–6
  tax, 5
accounts, 41–50
  asset, 43–44
  balance sheet, 49
  capital, 44
  expense, 44, 110–116
  liability, 43
  nominal, 49
  owners' equity, 44
  revenue, 44, 110–116
accounts payable, 43
  subsidiary ledger, 261
accounts receivable, 42
  subsidiary ledger, 261
accounts receivable turnover
  ratio, 522–524
accrual adjustments, 81, 85
accrual income, 482–484
accrued expenses, 43
accrued interest receivable, 42
acid-test ratio, 521–522
activity ratios, 528–535
actuary, 450
ad valorem taxes, 391
additional paid-in capital,
  214, 429–431
adjusted trial balance,
  108–109
adjusting entries, 23, 79–95
advance deposits, 43, 85

aging of accounts receivable
    method, 320–322
allowance journal, 279
allowance method, 319–322
American Accounting
    Association, 3, 13
American Institute of
    Certified Public
    Accountants, 6, 13
amortization, 365, 447–448
asset turnover ratio, 531–532
assets, 19, 23, 25,46
  accrued, 87–88
  current, 14
  depreciable, 83–84
  fixed, 14–16
  intangible, 364–365
  other, 365
auditing, 5
available-for-sale securities,
    467–468
average daily rate, 543
average food service check,
    545
average occupancy per room,
    534–535

B

bad debts, 318–322
balance sheet, 19–20, 201–217
  account format, 204
  limitations of, 203–204
  purpose of, 201–202
  report format, 204
bank reconciliation, 301–305
  preparation of, 302–303
bearer bonds, 442
beverage cost percentage, 546
bond indenture, 439
bonds, 439–449, 460
  advantages of, 440
  amortization of, 447–448
  bearer, 442
  callable, 443
  classification of, 441–443
  convertible, 448–449
  coupon, 442–443
  debenture, 441–442
  disadvantages of, 440
  discounted, 445

face value, 444–446
  journal entries for, 443–449
  market value, 444–446
  mortgage, 441
  payable, 212
  premium, 446
  registered, 442–443
  retiring, 440, 449
  serial, 441
  sinking fund, 448
  subordinated, 442
  term, 441
book of final entry, 52
book of original entry, 52
book value per share, 430–431
bookkeeping, 4
business entity principle, 16

C

callable bonds, 443
capital, 24
  expenditures, 355–356
  leases, 450
  stock, 212
carrying value, 84, 320
cash, 19, 42, 295–309
  disbursements journal,
    272–274
  equivalents, 477–478
  inflows, 479
  internal control of, 295–297
  outflows, 479
  receipts journal, 266–270
charge, 45
chart of accounts, 49
city ledger, 264, 317
clearing accounts, 112
closing, 21
  entries, 110–116
common stock, 423–424
common-size statements, 511
comparative financial
    statements, 510
complimentary occupancy,
    534
computerized accounting
    systems, 280–281
conservatism principle, 18–19
consigned goods, 340
consistency principle, 18

consolidated financial
    statements, 216–217,
    462–465
contingent liability, 326, 375
continuity of the business
    unit principle, 16
continuous events, 80
control account, 261–264
conversion parity price, 448
conversion ratio, 448
convertible bonds, 448–449
copyright, 364
corporate accounting,
    421–431
corporations, 9–10
    advantages and
        disadvantages of,
        421–422
    formation of, 423
    organization of, 422
    S, 10
    taxes and, 422
cost method, 461
cost of goods sold, 144–146
cost principle, 14
coupon bonds, 442–443
credit balance, 45
credit cards, 307–308, 322–323
credit checks, 317
creditors, 24
credits, 44–45
current assets, 205, 207–209
current liabilities, 205,
    209–210, 375–378
current ratio, 202, 210,
    520–521

D

debenture bonds, 441
debit balance, 45
debit cards, 322–323
debits, 44–45
debt-equity ratio, 526
debt securities, 460
deferrals, 81, 82–85
deferred charges, 365
deferred income taxes, 211,
    365
demand deposits, 300
departmental statements,
    157–160
depreciation, 23, 83–84,
    358–364
    accelerated, 358
    double declining balance,
        360
    fractional periods, 360–361

straight-line, 358–359
sum-of-the-year's-digits,
    359
tax reporting of, 361–362
units of production, 359
direct operating expenses, 153
direct write-off method,
    318–319
discounting, 325–326
dishonored notes, 324–325
dividends, 424–425, 460
    dates, 424
    journal entries for, 424–425
    stock, 428–429
double occupancy, 535
double taxation, 10

E

earnings per share, 149–150,
    539–540
earnings statement, 21
effective interest rate method,
    447–448
electronic funds transfer, 296
eliminating entries, 462–465
employee's earnings record,
    380
equities, 23, 25
equity investments, 460–461
equity method, 461
expenses, 21, 47, 146–147
external users, 141, 150–152
extraordinary items, 149

F

federal income tax, 383
FICA, 384
FIFO method, 342
Financial Accounting
    Standards Board, 6, 13,
    450, 462, 466
financial audit, 5
financial statements, 22
    analysis and interpretation,
        509–550
    corporations and, 421
financing activities, 479,
    490–491
fixed charge coverage ratio,
    527–528
fixed charges, 153
food cost percentage, 545
footnotes, 17, 150, 215
franchise, 264

front office cash receipts and
    disbursements journal,
    278
full disclosure principle, 17
fundamental accounting
    equation, 23–27

G

gains, 147
general journal, 274
general ledger, 274
general partners, 8
generally accepted
    accounting principles
    (GAAP), 6, 13
going concern, 16
goodwill, 46, 211, 364
gross operating profit, 153
gross operating profit per
    available room, 544
gross pay, 383
gross recording method, 305,
    307
guest ledger, 264, 317

H

held-to-maturity securities,
    467
Hilton Hotels Corporation,
    203
horizontal analysis, 510,
    513–514
Hospitality Financial and
    Technology
    Professionals, 6

I

imprest payroll account, 379
income statement, 20–21, 79,
    141–163
    balance sheet and, 143
    internal, 152–157
income taxes, 148–149
inflation, 16
intangible assets, 211, 364–365
interest-bearing notes,
    323–326
Internal Revenue Service, 6
internal users, 141, 150–152
International Association of
    Hospitality
    Accountants, 6
inventory, 43, 208, 337–347

control of, 337
merchandise, 337
periodic, 337–339
perpetual, 345–346
physical, 339–340
turnover ratio, 528–531
valuation methods,
341–345
investee, 461
investments, 43, 210, 479,
489–490
long-term, 459
short-term, 459
valuation of, 465–468
investor, 461

J

journalizing, 50–53, 58–63
journals, 50–53
general, 52–53

L

labor cost, 146–147
labor cost percentage, 546
leasehold, 364
improvements, 357
leases, 212, 449–450
capital, 450
operating, 449–450
ledgers, 49
general, 49
lessee, 449
lessor, 449
leverage, 525
liabilities, 19, 25, 46
contingent, 375
current, 375–378
payroll, 378–392
LIFO method, 342
limited liability companies, 9
limited partners, 8
liquidity, 202
ratios, 520–525
long-term debt to total
capitalization ratio, 526
long-term liabilities, 211
loss contingency, 375
losses, 148
lower of cost or market, 345
lump sum purchase, 357

M

management fees, 156
market value per share, 431

marketable securities, 43, 207
Marriott International,
150–151, 163
master payroll file, 379
matching principle, 18, 79
materiality principle, 19
maturity date, 324, 439–440
maturity value, 323
minority interest, 464
mix of sales, 542–543
mortgage bonds, 441
mortgages, 451
payable, 43, 212
multiple occupancy, 535

N

net book value, 84
net income, 21
net pay, 385
net recording method,
306–307
net working capital, 210
net worth, 25
noncash activities, 480–481
noncurrent receivables, 210
non-interest-bearing notes,
327–329
normal balance, 48–49
notes payable, 43, 211–212,
326–329, 376–378
notes receivable, 42, 323–326
NSF checks, 302
number of times interest
earned ratio, 526–527

O

objective evidence principle,
17
occupancy percentage, 534
office supplies, 43
operating activities, 479,
485–489
operating cash flows to
current liabilities ratio,
522
operating cash flows to total
liabilities ratio, 528
operating cycle, 205–207
operating efficiency ratio,
537–538
operating leases, 449–450
other assets, 211
owners' equity, 19, 25, 46,
212–215
owners' withdrawals, 47–48

P

paid occupancy percentage,
532–534
par value, 423
parent company, 462
partnerships, 8, 401–412
advantages of, 401–402
disadvantages of, 402
division of income,
404–406
formation of, 403–406
general, 402–403
limited, 8–9, 403
liquidation of, 409–412
patent, 364
payables, 317–330
payroll, 378–392
control of, 378–379
journal, 274–278, 380, 391
records, 379–381
taxes, 385
pensions, 450–451
defined benefit, 450–451
defined contribution, 450
percentage of sales method,
322
periodic inventory, 337–339
perpetual inventory, 345–346
petty cash, 299–301
physical inventory, 339–340
post-closing trial balance, 116
posting, 54
preferred stock, 427–428
prepaid expenses, 43, 208
prepaid insurance, 82
price earnings ratio, 540–541
prior period adjustments, 162,
425
profit and loss statement, 21
profit centers, 147
profit margin, 537
profitability, 19
ratios, 535–541
property and equipment, 43,
210–211, 355–364
disposal, 362–363
exchange, 363–364
turnover ratio, 531
property taxes, 391
purchases journal, 270–272

R

ratio analysis, 517–550
limitations of, 547
standards, 517–518

ratios, 512
  accounts receivable
    turnover, 522–524
  acid-test, 521–522
  activity, 528–535
  asset turnover, 531–532
  classes of, 519–520
  current, 520–521
  debt-equity, 526
  fixed charge coverage,
    527–528
  inventory turnover,
    528–531
  liquidity, 520–525
  long-term debt to total
    capitalization, 526
  number of times interest
    earned, 526–527
  operating, 541–547
  operating cash flows to
    current liabilities, 522
  operating cash flows to
    total liabilities, 528
  operating efficiency,
    537–538
  price earnings, 540–541
  profitability, 535–541
  property and equipment
    turnover, 531
  solvency, 525–528
receivables, 317–330
registered bonds, 442–443
relative change, 510
residual value, 83
responsibility accounting, 152
restricted cash, 209
retail method, 343–344
retained earnings, 214,
  425–426
return on assets, 538–539
return on owners' equity, 539
revenue, 21, 47
  expenditures, 355
  per available room,
    543–544
reversing entries, 120–121

S

S corporations, 10
sales, 143–144
sales journal, 264–266
salvage value, 83, 358
seat turnover, 532–534
Securities and Exchange
  Commission, 6

securities
  available-for-sale, 467
  held-to-maturity, 467
  trading, 467
security deposits, 365
serial bonds, 441
service centers, 147
short-term investments, 207
sinking fund, 441, 448
Social Security tax, 384
sole proprietorships, 7–8
solvency, 19
  ratios, 525–528
specialized journals, 264–274,
  278–280
specific identification
  method, 341
state income tax, 384
statement of cash flows,
  21–22, 477–496
  interpretation of, 493
  preparation of, 484–493
  relationship to other
    statements, 478–479
statement of financial
  position, 19
statement of income and
  expenses, 21
statement of owners' equity,
  110
statement of retained
  earnings, 162
stock
  splits, 429
  subscription plan, 426–427
  callable, 427–428
  common, 423–424
  cumulative, 427
  preferred, 427–428
  treasury, 429–430
subordinated bonds, 442
subsidiary company, 462
subsidiary ledger, 261–264
summary operating
  statement, 153, 154–157

T

T-accounts, 42–43, 58–63
taxes, 43
  ad valorem, 391
  federal income, 383
  payroll, 385
  property, 391
  Social Security, 384

  state income, 384
  unemployment, 385–386
term bonds, 441
tips, 389–391
total departmental income,
  153
trademark, 364
trading securities, 467
transfer journal, 279
transportation costs, 340–341
treasury stock, 214, 429–430
trend analysis, 515–517
trend percentages, 510
trial balance, 56, 61
  adjusted, 108–109
  post-closing, 116
trustees, 439

U

uncollectible accounts,
  318–322
underwriting firm, 439
undistributed operating
  expenses, 153
unearned revenues, 84
unemployment taxes
  federal, 385–386
  state, 385–386
Uniform System of Accounts
  for Restaurants, 160–162
Uniform System of Accounts
  for the Lodging Industry
  (USALI), 7, 50, 152–154,
  158, 201, 212–215, 355,
  361, 365, 459
uniform systems of accounts,
  152
unit of measurement
  principle, 16

V

vertical analysis, 512, 514–515
vouchers, 297–299
  preparation of, 299

W

Wall Street Journal, 439
weighted average method,
  341–342
worksheet, 116–120